SELECTED READINGS
IN ECONOMICS

C. Lowell Harriss
COLUMBIA UNIVERSITY

SELECTED
IN

PRENTICE-HALL, INC., Englewood Cliffs, N. J.   1962

READINGS
ECONOMICS

Second Edition

C. Lowell Harriss
SELECTED READINGS IN ECONOMICS, SECOND EDITION

© 1958, 1962 by PRENTICE-HALL, INC., Englewood Cliffs, N. J.
All rights reserved. No part of this book may be reproduced in any form, by mimeograph or any other means, without permission in writing from the publishers.

Library of Congress Catalog Card No.: 62-9587

Printed in the United States of America

80196—C

PREFACE

This book is for the student of elementary economics—and for his teacher. It is a supplement to standard textual material. Instructors know and students sense that textbooks do not contain all that a basic course should provide—illustrative material, a variety of points-of-view, application of tools of analysis, contact with classics, different ways of stating an important point. A wealth of material with which to enrich the course exists, but searching out the best of it is not easy. Making it readily accessible is even more difficult, for seldom is it available in edited form; nor can libraries often furnish sufficient copies. Thus, a real need exists. This volume is designed to help meet it.

Drawing upon the experience gained from many years spent both in teaching and in working with others who teach elementary economics, I have chosen selections to appeal to a wide range of student capacities and enthusiasms. As students vary, so do these readings. Yet no selection seems to me to be unworthy of the best student (and I know some of the best). Nor are there more than a dozen readings which the student of somewhat different potential and less intense motivation (and I know *him,* too) will find unduly difficult. The more difficult selections will provide that unusual challenge which is good for everyone and proves wonderfully stimulating to many.

The scope is cosmopolitan. Admittedly, the book does not touch upon *all* aspects of economics, nor does it reveal *all* important sources or introduce *all* leading economists. Yet, here are hundreds of pages of fine material. Some views will seem to many of us to be misleading or wrong, but still worth consideration. Rarely, I suppose, will the student get from a reading all the significant things his instructor will see. But it is hoped that the instructor will find satisfaction as his total accomplishment benefits from the use of materials which will help him to take his students beyond the scope of the text.

This revision is more nearly a new book than I expected when the search began. I have retained the selections which instructors reported as being most useful—except when something better appeared. Many readings of unquestioned merit have been eliminated to make room for material which is more up-to-date, clearer, more challenging, or in some other respect more suitable. As previously, editing has been for the benefit of the student, not the scholar.

Adequate acknowledgement of the sources and the nature of the help and advice offered me during the preparation of this book is, at the least, difficult. Authors and their publishers have been magnanimously co-operative and have my most sincere thanks. So, too, do the hundreds of students I have been privileged to teach and who hardly recognized that they were simultaneously enlarging my knowledge of the teaching of economics. Most difficult of all would it be to cite all the teachers of economics who have so thoughtfully contributed suggestions; many of them, however, will see evidence of my agreement with, and deference to, their judgments. But to all—my deepest appreciation for advice which, in so many cases, space limitations alone prevented my accepting. Finally, I must thank members of that most helpful of professions—librarians—not only at my home university but also at the University of Strasbourg and the Council of Europe in Strasbourg; most of the fruits of their skillful searching—but certainly not my deep appreciation—have been sacrificed to keep the book from impractical size.

C. LOWELL HARRISS

TABLE OF CONTENTS

I · WHAT IS ECONOMICS?

1. Understanding the Economic Problem — **1** — BEN W. LEWIS
2. Economic Laws — **7** — ALFRED MARSHALL
3. The Business Economist — **9** — RALPH E. BURGESS AND ALBERT G. MATAMOROS
4. The Development of Economic Thought — **13** — JOHN MAURICE CLARK

II · THE BUSINESS SYSTEM

5. The "Unproductive Middleman" — **21** — ABBA P. LERNER
6. Ownership, Control, and Management Responsibility in Large Corporations — **24** — ERNEST DALE
7. Management Problems as Seen by the Head of the World's Largest Business — **37** — FREDERICK R. KAPPEL
8. Careers in Business Management — **48** — WILLIAM PASCHELL

II • THE BUSINESS SYSTEM—Continued

9. How to Understand Corporate Financial Statements　56　NEW YORK STOCK EXCHANGE

III • COSTS AND PRICES

10. The Economic Functions of Prices　70　MYRON WATKINS, HOWARD R. BOWEN

11. The Price System in Microcosm: A P.O.W. Camp　73　R. A. RADFORD

12. Demand-Supply Analysis: Has There Been a Shortage of Engineers?　83　DAVID M. BLANK AND GEORGE J. STIGLER

13. Pricing by Business　88　JOEL DEAN

14. When Is Price Reduction Profitable?　99　CLARE E. GRIFFIN

15. Cost Accounting and Marginal Analysis　108　JAMES S. EARLEY

16. Substitution: Competition Among Building Materials　113　LAURENCE G. O'DONNELL

17. Product Variety　118　E. H. CHAMBERLIN

18. Rent Control: An Example of Price Fixing　120　BERTRAND DE JOUVENEL

III • COSTS AND PRICES—Continued

19. *Use of Economic Theory in Business: Operations Research*   **122**   SVEN DANÖ

20. *The Equilibrium Conditions*   **127**   PAUL A. SAMUELSON

IV • DEALING WITH MONOPOLY

21. *Adam Smith on Monopoly*   **128**   ADAM SMITH

22. *Why Seek Competition?*   **129**   JOHN MAURICE CLARK

23. *Bigness in Business: Dangers and a Proposed Remedy*   **131**   GEORGE J. STIGLER

24. *Price-Fixing Conspiracy Sends Business Leaders to Jail*   **137**   U.S. NEWS AND WORLD REPORT

25. *An Economist Analyzes an Antitrust Decision: Cellophane*   **142**   GEORGE W. STOCKING

V • CONSUMPTION AND CONSUMER PROBLEMS

26. *Conspicuous Consumption*   **151**   THORSTEIN B. VEBLEN

27. *New Features of the Consumer Market*   **153**   LAWRENCE C. MURDOCH

28. *Product Testing*   **162**   CONSUMER BULLETIN

VI · DISTRIBUTION OF INCOME

29. Theories of Private Property	165	E. R. A. SELIGMANN
30. Justice in the Distribution of Income	167	KENNETH E. BOULDING
31. Wage Theory: Basic Forces	180	J. R. HICKS
32. Pure Rent: The Classic View	184	DAVID RICARDO
33. Profit	188	FRANK H. KNIGHT
34. Development of Human Resources	190	ELI GINZBERG

VII · POPULATION AND LABOR

35. The Theory of Population	200	THOMAS R. MALTHUS
36. Manpower: Challenge of the 1960's	202	U.S. DEPARTMENT OF LABOR
37. Unions as Monopolies	217	HENRY C. SIMONS
38. Abuses of Union Power	223	KENNETH O. GILMORE
39. A New Agenda for Labor Unions	227	SOLOMON BARKIN
40. How a Union Helped Raise Productivity	231	KARL DETZER

VIII · PROBLEMS OF AGRICULTURE AND NATURAL RESOURCES

41. Guidelines for a Constructive Revision of Agricultural Policy **234** KARL BRANDT

42. The Adequacy of Resources for Economic Growth in the United States **242** JOSEPH L. FISHER AND EDWARD BOORSTEIN

43. The Affluent Society **250** JOHN KENNETH GALBRAITH

44. The Sumptuary Manifesto **257** SIR EPICURE MAMMON

IX · MONEY, BANKING, AND INFLATION

45. The Value of Money: An Introduction **260** SIR DENNIS H. ROBERTSON

46. Inflation: Its Causes and Cures **263** GOTTFRIED HABERLER

47. Effects of Inflation on Management Efficiency **283** JOHN MAYNARD KEYNES

48. Hyper-Inflation in Germany **285** FRANK D. GRAHAM

49. Steel, Union Power, Administered Prices, and Inflation in the 1950's **287** M. A. ADELMAN

X · THE NATIONAL ECONOMY: CYCLES AND STABILITY

50. Uses and Limitations of Gross National Product Figures   **296**   WALTER W. HELLER, KERMIT GORDON, AND JAMES TOBIN

51. Progress Towards Economic Stability   **300**   ARTHUR F. BURNS

52. Keynes' General Theory of Employment: A Summary   **315**   DUDLEY DILLARD

53. Monetary Policy in Practice: Background and Problems   **318**   WILLIAM MCCHESNEY MARTIN, JR.

54. No More Depressions?   **327**   MILTON FRIEDMAN

55. Value of Wage Increases for Nation's Economy: A Union View   **336**   AFL-CIO

XI · GOVERNMENT FINANCE

56. Government Functions: Economic Aspects of Government Spending   **338**   O. H. BROWNLEE AND E. D. ALLEN
JOHN STUART MILL
JAMES A. MAXWELL

57. "Economy" in Government   **350**   THE CITY OF NEW YORK

XI • GOVERNMENT FINANCE—Continued

58. Investment in Public Works:
    Use of the Interest Rate   **354**   ARNOLD C. HARBERGER

59. A Business Program for
    Federal Tax Reform   **356**   NATIONAL ASSOCIATION OF MANUFACTURERS

60. Income Tax Rates:
    International Comparisons   **364**   FIRST NATIONAL CITY BANK OF NEW YORK

61. Progressive Taxation:
    A Justification   **370**   F. W. TAUSSIG
    A Criticism   **371**   HARLEY L. LUTZ

62. Functional Finance   **376**   ABBA P. LERNER

63. Fiscal Policy for Economic
    Stabilization   **377**   COMMISSION ON MONEY AND CREDIT

XII • INTERNATIONAL TRADE AND FINANCE

64. Petition of the Candlemakers   **386**   FREDERIC BASTIAT

65. Forces Changing the U.S.
    Export Outlook   **389**   ALBERT O. HIRSCHMAN

66. Gold in World Monetary
    Affairs Today   **392**   MIROSLAV A. KRIZ

XII · INTERNATIONAL TRADE AND FINANCE—Continued

67. Canadian-United States Economic Relations **404** W. EARLE MCLAUGHLIN / STEFAN STYKOLT

68. State-Controlled Economies and International Quarrels **415** JACOB VINER

XIII · ECONOMIC GROWTH: THE UNITED STATES

69. Economic Growth: A Discussion by Economists **423** A SYMPOSIUM

70. Automation—As Seen by Business Leaders **442** RUDOLPH F. BANNOW / D. J. DAVIS / PAUL A. GORMAN

71. Automation—Views of Labor Leaders **454** GEORGE MEANY / WALTER P. REUTHER / EDWARD SWAYDUCK

72. Why Research Spending Soars **465** LEONARD S. SILK

XIV · GROWTH OF UNDERDEVELOPED ECONOMIES

73. Basic Factors Affecting Economic Development **472** DAVID MCCORD WRIGHT

XIV · GROWTH OF UNDERDEVELOPED ECONOMIES—Continued

74. International Investment and the Growth of Underdeveloped Areas **479** RAGNAR NURKSE

75. Population Growth and Per Capita Income in Underdeveloped Areas **486** HENRY H. VILLARD

76. Latin America's Economic Problems and Outlook **493** THE ECONOMIST

77. United States Business Performance Abroad: A Case Study **511** THEODORE GEIGER AND LIESEL GOODE

XV · ECONOMIC SYSTEMS AND IDEOLOGIES

78. The Communist Manifesto **533** KARL MARX AND FRIEDRICH ENGELS

79. American Economists Report on Russia **540** GREGORY GROSSMAN FLOYD A. BOND

80. How Soviet Industrial Managers Do Business **544** HARRY SCHWARTZ

81. Comparisons of the United States and Soviet Economies **548** WALT W. ROSTOW

SELECTED READINGS
IN ECONOMICS

I • WHAT IS ECONOMICS?

The young person today, whether he likes the prospect or not, faces a life of economic decision. Can he (or she, for women have large economic responsibilities) decide more wisely after having studied economics? An Oberlin professor, Vice-President of the American Economic Association, deals with this and other questions as he discusses the need for studying economics.

1 • Understanding the Economic Problem

BEN W. LEWIS

. . . Democracy—and this we have on the very highest authority—means *government by the people*. But the affairs of government, in large and increasing measure are *economic* affairs. To be sure, they have political and other overtones, but no one who casts his glance even casually over the range of matters with which modern governments have to deal will doubt that these matters are economic in substance or in effect. Look for a moment: money, credit, commerce, corporations, tariffs, quotas, foreign aid, development, monopoly, fair trade, farm support, small business, oil prorates, highways, rails, communications, private power, public power, inflation, employment, management-labor relations, distribution of income, education, health, public debt—and taxes.

. . . . .

The simple business of living in the United States in our age calls increasingly upon men to participate actively with other men, in the gigantic undertaking of collective governmental decision-making on a vast array of complex economic problems and issues. It is demanded of these men that they have economic understanding. The stakes, to put the matter bluntly, are the survival of democracy and human freedom. Freedom will not remain if democracy expires, and democracy will not last beyond the day when it fails to discharge the political-economic tasks which we ask it to perform. Remember, democracy is government of and by the people, and the capacity of the people to perform will set the level of performance which it is possible for democracy to attain.

Freedom and democracy are abstract concepts, but the matter of their preser-

---

BEN W. LEWIS, "Economic Understanding: Why and What," *The American Economic Review* (May 1957). Used by permission.

vation is concrete and immediate. This is our democracy, and we are "the people" on whose economic understanding and economic sense the outcome of our epic adventure in self-government rests.

. . . I have resisted the temptation to speak of the need of each individual in our highly specialized and interdependent economy for knowledge and skills which will help him to operate more effectively as a buyer and seller of goods and services. Men need to know about credit facilities and practices, installment buying, insurance, tax forms, social security provisions and a host of other matters, in order to move intelligently in making and enjoying their living. But information about these matters is not to be accepted as economics, or in lieu of economics. Such information may come to the student as a by-product of his study of economics, and it is often both possible and productive to employ topics of this kind as a vehicle for developing economic understanding. It may be that many of these things should be taught for their own sake. . . . But the call for more and better economics in the schools does not derive from the need for formal instruction in whether to buy or rent a home, or the conditions under which term-insurance is to be preferred to an annuity. A man may be very shrewd in his personal dealings in these matters and still be sadly deficient in economic understanding.

. . . . .

. . . Economic understanding does not consist in the accumulation of a stock of economic information or of an array of useful economic facts. It does not consist of the possession of a "Do-it-yourself" kit of answers to public economic problems or of a package of rules of sound thinking for solving these problems. Nor does it consist of skills or precepts to be employed in the conduct of economic transactions. Economics makes use of all of these things, but we are talking here about economic *understanding,* and "understanding" means *understanding.* Understanding is concerned with "why"; its interest in "what" is strictly ancillary to its interest in "why."

I will venture the proposition that to have economic understanding is to have a genuine sense of "what it's all about" as far as the economic phases of our lives together are concerned—a "feel" for economic issues—a rather clear impression of "having been here before" in the presence of economic situations calling for policy judgments, and hence a sense of direction and a workmanlike touch.

I believe economic understanding is to be gained through an understanding of the central core of economics that dominates all economics situations and issues—THE ECONOMIC PROBLEM faced by all societies of men who live and make their living together. We have economic systems or economies because we are confronted by THE ECONOMIC PROBLEM; economies, all economies irrespective of characteristics or qualities, are fashioned, molded and maintained solely because this problem exists. To understand THE ECONOMIC PROBLEM is to know the purpose and functions of economic systems, and thus to have a clear unmistakable point of reference, a firm home base, from which to proceed in considering any and all questions of economic public policy. I do not claim eternal and universal economic salvation as the reward for such understanding, but I do not hesitate to say that, in its absence, only confusion can prevail.

THE ECONOMIC PROBLEM, let us be reminded, is simply "What disposition shall society make of its *limited human and natural resources* in light of the *unlimited needs and desires* which these resources can be used to satisfy?" . . .

Let me labor this thesis, lightly. But, first another precautionary negative before I am accused of treating you solely to a bill of thawed-out economic ideas chipped out of our nineteenth century deep-freeze, and of ignoring the shattering impact upon our thinking of today's dynamic flows, growth modeling and equation splitting. THE ECONOMIC PROBLEM is not confined to static division; it does not reflect an assumption that product is fixed in amount and that economic alternatives relate only to kinds and direction. The problem is "What *use* shall be made of our resources?", and I offer "use" to you as a *dynamic* concept which confronts us with choices bearing on fullness and growth as well as with choices of kind —with questions of "how much" and "how quickly," as well as with questions of "what?"

THE ECONOMIC PROBLEM emerges from two basic, interrelated conditions—(1) man's unlimited desires for goods *in the aggregate* and (2) the limited human and natural resources available to society for the production of goods in the aggregate.

. . . . .

Mankind has unlimited desires for goods in the aggregate. Each one of us wants at least a minimum of material goods and services to satisfy his basic needs—such things, for example, as food, shelter, household furnishings, clothing, medical services and so forth. But each of us desires much more than this basic minimum of essentials. Each would like more, and more varieties, of all of these things and many things in addition. The fact is that if each of us did not have to restrain himself by some notion of what he could afford, his individual desires or wants would run on endlessly. In the aggregate, such limitless desires, multiplied in volume by the number of individuals who inhabit the world—go far beyond anything that society can ever dream of actually satisfying from its limited resources.

Society's human and natural resources available for the production of goods in the aggregate are limited. The goods and services with which we satisfy our desires do not grow in limitless quantities upon limitless trees; they do not appear out of nowhere when we rub a magic lamp or utter a "secret word." Goods must be *produced* (even those few that do "grow on trees" have to be picked—or picked up—and prepared for use). Production requires the use of *human resources* (labor) and *natural resources* (land, water, ores, minerals, fuels, etc.), together with techniques and methods for organizing and combining and processing these resources. And we know that basically, these resources are *scarce relative to human needs and desires*. Despite our marvelous advances in technology and despite the fact that our standard of material living has on the average risen markedly over the centuries, we can never produce such an abundance of goods that everyone in the world can have all he wants of everything, with lots left over.

Let there be no confusion on this point. Occasionally in our society we are confronted by so-called surpluses of *particular* products (the "butter surplus," the "potato surplus," for example, or the "surplus of used-automobiles"). These represent supplies of particular goods in excess of the amounts which buyers with purchasing power at a particular time and place are willing to buy at prevailing prices. In an economic sense they represent particular overproduction in relation to effective demand for particular goods—mis-production or mal-production, or a use or allocation of society's resources of which society, by its market calculus, indicates it does not approve. In the world as we know it, "too many" potatoes means "too few" of other things; it can never mean "too much of everything." And even in the case of a particular surplus at a particular time and place, it does not necessarily follow that human desires for the particular goods are not going unsatisfied somewhere else in society at the very same time. Breakdowns in society's institutional arrangements for bringing goods and desires together are not to be interpreted as evidence of society's power to produce without limit. By the same token, we must not be misled by terms and phrases which suggest contradictions where none exist. Specifically, there is no contradiction between an "economy of scarcity" and an "economy of plenty," where "scarcity" is understood as a *condition* of economizing, and "plenty" is understood as its *goal*.

It behooves us, thus, to take care in the use we make of our resources—to be concerned about their use, to manage them, to "economize" them. The reason we bother to manage or "economize" our resources is simply that, since they are limited in supply relative to the uses to which we would like to put them—that is, since in an economic sense they are "scarce"—*it makes a difference* to us how they are used. The degree and manner and direction of their use and the disposition of the product resulting from their use have, of sheer necessity, been a primary, basic concern of all societies through the ages. This is what the study of "economizing," or *economics as a social science* is about—it is *all* that economics is about.

Presumably any society will want its scarce resources to be "fully" employed (particularly its labor resources), and so used that their power to produce is great and expanding, and that the "right" goods are produced in the "right" amounts and, in each case, by using the "best" combinations of resources. Any society will be concerned, too, that the goods which are produced from its scarce resources are divided fairly among its members.

But the use of such terms as "fully," "right," "best," "fairly," etc. in defining the disposition to be made of resources suggests that alternative uses are possible and that society is faced with the never-ending problem of making millions of continuous and simultaneous decisions in the management or "economizing" of its resources. Surely we want our resources to be used fully and in the right and best way, but how "full" is "fully"? Exactly which ways are "right" and "best" and "fair"? We must remember, too, that society's answers to some of the questions may condition and set limits on its answers to other questions: a decision to promote technological advance *may* make employment less stable, a decision to divide the aggregate product more evenly among everyone *may* have an adverse effect upon the total amount produced, and public policies designed to bring about full employment *may* also promote productive inefficiency and aggravated inequities as an undesired consequence. Nonetheless, answers *must be* provided by society to THE ECONOMIC PROBLEM faced by men who want to live in harmony and well-being in a world where not everyone *can* have all he wants of the goods and services that make up his material living, and where, hence, the use made of our limited, valuable economic resources is a matter of concern to every living person.

Thus it is that all societies of men who make their living together must inevitably establish and maintain (or acquiesce in) an *economic system* or *economy*—a set of man-made arrangements to provide answers to the all-important *economic* questions which make up the over-all economic problem:

a. How fully shall our limited resources be used?
b. How shall our resources be organized and combined?
c. Who shall produce how much of what?
d. To whom and in what amounts shall the resulting product be divided among the members of society?

It is the job of the economic system (*any* economic system) to make the decisions and turn out the answers *that society wants,* whatever they may be, to these questions; and economics as a discipline is a study of THE ECONOMIC PROBLEM in all its parts, and of the institutional arrangements which men have devised to grind out the necessary answers to the questions which it poses.

The data and materials, the concepts and the "principles" with which the study of economics is concerned and the problems to which it attends all stem from and bear on this central problem —how *do* we and how *might* we dispose of the resources upon which the level and quality of our material life depend? This is THE ECONOMIC PROBLEM; all other economic problems and issues—for example, the farm problem, the labor-management problem, the problem of taxation, the inflation problem, the problem of full employment, the anti-trust problem—are simply partial manifestations of it in particular quarters and under particular conditions, and can be dealt with effectively only in conscious relation to the central problem—the *core* of economics. This should be the starting point of our economics teaching, and its destination. Between the starting point and the terminus, students should become familiar with the significant features of our own mid-twentieth century economy with its ever-changing combinations of individual-markets and collective-governmental economic activities and processes. They should become aware of its rationale and of how it has come to be what it now is, and of how it contrasts with earlier and other economic systems. They need to know something of the structure and operations of our major economic institutions, and the mechanics of income determination, resource guidance and income distribution. They should experience the centering of issues and the marshalling and weighing of considerations involved in the determination of policy in one or two areas of public economic policy. But all of this—systems, processes, institutions, mechanics, policy problems— I repeat, all of this should be tied constantly to the core of economics—THE ECONOMIC PROBLEM—and related at every turn to the purposes for which men build economic systems because that problem exists.

. . . Our story can be told and it can be understood. To what purpose?

A person who possesses economic understanding will relate his consideration of public economic issues, easily and purposively, to the central core— to the starting point, to home base. He will have a sense of the interrelationship of economic phenomena and problems—the "oneness" of the economy —the tie-in between each sector of the economy and the whole, and between the economy and himself.

He will know his "way around" and his "way home" in the economy. He will face such choices as those between alternative satisfactions, between present and future goods, between alternative methods of production, between production and leisure, between stability and security and innovation and progress, and between economizing by the market and economizing by government, under whatever conditions and guises these choices may appear, with awareness and a balanced sense of consequences.

He will know that products come from production, and will have an appreciation of the contribution made by diverse groups to the totality of production.

Familiarity with the mechanics of economics will not blind him to the reality that the operating forces in any political economy are human. He will know that economic life involves, essentially, the rational living together of human beings—a constant adjustment and readjustment in economic matters comparable to, indeed a part of, the constant adjustment and readjustment that characterize the total business of living together. He will realize that these adjustments frequently bring discomfort, even pain, to those established (vested) interests that are required to adjust, but that failure of one group to adjust may mean privation for other groups and stagnation for the economy as a whole. And he will relate this to situations in which his own interest lies in resistance to change (tariff, price supports, "fair trade," "featherbedding") as well as to those in which his own interest would be served by the adjustment of others.

He will distinguish between areas where "scientific" economic answers are possible, areas where such answers are impossible because necessary information or data are absent, and areas where only value judgments are called for and possible. He will realize that it is not the function of economics to provide answers to ethical or value problems, but, rather, to help to define and identify such problems and to place them in sharper focus.

Finally, his realization that, in the very nature of the case, economic problems permit of very few "right" answers will be one measure of the depth of his economic understanding—and the realization will fill him with a sense not of futility but of purpose. It will point up for him his personal role in the political economy in which he lives.

. . . . .

The laws of economics are not like those of physics or those passed by a legislature. Their nature is the subject of the following selection by the great neo-classical economist Alfred Marshall, of Cambridge University.

2 · Economic Laws

ALFRED MARSHALL

Political Economy or economics is a study of mankind in the ordinary business of life; it examines that part of individual and social action which is most closely connected with the attainment and with the use of the material requisites of well-being.

Thus it is on the one side a study of wealth; and on the other, and more important side, a part of the study of man. For man's character has been molded by his everyday work, and the material resources which he thereby procures, more than by any other influence unless it be that of his religious ideals; and the two great forming agencies of the world's history have been the religious and the economic. . . .

Let us then consider more closely the nature of economic laws, and their limitations. Every cause has a tendency to produce some definite result if nothing occurs to hinder it. Thus gravitation tends to make things fall to the ground: but when a balloon is full of gas lighter than air, the pressure of the air will make it rise in spite of the tendency of gravitation to make it fall. The law of gravitation states how any two things attract one another; how they tend to move towards one another, and will move towards one another if nothing interferes to prevent them. The law of gravitation is therefore a statement of tendencies.

It is a very exact statement—so exact that mathematicians can calculate a Nautical Almanac, which will show the moments at which each satellite of Jupiter will hide itself behind Jupiter. They make this calculation for many years beforehand; and navigators take it to sea, and use it in finding out where they are. Now there are no economic tendencies which act as steadily and can be measured as exactly as gravitation can: and consequently there are no laws of economics which can be compared for precision with the law of gravitation.

But let us look at a science less exact than astronomy. The science of the tides explains how the tide rises and falls twice a day under the action of the sun and the moon: how there are strong tides at new and full moon, and weak tides at the moon's first and third quarters; and how the tide running up into a closed channel . . . will be very high; and so on. Thus, having studied the lie of the land and the water all round

---

ALFRED MARSHALL, *Principles of Economics,* 8th ed. (London: Macmillan & Co., Ltd., 1920), pp. 1, 31–33, 36. Used by permission.

the British Isles, people can calculate beforehand when the tide will *probably* be at its highest on any day at London Bridge or at Gloucester; and how high it will be there. They have to use the word *probably*, which the astronomers do not need to use when talking about the eclipses of Jupiter's satellites. For, though many forces act upon Jupiter and its satellites, each one of them acts in a definite manner which can be predicted beforehand: but no one knows enough about the weather to be able to say beforehand how it will act. A heavy downpour of rain in the upper Thames valley, or a strong northeast wind in the German Ocean, may make the tides at London Bridge differ a good deal from what had been expected.

The laws of economics are to be compared with the laws of the tides, rather than with the simple and exact law of gravitation. For the actions of men are so various and uncertain, that the best statement of tendencies, which we can make in a science of human conduct, must needs be inexact and faulty. This might be urged as a reason against making any statements at all on the subject; but that would be almost to abandon life. Life is human conduct, and the thoughts and emotions that grow up around it. By the fundamental impulses of our nature we all—high and low, learned and unlearned—are in our several degrees constantly striving to understand the courses of human action, and to shape them for our purposes, whether selfish or unselfish, whether noble or ignoble. And since we *must* form to ourselves some notions of the tendencies of human action, our choice is between forming those notions carelessly and forming them carefully. The harder the task, the greater the need for steady patient inquiry; for turning to account the experience, that has been reaped by the more advanced physical sciences; and for framing as best we can well thought-out estimates, or provisional laws, of the tendencies of human action.

. . . . .

Economic laws, or statements of economic tendencies, are those social laws which relate to branches of conduct in which the strength of the motives chiefly concerned can be measured by a money price.

There is thus no hard and sharp line of division between those social laws which are, and those which are not, to be regarded also as economic laws. For there is a continuous gradation from social laws concerned almost exclusively with motives that can be measured by price, to social laws in which such motives have little place; and which are therefore generally as much less precise and exact than economic laws, as those are than the laws of the more exact physical sciences. . . .

It is sometimes said that the laws of economics are "hypothetical." Of course, like every other science, it undertakes to study the effects which will be produced by certain causes, not absolutely, but subject to the condition that *other things are equal,* and that the causes are able to work out their effects undisturbed. Almost every scientific doctrine, when carefully and formally stated, will be found to contain some proviso to the effect that other things are equal: the action of the causes in question is supposed to be isolated; certain effects are attributed to them, but only *on the hypothesis* that no cause is permitted to enter except those distinctly allowed for. It is true, however, that the condition that time must be allowed for causes to produce their effects is a source of great difficulty in economics. For meanwhile the material on which they work, and perhaps even the causes themselves, may have changed; and the tendencies which are being described will not have a sufficiently "long run" in which to work themselves out fully. . . .

Business demand for the services of economists is booming. Why? Two business economists give at least part of the answer in explaining the work of the company economist. Mr. Burgess is chief economist of American Cyanamid Co., and Mr. Matamoros is the general manager of economic and marketing research of Armstrong Cork Co. Clearly, their major concerns are rather different from those emphasized in the first selection.

3 · The Business Economist

RALPH E. BURGESS
ALBERT G. MATAMOROS

Just what does the business economist in the modern industrial corporation do? This question is widely asked by the "captive" economist's sometimes suspicious colleagues in the academic world. The same question is probably in the mind of the corporation executive who is thinking of establishing a business research department in his company.

This question has taken on increasing significance in recent years as the number of professional economists working in the business research departments of industrial concerns has multiplied. In 1955 *Fortune* magazine reported: "Twenty-five years ago there were perhaps 100 economists employed in industry; today there are approximately 1,500. Sixty-five big companies, for example, which employed a total of only 20 economists in 1930, today have 270 economists on their staffs." This trend has probably accelerated since then.

Most business research staffs are relatively small, perhaps averaging four to six professional economists.

The question as to what the economist "does" in business also assumes importance because a company's business research staff is usually placed organizationally close to the policy makers. The company economist heading a business research department invariably reports to a senior officer of the company, usually the president.

What makes the business economist so important? What does he do? Essentially the task of the business economist is to improve the quality of policy formulation as it affects both short-term operation and long-range planning. And planning means making things happen that would not otherwise occur.

This involves, first of all, the need to determine where a company is in terms of recent sales trends, competitive position, profitability, financial position, labor relations, management development, etc. The next step is to make long-range plans which exploit the company's strengths and eliminate its

---

RALPH E. BURGESS and ALBERT G. MATAMOROS, "Forecast for Decision Making," reprinted from *Challenge*, The Magazine of Economic Affairs, published by the Institute of Economic Affairs (June 1960), New York University, pp. 55–59. Used by permission.

weaknesses. Business research plays a key role in both of these critical stages of planning.

Uncontrollable Forces

Implicit in every decision made by management is an assumption about the future. These assumptions, or forecasts, must necessarily relate to factors at work within the business such as personnel policies, products and processes. But they must also relate to external forces that are largely uncontrollable. Among these forces are general business conditions and trends, technological change, availability of resources, government policies, consumer and business attitudes, etc.

The question, then, is not, "Should a company forecast?" but, "How well will it forecast?" The business economist and his research staff gather, analyze and interpret all the data relevant to a given business situation so as to reduce to a minimum the margin of error in forecasting and, thus, in executive decision. A recent survey by the National Industrial Conference Board reveals that industrial executives who employ formal business research staffs were almost unanimous in believing that forecasting is the fundamental activity of their research staffs.

A typical corporate economist will be called upon regularly to prepare a short-term forecast of general business activity for the 12-month period ahead. Further analysis relates the general economic forecast to specific market trends which are likely to be of more immediate import to the company.

The broad purpose of short-term general economic and specific market forecasts is to provide the framework within which the sales and profits forecast will be developed. On the sales forecast rests management's planning and control of operations; the establishment of standard costs, budgets and expense control; the estimation of cash requirements; the scheduling of production and control of inventories; the planning of advertising and promotion; the formulation of sales goals, quotas and incentive programs; and the programming of labor requirements and training. The sales forecast thus assumes critical importance for the company. It is the link between the external, uncontrollable forces and the internal, controllable factors mentioned earlier.

Long-term forecasts of general economic, industry and market factors are another increasingly important assignment of the corporate business research staff. Such forecasts, which most frequently cover a five-year period, occasionally run 10 to 25 years. They provide the foundation for long-range planning.

The first consideration is, of course, the trend of general economic activity over the forecast period. The most common approach involves projections of population and labor force, the average work-week and productivity. As in short-term forecasts the purpose of this long-term economic and market forecast is to build the basis for a sales forecast.

Company Goals

Where the sales forecast is in accord with company goals, the long-range plan is built around: (1) the amount of capital expenditures required to support the indicated future sales level; (2) long-range personnel requirements; (3) the size and *direction* of the company's research and development program; (4) future raw materials requirements; and (5) financial requirements.

This is not easy. But even more difficult problems arise when the company's goals are at variance with the forecasts. In these circumstances, the company devises a long-range plan outlining operational and policy changes that are designed to bring such goals within the realm of realization. The goal-forecast gap can be closed via the new product development route or through acquisition. Both of these approaches can be designed to achieve more intensive coverage of existing markets or diversification into new markets. The business economist can influence the ultimate decision on a choice of these methods by introducing all the relevant facts, weighing them objectively and making necessary recommendations.

Business research can and does play an integral role in new product planning. It can give direction to research and development through systematic appraisals of individual and industrial consumer needs. The business economist is also responsible for estimating the total market potential and the company's prospective share in that market, as well as for analyzing the competitive factors and distribution methods.

But these are only the first steps. These findings must then be translated in terms of the profit that any new product will bring to the company. Moreover, the financial considerations of new product development must be weighed. How much fixed capital investment will be required? What are the inventory requirements and risks, and what are the credit and collection problems? What will be the effects on the company's over-all working capital position?

After all this has been determined insofar as possible, the company's human, financial, technological and raw material resources must be examined to assure that they can carry the burden of launching a new product. Perhaps, for example, the product requires a method of distribution that is entirely foreign to the company. Or perhaps the company's financial position is so inflexible that it is unable to acquire the investment funds required to launch it. Or perhaps the company's executives are spread so thinly across the organization that the talent required to foster the growth of the new product is just not available. A balance sheet of new product requirements and company resources, drawn together by the business research staff, should reveal how the company should handle the proposed development.

Another area where the business economist can prove useful to management is when mergers and new acquisitions are being considered. His principal task here is to recommend to top management the criteria for evaluating any company being considered. After these criteria have been agreed upon, the economist's role is to apply them to proposed acquisitions. Here again, the business research staff is interested in sales trends, return on investment, management strength, financial solidity and flexibility, distribution channels, technological "know-how," plant location and efficiency, the extent of unionization, the pattern of wage and benefit agreements, and a host of other factors. Business research, by establishing and objectively applying acquisition criteria, seeks to reduce the range of executive decision and thereby to enhance the probability of success.

Evolution and Acceptance

All these services—whether performed by a centralized business research department or divided among several staff groups or operating divisions—are today an important aid to management decision-making. Yet, business research, as a separate and distinct management function, is a relatively new development. The Great Depression of the early 1930s was one of the events that led to the evolution and acceptance of business research. The vast financial losses business incurred during the depression were due in part to management's lack of preparation for either the amplitude or the duration of the depression. Recognition of this unpreparedness and firm resolution to prevent, if possible, a repetition of the disastrous experience, led a number of industrial companies to establish formal business research staffs in the 1930s.

But during World War II and the early postwar years, business was too preoccupied with defense production and, later, with huge backlogs of consumer demand. Sales volume was likely to be limited only by productive capacity. With sales forecasts dictated by what could be produced, some of the impetus that had been imparted earlier to business research was lost. However, in the closing months of 1948 the strong "sellers' market" which had prevailed in many types of goods gave way to a more competitive climate. The 1949 recession revealed that the hectic postwar period of heavy consumer buying and capital formation had come to a close. With the return of more nearly normal competitive conditions, renewed emphasis was directed by industrial firms toward planning their futures.

Today, most large, progressive industrial companies employ their own business research staffs. . . .

In broad terms, the business economist serves his company as a constructive—sometimes stimulating and sometimes restraining—influence. His infusion of objectivity, broad perspective and the concept of alternatives into the decision-making process, as well as his focus on longer-term trends, have helped reduce fluctuations in capital formation. This in turn has helped to maximize profits and stabilize production and employment.

An industry becomes more complex, as the general level of economic literacy rises and as the use of electronic data processing widens, it seems safe to predict that professional economists will be in increasing demand by business.

In the next few pages, a former President of the American Economic Association and professor at Columbia University, sketches important highlights in the history of economic ideas.

4 · *The Development of Economic Thought*

JOHN MAURICE CLARK

Historical Evolution of Economists' Attitudes

1. THE MEDIEVAL PERIOD. Current attitudes of economists are explainable partly in terms of their roots in the past development of their tradition. In sketching some high points of this development we may take medieval

---

JOHN MAURICE CLARK, *Economic Institutions and Human Welfare* (New York: Alfred A. Knopf, Inc., 1957), pp. 46–60. Used by permission.

thought as a point of departure. Here social and ethical goals were frankly set for economic activity, under the leadership of the church, which had sufficient authority and power to give its standards a considerable degree of effect. It accepted the customary class structure of society, and sanctioned the income suitable to one's station in life, as against unlimited arbitrary exploitation or unlimited business acquisition. Wealth was a trust, charity a duty, usury forbidden, and exchange subject to the (elastic) doctrine of the "just price."

In the large, this thinking was suited to a nearly static handicraft system, set in a strong frame of custom and obedience to authority, temporal and ecclesiastical. Its defects and abuses were many. Its strongest point was its insistence that men were members of one body, with mutual duties. . . .

2. MERCANTILIST-NATIONALIST ATTITUDES. With the end of the fifteenth century a dynamic, nationalistic commercialism broke the bonds of medieval customary authority and ecclesiastical control. The goals of the new nationalistic states were dynastic and militaristic, with growing influence exercised by the mercantile class, who were making the first large modern accumulations of capital. A large population was a national asset. Colonial empires were sought, and managed, with a view to allowing the mother country to do the manufacturing, which would support a dense population, while the colonies sent home raw materials and took manufactured products in exchange.

One prominent aim was a favorable balance of trade, sometimes fortified by disapproval of imported luxuries. But liberal expenditure by the rich was generally approved, as giving employment to the poor, while for the mass of workers low wages were generally sought, in order that they might be under pressure to work hard for the benefit of the more fortunate classes. And a working class was coming into existence, free of both the trammels and the protections of medieval status and dependent on employment in what seems to have been a buyers' oftener than a sellers' market.

The mercantilists understood one thing which later economists ignored, and which still later economists have had to rediscover: namely, the importance of spending as conditioning the level of economic activity. They represent the earliest and crudest phase of the kind of economic thinking that seeks methods of increasing the "wealth of nations" (as they conceived it) by utilizing and channeling the "free" activities of private traders.

3. THE PHYSIOCRATS. The physiocrats (whose name signifies "the rule of nature") made a rather remarkable attempt, under the circumstances, to rescue the sick economy of France from the abuses of the decaying Bourbon monarchy. Quesnay, court physician to king and economy alike, urged that taxes should be paid by the landed aristocracy, instead of falling with hampering or crushing weight on peasant cultivators and on trade and industry. The great landowners should also plow back capital into the land, to restore and maintain the productiveness of agriculture. This idea of direct taxation was a permanent contribution to economic thinking, though nowadays we do not confine it to land taxes. It is linked to the idea of the "natural order" of *laissez faire,* since direct taxes do not distort and hamper economic activity as indirect taxes do.

The physiocrats were probably sincere in believing that the resulting increase in productiveness would more than repay the landed nobility and enrich the king. One need not take too seriously any implication that in the physiocrats' minds this was the purpose of it all. Nobles and king were the powers who had to be persuaded, and Quesnay exhibited the wisdom of the serpent in devising ways of lubricating the insertion of his ideas into the mind of Louis XV. . . .

4. ADAM SMITH. Adam Smith was a pioneer of the conception that the proper goal of economic policy was primarily the increase of goods for consumption by the common man, sold at the lowest prices the producers could afford and still have adequate incentive for vigorous production. His consumer standpoint was an antithesis to the sponsorship of producer interests by the mercantilists, who were his main object of attack. But for a quantitative concept he was forced to fall back on the total exchange value of the nation's products, though he had already concluded that the exchange values of goods are not in proportion to their use values. Another criterion was a selection of occupations under which a given capital would set a maximum amount of productive labor in motion—but natural liberty would bring this about.

Smith evidenced solicitude for those with low incomes. Increased wealth does not bring proportional increase in happiness. People who gain substantial wealth, hoping to gain happiness thereby, are disappointed; but in the process they improve productive methods, and this brings a modest gain in real income to the masses, which does count in the scale of happiness. It tends to be eaten away by a consequent increase of population; but with continuing progress wages can be kept above a bare subsistence, and this is desirable. It is well that those who feed and clothe the rest of society should be themselves tolerably well fed and clothed. . . .

A position of personal independence is a desideratum. Laws in favor of workers are always just, since they must run the gauntlet of a Parliament that represents the other classes. At one point Smith excoriated the deadening effect on workers' minds and characters of the monotonous jobs that the subdivision of labor was creating. His suggested countermeasure was education. He approved of the effect of small religious sects because, among other things, they gave more people a chance to count for something in the life of a group.

On the ground that "defense is more important than opulence," he justified some deviations from "natural liberty"; but, in the conditions of the time, a few minor exceptions were sufficient. Perhaps his greatest departure was his approval of the navigation acts, which had ruined the carrying trade of Britain's rival, Holland. His many-sided thinking included some mercantilist elements. He did not question the "natural right" of landowner and capitalist-employer to their shares of the product at their "natural levels," which in the case of capitalist-employers meant the necessary supply price of capital and enterprise. But his arguments for individualism were not applied to joint-stock companies.

As the physiocrats spoke for a sick economy in which agriculture was basic, and the mercantilists spoke for trade and protected manufactures, Smith spoke, in the infancy of the industrial revolution, for a freely balanced economy in which manufacturing was the most dynamic element, needing no leading strings. . . .

5. BENTHAM. Bentham rejected intuitive concepts of natural right as a standard of appraisal and insisted that insti-

tutions should justify themselves by a rational scrutiny of their results. These were to be measured by maximum happiness, conceived as an algebraic sum on a scale of pleasure and pain, which in turn are the things which people actually seek or avoid. The task of the legal framework of economic life is, by rules of general application, to prevent people from pursuing their interests to the injury of others, leaving them free to pursue them in any other way. Since each is supposed to pursue his own interest more faithfully than others can be trusted to do it for him, this system leads to the maximum result. Thus Bentham laid the basis for a more rationalistic and doctrinaire system of *laissez faire* than did Smith. But it was built of elements that could lead, equally rationally, to quite different results; partly because law could not perform, or closely approximate, the miracle which the Benthamite system required.

In the Benthamite social sum of happiness every person counted as one; and Bentham assumed that the pleasures of different persons could be compared and added. He felt that this, while not strictly accurate, came nearer to the truth than any other practicable assumption; furthermore, without it his whole social mechanics of happiness became impossible. It afforded a strong case for distribution according to need; but he rejected this on the ground that it was more important to promote a progressive increase in the total income, through the stimulus afforded by the assurance that the person investing capital and assuming risk would reap the rewards that might come from ownership of the results. . . .

Bentham laid the basis for economics as a science of subjective feelings. And his optimistic confidence in the possibility of devising institutions as mechanisms to produce calculated results has been irresistibly attractive, despite difficulties and disappointments. This view of institutions has refused to stop with *laissez faire,* and has moved on to new deals and collectivist utopias. The Benthamite idea of the negative function of law—the "policeman state" (not to be confused with the totalitarian "police state")—has been buried under the growth of more positive state activities.

6. MALTHUS. Malthus's *Essay on Population* gave currency to the idea that limiting population was a prerequisite to any large and lasting raising of the standard of living of the masses, together with considerable skepticism as to the feasibility of such large improvements. With this went a hardening of poor-law policy. In a more general way he may be said to have established, as a characteristic of the economic profession, the principle of hard-headed exclusion from economic goals of anything seen not to be feasible. (But some of the things that economists proved impracticable have subsequently come to pass.)

After Napoleon's blockade Malthus wanted England to be less dependent on imported food, and to that end he favored moderate agricultural protection. He also had the hardihood to suggest the need for a due balance between saving and consumption, and the possibility that saving might go too far. . . .

7. RICARDO. From our present standpoint, perhaps, Ricardo's chief impact was to reinforce the classical tendency to hold that ambitions for social betterment are narrowly limited by economic laws, which are independent of human institutions and which society transgresses at its peril. He emphasized national net income—surplus above subsistence—as an objective measuring of a country's power to pay taxes and to

support a war. Cheap food would increase this margin, resulting in lower money wages without reducing real wages; and on this ground he opposed agricultural protection. But his recommendations on policy are frequently bare of explanation of the criteria that underlie them.

8. JOHN STUART MILL. John Stuart Mill represented a transition from Benthamite-Ricardian orthodoxy to broader conceptions of human values, of institutions, of what is feasible, and of what government can and should undertake to do. Raising of real wages by trade-union action would be desirable if possible, but it is impossible (wages being limited by the ratio between the working population and the wages fund). In other ways, however, working with and not against economic law, gains may be made; and some of these may be substantial enough to become embodied in the standards of living which people will protect by restricting their birthrate, and may thus be perpetuated, in the face of the Malthusian law of population.

Mill sought to escape from the fatalism of economic laws independent of human institution, searching for an area of laws that were matters of human institution and therefore modifiable. His charter of justified functions of government accepts private activity as the general rule. But Bentham, in the act of defining the logical basis of *laissez faire*, had also provided Mill with opportunity and grounds for a list of exceptions, which we can now see to be pregnant with possibilities of almost indefinite expansion under changed conditions or changed attitudes. His specific suggestions were modest, and his chief restriction was that only highly important values justify the compulsory variety of governmental interference. But with Mill, as with Smith, the presumption in favor of *laissez faire* did not apply to joint-stock companies.

Mill discusses collectivism tolerantly, and suggests that the decisive consideration might be which system affords the great freedom, indicating that this does not automatically settle the issue in favor of private enterprise. Another criterion is a healthy balance between the public and private spheres, in terms of the levels of ability they are able to enlist, and the scope for its exercise. In addition to the gratification of wants Mill appeared to be deeply concerned that individuals should exercise and develop their capacities in caring by their own efforts for the things that are important to them.

9. OTHER IDEAS OF THE CLASSICAL PERIOD. The thought of the early nineteenth century included forerunners of the historical school, institutionalists, aesthetic critics of early industrialism, early socialists, and other reformers. Sismondi noted that the Middle Ages afforded the security of belonging to a place in the community, a security which participants in the modern struggle lacked. The Middle Ages built enduringly, as modern builders did not. He was ahead of his time in viewing depressions as an inherent illness of the system. Fourier revolted against the waste and chicanery he saw in business. Robert Owen, successful industrialist, pioneered in welfare work and dissipated his fortune in collectivist experiments. Historical students envisioned social evolution, not bound by Benthamite specifications. Carlyle called economics the "dismal science" and blamed it for accepting poverty too calmly. But he had no sympathy for plodding utilitarianism or for "democratic" rule by the drab values of industrialized masses. He would not make them kings. . . .

The dissents influenced somewhat the attitudes of regular economists, without radically diverting their current of thought. To Marx, the actual goal of the existing system was exploitation of the workers; and the Marxian goal was the workers' seizure of the economy, without detailed attention to the ends to which they would subsequently put it.

10. EARLY MARGINAL THEORY, 1871–1900. With the aid of Ricardo's great tool, the marginal method, an answer was found to the difficulty that had baffled classicists—the apparent lack of correspondence between use value and exchange value. The solution hinged on the use value (or utility) dependent on the presence or absence of a little more or less of a commodity—a "marginal unit." Bentham's pleasure-pain mechanics could now be fulfilled in an economics of subjective values or utilities. Individuals' comparisons of utilities were accepted as meaningful, though the relative utilities of things to different individuals remained a problem, the more cautious theorists insisting that nothing can be known, scientifically, about it. (But when it comes to policy, most economists believe—scientifically or not—in reducing the inequalities of wealth and income which an unmitigated *laissez-faire* system would create.)

In the matter of incomes, the marginal-productivity theory—companion of marginal utility—rounded out a system in which, under competition, factors of production were allocated where they would be most productive, and their owners, including laborers, received the worth of their marginal contribution to the joint product. And this is not without an ethical element, though few would claim that it settles all ethical problems. . . .

Under this theory, the bulk of the gain from improvements was seen as filtering rather quickly through to the workers (manual and directive) while business kept as profits no more than the minimum needed to attract capital and afford enterprise the necessary incentive to take the risks of pioneering. The industrial revolution in the Western world had progressed to the point of emancipating this area from the pressure of population as an insuperable barrier to prospects of progressive raising of the level of living of the masses. This and many related values were lifted out of the limbo of the unattainable, and became accepted goals of endeavor. Thus the tone of the period was optimistic.

The individual worker had the responsibility, as well as the opportunity, of finding employment and keeping it by satisfactory performance in a competitive struggle with others. It was assumed that he could always find some job, at some rate of pay. It was only later that this view was progressively altered by the impact of cycles of mass unemployment, arising from causes largely inherent in the business system and beyond the power of individual workers to remove.

The marginal economists were, however, moving in the direction of a moderate interventionism. They prevailingly viewed the system of private enterprise as basically sound, though with particular defects. These should be remediable by piecemeal methods, which would not alter the fundamental character of the system. Like John Stuart Mill, they found exceptions to the *laissez-faire* theory, or necessary conditions unfulfilled; and the exceptions multiplied. Nevertheless, a good deal—though not all—of the public intervention which was approved could be characterized as trying to make the actual system work more nearly like the ideal model of free and fluid competition. With limitations, this was accepted as the most pertinent economic objective for a society made up mostly of everyday human beings, neither saints, geniuses, nor criminals; ready to give value for value received but not to make a charity of business; people with many and important generous impulses, but people to whom the most dependable stimuli to daily toil were stimuli of self-interest.

. . . The story reflects the liberation of great productive forces by an individualism, not wholly undisciplined, but often ignorantly disruptive of the values of the society it replaced. Then came belated recognition that something more was needed, and attempts to rectify defects and abuses. As we go on into the twentieth century, this movement gathers momentum, until ways of thinking are surprisingly transformed.

The Current Century: Moving Toward a New Balance Between Individual, Group, and Community

INSTITUTIONAL THEORY. While piecemeal exceptions to *laissez faire* multiplied in the realm of policy, so also did divergent heterodoxies in the realm of theory. The term "institutionalism" has been applied to a number of such theories, some of them having little in common except departure from "marginalist" orthodoxy.

Charles H. Cooley performed the great service of showing that the mechanism of the market, which dominates the values that purport to be economic, is not a mere mechanism for neutral recording of people's preferences, but a social institution with biases of its own, different from the biases of the institutions that purport to record, for example, aesthetic or ethical valuations. Policy-wise, his theories looked largely in the direction of making the market responsive to a more representative selection of the values actually prevalent in the society.

By way of contrast, Thorstein Veblen combined a merciless deflation of the pretensions of the business sytsem with an Olympian detachment from questions of what to do about it. His critique had much more of Marxian thought in it than Veblen himself would have willingly recognized, and it centered largely on failures in serviceability to the "material" interests of the common man. He appears to have taken democratic values as seriously as he took anything; but his final suggestion of a "soviet of technicians"—the germ of "technocracy"—was hardly a democratic proposal. . . .

John R. Commons was at the opposite pole from the detachment of Veblen. A practical crusader, his thought was frankly purposive, and he defined institutions as "collective action in control of individual action." His dominant purpose was to make the business system serviceable enough to deserve to survive; though he was not certain this effort would succeed. His main emphasis was on labor conditions, including the maintenance of employment. In the field of theory he wanted "to give collective action, in all its varieties, its due place throughout economic theory"[1]—a place which would be something more than a list of specific abuses or exceptions to *laissez faire*. With this in view he broadened the concept of a "transaction" to include social action, and added the conceptions of a "going concern" and its "working rules"—similarly broadened to include both private and social forms.

What these very different thinkers had in common was a refusal to accept the market as an adequate vehicle for expressing the importance of things to society. They looked beyond it in varying ways, according to their differing personalities.

---

[1] John R. Commons, *Institutional Economics* (New York: The Macmillan Company, 1934), p. 5.

WELFARE ECONOMICS. The reason for a separate subdiscipline labeled "welfare economics" arises as economics becomes growingly self-conscious in its attempt to separate its analysis of what actually is, from judgments of what is desirable. A. C. Pigou, in his *Wealth and Welfare,* published in 1912, proceeded on the basis of an "unverified probability" that welfare would be increased by an increase in the size of the national dividend, by a more equal distribution (unless it resulted in too great a reduction in the total), and by greater steadiness. But the use the poor make of relief funds should be supervised, or else the funds will be largely wasted. He justified, in principle, policies that would increase and regularize employment, but he had only cautious and limited suggestions to offer.

One sector of his analysis was a form of social accounting, aiming to identify cases in which a given added use of resources would add either more or less to the national dividend than to the income of the person making the outlay. He also justified some forms of negative eugenics, and raised the question whether some economic policies aiming at welfare might not have their effects canceled by a resulting deterioration of the biological stock of the population.

Two years later John A. Hobson brought out a welfare study of a very different kind, stemming from Ruskin's theme, "There is no wealth but life,"[2] Hobson did not try, as Pigou did, to isolate *economic* welfare, but asked simply, "What is welfare, and how is it affected by existing methods of producing and circulating wealth?" His answer held that welfare is an organic whole, not an arithmetic sum of marginal units of gratification; and his particular contribution lay in giving primary emphasis to the effect of the character of work on the worker. Much earlier he had ventured an underconsumption theory of depressions. Thus he put his finger on the two biggest blind spots in conventional economics. But economists were not impressed, regarding his treatment as nonscientific.

If Hobson's welfare economics left the scientific economics out, the form of theory which now bears the name can without real unfairness be described as welfare economics with the welfare left out, in a remarkably resolute attempt to meet the real or supposed requirements of economic science. Rejecting "interpersonal comparisons," this body of theory seems to end in rather complete agnosticism, aside from policies that increase the national dividend without making anyone worse off. But the existence of a single disadvantaged person acts as a veto on scientific approval of any policy—one cannot be scientifically certain that his loss does not outweigh the gains of many. Such a theory cannot recommend that we install tax-supported poor relief or a progressive income tax; but equally it could not recommend that they be not established. It seems clear that this theory has not reached satisfactory final form.

Meanwhile, no one has disproved the hypothesis that society cannot afford to let its less fortunate members starve, or that many highly important effects of industrialism are nonmarketable byproducts, so that it appears almost a matter of chance whether they are beneficial or the opposite—almost, but not quite, since men, even in economic life, have not wholly lost their moral sense, and are not completely indifferent to the diffused good or harm they do. State action is no automatic panacea. Extensions of state power have unintended byproducts also. And unmoral politics,

---

[2] J. A. Hobson, *Work and Wealth* (New York: The Macmillan Company, 1914), pp. 10–12.

like unmoral business, can fail to be directed to socially valid ends. Further, no one has disproved that if the moral fiber of the people deteriorates, and if the ethics of voluntary co-operation is submerged in self-seeking struggles, the material national dividend will suffer.

. . . . .

II • THE BUSINESS SYSTEM

The middleman gets more than his fair share of criticism. He is often thought of as a kind of parasite sucking his living from the "productive" elements of society. Here, however, a leading economic theorist describes the constructive nature of the services rendered by middlemen. In doing so, he also helps us see more clearly the essence of "production."

5 • The "Unproductive Middleman"

ABBA P. LERNER

The charge is well known: the middleman is nothing but a go-between. He is a trader who does not produce anything. He buys goods from the producer and sells them to the consumer at a profit; he is therefore an excrescence on the body economic, the profiteer, the "exploiter" *par excellence*.

The charge rests on a distinction between the "productiveness" of work and the "unproductiveness" of trade. But on what is this distinction based—apart from confused thinking?

Consider, for example, the question of the so-called "gray market," which was recently blamed for encouraging inflation. A moment's thought will serve to make one realize that the "gray marketeers" performed a useful social function; they broke through monopolistic practices and supplied vital materials like steel, sorely needed to keep vital productive processes going, which could not be obtained by any other means. Is it not perhaps because we are uneasily aware of this fact that we changed the color from black to gray?

Yet even the middlemen themselves plead guilty: often they are the first to deprecate their own social usefulness, to admit that they are parasites who not merely fail to do their fair share of work but are actually engaged in socially harmful activities.

. . . . .

This apologetic attitude is quite uncalled for. Viewed from a fundamental standpoint, the work of the middleman or trader has more than the ordinary usefulness: it consists in facilitating a socially desirable movement of things from one place to another. The trader buys something in one place for less than he can sell it for in another.

ABBA P. LERNER, "The Myth of the Parasitic Middleman," *Commentary* (July 1949), pp. 45–46, 49–50. Copyright, the American Jewish Committee. Used by permission.

That the commodity is dearer in the second place simply indicates that it is needed there more. The middleman, therefore, moves things from where they are needed less to where they are needed more.

. . . . .

Now it is common for people to understand and accept the foregoing analysis and then, nevertheless, repeat the old accusation: the middleman does not "produce" anything. He "merely" moves things from one place to another.

Those who persist in making this statement have overlooked something both obvious and startling. For what we have defined as the peculiarity of the middleman—that his activity consists in moving things from one place to another—is actually true of all economic activity. *All* the "real" or "direct" production with which the middleman's activity is unfavorably contrasted boils down to exactly the same thing.

Workers cannot create material things; they can only manipulate materials that already exist. A worker moves coal from the face of the mine to the truck which takes it away; he moves it on the truck from the mine face to the mine shaft, from below ground to above ground, from the coal-producing area to the homes and factories where it is needed. The farmer moves small pieces of earth with spade or plow; he moves fertilizer to where it is needed; he moves seeds from his bins to his fields; and, finally, he moves the ripe crops from the field to the barn. The automobile worker moves one piece of metal to join it to another piece and moves the screws so that they hold tight. The textile worker draws cotton or wool into threads, or arranges the threads so that they are entangled with each other to form cloth or joined with other pieces of thread to form suits and dresses and shirts.

Thus, since all work can be reduced to "shifting dirt from one place to another," there can be no *physical* way of distinguishing between productive and unproductive occupations. Only one significant test exists: whether the results are *useful*—how much they contribute to the needs and desires of human beings.

. . . . .

Nowhere is the special usefulness of the middleman seen more clearly than in Russia, where his activities are prohibited by law. The trader who buys screws or nails or other such small items in one Russian town and sells them in another at a profit has to brave severe punishment for "speculation." Yet his work is probably as productive as that of any worker in Russia. Many a huge Russian factory has had to curtail its work because it could not get some small items; and for these [items] to be obtained by the regular bureaucratic methods would take an unconscionably long time. The trader who illegally transports these small but essential items is performing a service of the highest importance in keeping the wheels of industry turning. Nevertheless, his critics claim that he is "exploiting" the workers when he makes a profit.

The condemnation of such useful trading as "speculation" rests on a confusion between two different kinds of activity which unfortunately have been given the same name—speculation. The kind of trading discussed above may be called *competitive* speculation, to distinguish it from *monopolistic* speculation. Monopolistic speculation consists in *creating* scarcities and thus causing prices to rise to the speculator's profit. Sometimes this is done by *destroying* goods in order to sell the remainder at higher prices. But much more important even than this destruction, since it occurs more frequently and on a larger scale, is the harm done in creating scarcity simply by limiting production. The greater part of the evil done by the monopolistic speculator thus lies not in what he takes out of the social product for himself, but in the part he destroys (mainly by preventing its production) in order to be able to take a larger share of what remains. As a result, the rest of society is doubly impoverished—first by what the monopolist takes for himself and again by the reduction in the total output.

This kind of speculation cannot be carried on by the ordinary middleman. It involves an extensive control over productive resources, for without this control it is impossible to bring about artificial scarcity and the concomitant higher prices. The competitive speculator—the middleman—has no such powers. He cannot influence prices, for he is too small in relation to the total market; on the contrary, he must accept the prevailing prices. His activity can therefore only be the moving of goods from where he finds them cheap to where he finds them dear, to the net benefit of society.

It is true, of course, that the economy could not live if everybody were a middleman and nobody engaged in direct production. But neither could the economy live if everybody became a coal miner or if everybody became a farmer.

It is also true that if there were a very good distribution of goods and services between different places and between different dates, and if this were brought about by a social authority without the use of middlemen, then there would not be much for middlemen to do. But this does not mean that middlemen should be discouraged or restricted. It means only that the authorities should try to bring about such a perfect distribution that the middlemen would be unnecessary. A perfect distribution would show itself in balanced prices throughout the economy. The middleman would then not be able to find any places where goods were relatively plentiful and cheap or where they were relatively scarce and dear. To have such a perfect distribution of goods would of course be a good thing, quite apart from its effects in diminishing the need for middlemen and setting them free for other useful activities. But so long as middlemen can make a living by competitive speculation, this stands as proof of an insufficiently perfect distribution, and shows that they have not been rendered unnecessary.

The fact that middlemen would not be needed if distribution were perfect is no more significant than the fact that plumbers would not be needed if pipes never leaked. In actuality our water and gas pipes are not perfect and we do suffer from leaks. Yet no one supposes that the plumbing situation would be improved by decrying the usefulness of plumbers and imposing restrictions on their activity in repairing the leaks that do occur. If we don't want plumbers and middlemen, then let us improve the quality of piping and the efficiency of goods distribution so that plumbers and middlemen will find little to do and will be available for other jobs. The man hours needed for all sorts of operations are continually being reduced by increased efficiency and technological advances, and they would be reduced still further by the abolition of "feather-bedding" practices. The ultimate in mechanization is presumably the complete elimination of the need for work, altogether. Yet nobody has argued that this proves that workers are useless members of society.

. . . . .

The middleman's function is to bring together the producer and the consumer. Those who do not understand his usefulness sometimes conceive of him as *separating* producers from consumers rather than joining them together, much as one might say that the mortar in a wall separates the brick rather than joining them to each other. Actually, of course, what makes the wall stand is the way the mortar holds the bricks together. . . .

Much of America's productive wealth is no longer managed by its owners. This condition, of course, is inevitable where governmental property is involved; only in the very smallest communities can the public exercise more than a remote and indirect influence upon the operation of governmental property. The problems have increased. Growth of large corporations and the spreading of the ownership of even smaller corporations have separated the owners of business facilities—the stockholders—from control. In effect, managers are often largely free from significant stockholder influence. Professor Dale of Cornell, a specialist in problems of business management, discusses some of the problems here.

6 · *Ownership, Control, and Management Responsibility in Large Corporations*

ERNEST DALE

• What happens when control of business is allowed to seep away from those who risk their capital and to dam up legally in the reservoirs of professional management?

• Have recent legal and economic trends made it possible for self-perpetuating managements to sit as judge and jury over their own actions?

• Is it now very likely that uncontrolled management will voluntarily restrict its own powers?

• Are there forces in society—e.g., stockholders or institutional investors —that potentially have the power to bring irresponsible management groups to account?

• Is governmental control over management's actions desirable?

Management's reaction to the recent Supreme Court decision in the *General Motors-Du Pont* case has been that here is another mortal blow to free enterprise. In this, they were right but for

---

ERNEST DALE, "Management Must Be Made Accountable," *The Harvard Business Review*, March—April 1960. Used by permission.

the wrong reason. The ruling was that one company cannot hold a controlling interest in another if there is "incipiency" (that is, potential monopoly). Although management's opposition stems from the impression that one more restriction has been imposed on management conduct, just the reverse is true.

Actually, the ruling endangers *free enterprise* rather than management, because it may mean *more* rather than less freedom for *managers*—freedom from the influence of the owners whom they are supposed to represent. A company like Du Pont which as a partial owner could exercise appreciable rebuttal power over GM management's decisions has now been forced to cease voting its GM stock. If the link between the owners and managers is ever entirely dissolved, management will lose the legal basis for its existence! What real claim will it have to its position unless it owns the company it manages or represents the owners?

Atomizing of Ownership

In the large corporation the controlling influence of owners was disappearing even before the Supreme Court decision. In perhaps one third of the 200 largest (with approximately 50% of total manufacturing assets), none of the stockholders owned enough shares to be able to exercise influence on management. In other words, the so-called "management revolution" was just about complete in these cases.

In the remaining two thirds of this group, however, ownership has not yet become completely diffused, and there is still a measure of control by the actual risk takers. True, the owners or families of owners who control a large enough proportion of the shares to be able to control the board of directors are rare. They exist, it may be estimated, in perhaps 10% of the 200 companies, among which are the Ford Motor Company and the Sun Oil Company. But, in a great many cases, an owner may hold enough shares to obtain a seat on the board of directors and exercise substantial though not controlling power. Examples are the Mellon directors on the Gulf Oil board, or the Block directors at Inland Steel, and until recently the five Du Pont directors on the General Motors board. Such "partial proprietors" are represented on the boards of approximately half the 200 largest companies, and the percentage is probably larger in the case of smaller enterprises.

While our folklore and textbook economic theory assume an identity of interest between management and stockholders, such agreement is by no means always the case. Both the personal financial interests of the managers and their yearnings to acquire a higher status in the community at large may tend to make them, quite humanly, think of themselves first. Especially this might be so when the actual owners are a faceless, voiceless group of small stockholders.

PARTIAL PROPRIETORS. Such would not be so, however, in the case of partial proprietors who possess substantial amounts of stocks themselves. Here the interests of the partial proprietors tend to coincide very closely with those of the other, smaller owners. Therefore they have one of the best possible reasons, self-interest, for lending their support to measures that will benefit small owners, rather than managers, and for checking any management tendency to put its own interests above those of the stockholders.

Small shareholders, of course, have their representatives in the supposedly controlling body of the corporation, the board of directors. But the directors do not always act as fiduciary trustees for the owners, and in quite a few cases it is actually difficult for them to do so. In many cases, companies have what are known as "inside boards," made up of active members of management. There may be individuals who can properly play the double role of member of management and representative of owners, but it is difficult to see how it is possible for the average manager to split his personality in this way.

Hence, the partial proprietor is actually the only true remaining legitimate representative of the owners in many companies; and if he disappears, management will be in complete control unless substitutes can be developed. And it is likely that he *will* disappear, at least in larger companies.

Individuals in a position to become partial proprietors are becoming fewer and fewer. The breaking up of large estates through division among descendants reduces their number. So do inheritance taxes, which often make it necessary for family holdings to be turned into cash. And the GM-Du Pont Supreme Court decision is likely to have a deterrent effect on companies in a position to acquire stock in other corporations. Companies are still free to do so if there is no taint of "potential" monopoly, but the danger of legal action against a corporate partial proprietor has been increased, and many companies may prefer not to run the risk.

Possible Consequences

Let us set aside for the moment the possibility of checks being exercised by forces other than ownership and competition, and consider what will happen if management in most big companies eventually reaches a position where its power over the organization is to all intents and purposes beyond review. What moral and economic consequences are likely? Will a situation like this one invite intervention from the government?

IN THE MORAL SPHERE. The essence of the moral issue is, of course, the potential abuse of unchecked power. Mr. Justice Stone in a series of opinions recognized clearly that:

> There is no place in a democracy for the exercise of irresponsible power. Where it exists, it must be broken up or directed to the public good. Those who have the power, in the words of the Constitution, "have to answer in another place" for their acts. If there is no other place in which to answer, the power itself must be denied.[1]

Any given *individual* in management, of course, can be trusted as much as any other individual to act according to high ethical standards despite the absence of sanctions of any kind. But the same cannot necessarily be said of managements in general, any more than it can be said of any other large and diversified group of human beings. As one of the foremost champions of the free enterprise system, the late Henry C. Simons, pointed out, "Monopoly power must be abused. It has no use save abuse."[2]

Even in the case of offenses for which legal sanctions exist (ordinary misappropriation of funds, for example, or conspiracy with gangster leaders of unions against employees), restraint is far less likely to be exercised if management is absolute. Where management is not accountable to anyone, it finds it all too easy to conceal the truth.

And what of perfectly legal though unethical conduct—for example, unreasonably high bonuses and other benefits for the top managers to the

---

[1] Walton Hamilton, "Legal Tolerance and Economic Power," *The Georgetown Law Journal,* Volume 46, No. 4, 1958, p. 563.
[2] "Some Reflections on Syndicalism," *Journal of Political Economy,* March 1944, p. 6.

detriment of stockholders' income and equity? . . .

Another moral hazard is the danger that the top group will fall prey to the delusion of infallibility. For the man who has no equals, only subordinates, is almost bound to be touched by it to some extent. One consequence is likely to be a tendency to enforce conformity, even in the smallest matters, with resulting frustration and unhappiness for those down the line.

And still another consequence of the absence of the moral check is likely to be the insensitivity of the chief executive to the outcome of his acts, a tendency which is aggravated the further removed the chief is from the impact of his actions. Hence it is not surprising that the head of one of our largest companies recently complained of being "a lonely wanderer on the wrong side of the fence, unable to learn of the consequences of my acts." [3]

IN THE ECONOMIC AREA. A recent study I have made, which is too long to recount here . . . indicates that in large companies economic results (profits as a percentage of investment) tend to be better when partial proprietors have a say than when companies are controlled by either independent managements, or sole owners. It is easy to postulate reasons why this is likely to be true:

(1) Fundamental business decisions—on major expansions or contractions, new products, financing, and selection of key personnel—are essentially matters of judgment that cannot be settled on the basis of figures or technical data alone. There are always intangibles that cannot be quantified. And since no one person can ever have full knowledge of all the intangibles involved, the chief executive is more likely to decide wisely if he checks with others who are not wholly dependent on him and can state their views freely.

In addition, the very fact that there will be a review by persons not dependent on him will make the chief executive more disposed to reach the best possible decision himself. Knowing that he can be called to account, the chief executive will be inclined to think his proposals through more carefully. He will then judge them more by what they contribute to the company's success than by what they contribute toward furthering his personal goals. Moreover, the outside check provides an opportunity to institute positive as well as negative incentives. There is little real satisfaction in self-praise, but the praise and respect of a group of qualified and independent associates can be very satisfying.

(2) The danger that personal goals will be at variance with company goals is great, for in the absence of an independent review the importance of an executive in his own eyes often depends on the size of the activities he manages. Such things as the volume of sales, the magnitude of his staff and his budget, the impressiveness of the company buildings and of his own executive suite, and other perquisites and status symbols may all become goals in themselves.

There have been a rapidly growing number of instances in recent years in which companies have apparently expanded for expansion's sake alone. The acquiring of new divisions and subsidiaries that actually resulted in a drain on company resources rather than in larger profits and had to be disposed of later at a loss is not uncommon.

An undue expansion of the capacity of existing divisions has been another manifestation of the same tendency in recent years. In the durable goods industries, for example, there have been a number of cases in which the forecasts of industry sales and company share of the market were based on what the chief executive wanted to happen rather than what the facts justified. The resulting overexpansion of capacity and budgets eventually produced severe losses and an expense-cutting panic.

---

[3] Ernest Dale, *Dynamics and Mechanics of Organization,* AMA Personnel Series, No. 141 (New York, American Management Association, 1951).

(3) The unchecked executive is also subject to heavy temptation to exemplify the working of Parkinson's Law by increasing administrative expense beyond a reasonable point. The more "assistants to" and staff advisers he has, the more important he seems. Such increased administrative expense, of course, may often be justified. Staff people can, and sometimes do, contribute as much to profitability as line executives. For example, a tax counsel may produce a major saving, or a safety expert prevent costly accidents.

But much of the administrative expense incurred in recent years has been for services as yet so new or so intangible that it is hard to measure thier real contribution. Certainly there is a wide margin between the potential contribution of entertainment and the amounts spent for it.

In an increasing number of companies administrative expense is greater than operating expense, and in most it is tending to rise both absolutely and relatively. . . .

(4) Finally, management inefficiencies may be hidden by a protective tariff, an "administered" price structure, a partial monopoly situation created by patents, or by the high capital investment needed to enter the industry. A company, furthermore, may be temporarily earning satisfactory profits because of the momentum established by an outstanding chief executive of the past. Thus, management may have a special source of income to which it may have contributed little or nothing and which it can use as a means of masking its own shortcomings.

In all these cases, the absence of an independent check makes it possible for companies to keep their stockholders and the general public in the dark for a long time, and even for the chief executives to deceive themselves.

Inherent Checks?

Can the potential moral and economic failures of management be checked if there is no restraint exercised by partial proprietors? Many of those who have hailed "the managerial revolution" (not to mention many of the managements that have attained a position of complete control) believe that a number of restraints do exist, and that these restraints are adequate to enforce proper management behavior.

PROFESSIONALISM OF MANAGEMENT. Often cited as an internal check is the growing professionalism of internal management. As professionals, it is argued, managers will be more and more interested in doing a good job of management in all its phases. Furthermore, the very freedom they have from pressure by owners will enable them to shape their conduct more nearly in the direction of the standards demanded by their profession.

But is management actually a profession at the present time? Professionalism requires a body of knowledge that can be taught and applied with at least some degree of universality. And it implies that the application of that knowledge will produce more or less predictable results. In support of the view that management is a profession, it has been claimed that there are certain "management skills"—planning, coordinating, controlling, and so on—that are equally applicable to any business, military, or government organization. It is also believed by many that the man who possesses these skills will be able to manage any type of operation with equal success.

But actually there has been little transfer of management skills from one major sphere of administrative activity to another—from, say, military organizations to business or vice versa. What has occurred has not always been successful, and where the transfer has been accomplished with apparently successful results, those results may well have been due mostly to factors other than knowledge of "management skills." A fortunate combination of circumstances or an extremely versatile personality may accomplish wonders.

There is even relatively little transfer of general managers from one industry to another. It is almost impossible to transfer in or out of some industries, or even in or out of some companies, and often for very good reasons. The knowledge required to fill a management position satisfactorily is not only managerial. Familarity with technical matters, products, personalities, and tradition, a type of knowledge that can be acquired only through long and painstaking experience in the actual situation, is also required in most cases. An analysis of the common qualities of leaders, based on a large number of leadership studies, found, in fact, that the one quality possessed by all the leaders was excellence in the technical specialties with which they were concerned.

Frequently the *sine qua non* in the selection of the head of an enterprise is his technical knowledge. For example, the top men in many oil companies have been geologists simply because the principal way in which such a company makes money is through finding more oil. Even when a knowledge of a specific more or less technical management function such as production, marketing, or accounting is also required, the selection of the top man will depend largely on the area in which the company's most important problems happen to lie at the moment. This is illustrated by the story of how the top leadership in the General Motors Corporation has changed over the years:

The first head of the corporation was W. C. Durant, who may be said to have invented the idea on which the corporation was based—a car for every purse. This concept required the acquisition of new capital for the purchase of other companies, and Durant was a good money raiser. After two years, a period of consolidation was necessary and a new president, C. W. Nash, took Durant's place, introducing the beginnings of systematic management through staff specialists. But in 1916, when a new period of acquisition started, Durant came back again.

Four years later, overexpansion, coupled with a recession, had brought GM to the verge of bankruptcy. To fight this problem, Pierre du Pont, who had performed similar lifesaving operations at E. I. du Pont de Nemours, became president. In 1923, du Pont turned the company over to A. P. Sloan, Jr. and a group of associates who excelled in engineering and marketing techniques designed to solve GM's current problems. When it came time to select Sloan's successor in 1947, the company's main troubles centered around union and governmental relations; thus, C. E. Wilson, who was considered especially competent in these particular fields, was chosen.

Five years later—after the first postwar demand for cars had been satisfied—marketing problems came to the fore again, and H. C. Curtice, whose main talents were considered to be in styling and merchandising, became president. Finally, in 1958, when the declining auto market appeared unlikely to resume great expansion immediately, no matter how persuasive the marketing effort, great importance was given to the need for cost reduction. In addition, the Supreme Court's antitrust decision imposed an additional technical financial problem—the disposition of the Du Pont stock in GM. Hence, a financial man, F. C. Donner, became chief executive.

Obviously, many of these managers supplemented their technical ability with the management skills of forecasting, planning, organizing, and controlling, as well as with leadership ability. But it is equally obvious that intensive technical experience in current and crucial phases of the business was also a ruling factor in their selection.

SOFT SCIENCE. The "managerial skills" and "leadership qualities" supposed to be universally applicable are as yet poorly defined. So are the "principles of management" that have been laid down by various writers. In the field of management it is rarely possible to predict with certainty that certain steps are likely to produce certain results. And the social sciences on which management must draw for aid in its strictly managerial role are themselves "soft" sciences in which there are few if any hard-and-fast rules directly applicable to the guidance of action.

These reflections on the state of management as a profession are not intended as criticism of those who are working to develop management as a science. There is a small but growing body of knowledge in the field with which every manager needs at least a nodding acquaintance. It must be pointed out, however, that while much of the research in this field has been valuable in providing bricks and stones, "the house of management" has not yet been built; not even the foundations have been laid.

This lack of real science in management is not surprising when we reflect that the study of management is at best only about half a century old, and that the other sciences took centuries to attain their present bodies of exact knowledge. Even if management arrives at professional status will there be any substitute for an external check on the authority of those in high places?

SOCIAL RESPONSIBILITY. Many of those who hold the view that management is a profession have also, as a concomitant, espoused the idea that the manager's responsibility is not entirely, or even primarily, to the stockholders who pay his wages. Rather, they hold that his job is to allocate the returns of the enterprise among all the groups whose interests may be affected by corporate activities: stockholders, employees, government, suppliers, customers, members of the communities in which plants and offices are located. Management's job, in this view, is to reconcile the interests of these groups where possible, or where there is a conflict of interest, to dispense even-handed justice.

Those who regard the management job in this way are also of the opinion that managers are fast developing a sense of "social responsibility" which acts as a check on their conduct as potent as any check the owners could provide, or even more potent.

There are two questions that may be asked of the promoters of this concept:

1. Is it possible to rely entirely on the manager's sense of social responsibility to provide an adequate check?

2. Is it desirable either from the viewpoint of the economy as a whole or from the standpoint of management itself that managers be given the broad social responsibility for allocating resources among the various interest groups?

In the allocation of the returns, of course, some portion is reserved to the manager himself—his salary, bonuses, and various perquisites, but it is contrary to all notions of equity that an arbiter should also be a party at interest. Furthermore, there is no general agreement on the exact size of a "fair" wage, a "fair" return to stockholders, a "fair" salary for a manager, and no "scientific" way of determining any of the figures. To put any man in such a position is to subject him to many of the moral hazards discussed earlier.

If managers abandon their traditional role as profit-maximizers in favor of the role of an arbiter whose main job is to keep things running smoothly, what becomes of the dynamism of the American economy? If "smoothness" and the reconciliation of conflict are the main aim of the former profit makers, who will be interested in developing new methods and new machinery, and in taking chances which are the spark of a growing economy?

Moreover, if the manager abrogates to himself authority over so many segments of the economy, he is, in effect, setting himself up as a czar rather than as the representative of one of the parties at interest (the owners) in the continuing struggle of countervailing powers.

If managers really begin to function in this way, all the various parties at interest, and the general public, may well begin to ask for a voice in selecting them. It is contrary to all democratic tradition for constituents to have no say in the selection of their representatives and no way of calling them to account.

. . . . .

Alternative Solutions

As the partial proprietors on the boards of large corporations inevitably pass from the scene, who is to take their place? Who is to serve as a check on the unrestricted authority of corporation managers? By and large, these partial proprietors (who may be aptly named "corporate dinosaurs") give us no answers. They enjoyed their role and they believed in it. Now they speak nostalgically of the opportunities they had, but feel that the world of today no longer provides room for them or for others like them.

But there is one legacy that this almost extinct breed has bequeathed to self-perpetuating managements which, if utilized, could help to keep the delusion of infallibility within bounds. That legacy is the atmosphere of free discussion which has tended to prevail in the companies they helped to manage.

FREE DISCUSSION. The practice of free discussion may, in fact, have been a key factor in the success of both Du Pont and General Motors. Very clearly it served in both as a shield against the dangers of ingrown management during the years of greatest growth. . . .

. . . . .

The tradition was carried over into General Motors by former Du Pont executives and reinforced when the GM management received a strong object lesson in the consequences of ignoring it. When GM was practically bankrupt in 1921, its management believed that C. F. Kettering's plan for a copper-cooled engine would provide salvation and was prepared to spend as much as $100 million on it. The protests of the GM engineers (some of them resigned, and others had nervous breakdowns) reduced the investment considerably, but the management held to the plan until it turned out that the engineers were right: the engine did not perform as expected. Then it was Kettering who had the nervous breakdown, and management was convinced that it should never force a major change without thorough discussion and careful weighing of opposing opinion.

Later, Pierre S. du Pont, who served as president from 1920 to 1922, established the practice of free discussion. He used board meetings, and especially the meetings of board committees, to inform directors of contemplated changes and the reasons for them, and invited the opinions of his fellow directors. To ensure against rubber-stamping, he chose as directors (both inside and outside) men who had proved themselves independent thinkers and were willing to stand up for their viewpoints. In addition, Alfred P. Sloan and his associates set up organizational mechanisms that made it possible to resolve major issues by free discussion.

Moreover, freedom of speech was carried far down in the ranks of management. In discussing proposals with individual executives Sloan would listen and ask searching questions rather than attempt to impose his own opinion. Often he would conceal his own viewpoint to avoid biasing the answers.

For example, he favored a plan—worked out by Donaldson Brown and a group of associates—to adapt production to dealers' sales as fast as possible instead of overloading the dealers. But in subsequent meetings with division managers he took the opposing view in order to be sure that none of the arguments against the plan were concealed from him. And his subordinates in turn were expected to carry free discussion down the line, even to the foreman level.

Walter S. Carpenter, Jr., one of the top group in the 1920's and a director of the corporation until 1959, reports that Sloan's methods of eliciting opinion made it possible to do many things that could not be done in any other way. "Sloan might argue his point for hours," Carpenter says; "then he would sit back and say: 'Maybe I'm wrong and we shouldn't do as I think.' And he would bear no grudge if his opinion didn't prevail." Charles E. Wilson has also commented that he could tell Sloan frankly of any facts that Sloan overlooked.

The tradition of free discussion was carried on by Pierre du Pont's brother who succeeded him as GM chairman. Lammot du Pont even argued that his vote should count no more than that of any other director and let himself be not only persuaded but sometimes overruled.

Thus "consultative management" at GM was genuine rather than make-believe and was established by the example of the chief executive. Moreover, there was an independent audit of management performance through a financial and accounting group that reported directly to the finance committee and the board of directors rather than to the president.

STOCKHOLDERS' VOICES. If ingrown managements refuse to allow internal freedom of discussion, there of course will be an even greater need to establish objective evaluations of their actions. Can the "still, small voice" of the stockholder, if he is well-informed, act as a check? Many small stockholders are well-informed and articulate enough for anyone who wishes to listen to them.

Such things as the pertinent letter (marked "personal") to the chief executive, the question asked at a stockholders' meeting, the letter to a courageous member of the board of directors detailing company sins of omission or commission evoke surprising responses sometimes. If more stockholders took the trouble to make themselves heard, they might provoke some action in many instances.

But once management has become completely ingrown, the voices crying in the wilderness seldom penetrate its soundproof rooms. Many managements point proudly to the small number of shares actually voted against them on given issues as evidence that the majority of stockholders support them. But there is probably no single case on record where stockholders have voted against management without an organized effort. In general, the stockholder owns but does not control; he elects (directors) but does not select. Hence, organized rebuttal power is likely to be effective only if there are sufficient funds available.

Securities and Exchange Commission proxy rules give any stockholder the right to present an issue to other stockholders through a statement on the proxy and ensure that the matter is brought to a vote. But the rules require only that management include a statement of 100 words—scarcely enough for the dissenter to present his arguments. Hence he must incur considerable cost if he is to circularize other stockholders at length.

Cumulative voting—under which a

stockholder may cast, say, twelve votes for one director instead of one vote for each of twelve directors—also strengthens the stockholders' hand. This is now mandatory in a number of states and permissible in others. But cumulative voting, if small stockholders are to gain by it, also requires an organized effort and some expenditure of money.

It has been suggested that stockholder rebuttal power might be made more effective by a change in the 1940 Investment Company Act and the Securities and Exchange Commission Act. This change would give the SEC power to express an opinion (if requested to do so by management or by holders of 25% of any class of a corporation's securities) on any controversy between stockholders and management made subject to a vote at a stockholders' meeting. A similar, though more liberal, provision is found in the recent Companies Act of India.

All these provisions could be made more effective by providing that stockholder representatives engaged in a proxy fight would receive reimbursement for money spent in presenting their views—up to the amount management spends—provided they could muster the support of, say, 10% of the shares on a petition.

There is, however, one major disadvantage to all these proposals for strengthening stockholder rights: the power might well be abused by corporate raiders or by irresponsible people who tend to magnify mere hills into mountains.

OUTSIDE DIRECTORS. The appointment of "outside directors" has also been suggested as a way of providing accountability where there is no effective ownership control. This is a well-established practice in many companies, and it can have considerable value for the company and its internal management. Providing genuine accountability is, however, not necessarily among its virtues.

Despite his valuable counsel and contributions, the outside director is usually beholden to and dependent on the sufferance of the internal management that appointed him. If he displeases internal management, his name is merely omitted from the next slate. A chronic dissenter may find himself quickly eased off the board with no chance to rally stockholders to his cause. As a rule, the outside director who stands up to management will find himself in the position of Pope Gregory VII, who observed: "I have loved justice and hated inequity: therefore I die in exile." Hence if management really wants an independent review from an outside director, he should be secure in his appointment for at least several years.

There are, it is true, some exceptional outside directors. There is the apparently disappearing band of the trustee type. . . . Then there is the rising group that includes military heroes, college educators, and scientists —men who have shown unusual competence in fields other than business and who are believed to have a strong sense of public responsibility. But there are large areas in which men of this type cannot hold internal management accountable because they lack the knowledge necessary to do so in any real sense. Moreover, they hold no power except through the threat of resignation, and this is effective only in the rare case where their resignation might seriously endanger the reputation of the ingrown management.

FINANCIAL INSTITUTIONS. Thus, all the possibilities so far considered must be discarded since they fall short of providing the necessary accountability. The only workable alternative appears to many students to be the replacement of the vanishing partial proprietors by a new and important group of owners: the institutional investors. These investors

—mutual funds, life insurance companies, savings banks and pension funds, as well as individual trusts managed by bankers—have always been an important potential influence. Today they are often grasped at as the shareholder's last straw.

Their potential power *is* indeed impressive. The percentage of issues listed on the New York Stock Exchange held by institutions has risen from a value of $9.5 billion or 12.4% in 1949 to an estimated $30 billion or 15.3% of the total at the end of 1957. If the equities of the individual trusts that are institutional are included, the 1958 total comes to about 30% of the value of all issues on the New York Stock Exchange.

Pension funds have risen faster than any other institutional funds. According to SEC statistician, Vito Natrella, they have grown from $5.6 billion in 1950 to $22.0 billion in 1959 or more than half of all institutional holdings, and they are said to rise at any annual rate of $4 billion. By 1965, it is estimated, they will have reached $50 billion, and more if the pension coverage of the work force should rise beyond its present one-fourth.

To these figures must be added the equity holdings and purchases of educational endowment funds, private foundations, and union treasuries. (The last have not been widely invested in equities, but they could be.) Of the 1,500 companies listed on the New York Stock Exchange, the institutional investors have large holdings in about 200 "investment grade" issues that are also public favorites. Their combined funds, and their potential power in even the very large corporations . . . [have become substantial].

Use of Powers

The potential powers of the institutional investors are impressive, but the actual use made of them is insignificant. The "new tycoons" who control these vast funds are new all right, but they are in no way tycoons. They are, in fact, frightened by any comparisons with the dinosaurs and happiest when their passion for anonymity is undisturbed.

Hence, the opposition of the institutional investors of all kinds to the use of their powers to criticize managements is extremely strong. In a series of interviews that I conducted, they advanced these reasons for nonintervention:

1. If institutional investors buy shares in a company, they *ipso facto* have to be loyal to the management of that company. Otherwise they should not have bought the shares in the first place.

2. Officers of institutional funds may lack the competence or the time to take an active interest in the management of the companies with which they deal.

3. Participation, if unsuccessful, can be blamed on the institutional officer; if he does not participate, he cannot be blamed.

4. Voting against management raises a danger that "interlopers" and "incompetents" will find an opening. Managements, feeling threatened, may appeal to the public and Congress against the "bullies."

5. The institutional officer reaches and holds his position by being nice to everyone. It he starts snooping under the president's bed, he may be "joined in"—induced to become one of the boys —or smoked out.

6. If the trust officers disapprove of management's policies, they can signify their disapproval by selling the stock.

The main error in this reasoning, of course, is that management does not have all the right answers in matters of interest to the stockholders. Where there is a clear conflict of interests, it is the right and duty of the stockholders' representatives to support the interest of their principals.

It may also be asked whether just selling a stock without attempting to correct a remediable situation is not actually a counsel of despair. Such an action amounts, for the following reasons, to an abdication of the accountability that is inherent in trusteeship:

1. The trustees disfranchise their numerous and trusting clients without even consulting them.

2. They act illogically by refusing even to try to improve the price of their shares.

3. If they simply sell their stock, they let others "hold the bag." Management also is then enabled to point to a shorter holding period and to claim that "continuity of control" requires that it be supreme.

4. If the financial institutions hold a substantial block of the shares of a company, say 50% or 60%, and do not vote their shares at all (and many of them do not), then any marauding group could conceivably gain control with perhaps 5% to 15% of the stock.

If they vote blindly for management, their failure as trustees will surely be held against them.

5. These trustees may invite government intervention almost by default. If the trusts do not gradually modify their stubborn opposition to the exercise of rebuttal power, and if ingrown managements continue to move into the void left by the dinosaurs, the various public authorities may well be tempted to fill the vacuum.

VOICE FUNDS. Some of the institutional investors have, it is true, started to realize their obligations. Gingerly and cautiously they are beginning to ask questions, and if any kind of managerial sensitivity exists, searching questions and moral persuasion can lead to a subtle exercise of rebuttal power. Analysts for some funds have taken to calling on companies in which sizable amounts of stocks are held or additions to the portfolios are contemplated and asking some fairly sharp questions about various phases of the company's operations. Thus:

For example, one analyst recently asked the officer of one big Connecticut firm why it continued pouring money into a division that was a steady money loser. Apparently the question was asked by analysts from other groups having a position in the company's stock—mutual funds, investment companies and insurance firms. Before long, the company got rid of that division.[4]

In some cases, too, trustees have worked hard on a management for years and resigned only when their persuasion got nowhere—as the J. P. Morgan directors did at Montgomery Ward. In still other instances, trustees have been forced to take sides in proxy fights even though they were very reluctant to commit themselves, as was the Chase Manhattan Bank when confronted with a choice between an incumbent management and the insurgents for whose stock the bank was a trustee.

But these things do not happen often enough. One large investment trust with many shares in a well-known company dispatched emissaries to the management when things began to slide badly. But it held on until the price of the stock dropped substantially and then sold without making an outcry. The trustees were afraid to use a club on management lest it in some way return the compliment.

Giving the beneficiaries of the funds a voice in the voting of the shares does not seem to provide a workable answer, though it is being done in at least one case. Sharp Congressional questioning warned the trustees of the Sears, Roebuck pension trust that the setup would

---

[4] *Business Week,* January 31, 1959, p. 99.

perpetuate management control of the company because Sears directors appointed the trustees (usually company officers) and the trustees in turn always voted the fund's stock for management. Now the 95% of the employees who have vested rights in the pension plan are polled by an independent research organization to find out how they want to vote the fund's Sears stock that is credited to them, and the trustees are expected to follow the instructions. But this raises several difficulties: Who will frame the questions? And will the voters be given veto power over all major propositions? Will they be provided with an absolutely impartial résumé of the pros and cons? And by whom?

Thus, the institutional investors are either going to be thrown back into their original state or expose themselves to the threat of public control. How can they escape from this dilemma?

INVESTOR WATCHDOGS. One way might be through the formation of a nationwide association of institutional and individual investors. Its purpose would be the selecting and appointing of representatives to the boards of companies in which the combined holdings of the association are large, either absolutely in terms of total dollars, or relatively as a proportion of the outstanding shares. Men could be chosen for outstanding technical competence and made independent of the companies on whose boards they serve by paying them well and having each of them sit on several boards. Salaries might be a tiny fraction of the dividends received (investment counselors' pay is already calculated in this way) or the money might come from the part of the income set aside for administrative expense.

These professional directors would not, of course, be perfect substitutes for the dinosaurs, but they might be more adaptable to changing circumstances and so have greater power of survival. They might also be able to make a contribution to the development of professional management that would banish the threat of public intervention altogether. Companies with this type of independent review might then become leaders and pacesetters and perhaps force the reluctant ones to follow suit—if not to be competitive, then at least to be respectable.

Conclusion

Having said all this, let me admit immediately that merely admonishing management to accept an independent review of one of the types suggested will appear weak to some readers. Management itself will naturally be reluctant to admit to any conflict—actual or potential—between itself and its stockholders (or anyone else, for that matter). And few persons of power are likely to accept voluntarily any curbs on their own actions. Ingrown managements, in fact, are likely to view the whole problem as one of "public relations" and attempt to provide the shadow instead of the substance. As for institutional investors, they have not so far shown much interest in stepping into the gap.

Hence, our proposals to make self-serving managements more accountable to stockholders (as well as to the public) may not be taken seriously either by managements or by institutional investors. But would the only alternative be more effective? Clearly that alternative is federal intervention to enforce managerial accountability, going possibly as far as direct or indirect government participation in the deliberations of boards of directors.

One need only recall the many government agencies that now possess powers of intervention. In some cases, because of partiality and "politics," they have been worse than the managements they are supposed to admonish. And who will then admonish the monitors? Theoretically, of course, they are accountable to elected officials who appoint them, and the latter are accountable to the general public at election time. But the connection is tenuous in the public mind, and the actions of administrative agencies do not appear to sway many votes. That is the basic weakness in the idea of relying on government to exercise independent review of management.

Accordingly, the continued admonition of management to preserve and expand the independent review of its own actions—and of institutional investors to play a part—seems worthwhile, especially since both must ultimately realize that the only alternative is public intervention.

> *When the successful head of a successful business talks to the heads of other leading businesses, his thoughts will have broad interest. Here we have an example. The speaker, President of A. T. and T., in three lectures dealt with a considerable range of problems, only a few of which are touched upon in this reading.*

7 · Management Problems As Seen By the Head of the World's Largest Business

FREDERICK R. KAPPEL

In general, a goal is any kind of aim or objective. But in the sense that I am using the word, a goal is something presently out of reach; it is something to strive for, to move toward, or to become. It is an aim or purpose so stated that it excites the imagination and gives people something they want to work for —something they don't yet know how to do—something they can be proud of when they achieve it.

Certain larger goals have particular value because they give meaning to other aims. In my own business, for example, it is an important aim to find a better way to splice a cable, or a faster way to handle a telephone call. But the work we do to accomplish these things takes on much more meaning when we are moved by some deeper or broader purpose—such as the kind of job we want to do for the nation, the kind of business we want to be. The goals that build the future are the goals that establish these broader purposes. They relate the near to the far, the present to the future, the individual to the business, the interests of the business to the welfare of the country. So they have great social meaning.

In order to see the real significance

FREDERICK R. KAPPEL, *Vitality in a Business Enterprise*, McKinsey Foundation Lecture Series sponsored by the Graduate School of Business, Columbia University (New York: McGraw-Hill Book Company, Inc., 1960). Used by permission.

of goals that build the future, I think it is helpful, as I said, to look back. In two critical periods of my business it was under the leadership of a man of great foresight, who also had unusual ability to act as he saw the future would need. There is no question that the character of the Bell System owes a great debt to this one man. I do not want to overstate this and convey the impression that one man did everything, for this was not the case with Theodore N. Vail, to whom I am referring. . . .

He was the first general manager of the first telephone company in 1878. He left the telephone business in 1887 and returned to serve as head of the A. T. & T. Company from 1907 to 1920. The present make-up of the business—a family of operating telephone companies, a manufacturing arm, a research arm, and a parent company which maintains a central staff and operates the interconnecting long distance network—this concept was largely worked out under his leadership. But his great achievement was that he envisioned a boundless future, foresaw what would be needed in order to drive ahead, and set others working according to his vision. I say "vision" because he set goals that must at the time have looked visionary, but which, as we see them now, have been largely achieved.

In effect Mr. Vail said: We will build a telephone system so that anybody, anywhere, can talk with anyone else, quickly, cheaply, and satisfactorily. He said it for years and he said it in many different ways. He said it in the face of staggering technical problems—when in fact the available technology was insufficient to permit fully satisfactory service even over short distances. To contemplate at that time the physical and human resources required to reach such a goal was a fantastic dream. Yet it was not an unrealistic dream. What was then foreseen is now do-able, and we are doing it.

The point here is that a goal that builds vitality and works for future success is not a wishful fancy. It is not a speculation. It is a perfectly clear statement that you are going to do something. I would say that part of the talent or genius of the goal-setter is the ability to discern between the possible and the impossible. Another equally necessary ability is to know how to set action going and what direction to give it.

The big goal I have described set the stage for others and generated decisive action in several fields. I shall mention three.

Every advance in telephony, from the beginning right up to now, has been based on ever-increasing technical competence. But more than that, successive advances have needed *new knowledge*. Just doing a smarter job in using existing knowledge could never have produced, by itself, the kind of progress that has been made. Yet back in the last century, and the early years of this one, it wasn't the usual thing for a business to go into basic research. More likely, you did all you could with what you had, and kept your eyes open for what the scientists at the universities might have to offer.

I think this might have been our course—except for one thing. This was the goal, the big dream, stated without equivocation—the dream of good, cheap, fast, worldwide telephone service for all. With this in the picture we had only one choice; we were compelled by our own goal, and the high order of importance placed upon it, to go into basic research on a scale sufficient to make the dream a reality. Today basic research in our Laboratories is world-renowned and nothing in our scheme of things outranks it in importance.

Second, the goal of universal service meant a single interconnected network. This sounds self-evident today, but the fact is that it was not easy to achieve. The business of the Bell System was structured initially on the basic Bell patents. In the 1890's when the basic patents expired, there emerged extensive duplicate development by competing companies in a great many large cities. There were also a few competing long distance networks. This was obviously not in the public interest. If there is anything a community doesn't need two of, it is telephone systems. But they developed anyhow.

This was a basic problem, and it was one that couldn't be worked out under existing law, because the anti-trust laws were construed to prevent the merger of competing companies. But this was not the only difficulty. Public opinion could not countenance the existing situation, where every man had to have two telephones to be sure he could do business or call his neighbor. At the same time, public opinion was dead against monopoly, and generally anti-business as well. The vista of government ownership was wide open.

In the face of all this, Vail set out to convince the people of the United States that in the case of telephone service, monopoly is good. It was a tremendous undertaking. But ultimately this view prevailed. In 1921, an Act of Congress legalized the merger of competing telephone companies. Without this achievement at that time, the telephone service you have today could not be, and we would have lost vitality as a business. Certainly our country would not have led the world in communications, as it undoubtedly has. So here again, the big far-reaching goal was building the future.

A third consequence of the goal was closely related to the second. Vail's contention was of course that the only good service would be a single, unified service, and he won his case on the promise to deliver. But in his campaign he made another radical departure from the usual business practice of the times. That is, he affirmed that the right course for the Bell System was to make candid disclosure of information about the business. The public was the boss, he said, and ought to have the facts.

So there were two commitments—one to top-flight service, and the other to provide information. Add these two together and you have the conception of responsibility to the public that has invigorated the Bell System for half a century. In its beginnings, I dare say this conception was as much in the forefront of business thinking as was the integration of basic research into a commercial enterprise.

One other development of that period was not as spectacular, but has had a most significant result. Vail set up one of the first industrial staffs. Whenever a goal was set and a specific course of action indicated, he gave responsibility for the job to the appropriate line operating man. But in doing this he also said to a staff man: The operating men who are responsible for this are too busy to do all the thinking that might profitably be done. You think about it in depth and see that these operating fellows don't want for ideas. Furthermore, you make it your business to know how they are doing in a way that I can know.

This brought us quickly to the use of control statistics, and out of these grew the highly refined measurements of performance that make possible the kind of telephone service you now get. These are among the important tools we use to foster keen competition to excel between all Bell System operating units.

. . . . .

Let me give you now [an] illustration drawn from present thinking about our job ahead.

We have always actively promoted and sold telephone service. We have never thought we ought to wait for customers to come to us. After all, you can hardly have a goal of universal service and then expect your customers to take the initiative in realizing it for you.

During war periods, of course, we have temporarily had to stop promoting and selling. But these were interruptions. The long-run tradition has always been to go out and get business.

Now something new is being added—and I suspect the public is already beginning to get a glimmer of it. People are seeing and using a growing variety of new instruments and communciation systems for their homes, their offices, their factories, their farms. Today you are reading about pocket telephones and see-while-you-talk telephones; tomorrow, to the full extent that you need, will use, and can be sold these and many other new services, you are going to get them.

What is going on? I will tell you. The Bell System has a big new goal. For more than 80 years we have been working to bring the arts of transmission and switching to the point where we could serve everybody over a big, reliable, basic network and do it reasonably well. This was the first necessity, and it has taken that long. But now we have reached that point and we want to take off from there.

So we have a new goal. I can describe it in a very few words. It is to give our customers the broadest possible *range of choice* in services available through our network—and I mean a range of choice that will be fully comparable to the choices or options offered consumers by nonregulated, competitive industry.

Of course, we have no thought of stepping outside our proper sphere in providing communication services to the public. But our goal is to conduct our business in such manner that our customers will see in the result—in our "line" of goods and services—all the virtues of competition, *in addition* to all the values of a single, interconnected service. Can we accomplish this? I am sure there will be skeptics who will raise all sorts of questions. I say, let them raise them. I know we can do it—and we will.

We have a second new goal today that is closely related, and I should like to describe it briefly. This has to do with the profits of the Bell System.

One aspect of the public image of our business is sometimes expressed like this: "It must be nice," people say, "to be in a business where there are no problems, where money is plentiful, and the revenue flows in without your having to fight for it." And it sometimes seems to us that responsible people who should know better are doing all they can to heighten the impression that we "have it made." The fact is, we are deeply concerned about being able to earn enough so that we can do everything that you who buy services from us really want us to do.

Today it seems clear to us that to maintain the vitality of our business under modern conditions, and provide all the service and the kind of service the country needs in the times we live in, we need to earn more than the bare minimum required to attract capital. We are therefore working toward the goal of widespread acceptance of this position. The public will be better served, we are convinced, when the profits of our business are in reasonable relationship with the profits of successful, progressive, non-regulated industries. This relationship must take into account the contribution our enterprise and service make to the economy and to society as a whole, and the responsibility a business like ours has to help advance the national welfare.

This view is as new and different from the current prevailing public view, as the idea that a monopoly could be good was new in 1910. But we are convinced it is sound and our goal is to bring about its acceptance. Our continued vitality demands it. Every purpose we serve requires it. We are confident this point of view will prevail and that it will benefit everybody who is served by or has an interest in telephone enterprise.

. . . . .

In our own situation in the Bell System, offering as we do a personal, necessary, human service, one of the first obligations—I'd almost say the very first necessity—is this thing I call a feeling, a drive for quality. We *must* aim to do better than people expect of us. So to begin with we must set very high technical standards and try constantly to raise the level of performance. Then to help the effort, every day we measure little variations in performance that our customers would never detect. And yet we know we do sometimes fall short, we do slip. When that happens, we aim to know about it and fix it before anyone else is even aware of it. If our habit had been to wait until somebody complained about something before we did anything about it, this business would never have gotten off the ground. And if this ever becomes our attitude, we will fall on our face.

Please understand that I am not talking to the point of how good a job we do. We groan about our shortcomings. I am simply describing a *principle of effort*. Of course this principle makes a better product than we could turn out otherwise. Of course it is good business. But it does much more than bring in business. If you can get the idea of quality into people's blood and people's bones, they are alert and receptive to a goal that is beyond their present reach. This is the hope we build on for the future. This is how we know that when a new goal asks people to stretch further, they will do it—not because they were ordered but because it is in their very being to strive for quality. And they will grow and feel good about it too, and get great satisfaction from their accomplishment.

The principle of quality is at the heart of tradition in our business. We describe it in homely, time-honored, deeply felt words—"the spirit of service." But this is not something just to talk about. It is something we intend to live by, and we do. It becomes more visible under stress or disaster—hurricane or fire, earthquake or flood—but in order to show at those times, it must be deep in people at all times. This quality in human effort is what great goals are made of. This is what makes a great business.

The second situation that favors the setting of goals is when we make a mistake. Mind you, I am not advocating mistakes—far from it. We are in business to do things right. An error is an error. It costs money, hurts the service, and wastes time. But enterprise means risk and there will always be some failure. What is then essential is to *learn* from it. . . .

I sometimes hear people say that there is just one goal—profit—that wraps up everything. I hope I have made clear how important I think profit is. But it doesn't wrap up everything. It is possible to be profitable today—or even for some time in the future—without doing some of the things necessary for the long pull. So I feel I must also ask, "What *are* these things on which I ought constantly to be checking myself?"

I would like to enumerate fifteen criteria that seem useful to me for judging whether any business is currently doing the things that build vitality. These are the product of about ten years of exploration during a course for executives in the field of credit and financial management. . . .

The list I am going to give you now represents their consensus. I shall run through it quickly, with only a few comments, and then I want to make some general observations.

The first four items cover the general

areas of financial and product development:

- Does the business make a satisfactory profit?
- Is it protecting its assets and using them efficiently?
- Is it strengthening its position in the industry and the economy?
- Is it developing new products, new fields, new techniques, new demands?

You will note that number one is a satisfactory profit. What is satisfactory? There are a number of tests, of course, but I would like to make a basic point. If "satisfactory" is judged *only* by rate of return, dividends, or comparisons with other companies or industries, an important element will be overlooked. It is today's profit that enables a business to do the things today that are needed for success tomorrow. Most of the fourteen items listed after profit depend on profit. In short, a satisfactory profit means a proper rate of return *after*—and this is the important word—*after* proper attention has been given to all the other items. If we skimp on the money and effort devoted to these purposes, the business will suffer in the future. We need a clear understanding and support of this position from every segment of society.

The next eight criteria have to do with relationships—that is, the rights and duties that exist between the business and the people whose lives it affects.

- Does the business conform fully with laws and ethical standards?
- Is it maintaining good shareholder relations?
- Is it alert to satisfy the wants of customers?
- Does it maintain good relations with competitors, to improve the industry?
- Is the business earning the respect of the communities in which it operates?
- Is it helping to influence favorably the climate in which all business operates?
- Are the people in the business growing—in terms of morale, attitude, ability, initiative, self-reliance and creativity?
- Is the business contributing as it should to the welfare of its people —in terms of their opportunity to do for themselves in such matters as economic security, health, safety, family stability, and community responsibility?

Here I shall comment briefly on only one item, namely, improving the general climate in which all business operates.

In my judgment, American business over the years has done at least as well in meeting its obligations as has any other segment of American society. Certainly our business system is not perfect. Nevertheless its achievements are great and I wholeheartedly believe that the facts justify a much better climate of public opinion than we have had. The unfortunate thing about the rather mediocre climate we do have is of course that it reduces incentives to do the best possible job, and makes it harder for a business to do what is right—right for the public, I mean, right for everybody.

I can't help thinking however that we businessmen have not been very effective in our efforts to improve this climate we work in. Are we really trying to bring about an atmosphere in which all business can operate better? Or do we tend to think mainly of our own interests? Do we speak out often enough? And when we speak on public issues, do we tend to adopt currently fashionable positions—or do we develop and state our own independent and informed opinions? I believe that when we discuss public issues, we must prepare ourselves thoughtfully and speak forcefully with the intent of making a constructive contribution. As I have said, I am certain that the facts warrant a better public view of what business does and what it stands for; but this will come about only with our best performance in all we say, as well as in all we do.

The final three items in my list of fifteen concern carrying on and improving the management of a business:

- Is the company improving its knowledge of, and control over, its business?
- Is it providing for future top management?
- Is it contributing to the available knowledge about managing?

. . . . .

One of my reasons for taking this time to talk about a common set of criteria as a basis for keeping our goals sharp is that I represent a regulated industry. We have considered ourselves different from non-regulated industry for so long that we may not have noticed how the gap is narrowing. When our successors meet to discuss such matters in a few years, they may search hard to find real differences. So I believe we should all begin to consider the common criteria by which we all will be judged.

. . . . .

I believe competitive strength in the future will rest even more on the quality of the management organization than it does today. Certain leveling influences tend nowadays to reduce other differences between competitors. Patent protection, for example, seems less certain than it did in the past. The weight of taxation and the severity of anti-trust actions make it more difficult for any one company to out-distance the field. The exercise of union power has a similar long-run effect. These trends suggest that we need to be increasingly concerned with developing strong, venturesome, competent management people.

So—whenever I am asked what is my number one challenge in my present job, there is no question about the answer. The answer is simply "people." I know it is trite. I suppose I could invent some elaborate language that would make it appear mysterious and un-trite. But the answer would still be the same, and I don't see how it could be anything else.

My number one aim is to have in all management jobs the most vital, intelligent, positive, imaginative men of brains and high character that it is possible to have. I want men who will outdo me and my associates. I want to get them into spots where their ability counts, and in so doing encourage and support their growth in ways that are important to them, to the business, to their families, and to the community. This is the way a business is built—by getting the right people into the right spots and giving them something to work for.

How is this done? First let me state a basic principle: I start from the conviction that the people we want and need are *whole men*—self-reliant *individuals*—and that everything we do that concerns their selection and development—the jobs we assign them, the way we train them, the way we boss them, *everything*—must be aimed at helping them increase their individuality and stature, their power of imagination, their ability to work effectively with associates, their independence, their command of themselves.

Perhaps this sounds as though the way

to build strength for the future is simply to fill the organization with perfect people. I guess that would be the way if it were possible. But looking at the matter realistically, I think the job of generating vital performance can be divided into two parts. One is to watch more carefully what people are hired, how they are developed, and who among them are moved into key spots. We can always do better at these things. The other half is to accept the fact that we are none of us perfect today and our successors won't be either. We must accept and respect people as they are, help them make the most of their strengths, and leave a tradition that will help our successors do likewise.

At this point I would like to make a comment. There has been a lot of talk about how the needs and drives and processes of business organizations smother individuals. The word that pops up most often in these discussions is "conformity," which many people apparently see as something evil. I think this is too bad, for in my judgment it only confuses the real issue.

Successful organized effort unquestionably depends on the power of individuals to make highly personal contributions. To make his best contribution, a man must be his own unique self and he must always know who he is.

But whenever two people come together to do something there must be some conformity. To some extent they must think and act alike. Otherwise any organized society would be impossible. There is a lot of conformity in every group effort—government, business, education, religion. To be against conformity is to be against order and for chaos.

The central problem today is no different from what it has always been. Between the need for conformity on the one hand, and the purely personal needs of individuals on the other, there is conflict—push and pull—stress and strain.

Is this bad? Of course it isn't. This is the conflict that makes men men, and it will be a sad world if we ever come to see it as bad.

Certainly some individuals in business *are* submerged—this happens because there is a weakness somewhere. Maybe it is basically in the person. Or it may be in the organization leadership which failed to draw out the strength he had. This is why I spent so much time in my first lecture talking about the organizational attitudes and actions that can weaken vitality. But our concern is not with conformity as such. Our concern is how to build individual vitality in every situation where some conformity is also required.

I have one other point to add here. Society today depends on large organizations much more than it did in the past. In consequence there *is* a greater need for the kind of conformity that enables people working together to get big jobs done. And I wonder if some of the current hullabaloo on this subject may not arise from the fact that many people just don't care for the idea that there have to be large organizations. Maybe they just don't want to face up to the difficulties of this conflict that separates the men from the boys. But the difficulties must be faced—there is no possible way to avoid them—and every man who elects to join a business must accept the challenge to him personally. He can't leave it to his company to find ways to keep him whole. He must work at it equally himself. This is what vitality is all about—the power of the individual to handle his conflict with any organization he happens to get involved with, and be a better man because of it.

Right here, I believe, is where the issue is joined in the battle for men's minds. We in the free world are opposed by a system that completely subjects the individual to organized authority. Our faith is that vital individuals, who are no less individuals because they work together for common purposes, will maintain a free society in any kind of competition.

With this background of basic principle and belief, I'll go on now to some of the particulars that seem to me most important in building the kind of organization—made up of the kind of individuals—that I think a business like mine ought to have.

I'll divide these matters into four parts.

The first has to do with the feelings of personal significance. If people are to develop vitality in a business, the work they do and their business relationships must help them achieve a feeling of personal worth. A man's career must make a positive contribution to balance in his personal life, in which family, community, church, friends, recreation are all part of the whole. When I said earlier that we want whole men, I used the word in this sense. But if these are the men a business wants, then the business must understand their need for wholeness and its leaders must show in their own lives that they have this understanding. I firmly believe that a human institution in which people do not achieve personal significance is not adequate, no matter how glittering its external accomplishments; and it does not have a good prospect for future success.

Second, I'd like to state a point of view about business ethics that I came across recently. This seems to me to offer considerable food for thought. Usually when we talk about business ethics we have in mind things like honesty and fair dealing. However the need for these is self-evident. The thought I wish to express goes deeper —and it is closely related to vitality because it deals with the obligation of managers to everlastingly grow and *prepare* themselves for right actions.

To manage is to make decisions—to choose among different courses of action. Unless we are willing to say that decisions are purely matters of expediency, then I think we have to agree that the choices we make are really ethical choices. The conscientious manager may not always be aware of this, but it is implicit in the very fact that he considers himself conscientious.

. . . . .

. . . In the Bell System, we are coming more and more to realize that the influence of the first years of work is of utmost consequence. The fact is, people learn fast—and if you are lax about helping them learn the things that are most worth learning, they will learn far too much of the opposite.

So in our business we feel this way: From a man's first day in the business, he must be given responsibilities that tax his current ability. His early years should constitute a genuine test. The company needs to know quickly how much he has on the ball. He, in turn, wants to know quickly whether the opportunities the company gives him measure up to his hopes and aims. Neither test can take place unless his job assignments are truly challenging—and I mean challenging in his judgment, not the company's.

I have heard that some companies are fearful of hiring men who have high aspirations and great self-confidence—cocky young fellows, some of them may be. Personally I think I would want to get the benefit of those good qualities they have. But I would also want to be sure that we put such a man into a work situation that will bring home to him fast how much he has to learn.

. . . People learn to manage by managing and by how they are managed.

If a subordinate does not get a true delegation—if he is not made responsible for success or failure—I am afraid the desired development will not occur. So far as learning is concerned, the essential point in the delegation of responsibility is the chance to fail and the great test of ingenuity and judgment *not* to fail. Yet some bosses can hardly bring themselves to let a subordinate really take a risk. The only cure I know for this is to bring home to such bosses that their own worth to the business will be judged largely on the basis of their ability to help people grow.

[A] basic problem is this: We need a better definition of what excellent management performance really is. This definition must include not merely the actions that bring current success; it must also take into account the things that need to be done to build vitality—for instance, the ability of managers to give subordinates a true delegation of responsibility, as I was saying a moment ago, their ability to choose people, to develop people, to set goals, and all the rest. When we get such a definition—when we have comprehensive standards of performance that describe accurately *all* that we really want—then and only then are we in the proper position to insist that every management person be judged according to what the standards call for.

By incentives I mean all the ways a company can take to tell a man how he is doing. These may be tangible or intangible, praise or criticism, a raise or no raise, promotion or demotion. The way incentives are handled ultimately determines the character of a management organization. First there must be high standards of performance, and second, willingness and astuteness in using the available incentives to bring about what is wanted. If top performance brings no more reward than performance that is merely adequate, then merely adequate performance will surely become the way of life.

. . . .

To a young man, a large company may look rather like a continuation of the educational system he grew up in. But it isn't. There are fundamental differences. The main drive of the people in a business is not to teach—although that is important—but to get the work done well. Then too, the requirements for individual success cannot be spelled out as they are in a school marking system. The danger, I think, is that a young person may not see the differences between a business and an educational system until it's too late.

It seems to me that we in business must take a good deal of the blame when young people come into our companies without realistic notions to what to expect. In the competition for top talent, we have often tended to overplay how men will be trained and coached for management careers. If some of them get the idea that all they have to do is to put their careers in our hands, this is not surprising—especially when their educational experience has conditioned them to think in these terms.

What then should we in business do about this situation? Several things, in my judgment. We should give young people a much clearer picture of business reality before they come to work, as well as after. We should watch out for, and make the most of, every man who has this self-development drive to begin with. But most important, we need to make it plain to all, by acts as well as words, that people *must* be self-developers if they are going to be successful managers.

We ought not to spoon-fed information. Let men work on their own initiative to get it. Give them assignments that call for imagination and ingenuity.

Make formal courses difficult and include a staff evaluation of individual performance. Be courageous in separating those who cannot meet the standard. In the end this is better for all concerned.

These ideas may sound harsh. I do not mean them that way. But we all know that management responsibilities take backbone. We have to have men who face up to tough problems and persist in the face of discouragement. This kind of strength doesn't grow overnight —it is a long, hard process. Some otherwise capable people never develop it. They do well in subordinate spots and every business needs many of them. But the heavier loads do require it, and this must be tested *from the start*. Any other course really does a disservice both to the business and to the individuals concerned.

. . . . .

We are immersed in one of the great ideological struggles of all time. We are so deep in it that it is hard to see in perspective. But essentially it is a contest between two quite basic concepts. One is that men are capable of faith in ideas that lift their minds and hearts, ideas that raise their sights and give them hope, energy, and enthusiasm. Opposing this is the belief that the pursuit of material ends is all that life on this earth is about. The future of American business institutions is at issue in this struggle. And I would also say—the vitality of American business may well be the decisive force. How wisely we shape our goals, how skillful we are in leadership that brings out the best in people and increases their vigor, how ably we set forth our purposes and win respect for our efforts—these things are the essence of business vitality; and these can spell the difference.

Career planning must be among the highest priority of any wise young person's responsibilities. The variety of opportunities grows. But this increasing richness in itself makes intelligent selection more difficult. Fortunately, the Bureau of Labor Statistics offers extensive help. Every two years it publishes its Occupational Outlook Handbook *and every three months a report,* Occupational Outlook Quarterly, *which provides more up-to-date facts. The selection here is from the* Quarterly—*a sample of the many kinds of articles made available. In this case, as in many others, the article is itself a summary of a longer report which the serious student can get from the Superintendent of Documents at the Government Printing Office if the library does not have a copy.*

8 · *Careers in Business Management*

WILLIAM PASCHELL

Success stories about corporation presidents who quit school and started work as messengers in their companies appear now and then in magazines and books. Such stories make fascinating reading and lead boys and girls to dream of similar accomplishments. However, ... the "self-made" man may soon become a rarity. It is increasingly difficult for persons without a formal educational background to move up through the ranks of a company to top management positions. Many modern businesses have become so complex that new entrants must, in many cases, have preparation in some specialized field. For meaningful career planning, young people interested in management positions need to know as much as possible about the nature of the work to be performed and the training required. This report was prepared to provide an overall view of the different types of management positions, the education and other qualifications required for entry, the ladders of advancement, future employment prospects, earnings, and other aspects of administrative work in private industry.

Nature of Work

Business management is one of the largest fields of employment for young men with college degrees; it also offers numerous opportunities for those with less education. Approximately 3 million salaried workers—85 percent of them men—were employed in 1959 to manage the business activities of enterprises ranging from aircraft manufacturing to zinc mining. In addition, many persons designated as professional workers such as engineers, scientists, and accountants, also have administrative responsibilities. Likewise, some foremen and supervisors in factories or offices may perform functions which overlap managerial activities. There are also large numbers of

---

WILLIAM PASCHELL, "Careers in Business Management," *Occupational Outlook Quarterly* (December 1959). Used by permission.

proprietors who carry on all or a part of the activities necessary for the management of their own businesses. However, this report is limited to a discussion of salaried management workers in private industry.

The management setup differs widely among companies, depending on the size of firm, volume and type of business, and a variety of other factors. Regardless of such differences, most business firms hire young people as management or business trainees in order to insure an adequate supply of experienced personnel to fill vacancies as they occur at higher levels. Most large companies recognize two levels of management positions above that of supervisor and manager-trainee—the middle-management group and the top-level executives and officials. In the biggest companies, a typical managerial setup would include a president, several vice presidents —each in charge of one or more broad functions, such as production, sales and marketing, or finance—and several middle or department managers who report to the vice president in charge of their area of work. A department head may have several managers in specialized areas. For example, the labor relations manager, hiring and placement manager, wage and salary administrator, training manager, director of safety, and pension plan manager may report to the head of the personnel and industrial relations department.

Middle-management personnel are responsible for operating their departments at peak efficiency. To do this, they must usually apply their knowledge of one or more specialized fields—accounting, economics, statistics, and engineering, to name a few—and utilize their practical business experience to make decisions on a variety of nonroutine problems within the framework of company policy. They must also have a broad understanding of such matters as costs, personnel practices, methods and procedures, and other matters related to their work. For example, a market research manager may have to draw up estimates of project costs, participate in interviewing and hiring personnel, and assign work to a staff of economists, statisticians, and others. As work progresses, he may evaluate and make a written report on studies made by the staff, discuss the findings with top executives, and make recommendations for changes in products, plant location, or other company policy.

Top-level executives set company goals and make major decisions on companywide policy. They may decide, for example, how the company should prepare to meet customer demands 5 or 10 years hence; whether new plants should be built and, if so, where and how they should be financed. Top company officials also make decisions on broad organizational problems. They identify the major functions to be performed, assign them to the various department managers, and clearly indicate the authority and responsibility for getting the work done. In many companies, final policy decisions on major problems are made by committees of high-level officials including the president, who, in turn, reports to a board of directors.

Where Employed

Every industry employs some management workers. However, the greatest proportion of such workers (nearly 30 percent in 1950) are employed by retail trade establishments. (See chart.) Food and department stores (including general merchandise stores) together employ more than a third of all retail management personnel. Among these workers are thousands of buyers and heads of merchandise departments, as well as many other persons who perform managerial functions but who do

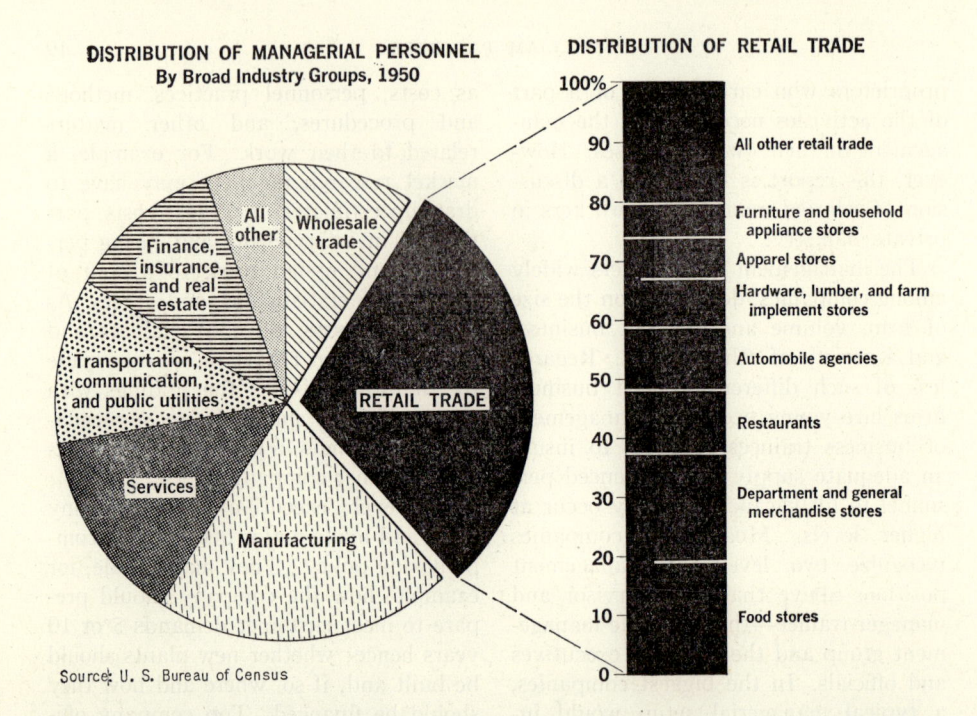

DISTRIBUTION OF MANAGERIAL PERSONNEL
By Broad Industry Groups, 1950

- Wholesale trade
- All other
- Finance, insurance, and real estate
- Transportation, communication, and public utilities
- Services
- Manufacturing
- RETAIL TRADE

Source: U. S. Bureau of Census

DISTRIBUTION OF RETAIL TRADE

- All other retail trade
- Furniture and household appliance stores
- Apparel stores
- Hardware, lumber, and farm implement stores
- Automobile agencies
- Restaurants
- Department and general merchandise stores
- Food stores

not have the title of "manager." Other retail establishments employing large numbers of management workers are restaurants and other eating and drinking places, and automobile agencies and accessories stores.

Manufacturing firms provide employment for about one-fifth of all management personnel. Large manufacturing establishments have a wider range of management jobs than do most other types of businesses. In addition to managers in such functions as personnel, finance, and advertising, which are carried on in most types of businesses, manufacturing companies generally employ managers in a variety of planning and production operations, in basic and applied research, purchasing, transportation or traffic functions, marketing, and sales.

Other broad industry groups employing many management workers are services (including automobile and other repair services, business services, hotels and other personal services, entertainment services, and educational and other professional services), transportation, and the finance-related industries.

Although the largest industries employ the greatest number of management workers, these industries do not necessarily have the greatest proportion of management employees in relation to their total employment. The finance-related industries (banking, insurance, and real estate) have the highest proportion of managerial-type personnel—one manager for every six workers. On the other hand, the manufacturing industries, as a group, employ only 1 manager for every 29 workers. A major reason for the difference in ratios is the existence of many thousands of small insurance agencies and small branch banks each requiring the services of one or more managers, whereas, manufacturing companies usually employ large numbers of workers in a plant and need relatively few managers. In addition, many management functions in factories are performed by engineers, foremen, and others who are not classified as managers.

Training and Other Qualifications

Inexperienced young people are seldom able to enter managerial positions directly. However, to an increasing extent, large companies recruit college graduates specifically as business-trainees. Each year, company representatives visit colleges throughout the country and interview students who are interested in jobs that may eventually lead to middle- and top-management positions. Although some employers prefer persons with specialized training, such as engineering, chemistry, or accounting, for certain types of entry positions, they are often less concerned with the student's major field of study than with his interests, initiative, judgment, maturity, and other personal characteristics. Leadership qualities, as evidenced by holding a class office, participating in sports, or taking part in other extracurricular activities, are sometimes given great weight. School grades are usually considered less important for business-trainee positions than for technical-type jobs. The young person who has worked part time while attending school or during summer vacations is often given preference.

A college degree with a major in the field of business administration is considered excellent preparation for prospective managers. Many employers hire persons with this educational background because it can be utilized in a wide variety of business functions. Students in schools of business may specialize in one subject field or they may take a few courses in several fields such as accounting, economics, finance, marketing, salesmanship, advertising, and insurance, as well as business management. Some universities have special schools which stress training for managerial and other types of work in certain industries, such as retail trade or hotels and restaurants. . . . There is also a growing trend in colleges of business administration to broaden students' background by requiring more courses in subjects such as philosophy, history, English, psychology, and sociology. An increasing number of graduates who have majored in engineering or other technical fields take graduate work in business administration and thereby improve their chances of being selected for choice management jobs.

. . . . .

. . . Prospective managers learn a great deal by working under competent managers who try to instill good work habits in young people, encourage them to improve themselves, and give increasingly difficult assignments to promising individuals. Through experience, these employees gradually gain the required know-how concerning company policy, operations, procedures, customer relations, and other matters.

Various types of formal training programs for management trainees have been set up by companies. The most well-defined and usually the lengthiest programs are available in the larger companies. In these programs—some lasting as long as 3 years—individuals may receive formal classroom instruction in combination with rotation among jobs in the particular function where they may work. The instruction received is designed to give trainees an overall view of the manager's job and an understanding of how the work of the different sections in a department fits together to produce results. In training for marketing, for example, trainees may first attend lectures in order to become acquainted with overall company policies, procedures, and operations. They are then given on-the-job assignments in specific areas such as market research, product planning, sales, or advertising. Experienced managers supervise and rate the trainees, and make suggestions for improving the quality of their work.

Training for experienced managers is available from many different sources —within companies, at colleges and universities, and in special courses sponsored by various organizations. Executives of many companies participate in the training program of the American Management Association (AMA)—the largest professional management organization. The AMA conducts a continuing educational program for managers at all levels, ranging from lecture and workshop-type meetings lasting a few days to formal classroom courses lasting several weeks. . . . The Society for the Advancement of Management (SAM) also sponsors educational-type meetings to help train managers. Membership in this Society is open to experienced managers in regular chapters. The Society also has chapters for students on college and university campuses. The American Institute of Management (AIM) is an organization which sponsors programs primarily of interest to experienced management personnel. Other professional organizations and trade associations distribute literature and sponsor meetings, conferences, and specialized training activities for managerial personnel, in a variety of industries and occupational fields. Active participation in such programs is valuable to managers not only because of knowledge that may be gained but also because of the contacts that may be made with businessmen in other companies.

Promotion to higher level management positions depends not only on the educational preparation and demonstrated ability of the individual, but also on his personal characteristics. Since an important aspect of the management function is getting work done through the efforts of others, the successful administrator must have outstanding leadership qualities and be able to get along well with people. Sometimes special personality tests are given the employees being considered for promotion, and several supervisors or managers may interview the candidates.

The rate of promotion in management positions depends also on the number of openings which may arise within a company as a result of expansion and turnover among experienced management personnel. Frequently, young people in large companies receive their first promotion within a year or two after completing management training programs. However, it usually takes several years to advance to a middle-management position involving considerable responsibility. The best opportunities for promotion are generally in companies that have a number of plants or branches in different areas, and in those that are expanding rapidly.

Employees may be promoted in one function, such as in a series of increasingly responsible accounting jobs, or, if they show special aptitudes, they may be transferred and advanced among different functions—personnel work, marketing, and public relations, for example. A typical line of promotion in a big company is from a supervisory job in a section to assistant department manager, department head, assistant division director or manager, and division director or manager, with the possibility of further promotion to vice president and, for some outstanding individual, to company president. Able managers with broad contacts may shift to better jobs in other firms, in the same or other industries.

Growth in Employment of Management Workers

In the past 20 years, employment of managers and related workers in private industry has more than doubled. . . . In the past 5 years (1954–59), managerial employment has increased by about 25 percent, a rate 3 times greater than for total nonfarm employment.

The rapid increase in the employment of managers and other salaried administrative personnel is largely the result of the enormous expansion in the size of business firms. The growth of companies and the establishment of many branches have reflected the demands of a rapidly increasing urban population for more products and services. As business enterprises become larger and establish more plants, they tend to employ higher proportions of management personnel. In 1940, slightly less than 4 percent of all nonfarm workers were in management positions; in 1959, approximately 5 percent were in this type of work.

In general, the larger and more complex a company becomes, the more specialized are its management functions. For example, a large firm needs specialists to control its fiscal department, direct personnel and industrial relations activities, guide research programs, plan and develop additional branches, locate new markets, organize advertising and other publicity projects, and give legal counsel, as well as to manage the various departments concerned more directly with production and distribution.

The growth in managerial occupations has been accompanied by an increase in the number of women entering this type of work. During the 1940's, employment of women in management positions grew at a rate twice that for men. . . . Major factors contributing to the increase in the employment of women managers were rising levels of economic activity, the greater participation of women in all types of employment, and the shortage of male workers during the World War II period. The largest area of employment for women managers is in retail trade which, in 1950, provided jobs for more than 100,000 female managerial workers, or over 40 percent of all women managers. . . .

Employment Outlook

Employment opportunities are expected to be very good during the early 1960's for young people to enter and advance in management careers. Many openings will arise in new and rapidly expanding functions and industries. There will also be numerous opportunities for management trainees in established areas of business activity. Among the major factors underlying this favorable outlook are the anticipated rise in population, economic growth, and continuing increase in the size of companies; emergence of new products, markets, and even new industries; and the ever-increasing complexity and specialization of managerial functions. Businessmen, keenly aware that successful competition depends largely on the competence of management staffs, are expected to hire and train many thousands of young people each year and promote them to managerial positions.

If the recent high rate of employment growth of salaried managers in private industry continues, more than 100,000 managers will be employed in new jobs each year, on the average, during the early part of the 1960 decade. Moreover, additional thousands will be needed annually to fill vacancies arising from turnover. Such vacancies occur mainly among young management workers who are not suited for this type of work, and among older managers who retire or die. The average age of managers is higher than for any other salaried occupational group. It is estimated that between 50,000 and 75,000 managers will be required annually for the next several years just to replace those who die or retire. The vacancies will provide advancement mainly for experienced managers. Nevertheless, for every manager promoted, a vacancy is usually created farther down the managerial ladder.

The most rapid advancement and the best managerial jobs will, in most cases, go to college graduates who have the necessary personal qualifications, including evidence of leadership, drive, imagination, integrity, and skill in human relations. Graduates of schools of business administration are expected to continue to be in strong demand for managerial jobs, particularly in such areas as finance, marketing, and purchasing. However, graduates with degrees in the liberal arts, law, and many other subject fields will also continue to find opportunities in a number of management-type jobs.

Demand is expected to be above average for college graduates with majors in scientific and engineering fields who also have the qualities necessary for good administrators. An important factor in the employment outlook for this group is the likely continuation of a high level of expenditures for research and development work.

A growing number of women are expected to enter management occupations in private industry. However, their employment in this area of work is likely to remain limited owing to the fact that many women do not stay in the labor market long enough to make a career in management. . . . Business firms are reluctant to train either men or women for management positions unless they plan to stay with the company.

. . . . .

Earnings and Working Conditions

Starting salaries averaged nearly $5,000 a year for business trainees hired by large companies in mid-1959, according to reports from college placement officials. Most beginning salaries were within the range of $4,500 to $5,500 in large firms. Men with advanced degrees in business administration—especially those who also had bachelor's degrees in engineering, mathematics, or science—generally received premium starting salaries.

A private survey indicated that an average annual salary of about $7,600 was earned in 1958 by graduates in business administration who had started in beginning jobs 5 years earlier. According to limited reports, persons with considerable experience who were employed in such jobs as production manager, plant manager, district sales manager, tax department manager, public relations manager, or manager in charge of electronic data-processing earned salaries of about $10,000 in small companies up to about $25,000 in large companies in 1958. Salaries of managers in a few large companies were between $30,000 and $40,000 annually. Within each company there may be a difference of several thousand dollars between the lower and upper limits of pay for a particular type of management position; pay raises within this range generally depend on how well an individual performs his job.

Earnings of top executives depend largely on company size and sales volume. The highest paid executive—usually the company president—may receive total compensation (including salary and bonus) of $50,000 to $75,000 a year in companies with an annual sales volume between $50 and $75 million, and from $100,000 to $150,000 in firms with annual sales between $300 and $500 million. Only a few top executives in giant industrial corporations earned more than $300,000 (before taxes) in 1958. Top executives having overall charge of functions such as marketing, sales, or engineering generally receive compensation amounting to from one-third to one-half that of the company president. . . . Compensation levels of high-ranking management officials, especially the amounts paid as bonuses, are greatly affected by a company's profits; bonuses normally average about 45 percent of salary.

Management trainees usually work the standard workweek of the company —generally from 35 to 40 hours a week. When assigned to more responsible jobs, they often work extra hours to handle nonroutine assignments. They may make special reports, attend special meetings, deal with customers, or travel for the company on their own time. Trainees receive paid holidays and generally are given 2 weeks' annual vacation with pay. Related benefits generally include life insurance, hospitalization and surgical insurance, and pensions. Many companies pay tuition and other fees for managers who enroll in specialized education and training programs. A number of companies also provide free recreational facilities to company officials.

Company executives are usually reimbursed for expenses arising in the conduct of business matters, for example, amounts spent for hotel bills, transportation on business trips, customer entertainment, and secretarial services. Employers often provide a company car or pay taxi fares for local trips and many even provide a company plane for travel about the country. The working arrangements of managers and executives usually reflect the prestige of their position. For example, a beginning management worker may share an office with other management workers and have letters and reports typed in a central stenographic pool. On the other hand, a higher level manager or executive may have his own well-furnished office, a private secretary, a receptionist, and other office assistants.

Men and women in important company positions frequently add to their own prestige and to that of their companies by becoming active in community organizations, trade associations, professional societies, and other organizations. They may give speeches, help on special projects such as fund-raising campaigns, write articles for the organization's magazine, or be active in other ways. As a result of the broad contacts made in such activities, executives sometimes receive job offers which may advance their careers.

Leading corporations, and many which are of only modest size, publish considerable information about their affairs. What can one expect to find in the typical financial statements? How can one go about using the data? It is questions such as these which the New York Stock Exchange attempts to answer in one of its many booklets of information.

9 · How to Understand Corporate Financial Statements

NEW YORK STOCK EXCHANGE

The Annual Report

The annual report is an account of American industry in action. It is economics come to life. The annual report records the past, reflects the present and often looks to the future.

For thoughful Americans who are interested in the corporate enterprises which produce a large share of the nation's goods and services, the annual report amounts to meaningful—and often exciting—reading. . . .

. . . For a period of many years some companies simply did not publish reports regularly.

In a way, there was little or no justification for elaborate annual reports. Corporations such as banks and mills were largely local enterprises with only a handful of stockholders. These owners were generally either affiliated with the company or else they were on intimate terms with the management. The state of business was one of the town's chief topics of conversation, and the annual meeting could be attended by nearly everyone. Under these circumstances, an annual report no bigger than a single sheet containing the financial statement sufficed.

But as the times began to change, the need for more complete reports was obvious. Corporations expanded, capital needs increased, the number of shareowners grew far beyond the boundaries of a particular region. The expense or trouble of attending an annual meeting, especially for smaller stockholders, hardly seemed worthwhile.

Financial Statements

At the turn of the century the Stock Exchange got the first industrial company to agree to publish an annual statement. The report would include statements of income and expenditures, along with a balance sheet showing a statement of the company's condition. An age of greater financial disclosure had set in. One after the other, companies listed on the Stock Exchange brought out annual reports. Companies which wanted to qualify for listing agreed to publish reports of their earnings, and the Exchange gradually applied more rigid requirements. Later, the Securities and Exchange Commission adopted

---

NEW YORK STOCK EXCHANGE, "How to Understand Financial Statements" (New York: 1959). Used by permission.

similar rules to protect the investors of companies registering under the Securities Acts.

. . . . .

... And anyone—whether he owns securities or not—can usually obtain an annual report merely by mailing a written request to the company.

Financial Ratios

In this booklet the items in the balance sheet and income account of a hypothetical company are explained and a running commentary highlights the results in the year of the annual report and the preceding year. Some significant financial ratios often used in analysis appear under "7 Keys to Value." These ratios are developed from the company's financial statements.

Sometimes there is disagreement on the conclusions which can be drawn from an interpretation of these financial ratios. Moreover, investment analysis naturally takes into account many other factors concerning the industry, company and security under consideration. In fact, financial ratios themselves vary among different industries and the significance of the various ratios may change from time to time.

Since financial statements covering a single year are not by themselves especially meaningful, two successive statements are employed for the purpose of our hypothetical study. Most annual reports now include statements for both the current and the previous year, and in many instances summaries for 5-to-10 year periods are provided. By measuring one against another, a pattern may emerge that can be helpful to the investor.

As professionals in the financial community realize, both the income account and balance sheet must be carefully analyzed. All too often people get a distorted picture by reviewing only the earnings statement. What may appear to be "good" earnings may not be especially healthy if the company concerned has borrowed too heavily. Similarly an improvement in earnings may not necessarily be commensurate with additional investments which have been made.

. . . . .

Assets

CURRENT ASSETS

Your Company had current assets on December 31, 1959 of $48.4 million—"current" because they may be turned into cash more readily than fixed assets.

Cash requires no explanation. The bulk will be in the form of bank deposits.

Receivables are usually amounts due from customers for goods sold or services rendered. In different industries, the ordinary terms of payment vary. It is conservative practice to set up a reserve to cover any amounts that may not be collectible.

Inventories are the raw materials, work in process, supplies used in operations and the finished goods ready for sale. Sometimes these items are shown separately. Since the value of inventories changes with price fluctuations, it is important to know how the inventories are valued. Statements usually indicate the basis, which generally is cost or current market price, whichever is lower. This method avoids overstating earnings and assets as a result of sharp increases in prices on the commodity markets.

A steady drop in the relation of sales to inventories, the so-called "inventory turnover" many be a warning: (a) that inventories are too heavy for the best results, adding to the dangers from falling prices; (b) in the case of merchandising companies sales policy is not aggressive enough; (c) buying is not skillful and a large part of the goods on the shelves may depreciate in value

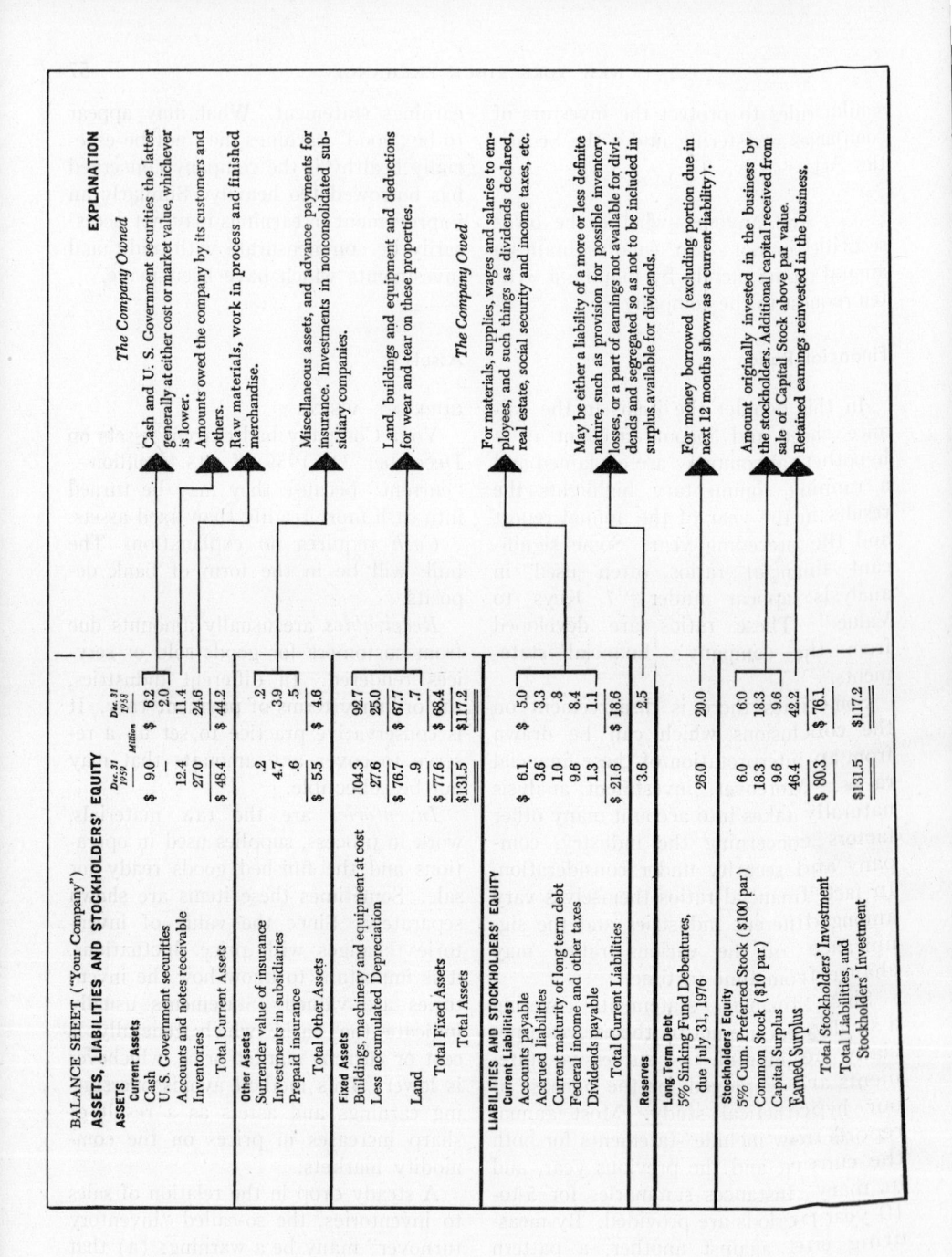

BALANCE SHEET ("Your Company")
ASSETS, LIABILITIES AND STOCKHOLDERS' EQUITY

ASSETS	Dec. 31 1959 Million	Dec. 31 1958
Current Assets		
Cash	$ 9.0	$ 6.2
U. S. Government securities	—	2.0
Accounts and notes receivable	12.4	11.4
Inventories	27.0	24.6
Total Current Assets	$ 48.4	$ 44.2
Other Assets		
Surrender value of insurance	.2	.2
Investments in subsidiaries	4.7	3.9
Prepaid insurance	.6	.5
Total Other Assets	$ 5.5	$ 4.6
Fixed Assets		
Buildings, machinery and equipment at cost	104.3	92.7
Less accumulated Depreciation	27.6	25.0
	$ 76.7	$ 67.7
Land	.9	.7
Total Fixed Assets	$ 77.6	$ 68.4
Total Assets	$131.5	$117.2
LIABILITIES AND STOCKHOLDERS' EQUITY		
Current Liabilities		
Accounts payable	$ 6.1	$ 5.0
Accrued liabilities	3.6	3.3
Current maturity of long term debt	1.0	.8
Federal income and other taxes	9.6	8.4
Dividends payable	1.3	1.1
Total Current Liabilities	$ 21.6	$ 18.6
Reserves	3.6	2.5
Long Term Debt		
5% Sinking Fund Debentures, due July 31, 1976	26.0	20.0
Stockholders' Equity		
5% Cum. Preferred Stock ($100 par)	6.0	6.0
Common Stock ($10 par)	18.3	18.3
Capital Surplus	9.6	9.6
Earned Surplus	46.4	42.2
Total Stockholders' Investment	$ 80.3	$ 76.1
Total Liabilities, and Stockholders' Investment	$131.5	$117.2

EXPLANATION

The Company Owned

Cash and U. S. Government securities the latter generally at either cost or market value, whichever is lower.

Amounts owed the company by its customers and others.

Raw materials, work in process and finished merchandise.

Miscellaneous assets, and advance payments for insurance. Investments in nonconsolidated subsidiary companies.

Land, buildings and equipment and deductions for wear and tear on these properties.

The Company Owed

For materials, supplies, wages and salaries to employees, and such things as dividends declared, real estate, social security and income taxes, etc.

May be either a liability of a more or less definite nature, such as provision for possible inventory losses, or a part of earnings not available for dividends and segregated so as not to be included in surplus available for dividends.

For money borrowed (excluding portion due in next 12 months shown as a current liability).

Amount originally invested in the business by the stockholders. Additional capital received from sale of Capital Stock above par value.
Retained earnings reinvested in the business.

58

STATEMENT OF INCOME

	Year Ended December 31	
	1959	1958
	Million	
SALES	$115.8	$110.0
Less:		
Costs and Expenses:		
Cost of goods sold	74.8	73.2
Selling, general and administrative expenses	14.2	13.0
Depreciation and depletion	4.2	3.5
	$ 93.2	$ 89.7
Operating Profit	$ 22.6	$ 20.3
Interest Charges	1.3	1.0
Earnings before Income Taxes	$ 21.3	$ 19.3
Provision for Federal and State Taxes on Income	11.4	9.8
Net Income for the Year	$ 9.9	$ 9.5
Dividend on Preferred Stock	.3	.3
Balance of Net Income Available for Common Stock	$ 9.6	$ 9.2

EXPLANATION

→ Amount received or receivable from customers.

→ Part of income used for wages, salaries, raw materials, fuel and supplies and certain taxes.

→ Part of income used for salesmen's commissions, advertising, officers' salaries and other general expenses.

→ Provision from income for the reduction of the service life of machinery and buildings and the use of minerals in mines.

→ The remainder after deducting the foregoing expenses from sales, but before providing for interest charges and taxes.

→ Amount required for interest on borrowed funds.

→ Amount paid or payable for taxes.

→ This amount was earned for stockholders.

→ Amount paid to preferred stockholders.

→ Amount remaining for common stockholders.

STATEMENT OF EARNED SURPLUS

	Year Ended December 31	
	1959	1958
	Million	
Balance at beginning of year	$ 42.2	$ 37.6
Add – Net Income for the year	9.9	9.5
	52.1	47.1
Less Dividends Paid on		
Preferred Stock	.3	.3
Common Stock	5.4	4.6
Balance at End of Year	$ 46.4	$ 42.2

→ Surplus or retained earnings reinvested in the business. Usually not all of the year's earnings can be paid out in dividends, a part being retained in the business for expansion or other purposes.

59

because of shifts in public taste or style.

There are a number of methods of valuing inventories. The most widely used is the first-in-first-out method, in which it is assumed that the oldest items are used or sold before later purchases or productions. Unavoidably, this method leads to the inclusion in income of unrealized appreciation in the value of inventories when commodity prices are rising. This increase is sometimes known as inventory profits or "fool's profits" because if rising prices are followed by a fall the price appreciation may never be realized.

To cushion the impact of rapid price changes, the last-in-first-out method (LIFO) of inventory valuation has been adopted by many companies. LIFO is intended principally to match current costs against current revenues. Sales are costed on the basis of inventory acquired most recently, or last-in, while first-in inventory is regarded as unsold. Consequently, in a period of rising prices, LIFO results in the application of a higher unit cost to items sold and a lower unit cost to inventory still unsold. The converse is true in a period of falling prices.

The rate of inventory turnover varies considerably among different industries. It is much higher in foods and automobiles, for example, than in tobacco or farm machinery.

Your Company's current assets increased during the year by $4.2 million mainly because of a $2.4 million increase in inventories and a $1.0 million rise in receivables. Normally these increases would result from a larger dollar sales volume due to the sale of a larger number of units, to higher prices, or to a combination of both.

Studies of industrial companies that failed showed that the proportion of total current assets to fixed assets usually declined persistently. In other words, it may not be wise to expand plant facilities at the sacrifice of current assets.

Fixed Assets, Buildings, Machinery and Equipment (less accumulated depreciation)— Land

Your Company has plants in Connecticut, Ohio and North Carolina, but all are lumped together in the balance sheet. This item includes the structures, the machinery and equipment, and such assets as tools and motor vehicles.

Except for land, fixed assets have a limited useful life. Each year a provision is made for depreciation due to wear and tear so the value of the assets will not be overstated.

Usually, gross fixed assets are carried at cost, although such cost usually will be different than the sum for which they could be sold.

An increase in fixed assets is the expected companion of expansion and increased sales. Also, an additional investment in equipment may be made, or new plants built, to cut costs.

If a large gain in fixed assets is not followed by a more or less corresponding gain in sales, management may have overestimated the ability to sell a larger volume of goods, or the industry may have reached overcapacity. However, if a company's fixed assets show little change for several years during a period of expanding business, the stockholder may have reason to worry about the company's competitive position or about management's keeping up with technological changes and innovations. A company often will tell you in the annual report that an addition has been made to its plants which will provide so many feet of additional floor space, and that a new warehouse has been acquired, or new equipment is being installed at a plant for the production of a new product.

Your Company's capital expenditures (outlays for new plant and equipment) amounted to $14 million, and during the year a provision for depreciation of $4.2 million was made for wear and tear. Gross fixed assets show an increase of $11.8 million.

The accumulated depreciation reserve also may be for obsolescence and may include an estimated amount for loss of value due to technological and other changes. Oil and gas and mining companies, as well as other natural resource enterprises having what are known as "wasting assets," also provide for depletion.

It would be fine if a company could continually produce and sell more merchandise, or mine more ore without adding to its investment. This is practically impossible. Sustained growth almost invariably requires an investment in additional facilities—either additional plant structures, machinery and equipment, or in the case of oil and gas companies, additional acreage for exploration.

What the investor likes to see is additional production or more efficient production as a result of capital expenditures. Failure to spend to obtain the most efficient equipment in our highly competitive economy can lead to higher costs and thus to the loss of business.

Your Company's balance sheet does not contain one class of assets, i.e., those known as intangibles because they represent non-physical items. Intangibles include good will, trademarks, patents and copyrights, among others. Years ago, it was more common than at present to show items of an intangible nature. In computing the company's net worth or the book value of the stock, the value at which any intangible item is carried in the balance sheet is omitted. It is the tangible net worth or tangible book value that is used for purposes of financial analysis.

Liabilities and Stockholders' Equity

CURRENT LIABILITIES

Your Company's debt is divided into two classes: "current" or money due and payable within a year, and "long term" debt that need not be paid until after one year.

Your Company's current liabilities as a rule are made up of several classes.

Accounts payable, i.e., money owed to suppliers of raw materials, and other costs that have to be met in the usual course of business. Ordinarily, when sales are expanding, there will be some increase in this item.

Accrued liabilities, which may represent such items as unpaid wages, salaries and commissions. This item is also likely to vary with the volume of business and many other factors.

Current maturity of long term debt, merely indicates the amount of such debt due in the next year. Often, a term loan due over a period of many years may provide for serial payments.

Federal income and other taxes include all accrued taxes. Sometimes the amount due for federal income taxes is shown separately. Through payment of local taxes of various kinds, which are not generally set forth in detail in financial statements, corporations make important contributions to the welfare of local communities.

Dividends payable represent preferred or common dividends, or both, declared by the board of directors, but not yet paid. Once a dividend has been declared it becomes an obligation.

Your Company owed $3 million more at the end of 1959 than at the end of the preceding year. Management has to plan carefully to meet current liabilities or obligations. Sometimes rapid growth makes planning all the more difficult. In recent years, a business in a sound financial position has had little or no difficulty in obtaining necessary bank credit. . . .

RESERVES

These reserves, if any, are not to be confused with the accumulated depreciation and depletion, which in the case of Your Company has appeared as a deduction from fixed assets. These reserves earmark appropriations from surplus not to be used for dividend payments. Such reserves may be set up against possible losses from declines in inventory value, or for various other contingencies. Ultimately, contingent reserves may be restored to surplus and become available for dividends.

Sometimes reserve funds are confused with reserves. Reserve funds are assets. For example, a company may set aside a sum in cash for a special construction program.

CAPITAL (LONG TERM DEBT AND STOCKHOLDERS' EQUITY)

Capital includes all sums used in the business, i.e., the funds invested by lenders and stockholders as well as the funds representing reinvested earnings. In the financial world, the term "capital structure" is used frequently and simply means the total of all long term debt, preferred stock, common stock and surplus:

The company may have raised funds through the sale of long term debt (mortgage bonds or debentures), preferred stock and common stock; or it may have outstanding only bonds and common stock, or preferred stock and common stock, or common stock only. In the last case it is said the capital structure is "simple" or that the company has a "one stock capitalization."

The point to note is that whatever the combination may be, a company *must* have common stock—it *may* have other securities. This results from the nature of common stock, which represents ownership. The common stockholder takes the greatest risk and stands to gain most from a company's prosperity. A holder of a bond or debenture is a creditor. Preferred stockholders have certain priorities over the common shareholders. The investor will learn, however, that legal relationships do not determine values. Bonds and preferred stocks of one company may be inferior in quality to common stocks of other companies.

LONG TERM DEBT

The amount included in this caption is the face or principal sum due at maturity, less any amount that is payable in less than a year. Sums repaid in the past, of course, have already been eliminated. In the case of Your Company, the original issue of debentures was $35 million which had been reduced to $20 million in 1958. A new period of expansion during 1959 involved the issuance of an additional $7 million dollars of debentures. Debt may consist of several different issues, representing money borrowed at various times and at different rates of interest.

Usually, long term debt may be called or redeemed by the company prior to maturity at a premium of three to five per cent over the principal amount.

STOCKHOLDERS' EQUITY

Preferred Stock. At one time Your Company raised funds through the sale of preferred stock. The rights of the preferred stockholder, like those of a holder of debt securities, are determined by contract. Usually a preferred stockholder is entitled to a fixed dividend before common stockholders may receive dividends, and to priority in the event of dissolution or liquidation. During the past fifty years dividends on preferred stocks usually have been "cumulative," i. e., no dividends can be declared on the common stock if there are any dividends in arrears on the preferred. Most preferred stocks now have voting power in the event that four quarterly dividend payments have not been declared.

Like bonds and debentures, preferred

stocks usually are redeemable at the company's option at fixed prices.

Common Stock. Common stock may be shown on the books at "par value" or, if the stock has no par value, at a "stated value." The thing to remember is that the par value or the stated value of "no par common stock" is an arbitrary amount, having no relation to the market value of the common stock, or to what would be received in liquidation. Market value is determined by buyers and sellers who take into account earnings, dividends, prospects, the caliber of management and general business outlook.

Surplus. Capital surplus includes such items as contributed assets or the premium received from the sale of stock over the par value.

Earned surplus represents past retained earnings, i.e., earnings not paid in dividends.

In other words, surplus is the excess of the total stockholders' equity, or net worth, over the total par value, or stated value, of the capital stock outstanding. *It is not a tangible sum or an amount on deposit in a bank.* Past earnings may have been used in part for the purchase of new machinery. To avoid misunderstanding, more and more companies no longer use the term "surplus" in their financial reports but use "earnings retained and invested in the business" or some similar phrase. Theoretically, at least, the surplus is available for dividends, but the ability of a company to pay dividends depends as much on its financial position as on the amount of surplus in the balance sheet. Sometimes, the creditors place a restriction on the extent to which surplus is available for dividends. Such limitations are usually referred to in a footnote to the balance sheet.

There is no "ideal" capital structure. Even so, the investor should be on guard against too heavy an amount of long term debt and preferred stock in relation to common stock and surplus. Your Company's capital structure at the end of 1959 was:

	Million	Percent of Total
Long Term Debt	$26.0	24.4%
Preferred Stock	6.0	5.7
Common Stock Capital Surplus Earned Surplus	74.3	69.9
TOTAL	$106.3	100.0%

As an ordinary manufacturing enterprise, Your Company has a "sound" or well-balanced capital structure. In other words, the relative amount of different securities gives the senior security holders protection without placing the common stock in a dangerous position.

A one-stock capitalization may be attractive because there are no prior claims ahead of the common stock. But, there may be an advantage in using senior securities provided the funds borrowed can earn more than is needed to pay the interest on debt or dividends on the preferred stock. Long term debt and preferred stock add what is called "leverage" to a company's capital structure. The degree of leverage is the percentage of the common stock and surplus to the total capitalization. After paying fixed charges and preferred dividends, increased earnings benefit the common stock. Therefore, leverage is an advantage to the common stockholders while earnings are increasing. But a high degree of leverage may be dangerous if a company's earnings are irregular or it is engaged in a cyclical industry. For industrial companies, a rough maximum for bonds and preferred stocks is that they should not exceed 50% of the total capitalization.

The smaller the year-to-year fluctuations in earnings, the larger the amount of senior securities outstanding may be without incurring danger. That is why electric and gas utility companies may properly have a 25–30% common stock equity (ratio of common stock and surplus to total capitalization) whereas this would be considered undesirable for a meat packing or steel company, or a railroad. A 50% common stock equity is generally regarded as a minimum for a manufacturing or retail business.

Income Statement

SALES

There was a time when quite a few companies did not publish their sales figures, generally because of the mistaken notion that such data would help their competitors. But today no one would think of investing in a company without asking "How much business does the company do?" An income statement begins by providing this information. For public utility and railroad companies, "revenues" or "operating revenues" are the terms used.

In 1959 Your Company had an increase in sales of $5.8 million. The investor likes to see a year-to-year increase in sales. That usually means progress, if the increase also represents increased profits, although it is not always possible to expand sales regularly. In addition, a favorable showing depends on what other companies in the industry have done in the same period. If the whole industry has increased sales by 12% and a specific company only 6%, the company's results might not be regarded as very satisfactory.

It is always well to determine whether unit sales have expanded or if the larger dollar volume is derived entirely from price increases. More companies now publish unit sales as supplementary information.

Cost of goods sold. The expenses of doing business involve outlays for raw materials, wages and salaries, supplies, power and light, and other costs.

Your Company was able to keep its expenses down relatively well so that the gain in sales was not entirely eaten up by rising costs. Some companies segregate various parts of the total costs of goods sold. For management purposes costs are broken down further into fixed costs, or those which do not change with volume and variable costs, or those which are flexible.

The lower the cost of goods sold, or the operating cost as it is also called, the larger is the gross profit margin. The investor likes to see a declining operating ratio (percentage of cost of goods sold to sales).

Selling, general and administrative expenses. Costs more directly involved in production, such as wages and raw material purchases are differentiated from selling, general and administrative expenses. Your Company spent a somewhat larger part of last year's receipts for the latter group.

This group of expenses varies considerably with the kind of business. For example, companies selling to consumers usually spend larger sums for advertising than companies selling to other manufacturers or companies that obtain a large part of their orders from government.

Depreciation and depletion. These expenses as well as amortization of various types—differ in a very important respect from the other expenses already considered. While looked upon properly as a cost item, the provision for depreciation does not represent—like other costs—an actual cash outlay. Every piece of machinery and equipment has a limited period of usefulness even when kept in good repair. Thus, Your Company makes a provision for "using up" the service life of each asset, depending on its characteristics. The U. S. Treasury Department holds that depreciation for tax purposes can be related only to cost. It sets forth maximum depreciation allowances in computing a company's taxable income. If a company did not provide for the wear and tear on its production facilities, its profits and net worth would be overstated.

Depletion is somewhat similar to depreciation. It is not a cash outgo and provides for the reduction in the value of natural resources as they are used. Timber, coal, copper, oil and gas are examples of the types of assets which are subject to depletion.

The higher the amounts provided for depreciation and depletion, the lower is the net reported income. Conversely, large deductions make for a high "cash flow," which is the total of net income plus the deduction for depreciation and depletion. "Cash flow" is sometimes considered a better guide to future dividend policy than net income. However, working capital and projected capital expenditures should always be considered.

OPERATING PROFIT

This is sometimes referred to as the pre-tax profit. As a percentage of sales, it indicates the pre-tax profit margin. In 1959 and 1958 the pre-tax profit margins were 19.5% and 18.5%, respectively. For a check on management efficiency, some analysts exclude depreciation and depletion in calculating pre-tax profit margin.

Manufacturing companies in 1959 had pre-tax profit margins (after depreciation and depletion) of around 10%. Incidentally, small companies do not necessarily have the smallest pre-tax profit margins, nor the big companies the widest.

INTEREST CHANGES

This is the amount required to meet interest payments on debt. Interest being deductible as an expense before taxes, it is often less costly to borrow money than to have funds supplied by stockholders.

The bondholder likes to see at least three dollars of available earnings for each dollar's interest the company must pay. That would mean interest charges were "covered" three times. Your Company's debenture holders can sleep well, for interest charges in 1959 were covered over 17 times before provision for federal income taxes.

EARNINGS BEFORE INCOME TAXES

In the case of Your Company, this is simply the operating profit minus interest charges.

PROVISION FOR FEDERAL AND STATE TAXES ON INCOME

The federal tax collector, at a 52% corporate profits tax rate, has more than a half interest in the earnings of Your Company (and others too). Some readers may remember when a $12\frac{1}{2}$% rate seemed too high to bear.

The full implications of a 52% tax rate have yet to be explored. Some economists and businessmen are sure higher tax rates are passed on to the consumer, but others contend prices are determined in other ways. For obvious reasons, virtually everyone would like to believe that sincere efforts will be made to reduce the tax burden on earnings. If for no other reason than that present tax rates unquestionably hinder small companies more than large businesses it is often more difficult for a small business to raise needed capital. Thus the taxes lessen competition by acting as a barrier against the entry of new firms into business.

NET INCOME FOR THE YEAR

This item, also known as earnings or profits is, after all, the acid test of business management. Earnings over the years sum up all the effort, achievement, progress, mistakes and problems of the business. Your Company's net income in 1959 after all expenses and deductions, including taxes, was about 4.2 per cent higher than for the previous year. So far, so good. Since dividends are paid out of profits a healthy state of affairs requires "good" earnings. But that doesn't necessarily mean earnings must increase each year. Some years will be better than others, although there are valid reasons to believe that the extremes of boom and bust on the scale of 1929 and 1932 can be avoided.

There are two standard tests of how good earnings are. The first is the relation of net income to sales. Your Company in 1959 earned 8.5 per cent on each dollar's sales against 8.6 per cent in 1958. It will be noted that net income may increase largely because sales have risen, or, on the other hand, mainly because expenses have been reduced in relation to sales.

Average net income to sales varies considerably among different industries and the investor must consider other factors in judging results. For example, chain store grocery companies earn less than 2 cents on each sales dollar, whereas the recent average in manufacturing is about 6 cents. This does not mean, however, that food distribution is necessarily a poor industry for investment.

The second test concerns net earnings in relation to the amount of the stockholders' investment. Grocery chains earn about 10 per cent on the funds the shareholders have in the business. In 1959 Your Company's earnings on the stockholders' investment (net worth) amounted to 12.3 per cent.

DIVIDENDS ON PREFERRED STOCK

The investment quality of a preferred stock is determined largely by the size of net income in relation to annual dividend requirements. Your Company's 1959 net income, in financial language, "covered" the preferred dividends 33 times. That means earnings could shrink drastically without creating any danger signs regarding payment of preferred dividends.

Careful investors also take note of the amount of interest required on a company's indebtedness, for interest comes ahead of the preferred stockholders' dividends. The dividends requirement on the preferred stock is not an obligation in the same way as the interest due a creditor. In a sense, a preferred stockholder is a "limited partner."

On cumulative preferred stocks, dividends that have not been paid in the past, in addition to current dividends, must be cleared up before dividends may be paid on the common stock.

BALANCE OF NET INCOME AVAILABLE FOR COMMON STOCK

After deducting preferred stock dividends, the remainder represents the balance available for common stocks.

This is the most commonly used item to indicate earnings for the common stockholder when reduced to a per share basis. Your Company earned $5.24 per share on the common stock in 1959 compared with $5.03 per share in 1958. Of course, if a company does not have preferred stock, the common stockholders' per share results are found by merely dividing the net income by the number of outstanding shares, or the average number of shares outstanding if there has been a substantial change during the year.

Earned Surplus

This is also known as income retained in the business. The amount retained from year to year depends on both net income and dividend payments.

Reinvested earnings, it is emphasized, are not as a rule retained in the form of cash. Normally, such reinvested earnings become part of the company's other assets—such as inventories and receivables—or are used for capital outlays to add to plant and equipment. Or they may be used to repay indebtedness. Over a period of time reinvested earnings should add to a company's earning ability.

ACCOUNTANT'S OPINION

The accountant's report that accompanies a financial statement expresses an opinion, not a guarantee, because the values of many items in financial statements are not subject to precise measurement. Nevertheless, the opinion of an independent expert, with experience and skill in auditing and accounting, serves three important purposes: It usually states that: (1) the statements presented have been prepared in accordance with generally accepted principles of accounting; (2) the financial statements present fairly the financial condition at the end of the year and the results of operations during the period covered; (3) the accounting principles followed are consistent with those of the preceding year.

7 KEYS TO VALUE

	1959	1958
1. Pre-tax Profit Margin	19.5%	18.5%
2. Current Ratio	2.24	2.38
3. Liquidity Ratio	41.7%	44.1%
4. Capitalization Ratios:		
Long Term Debt	24.4%	20.8%
Preferred Stock	5.7	6.3
Common Stock and Surplus	69.9	72.9
	100.0%	100.0%
5. Sales to Fixed Assets	1.1	1.2
6. Sales to Inventories	4.3	4.5
7. Net Income to Net Worth	12.3%	12.5%

Over the years, security analysts, brokers and investors have found that more can be gotten out of financial statements by applying ratios that focus attention on significant relationships in the income account and balance sheet. Those used here are not the only ratios that have been developed, of course, and they are applicable mainly to industrial companies. But even so, the ratios chosen are basic.

. . . . .

The approach used here is only one of several and necessarily omits broad economic factors, market analysis, psychology and such a vital element as technology in the struggle for industrial survival. The importance of management cannot be overestimated, but this discussion is confined to understanding financial statements, a step in the final judgment of management.

1. *Pre-tax profit margin.* This is the ratio of profit, before interest and taxes, to sales. It is expressed as a percentage of sales and is found by dividing the operating profit by sales. Some analysts compute the pre-tax profit margin without including depreciation and depletion as part of cost—because the provision has nothing to do with the efficiency of operations. For 1959, Your Company's pre-tax profit margin was 19.5%. In 1958, pre-tax profit margin was 18.5%. It is usually assumed that a material increase in sales will help widen the profit margin. Certain costs are fixed, i. e., they do not rise or fall in the same proportion as changes in volume. Such costs are interest, rent and real property taxes. Ordinarily, because of these fixed costs, profits tend to increase and decline more rapidly percentagewise than sales.

2. *Current (or working capital) ratio.* Probably the most generally used for industrial companies, this is the ratio of current assets to current liabilities. A 2-for-1 ratio is the standard. Your Company's current ratio at the end of 1959 was approximately 2.24 compared to 2.38 in 1958. The change was minor.

A gradual increase in the current ratio usually is a healthy sign of improved financial strength. Ordinarily, a ratio of more than 4 or 5 to 1 is regarded as unnecessary, and may in fact be the result of an insufficient volume of business to produce a desirable level of earnings. . . .

In 1958 Your Company did not improve its position in this regard because it used substantial funds to increase its plant and equipment. The ratio could have been better if Your Company had spent less for additions to its productive facilities, or had raised more funds for this purpose through the sale of securities, or paid less in dividends. But for one reason or another, none of these alternatives was deemed either necessary or desirable. This particular case illustrates why the entire annual report must be examined and the whole financial statement should be examined.

3. *Liquidity ratio.* This is the ratio of cash and equivalent (marketable securities) to total current liabilities. It is also expressed as a percentage figure and results from dividing cash and equivalent by total current liabilities.

This ratio is important as a supplement to the current ratio because the immediate ability of a company to meet current obligations or pay larger dividends may be impaired despite a higher current ratio. At the close of 1959, Your Company's liquidity ratio was 41.7% compared with 44.1% in 1958. A decline in the liquidity ratio often takes place during a period of expansion and rising prices because of heavier capital expenditures and larger accounts payable. If the decline persists, it may mean that the company will have to raise additional capital. . . .

4. *Capitalization ratios.* These are the percentages of each type of investment in the company to the total investment. As shown previously, the capitalization is made up of Long Term Debt, Preferred Stock, Common Stock and Surplus.

In financial circles, the word "capitalization" sometimes is loosely used to cover only the outstanding securities, but the surplus or retained earnings is an important part of the ownership interest.

The form of the capitalization results from the nature of the industry, the company's financial position, and in part from policy. Usually, the higher the ratio of common stock and surplus the more assured is the position of the common stock, as it has less "ahead" of it in the way of debt securities or preferred stock with prior claims. Companies in stable industries, such as electric light and power, may with safety have a higher proportion of debt financing than most industrial companies.

Your Company, at the end of 1959, had a common stock equity or ratio of approximately 70%. This is the total of common stock, capital surplus and earned surplus divided by the total of these items plus the outstanding debentures and preferred stock. The common stock ratio was somewhat smaller than in the previous year, because of the issuance of additional debentures during the year. Since the surplus was also larger, due to reinvested earnings, the change was slight and the common stock equity remained high.

5. *Sales to fixed assets.* This ratio is computed by dividing the annual sales by the value before depreciation and amortization of plant, equipment, and land at the end of the year. The ratio is important because it helps point up whether or not the funds used to enlarge productive facilities are being spent wisely.

In most cases, of course, a sizable expansion in facilities should lead to larger sales volume. If it doesn't, the added money tied up in the plant, equipment, and land is not producing properly or is not being utilized fully. Or, it may be that sales policies should be altered. After a big increase in capacity, it often takes time for demand to grow up to capacity, and in the meantime, the ratio of sales to fixed assets will naturally suffer.

In 1959 Your Company's ratio of sales to fixed assets amounted to approximately 1.1 to 1 compared with 1.2 to 1 in the previous year. But we learn from the annual report that there were delays in getting production under way at the new plant, which isn't uncommon.

In Your Company's balance sheet the fixed assets are shown both as a gross figure, and as a net figure, i.e., before and after accumulated depreciation. Sometimes, the details appear in a footnote to the balance sheet which sets forth the cost of the buildings, machinery, equipment and land. For our computation we have used the gross figure for all fixed assets, $105.2 million in 1959 and $93.4 million in 1958. The ratio is low, indicating that Your Company probably is in a "heavy" type of industry—possibly steel or paper rather than textiles or drugs, which ordinarily have a larger sales volume in relation to plant investment.

6. *Sales to inventories.* This ratio is computed by dividing the year's sales by the year-end inventories. The so called "inventory turnover" is important as a guide to whether or not the enterprise is investing too heavily in inventories. In this event a setback in sales or a drop in commodity prices would be particularly unfavorable. A more accurate comparison would result from the use of an average of inventories at the beginning and at the end of the year.

Because inventories are a larger part of the assets of a merchandising enterprise than of most manufacturing companies, this ratio is especially worthy of note in the analysis of a retail business. A high ratio denotes a good quality of merchandise and correct pricing policies. A definite downtrend may be a warning signal of poor merchandising policy, poor location, or "stale" merchandise on the shelves. The nature of the industry has an important part in determining whether a ratio is "high" or "low."

Your Company's sales-to-inventories ratio in 1959 was approximately 4.3 to 1 compared with 4.5 to 1 in 1958. This decline could have resulted from purchases of raw materials in anticipation of an increase in prices or a falling off in sales toward the end of the year.

7. *Net income to net worth.* This is another ratio given as a percentage and is derived from dividing net income by the total of the preferred stock, common stock and surplus accounts. This is one of the most significant of all the financial ratios. It supplies the answer to the vital question: "How much is the company earning on the stockholders' investment?" Naturally, a large or increasing ratio is favorable. In a competitive society, of course, an extraordinarily high ratio may invite more intense competition. An increase due to "inventory profits" may be shortlived because of rapid changes of commodity prices.

Broad economic forces may change the general direction of net income to net worth. A higher rate may be due to general prosperity and a decline to a recession or less favorable conditions, or to higher taxes.

Your Company's net income was equivalent to 12.3% on net worth in 1959 compared with 12.5% in 1958. The change didn't amount to much. According to general surveys of all manufacturing corporations in the United States a return of over 10 percent appears to be better-than-average. Executives often hesitate to embark on outlays for new plant and equipment unless they feel that an annual return of at least 10% on the new investment may be expected.

It will be observed that Your Company's ratio of return on net worth last year exceeded that of net income to each dollar's sales, which was about 8.6%. While the latter ratio is of interest, it is not as significant as the return on the stockholder's investment, as already pointed out.

. . . . .

III • COSTS AND PRICES

We live in a world of prices; an annoying situation, perhaps, for prices often seem unsatisfactory—too high for what we buy, too low for what we sell. The two selections following discuss the general functions of price.

10 • The Economic Functions of Prices

MYRON WATKINS

The price system may be conceived as a device for limiting the use of resources and the consumption of goods, which have alternative applications, to those particular applications which are deemed to deserve precedence. . . . In other words, prices are a means of directing and checking both production and consumption. In themselves these prices are simply the monetary values of goods and services. They may be determined by custom, by an arbitrary authority enjoying some broad social sanction, by higgling in each separate transaction, by a privileged monopolist either buyer or seller, or in an open market with free bargaining in full competition on both sides. But by whatever method prices may be fixed, their ultimate *raison d'etre* is to be found in the advantages afforded by the division of labor which they presuppose and the progressive development of which is predicated upon means for facilitating and expediting exchanges.

. . . What has to be accomplished is the enforcement of the negative checks upon and positive directions to productive and consumptive activities in such a manner as, at the minimum, to make the system of control tolerable and, at the optimum, to realize the prevalent disposition of the community. In certain circumstances a large measure of authority in price fixation, with enforced adherence to arbitrary and more or less inflexible price relationships, may alone suffice to insure a workable fit between productive inclinations and productive opportunities, between productive output and consumptive intake or between consumptive dispositions and consumptive opportunities. In other circumstances a large measure of freedom in the price adjustment process in the market, affording wide scope for the spontaneous expression of individual

---

MYRON WATKINS, "The Price System," *Encyclopedia of the Social Sciences* (New York: The Macmillan Company, 1934), XII, 366–367. Used by permission. This encyclopedia is a most useful source of information on economics, history, sociology, political science, and other branches of social science.

choices, may be quite compatible with, indeed better calculated to procure, an effective performance of this fitting function. . . .

. . . This superiority [of price freedom over autocratic direction by authority] appears to have rested upon two distinct considerations. First, the employment of money as a conventional unit of reckoning values facilitated comparison and presumably therefore made choice more informed and accurate. The use of prices, or money values, as guides to the selection of occupations, the purchase of goods and generally in the organization of productive and consumptive activities has tended accordingly to sharpen economic judgment and to make choice more fruitful. Secondly, the market price system afforded a convenient means of enforcing those checks upon the use of resources which in any case are inescapable, but the incidence of which may be borne with greater equanimity in so far as it appears to be the handiwork of fate. The application of scarce means to specific ends unavoidably excludes to that extent their application to other ends. Frustration and denial are thus inexorable features of the economic process. But these deprivations seem to be less onerous when they are not enforced by the arbitrary will of some human authority. . . .

HOWARD R. BOWEN

. . . The problem has been to determine what prices must be established if given supplies of goods and given supplies of the factors are to be used economically. The basic hypotheses were (1) that price is a measure of marginal satisfactions, and (2) that goods or factors are used to greatest advantage when greater marginal satisfactions are provided ahead of lesser marginal satisfactions.

It was concluded that a given supply of goods would be used most economically if a uniform price were placed on all the units of each good so that the amount which people would wish to buy would be equal to the amount available. Price established according to this rule, however, would only guide the use of goods already produced and would not aid in achieving a correct allocation of the factors of production. To accomplish this purpose, and at the same time to guide the use of goods already produced, four rules were found necessary: (1) A uniform price must be placed on all units of each factor, (2) The price of each good must be equal to its average cost of production, (3) The factors must be organized, for the production of each product, in the least costly manner; and (4) The price of each factor must be set so that the demand for it is equal to the available supply. These four rules boil down to the following statement: Uniform prices must be placed upon the factors so that the demand for the factors, when they are combined in the least costly manner, will be equated with the available supply.

The technique of *pricing* is a paramount element in each of the four conditions. The central significance of pricing is explained by the fact that economic calculation requires a technique of measurement whereby it is possible to compare the results from alternative uses of resources. Prices provide a common denominator or common measure of the relative importance of different factors and of different goods

---

HOWARD R. BOWEN, *Toward Social Economy* (New York: Holt, Rinehart and Winston, Inc., 1948), pp. 144–146. Copyright 1948 by Howard R. Bowen and used by permission of Holt, Rinehart and Winston, Inc.

in contributing to human satisfactions. With the use of prices, therefore, it is possible to establish rules which, if followed, will lead to the most economical use of resources.

Although these four conditions relate directly to the *pricing* process, yet at the same time they all have to do with the *allocation* of the factors of production among the many possible alternative uses of these factors. The fulfillment of the four conditions means that the factors of production are being used in the most economical manner in relation to the valuations of consumers.

Any change in these valuations would, of course, alter the allocation of the factors necessarily to meet the four pricing conditions. For example, assuming economy to begin with, suppose that the demand for shoes is increased, while that for suits is correspondingly decreased. This would mean that some of the factors used in producing shoes would be in greater demand than similar factors used for other purposes, that the price of shoes would rise above cost of production, and that, therefore, the prices paid for the use of the factors employed in the shoe industry would be greater than the prices paid for similar factors elsewhere. To maintain the original allocation of the factors would mean that factors capable of being used in producing shoes would be more urgently demanded for this purpose than for other purposes. At the same time, the demand for some of the factors used in producing suits would be decreased, and the price of suits would fall below cost of production. Therefore, in order to correct the dis-economy, a reallocation of the factors would be required. It would be necessary to transfer factors out of the suit industry; as a result, the supply of suits would be curtailed until the price would rise to a point of equality with cost of production. On the other hand, it would be necessary to transfer factors into the shoe industry, until the output of shoes was increased sufficiently for the price of shoes to fall to the point of equality with cost. These changes in demand would also probably require changes in the prices of the factors. The increase in demand for shoes would be basically an increase in the demand for the particular factors used in producing shoes. A reduction in demand for suits would at the same time be a reduction in demand for the particular factors used to produce these goods. If in shoe production we assume the use of factors totally different from those used for producing suits, then an increase in the price of the "shoe factors" and a decrease in that of the "suit factors" would be required. These changes in prices would affect the costs of producing all goods using either group of factors; this in turn would tend to vary, in all fields, the combinations which would be least costly. To the extent, however, that the same factors were used to produce shoes and suits, the reallocation would be a mere transfer of factors from the fields of decreased demands to those of increased demands without any change in prices of the factors. When, however, the four pricing conditions had been re-established, the available supply of factors would again be employed in the most economical manner.

In the little world of a prisoner-of-war camp there developed a trading system surprisingly similar to that prevailing in the business world. The workings of basic economic forces were demonstrated clearly: fluctuations of individual prices; the emergence of a currency unit (cigarettes); general inflationary and deflationary movements in prices; and the difficulties of price-fixing.

11 · *The Price System in Microcosm: A P.O.W. Camp*

R. A. RADFORD

Introduction

After allowance has been made for abnormal circumstances, the social institutions, ideas and habits of groups in the outside world are to be found reflected in a Prisoner of War Camp. It is an unusual but a vital society. Camp organization and politics are matters of real concern to the inmates, as affecting their present and perhaps their future existences. Nor does this indicate any loss of proportion. No one pretends that camp matters are of any but local importance or of more than transient interest, but their importance there is great. . . .

One aspect of social organization is to be found in economic activity, and this, along with other manifestations of a group existence, is to be found in any P.O.W. camp. True, a prisoner is not dependent on his exertions for the provision of the necessaries, or even the luxuries of life, but through his economic activity, the exchange of goods and services, his standard of material comfort is considerably enhanced. . . .

Naturally, entertainment, academic and literary interests, games and discussions of the "other world" bulk larger in everyday life than they do in the life of more normal societies. But it would be wrong to underestimate the importance of economic activity. Everyone receives a roughly equal share of essentials; it is by trade that individual preferences are given expression and comfort increased. All at some time, and most people regularly, make exchanges of one sort or another.

. . . But the essential interest lies in the universality and the spontaneity of this economic life; it came into existence not by conscious imitation but as a response to the immediate needs and circumstances. Any similarity between prison organization and outside organization arises from similar stimuli evoking similar responses.

The following is as brief an account of the essential data as may render the narrative intelligible. The camps of which the writer had experience were Oflags and consequently the economy

---

R. A. RADFORD, "The Economic Organization of a P.O.W. Camp," from *Economica*, XII, No. 48, New Series (London: November 1945), pp. 189–201. Used by permission.

was not complicated by payments for work by the detaining power. They consisted normally of between 1,200 and 2,500 people, housed in a number of separate but intercommunicating bungalows, one company of 200 or so to a building. Each company formed a group within the main organization and inside the company the room and the messing syndicate, a voluntary and spontaneous group who fed together, formed the constituent units.

Between individuals there was active trading in all consumer goods and in some services. Most trading was for food against cigarettes or other foodstuffs, but cigarettes rose from the status of a normal commodity to that of currency. Reichmarks existed but had no circulation save for gambling debts, as few articles could be purchased with them from the canteen.

Our supplies consisted of rations provided by the detaining power and (principally) the contents of Red Cross food parcels—tinned milk, jam, butter, biscuits, bully, chocolate, sugar, etc., and cigarettes. So far the supplies to each person were equal and regular. Private parcels of clothing, toilet requisites and cigarettes were also received, and here equality ceased owing to the different numbers despatched and the vagaries of the post. All these articles were the subject of trade and exchange.

The Development and Organization of the Market

Very soon after capture people realized that it was both undesirable and unnecessary, in view of the limited size and the equality of supplies, to give away or to accept gifts of cigarettes or food. "Goodwill" developed into trading as a more equitable means of maximizing individual satisfaction.

We reached a transit camp in Italy about a fortnight after capture and received one-quarter of a Red Cross food parcel each a week later. At once exchanges, already established, multiplied in volume. Starting with simple direct barter, such as a non-smoker giving a smoker friend his cigarette issue in exchange for a chocolate ration, more complex exchanges soon became an accepted custom. Stories circulated of a padre who started off round the camp with a tin of cheese and five cigarettes and returned to his bed with a complete parcel in addition to his original cheese and cigarettes; the market was not yet perfect. Within a week or two, as the volume of trade grew, rough scales of exchange values came into existence. Sikhs, who had at first exchanged tinned beef for practically any other foodstuff, began to insist on jam and margarine. It was realized that a tin of jam was worth one-half pound of margarine plus something else; that a cigarette issue was worth several chocolate issues, and a tin of diced carrots was worth practically nothing.

In this camp we did not visit other bungalows very much and prices varied from place to place; hence the germ of truth in the story of the itinerant priest. By the end of a month, when we reached our permanent camp, there was a lively trade in all commodities and their relative values were well known, and expressed not in terms of one another—one didn't quote bully in terms of sugar—but in terms of cigarettes. The cigarette became the standard of value. In the permanent camp people started by wandering through the bungalows calling their offers—"cheese for seven" (cigarettes)—and the hours after parcel issue were bedlam. The inconvenience of this system soon led to its replacement by an Exchange and Mart notice board in every bungalow, where under the headings "name," "room number," "wanted," and "offered" sales and wants were advertised. When a deal went through, it was crossed off the board. The public and semi-permanent records of transactions led to cigarette prices being well known and thus tending to equality throughout the camp, although there were always opportunities for an astute trader to make a profit from arbitrage. With this development everyone, including non-smokers, was willing to sell for cigarettes, using them to buy at another time and place. Cigarettes became the normal currency, though, of course, barter was never extinguished.

The unity of the market and the prevalence of a single price varied directly with the general level of organization and comfort in the camp. A transit camp was always chaotic and uncomfortable: people were overcrowed, no one knew where anyone else was living, and few took the trouble to find out. Organization was too slender to include an Exchange and Mart board, and private advertisements were the most that appeared. Consequently a transit camp was not one market but many. The price of a tin of salmon is known to have varied by two cigarettes in 20 between one end of a hut and the other. Despite a high level of organization in Italy, the market was morcellated in this manner at the first transit camp we reached after our removal to Germany in the autumn of 1943. In this camp—Stalag VIIA at Moosburg in Bavaria—there were up to 50,000 prisoners of all nationalities. French, Russians, Italians and Jugo-Slavs were free to move about within the camp: British and Americans were confined to their compounds, although a few cigarettes given to a sentry would always procure permission for one or two men to visit other compounds. The people who first visited the highly organized French trading center, with its stalls and known prices, found coffee extract—relatively cheap among the tea-drinking English —commanding a fancy price in biscuits or cigarettes, and some enterprising people made small fortunes that way. (Incidentally we found out later that much of the coffee went "over the wire" and sold for phenomenal prices at black market cafés in Munich: some of the French prisoners were said to have made substantial sums in RMk.s. This was one of the few occasions on which our normally closed economy came into contact with other economic worlds.)

Eventually public opinion grew hostile to these monopoly profits—not everyone could make contact with the French—and trading with them was put on a regulated basis. Each group of beds was given a quota of articles to offer and the transaction was carried out by accredited representatives from the British compound, with monopoly rights. The same method was used for trading with sentries elsewhere, as in this trade secrecy and reasonable prices had a peculiar importance, but as is ever the case with regulated companies, the interloper proved too strong.

The permanent camps in Germany saw the highest level of commercial organization. In addition to the Exchange and Mart notice boards, a shop was organized as a public utility, controlled by representatives of the Senior British Officer, on a no profit basis. People left their surplus clothing, toilet requisites and food there until they were sold at a fixed price in cigarettes. Only sales in cigarettes were accepted—there was no barter—and there was no higgling. For food at least there were standard prices: clothing is less homogeneous and the price was decided around a norm by the seller and the shop manager in agreement; shirts would average say 80, ranging from 60 to 120 according to quality and age. Of food, the shop carried small stocks for convenience; the capital was provided by a loan from the bulk store of Red Cross cigarettes and repaid by a small commission taken on the first transactions. Thus the cigarette attained its fullest currency status, and the market was almost completely unified.

It is thus to be seen that a market came into existence without labor or production. The [Red Cross] may be considered as "Nature" of the textbook, and the articles of trade—food, clothing and cigarettes—as free gifts—land or manna. Despite this, and despite a roughly equal distribution of resources, a market came into spontaneous operation, and prices were fixed by the operation of supply and demand. It is difficult to reconcile this fact with the labor theory of value.

Actually there was an embryo labor market. Even when cigarettes were not scarce, there was usually some unlucky person willing to perform services for them. Laundrymen advertised at two cigarettes a garment. Battle-dress was scrubbed and pressed and a pair of trousers lent for the interim period for twelve. A good pastel portrait cost thirty or a tin of "Kam." Odd tailoring and other jobs similarly had their prices.

There were also entrepreneurial services. There was a coffee stall owner who sold tea, coffee or cocoa at two cigarettes a cup, buying his raw materials at market prices and hiring labor to gather fuel and to stoke; he actually enjoyed the services of a chartered accountant at one stage. After a period of great prosperity he overreached himself and failed disastrously for several hundred cigarettes. Such large-scale private enterprise was rare but several middlemen or professional traders existed. The padre in Italy, or the men at Moosburg who opened trading relations with the French, are examples: the more subdivided the market, the less perfect the advertisement of prices, and the less stable the prices, the greater was the scope for these operators. One man capitalized his knowledge of Urdu by buying meat from the Sikhs and selling butter and jam in return: as his operations became better known more and more people entered this trade, prices in the Indian Wing approximated more nearly to those elsewhere, though to the end a "contact" among the Indians was valuable, as linguistic difficulties prevented the trade from being quite free. Some were specialists in the Indian trade, the food, clothing or even the watch trade. Middlemen traded on their own account or on commission. Price rings and agreements were suspected and the traders certainly co-operated. Nor did they welcome newcomers. Unfortunately the writer knows little of the workings of these people: public opinion was hostile and the professionals were usually of a retiring disposition.

One trader in food and cigarettes, operating in a period of dearth, enjoyed a high reputation. His capital, carefully saved, was originally about 50 cigarettes, with which he bought rations on issue days and held them until the price rose just before the next issue. He also picked up a little by arbitrage; several times a day he visited every Exchange or Mart notice board and took advantage of every discrepancy between prices of goods offered and wanted. His knowledge of prices, markets and names of those who had received cigarette parcels was phenomenal. By these means he kept himself smoking steadily—his profits—while his capital remained intact.

Sugar was issued on Saturday. About Tuesday two of us used to visit Sam and make a deal; as old customers he would advance as much of the price as he could spare then, and entered the transaction in a book. On Saturday morning he left cocoa tins on our beds for the ration, and picked them up on Saturday afternoon. We were hoping for a calendar at Christmas, but Sam failed too. He was left holding a big black treacle issue when the price fell, and in this weakened state was unable to withstand an unexpected arrival of parcels and the consequent price fluctuations. He paid in full, but from his capital. The next Tuesday, when I paid my usual visit he was out of business.

Credit entered into many, perhaps into most transactions, in one form or another. Sam paid in advance as a rule for his purchases of future deliveries of sugar, but many buyers asked for credit, whether the commodity was sold spot or future. Naturally prices varied according to the terms of sale. A treacle ration might be advertised for four cigarettes now or five next week. And in the future market "bread now" was a vastly different thing from "bread Thursday." Bread was issued on Thursday and Monday, four and three days' rations respectively, and by Wednesday and Sunday night it had risen at least one cigarette per ration, from seven to eight, by suppertime. One man always saved a ration to sell then at the peak price: his offer of "bread now" stood out on the board among a number of "bread Monday's" fetching one or two less, or not selling at all—and he always smoked on Sunday night.

The Cigarette Currency

Although cigarettes as currency exhibited certain peculiarities, they performed all the functions of a metallic currency as a unit of account, as a measure of value and as a store of value, and shared most of its characteristics. They were homogeneous, reasonably durable, and of convenient size for the smallest or, in packets, for the largest transactions. Incidentally, they could be clipped or sweated by rolling them between the fingers so that tobacco fell out.

Cigarettes were also subject to the working of Gresham's Law. Certain brands were more popular than others as smokes, but for currency purposes a cigarette was a cigarette. Consequently buyers used the poorer qualities and the Shop rarely saw the more popular brands: cigarettes such as Churchman's No. 1 were rarely used for trading. At one time cigarettes hand-rolled from pipe tobacco began to circulate. Pipe tobacco was issued in lieu of cigarettes by the Red Cross at a rate of 25 cigarettes to the ounce and this rate was standard in exchanges, but an ounce would produce 30 home-made cigarettes. Naturally, people with machine-made cigarettes broke them down and re-rolled the tobacco, and the real cigarette virtually disappeared from the market. Hand-rolled cigarettes were not homogeneous and prices could no longer be quoted in them with safety: each cigarette was examined before it was accepted and thin ones rejected, or extra demanded as a make-weight. For a time we suffered all the inconveniences of a debased currency.

Machine-made cigarettes were always universally acceptable, both for what they would buy and for themselves. It was this intrinsic value which gave rise to their principal disadvantage as currency, a disadvantage which exists, but to a far smaller extent, in the case of metallic currency—that is, a strong demand for non-monetary purposes. Consequently our economy was repeatedly subject to deflation and to periods of monetary stringency. While the Red Cross issue of 50 or 25 cigarettes per man per week came in regularly, and while there were fair stocks held, the cigarette currency suited its purpose admirably. But when the issue was interrupted, stocks soon ran out, prices fell, trading declined in volume and became increasingly a matter of barter. This deflationary tendency was periodically offset by the sudden injection of new currency. Private cigarette parcels arrived in a trickle throughout the year, but the big numbers came in quarterly when the Red Cross received its allocation of transport. Several hundred thousand cigarettes might arrive in the space of a fortnight. Prices soared, and then began to fall, slowly at first but with increasing rapidity as stocks ran out, until the next big delivery. Most of our economic troubles could be attributed to this fundamental instability.

Price Movements

Many factors affected prices, the strongest and most noticeable being the periodical currency inflation and deflation described in the last paragraphs. The periodicity of this price cycle depended on cigarette and, to a far lesser extent, on food deliveries. At one time in the early days, before any private parcels had arrived and when there were no individual stocks, the weekly issue of cigarettes and food parcels occurred on a Monday. The non-monetary demand for cigarettes was great, and less elastic than the demand for food: consequently prices fluctuated weekly, falling towards Sunday night and rising sharply on Monday morning. Later, when many people held reserves, the weekly issue had no such effect, being too small a proportion of the total available. Credit allowed people with no reserves to meet their non-monetary demand over the week-end.

The general price level was affected by other factors. An influx of new prisoners, proverbially hungry, raised it. Heavy air raids in the vicinity of the camp probably increased the non-monetary demand for cigarettes and accentuated deflation. Good and bad war news certainly had its effect, and the general waves of optimism and pessimism which swept the camp were reflected in prices. Before breakfast one morning in March of this year, a rumor of the arrival of parcels and cigarettes was circulated. Within ten minutes I sold a treacle ration for four cigarettes (hitherto offered in vain for three), and many similar deals went through. By 10 o'clock the rumor was denied, and treacle that day found no more buyers even at two cigarettes.

More interesting than changes in the general price level were changes in the price structure. Changes in the supply of a commodity, in the German ration scale or in the make-up of Red Cross parcels, would raise the price of one commodity relative to others. Tins of oatmeal, once a rare and much sought after luxury in the parcels, became a commonplace in 1943, and the price fell. In hot weather the demand for cocoa fell, and that for soap rose. A new recipe would be reflected in the price level: the discovery that raisins and sugar could be turned into an alcohol liquor of remarkable potency reacted permanently on the dried fruit market. The invention of electric immersion heaters run off the power points made tea, a drug on the market in Italy, a certain seller in Germany.

In August, 1944, the supplies of parcels and cigarettes were both halved. Since both sides of the equation were changed in the same degree, changes in prices were not anticipated. But this was not the case: the non-monetary demand for cigarettes was less elastic than the demand for food, and food prices fell a little. More important however were the changes in the price structure. German margarine and jam, hitherto valueless owing to adequate supplies of

Canadian butter and marmalade, acquired a new value. Chocolate, popular and a certain seller, and sugar, fell. Bread rose; several standing contracts of bread for cigarettes were broken, especially when the bread ration was reduced a few weeks later.

In February, 1945, the German soldier who drove the ration wagon was found to be willing to exchange loaves of bread at the rate of one loaf for a bar of chocolate. Those in the know began selling bread and buying chocolate, by then almost unsaleable in a period of serious deflation. Bread, at about 40, fell slightly; chocolate rose from 15; the supply of bread was not enough for the two commodities to reach parity, but the tendency was unmistakable.

The substitution of German margarine for Canadian butter when parcels were halved naturally affected their relative values, margarine appreciating at the expense of butter. Similarly, two brands of dried milk, hitherto differing in quality and therefore in price by five cigarettes a tin, came together in price as the wider substitution of the cheaper raised its relative value.

Enough has been cited to show that any change in conditions affected both the general price level and the price structure. It was this latter phenomenon which wrecked our planned economy.

Paper Currency—Bully Marks

Around D-Day, food and cigarettes were plentiful, business was brisk and the camp in an optimistic mood. Consequently the Entertainments Committee felt the moment opportune to launch a restaurant, where food and hot drinks were sold while a band and variety turns performed. Earlier experiments, both public and private, had pointed the way, and the scheme was a great success. Food was bought at market prices to provide the meals and the small profits were devoted to a reserve fund and used to bribe Germans to provide grease-paints and other necessities for the camp theatre. Originally meals were sold for cigarettes but this meant that the whole scheme was vulnerable to the periodic deflationary waves, and furthermore heavy smokers were unlikely to attend much. The whole success of the scheme depended on an adequate amount of food being offered for sale in the normal manner. To increase and facilitate trade, and to stimulate supplies and customers therefore, and secondarily to avoid the worst effects of deflation when it should come, a paper currency was organized by the Restaurant and the Shop. The Shop bought food on behalf of the Restaurant with paper notes and the paper was accepted equally with the cigarettes in the Restaurant or Shop, and passed back to the Shop to purchase more food. The Shop acted as a bank of issue. The paper money was backed 100 per cent by food; hence its name, the Bully Mark. The BMk. was backed 100 per cent by food: there could be no over-issues, as is permissible with a normal bank of issue, since the eventual dispersal of the camp and consequent redemption of all BMk.s was anticipated in the near future.

Originally one BMk. was worth one cigarette and for a short time both circulated freely inside and outside the Restaurant. Prices were quoted in BMk.s and cigarettes with equal freedom—and for a short time the BMk. showed signs of replacing the cigarette as currency. The BMk. was tied to food, but not to cigarettes: as it was issued against food, say 45 for a tin of milk and so on, any reduction in the BMk. prices of food would have meant that there were unbacked BMk.s in circulation. But the price of both food and BMk.s could and did fluctuate with the supply of cigarettes.

While the Restaurant flourished, the scheme was a success: the Restaurant bought heavily, all foods were saleable and prices were stable.

In August parcels and cigarettes were halved and the Camp was bombed. The Restaurant closed for a short while and sales of food became difficult. Even when the Restaurant reopened, the food and cigarette shortage became increasingly acute and people were unwilling to convert such valuable goods into paper and to hold them for luxuries like snacks and tea. Less of the right kinds of food for the Resturant were sold, and the Shop became glutted with dried fruit, chocolate, sugar, and so forth, which the Restaurant could not buy. The price level and the price structure changed. The BMk. fell to four-fifths of a cigarette and eventually farther still, and it became unacceptable save in the Restaurant. There was a flight from the BMk., no longer convertible into cigarettes or popular foods. The cigarette re-established itself.

But the BMk. was sound! The Restaurant closed in the New Year with a progressive food shortage and the long evenings without lights due to intensified Allied air raids, and BMk.s could only be spent in the Coffee Bar—relict of the Restaurant—or on the few unpopular foods in the Shop, the owners of which were prepared to accept them. In the end all holders of BMk.s were paid in full, in cups of coffee or in prunes. People who had bought BMk.s for cigarettes or valuable jam or biscuits in their heyday were grieved that they should have stood the loss involved by their restricted choice, but they suffered no actual loss of market value.

Price Fixing

Along with this scheme came a determined attempt at a planned economy, at price fixing. The Medical Officer had long been anxious to control food sales, for fear of some people selling too much, to the detriment of their health. The deflationary waves and their effects on prices were inconvenient to all and would be dangerous to the Restaurant which had to carry stocks. Furthermore, unless the BMk. was convertible into cigarettes at about par it had little chance of gaining confidence and of succeeding as a currency. As has been explained, the BMk. was tied to food but could not be tied to cigarettes, which fluctuated in value. Hence, while BMk. prices of food were fixed for all time, cigarette prices of food and BMk.s varied.

The Shop, backed by the Senior British Officer, was now in a position to enforce price control both inside and outside its walls. Hitherto a standard price had been fixed for food left for sale in the Shop, and prices outside were roughly in conformity with this scale, which was recommended as a "guide" to sellers, but fluctuated a good deal around it. Sales in the Shop at recommended prices were apt to be slow though a good price might be obtained: sales outside could be made more quickly at lower prices. (If sales outside were to be at higher prices, goods were withdrawn from the Shop until the recommended price rose: but the recommended price was sluggish and could not follow the market closely by reason of its very purpose, which was stability.) The Exchange and Mart notice boards came under the control of the Shop: advertisements which exceeded a 5 per cent. departure from the recommended scale were liable to be crossed out by authority: unauthorized sales were discouraged by authority and also by public opinion, strongly in favor of a just and stable price. (Recommended prices were fixed partly from market data, partly on the advice of the Medical Officer.)

At first the recommended scale was a success: the Restaurant, a big buyer, kept prices stable around this level: opinion and the 5 per cent tolerance helped. But when the price level fell with the August cuts and the price structure changed, the recommended scale was too rigid. Unchanged at first, as no deflation was expected, the scale was tardily lowered, but the prices of goods on the new scale remained in the same relation to one another, owing to the BMk., while on the market the price structure had changed. And the modifying influence of the Restaurant had gone. The scale was moved up and down several times, slowly following the inflationary and deflationary waves, but it was rarely adjusted to changes in the price structure. More and more advertisements were crossed off the board, and black market sales at unauthorized prices increased: eventually public opinion turned against the recommended scale and authority gave up the struggle. In the last few weeks, with unparalleled deflation, prices fell with alarming rapidity, no scales existed and supply and demand, alone and unmellowed, determined prices.

Public Opinion

Public opinion on the subject of trading was vocal if confused and changeable, and generalizations as to its direction are difficult and dangerous. A tiny minority held that all trading was undesirable as it engendered an unsavory atmosphere; occasional frauds and sharp practices were cited as proof. Certain forms of trading were more generally condemned; trade with the Germans was criticized by many. Red Cross toilet articles, which were in short supply and only issued in cases of actual need, were excluded from trade by law and opinion working in unshakable harmony. At one time, when there had been several cases of malnutrition reported among the more devoted smokers, no trade in German rations was permitted, as the victims became an additional burden on the depleted food reserves of the Hospital. But while certain activities were condemned as anti-social, trade itself was practiced, and its utility appreciated, by almost everyone in the camp.

More interesting was opinion on middlemen and prices. Taken as a whole, opinion was hostile to the middleman. His function, and his hard work in bringing buyer and seller together, were ignored; profits were not regarded as a reward for labor, but as the result of sharp practice. Despite the fact that his very existence was proof to the contrary, the middleman was held to be redundant in view of the existence of an official Shop and the Exchange and Mart. Appreciation only came his way when he was willing to advance the price of a sugar ration, or to buy goods spot and carry them against a future sale. In these cases the element of risk was obvious to all, and the convenience of the service was felt to merit some reward. Particularly unpopular was the middleman with an element of monopoly, the man who contacted the ration wagon driver, or the man who utilized his knowledge of Urdu. And middlemen as a group were blamed for reducing prices. Opinion notwithstanding, most people dealt with a middleman, whether consciously or unconsciously, at some time or another.

There was a strong feeling that everything had its "just price" in cigarettes. While the assessment of the just price, which incidentally varied between camps, was impossible of explanation, this price was nevertheless pretty closely known. It can best be defined as the price usually fetched by an article in good times when cigarettes were plentiful. The "just price" changed slowly; it was unaffected by short-term variations in supply, and while opinion might be resigned to departures from the "just price," a strong feeling of re-sentiment persisted. A more satisfactory definition of the "just price" is impossible. Everyone knew what it was, though no one could explain why it should be so.

As soon as prices began to fall with a cigarette shortage, a clamor arose, particularly against those who held reserves and who bought at reduced prices. Sellers at cut prices were criticized and their activities referred to as the black market. In every period of dearth the explosive question of "should non-smokers receive a cigarette ration?" was discussed to profitless length. Unfortunately, it was the nonsmoker, or the light smoker with his reserves, along with the hated middleman, who weathered the storm most easily.

The popularity of the price-fixing scheme, and such success as it enjoyed, were undoubtedly the result of this body of opinion. On several occasions the fall of prices was delayed by the general support given to the recommended scale. The onset of deflation was marked by a period of sluggish trade; prices stayed up but no one bought. Then prices fell on the black market, and the volume of trade revived in that quarter. Even when the recommended scale was revised, the volume of trade in the Shop would remain low. Opinion was always overruled by the hard facts of the market.

Curious arguments were advanced to justify price fixings. The recommended prices were in some way related to the calorific values of the foods offered: hence some were overvalued and never sold at these prices. One argument ran as follows:—not everyone has private cigarette parcels: thus, when prices were high and trade good in the summer of 1944, only the lucky rich could buy. This was unfair to the man with few cigarettes. When prices fell in the following winter, prices should be pegged high so that the rich, who had enjoyed life in the summer, should put many cigarettes into circulation. The fact that those who sold to the rich in the summer had also enjoyed life then, and the fact that in the winter there was always someone willing to sell at low prices were ignored. Such arguments were hotly debated each night after the approach of Allied aircraft extinguished all lights at 8 p.m. But prices moved with the supply of cigarettes, and refused to stay fixed in accordance with a theory of ethics.

Conclusion

The economic organization described was both elaborate and smooth-working in the summer of 1944. Then came the August cuts and deflation. Prices fell, rallied with deliveries of cigarette parcels in September and December, and fell again. In January, 1945, supplies of Red Cross cigarettes ran out: and prices slumped still further: in February the supplies of food parcels were exhausted and the depression became a blizzard. Food, itself scarce, was almost given away in order to meet the non-monetary demand for cigarettes. Laundries ceased to operate, or worked for £s or RMk.s: food and cigarettes sold for fancy prices in £s, hitherto unheard of. The Restaurant was a memory and the BMk. a joke. The Shop was empty and the Exchange Mart notices were full of unaccepted offers for cigarettes. Barter increased in volume, becoming a larger proportion of a small volume of trade. This, the first serious and prolonged food shortage in the writer's experience, caused the price structure to change again, partly because German rations were not easily divisible. A margarine ration gradually sank in value until it exchanged directly for a treacle ration. Sugar slumped sadly. Only bread retained its value. Several thousand cigarettes, the capital of the Shop, were distributed without any noticeable effect. A few fractional parcel and cigarette issues, such as one-sixth of a parcel and twelve cigarettes each, led to momentary price recoveries and feverish trade, especially when they coincided with good news from the Western Front, but the general position remained unaltered.

By April, 1945, chaos had replaced order in the economic sphere: sales were difficult, prices lacked stability.

Economics has been defined as the science of distributing limited means among unlimited and competing ends. On April 12th, with the arrival of elements of the 30th U.S. Infantry Division, the ushering in of an age of plenty demonstrated the hypothesis that with infinite means economic organization and activity would be redundant, as every want could be satisfied without effort.

Many people speak of the "law of demand and supply" without much notion of what they mean. Many use the term "shortage" loosely. In the selection following, two economists utilize the technical apparatus of "demand and supply analysis" to study a question of much interest.

12 · Demand-Supply Analysis: Has There Been a Shortage of Engineers?

DAVID M. BLANK
GEORGE J. STIGLER

To the economist—and he is the one person who has a professional obligation to use these concepts carefully—demand and supply are schedules or functions. Each denotes a whole array of quantities—quantities which will be offered, in the case of supply; quantities which will be asked for, in the case of demand—varying with certain governing factors as prices, incomes, consumer tastes, industrial techniques.

If these determining factors or variables of the supply and demand functions are allowed to vary (that is, if the market is free), they will move in such directions as will equate the quantity supplied and the quantity demanded. If, for example, the number of engineers that employers seek to hire is in excess of the number available, the salaries of engineers will rise. The higher salaries will invariably reduce the number demanded, and sooner or later increase the number seeking employment. In free markets, therefore, the actual number of engineers employed in a given past year represents both the number demanded and the number supplied.

. . . . .

Has There Been a Shortage? A Survey of Earnings

In recent years there has been much discussion of a shortage of engineers

---

DAVID M. BLANK and GEORGE J. STIGLER, *The Demand and Supply of Scientific Personnel* (New York: National Bureau of Economic Research, Inc., 1957), pp. 19, 22–23. Used by permission. Several accompanying tables have been omitted.

and natural scientists, and a variety of proposals have been made to alleviate a shortage that has been alleged to exist or to be imminent. We are not concerned in this study with public policy toward the technological professions, but we are deeply interested in the economic questions implicit in an allegation of a shortage.

The word "shortage" is seldom defined precisely in these discussions, but it appears to be used in a variety of senses. In one sense, there is a shortage of members of a particular profession if the actual number is less than the number dictated by some social criterion or goal. For example, one might use the criterion that we should have enough engineers to conduct a major war in a particular manner, or that we should have ten per cent more engineers than a hostile power is believed to have. Such a criterion could be important and fully developed, but normally it is left undefined in the literature. Since there is no consensus on any such criterion, and since we cannot construct one, we shall not discuss this type of shortage.

A second meaning of shortage is that the quantity of the labor services in question that is demanded is greater than the quantity supplied *at the prevailing wage*. In such a circumstance the wage normally rises, causing the quantity demanded to shrink and the quantity supplied to expand. The shortage vanishes as soon as the market can adjust to the excess demand. But if wages are regulated, and are not allowed to respond to the excess demand, the shortage will persist. Such a condition ruled in many labor markets, probably including engineering, during World War II, but there have been no general controls over engineering salaries since that time.

The third meaning of shortage, and the one that is most natural in an economy with a free labor market, is that a shortage exists when the number of workers available (the supply) increases less rapidly than the number demanded *at the salaries paid in the recent past*. Then salaries will rise, and activities which once were performed by (say) engineers must now be performed by a class of workers who are less well trained and less expensive. Such a shortage is not necessarily objectionable from a social viewpoint, but this is a separate question. In any event this is a well-defined and significant meaning of the word "shortage" and we propose to investigate now whether such a shortage has existed for engineers in recent decades. To this end we begin with a study of trends in earnings.

We begin with a comparison of engineering salaries with earnings or salaries in selected fields since 1929—the earliest year for which tolerably reliable engineering data are available. Ratios of engineering salaries to earnings of three groups of independent professional practitioners—doctors, dentists, and lawyers—rose during the thirties but declined sharply after 1939. By 1951 the salary-income ratio for engineers compared with physicians was 40 per cent below its level in 1929; for engineers and dentists, 16 per cent below; for engineers and lawyers, 3 per cent below. The decline was substantially greater when measured against a 1939 base. Salaries of engineers and full-time average earnings of manufacturing wage and salary employees and all wage and salary employees fluctuated in about the same manner between 1929 and 1939 but after 1939 wage earners increased their earnings more sharply than did engineers. From 1950 through 1954, the ratio of engineering salaries to earnings of wage and salary employees was about a third lower than in 1929.

. . . . .

The pronounced downward drift of earnings in all professions (except medicine) relative to earnings of the working population as a whole is well-known, and it is apparent that the engineers have fully shared in this relative decline. This downward drift is known only for the period since 1929, but one may plausibly conjecture that it began much earlier because the main force working in this direction—the rapid expansion in the number of trained professional workers —also began much earlier.

For the period 1939–1949 we can compare increases in engineering salaries with the increases in wages or salaries for selected occupations within the professional and technical worker group. These data . . . indicate a smaller income rise for engineers than for male employees in five out of six other professional or technical occupations. Only college teachers received smaller salary increases than the three main engineering branches, while chemists, clergymen, designers and draftsmen, and pharmacists had substantially larger increases. Public and private school teachers experienced larger percentage salary increases than two of the three engineering branches.

PERCENTAGE INCREASE IN AVERAGE WAGE OR SALARY INCOME, FULLTIME MALE WAGE OR SALARY WORKERS IN SELECTED PROFESSIONAL AND TECHNICAL OCCUPATIONS, 1939–1949

Engineers, civil	65.1
Engineers, electrical	56.5
Engineers, mechanical	56.8
Chemists	80.5
Clergymen	72.4
College presidents, professors and instructors (n.e.c.)	32.3
Designers and draftsmen	82.5
Pharmacists	120.0
Teachers (n.e.c.)	62.6

n.e.c.=not elsewhere classified.

SOURCE: Herman P. Miller, *Income of the American People* (New York: John Wiley & Sons, Inc., 1955), Appendix Tables C-2 and C-4.

Since the close of World War II, it is possible to trace out annual changes in salaries of engineers. We report the annual percentage increases in starting salaries for graduating engineers and in salaries at the starting level and at the 9–11 years' experience level for research scientists and engineers. The broad outlines of salary experience for these various groups are clear. After some declines in 1949 and early 1950, salaries for young engineers and scientists rose substantially under the impact of the Korean defense program. The largest increases took place in 1952, when apparently the full impact of the research and development programs of the federal government was felt. Smaller percentage increases were registered in 1953 and 1954, but there was a larger increase, especially for more experienced engineers, in 1955. Older research scientists and engineers experienced larger salary increases than younger scientists and engineers from 1948 to 1950 and in 1955, but on average the former's salaries have increased less rapidly in the postwar decade.

Only a few relevant salary or earnings series can be compared with those of engineers in the period since 1950. In the years immediately after the outbreak of the Korean War, salaries of new graduates in engineering rose at the same rate as those in fields like accounting and business, and as those of research scientists and engineers with little experience. All of these groups had larger increases than occurred in the average earnings of all manufacturing wage earners, but the difference was not large.

We may summarize these pieces of information on engineering earnings as follows. Since 1929, engineering salaries have declined substantially relative to earnings of all wage earners and relative to incomes of independent professional practitioners. Especially since 1939 engineering salaries have declined relative to the wage or salary income of the entire group of professional, technical and kindred workers, as well as relative to the working population as a whole. After the outbreak of the Korean War there was a minor increase in the relative salaries of engineers (and of other college-trained workers), but this was hardly more than a minor cross-current in a tide.

Relative to both the working population as a whole and the professions as a separate class, then, the record of earnings would suggest that up to at least 1955 there had been no shortage —in fact an increasingly amply supply —of engineers. But before we examine this conclusion more closely, it is necessary to consider whether the market for engineers' services is a good market in the technical economic sense. That is, do engineers fail to move to positions with higher salaries because of ignorance or inertia? Or do some employers have an appreciable degree of market control over salaries—an element of monopoly which distorts the movements of salaries over time? If the market for engineers' services has some imperfection such as these, movements of salaries are not an accurate index of scarcity in the economic sense.

More specifically, if engineers were not mobile among employers, then salaries would not be an accurate index of the state of the market because the offer of a higher wage would not necessarily attract an engineer away from another employer. There is no direct information on the mobility of engineers among employers. However, of those members of the engineering profession in 1939 who remained civilians in the United States between 1939 and 1946, 25 per cent changed at least once the industry in which they were employed during this seven-year period, 30 per cent changed their State of employment at least once, 22 per cent changed from one type of engineering activity to another, and an unknown percentage changed employers in the same locality and industry. Fourteen per cent changed their branch of engineering and more than 20 per cent of all engineers worked at some time in their lives in a branch of engineering other than that in which they were trained. The mobility of engineers among employers was undoubtedly higher than any of these indirect measures although less than their sum by the proportion of engineers who participated in two or more of the kinds of moves listed. . . . Some immobility undoubtedly exists, but in view of this level of mobility among engineers and the substantial flexibility of choice open to new entrants into the professions, one would expect major salary and other inducements to be offered in industries or geographic areas with rapidly increasing demands for engineers.

Again, there might be a failure of competition, so that an increased demand for engineers did not lead to a rise in salary offers. The suggestion that employers may have been reluctant to compete on salaries presupposes some type of monopsonistic situation in the market, i.e., that some firms employed such a large portion of the engineering profession that any action on their part with respect to hiring and salaries would significantly affect the market price for engineering services. But the fact is that the largest nongovernmental employer of engineers probably accounts for only about 2 per cent of the total number of engineers in the country, and other major employers account for substantially smaller percentages. Most engineers work for firms which employ insignificant proportions of the profession. Under these conditions, probably all firms have to match in some form or other the general market price for engineering services. Accordingly, general salary movement of engineers relative to those of other occupations should indicate the relative supply-demand in this market compared to that in the markets for other occupations.

It has been suggested that there may be an exception to the general prevalence of competition in the governmentally controlled industries. The Air Force retains the formal right to review the salaries paid by its contractors, and thus might hold down salaries in a substantial (but far from dominant) portion of the market. There is no evidence to suggest that this power is vigorously exercised. . . . But in any event such controls, whether public or private, over salaries paid by employers of a minority of engineers could not give rise to a shortage outside the industries practicing the salary control; i.e., there could be no general market shortage because of the salary control.

So we find no reason to reject the main implications of the data on the trend of relative earnings: the number of engineers has been growing more rapidly relative to the demand, in the past two and a half decades, than has been the case in the labor force as a whole. And since the differentials of engineers' earnings above those of the academically untrained labor force are still in excess of the costs of obtaining an engineering degree, we may expect this trend to continue in the future.

It is true that after 1950 there was a short, and relatively minor, reversal in this movement of relative earnings of engineers. Engineers' salaries rose substantially for at least two years, and at a rate exceeding that in the independent professions and the labor force as a whole. This movement, obviously related to the expansion of military procurement after the outbreak of the Korean War and the associated increase in government expenditures for private and public research, is the only basis we can find for the popular view that there was a shortage of engineers at that time, in comparison with other occupations.

It is clear that the increased demand for engineers for a short period after 1950 was not fully matched by a corresponding increase in supply. It is difficult, of course, to increase substantially the supply of engineers or other scientists with long academic training periods in a relatively short period. The major portion of current additions to the supply of engineers enter the profession via college training and the number of current graduates are determined by expectations ruling three or four years earlier. On the other hand, the number of nongraduates entering the profession through on-the-job training and upgrading can be speeded up more rapidly. And even a minimal degree of increased efficiency in the utilization of existing engineers substantially offsets a considerable degree of shortage in the production of new engineers, since the annual additions of new engineers to the profession are running at less than 5 per cent of the total.

Despite the temporary difficulties involved in meeting the increased demand for engineers and scientists after 1950, the modest relative increases in salaries of this group over the recent period cast considerable doubt on the existence of a shortage of such personnel of the magnitude that is implicit in much recent and some current discussions. A shortage of the dimensions often suggested would clearly have evidenced itself in perceptible changes in relative earnings of engineers and scientists since the late forties when the fear was just the reverse, i.e., that there were too many engineers. . . .

Our conclusion that there is no evidence of a shortage of engineers will strike many readers as surprising and some as patently wrong. Although there always remains a range of defensible positions in matters like this, most disagreements probably stem from one of three sources. First, a "shortage" may mean a deficiency by some standard other than the market's. Since we have not investigated nonmarket concepts of shortages (which may be very important), our conclusion has no relevance to them. Second, the finding that earnings of engineers have fallen relative to most other professions and to the general working population may be challenged. One would naturally wish that it rested upon fuller data—in particular, there is an urgent need for comprehensive data on the earnings of college graduates in business—and be supplemented by more precise analyses of "fringe" benefits. But the present statistical basis for the findings is impressive, and when that basis is widened, it is hardly probable that they will be so radically modified as to reverse direction. Finally, the conclusion rests upon the fundamental economic principle that increases in demand relative to supply will manifest themselves, in a free market, in a rising price relative to prices in other markets. . . .

. . . . .

Setting the prices it will charge, or try to charge, is one of the most important jobs of a firm's management. It is also one of the most difficult to do well. Some aspects of the problem are discussed in the following selection. Joel Dean is Professor of Business Economics in the Graduate School of Business, Columbia University, and an experienced management consultant.

13 · Pricing by Business

JOEL DEAN

PRICE POLICIES AND OBJECTIVES. From the modern firm's-eye view, competitive action can generally take three forms: (1) product improvements and new products; (2) sales promotion—advertising, introductory offers, etc., and (3) adjustments of selling prices.

A policy approach, which is becoming normal for other sales activities, is comparatively rare in pricing. Most well-managed manufacturing enterprises have a clear-cut advertising policy, product policy, customer policy, and distribution-channel policy. But pricing decisions remain a patchwork of *ad hoc* decisions, and are dealt with on a crisis basis. Price management by catastrophe discourages the systematic analysis needed for clear-cut pricing policies.

Since different competitive situations

JOEL DEAN, "Managerial Economics," in *Handbook of Industrial Engineering and Management*, ed. W. G. Ireson and E. L. Grant (Englewood Cliffs, N.J.: Prentice-Hall, Inc., 1955), pp. 81–93. Used by permission. In preparation of this section, Mr. Dean was assisted by Stephen Taylor. "Managerial Economics" is drawn largely from two books: Joel Dean, *Managerial Economics* (Englewood Cliffs, N.J.: Prentice-Hall, Inc., 1951); and Joel Dean, *Capital Budgeting* (New York: Columbia University Press, 1951).

require quite different pricing, good solutions for pricing problems require an understanding of the competitive environment in which the company sells its various products.

In pure competition, sellers have no pricing problems because they have no price discretion; they sell at the market price or not at all. Price policy has practical significance only when there is a considerable degree of imperfection in competition, enabling the firm to make some sales in spite of disparities with competitors' prices.

In our analysis of pricing, we shall be concerned with only those kinds of competitive structures that are thus marked by a zone of price discretion. On the basis of product, such competitive structures can be broken into three types, depending on whether the product has: (1) lasting distinctiveness, (2) perishable distinctiveness, or (3) little distinctiveness and a few competitive sellers. . . .

Since product differentiation is of critical importance in price competition, it should be understood that the only kind of product distinctiveness or differentiation that is important in competitive relationships exists in individual buyers' minds, not in technical factual difference. Some people choose television sets on the basis of price alone, because all sets look alike to them; others choose on the basis of cabinet design alone, since they can understand appearance but not performance, and are willing to pay whatever price is asked; still others may choose on the basis of performance alone. Most of us, of course, care about several such product characteristics, or, if you please, product dimensions, and have to establish an optimum compromise position among them. Thus each seller can usually have a monopoly with a few buyers and, at the same time, be in strong competition for sales to others.

PRICING PRODUCTS OF LASTING DISTINCTIVENESS. A product with strong and durable distinctiveness—that is, a rock-ribbed monopoly—is so rare in our economy that we shall not take the space to discuss its appropriate price policy, which is well established in economics as the theory of monopoly pricing. The traditional keystones of monopoly—control of scarce raw materials, patents, economies of large-scale production—have become steadily weaker in the face of the recent advances of industry in substituting one material for another, one design for another, and one process for another to achieve a given objective. Many industries have found that inadequacies of patent protection make it more profitable to pool technical advances among firms than to try to exploit individual discoveries. It is often best to assume, therefore, that new products that are distinctive at the outset will inevitably degenerate over the years into common commodities, with the entry of competition.

PRICING PRODUCTS OF PERISHABLE DISTINCTIVENESS. The real monopoly pricing problem starts when a company finds a product that is a radical departure from existing ways of performing a service and that is temporarily protected from competition by patents, secrets of production, control of a scarce resource, or by other barriers. Since price policy will inevitably have a serious influence on the rate of degeneration in the product's distinctiveness, price policy must integrate a forecast of that decline with company objectives as to its ultimate market position for the product.

Forecasting the progress of the new product is actually forecasting three approximately parallel time paths: (1) technical maturity, indicated by declining rate of product development, increasing standardization among brands, and increasing stability of manufacturing processes and knowledge about them; (2) market maturity, indicated by consumer acceptance of the basic service-idea, by widespread belief that the products of most manufacturers will perform satisfactorily, and by enough familiarity and sophistication to permit consumers to compare brands competently; and (3) competitive maturity, indicated by increasing stability of market shares and price structures.

. . . . .

What are the factors that set the pace of degeneration? An overriding determinant is technical—the amount of capital investment needed to use the innovation effectively. But aside from technical factors, the rate of degeneration is controlled by economic forces that can be subsumed under (1) rate of market acceptance, and (2) ease of entry.

"Market acceptance" means the extent to which buyers consider the product a serious alternative to other ways of performing the same service. The speed of market acceptance varies widely, from the slow growth of garbage-disposal units to the spectacular acceptance of anti-histamine cold tablets, ball-point pens, and soil conditioners. Low unit cost (25¢ rather than $300) probably favors growth, and a past record of successful product innovations aids in giving consumers faith in the company's technical ability and honesty.

Ease of entry is even more difficult to analyze than market acceptance, but probably the most important factor to consider is competitors' capital resources for research and promotion. And of course the bigger the opportunity in a new product, the more capital there is available to invade your field.

POLICIES FOR PIONEER PRICING. The strategic decision in pricing a new product is the choice between: (1) a policy of high initial prices that skim the cream of demand; and (2) a policy of low prices from the outset serving as an active agent for market penetration. . . .

SKIMMING PRICE. For products that represent a drastic departure from accepted ways of performing a service, a policy of relatively high prices coupled with heavy promotional expenditures in the early stages of market development (and lower prices at later stages) has proved successful for many products. There are several reasons for the success of this policy:

1. Demand is likely to be more inelastic with respect to price in the early stages than it is when the product is full-grown, particularly for consumers' goods. The public is still ignorant about the uses and limitations of the product, and there are frequently no readily apparent substitutes. Hence the people who are willing to buy tend to be adventuresome types who want to try out new ways of raising their living standards, and who are more susceptible to promotional effort than to price advantages.

2. Launching a new product with a high price is an efficient device for breaking up the market. This is actually a form of price discrimination. After selling to the market described in (1) above, the price is slowly lowered to reach successively less daring customers until market saturation is sufficient to rob the product of all novelty.

3. The skimming-price policy is safer, or at least appears so. That is, the company will not market the product at all unless initial prices cover the early high costs of product and selling—costs that, if success were certain, would be considered part of the investment outlay in the new product.

4. Many companies are not in a position to finance the product flotation out of distant future revenues, even when

the effects on market expansion make a low initial price clearly more profitable than a high price. High initial prices thus finance the costs of raising a product family when uncertainties block the usual sources of capital.

PENETRATION PRICE. The alternative policy is to use low prices as the principal instrument for penetrating mass markets early. . . . The orthodox skimming policy . . . prevents quick sales to the many buyers at the lower end of the income (or preference) scale who are unwilling to pay any substantial premium for novelty or reputation superiority. The active approach in probing possibilities for market expansion by early penetration pricing requires research, forecasting, and courage. The low-price pattern should be adopted with a view to long-run rather than to short-run profits, with the recognition that it usually takes time to attain the volume potentialities of the market.

What conditions warrant aggressive pricing for market penetration? First, there should be a high responsiveness of sales to reductions in price. Second, savings in production costs as the result of greater volume should be substantial. Third, the product must be of such a nature that it will not seem bizarre when it is first fitted into the consumers' expenditure pattern. Fluorescent lighting, which exemplifies these three traits, showed a dramatic growth of sales in response to early penetration pricing.

A fourth condition that is highly persuasive for penetration pricing is the threat of potential competition. One of the major objectives of most low-pricing policies in the pioneering stages of market development is to raise entry barriers to prospective competitors. But stay-out pricing is not always appropriate; its success depends on the costs of entry for competitors and on the expected size of market. When total demand is expected to be small, the most efficient size of plant may be big enough to supply over half the market. In this case, a low-price policy can capture the bulk of the market and successfully hold back low-cost competition, whereas high prices are an invitation for later comers to invade established markets by selling at discounts. In many industries, however, the important potential competitors are large multiple-product firms for whom the product in question is probably marginal. For such firms, present margins over costs are not the dominant consideration, because they are normally confident that they can get their costs down as low as competitors' costs if the volume of production is large. Thus, when the total market is expected to stay small, potential competitors may not consider the product worth trying, and a high-margin policy can be followed with impunity.

On the other hand, when potential sales appear to be great, there is much to be said for setting prices at their expected long-run level. A big market promises no monopoly in cost savings, and the prime objective of the first entrant is to entrench himself in a market share. Brand preference costs less at the outset than after the competitive promotional clamor has reached full pitch. An off-setting consideration is that, if the new product calls for capital recovery over a long period, there is a risk that later entrants will be able to exploit new production techniques which undercut the pioneer's original cost structure.

Profit calculations should recognize all the contributions that market-development pricing can make to the sale of other products and to the long-run future of the company. . . .

An example of market-expansion pricing is found in the experience of a producer of asbestos shingles. Asbestos shingles have a limited sale in the high-price house market. The company wanted to broaden the market in order to compete effectively with other roofing products for the inexpensive home. It tried to find the price of asphalt shingles that would make the annual cost per unit of roof over a period of years as low as the cheaper roofing that currently commanded the mass market. Indications were that the price would have to be at least this low before volume sales would come. Next, the company explored the relation between production costs and volume, far beyond the range of its own volume experience. Variable costs and overhead costs were estimated separately and the possibilities of a different organization of production were explored. Calculating in terms of anticipated dollars of profit rather than in terms of percentage margin, the company reduced the price of asbestos shingles and brought the annual cost down close to the cost of the cheapest asphalt roof. This reduction produced a greatly expanded volume and secured a substantial share of the mass market.

PRICING STANDARD PRODUCTS WHEN COMPETITORS ARE FEW. In this section we discuss oligopoly, the third competitive situation where price policy is an important management problem. Oligopoly is competition where three, four, or fifteen firms have not only similar products but roughly similar production costs. Usually, rivals' products are sufficiently different in buyers' minds to make brands an important feature in marketing and to allow differences in prices, yet sufficiently similar to make a seller watch rivals' prices closely.

In industries where a few competitors dominate the supply of relatively uniform products, periods of low demand and excess capacity create serious competitive problems. This is particularly so in industries with heavy plant investments, and high barriers to entry.

Each manufacturer is aware of the disastrous effects that an announced reduction of his own price would have on the prices charged by competitors. As a result, these companies have by experience developed a pronounced aversion for attempting to gain market share by open price cutting. Under these circumstances, market share is largely determined by secret price concessions and by non-price competition.

When the dynamic changes in demand and cost conditions that prompt a given price change are viewed in much the same way by all rivals, they do not cause serious uncertainties concerning rivals' reactions. But these uncertainties do become serious: (a) when rivals are quite differently affected by the same general changes in conditions, (b) when rivals differ in their estimates concerning the future conditions for which they are pricing, and (c) when rivals have drastically different notions about the effectiveness of price changes.

Since these disruptive influences are continually at work to some degree in many industries, a critical problem of oligopoly is to devise industry practices that can reconcile the need for adjustments to changing industry demand with the need to maintain the precarious price structure that has been established.

Two important releases from this dilemma are (1) non-price competition and (2) price leadership. . . .

NON-PRICE COMPETITION. Non-price competition is viewed with far more equanimity than price-cutting, and is frequently quite unrestrained. The basic reason may be that retaliation is much more difficult against advertising or product improvements than against price-cutting. The great variation in efficiency of marketing activities demonstrates the importance of "know-how" barriers to retaliation. The best way of doing things is too peculiar to each firm's situation to permit speedy imitation. Retaliation therefore often takes a different route. A sampling campaign by one soap manufacturer is met by a contest rather than by a duplication of the sampling campaign. Furthermore, the sales effects of a particular promotional stratagem are far less clear than the effects of price-cutting, and there is usually a less compelling necessity to retaliate.

PRICE LEADERSHIP. The institution of price leadership is another way for oligopoly competitors to achieve the delicate adjustment to changing cost and demand conditions without precipitating a price war. One firm takes the initiating role in all price changes, and the other firms follow along, matching the leader's price exactly, or with established differentials. Price leadership in action may be seen most clearly in a mature and stable industry with a standardized product, such as steel, oil, cement, or building materials. But it plays an important part in many industries that have considerable product differentiations.

Price leadership greatly reduces the number of possible reactions to a price change, and thus gives a modicum of certainty to the pricing aspects of market forecasting. All that is needed is one firm whose price policy is consistently acceptable to most of the industry. . . . In the more sophisticated industries, there is a feeling of mutual responsibility of the leader to set prices that other firms can live with, and of the followers to follow the leader in the best interests of the group.

PROBLEMS OF THE PRICE LEADER. Broadly conceived, the problem of the price leader is a problem of industrial statesmanship, particularly when industry conditions are changing rapidly. If he fails to reconcile his own and the industry's interests with those of the followers, he may easily impair his own position in leadership and market share.

In many industries, price leadership has been fairly responsive to changes in cost and in demand, and at the same time has managed to dampen the amplitude of cyclical fluctuations. Under leadership, prices have not gone as high in boom periods or as low in depressions. Price leadership usually produces few, but large and dramatic, price changes in the industry over the cycle. After World War II, a few leaders, notably International Harvester and General Electric, tried lowering prices in an attempt to curb inflation, but they were too far out of line with market conditions to be followed. They subsequently raised their prices again.

Even in normal conditions, however, the leader usually leads only in price rises. Any competitor can lead real prices down, and usually nominal followers take the initiative here.

It is important for the leader to know how long the lower price level will last. A temporary drop should be met only by informal concessions from the official price, since frequent changes in announced prices disrupt the followers' adjustments and weaken the leader's prestige. Only when market weakness indicates a fairly long-run shift in conditions should the major move of changing official prices be made. The price leader often merely formalizes what is generally recognized as inevitable in the trade, or merely forecasts sooner, and more accurately, what later becomes recognized. Forecasting is thus a critical part of leadership. . . .

UNDERGROUND PRICE COMPETITION. The discussion of price leadership has indicated that the most important device for short-run sales expansion is the secret price concession. The form of the concession is not important, so long as the buyer understands the real offer. It may take the form of high turn-in values, down-grading of high-quality lines, better payment terms, and so forth. Underground price competition in the tire industry takes such forms as concessions to mail-order houses and filling-station chains, and special prices for "test tires" (allegedly slightly used).

The industry leader has the problem of determining whether and how to reduce the level of official prices to meet undercover concessions. When are undercover concessions significant enough to warrant open reduction of prices? Here are a few strategic indicators:

1. When they spread over a wide geographic area.
2. When they continue for several months.
3. When first-line competitors indulge quite generally in undercover cutting.
4. When the price-cutter is out to broaden the market. If his motive seems to be to capture a bigger market share by secret concessions, the leader may merely meet these informal concessions.

The main economic function of underground price competition is to give resilience and stability to an otherwise brittle oligopoly situation. . . .

COST-PLUS PRICING. Surveys of actual business practice in setting prices have indicated that the most pervasive pricing method used is to make a cost estimate and to add a margin of some kind for profit—what is known as cost-plus pricing. Cost-plus pricing is so extensively used and at the same time so difficult to reconcile with economic theory that it deserves special attention.

DETERMINATION OF PROFIT MARK-UP. The percentage that is added for profit in cost-plus formulas differs strikingly among industries, among member firms, and even among products of the same firm, although it has been suggested that 10 per cent is a typical figure. Some of this variation may be due to differences in competitive intensity, some to differences in cost base (e.g., the degree to which profit has already been included by padding of overhead), and some to differences in turnover rate and risk. The size of this profit factor, however, often reflects habits or custom and some vague notion of a "just" profit.

The size of the mark-up can be determined rationally only in terms of sales forecasts, cost forecasts, and some criterion of an acceptable or goal rate of return. But any rate-of-return standard is essentially arbitrary—i.e., there are no economic guides to rate-standards except "all you can get"—and cost-plus pricing is fundamentally a denial of this economic doctrine. Within the cost-plus framework, perhaps the most sensible standard is a recent average return of companies that are comparable in products, processes, and risks. Such a standard provides some measure of the competitive return that is allowable in the industry without loss of market shares or invasion of markets.

INADEQUACIES OF COST-PLUS PRICING. The popularity of the cost-plus method does not mean that it is the best available method. In most situations it is not, for several reasons:

1. It ignores demand. What people will pay for a product bears no necessary relation to what it costs any particular manufacturer to make it.
2. It fails to reflect competition adequately, especially the effect upon the birth of potential competition.
3. It overplays the precision of allocated costs—that is, costs that are common to several products and must be distributed among the products by some arbitrary rule.
4. It is based upon a concept of cost that is frequently not relevant for the pricing decision. For many decisions, incremental costs rather than full costs should be controlling, and opportunity costs—i.e., alternative uses of facilities

—are not reflected in accounting systems.

5. It involves circular reasoning in some degree if current full cost is used as the base. To the extent that unit costs vary with output, and thus with sales volume, this cost depends partly on the price charged, provided that demand has significant elasticity and fixed overhead is important.

JUSTIFICATION OF COST-PLUS PRICING. In defense of cost-plus pricing, the following arguments have been marshaled for particular situations:

1. It is a resort of desperation, in the absence of the knowledge required for more reasonable methods. It is difficult to estimate at all precisely the impact of price upon sales volume. Ignorance of the firm's demand curve obviously makes it impossible to take its influence on price into account. The reaction of rivals to a given price policy that has a pronounced effect upon volume is also hard to forecast. The effect of today's price on tomorrow's demand and upon potential competition may also be hard to estimate. . . .

2. It is the safest though not the most profitable method of pricing. In pricing a new, made-to-order article, a cost-plus formula may set what amounts to a refusal price. The seller automatically saves himself from tying up facilities with work that would yield subnormal profits.

A major uncertainty in setting a price is the unknown reaction of rivals to that price. When the products and production processes of rivals are highly similar, cost-plus pricing may offer a source of competitive stability by setting a price that is more likely to yield acceptable profits to most other members of the industry.

Another kind of cost-plus safety pricing is based on some sort of Jeremiah criterion. By envisioning the worst probable cyclical demand shift, a price is built up that will produce a predetermined profit level under these circumstances. An example is pricing to break even at 30 per cent capacity. . . .

3. Most new products are molded to meet a zone of competitive price, and much selling effort goes into giving the maximum quality in that price range. In an extreme form, a selling price is predetermined exactly, and by working back from this, product cost, and hence design, are arrived at.

4. Another situation in which cost is an unusual limiter of price is in selling to a few powerful and knowledgeable buyers. An example is the automobile parts industry, where buyers know a great deal about suppliers' costs and are in a position to make the product themselves if they don't like the seller's prices.

PRICE DIFFERENTIALS. There are at least two parts to a complete price policy. The first is the method for determining the basic list price of a product, which has been the subject of this article so far. The second part, the subject of the rest of the article, is the system for determining the net price actually charged particular customers, that is, the system for price variation related to *conditions of sale:* (1) the trade status of the buyer, (2) the amount of his purchase, (3) the location of the purchaser, (4) the promptness of payment.

The average net realized price per unit obtained by the manufacturer depends not only upon the formal structure of price differentials for various classes of purchases, but also upon the proportion of sales made in each class. . . .

. . . . .

GOALS OF DIFFERENTIAL PRICES. From the seller's standpoint, the differential prices that result from the application of various discount structures and from product-line pricing may serve several purposes. It is, therefore, desirable to look first at the company's whole structure of price differentials in terms of these purposes, which may be grouped as follows:

1. *Implementation of marketing strategy.* The patterns of price differentials (product-price differentials and the various discount structures) should implement the company's over-all marketing strategy. These price differentials should be efficiently geared with other elements in the marketing program (e.g., advertising and distribution channels) to reach the sectors of the market selected by strategy. In doing so, the job of a particular structure of discounts may be quite specific. For example, an oil company whose strategy was directed at large and few service stations served by giant transport trucks would grant large quantity discounts for big purchases.

2. *Market segmentation.* A major objective of differential prices is to achieve profitable market segmentation when legal and competitive considerations permit discrimination.

The practical problem of putting price discrimination to work involves breaking the market into sectors that differ in price elasticity of demand. To the extent that it is feasible to seal off such segments of the market, charging different prices for different sectors can increase the total volume of sales. Price discounts of various sorts are a major means of achieving market segmentation.

3. *Market expansion.* Differential pricing that is designed to encourage new uses or to woo new customers is a common goal of product-line pricing, but it also extends over various phases of the discount structure, depending upon the circumstances of a purchase by a new user.

4. *Competitive adaptation.* Differential prices are a major device for selective adjustment to the competitive environment. Discounts are often designed to match what competitors charge under comparable conditions of purchase, in terms of net price to each customer class. When products are homogeneous, competitive parity is a compelling consideration.

5. *Reduction of production costs.* Differential prices can sometimes help solve problems of production. Seasonal or other forms of time-period discounts may be partly for the purpose of regularizing output by changing the timing of sales. For example, since electricity cannot be stored, classifications of electric rates are designed to encourage off-season uses and to penalize uses that contribute to peaks.

. . . . .

DISTRIBUTOR DISCOUNTS. Distributor (or trade-channel) discounts are deductions from list price that systematically make the net price vary according to the buyers' position in the chain of distribution. These differential prices distinguish among customers on the basis of their marketing functions (e.g., wholesaler vs. retailer), and are thus also called "functional discounts." Special prices given to manufacturers who incorporate the product in their own original equipment (e.g., tires and spark plugs sold to automobile manufacturers), special prices to other members of the same industry (e.g., gasoline "exchanges" among petroleum companies), and special prices to the Federal Government, to state governments, and to universities, are examples of common forms of discounts that are close enough to trade-channel discounts to be grouped with them. . . .

The economic function of distributor discounts is to induce independent distributors to perform marketing services. To build a discount structure on a sound economic basis, it is necessary to know:

(1) the objectives of the discount structure, (2) distributors' operating costs, (3) discount structures of competitors, (4) opportunities for market segmentation.

OBJECTIVES. To find out exactly what services the manufacturer wants from each type of distributor requires a broad, carefully thought-out distribution plan that fits the product, the competitive position of the seller, and the folkways of the industry. The primary consideration in working out such a plan is the allocation of marketing functions between the manufacturer and the distributing chain and among the links in that chain. The problem is to find which functionary can do each specific job most economically and effectively. . . .

DISTRIBUTORS' OPERATING COSTS. The most important function of trade-channel discounts is to cover the operating costs and normal profits of distributors. Discounts should be closely aligned to these costs if distributors are to play the part planned for them. Margins that are too rich produce excess selling effort or too many distributors, while margins that don't cover costs will not move the goods.

Should trade discounts be determined by the costs of the inefficient distributor or by the costs of the efficient distributor? One solution to this problem is to set trade discounts to cover the estimated operating costs (plus normal profits) of the most efficient two-thirds of the dealers. When cost estimates are uncertain, a practical test of excessive margins is the extent to which rehandlers pass margins on by knocking down realized prices.

Another check on distributors' costs is an estimate of the manufacturer's cost of performing the distributive function himself. Many companies periodically consider doing more of the marketing job themselves (e.g., bypassing the wholesaler), and such estimates are frequently available as by-products of these trade-channel policy studies. Moreover, some companies operate through different channels in different sections of the country, and thus have some cost experience in performing distributive functions.

COMPETITORS' DISCOUNT STRUCTURES. In a sense, dealer discounts are a means of purchasing the dealers' sales assistance in a competitive market. In many industries the actual (as opposed to the nominal) discounts granted by rival sellers vary. The manufacturer must decide whether he is to be guided by the higher or by the lower discounts. Specifically, a manufacturer whose product is at some disadvantage in consumer acceptance may consider making an attempt to buy distribution by granting larger margins than do competitors. The success of such an effort usually depends on whether the margin incentive will actually induce the distributor to push the product; and whether competitors are likely to meet the wider margins.

Price discrimination among individual consumers in the retail market is a common form of market segmentation. The manufacturer's pricing problem here is whether to keep the initial margins high enough to permit dealers to make individual concessions to customers. Realized margins that are substantially lower than official margins do not necessarily mean that the official margins should be reduced. This disparity may be justified in industries where competition at the dealer level is strong and where opportunities for personal differentiation are important. A dealer can then get the full price from some customers who are averse to shopping and bargaining and can give substantially lower prices, with the flavor of a bargain, to more careful shoppers. This kind of individual pricing can yield a higher dealer profit than can uniform pricing. A conspicuous example of such pricing is found in the operation of automobile dealers under normal competitive conditions. It is normally appropriate to permit the dealer considerable latitude when the unit cost of the article is high, when trade-ins and service concessions provide a convenient mechanism for veiled price reductions, and when the customer is not tied tightly to the dealer by strings of continuity of service or by customer relations.

QUANTITY DISCOUNTS. . . . The essential problem for management in quantity discounts is to decide how big they shall be. What merchandising job do we want quantity discounts to do? One important job of quantity discounts is to reduce both the number of and the losses from small orders. It is common for a firm to find that 80 per cent of its orders account for only 20 per cent of its sales, and the cost of making these sales frequently causes an actual out-of-pocket drain of cash. Quantity discounts can help correct the size-distribution of orders in three ways: (1) They may stimulate a given set of customers to order the same amount of business in bigger lots. (2) They may induce the same customers to give the seller a larger share of their total business in order to get savings of quantity buying. (3) They may turn away small accounts and attract bigger accounts, thus altering the size-distribution of the customers themselves.

. . . . .

LEGALITY. Quantity discounts have been a question of much litigation by the Federal Trade Commission . . . legality hinges largely on proved cost savings resulting from large orders, and that, by and large, cost savings are provable only in the selling and distribution expenses of filling the order.

. . . . .

When a business has some control over the prices it will charge, the management faces the question which is the title of this reading. Here a professor of business economics at the University of Michigan answers the question with special reference to the automobile industry. We see, among other things, the significance of differences in degree of elasticity of demand, the relative importance of fixed and variable cost, and the bearing of durability and of the existence of a used car market on price-output decisions. The brief summary of historical backgrounds is also of interest.

14 · When Is Price Reduction Profitable?

CLARE E. GRIFFIN

How often we have heard, at Congressional hearings or other public meetings, criticism of businessmen for failing to reduce prices, especially in the face of declining demand. This criticism is directed in particular at large firms operating under conditions of oligopoly (i.e., where a few large concerns share most of the market). A specific target for this criticism has been the automobile industry. For example:

• Walter Reuther proposed, about two years ago, that the automobile manufacturers should reduce prices by $100. This, he argued, would be good for the country and would actually be profitable to the companies.[1]

• John Blair, at one time chief economist to the Kefauver Committee on Antitrust and Monopoly, has taken the position that if automobile producers fully recognized the elasticity of demand, they would be more likely to reduce prices in their own interest. Blair quoted with approval Sir Denis Robertson as saying that in his experience businessmen almost invariably regard the demand for their industry's product as extremely inelastic.[2]

How much truth is there in such assertions? That is what I would like to examine in this article. Specifically, I shall discuss, from the point of view of business policy, the feasibility of price reduction as a means of stimulating sales in the short run. Even more specifically, I want to question the feasibility of price reduction for maintaining profits or reducing losses in an oligopolistic industry in the face of a real or threatened general decline in consumer purchases of the product in question.

Exaggerated Elasticity

It is difficult to know whether businessmen do, in fact, underestimate the

---

[1] *Hearings before the Senate Subcommittee on Antitrust and Monopoly*, 85th Congress, Second Session (Washington, Government Printing Office, 1958), p. 2225.

[2] *American Economic Review*, papers and proceedings of December 1958 meeting of the American Economics Association, May 1959, p. 444.

CLARE E. GRIFFIN, "When is Price Reduction Profitable?" *Harvard Business Review* (September–October 1960), pp. 125–132. Used by permission.

degree to which sales volume will increase as a result of reduced prices. But it is true, in any event, that business critics do exaggerate the effects that price elasticity of demand has or should have on price reduction. The chief reason for this is a relative neglect of the cost side of the problem.

In an industry where there are few producers of products that consumers regard as closely comparable, a price reduction by one important producer will almost necessarily be met by the others. Whether, under these circumstances, a price reduction would maintain or increase profits depends on two questions:

1. What will be the effect of the price reduction on demand and thus on revenues? (This is the problem of demand elasticity.)
2. What effect will this change in volume have on costs? (This is the problem of cost elasticity.)

Naturally, both questions must be considered by a manufacturer in determining whether a price reduction will be in his own interest.

I would argue that in most manufacturing industries the elasticity of demand would have to be very high indeed to lead producers into price reductions. Further, in most cases where manufacturers refrain from reducing a price when they know the reduction will be matched by competitors, this decision does not imply a general tendency to underestimate the elasticity of demand.

Of course, when I refer to price elasticity, I mean the relation of demand* to price in a moderate range around existing prices—say a 10% price change up or down from the existing

---

* Here and at numerous other points the author uses the term "demand" to mean "quantity demanded." *Ed.*

market price. Similarly, when I discuss the ratio of fixed to variable costs subsequently, I refer to production within a restricted range around the usual percentage of theoretical capacity. No practical purpose is served by departing unrealistically from reasonable price changes and from usual capacity percentages.

INCREASING REVENUE. Let us consider in some detail the automobile industry which, in many ways, is fairly representative of American heavy industry. It will be illuminating if we work out the implications of the studies of demand mentioned by John Blair, which indicate a price elasticity for new automobiles ranging from 1.2 to 1.5. These studies seem to imply that this would justify a price reduction. What the 1.5 figure means, for example, is that the increased demand will be one and one-half times as great as the decreased price, or that a 1.0% decrease in price would produce a 1.5% increase in demand. (Strictly speaking, the coefficient is a minus quantity, for the quantity bought varies inversely with price. However, it seems easier to neglect minus signs, and this fairly common practice will be followed here.)

This particular estimate for automobiles represents the limit that has been mentioned by independent researchers; the usual estimate is substantially less than this. . . .

Let us accept for the moment the largest of these figures as an indication of the reaction of demand to a price change and ask whether it would be profitable for an automobile manufacturer to reduce the list price of a line of cars by, say, $100. Assuming that the average price of the line is $2,500, let us place the anticipated sales volume at this price at 1,000,000 cars. We will also assume that a price reduction by one producer will be met by others, so that we are not considering a relative price advantage but the effect of a general price change. How will volume and revenue be affected? Consider this:

A price reduction from $2,500 to $2,400 is 4%. With a demand elasticity of 1.5 this would indicate a resulting increase in sales of 6% (i.e., 1.5 × 4%). So volume would be increased from 1,000,000 to 1,060,000 cars, and sales and revenue would be affected as follows:

At price of $2,500,
 1,000,000 cars × $2,500 = $2,500,000,000
At price of $2,400
 1,060,000 cars × $2,400 = $2,544,000,000

Thus, we would have increased revenue by $44,000,000. This is where much popular reasoning, as well as that of some economists, ends. The conclusion is hastily drawn that if the manufacturer really recognized the degree of elasticity, or if he were not overly cautious or just plain stupid, he would seize this opportunity to increase revenue.

THE KEY IS COSTS. Of course, revenue alone is not the objective; rather the maintenance of profit is the ultimate goal, and to estimate this we must consider costs as well. This is the point often overlooked by those who criticize business, especially the mass-production industries. Overestimating the role of increased volume in reducing unit costs, they forget that the true effect on total costs of producing the additional 60,000 cars will depend on the ratio of fixed costs to variable costs.

What is a reasonable estimate of the ratio between fixed and variable costs in heavy industries? Here are some good approximations:

• In the automobile industry, my own interviews indicate that the ratio would be on the order of 15% to 20% for fixed costs and 80% to 85% for variable.

• For the United States Steel Corporation (when operating at 80% of capacity), the ratio has been estimated at 18.5% for fixed, 81.5% for variable.[3]

• In the production of pig aluminum, the ratio has been placed at 15% for fixed and 85% for variable.[4]

In order to consider what happens to costs in our illustrative case, let us accept, for purposes of our analysis, a fixed-variable cost ratio of 20 to 80, thus taking again the upper limit of the estimated range which would be most favorable to the price reduction proposal.

We assumed as our starting point a price of $2,500 and a volume of $1,000,000, thus yielding a revenue of $2,500,000,000. Now if we assume that unit costs are $2,300, there is a total cost of $2,300,000,000 and a profit of $200,000,000. If the 20 to 80 ratio of fixed to variable costs exists, this total cost then breaks down to fixed costs of $460,000,000 (20% of $2,300,000,000) and variable costs of $1,840,000,000 (80% of $2,300,000,000), or $1,840 per car.

If we reduce the price to $2,400, revenue will, as indicated before, become $2,544,000,000, but the number of cars produced and sold is increased from 1,000,000 to 1,060,000. Costs will become:

Fixed cost	$ 460,000,000
Variable ($1,840 × 1,060,000)	1,950,400,000
Total cost	2,410,400,000

Profits can be determined thus:

Revenue	$2,544,000,000
Costs	$2,410,400,000
Profit	$ 133,600,000

---

[3] Study by Theodore O. Yntema included in *Hearings before the Temporary National Economic Committee,* Part 26, p. 14058.
[4] Nathanael H. Engle, *Aluminum, An Industrial Marketing Appraisal* (Homewood, Illinois, Richard D. Irwin, Inc., 1944), p. 208.

Thus, while the price reduction produced an increase in revenue of $44,000,000 (from $2,500,000,000 to $2,544,000,000), it reduced profits by $66,400,000 (from $200,000,000 to $133,600,000). Expressed in unit terms, the price reduction led to reduced revenue per car of $100, and to reduced cost per car of only $26.42. Cost at the larger volume, therefore, would be $2,273.58 instead of $2,300 at the old volume. Obviously, *the additional cars are not free goods,* and anyone who makes recommendations as to price policy on the basis of revenue only—or on the assumption that the reduction in revenue per car will "naturally" be offset by the larger volume—is being decidedly unrealistic.

THEORETICAL PROFITS. It is true that there might be some theoretical demand elasticity that would justify a price reduction even when considering the cost factor. It is true, also, that the higher the percentage of costs remaining fixed, the lower would have to be the coefficient of elasticity. However, assuming the 20% fixed and 80% variable cost ratio, the elasticity of demand under the conditions assumed above would have to be 4.46, in order to justify a price reduction.[5] This is about three times the elasticity found in any of the studies of the automobile industry.

In concrete terms, an elasticity of demand of 4.46 would mean that the effect of adopting a price of $2,400 instead of a price of $2,500 would be to increase the purchase of new cars by 17.84%, that is, from the assumed 1,000,000 cars to 1,178,400 cars (4.46 × 4% reduction = 17.84%).

In determining whether (on a common-sense basis) this result might possibly follow, we must bear in mind that this is not a question of cross elasticity, which expresses the effect of a price change by one competitor which is *not* met by the others. What would happen if one manufacturer of a large proportion of the cars in a certain price class were to set this lower price and his competitors, conveniently for him, chose to remain at the higher price? This is indeed another question, but not a very realistic one, for the other manufacturers almost surely would meet the lower price.

At any rate, when Reuther and economists refer to elasticity of demand, they mean general elasticity for the product of an industry—not cross elasticity which arises from a competitive differential in prices. Thus, the conclusion is inescapable that if businessmen deny that a price reduction of 4% by all the producers would probably increase demand by 17.84%, they are neither stupid nor ignorant of the workings of demand elasticity.

From a consideration of elasticity and

---

[5] The following equation can be used to determine the elasticity of demand required for a given price reduction (leaving profits unimpaired) when the ratio of fixed and variable costs within the range of volume contemplated is known:

X = per cent increase of volume required
Y = price reduction in dollars
P = profit per car at the old price
C = cost per car at the old price
V = per cent of variable cost at present level of production

Therefore $X = \dfrac{Y}{P - Y + (1 - V)C}$

and the coefficient of elasticity will be
$$\dfrac{X(P + C)}{Y}$$

In the above example, then:
$Y = \$100 \quad P = \$200$
$C = \$2,300 \quad V = .80$

Then $X = \dfrac{100}{200 - 100 + .20 \times 2,300} = 17.86\%$

and the coefficient of elasticity will be

$$\dfrac{17.86\,(200 + 2,300)}{100} = 4.465$$

fixed and variable costs, some other observations can be offered:

1. *The elasticity required to maintain profits varies inversely with the margin of profit at the point of departure.* If, in the above illustration, we had assumed the same original price of $2,500, a cost of $2,000 (instead of $2,300), a profit per car of $500, and the same ratio of fixed to variable costs, the elasticity required to maintain profits would have been 3.125 instead of 4.46.

2. *If in two situations the unit profit in dollars is the same, but in one instance it is a smaller percentage of cost or price, required elasticity in that case will be greater.* This generalization is suggested by the fact that if we assumed the original price to be $2,800, cost $2,300, and profit $500 (as in the immediately preceding example), the required elasticity would have been 3.256.

3. *The greater the price reduction, the greater must be the coefficient of elasticity.* Leaving all other factors the same as in the original example, let us contemplate a price reduction of $200 instead of $100. For profits to remain unimpaired in this case an elasticity of 5.42 would be required.

The fact that a higher elasticity is required to justify the larger price decrease follows, of course, from the fact that—with the relation of fixed and variable costs assumed here—the effect of a volume increase is greater increase in total costs than in total revenue. This divergence becomes greater as the price reduction is increased, and therefore a still larger elasticity would be required to offset this effect.

The conclusion is that the effect of a general price reduction on demand—what we have called price elasticity—is not great enough in the automobile industry to induce a price reduction when account is taken of the effect that increased demand has on costs.

There are, of course, many factors affecting people's demand for new cars. One of these (which, unfortunately for policy makers, is not subject to direct influence by the companies) is the level of consumer income. This effect of income on demand can be called "income elasticity," and for this too the coefficients have been estimated. All five of the studies cited at the Kefauver Committee hearings also estimated income elasticity, and in every case it was more pronounced than price elasticity. The estimates ranged from a low of 2.1 to a high of 4.2.[6]

This coincides with the common-sense observation that people will buy more new cars when their incomes are going up and, I would add, when their confidence in the future is high; in the opposite conditions, a price reduction will not do the trick. This is especially true in the automobile industry because most prospective customers have a car; therefore their refusal to buy a new one this year does not deprive them of transportation. In a sense, a new car for such persons is a luxury, and durable luxuries are not purchased even at reduced prices when the public is uneasy about the future. For this reason, it is difficult to buck the effect of a recession with a price reduction.

Price Dynamics

The concept of elasticity is commonly and properly used in economics in a static sense: i.e., it is concerned with the effect of price on effective demand at a given time with all other factors remaining inactive. Consistent with this concept, it is better to think of alternatives at a certain point in time rather

---

[6] *Hearings before the Senate Subcommittee on Antitrust and Monopoly,* 85th Congress, Second Session pursuant to S. Res. 57 and S. Res. 231, p. 3215.

than while changing from one time to another. When we phrase the problem in this way and give due attention to the costs incurred in producing the additional units, I think we must conclude that it is vain to expect voluntary price reductions in most oligopolistic industries purely in the hope of increased demand resulting from the price change itself. There are, of course, other reasons that may prompt a price reduction, but that is another story.

EXPANDING THE MARKET. But prices and price elasticity can also be viewed in a dynamic sense, and businessmen frequently do view them in that way. Thus, a price reduction, especially a radical one, may under some circumstances have a profound effect in expanding the market over a period of time. The expansion may be one not only of degree but of kind. For example, if a new product is put on the market at a high price (fully justified by unit costs), it may tap but one level of potential demand. There may be other, much larger potential demand levels in lower price ranges. A bold and imaginative policy of reaching to those lower levels could bring rich returns. Consider the chemical industry as an illustration:

> A new synthetic fiber, for example, may be so costly and high priced that it is used only for surgical and other very limited purposes. By dropping the price in anticipation of reduced costs, the hosiery and fine apparel markets may be reached; still further down the price scale, the rug, carpet, and industrial markets may be tapped.

This familiar story is basic to the epic of Henry Ford and other pioneers in the automobile industry who sharply dropped the prices of automobiles in the second decade of this century. The decline in the price of automobiles from 1909 to 1916 was radical indeed: the national average of wholesale prices dropped in this period from $1,250 to $604. And the revenue of the industry (wholesale value of U.S. production), rose from $160 million to $921 million.[7]

This is a story that has fired the imagination of generations of businessmen, greatly to our national advantage. It is also the favorite example of critics who urge present-day businessmen to act along the same lines. It is good that the example should be remembered, but like any prescription it cannot be applied indiscriminately. The situation that existed in the early days of the automobile industry was a very special one that ordinarily comes but once, if at all, to an industry.

CHANGED CONDITIONS. It is quite apparent that special conditions did exist in the automobile industry prior to World War I. First, look at some of the market facts. The automobile in its earliest days had been sold as a high-price sporting item, mainly for pleasure, and appealed strongly to social prestige. It was apparent (or at least it is now), that the large sectors of demand based on the utilitarian idea of the automobile as transportation had not been touched. Reaching those areas of demand required reliability and ease of operation in the product and, above all, radically lower prices. The movement in this direction was accompanied by cost-saving simplifications in the car—a downgrading of certain nonutilitarian features.

Moreover, one of the most important facts about the present economics of the automobile industry—the large used-car market—did not exist at that time, partly because very few cars had been produced to supply such a market and also because a 1906 car in 1916 was so

---

[7] Ralph Epstein, *The Automobile Industry* (Chicago, A. W. Shaw Company, 1928), p. 314.

outdated as to be unattractive. Today, the potential first buyer has the option of buying a very serviceable used car which is far below the price of the new cars. The fact that a good car of recent vintage is available at, say, 40% below the price of that same car new reduces materially the number of buyers who can be attracted by a 10% price reduction in a new car.

And no one suggests that a reduction of that magnitude today could lead to a commensurate reduction in cost unless it were accompanied by cost-reducing changes in design. The fact seems to be that the buyer of a new car must be motivated by the desire to get something better than, or at least different from, that offered in the one- and two-year-old cars. Thus, the decision to buy a new car is not ordinarily based on a desire for economy. This, incidentally, tends to explain the importance of the annual model and to indicate one reason why innovations are more important than slight price reductions.

On the marketing side, the large used-car market also introduces indirect effects which are in marked contrast to the market conditions of the early days of the century. Thus, a price reduction in this year's model will depress the price of the cars of previous years on the used-car market. Since the typical buyer of a new car today has a used car to trade in, he will find that his net cost, the amount he has to pay in addition to his old car, has not declined as much as the price of a new car. Thus, the manufacturer who reduces his price will find that the effect has been partly neutralized by the resulting decline in the value of the prospective customer's old car. Such problems were of minor concern to the early producers, because most of their customers were buying first cars and a large used-car market did not exist.

Moreover, those who argue that price reductions today in the automobile industry will have the same beneficial effect on demand that the reductions had in the first decades of this century overlook the fact that the early increase in production took place over a period of seven years—from 127,000 cars in 1909 to 1,525,000 in 1916. It is doubtful if any heavy industry could handle an increase of that magnitude—involving as it would new plants, equipment, and sources of supply—in any one year. Furthermore, some time interval must be allowed for consumer habits and attitudes to change. Realization of facts like these takes some of the steam out of the arguments for immediate increased demand through immediate reductions in price.

PRODUCTION DIFFERENCES. Radically new methods of production—continuous production lines and other features of mass production—were invented by the ingenuity of the early producers and made economically possible by the great increase in volume that took place. The 45-fold increase in the industry total brought revolutionary changes in production costs; it was not just a matter of spreading overhead over a larger volume, but also of making possible an entirely new producing complex.

The present situation stands in sharp contrast to this—in the matter of costs, for one thing. Today, even if lower prices did lead to much greater volume —say, at the extreme, a 50% increase —the unit cost reductions would be rather small. For any of the larger companies such an increase would not be possible simply by utilizing present capacity more fully. New plants would have to be built, and they would be substantially like the present ones. Some improvements might conceivably be made, but they would not be of comparable importance to the earlier introduction of the continuous production line. The extension of automation today would be of a lesser magnitude, because the present volume of the major companies is already sufficiently exploiting it.

Further improvements in production may and indeed probably will come, but *they are not dependent on increased volume*—nor would they be particularly hastened by such increased volume. Partial evidence for this is that existing assembly plants and other major plant units of the larger companies have apparently already reached optimum size. Hence, increased volume would presumably result in more, rather than larger, plants. An increased number of these units would probably "spread the overhead" somewhat; e.g., costs represented by the central office and research activities. Also, increased volume of any given model would reduce the unit cost of retooling for the annual model change. Primarily, however, a volume increase today would mean that more tons of steel, more days of labor, and perhaps more "overtime" would be expended and that more plants would be erected. In summary, hoped-for economies in all such industries will neither come from sheer increase in volume, nor be dependent on it.

The fact is that the automobile industry as a productive organization is now mature. It is 50 years old. This does not mean that it has no growth potential. It means rather that growth will presumably be a function of imaginative innovations in the product; the offering of greater variety in types and price classes as well as growth of the population and the advance of national productivity and affluence. In short, much the same growth potential exists here as in many mature industries like housing where the products have become established in the American pattern of consumption. In this respect, today's automobile industry is entirely different from the industry of the first quarter of this century, and the effects of price reductions are correspondingly different.

Some of these differences have been spelled out here because members of Congressional committees and their staffs have at times made unfavorable comparisons of the present-day industry and its leaders with "old Henry" and the other pioneers. And it is not to detract from the credit of early leaders to point out that even the exploits of the greatest of pioneers are conditioned by their times and that the lessons of the early period have only limited application to the detailed policies of today.

Mass Production Myths

Now what about the ratio of fixed and variable costs for U.S. manufacturing industries generally? We have become so impressed with the advantages of mass production that we assume additional products can be manufactured with very little incremental cost. The real advantages of mass production do not properly lead to this conclusion; they concern the effectiveness with which labor can be employed, supplies obtained, and the production process arranged. They do not imply that once plants and equipment are set up, additional output units will roll off the machines at very little extra cost. This misconception leads to much fallacious reasoning on the part of the public.

In manufacturing industries generally —even where there is a large investment in plant and equipment—the variable costs greatly exceed the fixed costs. In the automobile industry, the estimate has already been made of 15% to 20% for fixed costs and 80% to 85% for variable costs. That some ratio of this kind should be expected is suggested by the published figures of the automobile companies which indicate the distribution of the revenue dollar. Specifically:

It is indicated that 50% or more of every dollar taken in by the larger companies is spent on materials and supplies purchased from outside sources. The figures also suggest that another large item, around 25%, is the payroll, most of which, of course, is for hourly rated workers and will be influenced by the number of workers employed and the hours for which they are employed. Thus, both of these items vary almost directly with volume. On the other hand, salaries, depreciation, maintenance, and interest payments are in the short run relatively fixed. But the total of these items is proportionately small. These comments suggest why, contrary to wide popular opinion, the fixed costs in this industry play a minor role.

I stated earlier that these figures seem to be fairly representative of American manufacturing industries. True, in some industries the ratios will be affected by the degree of integration. For example, we would expect a petroleum company that limits itself to refining to have high variable costs represented by its purchases of crude oil. On the other hand, the consolidated statements of some of the larger integrated companies, covering costs and expenses of production and distribution, indicate a pattern not radically different from that shown by the industries mentioned.

Again, outside of the industrial field, public utilities do, of course, show a higher percentage of fixed costs, as do the railroads. But in most heavy industries the fixed-variable cost ratio will approximate that of the automobile industry.

All these comments on fixed and variable costs have assumed a moderate range of volume. If the proposed price reduction has a *very* extensive effect on volume, new facilities will be required. Probably this would mean new plants; and, if optimum plant size has been attained, this would not lead to lower unit costs. Indeed, during a period of inflation, the addition of new facilities would raise costs. Also, unit costs might advance because of increased pressure on suppliers, the necessity of attracting to the area a large number of new workers, and more overtime work. Three points of caution, however, should be noted:

1. Just because increased volume in manufacturing industries is not usually a sufficient reason for voluntary, industry-wide price reduction, advantages of large volume production should not be questioned. The major economies of scale, which explain the effectiveness of large firms in some industries, rest on a multitude of factors such as greater specialization of functions, the nature of the market, distribution methods made possible by large-scale operations, and the like. But a moderate increase in volume such as might result from a feasible price reduction will neither make possible nor enhance these normal advantages of scale.

2. The low price elasticity which may preclude a price reduction under conditions of oligopoly does not imply that a price advance is feasible. One reason for this is that a price reduction will almost certainly be met by competitors, while a price advance may or may not be followed. Herein lies an essential difference between monopoly and oligopoly. The monopolist is free to move his price up or down at will. The oligopolist may move his price *down*, but he may increase it only if such a move gains the approval of his competitors who may have different ideas about the economically feasible price.

3. Although the above argument throws doubt on certain reasons for

price reduction as a means of combating declining sales, it by no means implies that there are not any reasons for expecting oligopolists to reduce price. Actually, there are many such reasons. Most of them involve some of the various, subtle competitive pressures which exist in modern industry and which some think are more potent and socially useful than the simple price competition of "like with like" envisioned in the model of perfect competition.

Accountants and economists have not always talked the same language. They have often disagreed in discussing the relations between cost and price. Economic "theory of the firm" has shown (at least to the satisfaction of many economists) that the largest profit, or least loss, will result from decisions made on the basis of marginal rather than average costs. The following selection by a professor at the University of Wisconsin shows that new developments in cost accounting are emphasizing the management utility of marginal concepts.

15 · Cost Accounting and Marginal Analysis

JAMES S. EARLEY

In "management economics" and in business practice, . . . one finds growing evidence of new techniques—notably "management accounting," new forms of budgetary control, and so-called "profit-planning"—which singly and in combination display interesting marginalist properties, essentially "objective" and predominantly "short run" in nature. . . .

It is the purpose of this article simply to outline recent developments in one of these management techniques—cost accounting—and to demonstrate the extent to which leaders of that profession have of late been embracing marginalist principles. Elsewhere I shall set forth the results of some empirical investigations I have undertaken to ascertain the extent to which these newer accounting principles are actually becoming employed in American industry, analyze certain related managerial techniques, and suggest some appropriate modifications in economic theory. . . .

. . . Historically . . . cost accounting was designed for purposes unrelated to decision-making on marginal principles: namely, (1) valuation of inventories; (2) estimation of enterprise income; and (3) control of operating expenses. Because of this orientation, it is claimed, cost accounting obliterates the distinctions needed for "marginal" costing and tends to lead management toward "full-cost" bases for decision-making. . . .

JAMES S. EARLEY, "Recent Developments in Cost Accounting and the 'Marginal Analysis,'" *The Journal of Political Economy* (June 1955), pp. 227–245. Used by permission. Most of the many footnotes have been omitted here.

The defects of cost accounting for marginal analysis are considered especially serious for the multiproduct, multiprocess enterprise, to which any satisfactory modern theory must of course apply. In such enterprise, it is said, "attempts to apply the marginal type of analysis . . . leads to hopeless complexity."[1] It is widely believed, with Gordon, that

the assumption of marginal adjustment becomes more and more unrealistic as the number of variables is increased. . . . The existence of many variables subject to manipulation by the business man has an effect upon the latter's decision-making similar to that created by uncertainty as to future events. Both destroy the possibility of knowing what the effects of marginal adjustments would be and force upon him adherence to "short-cut" objectives. . . . For both the long and short period, the existence of common costs—particularly if numerous products are involved—creates an almost irresistible tendency to price on an average cost basis.[2]

THE EMERGENCE OF "MANAGEMENT ACCOUNTING." The evolution of cost accounting appears to be fast outdating these criticisms. Economists, it appears, have viewed this evolution in midstream. Originally, it is true, the prime purpose of cost accounting was to "accrue" the costs incurred through the production process—"distributing" them among products and through time—so as to place a "proper" value upon inventories and upon enterprise income. This is so-called "historical" or "financial" accounting. Somewhat later cost accounting's more crucial function came to be viewed as the control of operations for efficiency—so-called "control accounting." While these functions persist, a third has been added in still more recent years: assistance to management in "planning" and "decision-making," often referred to as "management accounting." This type of accounting appears to be the "new frontier" of the profession, especially in this country, as reflected in recent accounting periodicals, the proceedings of cost-accounting associations and even, to some extent, in the textbooks. . . .

Explicit reference, in this article, will be confined mainly to the recent studies of the Committee on Research of the National Association of Cost Accountants, since this group can be used as a "semi-authoritative" reference point. . . . [The Committee has published its views and findings in a series of research studies in the Association's *Bulletin*. Significant references are indicated simply by "RS," for Research Series, and the appropriate issue-number and page. *Ed.*]

The following principles run through these studies and also characterize the other literature of management accounting: (1) Accounting analysis should be designed to provide control and evaluation of specific operations and policies and help guide management in "choosing among alternatives," functions which "conventional" accounting performs very imperfectly. (2) For these purposes "cost" is not a unitary concept but takes different forms in different problems. (3) For most such problems it is *differences* in costs (and in profits) rather than their "absolute" levels that should be the focus of accounting analysis. (4) It is hence frequently advisable to avoid or ignore cost "allocations," ascertaining instead specifically "assignable" or "escapable" costs. (5) Whether the problem is short or long range, accounting analysis is aided by retaining the distinction between "variable" and

---

[1] W. J. Eitman, "The Equilibrium of the Firm in Multi-process Industries," *Quarterly Journal of Economics*, LIX (February 1945), 284.
[2] R. A. Gordon, "Short-Period Price Determination in Theory and Practice," *American Economic Review* (June 1948), pp. 267, 274.

"fixed" costs and by giving attention to the behavior of the former.

Management accounting involves a number of analytical and operational techniques, but the basic ones can be reduced to the following: (1) the maximum practicable "decomposition" of costs into their separate "elements" and among separate *"segments"* of an enterprise—"segment" here meaning any "subdivision" or "activity" (including volume variation) for which separate determination of costs and income is wanted; (2) the advance setting of "standards" for each cost element and segment; (3) the assignment of *"differential"* costs to "segments" in accordance with their *specific responsibility* for them—"responsibility" here meaning that, if the segment were not included, the costs would be avoided; (4) the marshaling of differential segmented costs, together with related revenue data, in ways designed to give management maximum insight into the advantages of alternatives; and (5) comparison of *actual* costs (and in some cases also incomes) with "standard" levels, for control, evaluation and the revision of plans.

"Differentiation by specific responsibility" constitutes the most significant departure from conventional cost accounting. Whereas the older (financial) accounting seeks the *aggregation* of costs (for valuing inventory, determining enterprise profit, or establishing "total unit costs" of operations or products), management (as well as control) accounting is *directly* interested in their decomposition. The motif of financial accounting is "allocation," that of management accounting "differentiation." The mecca of the older cost accounting was "average" and "total" cost; that of management accounting "marginal" cost (and benefit). . . .

. . . . .

The first step is the breaking-apart of the "variable" and "fixed" costs of operations. The committee expresses confidence in the substantial accuracy with which most costs can be so differentiated. . . .

The committee notes no special difficulty in carrying through the separation of fixed from variable costs in multiprocess production operations or in assigning variable production costs to product lines and individual products. In selling operations the difficulties are greater, and here fixed-variable cost breakdowns are more likely to be by product lines than by individual products, although there are exceptions to this rule.

A second operation is the segregation, wherever possible, of "separable" from "common" *fixed* costs. There are, of course, serious difficulties in assigning separable fixed costs to processes, products, and market areas in multidimensional enterprises; this is indeed part of the rationale for recommending that assignments and allocations should be eschewed except where the relation of costs to segments is clear-cut. Where the effect of a decision upon the level of fixed costs cannot be estimated with reasonable reliability, the principles of "marginal" accounting call for their being omitted from calculations. On the other hand, the committee finds that many such "separable" fixed costs can be identified and assigned, and that such assignments improve decision-making, especially on "longer-range" problems. As with variable costs, great accuracy frequently may not be necessary; the discovery that certain products or other segments have substantially *greater* assignable costs than others may be sufficient for intelligent decisions regarding them. . . .

. . . . .

THE USE OF MARGINAL ACCOUNTING IN PRICING. Because of its prominence in the "marginalist controversy," pricing is a matter on which the views of the proponents of the new accounting are especially interesting. . . . The committee clearly recognizes the superiority of marginal accounting principles over those of conventional accounting and calls at the least for supplementing the latter by . . . marginal income analysis in determining price policies and making specific pricing decisions.

Mechanical "full-cost-plus" pricing is emphatically and repeatedly rejected, for long-range policy as for short. "Rigid adherence to a full-cost-plus approach," it warns, "may result in loss of business to competitors and failure to obtain most profitable utilization of a company's facilities."[3] "In addition to cost, it is necessary to consider competition and customer demand so selling prices seldom have a rigid relationship to cost . . . cost has a role which differs according to whether the product being priced has an elastic or inelastic demand, whether competition is strong or weak."[4] While "in practice, cost is looked upon as a starting point in pricing," "often the principal use of costs . . . is to aid in forecasting the profit consequences of alternative prices, conditions of sale, methods of sale, etc."[5]

The appropriate relationship between "full cost" and price, the committee notes, is especially nebulous in multiproduct, multimarket enterprise, and here marginal accounting analysis can make an especially valuable contribution. "Total" costs of the separate products can almost never be estimated satisfactorily, and the optimal relationship between costs and prices will vary substantially both among products and among markets. Determination of variable and "specific" fixed costs is needed, moreover, to carry out intelligently the "market segmentation" that is such an important element in the success of the multiproduct, multimarket company.

SHORT-RANGE PRICING DECISIONS. The committee is not disposed to draw a sharp distinction between "short-run" and "long-run" pricing problems, and its advocacy of "marginal" principles extends to both. It is especially pointed, however, with respect to "short-range" pricing. Here, following the principle that costs not affected by decisions can often best be disregarded, the committee stresses the advantage of an alert pricing policy and advocates paying close attention to variable cost functions and marginal income computations. . . .

The committee specifically warns against the notion that short-run marginal cost analysis is useful "only as a tool for determining how far a company can go in meeting price cutting competition in a period of low sales volume." "The field study showed," it reports, "that it is equally useful under conditions of capacity production." While under these conditions it is most used "to decide which products are to be made and what markets to serve" (in accordance with relative marginal income ratios), such analysis can also be used to decide what prices shall be fixed on job orders and on orders of different volume and in considering possible shifts in relative product prices.

"LONG-RANGE" PRICING POLICY. Consideration of variable costs and use of marginal income analysis are also essential parts of intelligent long-range pricing policy, especially for multiproduct firms. In a section explicitly entitled "Costs for Long-Range Pricing Policy," the committee observes:

> Different prices for a given product result in different sales volumes, different unit costs, and different amounts of profit. . . . A multiproduct company has a variety of possible combinations to study. . . . The product price pattern that yields the greatest overall net profit can only be approximated because methods are lacking for determining what volume of goods could

---

[3] RS 20, p. 1588.
[4] RS 24, p. 1671.
[5] RS 24, pp. 1671, 1673.

be sold at different prices. However, it is possible to determine how costs vary with volume and thus management needs to deal with only one unknown rather than two.[6]

The fact that "long-run *fixed* cost" may vary as a function of scale or methods is also recognized, along with the implications of such variation for pricing policy:

> Over the long run, management has opportunities to change products, manufacturing methods and capacity, markets and methods of selling. Under such conditions, the costs associated with providing capacity to produce and sell are flexible with volume rather than fixed. When considering such changes, management is often interested in the probable effect of volume on product costs with reference to possible changes in selling prices. For example, larger scale production may reduce unit cost and make possible both lower selling prices and greater aggregate net profit.[7]

Such calculations, of course, require not only estimates of "fixed costs" as a function of capacity and methods, but also the variable cost functions associated with each. Break-even and profit charts for projected investment programs provide, analytically, just these kinds of data.

OBJECTIONS AND "CAUTIONS." The committee takes note of the objections made to "marginal costing" for pricing purposes and concludes that the objections can be met. It does, however, specify "cautions." The first is the obvious point that price must exceed variable cost if overheads are to be met and profits earned. This, the most frequent objection to marginal accounting, apparently worries the committee relatively little. Its more serious cautions are the following: (1) Where as a result of a decision "some increase in fixed costs is anticipated, the amount of the increase should be estimated and added to the variable cost in order that provision for its recovery may be made in pricing." (2) Not all "fixed" costs are irreducible; some—salaries, for example—can be reduced, and it may in some cases be more profitable to do so than to cut prices in slack markets. (3) "Control over sales mix must be maintained in order to make sure that prices are not cut or low margin items sold when factory and distribution capacity could be used for more profitable work." (4) "When market segmentation is practiced, care must be taken to avoid actions which may make it difficult to maintain prices in the more profitable segments of the market." (5) "It is essential to distinguish between volume increments which add to the peaks and those that fill the valleys in output . . . which improve balance and . . . [those which] create bottlenecks . . . business which is permanent and business which can be abandoned." [8]

In short, the committee recognizes that correct interpretation of costs and the use of judgment remain necessary when marginal accounting analysis is used, in pricing as in other fields. The "new accounting" is not put forth as a magic formula for managerial infallibility. But the members of the committee do credit it with making signal contributions to managerial excellence and conclude by calling upon their fellow-accountants to join in an educational venture:

> The breakdown of costs into fixed and variable categories and the use of marginal income rather than gross margin figures has been limited to a few companies until quite recently. For this reason, it is necessary for executives who make pricing decisions to learn to use the new cost concepts. The accountant, as an expert on

---

[6] RS 24, p. 1708.
[7] *Ibid.*, p. 1709.

[8] *Ibid.*, pp. 1728-9.

costs, should be able to take the lead in this process of education.[9]

CONCLUSIONS. Cost-accounting principles appear to be fast incorporating the wisdom of the economists. Far from constituting an impediment to profit maximization via marginal principles, the new accounting is providing techniques by which these estimated principles can at last be properly applied to modern business. The present, consequently, is not a time when economists should be retreating from "objective" marginal analysis. They will do better to study the new management techniques very carefully and rebuild their models to fit the logic of the newer forms of "scientific management."

[9] *Ibid.*, p. 1729.

Technological progress, price, and salesmanship create ever-changing forces of competition. Business men and economists point out that a highly important "dimension" of competition today is the substitution of one product for another. The building industry presents examples which are described here.

16 · Substitution: Competition Among Building Materials

LAURENCE G. O'DONNELL

Next fall a 35-story office building will start rising in downtown Los Angeles. Though it will resemble many other buildings outwardly, the structure will have an unusual characteristic for an office building of its size. It won't contain any structural steel.

Replacing steel will be a framework of pre-stressed concrete. This will consist of prefabricated concrete structural members strengthened by taut steel wires running through them. By using pre-stressed concrete instead of structural steel, the architects designing the building expect to save as much as $2 million.

The displacement of structural steel by pre-stressed concrete in this skyscraper—a class of building long assumed to be a sure market for steel—underscores the increasingly fierce rivalry between producers of basic building materials. In addition to steel and concrete, aluminum, glass, plastic and lumber are all engaged in lively competitive battles. Largely responsible for roiling the $15 billion-a-year building materials industry are a number of relatively new products and techniques which are competing vigorously for the construction dollar and which are spurring producers of traditional materials to redouble their selling efforts.

Siding and Flooring Contests

Consider a few of the contests now under way. Makers of aluminum siding

---

LAURENCE G. O'DONNELL, "Materials Melee," *Wall Street Journal* (March 23, 1961), Copyright 1961 by Dow-Jones & Co., Inc., p. 1 ff. Used by permission.

are trying to grab a bigger portion of the home-siding business from lumber producers. Plastics are taking flooring orders from asphalt and hardwood flooring. Aluminum, stainless steel, glass and pre-cast concrete are challenging each other for dominance in "curtain-wall" construction, a building technique in which thin panels are bolted to the framework of a structure. All these curtain-wall products are competing with masonry. Steel producers, smarting over losing construction business to pre-stressed concrete, are urging builders to use steel framing instead of lumber in homes.

The intensity of the competition is pointed up by the increase in the materials options available to builders. Gerald J. Carey, general manager of the New York City Housing Authority, says the specifications his agency drafts for its projects nowadays allow contractors 30% to 40% more such options than they were permitted a decade ago.

Despite counterattacks by older materials and occasional roadblocks thrown up by local building codes or labor unions, new construction materials are making headway. The aluminum industry claims the average new home now uses close to 200 pounds of aluminum for such things as window frames and gutters, compared with only about 80 pounds in 1955. As for plastics, Dow Chemical Co. asserts use of plastics in construction has risen to 1.1 billion pounds a year now from 683 million in 1957. Besides winning a share of flooring business, plastics are used increasingly in counter tops and wall coverings.

Hurrying the development of new products is pressure from builders for materials that will cut their costs. The average cost of materials to builders has risen 26% in the past decade, and average construction labor rates have jumped 56% over the same span, according to F. W. Dodge Corp., construction news service. Builders are particularly eager for prefabricated components, such as large wall or roof panels. The theory behind such prefabrication is that the components can be produced in factories by mass-production techniques far more cheaply than they could be assembled on the site by high-priced building trades workers.

Savings from "Sandwich" Panels

Arousing interest among home builders, for example, are prefabricated, three-layer panels consisting of exterior and interior walls of plywood or composition board, with a plastic foam insulating core sandwiched between them. The panels can eliminate on-site application of 10 to 12 layers of materials, ranging from exterior bricks or shingles to the interior plaster, according to some builders who have tested them. Because they are rigid and need little support, the panels also do away with much wood framing, their developers claim. Koppers Co., one of the producers of the "sandwich" panels, claims an average-sized three-bedroom house made with its panels cost up to $500 less than a comparable dwelling with lumber framing and siding. Industry authorities expect this saving at least to double as competition and mounting volume trim prices.

The $375 million-a-year commercial curtain-wall market is the scene of some of the most spirited competition currently. Modern curtain walls are employed in the construction of many factories, office buildings and apartments. Pre-cast concrete curtain-wall panels have found wide use in factories, while aluminum, stainless steel and glass panels are employed in more glamorous structures. A prime advantage of curtain-wall buildings, according to advocates of this construction technique, is that they can be put up faster than structures of brick or concrete block.

The spotlight currently is on a struggle for curtain-wall business between aluminum and stainless steel producers. The availability of color coatings, along with lower prices, has given aluminum the lead so far. But recently a stainless steel producer, Washington Steel Corp., began offering stainless panels in 11 colors. And a $100,000 study sponsored by major stainless steel makers not long ago concluded that architects have been specifying curtain-wall panels twice as thick as actually required, thereby making the price needlessly high.

"We didn't educate the architects," says an executive of one steel company. "They would design in aluminum, then substitute stainless in the same thickness. Then they'd say stainless cost twice as much. Now they can cut the cost of stainless in half in some cases." A Washington Steel spokesman claims the cost of stainless walls is now within 7% to 15% of that of aluminum walls. "If the architect has budget problems, he can argue that stainless is more durable," claims the spokesman.

Two big aluminum producers have plunged into real estate development in hopes of expanding the market for their curtain-wall products and other aluminum building items. Aluminum Co. of America holds a 40% interest in a joint venture it is undertaking with Webb & Knapp, Inc., a large real estate firm. The partners will build two apartment projects, one in Los Angeles and another in New York. Alcoa has control over the design of the structures and, notes an Alcoa spokesman, "the buildings, of course, will be all aluminum."

In partnership with local developers, Reynolds Metals Co. is sponsoring residential building projects in several cities. In Washington, for instance, construction of 518 residential units, including a high-rise apartment building, will start in May. The project will cost $9 million and will use aluminum curtain walls throughout. Projects scheduled to be built later on in Philadelphia and Kansas City will also make extensive use of aluminum curtain walls. In all, Reynolds figures the building projects in which it has a stake will consume 35 million or more pounds of aluminum.

Dramatic Changes

New materials and techniques are stirring up competition in the individual home market almost as intense as that in the commercial and apartment curtain-wall field. Among the most spectacular new products are the large prefabricated wall and roof panels, such as the sandwich panels turned out by Koppers. These prefabricated panels especially suitable for some of the clean-lined modern design homes now being built, open up possibilities for dramatic changes in home building. Johns-Manville Corp., which recently announced it had developed a new factory-assembled panel for house walls, termed its new product a "major technological breakthrough" which "could have far-reaching effects in lowering costs for quality homes." Some contractors report it's now possible for a five-man crew using prefabricated panels to erect the shell of a solidly built, individually designed home in two days. The day is coming, they suggest, when the bulk of the on-site manual labor now required to build a house will be supplanted by swift economical assembly-line production of house components which will be fitted together quickly at the site.

Lumber producers naturally aren't sitting on their hands while Koppers, Johns-Manville and others invade their market with products that could affect sales of both lumber framing and siding. The National Lumber Manufacturers Association trumpets the virtues of traditional wood siding for houses, praising, among other things, its compatibility "with people, giving a warm and friendly look to their finest dwellings."

Lumber men are also fighting prefabricated panel producers' contention that rigid panels can do away with wood framing. The . . . Association is backing efforts to develop prefabricated panels that have wood frames, and it's also trying to convince builders sturdy wood framing is an asset, no matter what type of siding is used. Appealing to builders' cost consciousness, however, the lumber group now suggests that wood uprights can be placed 24 inches apart instead of the 16 inches customary in the past; the association claims this change can save builders over $200 on an average house.

Easy Maintenance

Aluminum concerns are pressing hard for home siding business. They claim their product, which is formed to look like wood siding and has enamel baked on t can go for 15 to 20 years with no maintenance other than an occasional hosing down. And, asserts . . . an aluminum fabricator, aluminum siding can meet "the price schedules of all competitive materials."

[The] firm supplied the siding for an Akron suburban development in which 1,200 houses sheathed in aluminum of assorted colors have already been completed and another 300 are scheduled to rise shortly. Sizing up the national outlook for sales of aluminum siding, [the company's president] says: "Aluminum siding was not in over 20,-000 starts in 1960. We expect 100,000 aluminum starts in 1961, and we are shooting for 200,000 starts with baked enamel siding within five years."

So far, pre-stressed concrete has made its deepest penetration of structural steel markets in bridge construction. But now, as the Los Angeles office building illustrates, pre-stressed concrete is challenging steel on new fronts. Edward K. Rice, vice president of the architectural firm planning the Los Angeles building, claims savings attributable to pre-stressed concrete will not be limited to a reduction in the cost of basic structural components. The building will be 385 feet tall, compared with 437 for a comparable steel structure, explains Mr. Rice, because the floor slabs will be a third thinner than if structural steel were used. This will result in savings on plumbing lines, heating and air-conditioning ducts, electrical wiring and elevator shafts because all will be shorter than they would be if the building had a structural steel framework.

Concrete for Factories and Stores

Though towering office buildings draw more attention, factories, supermarkets and other single-story commercial buildings are currently providing more important markets for pre-stressed concrete. Pre-stressed concrete structural members have the advantage of requiring fewer support columns than steel, thereby allowing large, unobstructed bay areas.

Cement makers claim pre-stressed concrete is displacing a growing tonnage of steel. They say pre-stressed concrete will be used this year in projects that would consume over 400,-000 tons of structural steel, while the comparable figure for 1955 was 70,000 tons. Steel men are generally reluctant to discuss how they are faring in this competition, but the chief market researcher for one major steel company concedes that since pre-stressed concrete began to compete with steel the amount of steel business lost has been "in the hundreds of thousands of tons."

Steel producers are, however, achieving a measure of success in narrowing the gap between the prices of structural steel and pre-stressed concrete. A New York engineering firm which specializes in pre-stressed concrete bridge construction says pre-stressed bids for bridge jobs now average only 5% less than steel, compared with as much as 18% less a few years ago.

Cutting Steel Requirements

But some steel men suggest this achievement hasn't bettered their position much. For, they note, steel fabricators are able to submit lower bids only by using new designs that require less steel than old methods. Helping to lower steel requirements are new, more efficiently designed structural shapes which are lighter than conventional structural steel but equally as strong.

The attempt to win a role for steel in home framing, aimed at counterbalancing the trends toward more pre-stressed concrete and designs using less steel, is being pushed by Bethlehem Steel Co., among others. Concentrating its efforts on the West Coast currently, Bethlehem is promoting light steel beams as the most economical way to build houses on hillsides. It doesn't view the market as restricted to hillside homes, however.

Steel men claim steel framing costs no more than lumber. But they concede it's not an easy task to increase the use of steel in home framing. Many people assume it costs too much, and some frown on using steel in houses in which structural members are exposed, deeming the metal too cold and institutional Nevertheless, Bethlehem feels the market has "tremendous potential." With conventional wood construction, steel consumption averages less than two tons per house, according to Bethlehem researchers; a steel frame they say, would increase this by 8 to 12 tons.

Economists often criticize product differentiation. Sellers, in offering products which are somewhat—but not entirely—similar, incur higher production costs because lack of standardization entails extra, duplicated overhead. Incurred, too, are higher selling costs. Professor Chamberlin of Harvard, developer of the theory of monopolistic competition, here indicates ways in which public welfare is enhanced by product differentiation.

17 · *Product Variety*

E. H. CHAMBERLIN

. . . . human beings are individuals, diverse in their tastes and desires, and moreover widely dispersed spatially. Sofar as demand has any force as a guide to production, one would expect entrepeneurs to appeal to them in diverse ways, and thus to render the output of the economy correspondingly heterogeneous, using this term in its broadest sense to embrace not only the qualitative aspects of the product itself, but also the conditions surrounding its sale, including spatial location. And since what people want—an elaborate system of consumers' preferences—is the starting point in welfare economics, their wants for a heterogeneous product would seem to be as fundamental as anything could be. Heterogeneity as between producers is synonymous with the presence of monopoly; therefore monopoly is necessarily a part of the welfare ideal.

It must be emphasized that any and all monopoly is included within the general concept of heterogeneity or differentiation (although there is no implication of an identity between the actual and the ideal). . . . equally for a patent, a cement producer separated in space from others, a local gas utility, a toll bridge, or the A & P. And they are, of course, all without exception engaged in competition with others nearby on the chain of substitutes and with others generally in the system. "Industry" or "commodity" boundaries are a snare and a delusion—in the highest degree arbitrarily drawn, and, wherever drawn, establishing at once wholly false implications both as to competition of substitutes within their limits, which supposedly stops at their borders, and as to the possibility of ruling on the presence or absence of oligopolistic forces by the simple device of counting the number of producers included. As for the *conventional* categories of industries, it seems increasingly evident to me that they have their origin, not primarily in substitution at all, but in similarity of raw materials or other inputs or of technical methods used. Glass, leather goods, drugs and medi-

---

E. H. CHAMBERLIN, "Product Heterogeneity and Public Policy," *American Economic Review* (May 1950), pp. 86–89. Used by permission.

cines are obvious examples. Apart from the wide diversity of products embraced by almost any so-called "industry," spatial separation of producers within it is an added prime obstacle to substitution in most cases. But the main point is that, even if lines were arbitrarily to be drawn, they would have literally nothing to do with the extent and character of the heterogeneity, either within such an "industry" or beyond it, which would be defensible from the point of view of welfare or of public policy.

. . . . .

. . . the term "differentiation" has taken on to many something of the superficial. (Hence the term "heterogeneous" in this paper.) It is often conceived as describing the reprehensible creation by businessmen of purely factitious differences between products which are by nature fundamentally uniform. In this vein, some have even gone so far as to attribute differentiation, and monopolistic competition generally, to "imperfect knowledge," as though the individuality of particular products could be dismissed as an optical illusion based upon ignorance—a purely psychic phenomenon. . . .

. . . . .

There is a case, of course, for improving knowledge . . . but no reason to think that improved knowledge would leave us with fewer or weaker preferences. In some cases it seems clear that increased standardization of certain products by public authority is indicated as when oligopolistic forces are supporting an unduly large number of producers, or when the gain in efficiency is judged by proper authorities to be more important than the losses in consumers' surplus through abandoning certain products. But the labeling of most preferences within an arbitrarily defined "industry" as "irrational" seems to me to indicate mainly a preference for the purely competitive ideal, and an attempt, perhaps largely unconscious, to salvage it. . . .

It might be added that no invidious distinctions are indicated either on the basis of whether or not the demands for particular products are influenced by selling expenditures. Here again, stress on irrational preferences makes an easy transition to the labeling of those established by advertising as irrational, and to conventional sweeping condemnation of advertising as a "competitive waste." Granted that the techniques of modern advertising are often a shocking affront to good taste, or objectionable on other grounds, it remains true, so far as I can see, that the question of whether advertising is wasteful or not, in the sense of being a misallocation of resources, simply cannot be answered by any criteria derived from market demand and cost curves—or from indifference curves either. . . .

The fact that equilibrium for the firm when products are heterogeneous normally takes place under conditions of falling average costs of production has generally been regarded as a departure from ideal conditions, these latter being associated with the minimum point on the curve; and various corrective measures have been proposed. However, if heterogeneity is part of the welfare ideal, there is no prima facie case for doing anything at all. It is true that the same total resources (either within some arbitrarily defined "industry" or within the whole economy) may be made to yield more units of product by being concentrated on fewer firms. The issue might be put as efficiency versus diversity—more of either one means less of the other. But unless it can be shown that the loss of satisfaction from a more standardized product (again, either within an "industry" or for the economy as a whole) is less than the gain through producing more units, there is no "waste" at all, even though every firm is producing to the left of its minimum point.

. . . . .

In this article a French economist observes the result of efforts to set prices below the equilibrium level. Rents have risen since this article was written. Although the basic problems remain, they are less acute.

18 · Rent Control: An Example of Price Fixing

BERTRAND DE JOUVENEL

A dollar a month pays a wage-earner's rent in Paris; quarters adequate for a family of six cost $2 (equivalent to 11 packages of the cheapest cigarettes). Middle-class apartments of three or four main rooms frequently cost from $1.50 to $2.50 per month. Important officials or executives pay from $3.50 a month to $8 or $10 a month.

This may seem a desirable state of affairs, but there are drawbacks. There are no vacant lodgings; nor is anyone going to vacate, nor can the owners expel anyone. Young couples must live with in-laws. . . .

The only opportunity to get quarters is to watch for deaths. Tottering old people sunning themselves in public gardens are shadowed back to their flat by an eager young wife who strikes a bargain with the *concierge* to be first in at the death. Other apartment-chasers have an understanding with funeral parlors.

There are two ways of obtaining an apartment made available by death. Legally, if you fulfill certain conditions which give you priority, you may obtain an order of requisition, but usually you find that the same order for the same apartment has been given to two or three other applicants. The illegal method is the surest—an arrangement with the heir that some pieces of your furniture be carried in immediately upon death of the tenant. As soon as you are in, your are the king of the castle.

Buying one's way into an apartment will cost anything from $500 to $1500 per room. Wage-earners might as well give up hope of setting up house; they have to stay with their families or live in miserable hotels.

Paris has 84,000 buildings for habitation, almost 90 per cent of them built before World War I. Even a very lenient officialdom estimates that 16,000 are in such disrepair that they should be pulled down. Nor are the others altogether satisfactory; 82 per cent of Parisians have no bath, more than half must go out of their lodgings

---

BERTRAND DE JOUVENEL, *No Vacancies* (Irvington-on-Hudson, N. Y.: The Foundation for Economic Education, October 1948). *The Reader's Digest* condensation (February 1949), pp. 43–46, copyright 1949 by the Reader's Digest Association, Inc. Used by permission of the Foundation for Economic Education, Inc., and *The Reader's Digest.*

to find a lavatory, and a fifth do not even have running water. Little more than one in six of the existing buildings is pronounced in good condition by the public inspectors.

Owners are not financially able to keep up their buildings, let alone improve them. To take an example of a very common situation, there is a woman who owns three buildings containing 34 apartments, all inhabited by middle-class families. Her net loss from the 34 apartments, after taxes and repairs, is $80 per year. Not only must her son take care of her, but he must also pay out the $80. She cannot sell; there are no buyers.

When the owner tries to milk a little net income from his property by cutting down the repairs, he runs great risks. One landlord postponed repairs on his roofs and rain filtering into an apartment spoiled a couple of armchairs. He was sued for damages and condemned to pay a sum amounting to three years of the tenant's paltry rent. Since 1914, rents at the most have multiplied 6.8 times, while taxes have multiplied 13.2 times, and repairs cost from 120 to 150 times the 1914 price!

An outsider may be tempted to think that only an incredible amount of folly can have led us to this condition. But it is not so. We got there by easy, almost unnoticed stages, slipping down on the gentle slope of rent control. And this was not the work of the Reds but of succeeding governments, most of which were considered rather conservative.

The story starts with World War I. It then seemed humane and reasonable to stabilize housing costs while the boys were in the Army or working for victory. So existing rentals were frozen. It was also reasonable to avoid disturbances at the end of the war lest the veterans' homecoming be spoiled by evictions and rent increases. Thus prewar situations hardened into rights. The owner lost—"temporarily," of course—the disposition of his property.

When the situation was reviewed in 1926, retail prices had trebled, and it was plain that lifting controls would bring huge rent increases. The legislators shrank from this crisis and decided to confirm the tenant's right to stay in possession but to raise rents slightly. A new owner-tenant relationship thus took shape. The owner was powerless either to evict the tenant or to discuss the rent with him. The State took care of the price, which rose slowly, while regulation was extended to bring in flats not previously regulated. Only buildings put up since 1915 were left unregulated, this to stimulate construction.

No systematic view inspired this policy. It just grew from the fear of a sudden return to liberty, which seemed ever more dangerous as prices stepped up. And, of course, if one must control the price of rent, one could not allow the owner to dismiss tenants, because in that case he might so easily have stipulated secretly with the new tenants.

As rent-control lawmaking continued —no single subject has taken up so much of the time and energy of Parliament—the real income from buildings crumbled from year to year. Then came World War II. The return to liberty which had been devised for 1943 was, of course, abandoned, and all rents were frozen, including those of recent buildings, which had till then escaped.

Since the Liberation, new laws have provided for increases in rents, but retail prices increased much more. To put it briefly, owners of new buildings (built since 1914) have been allowed, in terms of real income, less than a tenth of what they got before World War II. Owners of old buildings, that is, nine-tenths of all buildings, have been allowed in terms of real income either 12 per cent of what they got in 1939 or a little less than 7 per cent of what they got in 1914—whichever is less.

If today a builder were to put up apartments, they would have to rent for prices from 10 to 13 times present rent ceilings, in order to break even. Thus, according to a report of the Economic Council, a wage-earner's apartment of three small rooms and a kitchen now renting for $13 to $16 a year (!) would have to be rented for $166 to $200 a year. Obviously, construction will not be undertaken.

Such is the spread between the legal and the economic price of lodgings that even the most fervent advocates of freedom shudder at the thought of its return; the thing, they say, has gone too far and the right to dismiss tenants, if restored, could not be executed. The whole nation of tenants would go on a sit-down strike.

. . . . .

The French example may prove of some interest and use to our friends across the sea. It goes to show that rent control is self-perpetuating and culminates in both the physical ruin of housing and the legal dispossession of the owners. The havoc wrought in France is not the work of the enemy, but is the result of our own measures.

The practical, and profitable, use of economic theory by business firms offers attractive opportunities to an increasing number of young people. (We now refer to the portions of economics that involve the theory of the firm—microeconomics—not the portions that deal with national income—macroeconomics—which are the most important of the concerns discussed in the third selection of this book.) Because this work has already developed in a variety of directions; because it is continuing to grow; and because it is technical and difficult, no easily understood and full representative sample can be given here. Nevertheless, the following selection provides some indication of the nature of this practical application of theory. The author, a professor at the University of Copenhagen, was at the University of Illinois when he wrote this article.

19 · Use of Economic Theory in Business: Operations Research

SVEN DANÖ

Like so many other new branches of science, operations research—or operations analysis, as it is sometimes called—is hard to define. It covers a great many different problems and methods, and if a professional operations analyst is asked what operations research really is, he will often be inclined to overemphasize that particular field in which he himself happens to be working, giving sometimes less than full credit to what has been done in other branches of operations research. Furthermore,

---

SVEN DANÖ, "On the Nature and Significance of Operations Research," *Current Economic Comment* (Vol. 21, May 1959), College of Commerce, University of Illinois, Urbana, Ill., pp. 11–16. Used by permission.

some people seem to think of operations research as a mere cover for a pseudo-scientific jargon, intended to impress innocent businessmen. . . .

. . . However, it cannot be denied that when the slogans and the amateurishness are sorted out, there remains a core of genuine scientific achievements in *applying various mathematical and statistical methods to solving practical economic problems* in business and other large organizations. A vast number of new models and new methods have been devised during and since the war, and some of them have proved eminently useful when applied to such problems. The methods differ widely and so do the problems, but they nevertheless have certain elements in common which may well justify their being classified under the same heading, that of *operations research*.

I.

Let us first see if we can find a common denominator for the types of problems with which operations research is concerned. In rather abstract terms any problem of operations research can be described as a problem in *rational decision making*. This implies a situation where the management, or whoever is to make a decision, is facing a range of alternative feasible decisions and the problem is to determine which is the optimal decision—the optimal choice —that can be made under the given circumstances. This sounds at least vaguely familiar to an economist—and no wonder, because the existence of alternative possibilities from which an optimal choice is to be made is merely another way of saying that the problem has an economic aspect. Indeed, any problem in economics can be described as that of making an economically optimal choice from the possible alternatives—in other words, the science of economics is concerned with optimal utilization of resources. It is the possibility of *choice* that characterizes an economic problem as such. As an example, take the familiar problem of finding the least combination of certain factors of production for a given quantity of output. The factors, or inputs, are mutual substitutes, i.e., there exist a number of alternative input combinations which will yield the same quantity of the product, so we have a range of economic choice (whose geometric picture is an isoquant) and the problem is to find along the isoquant that particular combination which is optimal in the sense that it corresponds to minimum total cost. The whole economic theory of cost and production is based upon such considerations.

Thus, operations research is basically an economic discipline, though it is concerned with solving practical economic problems in business rather than with economic theory. Operations research is a normative branch of science in the sense that the ends are given and the means are the unknowns of the problem.

II.

Next let us look into the methods of operations research, still in broad and abstract terms. Operations research is a quantitative discipline, which means that the methods employed are mathematical, including of course statistical methods. Indeed, from a formal point of view, operations research can be classified as applied mathematics. The general procedure in operations research is, first, to formulate the concrete problem in terms of a mathematical model which takes all relevant factors into account and whose coefficients represent the technological, economic, and other data of the problem. Whenever risk, uncertainty, and the like come into the picture, the model will have to be formulated in stochastic terms. The feasible economically meaningful solutions to the mathematical model then represent the alternatives from which we have to select a solution—i.e., to made a decision—which is optimal with respect to some given criterion of optimality such as maximum profit, minimum total cost, and the like. Evidently this approach is closely related to that of econometrics, at least from a methodological point of view.

III.

All this has been rather abstract and general, and the reader is no doubt getting impatient to see some concrete practical examples. The nature of some of the more important types of problems which have been solved by operations research methods will be briefly indicated.

(a) One of the best known, and most useful, methods of operations research is that known as *linear programming*, a mathematical technique which has been extensively applied to problems of operations planning, in particular the planning of production. Mathematically, linear programming is the problem of finding a maximum (or a minimum) of a linear function, subject to linear side conditions and to the requirement that the variables shall be non-negative. A great many practical economic problems in industry and agriculture have turned out to fit into a model of this type.

The linear planning model may be illustrated by the following simplified example. A brewery has received an order for 100 gallons of 4 percent beer for prompt delivery. That particular type of beer is not kept in stock, so it has to be blended from such types as are available. There are four types in stock, and water may be added to dilute the mix if necessary; the respective alcoholic contents of these five possible ingredients and their prices are as follows.

Ingredient	Alcoholic content	Price per gallon
1 (water)	....	....
2	2.5%	$0.22
3	3.7	0.25
4	4.5	0.32
5	5.8	0.45

The problem is to find a combination of ingredients which will minimize total cost of ingredients. Clearly each of the possible combinations can be thought of as representing a particular solution to the two linear equations

$$x_1 + x_2 + x_3 + x_4 + x_5 = 100$$
$$0.0x_1 + 2.5x_2 + 3.7x_3 + 4.5x_4 + 5.8x_5 = 400.$$

Solutions involving negative values for one or more x's are clearly meaningless, so that only non-negative solutions are to be considered, whereas zero values in the solution merely imply that not all of the ingredients are used for that particular blend. The optimal solution is that combination for which total cost of ingredients is as small as possible, i.e., the one for which the linear cost function

$$c = 0.00x_1 + 0.22x_2 + 0.25x_3 + 0.32x_4 + 0.45x_5$$

has a minimum.[1]

Another example is the so-called "transportation problem." Suppose that a company produces the same commodity in two factories, one in the East and one on the West Coast, and distributes the product from three warehouses scattered across the country. Total production per week, 600 tons, is to be distributed among the ware-

---

[1] The optimal solution turns out to be a combination of only two ingredients: $x_3 = 62.5$, $x_4 = 37.5$, all other x's equal to zero, $c = 27.63$.

houses, the two factories producing 200 and 400 tons and the warehouses requiring 300, 100, and 200 tons per week respectively. The problem is to determine an optimal pattern of shipments, i.e., to determine the amounts to be shipped from each plant to each warehouse per week, with total cost of transportation to be as low as possible. Now let x_{ij} be the unknown quantity to be shipped from factory i to warehouse j. The corresponding freight rates c_{ij} —the costs of shipping one ton from factory to warehouse—are displayed in the following tabulation.

To From	Warehouse		
	1	2	3
	c_{ij} (dollars per ton)		
Factory 1	3	2	1
Factory 2	2	4	7

Then the problem is to find a minimum of the linear cost function

$$c = 3x_{11} + 2x_{12} + 1x_{13} + 2x_{21} + 4x_{22} + 7x_{23}$$

subject to the linear restrictions

$$\begin{aligned}
x_{11} + x_{12} + x_{13} &= 200 \\
x_{21} + x_{22} + x_{23} &= 400 \\
x_{11} + x_{21} &= 300 \\
x_{12} + x_{22} &= 100 \\
x_{13} + x_{23} &= 200.
\end{aligned}$$

This is a typical linear programming problem.

(b) Other methods of operations research are concerned with solving problems of *inventory planning and inventory control*. Some problems of optimal inventory planning have been successfully solved by linear programming, while others require more conventional mathematical tools; in many cases the model will, of course, have to be a stochastic one because the demand for the company's products is not known with certainty. A very simple inventory model (which does not involve the use of statistical methods) is the following.

A manufacturer supplies a given total number of units of his product to a customer during a given period of length T. Deliveries are made at a constant rate, and delays in meeting the demand are not to be tolerated (see diagram). The problem is to determine in how many production runs the total numbers of units desired should be made if total cost of production and inventory is to be minimized. (Clearly this is equivalent to determining the time interval between runs, t, or the optimal lot size, x.) There are two types of costs that are variable in respect to this situation: the total cost of carrying the inventory, and the total setup costs associated with the production runs. The former can be expressed as an increasing function of x, whereas the latter will decrease for increasing x. The problem can be solved either analytically— by setting the "marginal" cost, i.e., the derivative of total cost with respect to x, equal to zero—or graphically as the minimum point on the total cost curve.

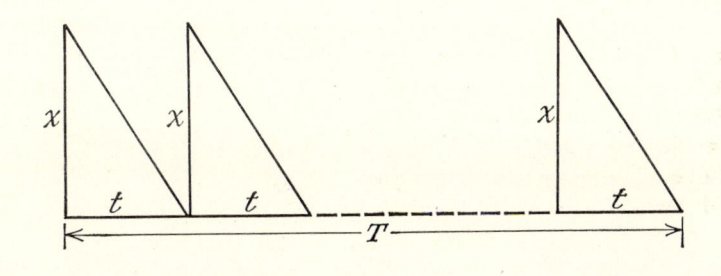

(c) Still another branch of operations research is the so-called *queuing (or waiting-line) theory*. When a number of customers requiring a certain kind of service arrive at random points of time, we have the problem of balancing costs due to waiting (e.g., loss of business) against the increased costs of investment and operation by which waiting time can be reduced. Problems of this type are mathematically fairly complicated. Waiting-line models are, of course, particularly important to problems in traffic and communications . . . but since World War II the queuing models have been extended to cover related problems in many other fields.

(d) A somewhat related type of problem is that of *scheduling* a number of operations through the facilities performing the operations (e.g., machines) in such a way as to minimize idle (machine) time, a type of problem frequently met in production planning.

(e) Finally I might mention the *theory of games,* which is relevant to certain competitive situations where the behavior of each party affects the subsequent behavior of the opposite party.

IV.

These various models are widely different both with respect to the type of problem and with respect to the technique used in solving them. However, they are all problems of economic balance, problems in rational decision making. All of them require mathematical or statistical tools for their solution. Of course the problems have always been there, and they have been solved somehow. Many of them can be solved approximately by various common-sense methods, from inspired guesswork to systematic trial-and-error procedures. Any large organization has its own rules of thumb for dealing with problems of optimal decision making. It may be difficult to give precise explicit grounds for their application, let alone "proofs," but there is a general feeling that they will often lead to fairly acceptable results, based as they are on practical experience, special insight, intuition, and businessman's flair. Nevertheless, a great many such optimization problems, particularly those of large enterprises, are so complicated that it will pay to employ more scientific methods—and by scientific methods is meant formulating and solving the problem within the framework of a formal mathematical model. This was the basic idea behind a great part of what in the interwar period was called scientific management, as it is the basic idea behind what we now call management science or operations research. The slogans may change, but the underlying basic idea is sound and fruitful. There is no doubt that production technology is far ahead of management economics, so far as application of scientific method is concerned. It is the job of operations research to eliminate this time lag, and it seems certain that we may expect great things to happen within this field in the years to come.

In the following brief selection Professor Samuelson of Massachusetts Institute of Technology brings together key conclusions of economic theory.

20 · *The Equilibrium Conditions*

PAUL A. SAMUELSON

I. The first fundamental assumption is that the firm tries to maximize its profits, and from this the following internal conditions of equilibrium can be deduced:

A. Any output which is produced must be produced with factor combinations such that total cost is a minimum. As a result of this, we have two corollaries:

 1. The marginal productivity of the last dollar must be equal in every use.
 2. The price of each factor of production must be proportional to marginal physical productivity, the factor of proportionality being marginal cost.

B. That output will be selected which maximizes net revenue, total cost being optimally determined by the previous conditions. This implies:

 1. The equality of marginal cost and marginal revenue, the slope of the latter being the smaller.
 2. In combination with the previous conditions under "A" we also have the marginal value productivity of each factor equal to its price, the first term being defined as marginal revenue times marginal physical productivity.
 3. The total cost must not exceed total revenue, since otherwise the firm would go out of business.

II. If we impose by arbitrary assumption or hypothesis the external conditions that entry be free, *i.e.*, that total revenue be equal to cost, then:

A. Product will be exhausted by definition.
B. The demand curve must be tangent to the unit cost curve. In the case of pure competition, this implies minimum average cost.

PAUL A. SAMUELSON, *Foundations of Economic Analysis* (Cambridge, Mass.: Harvard University Press, 1947), p. 88. Copyright 1947 by the President and Fellows of Harvard College.

IV • DEALING WITH MONOPOLY

Adam Smith, the great advocate of laissez-faire, did not welcome everything he would expect to occur if businessmen—or workers' organizations—were left free to indulge their inclinations to monopolize.

21 • *Adam Smith on Monopoly*

ADAM SMITH

A monopoly granted either to an individual or to a trading company has the same effect as a secret in trade or manufactures. The monopolists, by keeping the market constantly understocked, by never fully supplying the effectual demand, sell their commodities much above the natural price, and raise their emoluments, whether they consist in wages or profit, greatly above their natural rate.

The price of monopoly is upon every occasion the highest which can be got. The natural price, or the price of free competition, on the contrary, is the lowest which can be taken, not upon every occasion indeed, but for any considerable time together. The one is upon every occasion the highest which can be squeezed out of the buyers, or which, it is supposed, they will consent to give: the other is the lowest which the sellers can commonly afford to take, and at the same time continue their business.

The exclusive privileges of corporations, statutes of apprenticeship, and all those laws which restrain, in particular employments, the competition to a smaller number than might otherwise go into them, have the same tendency, though in a less degree. They are a sort of enlarged monopolies, and many frequently, for ages together, and in whole classes of employments, keep up the market price of particular commodities above the natural price, and maintain both the wages of the labor and the profits of the stock employed about them somewhat above their natural rate.

. . . . .

People of the same trade seldom meet together, even for merriment and diversion, but the conversation ends in a conspiracy against the public, or in some contrivance to raise prices. It is impossible indeed to prevent such meetings, by any law which either could be executed, or would be consistent with liberty and justice. But though the law

ADAM SMITH, *The Wealth of Nations* (1776), Book I.

cannot hinder people of the same trade from sometimes assembling together, it ought to do nothing to facilitate such assemblies; much less to render them necessary.

Why, really, is competition to be preferred to monopoly? Professor John Maurice Clark of Columbia University, a long-time student of the problems of competition and monopoly, and a member of the Attorney-General's National Committee to Study the Antitrust Laws, discusses here in simple terms the benefits we seek from competition.

22 · Why Seek Competition?

JOHN MAURICE CLARK

Benefits of Competition

What do we want competition to do for us? What benefits do we expect from it? The main economic benefits may be listed under four heads.

1. We expect competition to furnish incentives to increased productive efficiency that are more compelling than the interest a monopoly has in improving its processes. To get the benefit of this incentive, where progressive increase in efficiency depends on expensive research and experimentation, requires that business units of large size shall still feel this competitive incentive.

2. We expect the rivalry of independent producers to give us an ample variety of types and qualities of products to choose from, including new varieties. This competition in quality implies that the offerings of different producers shall be distinctive; that is, they shall be in some respect unique. And I would contend that this uniqueness is a competitive fact, not a monopolistic one, so long as others are free to imitate or not, whichever seems to them more advantageous.

3. We want the gains from all this to be diffused as widely as possible and as rapidly as consistent with business enterprise having the incentives to the necessary pioneering. As fast as the "state of the arts," or the knowledge of what kinds of products consumers want, become common property, no one can make a special profit by merely equaling this standard. But if he excels it, in productive efficiency or in the quality or attractiveness of his product, he can still make a special profit—for a time, until others catch up and his achievement is in turn absorbed into the "state of the arts." If instead of excelling he falls behind, he will make losses; and unless he can better his position, he may end by being forced out of business.

Gains may be diffused to customers

JOHN MAURICE CLARK, *Economic Institutions and Human Welfare* (New York: Alfred A. Knopf, Inc., 1957), pp. 158–166. Copyright 1957 by Alfred A. Knopf, Inc. Used by permission. Adapted from "Economic Welfare in a Free Society," *National Policy for Economic Welfare at Home and Abroad,* ed. R. Lekachman (New York: Doubleday & Company, Inc., 1955).

in lower prices, or they may go in paying standard rewards to added capital that is used in making improvements, but historically the greater part of the diffusion has been to workers in higher real wages. And this is as good a way of diffusion as any other, on two conditions. One is that wage increases do not amount to more gain than there is available to diffuse. This would be inflationary. The other is that the structure of wages maintains equity between different occupations, and does not give some an enduringly favored status because the industries that employ them have made more than the average rate of progress. The fulfillment of these conditions would be impaired to just the extent that either employers or workers in a particular industry possessed and exercised the power of a privileged monopoly position.

This indicates the limits of the useful role of "countervailing power," which J. K. Galbraith has recently suggested as a substitute for competition. If this meant that competition were completely displaced, "countervailing power" would take the shape of bilateral monopoly, which Galbraith apparently regards as a response to unilateral monopoly and a rough remedy for it, diffusing its gains at least in part. A more common view regards bilateral monopoly as an aggravation, operating as an unholy alliance in which, if a union grabbed an employer's monopoly gains, the employer could get them back from the customers. But in practice there may be enough competitive pressures or enough resistance to price increases to prevent the employer from recouping his gains in this way; thus imperfect competitive forces may set limits on the gains available for a strong union to grab, even if competition is not strong enough to diffuse all the gains to the customers in the first place.

On the buyer's side, what a strong buyer does is generally to get access to some alternative source of supply and make the most of it as a bargaining leverage, thus bringing to bear competitive alternatives of which weaker buyers would not be able to take advantage. When it acts in this way, "countervailing power" would seem to be, not a substitute for competition so much as a complementary factor, activating competitive alternatives that would otherwise be ineffective, or, if competitive forces are sluggish, bringing about a condition in which sluggish competitive forces are sufficient. Gains may still be diffused, though less completely and less evenly than active and two-sided competition is supposed to diffuse them.

This diffusion of gains results in keeping the over-all level of profit down to the minimum necessary for healthy incentives; and this is important. But it is important largely for a different reason from the one economists tend to emphasize and which has at times led business men to characterize the economists' ideal as one of "profitless prosperity." A scaling-down of the over-all rate of profit, if it has been unnecessarily high, is a social gain, but if that were all, it would be a strictly limited gain, which could be secured only once. It seems more than likely that its more important effect is on the incentives to progress; because industrialists who are capable of making improvements are placed in a position in which, if they are to renew their profits, they must go on making more improvements in a progressive series. And such a continuing series is bound to outweigh any once-for-all gain; the resulting profits can be absorbed repeatedly, as long as the improvements continue. The mark of effective competition is not absence of differential profits, but their successive creation, erosion and re-creation as one of the incidents of progress.

4. Competition frees the customers,

and others who deal with business, from dependence on the good will or benevolence of business for the diffusion of the gains it makes, giving them instead the leverage that comes from a chance to choose between rival offers in a field that is open to all who see a chance to make some net gain. This does not deprive business of all discretion as to price and policy, but it keeps it within the limits that the rival offers set.[1] A further incidental benefit is that a "market" may result in which many buyers who do not themselves canvass all the rival offers may get the benefit of others' canvassing in the shape of fairly standardized terms. Obviously, if too many buyers rely on others' canvassing, the benefits may be impaired or even lost. If people are completely negligent in protecting themselves, even efficient antitrust laws may not give them full protection.

[1] One sometimes sees an overstatement of this goal, implying that any margin of discretion in private hands is an improper degree of power, and that impersonal economic forces should determine the result so completely as to eliminate this private "power." This seems to imply that no one should have any discretion—except government officials. The exception exposes the fallacy of the rule.

Bigness, we are often told, is necessary for mass production, great industrial research, and risk-taking in large projects. Criticism of bigness as such tends to be uninformed and often more emotional than rational. The following selection is a notable exception. The author is Professor of Economics at the University of Chicago and was a member of the Attorney-General's National Committee to Study Antitrust Laws.

23 · *Bigness in Business: Dangers and a Proposed Remedy*

GEORGE J. STIGLER

What is Bigness?

Bigness in business has two primary meanings. First, bigness may be defined in terms of the company's share of the industry in which it operates: a big company is one that has a big share of the market or industry. By this test Texas Gulf Sulphur is big because it produces more than half the sulfur in America, and Macy's (whose annual sales are much larger) is small because it sells only a very small fraction of the goods sold by New York City retail stores. By this definition, many compa-

GEORGE J. STIGLER, "The Case Against Big Business." Reprinted from the May 1952 issue of *Fortune Magazine* by special permission; © by Time, Inc. Legal citations and most of the footnotes have been omitted.

nies that are small in absolute size are nevertheless big—the only brick company in a region, for example—and many companies that are big in absolute size (Inland Steel, for example) are small. Second, bigness may mean absolute size—the measure of size being assets, sales, or employment as a rule. Then General Motors and U.S. Steel are the prototypes of bigness.

These two meanings overlap because most companies that are big in absolute size are also big in relation to their industries. There are two types of cases, however, in which the two meanings conflict. On the one hand, many companies of small absolute size are dominant in small markets or industries. I shall not discuss them here (although they require attention in a well-rounded antitrust program). . . . On the other hand, there are a few companies that are big in absolute size but small relative to their markets—I have already given Macy's as an example. These companies are not very important in the total picture, and I shall also put them aside in the following discussion.

For my purposes, then, big businesses will mean businesses that are absolutely large in size and large also relative to the industries in which they operate. They are an impressive list: U.S. Steel, Bethlehem, and Republic in steel, General Electric and Westinghouse in electrical equipment, General Motors, Ford, and Chrysler in automobiles, du Pont, Union Carbide, and Allied Chemical among others in chemicals, Reynolds, Liggett & Myers, and American Tobacco in cigarettes.

What bigness does not mean is perhaps equally important. Bigness has no reference to the size of industries. I for one am tired of the charge that the critics of the steel industry vacillate between finding the output too large and too small: at various times the industry's output has been too small; for fifty years the largest firm has been too large. Concerted action by many small companies often leads to over-capacity in an industry: it is the basic criticism of resale price maintenance, for example, that it encourages the proliferation of small units by fixing excessive retail margins. Industries dominated by one or a few firms—that is, big businesses—seldom err in this direction. Nor does bigness have any direct reference to the methods of production, and opposition to big business is usually compatible with a decent respect for the "economies of large-scale production" . . .

The fundamental objection to bigness stems from the fact that big companies have monopolistic power, and this fundamental objection is clearly applicable outside the realm of corporate business. In particular, big unions are open to all the criticisms (and possibly more) that can be levied against big business. I shall not discuss labor unions, but my silence should not be construed as a belief that we should have a less stringent code for unions than for business.

The Indictment of Bigness

There are two fundamental criticisms to be made of big businesses: they act monopolistically, and they encourage and justify bigness in labor and government.

First, as to monopoly. When a small number of firms control most or all of the output of an industry, they can individually and collectively profit more by cooperation than by competition. This is fairly evident, since cooperatively they can do everything they can do individually, and other things (such as the charging of non-competitive prices) besides. These few companies, therefore, will usually cooperate.

From this conclusion many reasonable men, including several Supreme Court Justices, will dissent. Does not each brand of cigarettes spend huge sums in advertising to lure us away from some other brand? Do not the big companies—oligopolists, the economists call them—employ salesmen? Do not the big companies introduce constant innovations in their products?

COMPETITION OF A KIND. The answer is that they do compete—but not enough, and not in all the socially desirable ways. Those tobacco companies did not act competitively, but with a view to extermination, against the 10-cent brands in the 1930's, nor have they engaged in price competition in decades. . . . The steel companies with all their salesmen, abandoned cartel pricing via basing-point prices only when this price system was judged a conspiracy in restraint of trade in cement. . . . The plain fact is that big businesses do not engage in continuous price competition.

Nor is price the only area of agreement. Patent licensing has frequently been used to deprive the licensees of any incentive to engage in research; General Electric used such agreements also to limit other companies' output and fix the prices of incandescent lamps. . . . The hearings of the Bone Committee are adorned with numerous examples of the deliberate deterioration of goods in order to maintain sales. For example, Standard Oil Development (a subsidiary of the Jersey company) persuaded Socony-Vacuum to give up the sale of a higher-potency commodity (pour-point depressant) whose sale at the same price had been characterized as "merely price cutting."

Very well, big businesses often engage in monopolistic practices. It may still be objected that it has not been shown that all big businesses engage in monopolistic practices, or that they engage in such practices all, or even most of, the time. These things cannot be shown or even fully illustrated in a brief survey, and it is also not possible to summarize the many court decisions and the many academic studies of big business. But it is fair to say that these decisions and studies show that big businesses usually possess monopolistic power, and use it. And that is enough.

For economic policy must be contrived with a view to the typical rather than the exceptional, just as all other policies are contrived. . . .

Second, as to bigness in labor and government. Big companies have a large —I would say an utterly disproportionate—effect on public thinking. The great expansion of our labor unions has been due largely to favoring legislation and administration by the federal government. This policy of favoring unions rests fundamentally upon the popular belief that workers individually competing for jobs will be exploited by big-business employers— that U.S. Steel can in separate negotiation (a pretty picture!) overwhelm each of its hundreds of thousands of employees. In good part this is an absurd fear: U.S. Steel must compete with many other industries, and not merely other steel companies, for good workers.

Yet the fear may not be wholly absurd: there may be times and places where big businesses have "beaten down" wages, although I believe such cases are relatively infrequent. (In any event, the reaction to the fear has been unwise: for every case where big business has held down workers there are surely many cases where big unions have held up employers.) But it cannot be denied that this public attitude underlies our national labor policy, the policy of local governments of condoning violence in labor disputes, etc.

Big business has also made substantial contributions to the growth of big government. The whole agricultural program has been justified as necessary to equalize agriculture's bargaining power with "industry," meaning big business. The federally sponsored milkshed cartels are defended as necessary to deal with the giant dairy companies. BUSINESS ACROSS THE BOARD. Big business is thus a fundamental excuse for big unions and big government. It is true that the scope and evils of big business are usually enormously exaggerated, especially with reference to labor and agriculture, and that more often than not these evils are merely a soapbox excuse for shoddy policies elsewhere. To this large extent, there is need for extensive education of the public on how small a part of the economy is controlled by big business. But in light of the widespread monopolistic practices—our first criticism of bigness—it is impossible to tell the public that its fears of big business are groundless. We have no right to ask public opinion to veer away from big unions and big government—and toward big business.

Efficiency and Big Business

Are we dependent upon big businesses for efficient methods of production and rapid advances in production methods? . . .

A company may be efficient because it produces and sells a given amount of product with relatively small amounts of material, capital, and labor, or it may be efficient because it acquires the power to buy its supplies at unusually low prices and sell its products at unusually high prices. Economists refer to these as the social and the private costs of production respectively. Big businesses may be efficient in the social sense, and usually they also possess, because of their monopoly position, private advantages. But the ability of a company to employ its dominant position to coerce unusually low prices from suppliers is not of any social advantage.

It follows that even if big companies had larger profit rates or smaller costs per unit of output than other companies, this would not prove that they were more efficient in socially desirable ways. Actually, big businesses are generally no more and no less efficient than medium-sized businesses even when the gains wrung by monopoly power are included in efficiency. This is the one general finding in comparative cost studies and comparative profitability studies. Indeed, if one reflects upon the persistence of small and medium-sized companies in the industries dominated by big businesses, it is apparent that there can be no great advantages to size. If size were a great advantage, the smaller companies would soon lose the unequal race and disappear.

When we recall that most big businesses have numerous complete plants at various points throughout the country, this finding is not surprising. Why should U.S. Steel be more efficient than Inland Steel, when U.S. Steel is simply a dozen or more Inland Steels strewn about the country? Why should G.M. be appreciably more efficient than say a once-again independent Buick Motors? . . .

. . . . .

If big businesses are not more efficient as a rule, how did they get big? The answer is that most giant firms arose out of mergers of many competing firms, and were created to eliminate competition. Standard Oil, General Electric, Westinghouse, U.S. Steel, Bethlehem, the meat packers, Borden, National Dairy, American Can, etc.—the full list of merger-created big businesses is most of the list of big businesses. A few big businesses owe their position to an industrial genius like Ford, and of course future geniuses would be hampered by an effective anti-trust law—but less so than by entrenched monopolies or by public regulatory commissions.

We do not know what share of improvements in technology has been contributed by big businesses. Big businesses have made some signal contributions, and so also have small businesses, universities, and private individuals. It can be said that manufacturing industries dominated by big businesses have had no larger increases in output per worker on average than other manufacturing industries. This fact is sufficient to undermine the easy identification of economic progress with the laboratories of big businesses, but it does not inform us of the net effect of monopolies on economic progress.

At present, then, no definite effect of big business on economic progress can be established. I personally believe that future study will confirm the traditional belief that big businesses, for all their resources, cannot rival the infinite resource and cold scrutiny of many independent and competing companies. If the real alternative to bigness is government regulation or ownership, as I am about to argue, then the long-run consequences of big business are going to be highly adverse to economic progress.

Remedies for Big Business

Let me restate the main points of the foregoing discussion in a less emphatic—and I think also a less accurate —manner:

1. Big businesses often possess and use monopoly power.

2. Big businesses weaken the political support for a private-enterprise system.

3. Big businesses are not appreciably more efficient or enterprising than medium-size businesses.

Few disinterested people will deny these facts—where do they lead?

A considerable section of the big-business community seems to have taken the following position. The proper way to deal with monopolistic practices is to replace the general prohibitions of the Sherman Act by a specific list of prohibited practices, so businessmen may know in advance and avoid committing monopolistic practices. The proper way to deal with the declining political support for private enterprise is to advertise the merits of private enterprise, at the same time claiming many of its achievements for big business. Much of this advertising has taken literally that form, apparently in the belief that one can sell a social system in exactly the same way and with exactly the same copywriters and media that one sells a brand of cigarettes.

GUARD THE SHERMAN ACT. The request for a list of specifically prohibited monopolistic practices will be looked upon by many persons as a surreptitious attack upon the Sherman Act. I am among these cynics: the powerful drive in 1949 to pass a law legalizing basing-point price systems is sufficient evidence that large sectors of big business are wholly unreconciled to the law against conspiracies in restraint of trade. Even when the request for a specific list of prohibitions is made in all sincerity, however, it cannot be granted: No one can write down a full list of all the forms that objectionable monopoly power has taken and may someday take. Moreover, almost all uncertainties over the legality of conduct arise out of the Robinson-Patman Act, not the Sherman Act, and I would welcome the complete repeal of the former act.[1]

We must look elsewhere for the solution of the problems raised by big busi-

---

[1] The prohibition against price discrimination was partly designed to cope with a real evil: the use by a large company of its monopoly power to extort preferential terms from suppliers. This exercise of monopoly, however, constitutes a violation of the Sherman Act, and no additional legislation is necessary if this act can be made fully effective. The Robinson-Patman Act, and certain other parts of the so-called "antitrust" amendments, also have another and objectionable purpose: to supervise and regulate the routine operations of businesses in order to ensure that they will display the symptoms of competitive behavior.

ness. . . . Our present policy is not a satisfactory solution. The Sherman Act is admirable in dealing with [the] formal conspiracies of many firms, but . . . it cannot cope effectively with the problem posed by big business. In industries dominated by a few firms there is no need for formal conspiracies, with their trappings of quotas, a price-fixing committee, and the like. The big companies know they must "live with" one another. . . . Any competitive action one big company takes will lead to retaliation by the others. An informal code of behavior gradually develops in the industry: Firm X announces the new price, and except in very unusual circumstances Y and Z can be relied upon to follow. So long as there are a few big businesses in an industry, we simply cannot expect more than the tokens of competitive behavior. Antitrust decrees that the big businesses should ignore each other's existence serve no important purpose.

This conclusion, I must emphasize, is not merely that of "economic theorists," although most (academic) economists will subscribe to it. It is also the conclusion our generation is reaching, for our generation is not satisfied with the behavior of big business. More and more, big businesses are being asked to act in "the social interest," and more and more, government is interfering in their routine operation. . . .

DISSOLUTION THE REMEDY. No such drastic and ominous remedy as the central direction of economic life is necessary to deal with the problems raised by big business. The obvious and economical solution, as I have already amply implied, is to break up the giant companies. This, I would emphasize, is the minimum program, and it is essentially a conservative program. Dissolution of big businesses is a once-for-all measure in each industry (if the recent anti-merger amendment to the Clayton Act is adequately enforced), and no continuing interference in the private operation of business is required or desired. Dissolution involves relatively few companies: one dissolves three or four big steel companies, and leaves the many smaller companies completely alone. Dissolution does not even need to be invoked in a large part of the economy: some of our biggest industries, such as textiles, shoes, and most food industries, will require no antitrust action.

A policy of "trust busting" requires no grant of arbitrary powers to any administrative agency; the policy can be administered by the Antitrust Division acting through the courts. It is sufficient, and it is desirable, that the policy be directed against companies whose possession of monopoly power is demonstrated, and that dissolution be the basic remedy for the concentration of control in an industry that prevents or limits competition. Indeed, the policy requires new legislation only to the extent of convincing the courts that an industry which does not have a competitive structure will not have competitive behavior.

The dissolution of big businesses is only a part of the program necessary to increase the support for a private, competitive enterprise economy, and reverse the drift toward government control. But it is an essential part of this program, and the place for courage and imagination. Those conservatives who cling to the status quo do not realize that the status quo is a state of change, and the changes are coming fast. If these changes were to include the dissolution of a few score of our giant companies, however, we shall have done much to preserve private enterprise and the liberal-individualistic society of which it is an integral part.

When high officials of giant corporations were sent to jail in 1961 for violating antitrust laws, what could the public conclude? One conclusion, certainly, would be that the antitrust laws had teeth which would really bite. Another conclusion would be that the laws are needed. The evidence left no doubt that prices had been fixed, not by accident nor by implicit "follow the leader" action but by conspiracy. If in spite of the law and in spite of the policies of the corporations directing employees to obey the laws, business men would do such things, what would they do if there were no law? The significance of the case summarized below may not be fully evident for many years. One prediction is safe, however: If somewhat similar practices have been limiting competition in other industries, unannounced but effective reforms will result from the jail sentences (and fines) imposed in this case.

24 · Price-Fixing Conspiracy Sends Business Leaders to Jail

U.S. NEWS AND WORLD REPORT

On a November day in 1955, a small group of men sat down in a hotel room in New York City to talk over a business matter.

To an outsider, the meeting might have seemed like a casual get-together of business acquaintances. In reality, court records show, it was part of a multimillion-dollar plan to control the marketing and pricing of products used by the electric-utility industry of this country.

The full dimensions of what the Government called a "combination and conspiracy" are just now coming to light. What went on, over a long period of years, resulted in the broadest set of convictions under the antitrust laws in the history of U. S. business.

The men who got together in the New York hotel room were officials of three of the country's biggest, most respected companies—General Electric Company, Westinghouse Electric Corporation and Allis-Chalmers Manufacturing Company.

UPSHOT: AN AGREEMENT. Before their meeting broke up, they had worked out a gentlemen's agreement to split up the market for three big turbine-generator orders for nuclear power plants.

Their quiet gathering, it turned out, was just one in a series of secret meetings that had been taking place for years at hotels, motels, private clubs and other places. Involved, in addition to GE, Westinghouse and Allis-Chalmers,

---

U.S. NEWS AND WORLD REPORT, "How 29 Companies Got Into Trouble," reprinted from *U.S. News and World Report,* published at Washington (February 27, 1961).

were 26 other manufacturers. All told, the 29 supply 95 per cent of all equipment sold in the U. S. for the generation, transmission and control of electric power. Their combined sales of this equipment amount to almost 2 billion dollars a year.

No one seems to know, for sure, when the first of the meetings took place. Testimony in one case involving circuit breakers indicated that collusion "was in effect for a quarter of a century."

The whole affair had many of the aspects of a mystery thriller. Official records give this picture:

The "conspirators" went to great lengths to avoid detection. They used a set of code numbers for identification, and addressed one another by first names only. They set up elaborate schemes for deciding who would get which orders. They never used company letterheads. They called each other at home, at odd hours, from telephone pay stations.

At hotels, the men registered separately and avoided chance encounters in lobbies or public places. After meetings in their suites, they were careful to destroy notes or memos that might prove incriminating.

The result of all this, according to evidence sifted by four grand juries, was that these makers of heavy electrical equipment had fixed and maintained prices, had allocated all available business among themselves, had met secretly to arrange bids and had rigged prices.

For Government agencies and private firms buying such electrical equipment, the effect was this: Over the years, these buyers had been asking for sealed bids, under the impression that, by doing so, they would get their needs supplied at the lowest competitive prices in a free and open market.

Instead, the whole bidding process was built around "collusive and rigged prices," court records show. The successful bidder, and the price he was to ask, had all been agreed upon in advance. Also, over the years, when equipment prices were changed by one company after another, what appeared to be spontaneous actions actually had been secretly planned.

IN 1957, COMPLAINTS. The investigation of the antitrust conspiracy started . . . in 1957. At that time, according to . . . the . . . Antitrust Division of the Justice Department, complaints had begun to dribble into [the] office reporting "something phony in the pricing structure" of the heavy electrical-equipment industry.

Federal Bureau of Investigation agents were assigned to the case. They worked for months, digging up fragmentary, but not conclusive, evidence of agreements to fix prices and rig bids.

In the spring of 1959, the Tennessee Valley Authority, one of the country's biggest buyers of electrical equipment, reported what it considered "flagrant examples of identical bidding" for its business.

The investigators stepped up their efforts. A grand jury was called into session in July of 1959. Company records were subpoenaed, and witnesses were called to testify in secret.

"TRAIL" OF EXPENSE ACCOUNTS. The records of the companies showed an intriguing pattern. By making comparisons of expense accounts, the investigators discovered that officials of various companies had been together in the same city at the same time, and frequently had been staying at the same hotels or motels.

Three other grand juries interviewed more than 100 witnesses. Some were promised immunity from prosecution in return for co-operation.

Out of all this came the indictment of 29 firms and 45 of their executives on charges of violating the Sherman Antitrust Act.

The cases did not go to trial.

All of the defendant companies and most of the individuals charged with Sherman Act violations pleaded either guilty or *nolo contendere* (no contest).

FINES AND SENTENCES. Early in February [1961], Judge J. Cullen Ganey of the U. S. District Court in Philadelphia pronounced sentence. The guilty corporations were fined a total of $1,787,000. Forty-four individual defendants were fined $137,500.

In addition, seven executives were sent to prison for 30 days each, and 21 others were given suspended prison terms and put on probation. . . .

Troubles of the defendant companies are by no means over. Still pending are 19 civil suits, and there is a possibility of scores of suits by municipalities and utility firms for triple damages.

Ralph J. Cordiner, chairman of General Electric Company, said . . . that he did not believe the firm's utility and industrial customers were damaged by the admitted price fixing, but, "if we've unwittingly damaged any customer anywhere we wish to make an adjustment." He added that since mid-December he has personally called on 24 utility customers, and "I've yet to encounter the first man who said, 'Cordiner, we've got a case, we've been damaged.'"

Allis-Chalmers Manufacturing Company said a preliminary check showed that the prices it charged during the four-year period covered by the suits "were not out of line."

What is described as "the big electrical-equipment antitrust case" actually embraced 20 separate indictments against various defendants, charging Sherman Act violations. The Sherman Act . . . forbids any actions in "restraint of trade," including the fixing of prices or the splitting up of markets.

Some of the "combinations and conspiracies," as Government lawyers noted, went back far into the past. Several were going on simultaneously, with different sets of company executives involved.

A FIVE-WAY SPLIT. In one case, centering on a type of equipment known as "power switchgear," a group of men met 26 times in 10 months to set prices and divide up sales territories. They met in expensive hotels in Chicago, New York, Pittsburgh, Detroit and elsewhere. One meeting was in a bar in Milwaukee.

There was no guesswork in the way the market for switchgear was divided up, according to the record in this case. Said the indictment:

Representatives of all of the defendant manufacturers would meet periodically and allocate bids to federal, State and local governmental agencies according to the following approximate percentage shares: General Electric Company, 39 per cent; Westinghouse Electric Company, 35 per cent; I-T-E Circuit Breaker Company, 11 per cent; Allis-Chalmers Manufacturing Company, 8 per cent; Federal Pacific Electric Company, 7 per cent.

As a way to quote nearly identical prices to electric-utility companies, private industrial corporations and contractors, the manufacturers used a sophisticated formula described by antitrust attorneys as the "phase of the moon" or "light of the moon" formula.

This formula had four phases, which were named for the four phases of the moon. The pricing scheme provided for automatic rotation of bidding positions every four weeks. The price spread between the manufacturers' quotations was kept narrow enough to eliminate any real price competition, yet wide enough to give the appearance of competition.

IN U. S., FOUR QUADRANTS. Another method for dividing markets, also described in court, was worked out by 16 manufacturers. This scheme, mapped at a secret meeting in Philadelphia in November, 1958, became known as the "quadrant" system. The country was divided into four separate geographical areas—the Northwest quadrant, the Southwest quadrant, the Southeast quadrant and the Northeast quadrant.

Four companies were assigned to each quadrant, and a representative from one particular company was picked as "secretary" to allocate business within the quadrant. This system was put into effect on Jan. 1, 1959.

CODE FOR CIRCUIT BREAKERS. In still another secret agreement involving the sale of circuit breakers, the principal participants were given code numbers.

Former Assistant Attorney General Robert A. Bicks, head of the Antitrust Division, who was responsible for the electrical-industry prosecutions, explained the code this way:

> There would be communication, either by phone to homes, with just the first names used, or by letter to homes with just first names of senders with no return address, and this wonderful code which appears for the first time in this case:
>
> The numbers were: 1, General Electric; 2, Westinghouse; 3, Allis-Chalmers; and 7, Federal Pacific. What happened to 4 or 5 and 6 until I-T-E came in remains a mystery. We don't know why 4 and 5 were left out. The communications referred only to 1, 2, 3. When I-T-E came in, in 1958, it got 6, and 7 [was given to] Federal Pacific.

SOMETIMES, PRICE CUTTING. All sorts of curious sidelights emerged as the antitrust cases were prepared for court action. Here are some examples:

- The company representatives, after a session to agree on certain price increases, sometimes went home only to find that some of their group failed to abide by the secret agreement. Then would come what Government lawyers described as a "dirty-linen-washing meeting," at which the participants would criticize each other for cutting prices.

- Company representatives involved in the suits used a variety of ways to decide who would get a particular order, or take the lead in announcing a price change. At a January, 1959, meeting in Philadelphia, the toss of a coin decided which company would initiate a plan for quoting prices on electrical equipment for the Navy and which would be low bidder.

- Secret talks involved introduction of new products, as well as prices and contracts for existing equipment. When one manufacturer decided to put out a new electrical product, a type of starter, the participants talked the firm out of marketing a "low quality" starter to sell at about two thirds the price of the starter then in existence. Instead, the company agreed to put out a "high quality" starter.

- In the case of at least one company, General Electric, the secret meetings were in direct conflict with a specific company directive first issued in 1946, and reissued several times since, that warned employes against talking with competitors or taking any other steps that might violate any antitrust law.

WORD FROM A RELAYMAN. In at least one instance described in court records, a company executive apparently wanted to avoid a face-to-face meeting with a group of competitors, yet still have a hand in price fixing. The court was told of a meeting at a camp near North Bay, Ontario, Canada. From the record comes this story:

> The defendants held the meeting at a particular cabin in this island resort. Mr. Oswalt, . . . who was representing General Electric during this period of time, was not attending meetings with the rest of the companies.
>
> However, Mr. Oswalt got himself a cabin in very close proximity to the cabin being occupied by the other defendant representatives. An individual at the con-

spiratorial meeting was sent periodically during the course of the meeting . . . to Mr. Oswalt's cabin [to] consult Mr. Oswalt as to his position on the various matters that were being discussed. It was a representative of one of the smaller companies that was delegated to be, in effect, the relayman between the two cabins.

Mr. Oswalt agreed to the price increase and so notified the relayman, who communicated this fact back to the remainder of the individuals at the first cabin.

A "PLAN OF ENFORCEMENT." After sentencing of the defendants Westinghouse Electric's president, Mark W. Cresap, Jr., announced the formation of a new antitrust section within the corporation's law department, with a "detailed plan of enforcement within the company to assure future compliance with antitrust laws."

Allis-Chalmers noted that its top management did not believe the men involved in the conspiracy acted with criminal intent. Said a company statement: "We think they were mistaken in their ideas as to what they ought to do to serve the company."

Judge Ganey, in sentencing the individual defendants, all of whom are men highly respected in their communities, said he was convinced, that, in the great number of the defendants' cases, "they were torn between conscience and an approved corporate policy, with the rewarding objectives of promotion, comfortable security and large salaries."

But Judge Ganey also repeated the prosecution's statement that the whole conspiracy "flagrantly mocked the image of that economic system of free enterprise which we profess to the country, and destroyed the model which we offer today as a free-world alternative to state control."

Copyright 1961 United States News Publishing Corporation.

A leading antitrust case involved the Du Pont Corporation and Cellophane. The Supreme Court decided that Du Pont had not violated the antitrust laws in its Cellophane operations. The judges placed heavy emphasis on economic evidence—evidence of price reductions; product improvement; vigorous and imaginative selling effort; cost reductions; and, especially, the existence of many alternative wrapping materials produced by other firms. An outstanding authority on antitrust, Professor Stocking of Vanderbilt University, differs with the interpretation of the evidence.

25 · An Economist Analyzes an Antitrust Decision: Cellophane

GEORGE W. STOCKING

Section 2 of the Sherman Act prohibits monopolizing, attempting to monopolize, or conspiring to monopolize. Monopolizing involves acquiring a monopoly and is basically an economic concept. Trying to monopolize involves motives and is basically a psychological concept. Conspiring is a matter of the law. A balanced interpretation of the Sherman Act would seem to embrace three disciplines—economics, psychology, and the law. Fortunately judges, versatile by training and experience and self-reliant by disposition, have not felt the need [for] psychologists in applying the Sherman Act. Since motives have economic significance only as they reveal themselves in business conduct, there is indeed little reason for the courts to call in the psychologists in administering Section 2. Only recently have they felt the need of economists. Economists perhaps can do double duty. Surely they know something about monopoly, and they should have special competence in determining whether business conduct—that is, business practices—is competitive or monopolistic in character. In short, the economists' function with reference to Section 2 should be to determine whether a defendant has really obtained a monopoly. It is for the courts to decide whether he has monopolized within the meaning of the Sherman Act, because the law bans only monopolies that have been unlawfully acquired or maintained.

Even for economists, determining the existence of monopoly is difficult. It was perhaps simpler when we knew less about it. In the good old days before we had learned of the purity and perfection of competition, when monopoly was merely an ugly, bloodthirsty Moloch, it was easier to recognize. Today we know that pure monopoly is no

---

GEORGE W. STOCKING, "Economic Tests of Monopoly and the Concept of the Relevant Market," *The Antitrust Bulletin* (March 1957). Used by permission.

less an abstraction than is pure competition and is rarely found in real markets. No market situation is apt to be entirely free from monopolistic restraints, and no monopolist can ignore the rivalry of substitutes.

Technical progress and mechanical ingenuity have so broadened markets and dimmed boundaries that among firms and products with previously isolated markets a vigorous rivalry has broken out. Aluminum was for many years a classic example of domestic monopoly. Today other materials are available for the uses it serves: copper for electrical cables and conductors, lead for tubes and cables, zinc, brass, and magnesium for alloys, steel for trucks, vans, and trailers, and wood, steel, and copper for construction. For the manufacture of cooking utensils aluminum meets the rivalry of glass, tin ware, stainless steel, cast iron, enamel ware, and copper. As uses for aluminum have multiplied, its exclusive domain has so diminished that today it has few markets in which it does not meet the rivalry of alternative materials. The same is true of most other products throughout industry. As firms have diversified their operations and broadened their product mix, they not only have intensified rivalry with each other but have created a rivalry within themselves by producing different products that serve the same general function.

These developments raise a challenging question for antitrust lawyers, economists, and the courts. Does rivalry among substitutes provide the protection to consumers contemplated by the antitrust statutes? Many people believe it does. Businessmen have noted these developments with pride, economists, with optimism. Businessmen have pointed to them as evidence not only of the virility of private enterprise but of the rejuvenation and intensification of competition. Economists in loftier language, more technical and abtruse, have seen in them a waning of oligopolistic power. . . .

But the optimism of the economists has not been matched by their ability to agree on the extent of monopoly power in particular situations or on the weight that should be given to various factors in identifying and measuring it. Economists like judges cannot free themselves of all preconceptions. Depending on their point of view, they have been willing to use their tools either for defendants or for the government in antitrust cases. And in independent analysis of antitrust proceedings, when they must select signiflcant facts from the multitude of data spread over thousands of pages of testimony and exhibits, what they find may unwittingly be influenced by what they are looking for.

With this acknowledgment of the frailities that affect us, I shall endeavor to indicate as objectively as I can what I regard as proper criteria for determining monopoly and to show their significance to the *Cellophane* case.

The Concept of Workable Competition

Economists, recognizing the imperfections of competition in the market place and the many and unique patterns into which it falls, have sought to differentiate the socially acceptable situation from the unacceptable by developing the concept of workable competition. According to this concept, a market structure is workably competitive if it yields acceptable performance that cannot be improved without abandoning the market entirely as a regulator of economic activity. In determining workability economists look to three factors: industrial structure, business conduct, and economic performance. . . . I do not believe that the standard of workability is an appropriate one by which to determine the legality of business arrangements under the antitrust statutes. The least acceptable of these criteria is performance. Bad performance may be an appropriate criterion for determining public policy towards a competitive industry, but good performance can scarcely justify private monopolies in a society dedicated to free enterprise. As Ben W. Lewis has expressed it,

> Results alone throw no light on the really significant question: have these results been *compelled* by the system—by *competition*—or do they represent simply the dispensations of managements which, with a wide latitude of policy choices at their disposal, happened for the moment to be benevolent or "smart"? This points up the real issue.[1]

Although I do not regard the principle of workability as an acceptable guide in antitrust cases, I do believe that the criteria that economists have developed for determining workability —structure, conduct, and performance —can serve a useful, perhaps indispensable, function in determining the existence of monopoly.

INDUSTRIAL STRUCTURE AND THE RELEVANT MARKET. In examining industrial structure one looks to the number of firms in an industry, their relative size, the extent to which a few dominate it, ease of entry, availability of substitutes, and similar characteristics that have relevance to economic behavior. Some economists have contended that structure does not have a definitive relationship to behavior. M. A. Adelman, for example, has argued that competition can be effective with only a few large firms in an industry, with many small firms, or with a mixture of large and small firms. This may be true, but most economists would probably admit that the fewer the firms in an industry the greater the likelihood of their following common pricing policies and common business practices calculated to maximize their earnings; in short, the greater the likelihood of their behaving like monopolists. In truth, structure may dictate behavior. Despite the vogue that the Chamberlinian theory of oligopolistic pricing attained shortly after its enunciation, economists generally would probably now accept the proposition that without tacit agreement oligopolists are as likely to behave like competitors as like monopolists. Uncertainties, as Chamberlin pointed out, may make the outcome indeterminate. What is certain is that some structural patterns are more conducive to tacit agreement than others. When only a few sellers dominate a market they need no formal agreement to insure their acting in a way to promote their mutual interests. And they can readily find pricing devices—basing point pricing, price leadership and the like—that will insure their doing so.

Students of industrial structure who emphasize the role that substitutes play in determining the effectiveness of competition believe that the relevant market for any product may be broader than that of the firms producing it. Ross M. Robertson, an able exponent of this view, has declared,

> To assess the competitive situation of a firm we must still resort to counting. . . . Yet counting only those firms which are within the "industry" tells us very little. We must do our counting by taking categories of uses for the output of an industry, considering what products of other industries directly compete within these categories.[2]

---

[1] LEWIS, "The Effectiveness of the Federal Antitrust Laws: A Symposium," Keezer, organizer, 39 Am. Econ. Rev. 689, 707 (1949).

[2] ROBERTSON, "On the Changing Apparatus of Competition," *American Economic Review* (March 1954), pp. 53–54.

But if counting substitutes is to have any real significance, some method of calculating the substitutability of the so-called substitutes is required. All products compete with each other for the consumer's dollar, and in this sense each product is a substitute for any other. Substitutes regarded in this light have no significance to the monopoly problem. To have meaning they must be close enough to insure an ecomonical allocation of resources and to protect consumers from exploitation. Economists have developed the concept of cross-elasticity to measure substitutability, and the courts have borrowed it in trying to determine a product's relevant market. . . . I believe this concept alone cannot be of much use in antitrust cases and that its use by those not trained in economics will lessen the effectiveness of Section 2 of the Sherman Act.

BUSINESS CONDUCT AND THE RELEVANT MARKET. Conduct or business strategy may be not only designed to insure common policies among business rivals but may be used by a single firm to protect some advantage—that is, some monopoly power—that it possesses. Some economists, notably Joseph A. Schumpeter, have argued that temporary monopolistic advantages are essential to economic progress. Every innovation represents a monopoly and if it meets with popular acceptance is likely to bring to the innovator, for a time at least, monopoly profits. Without the promise of such profits, Schumpeter argues, innovations would cease and progress would be stifled. But while Schumpeter would apply a performance test to the acceptability of monopoly, he would not deny that the innovator possesses monopoly power.

This country's patent policy was based on the Schumpeterian theory long before Schumpeter advanced it. That business firms acquire patents is indicative of their belief that the patented process or product has unique qualities that so differentiate it from rival processes or products as to enable the possessor to make gains greater than he could make if everyone were free to use it. Patents may legalize monopoly power, but that they create it can scarcely be denied. Other forms of business strategy designed to give a business firm power in the market do not enjoy legal status, but they similarly reflect an effort to isolate firms from the unrestrained competition of their rivals. Dividing territories, setting market quotas, and the like are devices of the monopolist or of the would-be-monopolist. That businessmen resort to such devices makes them suspect under both Section 1 and Section 2 of the Sherman Act. When they do, both the economists and the courts may find their task simplified.

Where monopolistic strategies are entirely lacking, it may be necessary to determine the precise boundary of a seller's market as a step in determining whether he has monopoly power. But when business strategy provides the answer to the question whether a firm has monopoly power, the difficult task of determining the boundaries of the revelant market may be avoided. Businessmen do not try to protect a position that has no value. When they act with respect to their position as though they believe it possesses elements of monopoly, this is persuasive evidence that it does. Business conduct, in short, can be a significant factor in determining the existence of monopoly.

BUSINESS PERFORMANCE. Judges may regard business conduct as a slender reed on which to [hang] the determination of antitrust violation. But rarely will they have to rely on it alone. Business performance may so reinforce a judgment on structure and conduct as to leave little doubt that a firm in fact has power over the market. The economist's interest here is not whether a firm with monopoly power serves society well, but whether a firm has monopoly power. The aspects of performance most relevant to determining whether a firm possesses monopoly power are its pricing policy and its profits record. The courts have defined monopoly power as the power to exclude competitors and the power to control price. . . .

To distinguish competitive pricing from monopolistic pricing is not always easy. In a perfectly competitive market rivals will sell at identical prices at any moment of time, but prices will change frequently in response to changing consumer wants and consumer evaluations of the relative importance of different products and in response to changing conditions of supply. In a market of pure monopoly, prices will similarly change in response to changes in consumer evaluations and in response to changes in cost. The difference is that in competitive markets the average cost of production (including a normal rate of return on investment) sets the limit to long-run price, while in a monopolized market the monopolist continuously reevaluates demand and cost functions and tries to so adjust output as to maximize earnings by keeping price above cost. The greater the power of a monopolist the greater the likelihood that his prices will be flexible. The limitations on monopoly power in most industrial markets are such that noncompetitive or quasi-monopolistic pricing is apt to result in identical pricing by business rivals, with prices stable over a long period. In short, the closer markets are to perfect competition or to perfect monopoly the greater the similarity in their price behavior.

The characteristics that distinguish monopolistic from competitive markets where both have flexible prices are their cost-price ratios and their rate of earnings. In competitive markets prices tend to equal costs—marginal in the short run, average in the long run. In monopolistic markets prices tend to exceed marginal costs in the short run and average costs in the long run. The excess shows up in abnormal, that is, noncompetitive profits. Because economists rarely have access to cost data they may be forced to rely on profits data in determining the existence of monopoly. Pure profits of course are not confined to monopolistic markets. Competitors who respond to a rapidly expanding demand may realize earnings in excess of normal competitive rates. That they do so reflects the frictions that retard shifts in the use of resources. But such earning rates are apt to be short-lived. Long-term profits rates may be an aid in determining the existence of monopoly.

Economic Tests of Monopoly and the Cellophane Case

Let us now examine the *Cellophane* case in the light of the several criteria for determining the existence of monopoly outlined above—structure, conduct, and performance. My task is to answer [the question] . . . Does Du Pont have a monopoly in making and selling Cellophane?

STRUCTURE. Only two domestic firms made and sold Cellophane in the domestic market when the Government filed its antitrust case in 1947—Sylvania Industrial Corporation of America and the Du Pont Company, [together] . . . accounted for over three-fourths of domestic sales. The structure of the industry was clearly not conducive to effective competition in selling Cellophane if Cellophane be considered a differentiated product. But is not Cellophane's relevant market determined by the products that serve a similar function? Judge Leahy concluded that it was. In doing so he decided, and the Supreme Court sustained him, that Cellophane was not a unique product, that in most of its end uses it met the competition of other wrapping papers, and hence that its relevant market was that for flexible wrapping materials. Of this broader market Du Pont obviously had no monopoly. In food packaging, for which Du Pont sold 80 per cent of its Cellophane output, its percentage of total sales of Cellophane, aluminum foil, glassine, waxed and other specialty wrapping papers, and films by nineteen major converters in 1949 varied from 6.8 per cent in bakery products to 47.2 per cent for wrapping fresh produce. For every important food except fresh produce, foil, glassine, and waxed and other specialty papers outsold Cellophane. In finding that these several flexible wrapping materials gave vigorous competition to Cellophane, Judge Leahy noted that shifts in business between Cellophane and other materials were "frequent, continuing and contested." From this the district court and the Supreme Court concluded that cross-elasticity was high. By delimiting Cellophane's market according to the areas in which it met the rivalry of substitute products and by applying the concept of cross-elasticity, this decision brings the law into harmony with recent concepts of competition. Nevertheless I find the courts' analysis and their conclusions unsound. As I have indicated, I do not believe the concept of cross-elasticity is of much use in determining whether a firm has a monopoly. In the first place, it calls for more precise information than antitrust cases can be expected to provide. Cross-elasticity defines the extent to which a change in the price of one commodity, for example, A, affects the sales of another commodity, B. If a decrease in the price of A diminishes the sales of B, cross-elasticity is positive. All that this tells us is that one product can be substituted for another, and that some consumers will make the substitution if their evaluation of the two products warrants it. If a given percentage change in the price of one product causes a relatively large change in the sales of the other product, cross-elasticity is high. On this question the record in the *Cellophane* case is necessarily silent; to answer it would involve disclosure of confidential information by business rivals. In the second place, even if the data were available, positive cross-elasticity, alone may not warrant the conclusion that the seller of neither product can be a monopolist. To determine the existence of monopoly power, economists and the courts must examine both the price response of the firms losing business and the cost-price relationships of firms selling both products. If a price decrease by a firm selling product A shifts business from B to A, firms selling B must reconsider their pricing policies. To recapture lost business or, where cross-elasticity is high, to prevent the loss of what they have, they must lower their prices. If price changes by producers of one commodity are unaccompanied by price changes in the rival commodity, this indicates a lack of competition between the two commodities. Either the loss of business is too slight to matter—the cross-elasticity is low—or the firm cutting prices has a monopoly advantage not possessed by those not cutting prices. The firms not cutting prices must already be selling their product at a price equal to their marginal cost, while the firm that cut may have been getting a price in excess of its marginal cost.

So much for the principles. What are the facts? Between 1924 and 1938 Du Pont through a series of price cuts reduced the average price of Cellophane by over 80 per cent. During this same period the average price of glassine and waxed paper remained virtually constant. Between 1938 and 1940 Du Pont decreased the price of cellophane a further 8.6 per cent, while the prices of glassine and waxed paper actually increased. Obviously the cross-elasticity of demand was very low. In selling Cellophane Du Pont was able to ignore the prices of rival wrapping papers. Between 1924 and 1950, as Du Pont dropped its average prices of Cellophane from $2.51 to 49 cents a pound, prices for the principal type of moistureproof Cellophane were from two to seven times the price of 25# bleached glassine and from two to four and one-half times the price of 30# waxed paper. That Du Pont could continuously sell Cellophane in so-called competition with glassine and waxed paper, never charging less than twice as much, is sufficient evidence that Cellophane was a unique product. As the Supreme Court dissenting opinion put it,

> We cannot believe that ... practical businessmen would have bought Cellophane in increasing amounts over a quarter of a century if close substitutes were available at from one-seventh to one-half Cellophane's price. That they did so is testimony to Cellophane's distinctiveness.[3]

That marginal buyers, candymakers, for example, shifted their purchases from one product to another from time to time does not indicate that Du Pont had no monopoly in selling Cellophane. No monopolized product is completely isolated from rival products, and consumers anxious to get their money's worth are constantly comparing values and shifting purchases. They are not dissuaded from doing so merely because one of the products they desire is sold by a monopolist and another by competitors.

CONDUCT. Du Pont officials themselves are on record as believing that they had in Cellophane a unique product for which there was no effective substitute,[4] and they adopted a strategy to protect Du Pont's monopoly. Du Pont entered the business in 1923 by joining with La Cellophane, a French company that owned the original patents, to form the Du Pont Cellophane Company, which acquired the exclusive right to exploit the patents in the American market. In 1929 Du Pont Cellophane Company entered into a patent exchange agreement with Kalle & Company of Germany, and in 1935 it entered into one with British Cellophane, Ltd. In effect these agreements were also divisions of territory. While not signers of the 1930 cartel agreement dividing world markets, Du Pont representatives attended the Paris cartel conference, and Du Pont Cellophane Company later relied on the cartel agreement to protect its claim to the West Indies market. It took steps to obtain tariff protection that eventually excluded virtually all imports of Cellophane. It settled its patent-infringement suit against Sylvania by a patent exchange and cross-licensing agreement that geared Sylvania's production to its

---

[3] *United States* v. *E. I. du Pont de Nemours & Co.*, 351 U.S. 377, 417 (1956).

[4] ... Olin Industries, Inc., a company that Du Pont in 1948 decided to encourage to enter Cellophane production (and that did so in 1951), after investigation reported: "According to du Pont, Cellophane is considered the only all purpose film, and any product to be truly competitive with Cellophane must have the following attributes: (1) low cost, (2) transparency, (3) operate with a high efficiency on mechanical equipment, (4) print well both as to speed and appearance. There are no films currently marketed which are potentially competitive to any substantial degree in Cellophane's major markets when measured by the above attributes necessary for wide usage. ..."

own. It launched a research and patent-accumulation program that, according to President Yerkes, was designed as a defense measure to protect "the field of moistureproofing agents other than waxes." By these steps it forestalled genuine competition in selling Cellophane in the American market. Its strategy was that of a monopolist.

PERFORMANCE. The district court found Du Pont to be an aggressive and progressive competitor of all flexible packaging material producers, quick to improve its product and processes, quick to lower its prices, and quick to promote its sales by acquainting potential users with Cellophane's superior qualities. In the broad market for flexible wrapping materials Judge Leahy found a vigorous and healthy competition, and for its farsighted, aggressive management in meeting this competition he thought Du Pont deserved praise, not censure. From the same record I find that Du Pont behaved as any intelligent monopolist might have behaved. Through research and experience it improved the quality of its product and the processes for making it. It was continuously alert to the market potentialities of Cellophane, and it took aggressive steps to acquaint potential users with its peculiar qualities.[5] Its management periodically re-examined its costs and sales, actual and potential, and shaped its price and production program to improve its earnings. In doing so, as I have indicated, it was able to ignore the pricing policies of producers of rival wrapping materials. Du Pont officials recognized that they had control over Cellophane prices, and the record shows they used it to achieve specified profit goals. In May 1948, with earnings on investment in Cellophane averaging 31 per cent before taxes, a division manager suggested that if such earnings were considered inadequate Du Pont should raise its prices; and he proposed a schedule of prices calculated to yield 40 per cent. After adoption of the schedule Du Pont's earnings rate increased to 35.2 per cent in 1949 and to 45.3 per cent in 1950. An intracompany memorandum indicates that in considering a price increase during the postwar inflation Du Pont was more concerned about its effect on public relations than on rivals or customers. Du Pont's pricing policies were clearly those of a monopolist.

Du Pont's earnings were likewise monopolistic. Its annual rate of earnings on investment, before taxes, in cellophane ranged from 18.0 per cent to 62.4 per cent and averaged 35.6 per cent during the period 1925 to 1938. Du Pont's earnings on its investment in rayon during the same period ranged from —0.9 per cent to 34.2 per cent and averaged only 12.9 per cent. During the nine years from 1930 to 1938 inclusive, when competition had become vigorous, earnings on rayon averaged only 6.6 per cent. This comparison has unique significance. Cellophane and rayon stem from the same basic raw materials. Both were innovations appearing about the same time. Both were initially manufactured under noncompetitive conditions and both enjoyed substantial tariff protection. Du Pont produced both. Both have reasonably close substitutes. As output increased

---

[5] [The following example is taken from the longer study. *Ed.*] Du Pont showed great ingenuity and aggression in developing new uses for Cellophane and expanding old ones. R. R. Smith, assistant director of sales of Du Pont's film department, testified that in 1934, when white bread regularly sold for 10 cents a loaf and its profit margin was small, he and other salesmen actually created the specialty breads industry—new varieties of bread which could be sold at a price large enough to cover the higher cost of wrapping them in Cellophane. . . .

both were the beneficiaries of continuing improvements in production, a rapid reduction in costs, and a rapid decline in price. The significant difference in making and selling the two products is the structure of the two industries. Both began as monopolies, but in rayon rival producers quickly appeared. By 1930 American Vicose Corporation, the country's first producer, and Du Pont, its second, met the rivalry of eighteen other rayon makers. This intensification of competition eventually resulted in competitive pricing and the disappearance of monopoly earnings.

The basic issue in the *Cellophane* case really boils down to this: Would freedom of entry have brought in a larger number of cellophane producers and ultimately lower prices and earnings than have prevailed? I believe it would have. Moreover, if the rivalry of substitute packaging materials, particularly glassine and waxed paper, had in fact forced competitive pricing on Du Pont, as the court concluded, Du Pont should have been indifferent to the entry of rival cellophane producers. Competition from either cellophane or waxed paper would have resulted in precisely the same cost-price ratios in selling cellophane. As judged by structure, conduct, and performance, Judge Leahy erred in giving a negative answer to his first question: Does Du Pont have a monopoly in making and selling Cellophane?

What can be said about the broader significance of the Supreme Court's opinion affirming Judge Leahy's decision? If it becomes a precedent, the Supreme Court minority is right in declaring that the Court has emasculated Section 2 of the Sherman Act. If Cellophane is merely a flexible wrapping material, then airlines, railways, bus lines, and river steamers are merely transportation facilities; aluminum, copper, brass, and steel are merely metals; and cotton rugs, linen rugs, nylon rugs, woolen rugs, linoleum, and similar substitutes are merely floor coverings. Under the Supreme Court's *Cellophane* ruling a monopoly in any one of them need not violate Section 2 of the Sherman Act, and in denying the existence of monopoly the courts need only ascertain that people choose among alternative products serving similar functions in trying to get their money's worth.

. . . . .

V · CONSUMPTION AND CONSUMER PROBLEMS

One of the most famous books in the literature of American economics develops as a major theme the point that much consumption, and especially by persons with large incomes, is futile, socially wasteful, and motivated essentially by a desire to at least keep up with the Joneses, to get ahead of them if possible. The selected paragraphs below indicate the general sense of the book.

26 · *Conspicuous Consumption*

THORSTEIN B. VEBLEN

With the exception of the instinct of self-preservation, the propensity for emulation is probably the strongest and most alert and persistent of the economic motives proper. In an industrial community this propensity for emulation expresses itself in pecuniary emulation; and this, so far as regards the Western civilized communities of the present, is virtually equivalent to saying that it expresses itself in some form of conspicuous waste. The need of conspicuous waste, therefore, stands ready to absorb any increase in the community's industrial efficiency or output of goods, after the most elementary physical wants have been provided for. Where this result does not follow, under modern conditions, the reason for the discrepancy is commonly to be sought in a rate of increase in the individual's wealth too rapid for the habit of expenditure to keep abreast of it; or it may be that the individual in question defers the conspicuous consumption of the increment to a later date—ordinarily with a view to heightening the spectacular effect of the aggregate expenditure contemplated. As increased industrial efficiency makes it possible to procure the means of livelihood with less labor, the energies of the industrious members of the community are bent to the compassing of a higher result in conspicuous expenditure, rather than slackened to a more comfortable pace. The strain is not lightened as industrial efficiency increases and makes a lighter strain possible, but the increment of output is turned to use to meet this want, which is indefinitely expansible, after the manner commonly imputed in economic theory to higher or spiritual

THORSTEIN B. VEBLEN, *The Theory of the Leisure Class* (New York: The Viking Press, Inc., 1899), pp. 110–112, 131–133. Used by permission.

wants. It is owing chiefly to the presence of this element in the standard of living that J. S. Mill was able to say that "hitherto it is questionable if all the mechanical inventions yet made have lightened the day's toil of any human being."

The accepted standard of expenditure in the community or in the class to which a person belongs largely determines what his standard of living will be. It does this directly by commending itself to his common sense as right and good, through his habitually contemplating it and assimilating the scheme of life in which it belongs; but it does so also indirectly through popular insistence on conformity to the accepted scale of expenditure as a matter of propriety, under pain of disesteem and ostracism. To accept and practice the standard of living which is in vogue is both agreeable and expedient, commonly to the point of being indispensable to personal comfort and to success in life. The standard of living of any class, so far as concerns the element of conspicuous waste, is commonly as high as the earning capacity of the class will permit—with a constant tendency to go higher. The effect upon the serious activities of men is therefore to direct them with great singleness of purpose to the largest possible acquisition of wealth, and to discountenance work that brings no pecuniary gain. At the same time the effect on consumption is to concentrate it upon the lines which are most patent to the observers whose good opinion is sought; while the inclinations and aptitudes whose exercise does not involve a honorific expenditure of time or substance tend to fall into abeyance through disuse. . . .

. . . . .

The blending and confusion of the elements of expensiveness and of beauty is, perhaps, best exemplified in articles of dress and of household furniture. The code of reputability in matters of dress decides what shapes, colors, materials, and general effects in human apparel are for the time to be accepted as suitable; and departures from the code are offensive to our taste, supposedly as being departures from aesthetic truth. The approval with which we look upon fashionable attire is by no means to be accounted pure make-believe. We readily, and for the most part with utter sincerity find those things pleasing that are in vogue. Shaggy dress-stuffs and pronounced color effects, for instance, offend us at times when the vogue is goods of a high, glossy finish and neutral colors. A fancy bonnet of this year's model unquestionably appeals to our sensibilities today much more forcibly than an equally fancy bonnet of the model of last year; although when viewed in the perspective of a quarter of a century, it would, I apprehend, be a matter of the utmost difficulty to award the palm for intrinsic beauty to the one rather than to the other of these structures. So, again, it may be remarked that, considered simply in their physical juxtaposition with the human form, the high gloss of a gentleman's hat or of a patent-leather shoe has no more of intrinsic beauty than a similarly high gloss on a threadbare sleeve; and yet there is no question but that all well-bred people (in the Occidental civilized communities) instinctively and unaffectedly cleave to the one as a phenomenon of great beauty, and eschew the other as offensive to every sense to which it can appeal. It is extremely doubtful if anyone could be induced to wear such a contrivance as the high hat of civilized society, except for some urgent reason based on other than aesthetic grounds.

By further habituation to an appreciative perception of the marks of expensiveness in goods, and by habitually identifying beauty with reputability, it comes about that a beautiful article which is not expensive is accounted not beautiful. In this way it has happened, for instance, that some beautiful flowers pass conventionally for offensive weeds; others that can be cultivated with relative ease are accepted and admired by the lower middle class, who can afford no more expensive luxuries of this kind; but these varieties are rejected as vulgar by those people who are better able to pay for expensive flowers and who are educated to a higher schedule of pecuniary beauty in the florist's products; while still other flowers, of no greater intrinsic beauty than these, are cultivated at great cost and call out much admiration from flower-lovers whose tastes have been matured under the critical guidance of a polite environment.

. . . . .

The Federal Reserve System tries to keep abreast of changes in the economy. Its studies range from the passing events of each day to the broader and deeper trends of long-run importance. One topic of great significance is consumer buying. The Federal Reserve, among other things, has financed many consumer inquiries by the Survey Research Center at the University of Michigan. Such investigations of the intentions of a carefully chosen sample of consumers help in forecasting economic events in the months ahead. The selection here, however, deals with changes of a more general nature in the structure of consumer buying.

27 · New Features of the Consumer Market

LAWRENCE C. MURDOCH

In the American economy, every family is a royal family. Each consumer is a king, queen, prince, or princess. No mere figureheads, they dominate and rule the economy.

The royal family of consumers buys about two-thirds of all goods and services produced. And consumers wield despotic power. They can impose their wills on governments through the ballot box, and on businesses through free markets.

The royal family now seems to be getting restless after being relatively set in its ways through much of the postwar period. Consumers themselves are changing and so are their spending habits. Spending has shifted away from some old standbys and this could be an important cause of the current business setback. Some of our present excess plant capacity and unemployment cer-

---

LAWRENCE C. MURDOCH, "The Royal Family Grows Restless," reprinted from *Business Review*, a publication of the Federal Reserve Bank of Philadelphia (Philadelphia: February 1961). Used by permission.

tainly are located in industries whose products consumers no longer favor. Anthracite coal is the classic example but durable goods and houses should not be overlooked. . . .

The shift away from these "hard" goods may have a significant effect on the course of business. The products and services consumers covet today do not have the explosive impact on the economy that durables and housing have. The dollars spent in 1961 may not ripple out quite so far or so fast or create so many jobs as they once did. Compare the immediate effect on production of $3,000 spent for an automobile versus $3,000 spent for college tuition.

But if the new spending mix is not so stimulating neither is it so volatile. Durables and housing are subject to wide cyclical swings. By spending more of their money for other things, consumers may be adding a note of stability to the economy.

The royal treasury is bulging. Incomes should remain high in 1961 and consumers will spend record sums. But the royal family will probably remain restive for some time. Consumers are more sophisticated and have more complex wants. They are more choosy and harder to please. They are interested in real value and will pay to get it. Sharper shoppers, consumers should be harder to manipulate. The creation of artificial demands through frequent style changes and "hidden persuader" advertising is becoming more difficult. In short, the royal family is turning into something of a tyrant and businessmen will have to work harder than ever to serve by "appointment to their majesties." Yet the rewards will be great for the firms that make the grade.

Aside from the broad drift to services, no clear new consumer spending pattern has emerged. Instead there seems to be a churning of trends—a kaleidoscope of demands. This may be just a gusty interim before the winds of trade steady in a definite direction. Or it could be a permanent thing. It could be that consumer spending during the early part of the 1960's will be characterized by the lack of a neat pattern such as we have seen in the past. This is a real possibility for consumers are subject to some very complicated, somewhat contradictory forces.

In this article, we sketch, as we see them, a few of the many changes that have taken place in the consumer market. Some are psychological, some sociological, some economic, but all could affect the way consumers spend their money—which products they favor and which they banish to oblivion. It is difficult if not impossible to measure the extent of these changes or indeed to prove they actually have taken place. Furthermore, many of their impacts and effects must, of necessity, be based on conjecture. . . .

The Death of a Spokesman

The average consumer was a faceless spender who spoke for many millions of his fellows. Born of myriad surveys, he had been pried and probed by marketing men for decades. Know what the average consumer would do and you knew what consumers in general would do. In other words, the early post-World War II consumer market was relatively cohesive and predictable. Families tended to spend as units and the units often behaved in much the same ways.

The concept of the average consumer, the easy-to-understand model of all consumers, has much less validity today. The consumer market has begun to atomize—to split into many autonomous markets and submarkets. Family members are spending more as individuals and neither families nor individuals seem to fit neatly into any inclusive mold. No longer is the market well-gauged by over-all averages. . . .

The consumer market has divided many ways—by age, sex, marital status, race, region, and income, to mention but a few, and each group exercises discretion over increasingly larger sums of money.

WHAT MADE SPENDERS SPLINTER? The fragmentation of the consumer market has a number of causes. Most important, perhaps, is the great rise in discretionary income—income left over after the essentials of food, clothing, and shelter have been bought. This is income consumers can spend as they choose—for steaks, stereo sets, travel, etc. The National Industrial Conference Board estimates that discretionary income has risen 64 per cent since 1946.

The broad diffusion of income is another key feature. Increases in income have spread throughout the entire economy. Vast numbers of people have moved up from subsistence levels and now have money for other purposes. Many minority groups—Negroes are an example—have enjoyed greater-than-average income gains.

The rise in income has liberated individual spenders within families and has magnified differences among families. We don't mean to imply that consumer spending patterns were once all the same. There have always been important variations, of course. The point is that the patterns have grown considerably more diverse in recent years. . . .

Let's flash back to the end of the war. . . .

On the home front, 1946 was the year of the in-laws. There was a housing shortage and families doubled and tripled up. Returning servicemen and their brides moved in with parents who already may have been harboring a selection of grandparents and unmarried siblings. And don't forget Aunt Harriet who had moved East to do war work.

Incomes were partially pooled and much spending was done by the household for its members. Individual tastes and preferences tended to be laminated into a single market unit.

Most people didn't really like this communal arrangement. They put up with it because there was no choice. They were ready to move out when they got the chance. For many, the chance came in the late 1940's. A great number of houses were built . . . and many existing structures were converted into apartments. Young couples went to development "castles" financed on the "G. I. Bill." Aunt Harriet moved to her own apartment. Many people had hefty accumulations of wartime savings which were a big help in getting started on their own. This undoubling process is the reason that the average size of households has declined during the postwar period in spite of the prevailing high birth rates.

A lot of new spending units were created, amoeba-fashion, but families still had many needs and desires in common. Two things stand out above the others—automobiles and appliances. Many people had gone without these glamour goods during the depression for the lack of income, and during the war for lack of production. Again, families tended to spend as a unit. They devoted much of their incomes, savings, and borrowing power to get their automobiles and appliances and they didn't have too much left over for other items.

Consumers stocked up on durables during the latter 1940's and part of the 1950's. In the past several years, however, the original demand has become pretty much a replacement demand. There is now one car on the road for every two persons over 18 years. Of all wired homes, 98 per cent have refrigerators, 93 per cent have washing machines, and 90 per cent have television.

Replacement demand is much less dynamic. Purchases can be postponed almost indefinitely by judicious repairing. Furthermore, the mouth-watering excitement of durables has been reduced by ownership and familiarity. Today, consumers have larger portions of their ever-increasing income left over to spend as they wish. As we pointed out, no single-minded, new spending trend has taken the place of houses and durables. Instead, the flow of discretionary dollars seems to be darting like quicksilver in many different directions.

Other postwar developments also have helped shred the consumer market. . . . Increased education has changed tastes and diversified desires. Widespread travel has had a broadening effect, pulling many out of their buying ruts. The growth of leisure has given greater range to consumer demand.

MEET THE MARKETS. Not long ago teenagers were economically submerged in the family spending unit. They had only nickel-and-dime allowances to call their own. Now our 16 million high school students spend an estimated $6 billion a year. The youth market is highly specialized. Highschoolers emphasize sports and sport equipment, clothing, hobbies, movies, records, and, of course, food and more food. As one writer puts it, the current teenage greeting is often "take me to your larder."

The moppet market is growing in importance. Children up to ten years of age spend little themselves but they determine how hundreds of millions of dollars are spent. Television, the electronic baby sitter, has made this market. Small fry spend hours watching Yogi Bear, Captain Kangaroo, and other heroes plead "tell your mother to get a package of Super Crunchies." Food, candy, clothes, and toys are the mainstays of the moppet market.

It is hard to define the senior market. How do you tell when a person is old? One way we have heard is when a woman is more interested in the fit of her shoes than the fit of her sweater. Statisticians usually take a more prosaic approach and draw an arbitrary line at age 65. There are 16 million people over 65 and they spend approximately $30 million a year. They devote a relatively higher percentage of their income to housing, household operation, food, and medical care.

The Negro market is expanding rapidly as the economic status of the Negro improves. Negroes spend about $20 billion a year for goods and services. Their greatest need is for good housing for which, when available, they are willing to pay top dollar. An *Ebony* magazine survey indicates that Negroes spend a greater-than-average share of their income for clothing, automobiles, food, and cosmetics.

There are over 10 million single, adult consumers and their income is over $30 billion. They usually live alone in rented quarters, and they tend to gravitate to the cities. Clothes, entertainment, and eating out are big items in their budgets.

We also should mention the "country club" market, the 7 million families with incomes over $10,000 a year. These folks can afford many kinds of luxuries and are highly receptive to new products and ideas.

Then there is the newlywed market and the young parent market. People in the South have a distinctive spending pattern and so do Westerners, and those from other sections of the country. Suburban families have their own special needs. Spenders also differ by ethnic origin and, to some extent, by religion.

Finally, in many families husband and wife have turned into separate spending units. They both have more money to call their own. Dad may treat himself to a shotgun and mother may choose French perfume or a new hair style. It is said that one-third of all married women hold jobs and that they add nearly $30 billion to the family coffers. Working wives spend more than their stay-at-home sisters on clothes, personal care, restaurant meals, entertainment, and household conveniences.

SPLIT-LEVEL SELLING. The existence of many separate consumer markets makes merchandising more difficult. Many products do not appeal to all groups. Selection and variety are the "buywords."

Automobiles are a good example. Not long ago all available cars were much the same—big, chromy, and expensive. Now automobiles are highly specialized. There is a car for every purpose and purse. For the drive-to-the-station commuter there is the foreign "doodlebug"; for large families there are miniature buses; for the economy-minded there is a selection of compacts; for luxury-lovers and status-seekers there are several makes of "show boats"; for suburban hauling there is the station wagon; for city dwellers there is a variety of easy-to-handle and easy-to-park models.

Radio stations also cater to specific consumer markets. In Philadelphia, and no doubt elsewhere, there are many stations that offer nothing but specialized fare. One local station plays only "big band" music, principally the Tommy Dorsey, Glenn Miller, Benny Goodman recordings from the late 1930's and early 1940's. Several stations offer nothing but classical music, and still others fill the day with rock-and-roll for teenagers and culturally retarded adults.

The splintering of consumer demand has boomed the "doubles" market. Families who have everything now are getting two or more of it—TV sets, radios, telephones, cars, appliances, and even houses. Since the second item is usually to meet a specialized need—often for the children—it is likely to be of a different model or style than the first.

The growth of his-and-her products is further evidence of discretionary spenders within the family. Now mother and father may have their own separate types of deodorants, shampoos, electric razors, soda crackers. . . .

A legion of products is aimed directly at individual markets. Specifically for the older folks, there are health products, retirement cottages, golf clubs with more whip, watches with easy-to-read faces. Certain clothing styles, records, and books are slanted at teenagers. The moppet market is featuring space toys and cowboy guns this year. And so it goes in endless variety.

Firms will have to learn more about their customers—who they are and why they buy. This may mean increased expenditures for market research. Advertising also has become more complicated. With consumers behaving in unaverage ways, the effectiveness of mass media is weakened. There is, therefore, a trend to pinpointed advertising. Some companies are making extensive use of spot announcements on local radio stations. National magazines are accepting split-run ads that appear only in certain areas. The right market can be reached once it is known, but it may prove costly.

Producing goods for varied markets also may be more expensive. Specialized products must be researched and properly designed. And they often must be produced in smaller quantities than heretofore.

This matter of costs is the crux of the challenge businessmen face. As the magazine *Nation's Business* puts it, "We must shift from mass markets to custom markets for services as well as goods without losing the efficiency of mass production and mass merchandising methods."

The Bulldozer Effect

Powerful forces are working to bulldoze consumers into a vast, amorphous mass. These forces tend to submerge the individual and homogenize tastes and behavior. At first thought, it seems surprising that the consumer market has atomized at all while subject to such influences.

Television is one of the great levelers. Without getting into the controversy, we can report that many critics claim television is programmed for an egalitarian audience. If Madison Avenue feels that the mass likes westerns, private eyes, and situation comedies, that is what everybody gets, hour after hour.

Housing developments are another homogenizing force. Armies of similar box-houses stand in parade ranks on yesterday's farmland. Most development dwellers are about the same age, have the same income, and face the same problems—children, money, and crab grass, though not necessarily in that order. There is good reason for Suburbo-man to look, act, and think just like his neighbors.

Giant corporations and giant unions also can impinge on individuality. Workers, even managers, are small cogs subservient to the organization. In many cases they must conform to rigid codes of behavior—right down to the clothes they wear. How many bankers did you see last summer in sports shirts?

But consumers are resisting homogenization and refuse to be entirely squeezed into a mold. Without rebelling against established conventions they still are striving to express their individuality whenever they can. They have more income than ever before and they are willing to spend a good part of it to be different.

The splitup of the consumer market could be, in part, a reaction to these leveling forces. Original art and hand-made items, now enjoying a boom, also may be antidotes to the bulldozer effect. The desire to be different helps to explain why exotic imports are so popular and why gourmet foods are selling at a $250 million clip. "Anyone for chocolate-covered caterpillars?"

Interiors of development houses are as different as the outsides are similar. No two are decorated alike. Furniture styles have run riot in the past five years . . . and one reason is the housewife's desire to display her very own tastes.

Home from the office, "organization men" shed their grey flannel uniforms and become rugged individualists in their leisure activities. Do-it-yourself satisfies the urge for distinctive creation. Sports give the whole family ways to flex their identities. Good books and classical records provide ways to be different and they are also part of . . .

The "Egghead" Syndrome

Culture is a hot item. There are 42 major American symphony orchestras and hundreds of others associated with colleges and small communities. Phonograph record sales in 1959 were 316 per cent of their 1950 level and "serious" records have been doing at least as well as the total. About $1 billion is spent each year on books—one quarter of that on encyclopedias alone. About 55 million people visit museums each year. In 1959, twice as many New Yorkers visited the Metropolitan Museum of Art as saw the Yankees play baseball. The attendance at concerts has doubled since the war, and the opera and ballet never had it so good. Painting and sculpture have become hobbies for millions. Adult education courses are thriving all over the nation.

Not long ago the "egghead" was considered a fuzzy bumbler—a comic character who was always misplacing his glasses. Today he is something of a hero, more to be emulated than snickered at. We wonder how many people now become scholars, artists, musicians, and scientists in their "Walter Mitty" dreams rather than athletic heroes, sea captains, and soldiers of fortune.

A large part of the new interest in culture probably is genuine. People truly have become more intellectual. Many have a better appreciation of art, music, and the like than their parents did. Here, too, increased income, education, and leisure are important factors.

But not all the "culturephiles" are real. No doubt many adopt a veneer of culture for status purposes—a sort of aesthetic one-upmanship. Many like to think of themselves as intellectuals when by any realistic test, they are not. How many husbands yawn through a concert because attending is the thing to do? Self-imagery, however, can be just as important economically as real appreciation. If consumers picture themselves as cultured, "thinking men" or even if they want others to see them as such, they will spend willingly for the trappings of culture. . . .

No matter what their own appreciation and backgrounds are, many parents want their children to get genuine exposure to culture. This is part of the reason for the increasing popularity of higher education. Higher education, in turn, has a most important influence on consumer spending patterns. The total cost of a college diploma is estimated to average around $10,000. A budget-wrecking expenditure like this usually takes plenty of planning and scraping. How many families are struggling right now to send children to college and how many more are putting money aside in anticipation of the struggle? Certainly some of the shift away from "hard" goods is being forced by saving and spending for college. And since birth rates have remained at high levels through the postwar period, education will be a big item in consumer budgets for the foreseeable future.

The New Isolationism

We don't hear much about political isolationism these days. With distances shortened as the missile flies, it is hardly possible for America to snuggle down behind her oceans and ignore the rest of the world.

It is possible, however, for individuals to hide from the world. Some do it consciously and deliberately—hermits and beatniks—but they are a small minority. Experts say a far larger group of Americans is unconsciously trying to escape certain realities. This is the new isolationism—a psychological withdrawal from the world. Or perhaps we should say from several worlds. For the individual actually lives in at least four concentric worlds. The first is the international world, the planet, earth. The second is national, the United States. The third is the job world of farm, factory, or office. The fourth world encloses the home and family.

Proponents of the new isolationism theory claim the first three worlds have become more and more unsatisfactory to many Americans. Crisis follows crisis in the international world. As this is written, the morning paper headlines four critical areas—the Congo, Algeria, Cuba, and Laos. Others such as Berlin and Quemoy are smoldering ominously. And what happens when Red China gets The Bomb? Many people, however, are past the point of being afraid. The sharp pain of panic has worn into numbness. People worried for years and it did no good; conditions only became more depressing. Recently, the theory goes, many citizens have turned away from the international world and tried to shut it out of their minds. Readers bypass front pages and quickly turn to the sports and comics. At social gatherings, conversation usually runs to small talk rather than serious issues. There are exceptions, of course. The "New York Times set" and others are deeply concerned with international affairs but they are probably in the minority.

The national world is also beset with ugly problems—integration, inflation, juvenile crime, unemployment. Gold is a serious concern to some, and so is our alleged lack of national prestige and purpose. Although the tendency to withdraw is not nearly so great here as it is from the international world, many people are reluctant to think too much about national questions.

The job world also is often less than satisfactory. True, people are working shorter hours and earning higher pay than ever before but modern jobs can also be dull and stultifying. The old-time craftsman put in long hours but he enjoyed variety and creativity and took pride in his work. Today's mass production demands specialists. Workers make small contributions to giant projects and feel little sense of identity with their work. The emphasis is on the team and, as we mentioned earlier, the individual can often become frustrated.

The international, national, and job worlds are big worlds, driven by big forces. The individual, it is claimed, often feels powerless to do anything about them. As a result, many have tended to isolate themselves psychologically in the fourth world of home and family where things are more pleasant and manageable. . . .

The new isolationism may play a part in some basic sociological trends. Earlier marriages may be to some extent an attempt to get more out of life in uncertain, frustrating times. Alfred H. Williams, past president of this Bank, has suggested that the high postwar birth rate may be partially due to some "deep-seated drive to perpetuate our kind in the face of a daily diet of tension and trouble."

The sharper focus on home and family has had its effect on consumer spending. It probably is a factor in the rapid rise in home ownership. The new isolationism is a reason why homes are more important as status symbols and entertainment centers. It also helps to explain why people are spending heavily on furnishings, patios, and yards.

The desire to make the home and family world as pleasant as possible extends to the immediate community. Possibly as a result of this, there is a revival of interest in local affairs. Husbands and wives are said to be more willing to participate in community clubs, P.T.A.'s, church work, and local governments. Taking part in community groups carries quite a bit of status and prestige in some neighborhoods.

The new isolationism came to flower in the late 1950's. In the past several months, some of our associates here at the bank claim to have sensed a greater public interest in national problems, a greater willingness to face up to the international ugliness, especially on the part of our youth. If true, this could be the start of a major trend or it could be only a flurry associated with the recent elections and the change of Administrations. At any rate, it is not likely that the consumer's concern with home and family matters will diminish significantly in the near future.

The new isolationism is part cause, part effect of the last factor we shall discuss.

Linus' Blanket

Linus is a little boy in the comic strip "Peanuts." Like many small children, he is firmly attached to his blanket. For some reason, the feel of it against his check gives him a sense of cozy security.

Adults outgrow their blankets but not their need for security. It is economic security that concerns us here. The quest for economic security seems particularly strong these days. People are demanding and, to a large extent, getting freedom from poverty. They want assurance of a steady income both during their working years and after retirement.

This is one of the most natural desires, yet it is criticized by some. They say the price of economic security runs high, that sometimes one must settle for less chance of gain to minimize the chance of loss. The premium on security, it is claimed, can lessen initiative, ambition, and the desire to compete. Security also can reduce the mobility of the labor force as people become chained to jobs by seniority and pension rights. A less vigorous, less mobile work force can reduce our economy's ability to grow and, in the end, may undermine the very security people seek. It is a gloomy thought but it is only a thought. The quest for security has other, more definite effects on the economy.

Security-conscious consumers now squirrel away more money for rainy days and retirement and, as a result, spend less for immediate consumption than they otherwise might. Personal savings are at record levels and retirement funds of all types amount to about 100 billion dollars. Most consumer savings are invested and insofar as they become available to businesses, they serve to finance economic growth without inflation.

Relatively few consumers invest their savings directly. Rather they put their money in a financial intermediary, such as a commercial bank, mutual savings bank, savings and loan association, or insurance company which does the investing for them. It's the desire for safety and security again. Savers choose a smaller, surer income over the chance for a greater but riskier return.

Financial intermediaries are concerned with safety, too; they have to be for they are dealing with other people's money. With huge sums to invest, they tend to favor large blocks of "blue chip" securities. This policy, it has been said, diverts funds away from venturesome small and new businesses where the investment risk may be greater.

In their quest for economic security, many individuals turn to unions. Many others, however, turn to governments. Governments, particularly the Federal Government, are in the economic security business in a big way. Pensions, social security, unemployment compensation, veterans' benefits, agricultural programs all provide economic security for large groups.

Such benefits never can be manufactured out of thin air. Their cost is high and, no matter how you look at it, the public in general must pay. It could be through contributions or direct taxes, or through the cruel, hidden tax of inflation which just as surely and probably more inequitably takes away consumer spending power. Thus the desire for security has shifted funds to governments that might otherwise be spent by consumers. Whether one thinks this is good or bad depends on his own persuasions and political beliefs. Our point is that it has altered consumer spending patterns.

Conclusion

We have mentioned only a few of the factors we feel are influencing consumers. There are many more—some run at cross purposes and all are complex and complicated. The net result could well be that consumer spending patterns will grow more diverse and over-all demand will continue its restless churning. Not that consumers are becoming more flighty or faddish but they are enjoying the freedom of intelligent choice that goes with affluence, education, and a degree of satiation with goods.

As consumer preferences shift, they often leave unemployment and excess capacity in their wake. As a result, pockets of chronic unemployment may continue to plague the economy. The solution usually offered to this problem is to increase the mobility of productive resources. Let capital and labor move between companies or between industries to follow consumer demand. But this is often easier said than done. We have indicated how the desire for security tends to inhibit the mobility of labor and capital.

Consumers are playing an increasingly active role in determining the course of the economy. Once consumer spending was linked closely to production—how much consumers spent largely depended on how much they earned by producing goods. Consumers were relatively passive, and fluctuations in production caused the ups and downs in the economy. Today, however, the tie between spending and production has been loosened considerably by increased savings, the greater availability of credit, the growing importance of services, and by governmental income-generating programs. Thus, consumer market decisions —to buy or not to buy—are, more and more, a causative factor in the business cycle.

With this additional power in their hands it becomes more important to understand the royal family of consumers and to try to figure out what they are going to do. But, as we have attempted to show, consumers are complex and psychoanalyzing them is more difficult.

As we see it, the royal family will be a tremendous sustaining force in the economy during the rest of the year. But their shifting spending patterns do not seem to contain the ingredients for explosive growth. In fact, the royal family may decree little more than a gently rising economy for several years to come.

Spending money is easy, but spending it well is often very difficult. Some of our greatest difficulties arise in buying the complicated equipment or the new products which are so important in a rising standard of living. Scientific product-testing can help us, however; but even this is not so easy as one might suppose.

28 · Product Testing

CONSUMER BULLETIN

. . . Scientific research is a long and slow process. It is impossible to predict the course of a particular drug and its effect on a human being until *thousands of cases of its use* have been studied in carefully controlled experiments, and criticized, discussed, and interpreted over a considerable period of time. The person who wishes to take no chances with his health and pocketbook will take a conservative, show-me attitude toward

---

CONSUMER BULLETIN, from "Off the Editor's Chest," *Consumers' Research Bulletin* now *Consumer Bulletin* (February 1950), pp. 18-20. Reprinted by permission of Consumer Bulletin, Washington, N.J.

these advertised marvels, however persuasive the advertising may be. It is well to remember, too, that the true scientist is a modest and careful fellow who is not given to boasting about the results of his researches. Any claims that he sanctions will be restrained and conservative because his work has taught him that surface appearances are deceiving and that the long-time effects of a treatment or drug may be immeasurably more important than the result that follows immediately.

The belief that the scientist and engineer can always be relied upon to provide a ready answer to any problem that may appear to be in his field is one that Consumers' Research frequently encounters. As we have often pointed out, conducting a comprehensive test of an appliance or device is a time-consuming job that will often involve the recording, checking, and evaluating of literally thousands of measurements capable of being made correctly only by specially qualified engineers and scientists experienced in the use of certain specialized tools and instruments. In the test of washing machines alone, for example, a test run to determine effectiveness of the machine in removing artificial dirt from fabric test samples on five machines required 30 days, and that aspect constituted only a part of the complete study of the five washers. It takes about six months to complete laboratory tests and prepare a highly condensed report of the work done in testing mechanical refrigerators, vacuum cleaners, and electric and gas stoves.

CR has purchased a number of . . . [new] automobiles for test and will buy others as they become available. The actual task of studying their advantages and weaknesses and comparing their several performances is under way, but to provide CR subscribers with a careful appraisal will require several months of hard, detailed, painstaking observations and tests, followed by careful checking by several other qualified consulting experts before the reports can be prepared for presentation in CR's *Bulletin*. . . . There is no competent technical advice that *can* be provided speedily and at small or negligible cost, as some suppose. In reporting on automobiles, it is important, for example, to check with servicemen on the type of repairs or adjustments that are most frequently needed on the various new models. In a recent year the roof supports (door posts) of a well-known make of car had to be reinforced by welding on a considerable number of new cars within a month or two of their manufacture. No one could have predicted or foreseen that unusual type of weakness or failure on the basis of preliminary test runs, and only the test of time and a period of hard use on the road brought to light the structural weakness of the body design. The manufacturer's engineers with their superior facilities for study of their product did not, of course, know about the defect; neither did their test runs and road-abuse program reveal the fault soon enough to prevent a serious loss to the manufacturer and many of his customers.

Each time some new product is announced with a fanfare or advertising, we are flooded with inquiries about its performance and the validity of its advertising claims. It is pleasant to be credited with omniscience, but it will save our readers considerable effort if they will remember that even with an income of many millions of dollars a year, we should not be able to include in our test program all, or the greater part of the abundant variety of products that are available to the American consumer, as fast as the consumers would like to know about them. We do endeavor to test the brands and models that are in national distribution and that are most sought after by prospective purchasers of items, such as washers, refrigerators, and vacuum cleaners, that require a large initial outlay where performance, safety, and economy in use are especially important factors that can be measured by instrumental equipment.

In the case of a new invention such as television, it requires time to set up criteria for evaluating performance and to work out the testing procedure and select and procure the costly instrumentation needed.

It may be news to the nontechnically trained consumer, but it is not easy to arrive at a sure, dependable decision on just what constitutes a good product and what a poor product in an entirely new field. And the consumer who thinks about the problem will realize that opinions and judgments which are not reasonably trustworthy will not be of service to him, but may do more harm than good, besides doing an injustice to honest and competent manufacturers, in many instances.

Science has been defined as knowledge obtained by controlled quantitative investigation. In applying the method of scientific investigation to evaluation of products for consumers, we must proceed carefully, to make certain that all the factors most important to consumers (including convenience, adaptability, economy in use) have been taken into consideration, and second that the products have been subjected to testing procedures that are contrived properly to bring out important differences between the various makes or brands. It would be fine if it were possible to subject every article to a life test of sufficient duration to bring out good features or weaknesses such as would come to light in a long period of use in the home. Practically speaking, life tests cannot be made on most items since if they are carried on for a sufficiently long period, the findings will become available so late that the model is no longer current and the results would thus have only what is known as "academic" interest. On many items there is no possible way accelerated tests can be performed so that results of, let us say, five years' use of a toaster or electric range and its heating elements, switches, and thermostats can be telescoped into a month or two of operation in the laboratory.

It is important to remember that the fact of an advertiser's being able to prepare appealing copy or convincing demonstrations quickly does not mean that the reverse process of taking the claims apart and testing their truth can be carried out with equal speed or facility. The laboratory does not work with words but with expensive and exacting tools and instruments; *its* findings aim to secure dependable facts, where the advertiser's claims are designed to be persuasive and to "sell the goods." If we are unable to provide you with an immediate answer to your problem on a postcard, please remember that our trade is not the verbal magic of the advertiser and salesman but the difficult and time-consuming discipline of the professional expert and engineer. The end-result may seem simple and clear, but the process by which it is arrived at calls for time-consuming observations and measurements, exacting and often intricate correlations, and careful, responsible interpretation.

VI · DISTRIBUTION OF INCOME

Property law, a topic rarely included in the study of economics, has much to do with the distribution of income. In the western world most property is privately owned, though the exceptions are important. Here a distinguished professor of economics of an earlier era discusses theories which underlie the institution of private property.

29 · *Theories of Private Property*

E. R. A. SELIGMANN

The earliest theory of private property as found in some of the Roman writers is *the occupation theory*. The doctrine that property belongs of right to him who first seizes it is, however, one that can apply, if at all, only to the earliest stages of development. Where no one has any interest in the property, no one will object to the assertion of a claim by a newcomer. When property is without any discoverable owner, we still today assign it to the lucky finder. The occupation theory may explain how the present legal title to certain forms of property originated; it cannot serve as a justification of private property, except in the rare case of previously unoccupied or unutilized wealth. The mere fact that a person has seized a thing is no reason why he should retain it.

The next doctrine was *the natural rights theory*. Private property, so we were told by the philosophers of antiquity and the publicist of the later middle ages, is a natural right, a part of the law of nature. It will at once be asked, however, what is denoted by nature? The great philosophers of antiquity upheld private property in slaves as a natural right. Much of what we today consider natural, our descendants will deem unnatural. Our conception of nature in this sense is essentially ephemeral and mutable.

Driven from this position, the natural rights school took refuge in *the labor theory*, and maintained that the real title to private property is derived from the toil and trouble experienced in creating it. Surely, it will be said, a thing belongs of right to him who produces it. But at once comes the reply: no one has created the land. As a consequence, we find thinkers of all ages, from Phaleas of antiquity to the disciples of Henry George today, who contend that private property in land is unjust, while

---

E. R. A. SELIGMANN, *Principles of Economics* (New York: Longmans, Green & Co., Inc., 1905), pp. 131–134. Used by permission.

maintaining that private property in everything else is defensible. These critics, however, overlook the fact that the difference between land and so-called labor products is in this respect, at all events, one only of degree, because nothing is the result of individual labor alone. The carpenter, it is said, rightfully owns the table which he has made. But to what extent has he made it? The tree which affords him the raw material was not created by him; the axe with which the tree is felled is the accumulated result of centuries of invention expended by his ancestors; the stream along which the log is floated is not of his making. To pass over all the other intermediate processes, how long would he be secure in the possession of the tools he has used or of the product he has finished, were it not for the protection afforded to him by the law? And finally, of what use would the tables be unless there were a demand for them on the part of the community? The value of the table is as little the result of individual labor as is the value of the land. Society holds a mortgage over everything that is produced or exchanged.

Since, therefore, neither occupation, natural law nor labor gives an indefeasible title to private property, some philosophers were led to frame the so-called *legal theory* of private ownership which is in essence that whatever is recognized as such by the law is rightfully private property. Obviously, however, this is not an economic doctrine. Good law may be bad economics. The law generally follows at a respectful distance behind the economic conditions, and adjusts itself gradually to them. The legal theory tells us *what* property is, not *why* it is, nor what it should be.

Thus we are finally driven to *the social utility theory*. This is really implied in the preceding theories and supplies the link that binds them all together. In ancient as in modern communities, the individual is helpless as against society, however much under modern democracy society may see fit to extend the bounds of individual freedom. If we allow the individual to seize upon unoccupied wealth, if we recognize the existence of certain rights in what are deemed to be the products of labor, if we throw the mantle of the law around the elements of private property—in every case society is speaking in no uncertain voice and permits these things because it is dimly conscious of the fact that they redound to the social welfare. Private property is an unmistakable index of social progress . . . it has grown under continual subjection to the social sanction. It is a natural right only in the broad sense that all social growth is natural.

"Fair," "just," "equitable," and other such terms appear frequently in discussion of economic issues. Yet how often do we really know what we mean when we use one of these words? A leading economist shows some of the problems of using the concept "economic justice" in analysis of income distribution.

30 · *Justice in the Distribution of Income*

KENNETH E. BOULDING

JUSTICE AS POLITICAL DISCONTENT. The concept of justice has always been an elusive one, and has concerned man from the earliest times. For all its elusiveness it has been of enormous importance in the dynamics of human life and society, at least in a negative sense, for it is the sense of injustice that more than anything else drives men to political action of all kinds.

The sense of injustice is the feeling that something is wrong not merely with our personal condition but with the world at large. It is the sense of something needing amendment in the *world at large* that makes the feeling of injustice so important for *political* action. A merely personal discontent leads to merely personal policies and activities, within the existing framework of laws, customs, and institutions. If we don't like our job we look for another, if we don't like our house we look for another, if we don't like the town where we live we move to another. Political discontent, however, leads towards organization to change the framework of the society within which we move, by voting in a new party, by lobbying for new laws, or by fomenting a new revolution.

A "DISCONTENT" AS A DIVERGENCE OF "REAL" FROM "IDEAL." If, then, we are to understand the dynamics of the movement towards economic justice, we must look for the economic sources of political discontents. We must ask ourselves what aspects of the over-all economic system are perceived as "wrong." In order to answer this question we must ask what would be perceived as "right" —that is, what are the ideals by which existing situations are judged? A "discontent" is a perceived *difference* between an imagined ideal state of affairs and a perceived reality. The source of discontent, therefore, is found in the nature of the image of the ideal on the one hand, and of the perception of the real on the other.

"COMMUTATIVE" JUSTICE AS IDEAL DISTRIBUTION. Stated in this way, economic justice seems to include all the goals and ideals of economic life. There is, however, a more restricted use of the term in the sense of "justice in distribution"—sometimes called "commutative justice." . . .

KENNETH E. BOULDING, *Principles of Economic Policy* (Englewood Cliffs, N. J.: Prentice-Hall, Inc., 1958), pp. 83–109. Used by permission.

The particular discontent that gives rise to political activity directed towards redistribution also depends, of course, on a comparison of a perceived "real" state of affairs with some image of the ideal. In this case, however, the image of the ideal is hard to establish clearly and firmly. There seem to be several conflicting ideals among which some compromise must be made. This makes the problem of ideal distribution much more difficult than, say, the problem of progress or of stability. . . .

CONFLICTING IDEALS OF DISTRIBUTION: "MERIT" VS. "NEED." Let us consider, for instance, two conflicting, and yet plausible ideals of distribution. One, which goes back to an ancient notion of justice as a situation in which everybody gets what he deserves, may be called the *merit standard*. The other, which goes back to another ancient notion of justice as the situation in which everybody gets what he needs, may be called the *need standard*.

THE "CONTRIBUTIVE STANDARD" SUBSTITUTES FOR THE "MERIT STANDARD." The singleminded pursuit of either of these standards alone leads us into impossible contradictions. In both cases we find ourselves at the outset faced with the problem of an objective *measure*—of desert in the one case and of need in the other. This is a problem of agreement as to what constitutes information: how can we know, for instance, in a way that will be agreeable to all, what each deserves? "Use every man after his desert and who should 'scape whipping." Most of us probably have a somewhat inflated notion of our own merits, and the device of simply asking everyone what he thought he deserved would probably not result in a solution acceptable to all. Consequently the ideal of the merit standard inevitably gets pushed towards a somewhat different ideal, that of the *contributive standard* —to each according to his contribution. . . .

REWARD AS THE MEASURE OF CONTRIBUTION. Even the contributive standard presents the gravest difficulties of measurement. The most objective measure would seem to be obtained through the impersonal dictates of a free market. In such a market an equilibrium set of prices tends to be established for factors of production. The contribution to the total product made by any factor can then be estimated by multiplying the price of its services by the quantity rendered. Thus, if the market price of the services of my person is $2 per hour, and if I work 2,500 hours a year, the contribution I make to the total product and the value of the reward I receive are both equal to $5,000. Stated in this crude way it is clear that contribution has simply been measured by actual reward, and we have really said little more than "everybody gets what he gets."

PHYSICAL AND VALUE PRODUCTS. Attempts have been made to avoid the apparent tautology involved in measuring contribution by reward by supposing that contribution is measured by the marginal product, and that reward is only equal to marginal product under some circumstances, so that the possibility emerges that reward may not be according to contribution. The problems that emerge here are of a rather technical nature. The difficulty, however, can be grasped more easily than the solution. In a simple case of a workman producing with his own hands and tools a single product the concept of "contribution" is fairly clear: the cobbler has contributed the shoes on his shelves, the farmer the wheat in his barn. The "take" of the cobbler, however, is not shoes, nor that of the farmer wheat, except in small part, and if the shoes and the wheat and the million other products of economic activity are to be added up into a single measure of output or income, they must be priced or valued in terms of some common unit, say the dollar. Thus the value of any physical product depends on the whole price system, and for each set of prices there is a corresponding set of incomes of different contributors. We feel a little uneasy, however, in supposing that there is always *one* price system that is "right" from all points of view. But if there is not a single, unequivocal price system at which the various contributions and rewards are valued, physical product does not unambiguously determine either contribution or reward. Even if the physical productivity of the shoemaker does not change, a change in the price of shoes will change both his contribution and his reward.

THE MEASUREMENT OF NEED. The problem of the measurement of "need" is also a great obstacle to the establishment of a "need standard" as an ideal of distribution. Just as it is impossible to judge the deserts of another in a way that will command general acceptance, so it is impossible to judge his need. On these grounds alone the need standard as a single ideal breaks down. Nevertheless, there are situations in which distribution according to rough estimates of needs is possible. Such a situation is found generally within the confines of the family, where the total family income is spent according to some rough criterion of the needs of the members. In emergency situations, as among a group of castaways, or in time of war or famine in larger societies, rationing is used as an attempt to apportion according to need.

RATIONING. Nothing illustrates the difficulties of the need standard as clearly as the problems encountered in rationing. The simplest method of apportionment is, of course, to give everyone an equal share. This has been done—in wartime, for instance—in the case of sugar and coffee. Equal distribution, however, is clearly inequitable, for needs are not equal. Some like sugar, some do not; some bake cakes, some do not; some are diabetic, some are not. Hence, rationing means no hardship for some, and considerable hardship for others. The equal rationing of coffee is even more inequitable—a household where only one member drinks coffee feels no pinch, whereas a household of heavy coffee drinkers is sharply restricted. . . .

Even for the simplest needs, therefore, equal rationing is hopelessly unjust. Hence, there must be graduated rationing; special food rations for heavy workers, special gasoline rations for heavy drivers, and so on. The attempt to ration for individual needs, however, results in a piling of board on board and application on application until red tape engulfs everybody. Even in the case of such a basic "need" as food, rationing cannot be applied as a universal principle. . . .

. . . . .

DIFFICULTY OF ESTIMATING "NEEDS." If the criterion of need is so difficult to apply even in the case of basic necessities, how much more difficult would it be to apply it to the luxuries and conveniences of life! The thought of distributing phonograph records, books, travel, and the like according to individual need by some rationing authority is one before which the stoutest communist might quail. It may be objected that we can still permit goods to be allocated through the price system, so that there is a certain amount of consumers' choice, and yet ration *incomes* according to need. But what standards could we follow in such a case? Should we give all university graduates double the income of high school graduates, because presumably a college education breeds expensive tastes? There is simply no administrative solution to the problem of allocation according to need, once we get away from the barest necessities, and even there the administrative problem is almost insuperably difficult and can only be solved by rule-of-thumb methods.

THE "MERIT STANDARD" DENIES COMMUNITY. Even if the measurement problems could be solved, there are more fundamental reasons why neither the merit standard nor the need standard is satisfactory as a single criterion of ideal distribution. The merit standard, at least in the form of a contributive standard, breaks down because we are forced to recognize that society has certain obligations towards nonproducers, particularly towards children, old people, the sick, the insane, and the involuntarily unemployed. We must break down the criterion of "reward according to contribution" in some cases; hence, it loses its validity as a general formula. The reason for this seems to be that there is a certain sense of kinship that binds us all together and makes us feel in a measure responsible for the welfare of all. We must support the unproductive elements of society because in some sense they "belong" to us, just as a limb belongs to us. . . .

THE "NEED STANDARD" DENIES "SCARCITY." Even if there were no difficulties in the measurement of needs, the need standard would still face certain fundamental difficulties of application. The main difficulty here is that there is no particular reason to suppose that distribution according to needs would just exhaust the product: the sum of needs may be either less than or greater than the total product. We are less likely to encounter this difficulty in the case of the contributive standard. If everybody gets what he puts into the pot there is a certain presumption that this rule of distribution will just exhaust what is in the pot to be distributed. If everyone gets what he "needs," however, either there may be something left over in the pot, or the pot may prove to be not quite large enough to supply all the needs of those who are to be served from its contents.

THE "PURE COMMUNIST" CRITERION. The difficulties in the application of the need standard are brought out clearly when we examine the possible application of what might be called the "pure communist" criterion—"From each according to his abilities, to each according to his needs." There is much that is appealing about this standard, and a good deal of the ethical appeal of communism rests on it. Nevertheless, the attempt to apply it is tragically self-defeating, simply because abilities and needs do not usually correspond. The things we most want to do, and are best able to do—those activities miscalled "leisure"—do not in general produce a sufficient quantity of the commodities that we need. This is the fact that makes necessary the whole system of economic values and institutions. Suppose, for instance, that we had a society in which everybody liked fishing and had great ability in the art, but in which nobody liked fish, and in which, to make the case even stronger, fish did not agree with the people so that they had to live mainly on bread. It would require a remarkable act of chemical magic to transform the fish that the abilities produced into the bread that the needs demanded! Such a society would be forced to do something to make fishing unattractive relative to breadmaking. The price of fish and the wages of fishers would have to be low, and the price of bread and the wages of breadmakers high, even though the needs of the two groups might be identical. The logic of valuation would force the authorities to abandon any attempt to distribute solely according to need; they would have to distribute in order to encourage some lines of production and discourage others. This is what has happened in Communist Russia, where the desire for increased production continually thwarts the desire for equalitarian distribution.

THE "EQUALITY STANDARD": EQUALIZATION OF MARGINAL UTILITY. A special, and more sophisticated, case of the need standard is the "equality standard"— the claim that the ideal mode of distribution is to have all incomes equal. The theoretical foundations of this standard are worth examination, not only because of its historical importance as an element in political dynamics and as a mover of both men and nations, but also because some of the basic problems involved in a critique of standards emerge clearly.

Let us suppose first that it is possible to assign to any individual a number that measures his state of well-being or welfare. This is his "total utility." Suppose further that for each level of a person's income we can assign such a utility number. We then define the marginal utility of income as the change in total utility that results from a unit change in income. Now suppose that it is possible to add the total utilities of different individuals to get a total social utility for the whole society. On these assumptions we could say that total social utility was at a maximum when the marginal utility of income of all individuals was equal. Suppose, for instance, that for individual A the marginal utility of income was 5 "utils per dollar" and that for individual B it was 3 utils per dollar. Then if a dollar were taken from B and given to A, B would lose 3 utils and A would gain 5 utils, there being a total social gain of 2 utils. If now we suppose a law of diminishing marginal utility of income with increase of income, as we go on transferring income from B to A, A's marginal utility of income falls as he gets richer and B's marginal utility of income rises as he gets poorer until finally both are equal, say at 4 utils per dollar. At this point it no longer increases social utility to transfer income from one to the other, for the gain of one would be just equal to the loss of the other.

Equality of marginal utility does *not* imply equal incomes. It should be observed that the equality for all individuals of their marginal utility of income does not in itself imply that social utility is at a maximum when all incomes are equal. Thus in Fig. 1 we draw the marginal utility of income curves for two individuals. Individual I cares very little for riches, and his marginal utility of income diminishes rapidly as his income increases. Individual II enjoys riches a great deal: his marginal utility of income declines very slowly. If now both have the same marginal utility of income, O_1A_1 ($= O_2A_2$), individual I will have a much smaller income (A_1B_1) than individual II (A_2B_2).

An even more striking conclusion follows from this figure. If income in-

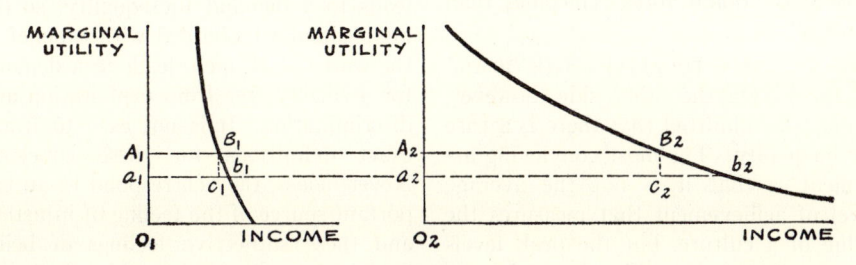

FIGURE 1

creases, the marginal utility of income will fall, say to O_1a_1. The increase in the income of the second individual (c_2b_2) then should be greater than the increase in the income of the first (c_1b_1). Not quite "to him that hath shall be given," but "to him that enjoyeth most what he hath, to him should be given more." In a society where individuals are unlike in regard to the slopes of their marginal utility curves, assuming that the marginal utilities of different individuals are roughly the same for subsistence levels of income, then an increase in the total income of the society should result in more unequal distribution as the increase in income should go mainly to those who will enjoy it most.

INCOMES SHOULD BE EQUAL ONLY IF ALL MEN ARE ALIKE. The conclusion that incomes should be equal, therefore, follows from the principle of equality of marginal utility of income only if the further assumption is made that all men are alike, at least in regard to their utility of income curves. . . . [The] assumption that men are all very much alike is the foundation of democratic institutions ("We hold these truths to be self-evident . . .") and we certainly do not attempt in politics to give the voter a number of votes in proportion to his intelligence and his ability to use them. The one-man-one-vote principle is forced upon us by the recognition of the practical impossibility of any other. So, the equalitarians argue, there is no good reason why one man should have more "dollar votes" (income) than another.

THE CASE FOR INEQUALITY—THE "PEAK" AS IDEAL. On the other side, however, it must be admitted that there is a case for inequality. The most convincing argument is that it is not the average level of achievement that measures the value of a culture, but the peak levels that it reaches. On this standard a society of mud huts and a great cathedral is better than a society of equal resources having stone huts and no cathedral. One perfect lyric is worth a million tons of trashy Sunday Supplements. It is by the quality of its saints and heroes, not its common men, and by its masterpieces and not by its domestic utensils, that a culture should be judged. This point of view is not to be dismissed lightly, even though it is capable of absurdity and perversion, and though it does not fit comfortably into the ideals and prejudices of a predominantly democratic society. . . .

THE OPTIMUM DEGREE OF INEQUALITY. . . . the notion that there is some "ideal" degree of inequality is a useful one. As we move away from this towards greater equality we lose "peakedness," interest, color, excitement, drama: the perfectly equal is the perfectly dull. As we move away from this imaginary ideal in the other direction, towards greater inequality, we lose democracy, brotherhood, the concern and responsibility of all for all which is what makes organization tolerable. Somewhere in the middle, at the blessed Aristotelian mean, is an optimum point from which any movement one way or the other costs us more than we gain. It is easy, of course, to postulate the existence of such a point—it is quite another matter to find it, or to agree on where it is. . . .

. . . . .

EXPLOITATION AND DISCRIMINATION. Just as the need-standard, coupled with a belief in the basic similarity of all men, leads to a demand for equality, so the merit-standard, coupled with a belief in the worth of all men, leads to a demand for a society free from exploitation and discrimination. It is not easy to frame exact definitions for these concepts. Nevertheless, they correspond to an important source of the feeling of injustice, and these subjective feelings of being exploited or discriminated against frequently are derived from the observation of objective realities.

In the broadest sense, exploitation may be said to occur whenever one receives less than his contribution and another receives more. As we have seen, however, the contributive standard cannot be applied rigidly because of the universally acknowledged necessity of supporting many noncontributors—children, old people, the sick, and so on. The definition of exploitation must therefore be narrowed, and yet at the same time it becomes more difficult to apply: we are thrown back in a sense on the vagueness of the merit-standard itself, and we have to say that there is exploitation when some get less than they "deserve" and some get more. Still another implication of the concept of exploitation is that of the relationship between the exploiter and the exploited —the exploiter "exploits" the exploited by taking away from them what they have produced. We see that the concept of exploitation runs into all the difficulties that we have previously observed in the contributive standard. Nevertheless, we cannot cast the concept aside. We can neither deny the possibility—indeed, the actuality—of exploitation, nor claim any very good way of recognizing it when we see it!

EXPLOITATION AND MONOPOLY. The economist has attempted to solve this problem by relating exploitation to the presence of monopoly, and this is at least a guide line. The monopolist gets more than he "deserves" because, if it were not for monopoly, what he supplies would be supplied cheaper. Because the monopolist is in a position to restrict output below what it would be if there were not a monopoly he can thereby obtain a higher price for what he sells. Monopoly, that is, represents an obstacle to the free flow of resources among occupations. On the monopolist's side of the obstacle there are fewer resources and therefore higher rewards than there would be if the obstacle were not present.

It is easy to see that a monopolist is an exploiter: it is more difficult to identify those whom he exploits. The question of the distribution of the losses of monopoly among those who are adversely affected by it is by no means easy to answer. On the one hand there is something lost by the purchasers of the monopolist's product, who have to pay a higher price than they otherwise would. Then there is something lost by those who would *like* to be making the monopolist's product at prices between the monopoly price and the competitive price, but who are excluded from this occupation because of the obstacle that is the source of monopoly power. Finally, we may have a situation known in economics as "monopsony," where resources receive a return less than they should, not because they are prevented from getting into some other occupation, but because there are obstacles to their leaving the occupation that they are now in.

[The author next discusses the difference between "natural" and "artificial" monopoly and then the role of education in weakening monopoly based on possession of knowledge. *Ed.*]

. . . . .

EXPLOITATION BY ARTIFICIAL IMMOBILITY. When the obstacle to movement consists of statutory regulations or prohibitions sanctioned by law or even by custom, the presence of exploitation may almost be taken for granted. . . . A craft union that sets up artificial barriers to entry and that can prevent non-union members from working at the trade "exploits" both those who would like to enter the craft but are prevented by the restrictions, and those who purchase the ultimate product of the craft. An employer who can "tie" his labor force to him, whether by reason of geographical isolation as in some isolated manufacturing or mining town, or even by quasi-benevolent schemes such as pension plans, may be in a position to exploit his workers "monopsonistically"—they may be paid less than the prevailing wage because they cannot leave the occupation.

DISCRIMINATION. An important aspect of the problem of exploitation is *discrimination*. This is the term given to the situation where certain *groups* or classes of individuals receive less than they "should" because of certain obstacles to movement into or out of occupations that they face as a group. Wherever, that is to say, an individual is exploited because of his membership in a group, we have discrimination.

There are many kinds of groups that suffer discrimination. Racial discrimination results in Negroes, Mexicans, Chinese, and certain immigrant groups receiving lower wages for a given job than native white Americans. Sex discrimination results in women receiving lower wages for a given job than men. Age discrimination results in the exploitation of children and old people. Caste discrimination results in lower wages for people with "inferior" language and manners.

It is a general economic principle that discrimination exists only in the presence of monopoly. If two different prices exist for the same commodity in a competitive market, all the buyers will rush to buy from the venders selling at the lower price, so that their price will rise, while the lack of buyers forces the high-price sellers to lower *their* prices, until everyone is selling at the same price. If the labor market were perfectly competitive, with large numbers of both workers and employers, and open knowledge of the wages and abilities offered, there could not be different wages for the same work, for employers would all rush to employ the low-wage workers, thus bidding up their wage, and would not employ the high-wage workers until their wage had come down to the general level. If the labor market were perfectly competitive, for instance, it would be impossible to maintain a higher wage rate for whites than for Negroes of equal ability in identical jobs, for in that case employers would rush to employ Negroes, and any employer who employed whites only would be forced out of business.

MONOPOLY MAY BE ON THE SIDE OF EMPLOYER OR WORKERS. Discrimination can exist only where there are elements of monopoly, either on the side of the employer, or on the side of organized labor. If, for instance, we have a situation in which a single employer is faced by two groups of employees, one of which is prepared to work for a lower wage than the other, he may be able to make greater profits by paying the less-favored group a lower wage, provided that he is in something of a position of monopoly. Or, on the other side, an organized labor group may be able to get higher wages for its members by the process of shutting out certain groups, classes, or races from its ranks. This again is really an exercise of monopoly power, and the story of trade unions is full of examples of it. The discrimination of a few unions against Negroes and against women, is a good example. If a union can keep Negroes or women out of a particular employment, a higher wage can thereby usually be ensured for the members. This is simply an example of the general method of exercising monopoly power—through the restriction of supply of the monopolized commodity by the ability to prevent "outside" resources from entering the occupation.

"UNEARNED" INCOME. One further aspect of the problem of exploitation . . . is the problem of "unearned" rewards. The attitude towards "unearned income" varies greatly. At one extreme we have the Marxist view that *all* income that is not derived from labor is unearned; this view would condemn all profit, interest, and rent as the result of the exploitation of the working class. At the other extreme we have the view that all property income is justified, or even the very extreme mercantilist view, which is hard to find expressed nowadays, that any income to labor above minimum subsistence is "unearned," labor merely being a passive resource which would produce nothing unless organized by the property owners.

ECONOMIC RENT. The view held by economists will fall somewhere between these two extremes. Economists have held almost without exception from the time of Adam Smith that there are some incomes that are "unearned" in the sense that they are greater than what is necessary to call forth the activity or contribution of the income receiver. This is what is known in economics as "economic rent." Ricardo, and for that matter Adam Smith, tended to identify economic rent with income from land, and this tradition found later expression in the proposals of Henry George for the taxation of rent and of any rise in land values. The modern view is that the situation is more complicated than either Ricardo or Henry George thought, and that though economic rent unquestionably exists in almost any society, it runs through all forms of income and is by no means easy to identify.

Thus, suppose we have a situation in which in equilibrium there are 1,000 people employed in a particular occupation. The "equilibrium" means that the wage of these people is just enough to persuade exactly 1,000 people to engage in this particular occupation. If we wanted 1,100 people, we might have to offer a somewhat higher wage; if we wanted only 900 people we might get them for a somewhat lower wage. The people who are only just attracted to the occupation at the going wage are said to be "marginal" to that occupation. If, however, we have to pay a wage high enough to attract the marginal men, this implies that unless *all* the people who work at this occupation are marginal, in the sense that they would leave the occupation if the wage were lowered even slightly, there will be some people who would actually be willing to work in this occupation for *less* than the equilibrium wage. The difference between the least wage for which they would be willing to work and the actual (equilibrium) wage is economic rent. This assumes, of course, that the same wage is paid to all workers.

DISCRIMINATION TO ELIMINATE ECONOMIC RENT. The only way to eliminate economic rent is to discriminate—to pay each worker the least he would be willing to work for. This is impossible in a competitive market, and is probably sociologically impossible even under monopoly, because of the effect such a practice would have on the morale of the organization. It is only in institutions such as universities where the conventions of polite society prevent the discussion of sordid matters like income, that employers are able to discriminate effectively among individuals in the extraction of economic rent. Where the individual's income is a dirty little secret between his employer and himself, discrimination may be practiced without danger to morale. A man who has to be paid well to keep him from seeking greener pastures elsewhere, is paid well; a man who may be of equal value and service to the organization, but who is willing to serve for less, is paid less.

It is clear that there is a real conflict here between the ideal of no discrimination ("equal pay for equal work") and the ideal of the elimination of private income that is economic surplus ("nobody should be paid more than is necessary"). In practice some compromise must be worked out among these various ideals, leaning to one side or the other according to the importance of the ideal in the value systems of the society.

THE DYNAMICS OF DISTRIBUTION. On the whole our discussion of distributional justice up to this point has been conducted in a static framework. We have conceived the problem in terms of the "best" distribution of a *fixed* total income among the various individuals and groups in society. We know, however, that total income is not fixed, and that in a developing society it grows and in a declining society it shrinks. In a dynamic theory of distributive justice, therefore, we must liberate ourselves from the narrow view of the problem that conceived it in terms of sharing a fixed "pie," and think of it in terms of sharing an expanding or possibly a contracting pie. We must, that is to say, try to bring together the ideals of distribution with the objectives of economic progress. . . .

We face, for instance, the problem of *who* are the sharers in the pie—how do we reconcile the claims of one generation against another, or of posterity against the present? This raises the whole problem of the conservation of resources as an ideal. We face also the problem of how present changes in distribution among present claimants may affect the future size of the pie that is distributed. Suppose, for instance, that we achieved what we thought was an ideal distribution of *current* income among the various claimants. Suppose further, however, that some other distribution would result in a higher rate of growth of total income. We would be in effect redistributing income from our children and descendants towards ourselves, or even from ourselves in old age towards ourselves now.

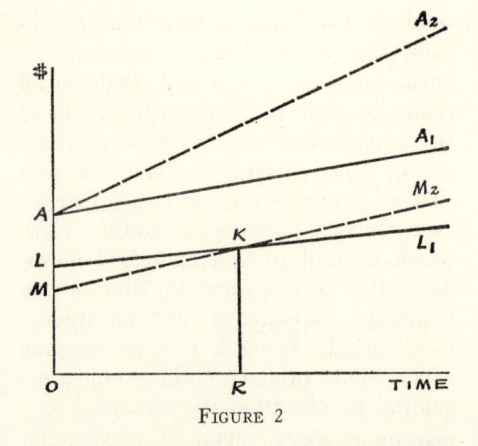

FIGURE 2

EQUALITY VERSUS PROGRESS. The dilemma is pointed up in Fig. 2. Here we measure time along the horizontal axis, with the present at the origin, O. Income is measured along the vertical axis. OA is total present income. We suppose this divided into two parts, OL and LA. To fix ideas, suppose OL represents labor income and LA nonlabor income—interest, profit, and rent. Suppose now that total income grows along the line AA_1, and that the same proportional distribution is maintained, so that labor income grows along the line LL_1. Now let us suppose a redistribution in the present, resulting in a permanent shift in proportional distribution, so that labor now gets a smaller relative share than before, and so that this smaller share persists into the future, but suppose also that as a result of the redistribution the rate of growth is greater. Total income now grows following the line AA_2. Labor income is reduced from OL to OM in the present, but also follows a faster growth curve, MM_2. It is clear from the figure that MM_2 and LL_1 must intersect at some point, K, at the time OR. From the date R forward not only is total income greater than it would have been without the redistribution, but labor income in absolute terms is also greater: KM_2 lies above KL_1.

Even if we took an extreme Marxist position, therefore, that only labor income possesses social utility and that therefore any transfer to labor away from nonlabor income is always desirable, we might well prefer the distribution M to L in the present provided that we estimate the "loss" involved in the triangle LKM to be less than the "gain" involved in the open-ended triangle KL_1M_2. The situation is complicated also by the fact that future incomes and distributions are uncertain and distant, and may be discounted on both these scores. It has long been recognized that a bird in the present hand may rationally be preferred to two birds in some future bush. For this reason the "gain" triangle KM_2L cannot be regarded as infinite. If it were not for uncertainty and time preference, however, no matter what our preferences in regard to distribution, *any* reorganization that was favorable to income growth, no matter what its impact in the present, would be preferred over one that was less favorable to growth. The sum total of income, no matter how weighted by our preferences as among different recipients, would always be greater with greater rates of growth. Uncertainty and time discounting, however, destroy the delightful simplicity of this proposition and make the problem of choice between the ideals of distribution and of progress both real and difficult.

RELATION BETWEEN DISTRIBUTION AND GROWTH IS LITTLE KNOWN. The problem of what in fact is the relationship between distribution and economic progress is one of the least known relationships in all of economics. In the illustration of Fig. 2 I supposed, purely for the sake of illustration, that a reduction in the proportion of income going to labor would increase the rate of income growth. This is certainly not always true, and under many circumstances the reverse might well be the case, and a shift in distribution towards labor income might increase the rate of income growth. The most general and most reasonable hypothesis would be that there is some distribution at which income growth is at a maximum, and therefore on the one side of this an increase in the proportion going to labor raises the rate of income growth, and on the other side of it the reverse is true. Where, however, in any actual society this maximum point is to be found, is almost impossible to discover. . . .

MONOPOLY AND GROWTH. In the light of this dynamic analysis, many of the propositions and prescriptions of the economist that are based on essentially static considerations become exposed to serious doubt. We may take as an example the general and almost universal condemnation of monopoly by economists. As long as we stick to static considerations, these condemnations are very securely founded. Monopoly results in both restriction of output and exploitation of society by the monopolist. The monopolist is like a greedy boy at the table who not only grabs more cake than he should, but in the process actually spills cake on the floor, so that there is less altogether. When, however, we take the dynamic viewpoint, the case against monopoly is much weaker. It may be, indeed, that economic growth tends to proceed outward from little shelters of monopoly in society, and that without these shelters growth would not take place. We give this hypothesis official recognition of sorts in the patent and copyright laws, the object of which is to reward the innovator by granting him a temporary monopoly. We do not really know, however, whether some other method of rewarding innovation, such as direct payments, would not be even more effective.

MONOPOLY MAY STIMULATE GROWTH BY REDUCING UNCERTAINTY. There is a good deal of evidence that *uncertainty* is itself an important element in preventing change, and especially in preventing investment. The investor who commits his resources in specific and definite forms—such as specialized equipment—is a hostage of the future; and the less certain that future, the less likely he is to commit himself. From this point of view, then it can be argued that stability of prices encourages economic development, and that therefore monopoly, by contributing to stability of prices, eventually results in a cheapening of the monopolized commodity even though at first the price may be higher than it would be in a competitive market. Thus by an argument akin to that of Fig. 2 we might balance the period from some point in the future when monopoly would give us lower prices against the period before this critical point when monopoly would give us higher prices. The questions we have just raised are extremely difficult to answer. They must be raised, however, if we are not to have illusions about the simplicity of the problem.

INTERPERSONAL COMPARISONS OF UTILITY. We should not omit from this discussion a very basic objection that has been raised against any attempt to give theoretical solutions to the problem of distribution. It is argued by the purists among the welfare economists [1] that any discussion of ideal distribution must involve what is called "interpersonal comparisons of utility," which are held to be illegitimate. An individual, it is argued, can judge fairly accurately whether one state of affairs is better or worse *for him*, because in this case he is comparing two things in his own mind. Nobody, however, can compare a state in his mind with a state in some other mind, and hence we can never make comparisons of utility from one individual to another. This means that a total social utility cannot be derived from adding up the individual utilities of the people composing the society, and that hence it is illegitimate to compare the marginal utilities of income of different individuals.

RESPONSIBLE DECISIONS NECESSITATE INTERPERSONAL COMPARISONS. The trouble with the above argument is that it seems to prove too much. Any responsible decisions—that is, any decisions that are made on behalf of others, whether by a parent, a businessman, a trade union leader, or a politician—do in fact involve interpersonal comparisons. On the fundamental principle, therefore, that anything that exists must be possible, interpersonal comparisons in some sense must be possible. The criticism that has been leveled against the simple summation of arithmetical utilities is justified—we cannot strap a galvanometer to the seat of the emotions and simply add up the figures obtained for different people. In throwing out a too simple and mechanical interpretation of the process of making interpersonal comparisons, however, economists have cut themselves off from the study of responsible decisions, which means they have really cut themselves off from any study of economic policy.

The dilemma can be resolved when we realize that comparisons between the welfares of different individuals are in fact made in the mind of a single

---

[1] See, for instance, Lionel Robbins, *Essay on the Nature and Significance of Economic Science*, 2d ed. (Toronto: The Macmillan Co., 1935). Marshall and Pigou had no particular qualms on this score—see A. C. Pigou, *The Economics of Welfare*, 4th ed. (London: Macmillan & Co., Ltd., 1938)—but what is called the "Paretian" welfare economics carefully eschews interpersonal comparisons. See Melvin Reder, *Studies in the Theory of Welfare Economics* (New York: Columbia Univ. Press, 1947).

individual—the responsible decision-maker—and do not, therefore, involve comparing things in one mind with things in another. The parent decides that one child needs a new coat worse than the other, the union leader sacrifices the younger men for the older in a contract for seniority, the businessman decides to expand one department at the expense of another, the politician votes for a progressive income tax or for subsidies to agriculture.

THE CONTROL OF RESPONSIBLE DECISION-MAKERS. A theory of responsible decision-making would carry us far beyond the usual confines of economics—it is, indeed, perhaps the most basic question of political science. In what way, for instance, is the responsible decision-maker made *responsive* to the wishes and opinions of those for whom he is responsible—those, that is, who are affected by his decisions? How in other words, are the decisions of the responsible decision-maker fed back to him from those whom his decisions affect?

There are, of course, a great many different answers to this question. The bad king may eventually get dethroned. The incompetent dynasty eventually is replaced by a more vigorous successor. The bad dictator may be eventually deposed, or even assassinated. In democratic societies the politician whose actions arouse discontent may fail to be reelected. In a free market economy the businessman who fails to satisfy his customers and his suppliers may eventually go bankrupt; the unsuccessful executive may be forced out by his superiors, or by a stockholders' revolt. In all societies there are *some* mechanisms for dealing with "unsuccessful" or irresponsible decision-making where these decisions affect the welfare of others. Some of these mechanisms, however, as in authoritarian societies, are slow, crude, clumsy, and may be almost as damaging in their consequences as the evils that they eventually try to correct. It is the great virtue of the invention of representative democracy, that it has permitted more rapid and exact feedbacks to the politician from those who are affected by his decisions. It is a great virtue also of a free market economy that the power of businessmen is sharply limited by the ability of their customers not to buy from them if they don't like the product, or if it is too expensive, and is limited also by the abilities of their suppliers of labor or materials to turn to other purchasers if the terms are not satisfactory. The feedbacks to the businessman in a competitive society are sharp, rapid, and frequently painful. Only when he has established a position of monopoly can he afford to be insensitive in some degree to the response of those who are affected by his decisions.

CONFLICT OF IDEALS RESOLVED BY RESPONSIBLE DECISION-MAKING. To return now to the question of the ideal distribution of income. It is clear that no simple mechanical definition of ideal distribution can be given. Nevertheless, there are responsible decisions to be made in this area, and these decisions are not reached wholly in the dark. [We do have] notions of what constitutes ideal distribution ... and where a divergence is felt between the ideal and actual distribution in the minds of responsible decision-makers and of those who are influential in affecting their behavior, action will be directed towards eliminating the divergence. There may be, as we have noticed, a certain conflict of ideals. Like all conflicts of ideals, these are usually resolved by compromise, each ideal being carried to the point where a further realization of it would not be judged worth the sacrifice of some other ideal.

THE LIMITS OF TOLERANCE—THE BASIC MINIMUM. We can, however, be more specific than this. Even though the exact compromise between these various ideals cannot be worked out in advance, but must depend on the nature of the political process by which it is achieved, nevertheless each of the ideals may be used to prescribe certain *negative* limits which give minimum standards of performance for the system. Thus, although the need standard is not, as we have seen, capable of being erected into a complete system of distribution, it does lead to the proposition that there should be in every society a basic minimum standard of life below which no one should be allowed to fall. This notion of a basic minimum level is an old principle—it is involved, for instance, in any "poor law." The practical problem—and the one that is likely to cause most controversy—is that of deciding where this minimum level should lie. . . . We have good reason to suppose that, in the Western world at least, we can now afford to set a basic minimum much higher than we have been accustomed to in the past, because of the rise in productivity and in the economic surplus. A flat basic minimum could only apply, of course, to a fairly homogeneous region. Over a large and heterogeneous area, it would be necessary to set lower basic minima in those areas less technically advanced and more accustomed to poverty.

THE CONTROL OF MONOPOLY. The merit standard likewise is not capable of universal application. Here also, however, it is possible to spell out certain gross violations as constituting a lower limit of tolerance. Monopolistic privileges should not be tolerated unless a strong case can be made for them on the grounds of their contribution to economic progress. . . . In the movement towards equality, however, we must beware of attempting to redistribute more than the economic surplus: if taxation, for instance, cuts below the supply price of some essential factor, that is, the minimum "reward" which is necessary to keep it functioning, the supply of this factor will be curtailed to the loss of the whole society.

. . . . .

Wages and the forces affecting their determination are examined by an outstanding British economist. This selection deserves careful study, for it develops principles that have broad application.

31 · Wage Theory: Basic Forces

J. R. HICKS

The interaction of supply and demand on the labor market is a problem which will have to occupy a good deal of our attention. All buying and selling have some features in common; but nevertheless differences do exist between the ways in which things are bought and sold on different markets. Organized produce markets differ from wholesale trade of the ordinary type; both of these

---

J. R. HICKS, *The Theory of Wages* (London: Macmillan & Co., Ltd., 1932), pp. 4–9, 14–19. Used by permission.

differ from retail trade, and from sale by tender or by auction. The labor market is yet another type. It has been the usual practice of economists to concentrate their attention on those features of exchange which are common to all markets; and to dismiss the differences between markets with a brief reminder that markets may be more or less "perfect." There is little doubt that in doing so they did seize on the really significant thing; the general working of supply and demand is a great deal more important than the differences between markets. But this course meant the almost complete neglect of some factors which appear at first sight very important indeed; the fact that they are really less important than those aspects which were discussed were really demonstrated clearly.

When an attempt is made to apply to the labor market the ordinary principles of price determination—without making allowance for the type of market—the result appears at first sight very odd. Wages, say the textbooks, tend to that level where demand and supply are equal. If supply exceeds demand, some men will be unemployed, and in their efforts to regain employment they will reduce the wages they ask to that level which makes it just worthwhile for employers to take them on. If demand exceeds supply, employers will be unable to obtain all the labor they require, and will therefore offer higher wages in order to attract labor from elsewhere.

Now this, as I hope to make abundantly clear, is quite a good simplified model of the labor market. So far as general tendencies are concerned, wages do turn out on the whole very much as if they were determined in this manner. . . .

We can begin by confining our attention to a labor market in equilibrium. Let us suppose that a level of wages is fixed so that demand and supply balance, and thus there is no tendency for wages to rise or to fall. Let us suppose, further, that this balancing of demand and supply is brought about, not by compensating fluctuations of the demand from particular firms, but by the demand from each firm being stationary, because no employer has any incentive to vary the number of men he takes on. It is necessary for us to adopt this abstract and rigorous conception of equilibrium, since otherwise we should not be effectively ruling out the difficulties of change, but should still be faced with very much the same kind of problem which confronts us in the case of a rise or fall in wages.

We have thus to examine the conditions of full equilibrium in the labor market, assuming the supply of laborers given, and their efficiencies given and equal. This enables us finally to isolate the pure problem of demand. It is true that we only achieve this isolation at the expense of a series of highly artificial assumptions; but in economics, as in other sciences, abstraction is usually the condition of clear thinking. The complications created by the things we have left out can be reintroduced later.

Conditions of Equilibrium

The first of the necessary conditions of equilibrium is that every man should receive the same wage—subject at any rate to allowances for "other advantages" and possibly for costs of movement (but these things also we neglect at present). If wages are not equal, then it will clearly be to the advantage of an employer who is paying a higher level of wages to dismiss his present employees, and to replace them by other men who had been receiving less. If he offers a wage somewhere between the two previously existing levels, he will both lower his own costs (and consequently improve his own situation) and successfully attract the new men, since he is offering them a higher wage than they received before. So long as such transfers can be made advantageously to both parties entering upon the new contract, there is no equilibrium; since someone can always disturb it to his own advantage. Equal wages are a necessary condition of equilibrium in a market governed by our present assumptions.

The second condition is much more critical. The only wage at which equilibrium is possible is a wage which equals the value of the marginal product of the laborers. At any given wage it will pay employers best to take on that number of laborers which makes their marginal product—that is to say, the difference between the total physical product which is actually secured and that which would have been secured from the same quantity of other resources if the number of laborers had been increased or diminished by one— equal in value to the wage. In this way the demand for labor of each employer is determined; and the total demand of all employers is determined from it by addition. Since in equilibrium it is necessary that the total demand should equal the total supply, the wage must be that which just enables the total number of laborers available to be employed. This must equal the value of the marginal product of the laborers available.

The conventional proof of the marginal productivity proposition is simple enough. It follows from the most fundamental form of the law of diminishing returns that an increased quantity of labor applied to a fixed quantity of other resources will yield a diminished marginal product. Thus if the employer were to take on a number of laborers so large that their marginal product was not worth the wage which has to be paid, he would soon find that the number was excessive. By reducing the number he employed, he would reduce his total production, and therefore (under competitive conditions) his gross receipts. But at the same time he would reduce his expenditure; and since the wage was higher than the marginal product, he would reduce his expenditure more than his receipts, and so increase his profits. Similarly, he would not reduce his employment of labor to such a point as would make the wage less than the marginal product; for by so doing he would be reducing his receipts more than his expenditure, and so again diminishing his profits. The number of laborers which an employer will prefer to take on is that number which makes his profits a maximum, and that number is given by the equality of wages to the marginal product of the labor employed.

It is thus clear that the wage at which equilibrium is possible will vary in the opposite direction to changes in the total number of laborers available. If the number of laborers available on the market had been larger, the wage must have been lower; since the additional product secured by the employment of one of these extra laborers would be worth less than the previously given wage, and consequently it would not pay to employ these men unless the wage-level was reduced. If the number had been less, employers would have had an incentive to demand more laborers at the given wage than would actually have been available, and their competition would therefore force up the level of wages. The only wage which is consistent with equilibrium is one which equals the value of the marginal product of the available labor.

This "Law of Marginal Productivity" is regarded by most modern economists as the most fundamental principle of the theory of wages. . . .

When an entrepreneur has to choose

between two different methods of producing a given output, he may be expected to choose that which costs least. For, at any rate in the first place, anything which reduces his costs will raise his profits. If employers are not using the cheapest method of production available to them, they have an incentive to change; and so there is no equilibrium.

It is this condition of minimum cost of production per unit of output which leads us directly to the law of marginal productivity. For if we suppose the prices of all the factors of production to be given, the "least cost" combination of factors will be given by the condition that the marginal products of the factors are proportional to their prices. If the

$$\frac{\text{marginal product of factor A}}{\text{price of A}}$$

is greater than

$$\frac{\text{marginal product of factor B}}{\text{price of B}}$$

then this means that it will be to the advantage of the entrepreneur to use a method of production which uses a little more of A and a little less of B, since in that way he will get a larger product for the same expenditure, or (what comes to the same thing) he will get an equal product at a lower cost.

This condition of the proportionality of marginal products is simply another means of expressing the necessity that the method employed in a position of equilibrium should be the cheapest method of reaching the desired result. No new principle whatever is introduced; so that in practical applications we can work with the condition of minimum cost, or with the condition of the proportionality of marginal products—whichever seems more significant in the particular case.

It must, however, be observed that the above condition only states that the marginal products are proportional to the prices of the factors—it does not say that the prices *equal* the values of the marginal products. So far as the choice of methods of production is concerned, it appears that the prices of the factors might exceed, or all fall short of, the values of the marginal products —so long as they do it in the same proportion. But if this were to be the case, it would be possible for the entrepreneur to increase his profits by expanding or contracting production without changing his methods. The condition of equality between price and cost of production would not be satisfied.

When we allow for the variability of methods of production, there is thus another way in which changes in wages may affect the demand for labor. A rise in wages will make labor expensive relatively to other factors of production, and will thus encourage entrepreneurs to use methods which employ less labor and more of these other factors. And this evidently applies in exactly the same way to industry as a whole, as it does to particular industries. The more extensive the rise in wages, the more substitution will take place. For exactly the same reason, a fall in wages will lead to substitution in the reverse direction.

The law of marginal productivity, in its usual form, is simply a convenient means whereby the statement of the two tendencies we have been discussing can be combined. On the one hand, the returns to other resources than labor tend to equality in their different applications (the tendency which alone is taken account of in the formulation of "net productivity"); on the other hand, employers can modify the methods which they employ in their businesses, and the relative profitability of different methods depends on the relative prices of the factors of production. For some purposes it is convenient to use the conventional formulation, which brings together the two tendencies, and enables us to manipulate them together; but for a good many other purposes it is convenient to treat them separately.

There can be no full equilibrium unless the wages of labor equal its marginal product; since, if this equality is not attained, it means that someone has open to him an opportunity of gain which he is not taking. Either employers will be able to find an advantage in varying the methods of production they use, or investors and other owners of property will be able to benefit themselves by transferring the resources under their control from one branch of production to another. But we cannot go on from this to conclude that this equality of wages and marginal products will actually be found in practice, for the real labor market is scarcely ever in equilibrium in the sense considered here. In actual practice, changes in methods are continually going on; and resources are continually being transferred from one industry to another, or new resources being put at the disposal of industry, which are not uniformly distributed among the various branches of production. This ceaseless change is partly a consequence of changes in the ultimate determinants of economic activity—those things which we have to take as the final data of economic enquiry—changes in tastes, changes in knowledge, changes in the natural environment, and in the supply and efficiency of the factors of production generally. As these things change, so the marginal product of labor changes with them; and these changes in marginal productivity exert pressure, in one direction or the other, upon the level of wages.

The theory of pure rent stated in this famous selection has played an important role in the development of economic thought. How might it help explain the urban real estate fortunes of the nineteenth century, or the oil fortunes of the twentieth?

32 • Pure Rent: The Classic View

DAVID RICARDO

Rent is that portion of the produce of the earth which is paid to the landlord for the use of the original and indestructible powers of the soil.

It is often, however, confounded with the interest and profit of capital, and, in popular language, the term is applied to whatever is annually paid by a farmer to his landlord. If, of two adjoining farms of the same extent, and of the same natural fertility, one had all the conveniences of farming buildings, and, besides, were properly drained and manured, and advantageously divided into hedges, fences, and walls, while the other had none of these advantages, more remuneration would naturally be paid

---

DAVID RICARDO, *Principles of Political Economy and Taxation* (1817).

for the use of one, than for the use of the other; yet in both cases the remuneration would be called rent. But it is evident, that a portion only of the money annually to be paid for the improved farm, would be given for the original and indestructible powers of the soil; the other portion would be paid for the use of the capital which had been employed in ameliorating the quality of the land, and in erecting such buildings as were necessary to secure and preserve the produce. Adam Smith sometimes speaks of rent, in the strict sense to which I am desirous of confining it, but more often in the popular sense in which the term is usually employed. He tells us, that the demand for timber, and its consequent high price, in the more southern countries of Europe caused a rent to be paid for forests in Norway, which could before afford no rent. Is it not, however, evident, that the person who paid what he thus calls rent, paid it in consideration of the valuable commodity which was then standing on the land, and that he actually repaid himself with a profit, by the sale of the timber? If, indeed, after the timber was removed, any compensation were paid to the landlord for the use of the land, for the purpose of growing timber or any other produce, with a view to future demand, such compensation might justly be called rent, because it would be paid for the productive powers of the land; but in the case stated by Adam Smith, the compensation was paid for the liberty of removing and selling the timber, and not for the liberty of growing it.

On the first settling of a country, in which there is an abundance of fertile land, a very small proportion of which is required to be cultivated for the support of the actual population, or indeed can be cultivated with the capital which the population can command, there will be no rent; for no one would pay for the use of land, when there was an abundant quantity not yet appropriated, and, therefore, at the disposal of whosoever might choose to cultivate it.

If all land had the same properties, if it were unlimited in quantity, and uniform in quality, no charge could be made for its use, unless where it possessed peculiar advantages of situation. It is only, then, because land is not unlimited in quantity and uniform in quality, and because in the progress of population, land of an inferior quality, or less advantageously situated, is called into cultivation, that rent is ever paid for the use of it. When in the progress of society, land of the second degree of fertility is taken into cultivation, rent immediately commences on that of the first quality, and the amount of that rent will depend on the difference in the quality of those two portions of land.

When land of the third quality is taken into cultivation, rent immediately commences on the second, and it is regulated as before, by the difference in their productive powers. At the same time, the rent of the first quality will rise, for that must always be above the rent of the second, by the difference between the produce which they yield with a given quantity of capital and labor. With every step in the progress of population, which shall oblige a country to have recourse to land of a worse quality, to enable it to raise its supply of food—rent, on all the more fertile land, will rise.

Thus suppose land—No. 1, 2, 3—to yield with an equal employment of capital and labor, a net produce of 100, 90, and 80 quarters of corn. In a new country, where there is an abundance of fertile land compared with the population, and where therefore it is only necessary to cultivate No. 1, the whole net produce will belong to the cultivator, and will be the profits of the stocks which he advances. As soon as population had so far increased as to make it necessary to cultivate No. 2, from which 90 quarters only can be obtained after supporting the laborers, rent would commence on No. 1; for either there must be two rates of profit on agricultural capital, or 10 quarters, or the value of 10 quarters must be withdrawn from the produce of No. 1, for some other purpose. Whether the proprietor of the land, or any other person, cultivated No. 1, these 10 quarters would equally constitute rent; for the cultivator of No. 2 would get the same result with his capital, whether he cultivated No. 1, paying 10 quarters for rent, or continued to cultivate No. 2, paying no rent. In the same manner it might be shown that when No. 3 is brought into cultivation, the rent of No. 2 must be 10 quarters, or the value of 10 quarters, whilst the rent of No. 1 would rise to 20 quarters; for the cultivator of No. 3 would have the same profits whether he paid 20 quarters for the rent of No. 1, 10 quarters for the rent of No. 2, or cultivated No. 3 free of all rent. ["Corn" in English usage means grain. *Ed.*]

It often, and, indeed commonly happens, that before No. 2, 3, 4, or 5, or the inferior lands are cultivated, capital can be employed more productively on those lands which are already in cultivation. It may perhaps be found, that by doubling the original capital employed on No. 1, though the produce will not be doubled, will not be increased by 100 quarters, it may be increased by 85 quarters, and that this quantity exceeds what could be obtained by employing the same capital, on land No. 3.

In such case, capital will be preferably employed on the old land, and will equally create a rent; for rent is always the difference between the produce obtained by the employment of equal quantities of capital and labor. If with a capital of £1,000 a tenant obtain 100 quarters of wheat from his land, and by the employment of a second capital of £1,000, he obtain a further return of 85, his landlord would have the power at the expiration of his lease, of obliging him to pay 15 quarters or an equivalent value for additional rent, for there cannot be two rates of profit. If he is satisfied with a diminution of 15 quarters in the return for his second £1,000 it is because no employment more profitable can be found for it. The common rate of profit would be in that proportion and if the original tenant refused, some other person would be found willing to give all which exceeded that rate of profit to the owner of the land from which he derived it.

If, then, good land existed in a quantity much more abundant than the production of food for an increasing population required, or if capital could be indefinitely employed without a diminished return on the old land, there could be no rise of rent; for rent invariably proceeds from the employment of an additional quantity of labor with a proportionally less return.

The exchangeable value of all commodities, whether they be manufactured, or the produce of the mines, or the produce of land, is always regulated, not by the less quantity of labor that will suffice for their production under circumstances highly favorable, and exclusively enjoyed by those who have peculiar facilities of production; but by the greater quantity of labor necessarily bestowed on their production by those who have no such facilities; by those who continue to produce them under the most unfavorable circumstances, the most unfavorable under which the quantity of produce required, renders it necessary to carry on the production.

It is true, that on the best land, the same produce would still be obtained with the same labor as before, but its value would be enhanced in consequence of the diminished returns obtained by those who employed fresh labor and stock on the less fertile land. Notwithstanding, then, that the advantages of fertile over inferior lands are in no case lost, but only transferred from the cultivator, or consumer, to the landlord, yet since more labor is required on the inferior lands, and since it is from such land only that we are enabled to furnish ourselves with the additional supply of raw produce, the comparative value of that produce will continue permanently above the former level, and make it exchange for more hats, cloth, shoes, etc., etc., in the production of which no such additional quantity of labor is required.

The reason, then, why raw produce rises in comparative value, is because more labor is employed in the production of the last portion obtained, and not because a rent is paid to the landlord. The value of corn is regulated by the quantity of labor bestowed on its production on that quality of land, or with that portion of capital, which pays no rent. Corn is not high because a rent is paid, but a rent is paid because corn is high; and it has been justly observed, that no reduction would take place in the price of corn, although landlords should forego the whole of their rent. Such a measure would only enable some farmers to live like gentlemen, but would not diminish the quantity of labor necessary to raise raw produce on the least productive land in cultivation.

Nothing is more common than to hear of the advantages which the land possesses over every other source of useful produce, on account of the surplus which it yields in the form of rent. Yet when land is most abundant, when most productive, and most fertile, it yields no rent; and it is only when its powers decay, and less is yielded in return for labor that a share of the original produce of the more fertile portions is set apart for rent. It is singular that this quality in the land, which should have been noticed as an imperfection, compared with the natural agents by which manufacturers are assisted, should have been pointed out as constituting its peculiar pre-eminence. If air, water, the elasticity of steam, and the pressure of the atmosphere, were of various qualities; if they could be appropriated, and each quality existed only in moderate abundance, they, as well as the land, would afford a rent, as the successive qualities were brought into use. With every worse quality employed, the value of the commodities in the manufacture of which they were used, would rise, because equal quantities of labor would be less productive. Man would do more by the sweat of his brow, and nature perform less; and the land would be no longer pre-eminent for its limited powers.

One of the outstanding works in economic theory in this century is Frank H. Knight's Risk, Uncertainty and Profit. *It tackled some of the more controversial elements of economic theory and reached conclusions which won wide acceptance. The following selection, from a more recent volume, presents the central ideas briefly.*

33 · Profit

FRANK H. KNIGHT

. . . . .
. . . profit is a difference—positive in the case of "profit" and negative in the case of "loss"—between the income realized from the sale of a product and the total cost incurred in producing it, including in cost payment at the ordinary competitive rates for whatever personal service or use of his own property the producer himself puts into the productive operations, as well as his actual outlays for the services and property of other persons. Such differences arise because the process of distribution, or evaluating the productive services entering into a product, does not work with perfect accuracy. If this process did work with unfailing precision, the product value would be exactly distributed among the productive services, including those furnished by the owner of the business, and no profit or loss outside of payment for the owner's services would exist. The whole theory of normal price rests on this "tendency" of price and cost of production to be equal which is the negation of profit.

. . . the reason for the inaccuracy of distribution and the occurrence of profit is essentially the inaccurate forecasting of demand by producers, and to a lesser degree the impossibility of predicting the physical result of a productive operation and so controlling it with precision. The latter cause applies especially to agriculture and industries affected by weather conditions. It is fairly apparent that if business men could foresee future conditions exactly, and if the relations between them were those of competition only, cost and price would always be equal, there would be no pure profit. We are concerned here with the first of these two phenomena, errors in estimating conditions and in making adjustments to them. The existence of conditions other than those of competition implies *monopoly gain,* a form of income often included under profit, but of a very different character from that now under discussion.

All that is here to be added to the discussion of the theory of profit is a few observations on the nature of risk and uncertainty or the reasons for inaccuracy in prediction. The first of these observations is that not all "risks" necessarily give rise to profit, or loss. Many kinds can be *insured against,* which eliminates them as factors of uncer-

---

FRANK H. KNIGHT, *The Economic Organization* (New York: Kelley & Millman, Inc., 1951), pp. 118–121. Used by permission.

tainty. The principle of insurance is the application of the "law of large numbers," that in a large group of trials the proportion of occurrences to non-occurrences of a contingent event tends to be constant. The death of a particular individual, burning of a particular building, loss of a particular ship at sea, etc., is uncertain; but in a group of a hundred thousand similar cases the proportion of losses is very accurately predictable. There are many ways of applying this principle, in addition to the various forms of insurance called by the name. A large corporation, by broadening the scale of its operations, distributes and reduces its risks. Concentration of speculation in the hands of a professional class tends to make errors in judgment largely cancel out. The essential point for profit theory is that insofar as it is possible to insure by any method against risk, the cost of carrying it is converted into a constant element of expense, and it ceases to be a cause of profit and loss.

The uncertainties which persist as causes of profit are those which are uninsurable because there is no objective measure of the probability of gain or loss. This is true especially of the prediction of demand. It not only cannot be foreseen accurately, but there is no basis for saying that the probability of its being of one sort rather than another is of a certain value—as we can compute the chance that a man will live to a certain age. Situations in regard to which business judgment must be exercised do not repeat themselves with sufficient conformity to type to make possible a computation of probability.

It is further to be observed that a large part of the risks which give rise to profit are connected with progressive social change. Changes in demand and in methods of production, especially, cause large gains to some enterprises, and losses to others. And the work of exploring for and developing new natural resources is fraught with the greatest unpredictability, with corresponding frequency of large profits or losses. It is to be kept in mind that such changes do not merely "happen," giving rise to profit. The possibility of securing a profit in consequence of a change induces business men to make large expenditures in bringing about changes in every field. In the main, no doubt, changes thus induced are improvements, and represent real social progress. This is true of the discovery of natural resources and of more effective productive methods. It is not so certain in connection with the promotion of changes in wants. . . . the theory of individualism is especially weak at this point and . . . a large fraction of the political interference found necessary has to do with safeguarding the maintenance and improvement of society. Where distinctively human values are involved, the working of the profit motive is likely to give very unsatisfactory results.

The nature and source of *monopoly* [*gain* are different]. . . . Where a producer can in any way prevent other persons from using productive resources in making a product equivalent to his own, or can bar them from using especially effective processes, he can make a gain by restricting output. It is to be observed that any individual rendering a unique personal service—such as an artist, or a professional man with a reputation causing his services to be in special demand—has a monopoly of a very distinctive and secure variety. . . . uniqueness is the very essence of monopoly. The greater part of advertising represents an effort to build up an impression of uniqueness, to establish what may be called a "psychological" uniqueness, in particular products, and thus to secure a degree of monopoly power.

In 1950 Columbia University's Conservation of Human Resources Project, along with the closely associated National Manpower Council, began research which has resulted in nearly two dozen volumes. The selection here includes portions of two chapters of a progress-report volume by the director, Professor of Economics at Columbia University.

34 · Development and Utilization of Human Resources

ELI GINZBERG

Talent and Superior Performance

. . . . .

Earlier generations believed that the progress of any society depends on the creativeness of a relatively small number who produce the ideas, the art, and the leadership that give direction and distinction to a nation, but we still understand very little about the creative process. . . .

Our interest in the creative few does not permit us to ignore the larger group from whom they draw their strength and whom they seek to nourish. This interdependence between the few and the many can be easily illustrated. The great difficulties which Great Britain faced in the years after World War I were the direct outcome of the losses it suffered during that war. The clumsiness with which the British set out to resolve their economic difficulties and the slow progress which they made can be largely explained by the long lists of names on the memorial tablets at Oxford and Cambridge—reminders that the nation's future leadership was killed off before it could flower. . . .

The interdependence of the exceptional man and his environment can be seen in the experience of Enrico Fermi, who shortly before the outbreak of World War II went to Washington to alert the United States Navy about the military potentialities of nuclear energy and to seek a grant so that he could speed his experiments at Columbia University. The responsible officer listened but did not understand. In terminating the interview he asked Fermi to please keep the Navy informed if anything worth while developed. . . .

The word *talent* has usually been used to describe that special ability of individuals who have made important contributions to the arts. But a modern society has need of many different types of superior performance not only in the arts, but in science, politics, business—in fact, in every domain of life. In appraising the amount of talent in a society and in analyzing the complex forces that contribute to or retard its development and utilization, a broad rather than a narrow use of the term is desirable.

ELI GINZBERG, *Human Resources: The Wealth of a Nation*, Copyright 1958 by Eli Ginzberg (New York: Simon and Schuster, Inc., 1958). Used by permission.

We know most about intellectual potential. For fifty years psychologists have been busy testing children and adults to determine their IQs. On the basis of these tests they have found that approximately one per cent of the population scores at 140 or above. Outstanding contributions to mathematics, science, and the social sciences are likely to be made primarily by individuals who score this high. In some fields, such as theoretical physics, a man can probably not even qualify, much less make a significant contribution, unless he scores in this range.

With more than 100 million adults it might appear that the nation has in its work force at least one million with a high order of intellectual ability. But that is not so. A sizable reduction has to be made in the estimated one million because many able women are not available for paid employment, but women account for about half of the country's top brains. And a much greater reduction has to be made because so many of both sexes fail to develop their full potential—and it is developed potential that counts. An important indication of the underdevelopment of high potential is the sizable group, about 5,000 soldiers, who scored in the top mental group on the Army's General Classification Test during World War II but who never had gone beyond the eighth grade! Currently almost one out of every three of the intellectually ablest fails to enter or graduate from college. Of those who do graduate, only a relatively small percentage goes on to acquire a graduate or professional degree. There are probably no more than 100,000 in the labor force with an IQ of 140 or over who are fully trained.

. . . . .

The assumption that talented persons probably start life with much the same type of basic endowment is perhaps less important than the recognition that the different education and training which they pursue early leads to a channeling of their original endowment into specific areas. A young person who prepares himself for one career inevitably closes out others. . . . The values of a culture will greatly condition which fields are stressed, which are neglected. . . .

. . . . .

With regard to the individual, the first point to note is that, although power can be transferred from father to son, excellence can never be bestowed. It must be earned. One must work to acquire it. Parents can smooth the way, but they can also make the way much more difficult.

Second, the process whereby an individual acquires a high order of competence is always long and difficult. It is misleading to use the word *talent* to describe the finger drawings of an eight-year-old or the singing of a ten-year-old. Precocity is not talent. Neither is aptitude. Whether a youngster with aptitude finally becomes a superior performer will depend on his personality and his opportunities. Mischa Elman prepared for his first European tour after the end of the war by playing scales on shipboard and exercises eight hours a day for five days! Superior performance is much more than winning a scholarship.

. . . . .

Excellence requires the individual early in life to trade current pleasure for future gain. He must be able to stay with his studies while others go out to play. He must be able to gain such buoyancy from what he hopes to accomplish in the distant future that he will not feel unduly deprived in denying himself current gratifications. . . .

One of the more startling transformations in American life is represented by today's lower age of marriage and the fact that many women have two or three children before they are twenty-eight. . . . Too little attention has been paid to the impact of these patterns on the development of talent. Although a wife may turn out to be a tremendous help to the young graduate student, for she can work while he studies, his freedom of choice and action are likely to be restricted once he secures his degree. Offered a choice between an instructorship at a university or a position with a large corporation that pays twice as much, he is likely to take the second and is almost certain to do so if there are children to consider.

We frequently overlook the family's role in the development of talent. For instance, no child ever decides on his own to become a virtuoso. At most he may confirm the choice that his parents originally made for him. But the child who devotes many hours a day to practicing is responding to a parental decision. The family is frequently responsible for a young person's closing out certain options. . . .

. . . . .

The more parents are handicapped in guiding their offspring because of their own deprived backgrounds, the more important is the role of the school in helping to develop and direct young people. The school should be able to guide these youngsters with or without the formal testing programs which are used to identify high potential. More important than testing instruments or other guidance techniques is the contribution the school can make by providing able teachers. A good teacher serves as a model of excellence and can thereby capture the imagination of the young. This is a difficult assignment and only the exceptional teacher will succeed. Fortunately, the student does not need many exceptional teachers to unlock his potentialities and to stimulate him to do his best. But regretfully many of the 123,000 elementary and 30,000 high schools of the country cannot boast of even a few outstanding teachers. Hence many students complete school without ever becoming aware of their own strengths or how they might develop them.

. . . . .

The absence of good teachers is that much more crippling if young people have need for special guidance and stimulation. This is the situation in which most young women find themselves today. Neither their fathers nor their mothers can help them to interpret the revolutionary changes under way in women's changing place in the world of work. The young Negro also has great need of special guidance and counseling to help him appreciate his widening opportunities and learn how he can best prepare himself to qualify for a better job. Once again it is the good teacher, more than anybody else, who can help him.

The home and the school provide the basic experiences that individuals of high endowment require to develop their potential. But neither the home nor the school can protect the individual against the turmoil of adolescence. If the pull of sex becomes very strong, it may seriously unsettle the young person. Many of the outstanding scientists on whom Anna Roe reported in *The Making of a Scientist* told a story of slow sexual maturation. They were not deflected, as so many are, from their books.

Another personality trait of great importance in the development of high potential that reveals itself during the educational cycle is the ability of an individual to go his own way, able to respond to his own internal standards and goals irrespective of whether his friends approve or not. This is particularly hard in adolescence, when most young people need support from their peers in their struggles to free themselves from the authority of their parents. Moreover, the American environment puts such a heavy premium on being "one of the gang" that the cards are stacked against deviation. Many able youngsters settle for second-best solutions because they cannot face the disapproval of their peers.

Even if the gifted individual surmounts the many difficulties of childhood and adolescence, his ability to reach high-level performance will depend on what happens to him after he enters the world of work. . . .

No matter how able one is, no matter how well one has been trained, unless a man can find—or make—opportunities in the world of work, he will never be able to demonstrate his full worth. . . .

Currently many large corporations are devoting much time and effort to programs of executive development in the hope of broadening and deepening the knowledge and understanding of those most likely to be selected in the future for top positions. Great enthusiasm prevails in business for this effort, which led last year to the enrollment of 75,000 executives in the programs sponsored by the American Management Association alone. Widespread enthusiasm has also been manifested toward the various training devices such as role-playing, developed to illuminate the decision-making process, and of course the time-honored formal lecture and informal discussion group.

. . . the core of development is to be found not in these formal learning situations but in the efforts that large organizations make, or should make, to assign men of ability to positions of challenge. Further, as they master one job, they should be moved to another where they are confronted with a new task. Obviously, men who remain in one groove for a decade or two will not broaden their competence. Men who are strictly supervised will not be able to develop their full potentialities. Men with abilities must be given adequate authority and held to account for their performance.

The early economists looked to the market place to differentiate between the competent and the incompetent. The former earned profits, the latter suffered losses or bankruptcy. Today it is difficult to assess the contribution of various executives when key decisions are usually made in committee. Top management's interest in executive-development programs grows out of its need to find some substitutions for the rough-and-tumble of the market place which used to bring the ablest to the top.

In science, sports, and the arts, it is much easier to appraise the worth of a man. If a leading university has an opening in mathematics or physics, the same names will appear on different lists of recommendation. At most, the ranking may vary. In sports, there is no problem of identifying the top tennis players or golfers, and the experts are usually in substantial agreement in selecting the all-American team in football, or even the most valuable player in baseball. The public leaves little doubt about how it appraises the talent of a Heifetz or a Horowitz. . . .

. . . . .

In every large organization, in corporations, universities, labor unions, hospitals, ecclesiastical institutions, the men who rise to the top usually get there through the exercise of political skills. But the men with political skills do not necessarily have the other qualities which will help the institution grow and prosper. The man of strong convictions, of fertile ideas, of lively imagination is likely to become a target for criticism long before he is within sight of the top. The hurdles in the contest for high position are many. And many men feel that the prize is not worth the game. They are unwilling to make the heavy sacrifices year after year to bring themselves within the orbit of eventual consideration. . . .

Although American folklore tells us that every boy desires to be president —if not of the United States, then at least of a small company—there is little evidence to back this up. The greater the progress of the economy, the less a man need struggle to live decently. The talented person has a tremendous range of options open to him; with a reasonable investment of effort he can go a long distance. But to go to the top usually requires an all-out effort. Many simply refuse to compete for the major prizes.

It is worth inspecting the proposition that a man's wife frequently exercises a restraining influence on his progress. Reference has been made to the handicapping impact of early marriage and early families on a young man's development. These responsibilities inevitably prevent a man from devoting himself exclusively to his work and they usually come at a period of his life when he still needs broadening and deepening experiences in order to mature fully. The insistence of many wives that their husbands play major roles within the home and participate fully in the upbringing of the children is surely not bad. Yet the results, no matter how beneficial for the wife, the children, and even the husband, must be paid for. The Church did not establish the rule of celibacy to try the flesh but because it recognized how difficult it is for a man to dedicate himself wholeheartedly to his work in the presence of family responsibilities. . . .

. . . The constant rise in the American standard of living and the ever larger number of families who find themselves in comfortable circumstances do not augur well for the continued development of excellence. The record of the recent past shows that the wealthy have only occasionally made important contributions to science, art, or politics. They had little incentive to strive very hard. For a man born to wealth and position life held sufficiently attractive alternatives that he was not encouraged to drive himself. It would be a statement of faith unsupported by reason to hold that as more and more Americans have the opportunity to live easily and well, the spur to fame will remain the same.

. . . . .

Human Resources and the General Welfare

Several years ago, when the American public was first becoming concerned with the shortage of scientists and engineers, a leading member of the Congress . . . prepared a paper for the annual meeting of the American Association for the Advancement of Science. Using Soviet Russia as a contrast, the Congressman bemoaned the way in which this country treated its scientists. We did not pay them large salaries, award them medals and other honors, or otherwise indicate that we hold them in high esteem. Contrariwise, the Russian scientist was in a coveted position at the very top of the occupational hierarchy. The Congressman urged that this country wake up and take a leaf from Russia's book before it was too late, since the future of our defense and of our national prosperity is increasingly in the hands of scientists.

Although the Congressman outlined sensible corrective actions to improve the attractiveness of science as a career, there was an incongruous note in his presentation. Here was a distinguished member of the House of Representatives—which has been appropriating huge sums for many years to enable this nation to meet the challenge of aggressive Communism, the arch-enemy of freedom and decency—holding up Soviet Russia as a model of sagacity and propriety. The speaker was silent about irreconcilable differences between the approach of America and the rest of the free world and that of the Communists toward human values, especially about the relations of man to the state.

Although the Congressman was right when he stated that we could learn something from the Russians about trained manpower, he completely ignored the fact that in a Communist society people are always the means, never the ends. If the Russian leaders decide to increase the number of scientists and engineers, they can set machinery in operation to recruit those with the required intellectual qualifications. The incentives attached to professional work can be strengthened. And the powerful apparatus of a controlled society can make use of the enthusiasm of the young to help accomplish the desired results.

Superficially it is esay to conclude that the advantages are with the Russians, who are able to open or close the sluices through which young people are channeled into various work areas, and who can alter the rewards that attach to different careers so as to bring about a better balance between national needs and manpower availabilities. But the manipulatory aspects of this type of occupational determination were passed over by the Congressman. Moreover, he did not mention that when it suited those in power they could and did place a leading physicist under house arrest for seven years; they could and did order the secret police to prepare false accusations of murder against a group of distinguished physicians; they could and did silence outstanding biologists and padlock their laboratories because they would not follow the interpretations of a colleague whose sole claim to distinction resided in his personal connections with an aging and brutal dictator.

. . . . .

The crucial point is that the Russians have already demonstrated sufficient strength to force us into a nuclear stalemate. This being so—assuming that we will not fall behind in the arms race—our security and prosperity will henceforth largely depend upon the leadership we can provide in helping the free nations of the world to prosper and in demonstrating the advantages of democracy in advancing the welfare of the individual citizen. To this end ministers and doctors, teachers and social scientists, artists and statesmen, will have as much to contribute as, and possibly more than, scientists and technologists.

Some might assume that a Communist, or controlled, society has no special difficulty in determining the shape of its manpower policy. After identifying its long-range goals and taking account of its available resources, it need only estimate the number and types of skilled manpower that it will require and allocate sufficient resources to training them. But in point of fact such a society does not have an easy task. The needs that Russia will have in 1965 or 1970 cannot be clearly estimated by the present leadership. And at that time they may encounter great difficulties in adjusting their availabilities to their requirements. In Communistic, as in capitalistic, societies the training of a professional man requires from ten to twenty years—long enough for the best-considered plans to go awry.

How does a democratic society provide for the large numbers of different types of trained people that it expects to use a decade or two hence? Unable to exercise direct control over the individual in training or at work, how does it ever succeed in getting the types of manpower it requires? The answer to this question must be sought in the mechanisms available to a democratic society to influence the ways in which individuals choose their occupations, the opportunities they have to become trained, and the considerations that determine their effectiveness at work. With respect to each of these facets—occupational choice, education and training, and manpower utilization—a democratic society influences the outcome. It cannot move as quickly as a controlled society to alter the occupational pattern, for it must work through a host of discrete mechanisms—business, education, government, voluntary groups, and the individual citizen. Yet it can meet any challenge that it recognizes.

A democratic society traditionally relies on the individual to undertake of his own volition the long cycle of education and training required to prepare him for a professional or scientific career. Presumably the rewards, monetary and psychic, are sufficient to draw the required numbers into each field. If too many or too few are attracted, the reward structure is altered until a more reasonable balance is achieved between supply and need. At any point in time there may be an imbalance between the numbers of trained personnel available and of those currently required. But this is inevitable in a dynamic economy in which demand can undergo much more rapid changes than supply.

. . . . .

The problems involved in attempting to adjust the demand and supply of trained manpower can be further illustrated by reference to engineering. Shortly before the outbreak of hostilities in Korea several professional engineering societies, in consultation with the United States Department of Labor, concluded that the outlook for engineers was not favorable; industry was unlikely to hire all of those who were in the educational pipeline. This informaton was widely broadcast, and many who had been considering engineering changed their occupational choice.

The partial mobilization which this country initiated after the fighting broke out in Korea turned the prospective oversupply into an imminent shortage, among other reasons because of substantial increases in the research and development expenditures of the Federal Government. For the next few years the engineering societies, aided and abetted by industrial and government leaders, warned that the United States was increasingly vulnerable because of the prospective shortage of young engineers. The campaign proved successful. The percentage of male college freshmen selecting engineering as a field of specialization increased from 11 per cent in 1950 to 17 per cent in 1956.

The arguments of those who, like the members of the National Manpower Council (*A Policy for Scientific and Professional Manpower*), questioned whether the shortage was one of numbers (the country had over 600,000 engineers) were viewed askance. It was easier to persuade more young people to enter engineering than to reform engineering education so that the average graduate would be better prepared or to convince industry to improve its utilization practices.

In contrast to the advocates of a large-scale expansion in the numbers to be trained as engineers, the Society of Consulting Engineers questioned the need and called attention to the possible selfish interests motivating the proponents of the proposal. The spokesmen for expansion were for the most part on the payrolls of the large industrial employers who would be in a better bargaining position if the supply were increased at somebody else's expense. . . .

. . . . .

In contrast to medicine, where the number of qualified applicants has for many years exceeded the training capacity, such important professions as the ministry, the military, and teaching have been striving for as long to attract adequate numbers of qualified individuals. These professions face similar difficulties. Each needs candidates who combine intellectual endowment with a commitment to a special scale of values. But ours is a society that, despite increases in church attendance, is not spiritually oriented; that despite international tensions remains basically anti-military; and that despite its professed respect for education considers teaching a poor career for an able male. Moreover, in each of these fields the salary scale is relatively low. The successful businessman can look forward to a substantial income. So can the successful entertainer. But the public is unwilling to pay more than a modest salary to those responsible for its souls, its minds, or its security.

Since free choice of a career is a hallowed value in a democracy, it is disquieting to see professional societies placing artificial barriers on entrance or, as has more recently been the case, using propaganda to increase the number of prospective applicants. Young people and their parents need objective information about the present state of professions and the probable trends in the demand for professional personnel in the years ahead. No one can make an intelligent choice without such reliable information. And the professional societies, government, and the educational institutions each have a responsibility in providing such information. But no one without the gift of prophecy should take it upon himself to bar young people from or entice them into a particular career. The individual should be provided with the best information available and then be permitted to make his own decision.

. . . . .

Several states have recently established scholarships to encourage more young people to enter teachers' colleges, in the hope that upon the completion of their training they will be available to teach school. The same practice is being followed for nursing and other shortage occupations. Many corporate scholarship plans follow the same general pattern except that their support is most frequently extended to young people selecting science and engineering.

There are several grounds for sounding a note of warning about this type of scholarship. Unless the total number of able people who attend college is increased, categorical scholarships rob Peter to pay Paul. Who can be sure that a bright boy who prefers to study biology but enters engineering because of a scholarship would not make a greater contribution to society if he remained with his first choice? How much useful service will the Navy get from a disgruntled college graduate who knows that if he were permitted to study graduate physics his eventual contribution to the security of his country would be much greater than as an ensign? And how sound can manpower planning be when it awards a scholarship for special training to individuals who have little intention of remaining within the field if they enter it at all? And what does it profit a society to improve its teaching of mathematics and chemistry in high school if this is done at the cost of instructing its pupils poorly in English and history?

What are the responsibilities of a democratic society toward helping its members decide about their life's work? First, as we have seen, a basic tenet of democracy is that everybody should have the right to choose his own work. Second, he should have access to the education he needs to qualify for that work. Third, he should be permitted to utilize effectively the education and training which he obtains. These are the essential responsibilities that a democratic society should assume and discharge.

The more an individual can be encouraged to develop his full potential, the better. No one should be prevented from selecting an occupation because of considerations of race, religion, sex, the economic circumstances of his family, or any other determinant which is not directly related to the question of his present or potential competence. Teachers and counselors have long been saddened by the considerable number of young people who because of their own neurotic needs or those of their parents choose occupations for which they are not suited either intellectually or emotionally.

But the major waste of potential occurs because young people aim too low, not too high. They do so because, among other reasons, they have no clear perception of their own potentialities or of the opportunities available to them in the world of work. There is great need for our society to improve the services to young people in order to help them appraise the complex occupational structure and the ways in which they can best qualify themselves for the fields of their choice. One of the most difficult challenges that the schools face is to know how to provide some understanding of this adult world for adolescents who are preoccupied with other, more immediate, problems.

. . . . .

The situation in our colleges and universities is, if anything, more serious. Here is the training ground for tomorrow's leaders—for science, business, education, government. And the men who do the training cannot support themselves and their families in even modest comfort. One insightful critic, David Riesman, has commented that the only way a man can afford to remain in academic life is to turn his wife into a drudge. At a recent faculty meeting we heard a report of the jobs obtained by our graduates of last spring. With one envious voice we asked whether the faculty could make use of the student placement service. Several of our students were earning more in their first jobs than members of the faculty were earning after ten or fifteen years of teaching.

In the nineteen thirties, the university was able to add to its teaching staff the best of its graduate students; in the forties, the second best. Today, with few exceptions, it can retain only the third best! Yet those whom it adds set the standards and are responsible for the instruction of the leaders of tomorrow.

. . . . .

A quite different aspect of utilization is suggested by the high turnover rates that characterize engineering personnel in the aircraft industry. Within any twenty-four months, approximately one third of the engineering staff leaves one company to find jobs with a competitor. This high rate of separation does not reflect a careful weeding out of the less competent engineers by management; it indicates the widespread dissatisfaction of the engineers with their working conditions and their hope to better themselves through relocation. Although some turnover is always necessary for efficient utilization, since men must experiment before they can find the work they like and can do best, the loss of one third of a professional work force every two years is preposterously high.

American corporations have been so busily engaged in scrambling for the limited number of new engineering graduates that they have paid relatively little attention to improving their utilization practices. Yet a five-per-cent improvement in the utilization of 700,000 engineers would represent a manpower gain greater than the total annual graduating class!

Another striking example of poor utilization is the failure of colleges and universities to provide adequate support for their faculty. Full professors must often write letters by hand or "hunt and peck" on the typewriter. Again, senior professors must frequently check bibliographical references when a research assistant could do this and much more for them. No businessman would pay an employee $8,000 to $10,000 annually and then permit him to waste his time in this manner. But since they operate in or close to the red, universities manage to ignore the obvious.

. . . . .

The outstanding economic progress of the Western world has been rooted at least as much in improvements that have taken place in the quality of the population as in increased investments of capital. The recent efforts of underdeveloped countries to industrialize suggest that investments in capital are not likely to yield significant returns unless they are paralleled by investments in people.

Only men and women can develop the ideas that serve as the foundations for scientific and technological progress; only men and women—even in an age of the giant computers—can manage organizations; only men and women can operate and repair the new automatic machines which produce the goods we desire; only men and women can provide services to the young and old, to the sick and well, to those seeking education or recreation. Only men and women, not financial grants or ballistic missiles, determine the strength of a government.

. . . . .

VII • POPULATION AND LABOR

Few writings have had as much influence on the development of economics as the one from which the following selection is taken. The passage here presents the main theme of the larger work.

35 • The Theory of Population

THOMAS R. MALTHUS

In an inquiry concerning the improvemen of society, the mode of conducting the subject which naturally presents itself, is, (1), to investigate the causes which have hitherto impeded the progress of mankind towards happiness; and (2), to examine the probability of the total or partial removal of these causes in the future. The principal object of this essay is to examine the effects of one great cause intimately united with the very nature of man. That is the constant tendency of all animated life to increase beyond the nourishment provided for it.

Through the animal and vegetable kingdoms Nature has scattered the seeds of life abroad with the most profuse and liberal hand. If the germs of existence contained in the earth could freely develop themselves, they would fill millions of worlds in the course of a few thousand years. Necessity, that imperious, all-pervading law of nature restrains them and man alike within prescribed bounds.

The effects of nature's check on man are complicated. Impelled to the increase of his species by an equally powerful instinct, reason interrupts his career, and asks whether he may not bring beings into the world, for whom he cannot provide the means of support. If he hear not this suggestion, the human race will be constantly endeavoring to increase beyond the means of subsistence. But as, by that law of our nature which makes food necessary to the life of man, population can never actually increase beyond the lowest nourishment capable of supporting it, a strong check on population, namely, the difficulty of acquiring food, must be constantly in operation. This difficulty must fall somewhere, and must necessarily be severely felt in some or other of the various forms of misery by a large portion of mankind. This conclusion will sufficiently appear from a review of the different states of society in which man has existed. But the subject will be seen in a clearer light if we endeavor to ascertain what would

THOMAS R. MALTHUS, *An Essay on the Principle of Population,* 6th ed., I (1826), pp. 1–24.

be the natural increase in population, if left to exert itself with perfect freedom.

Many extravagant statements have been made of the length of the period within which the population of a country can double. To be perfectly sure we are far within the truth, we will take a slow rate, and say that population, when unchecked, goes on doubling itself every 25 years, or increases in a geometrical ratio. The rate according to which the productions of the earth may be supposed to increase, it will not be so easy to determine. However, we may be perfectly certain that the ratio of their increase in a limited territory must be of a totally different nature from the ratio of the increase in population. A thousand millions are just as easily doubled every 25 years by the power of population as a thousand. But the food will by no means be obtained with the same facility. Man is confined in room. When acre has been added to acre [until] all the fertile land is occupied, the yearly increase in food must depend upon the melioration of the land already in possession. This is a fund which, from the nature of all soils, instead of increasing must be gradually diminishing. But population, could it be supplied with food, would go on with unexhausted vigor, and the increase in one period would furnish a power of increase in the next, and this without any limit. If it be allowed that by the best possible policy the average produce could be doubled in the first 25 years, it will be allowing a greater increase than could with reason be expected. In the next 25 years it is impossible to suppose that the produce could be quadrupled. It would be contrary to our knowledge of the properties of land.

Let us suppose that the yearly additions which might be made to the former average produce, instead of decreasing as they certainly would do, were to remain the same; and that the product of the land might be increased every 25 years, by a quantity equal to what it at present produces. The most enthusiastic speculator can not suppose a greater increase than this. Even then the land could not be made to increase faster than in an arithmetical ratio. Taking the whole earth, the human species would increase as the numbers 1, 2, 4, 8, 16, 32, 64, 128, 256, and subsistence as 1, 2, 3, 4, 5, 6, 7, 8, 9. In two centuries the population would be to the means of subsistence as 256 to 9; in three centuries as 4,096 to 13, and in two thousand years the difference would be almost incalculable.

In this supposition, no limits whatever are placed to the produce of the earth. It may increase forever and be greater than any assignable quantity; yet still the power of population, being in every period so much greater, the increase of the human species can only be kept down to the level of the means of subsistence by the constant operation of the strong law of necessity, acting as a check upon the greater power.

But this ultimate check to population, the want of food, is never the immediate check except in cases of famine. The latter consists in all those customs, and all those diseases, which seem to be generated by a scarcity of the means of subsistence; and all those causes which tend permanently to weaken the human frame. The checks may be classed under two general heads—the preventative and the positive.

The preventative check, peculiar to man, arises from his reasoning faculties, which enable him to calculate distant consequences. He sees the distress which frequently presses upon those who have large families; he cannot contemplate his present possessions or earnings, and calculate the amount of each share, when they must be divided, perhaps, among seven or eight, without feeling a doubt whether he may be able to support the offspring which probably will be brought into the world. Other considerations occur. Will he lower his rank in life, and be obliged to give up in great measure his former habits? Does any mode of employment present itself by which he may reasonably hope to maintain a family? Will he not subject himself to greater difficulties and more severe labor than in his present state? Will he be able to give his children adequate educational advantages? Can he face the possibility of exposing his children to poverty or charity, by his inability to provide for them? These considerations prevent a large number of people from pursuing the dictates of nature.

The positive checks to population are extremely various, and include every cause, whether arising from vice or misery, which in any degree contributes to shorten the natural duration of human life. Under this head may be enumerated all unwholesome occupations, severe labor, exposure to the seasons, extreme poverty, bad nursing of children, great towns, excesses of all kinds, the whole train of common diseases, wars, plagues, and famines.

The theory of population is resolvable into three propositions: (1) Population is necessarily limited by the means of subsistence. (2) Population invariably increases where the means of subsistence increase, unless prevented by some very powerful and obvious checks. (3) These checks which keep population on a level with the means of subsistence are all resolvable into moral restraint, vice, and misery.

36 · *Manpower: Challenge of the 1960's*

U.S. DEPARTMENT OF LABOR

In 1960 the Secretary of Labor made public a brochure-summary of a vast amount of research which his department, and others, had conducted. Highlights are presented on the following fourteen pages.

U.S. DEPARTMENT OF LABOR, "Manpower: Challenge of the 1960's" (Washington, D.C.: U.S. Department of Labor, 1960).

the United States has the manpower resources for a much higher standard of living during the 1960s

Our manpower potential is great enough, with an improving technology, to increase the production of goods and services by about 50% from 1960 to 1970.

This means that by 1970 we can provide our expanding population with a 25% increase in its standard of living.

our population will increase from 180 to 208 million up 28 million, or 15%, over the decade

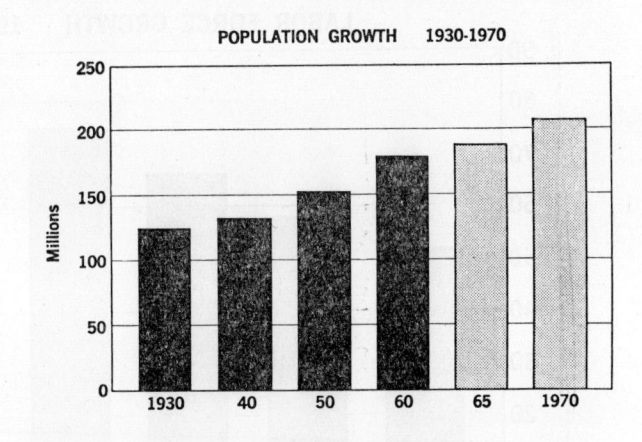

POPULATION GROWTH   1930-1970

ESPECIALLY RAPID POPULATION GROWTH WILL OCCUR AMONG YOUTH REACHING WORKING AGE

YOUNG PERSONS REACHING 18 ANNUALLY
1950 to 1970

The number of young people reaching 18 each year,
    ready to enter the labor force
    or go on to college,
will increase from 2.6 million in 1960 to 3.8 million in the single year 1965, a rise of nearly 50%.

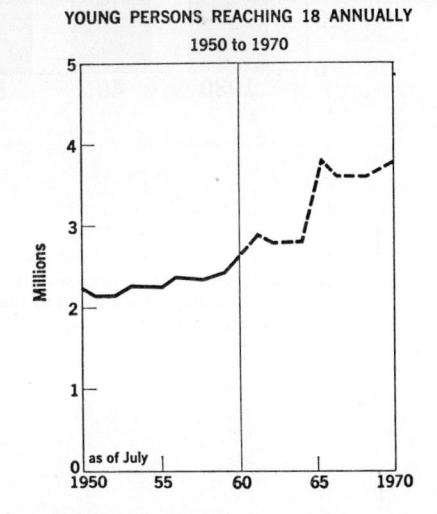

the number of workers will grow faster, by nearly 20%
up 13.5 million to 87 million in 1970

The increase in the number of workers during the 1960's will be by far the largest for any 10-year period in our history — 50% greater than during the 1950's.

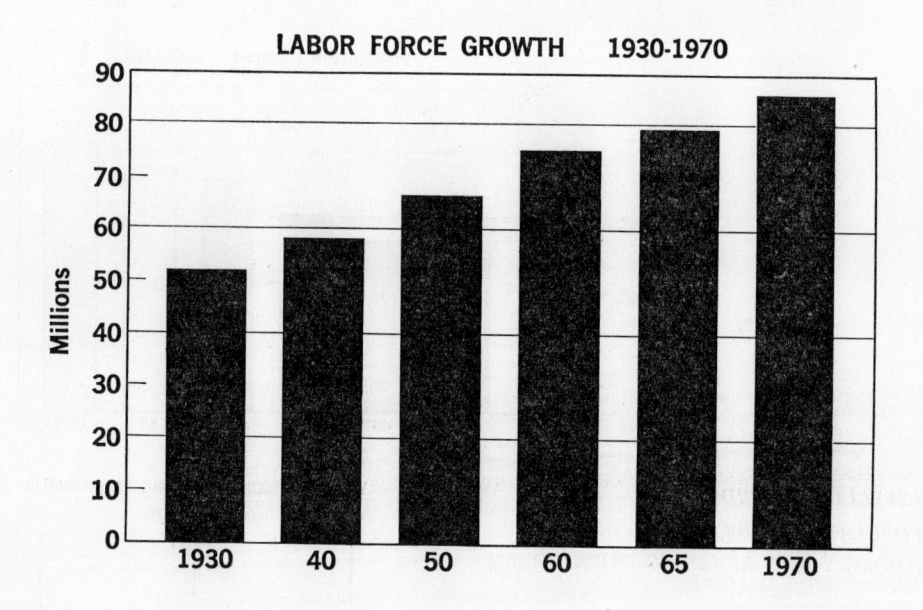

LABOR FORCE GROWTH   1930-1970

Along with this large increase in the total number of workers, major changes will take place in the composition of the labor force and in the kinds of jobs which the economy will demand.

young workers will account for a major share of the changes in the working population during the 1960s

THERE WILL BE:

MANY MORE YOUNG WORKERS
Workers under 25 will account for nearly half of the labor force growth during the 1960's, even though they will stay in school longer.

A RELATIVELY SMALL INCREASE AMONG WORKERS 25-34

ACTUALLY FEWER WORKERS AGE 35-44

Many of these persons were born during the depression of the 1930's when birth rates were low.

LARGER NUMBERS OF OLDER WORKERS

More workers will be 45 years and over in 1970 than in 1960, despite earlier retirements.

**CHANGES IN THE NUMBER OF WORKERS IN EACH AGE GROUP
1950 to 1960 and 1960 to 1970**

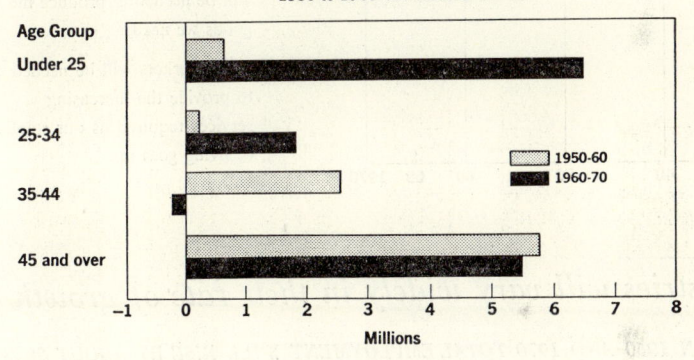

and the number of women workers will increase at nearly twice the rate for men

By 1970,
there will be about 30 million women workers,
six million more than in 1960. This represents a 25% increase for women, as compared to a 15% increase for men.
One out of every three workers will be a woman.

Except for teen-age girls (most of them still in school) and women 65 and over (most of them either retired or past working age), at least two out of every five women in 1970 will be in the labor force.

Among women whose children are in school or past school age, the proportion who work will be much higher than now.

as the economy grows, changes take place
in its industrial makeup

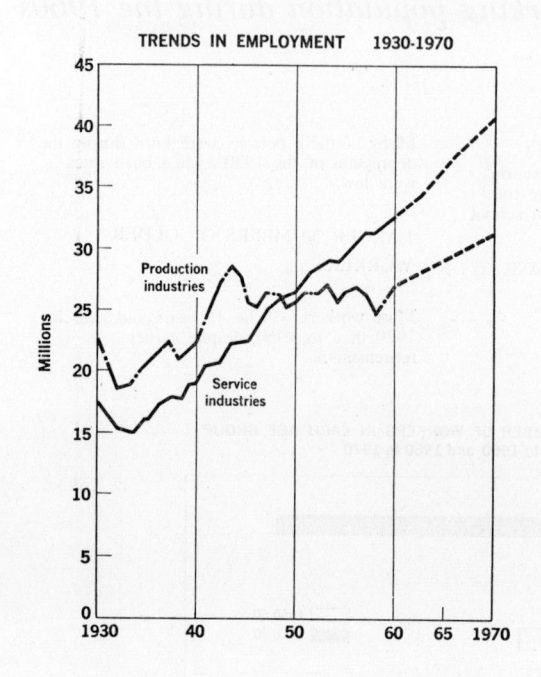

TRENDS IN EMPLOYMENT 1930-1970

(Chart showing Production industries and Service industries employment in millions from 1930 to 1970)

EMPLOYMENT WILL CONTINUE TO GROW FASTER IN THE SERVICE INDUSTRIES THAN IN THE PRODUCTION INDUSTRIES

As our technology advances, proportionately fewer workers will be needed to produce the goods we need.

More workers will be needed to provide the increasing services required as our standard of living goes up.

and industries will vary widely in their rate of growth

BETWEEN 1960 AND 1970 TOTAL EMPLOYMENT WILL RISE BY ABOUT 20%

Here is how the major industries in the United States are expected to grow in the next ten years, compared with the over-all rise in employment.

COMPARED WITH 20% RISE IN TOTAL EMPLOYMENT

ACTUAL DECLINE	INDUSTRY	MUCH SLOWER	ABOUT SAME	FASTER	MUCH FASTER
	Construction				→
	Finance, insurance, real estate				→
	Trade			→	
	Government services			→	
	All other services			→	
	Manufacturing		→		
	Transportation and public utilities	→			
	Mining	→			
← Agriculture					

the kinds of jobs industry will need workers for

are also changing

and the biggest increases will occur in occupations

requiring the most education and training

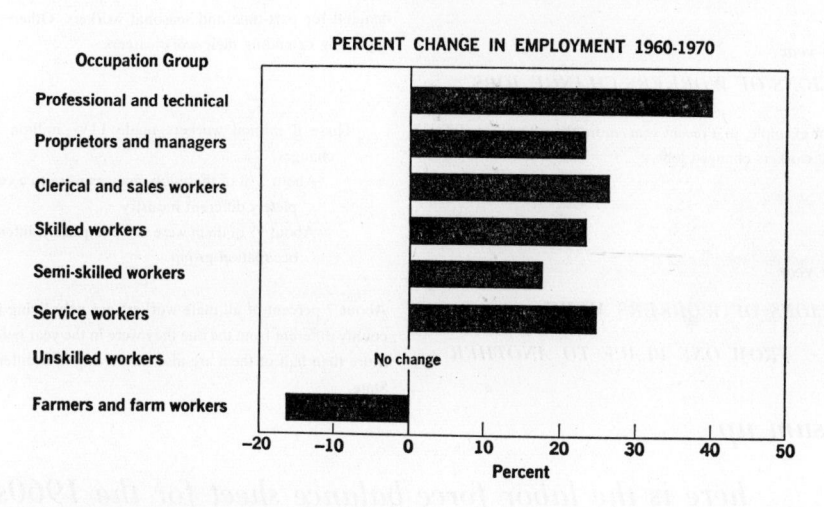

PERCENT CHANGE IN EMPLOYMENT 1960-1970

Occupation Group	Percent Change
Professional and technical	~40
Proprietors and managers	~22
Clerical and sales workers	~25
Skilled workers	~22
Semi-skilled workers	~18
Service workers	~25
Unskilled workers	No change
Farmers and farm workers	~-17

Average years of school completed of those working in 1959

Occupation Group	Years
Professional & technical	16.2
Proprietors & managers	12.4
Clerical & sales	12.5
Skilled	11.0
Semi-skilled	9.9
Service	9.7
Unskilled	8.6
Farmers & farm workers	8.6

These anticipated changes in employment in various occupation groups during the coming decade will result from several major causes:

√ The continuing shift from an agricultural economy to one that is predominantly industrial

√ The rapid expansion in research and development activities

√ The tremendously rapid increase in application of technological improvements

√ The increasing size and complexity of business organization

√ The widespread growth of record keeping among all types of enterprises

√ The growing need for educational and medical services

The United States has a highly mobile labor force

every year

MILLIONS OF WORKERS VOLUNTARILY COME IN AND OUT OF THE LABOR FORCE

Many more persons work at some time during the year than are employed at any one time. Most of them enter the labor force for a short while only, to help meet the demand for part-time and seasonal workers. Others are beginning or ending their work careers.

every year

MILLIONS OF WORKERS CHANGE JOBS

For example, in a recent year, more than 8 million different workers changed jobs.

These 8 million workers made 11½ million job changes.
- About 2/3 of these job changes were to a completely different industry.
- About ½ of them were to a completely different occupation group.

every year

MILLIONS OF WORKERS MOVE FROM ONE PLACE TO ANOTHER

About 7 percent of all male workers are now living in a county different from the one they were in the year before. More than half of them are also now living in a different State.

to sum up

here is the labor force balance sheet for the 1960s

	Millions
Number of workers in 1960	73.6
SUBTRACT:	
Withdrawals from the labor force because of death, retirement, marriage, child-bearing, etc.	−15.5
1960 workers still in labor force in 1970	58.1
ADD:	
Young workers coming into the labor force during the 1960s	26.0
Women returning to the labor force during the 1960s	3.0
Number of workers in 1970	87.1

BECAUSE OF THE MANY CHANGES EXPECTED IN OUR LABOR FORCE THE NATION WILL HAVE TO FACE MAJOR CHALLENGES IF IT IS TO MAKE THE BEST USE OF ITS MANPOWER

Here are some of the groups requiring special attention
- New young workers
- Middle aged and older workers
- Negro workers
- Farm workers
- Part-time workers, many of them working mothers

the number of new young workers

will increase sharply during the 1960s

By the late 1960s three million new young workers will enter the labor force each year, as compared with TWO MILLION A YEAR now starting their work careers.

Altogether 26 million new young workers will enter the labor force during the 1960s—almost 40% more than during the 1950s.

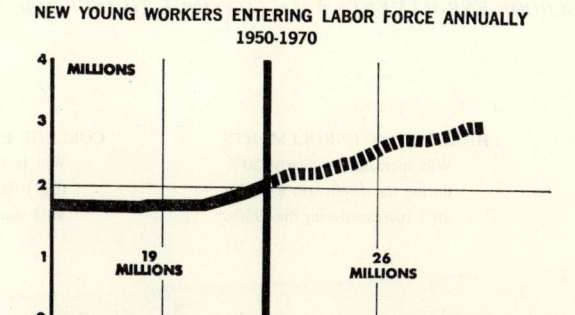

NEW YOUNG WORKERS ENTERING LABOR FORCE ANNUALLY 1950-1970

19 MILLIONS — 26 MILLIONS

THIS LARGE NUMBER OF NEW YOUNG WORKERS WILL MEAN THAT . . .

EMPLOYERS
- Will find they have even a bigger stake in a sound educational system
- Will have to employ a larger proportion of young and inexperienced persons
- Will have to provide more and better training on the job, and concentrate on supervision and safety education
- Will have to expect more turnover
- Will have to allow for more part-time workers

YOUNG WORKERS
- Will have to prepare themselves for a rapidly changing and more complex world of work
- Will need more education and training, with better guidance and counseling
- Will have to compete more keenly for the better jobs

education and training in the United States
will get even more emphasis during the 1960s

SCHOOL ENROLLMENTS WILL CONTINUE TO INCREASE SIGNIFICANTLY

HIGH SCHOOL ENROLLMENTS
Will increase by nearly 50% during the 1960s—on top of a 40% increase during the 1950s.

COLLEGE ENROLLMENTS
Will increase by 70% during the 1960s—as compared with 40% during the 1950s.

NEW YOUNG WORKERS WILL HAVE MORE EDUCATION

70% of new young entrants to the labor force in the 1960s will be high school graduates or better, as compared with 60% in the 1950s.

AMOUNT OF SCHOOLING OF NEW YOUNG WORKERS IN THE 1960s and 1950s

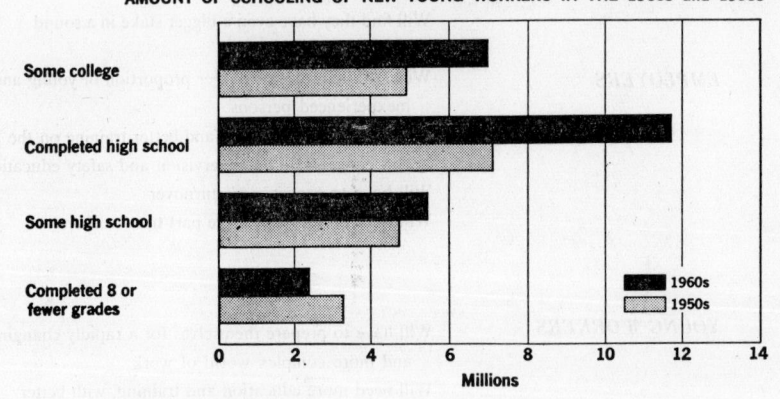

210

but, millions of new young workers will not have had a high school education

**EMPLOYERS WILL REQUIRE AT LEAST
HIGH SCHOOL DIPLOMAS FOR MORE AND MORE JOBS**

NEVERTHELESS

7.5 million young people entering the labor force during the 1960s will not have completed high school.

AND 2.5 MILLION OF THESE will not have completed even a grade school education.

THE PROSPECT THAT 30% OF ALL YOUNG WORKERS ENTERING THE LABOR FORCE DURING THE 1960s WILL LACK A HIGH SCHOOL EDUCATION — POINTS TO THE NEED TO:

Encourage boys and girls to get all the education and training possible.

Develop courses of training designed to meet the needs of these young people.

Provide guidance and counseling earlier in their school years.

the kind and amount of education young persons receive affect their lifetime careers

PEOPLE WHO WORK
    IN THESE OCCUPATIONS

HAVE THIS KIND OF EDUCATION
Percent with

	Less than high school graduation	High school graduation	Some college education
Professional and technical workers	6	19	75
Proprietors and managers	38	33	29
Clerical or sales workers	25	53	22
Skilled workers	59	33	8
Semi-skilled workers	70	26	4
Service workers	69	25	6
Unskilled workers	80	17	3
Farmers and farm workers	76	19	5

IN GENERAL, THOSE WITH MORE SCHOOLING HAVE HIGHER EARNINGS
MOREOVER
UNEMPLOYMENT IS MUCH HIGHER AMONG THOSE WITH THE LEAST EDUCATION

PERCENT UNEMPLOYED BY AMOUNT OF EDUCATION — 1959

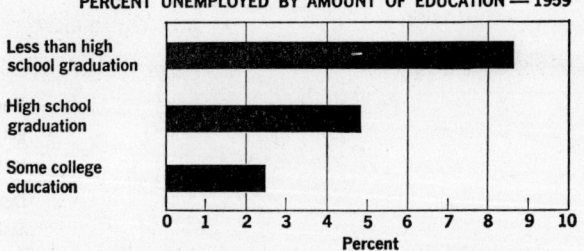

Less than high school graduation
High school graduation
Some college education

during the 1960s 2 out of 5 workers will be 45 years or older

By 1970, over 33 million men and women 45 years or older will belong to the labor force, 5.5 million more than in 1960.

OLDER WORKERS
Have the skill and work experience needed for our growing economy

They now account for a significant proportion of our managerial and skilled workers.

PERCENT OF WORKERS IN EACH MAJOR OCCUPATION GROUP WHO ARE 45 OR OLDER — 1959

- Proprietors and managers
- Farmers and farm workers
- Service workers
- Skilled workers
- Professional and technical
- Clerical or sales workers
- Semi-skilled workers
- Unskilled workers

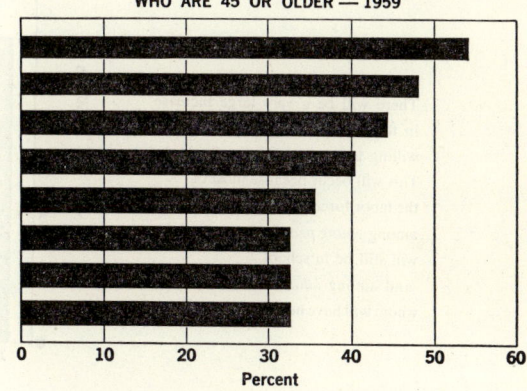

PERCENT UNEMPLOYED IN EACH AGE GROUP 1959

PERCENT UNEMPLOYED IN EACH AGE GROUP OUT OF WORK 15 WEEKS OR MORE 1959

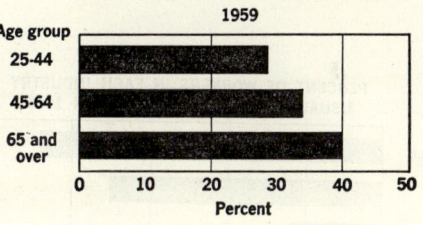

Age group
- 25-44
- 45-64
- 65 and over

OLDER WORKERS
Do not experience a markedly different rate of unemployment than do workers in other age groups.

BUT
Once out of work, they remain unemployed for longer periods of time.

THESE FACTS POINT TO

The need to eliminate discrimination in hiring on the basis of age.

The need for training and retraining of older persons to help them keep up to date on technological changes.

more people will choose to work part time

16 million persons will be part-time workers in 1970, a 30 percent increase from 1960.

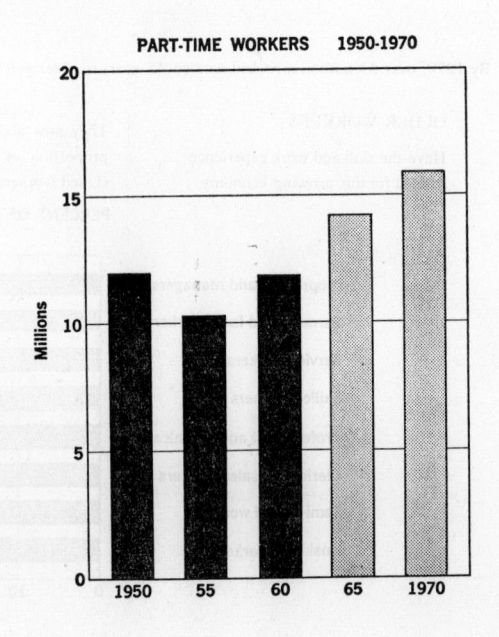

There will be a very large increase in the number of persons able and willing to work only part time. This will occur because most of the labor force growth will be among *young people*, many of whom will still be in school,
 and among *adult women*, many of whom will have home responsibilities.

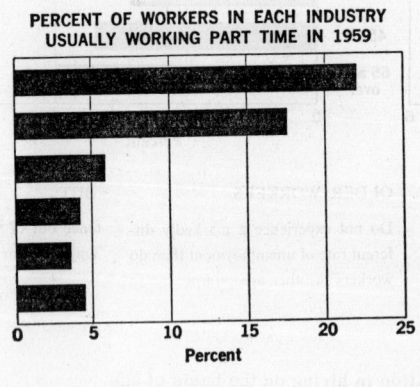

PART-TIME WORKERS 1950-1970

PERCENT OF WORKERS IN EACH INDUSTRY USUALLY WORKING PART TIME IN 1959

Industry
- Service and finance
- Trade
- Construction
- Transportation and public utilities
- Manufacturing
- Other

The increase in the number of part-time workers
will provide employers with a flexible manpower supply

BUT

other industries as well as trade and service
will have to reschedule more of their jobs to a part-time basis
if this large supply of workers is to be used effectively.

214

Negro workers represent an important manpower resource

One out of every ten workers is a Negro.

For a variety of reasons—lack of education and experience, discrimination—many Negro workers are not being used to their fullest capabilities.

The kinds of jobs in which Negro workers are employed are substantially different from those of white workers.

These job differences have become less pronounced in recent years.

For example, the percent of Negro workers in professional, clerical, sales and skilled jobs has doubled during the past 20 years.

NEVERTHELESS, THERE IS STILL A LONG WAY TO GO in the development and effective use of Negro workers.

OCCUPATIONAL DISTRIBUTION OF NEGRO AND WHITE WORKERS IN 1959

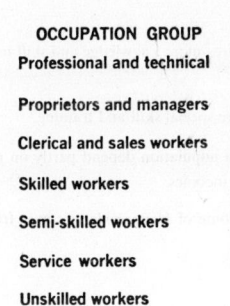

OCCUPATION GROUP	White	Negro
Professional and technical	11	4
Proprietors and managers	11	2
Clerical and sales workers	22	7
Skilled workers	14	6
Semi-skilled workers	18	20
Service workers	10	32
Unskilled workers	5	15
Farmers and farm workers	8	13

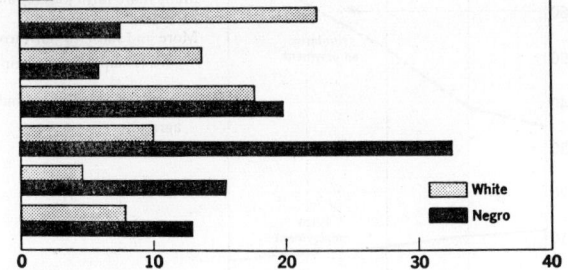

many of our manpower resources will come

from the farm population

The number of persons living on farms has decreased substantially over the years.

The movement of farm people to urban areas has been one of the major trends of this century, reflecting in part the continuing reduction in farm manpower requirements.

YOUNG PEOPLE, ESPECIALLY, ARE LEAVING THE FARMS IN GREATER PROPORTION THAN ANY OTHER AGE GROUP

They will need the kind of education and guidance that will help them adjust to work and to compete for the better jobs in nonfarm settings.

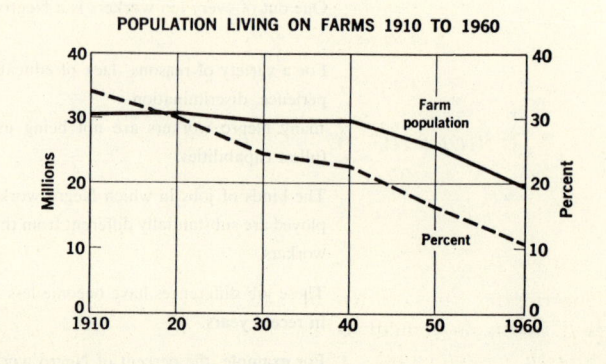

POPULATION LIVING ON FARMS 1910 TO 1960

PERSONS WHO REMAIN ON THE FARMS WILL ALSO NEED BETTER EDUCATION AND TRAINING

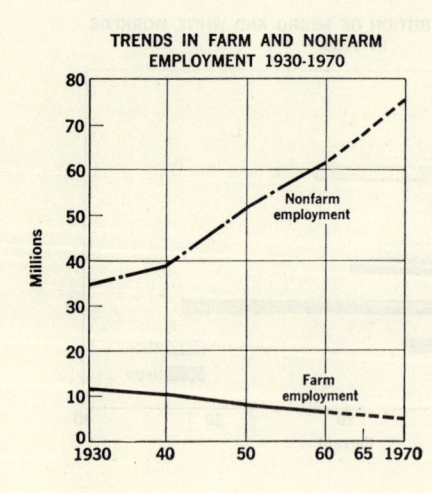

TRENDS IN FARM AND NONFARM EMPLOYMENT 1930-1970

Farming as a business requires more knowledge and skill to operate effectively.

Many more farm jobs require special skill and training.

More and more of our farm population depend partly on nonfarm jobs to supplement their incomes.

Almost one-third of all income of farm residents comes from non-agricultural sources.

216

Fundamental, but often ignored, economic and social problems arising from the development of large, strong labor organizations are analyzed in the selection that follows. The author was a Professor of Economics at the University of Chicago.

37 • *Unions as Monopolies*

HENRY C. SIMONS

Questioning the virtues of the organized labor movement is like attacking religion, monogamy, motherhood, or the home. Among the modern intelligentsia any doubts about collective bargaining admit of explanation only in terms of insanity, knavery, or subservience to "the interests." Discussion of skeptical views runs almost entirely in terms of how one came by such persuasions, as though they were symptoms of disease. One simply cannot argue that organization is injurious to labor; one is either for labor or against it, and the test is one's attitude toward unionism. But let me indicate from the outset that my central interest, and the criterion in terms of which I wish to argue, is a maximizing of aggregate labor income and a minimizing of inequality. If unionism were good for labor as a whole, that would be the end of the issue for me, since the community whose welfare concerns us is composed overwhelmingly of laborers.

Our problem here, at bottom, is one of broad political philosophy. Advocates of trade unionism are, I think, obligated morally and intellectually to present a clear picture of the total political-economic system toward which they would have us move. For my part, I simply cannot conceive of any tolerable or enduring order in which there exists widespread organization of workers along occupational, industrial, functional lines. Sentimentalists view such developments merely as a contest between workers who earn too little and enterprises which earn too much; and, unfortunately, there has been enough monopsony in labor markets to make this view superficially plausible, though not enough to make it descriptively important. What we generally fail to see is the identity of interest between the whole community and enterprises seeking to keep down costs. Where enterprise is competitive—and substantial, enduring restraint of competition in product markets is rare—enterprisers represent the community interest effectively; indeed, they are merely intermediaries between consumers of goods and sellers of services. Thus we commonly overlook the conflict of interest between every large organized group of laborers and the community as a whole. What I want to ask is how this conflict

---

HENRY C. SIMONS, *Economic Policy for a Free Society* (Chicago: University of Chicago Press, 1948), pp. 121–123, 129–131, 139–140, 142–148, 152–153. Originally published in the *Journal of Political Economy* (March 1944), pp. 1–25. Used by permission.

can be reconciled, how the power of strongly organized sellers can be limited out of regard for the general welfare. No insuperable problem arises so long as organization is partial and precarious, so long as most unions face substantial nonunion competition, or so long as they must exercise monopoly powers sparingly because of organizational insecurity. Weak unions have no large monopoly powers. But how does a democratic community limit the demands and exactions of strong, secure organizations? Looking at the typographers, the railway brotherhoods, and metropolitan building trades, among others, one answers simply: "It doesn't!"

In an economy of intricate division of labor, every large organized group is in a position at any time to disrupt or to stop the whole flow of social income; and the system must soon break down if groups persist in exercising that power or if they must continuously be bribed to forego its disastrous exercise. There is no means, save internal competition, to protect the whole community against organized labor minorities and, indeed, no other means to protect the common interests of organized groups themselves. The dilemma here is not peculiar to our present economic order; it must appear in any kind of system. This minority-monopoly problem would be quite as serious for a democratic socialism as it is for the mixed individualist-collectivist system of the present. It is the rock on which our present system is most likely to crack up; and it is the rock on which democratic socialism would be destroyed if it could ever come into being at all.

All the grosser mistakes in economic policy, if not most manifestations of democratic corruption, arise from focusing upon the interests of people as producers rather than upon their interests as consumers, that is, from acting on behalf of producer minorities rather than on behalf of the whole community as sellers of services and buyers of products. One gets the right answers usually by regarding simply the interests of consumers, since we are all consumers; and the answers reached by this approach are presumably the correct ones for laborers as a whole. But one does not get elected by approaching issues in this way!

. . . . .

I do not assert that our only monopoly problems lie in the labor market. Save for the monopolies which government is promoting in agriculture, however, no others seem comparably important for the future. It is shameful to have permitted the growth of vast corporate empires, the collusive restraint of trade by trade associations, and the gross abuse of patent privilege for extortion, exclusion, and output restriction. But enterprise monopoly is also a skin disease, easy to correct when and if we will, and usually moderate in its abuses, since its powers are necessarily small, and since the danger of political reckoning is never very remote. Enterprise monopoly, enjoying very limited access to violence and facing heavy penalties for unfair methods against rivals, is always plagued by competition, actual and potential, and must always operate against a deeply hostile, if lethargic, attitude of courts, legislatures, and the public. In exceptional cases it has acquired vast power and sustained power over long periods. In many cases it has transformed salutary price competition into perverse and wasteful "competition" in merchandising and advertising. But, to repeat, the proper remedies here are not very difficult technically or politically.

Labor monopolies are, now or potentially, a different kind of animal. If much violence has been used against them as they struggled into existence, this should not obscure the fact that, once established, they enjoy an access to violence that is unparalled in other monopolies. If governments have tolerated flagrant violations of law by employers, they are nearly impotent to enforce laws against mass minorities even if majority opinion permitted it. Thus, unions may deal with scabs in ways which make even Rockefeller's early methods seem polite and legitimate. They have little to fear from chiselers in their own midst; and they have now little to fear from Congress or the courts.

Patently restrictive practices are now commonly deplored and, perhaps because unnecessary, seem somewhat on the wane. But there have been many cases of severe limitations upon entry —high initiation fees, excessive periods of apprenticeship and restrictions upon numbers of apprentices, barriers to movement between related trades, and, of course, make-work restrictions, cost-increasing working rules, and prohibition of cost-reducing innovations, notably in the building trades—not to mention racial and sex discriminations against which effective competition in labor markets is probably a necessary, if not a sufficient, protection.

It is not commonly recognized, however, that control of wage rates *is* control of entry, especially where seniority rules are in force and, even failing such rules, where qualitative selection is important and turnover itself very costly to firms. If able to enforce standard rates, experienced, established workers can insulate themselves from the competition of new workers merely by making their cost excessive, that is, by establishing labor costs and wage expectations which preclude expansion of production or employment in their field. New and displaced workers typically migrate, not to high-wage occupations but to places where employment opportunities exist; high wages are less attractive if jobs cannot be had. Wage control, determining a major element in operating cost, also determines the rate at which a whole industry will expand or, more likely, with strong organization, the rate of contraction.

. . . . .

Consider also the untoward effects of standard rates on new and venturesome enterprise. The most vital competition commonly arises from firms content to experiment with new locations and relatively untrained labor. Such enterprises must offer workers better terms than they have received in alternative previous employment but cannot offer the wages paid to highly specialized, selected workers in established centers. If compelled to offer such terms, they will not arise. Yet it is obviously one of the finest services of new and venturesome enterprise to find better uses for existing labor and to employ more productively than theretofore labor resources that need not be confined to activities of low value. Indeed, every new firm must do this in large measure. Old established firms have skimmed off the cream of the labor supply and have trained their workers to a substantial superiority over the inexperienced. If potential competitors must pay the same wages as old firms, the established enterprises will be nearly immune to new competition, just as high-grade workers are immune to the competition of poorer grades. Here again one sees an alarming identity of interest between organized workers and employers and a rising barrier to entry of new firms, as well as to entry of new workers.

. . . . .

Organization is a device by which privilege may be intrenched and consolidated. It is a device by which the strong may raise themselves higher by pressing down the weak. Unionism, barring entry into the most attractive employments, makes high wages higher and low wages lower. Universally applied, it gets nowhere save to create disorder. Surely we cannot all get rich by restricting production. Monopoly works when everyone does not try it or when few have effective power. Universally applied it is like universal, uniform subsidy paid out of universal, uniform taxation, save that the latter is merely ridiculous while the former is also incompatible with economy of resources and even with order. But the dictator will be installed long before monopoly or functional organization becomes universal. Must we leave it to the man on horseback, or to popes of the future, to restore freedom of opportunity and freedom of occupational movement?

Unionism is only incidentally a means for raising labor incomes at the expense of profits or property income. Profits are usually a small moiety, sometimes positive and often negative; and all property income is a margin whose reduction by particular wage increases reacts promptly and markedly upon employment, production, and product price. Increased labor cost in particular areas has its impact upon earnings; but, as with excise taxes, the burden or incidence quickly transfers to the buyer of products, if not to sellers of services, via output changes.

Labor demands may be rationalized and popularized as demands for a larger share of earnings—as part of a contest over the shares of labor and capital in particular outputs. But enterprises remain essentially intermediaries between sellers of services and buyers of product. The semblance of struggle between labor and capital conceals the substantial conflict between a labor monopoly and the community; between organized workers and consumers; and especially between established workers in more remunerative occupations and workers elsewhere. The masses of the unorganized and unorganizable lose as consumers; they lose by being denied access to higher-wage areas; and they lose by an artificial abundance of labor in the markets where they must sell, that is, by being forced to compete with workers who should have been drawn off into the higher-wage occupations. And let no one infer that their problem would be solved if they too were organized. The monopoly racket, like that of tariffs and subsidies, works only so long as it is exceptional—works only to advantage minorities relatively, with over-all diseconomy and loss.

. . . . .

The situation here is especially alarming when one considers it from the viewpoint of enterprises or investors. In a free-market world, every commitment of capital is made in the face of enormous uncertainties. One may lose heavily or gain vastly, depending on unpredictable (uninsurable) contingencies. For reasonably intelligent investors, however, the gamble, with free markets, is a fairly even one, with chances of gain balancing roughly the risks of loss —relative to a conservative commitment, say, in government bonds. The willingness to take chances, to venture with one's property, especially in new and novel enterprises, of course, is the very basis of our whole economic and political system. It is now gravely jeopardized by developments that tend ominously to diminish the chances of gain relative to the chances of loss.

Much has been made of our taxes as factors inhibiting enterprise; but . . . we can, by proper reforms, mitigate the bias of taxes against venturesome investment, while strengthening the progressive principle and applying it more fully. But the bias against new investment inherent in labor organization is important and cannot be removed by changes in matters of detail. Investors now face nearly all the disagreeable uncertainties of investors in a free-market world plus the prospect that labor organizations will appropriate most or all of the earnings that would otherwise accrue if favorable contingencies materialized. Indeed, every new, long-term commitment of capital is now a matter of giving hostages to organized sellers of complementary services. Enterprisers must face all the old risks of investing in the wrong places—risks of demand changes, of technical obsolescence in plant facilities, and of guessing badly only because too many others guessed the same way. Besides, they must risk being unable to recover the productivity which their assets would have if there were freemarket access to complementary factors. The prospect for losses is as good as ever; the prospect of profits is, in the main, profoundly impaired.

If we are to preserve modern industrial production without totalitarian control, we must solve the problem of private investment. . . . I believe that investment opportunities were never so large as now, . . . if owners of new capital assets could be assured of free-market access to labor and other complementary factors (mainly indirect labor). But the prospect of such access has diminished everywhere. Every new enterprise and every new investment must now pay heavy tribute to labor (and other monopolies) in acquiring its plant and equipment; and it faces the prospect of increasing extortion in its efforts to utilize facilities after they are constructed. (Labor monopolies are highly concentrated in construction and in capital-goods industries generally; they are also peculiarly characteristic of the more capital-intensive industries.)

. . . . .

In the name of equalizing bargaining power we have sanctioned and promoted the proliferation of militant labor monopolies whose proper, natural function is exploitation of consumers. The ultimate burden of their exactions will not fall mainly upon industrial investors or enterprises; but enterprises, as intermediaries, will bear the impact of new exactions and may expect to see earnings continuously pressed down to such extent that the average expectations are utterly discouraging. For industrial investors, the result is much the same as though the state had promoted organized banditry and denied them all protection against it—while offering unusual safeguards to holders of idle funds (deposits) and large new investment outlets in government bonds (not to mention "tax-exempts").

. . . . .

To repeat, we have never faced the kind of minority problem which widespread, aggressive, national and regional unions and their federations present. They are essentially occupational armies, born and reared amidst violence, led by fighters, and capable of becoming peaceful only as their power becomes irresistible.

Other groups practice violence, of course; but few others practice it with general public approbation or employ it at all without grave risks of punishment or loss of power. Peaceful strikes, even in the absence of overt violence or intimidation, are a meaningless conception when they involve disruption of an elaborate production process with intricate division of labor. What is obvious in the case of railways and utilities is similarly true of coal-mining, steel production, and ultimately of every important industry and occupation.

Some conservatives will defend labor organization in terms of the right of voluntary association as a basic privilege in a democratic system, while deploring the use of violence and intimidation. Obviously, the practical problem would largely disappear if laws protecting persons and property were enforcible and enforced against strikers, pickets, and labor organizers. But there are no absolute rights; and the right of voluntary association must always be qualified, *inter alia,* by prohibitions against monopolizing—against collusive action among sellers. Failing ability to use violence or to threaten it effectively, particular organizations could not practice heavy extortion or sustain it indefinitely; but they could often tax the community substantially for a time and subject it to substantial, if minor, disturbances. The grave diseconomies of the theorist's pure cartel situation, in labor and other markets, are relevant to real situations, actual and possible; and protection of the public interest demands limitation of the right of association where the association is of people as suppliers of particular commodities or services.

. . . . .

[Compare Simons' 1944 statement with the following one from "Industrial Relations—1975," an address given at Michigan State University, April 1957, by J. S. Bugas, who has charge of labor relations of the Ford Motor Company. Ed.]

Examine the statements that union leaders make to their membership, read the literature aimed at their constituents, observe the activities and records of their conventions and one must realize that the power and tenure even of those union leaders who present the most calm and reasoned aspect to the outside world depend on appearing to their constituents as fighters defying all dangers and obstacles to advance the group interest. Indeed, so ingrained is this concept in the institutional dynamics of the mass union movement as it exists today that union leadership would have to invent an adversary if it did not have one.

An equally disturbing fact is that organized labor's power puts it in position to stifle some public criticism of its activities. Clearly the power to suppress adverse comment by those outside the movement who know labor best—the management people who have daily dealings with it—is a factor to be reckoned with. The reluctance of many people in management to speak out is not a mere matter of distaste for the vilification—the name-calling, the accusations of reaction and anti-unionism—which labor frequently heaps upon its critics. . . .

The real basis for this reluctance to speak out is the union's power of economic retaliation. Retaliation need not take the form of a dramatic strike, called for that purpose. It can be made effective in a countless variety of subtle ways—but they all add up to more trouble, more cost in the shop, more difficulty in getting along with the union. Too often management decides not to risk it, and this is not healthy. . . .

It is inherent in the nature of things that unions will make excessive demands which call for resistance. This, of course, exposes management to all sorts of charges by union leadership, which, as I remarked earlier, needs an "enemy."

It is important that there be general understanding of this union tactic. For it is essential to the preservation of the bargaining process that both the nature and the indispensability of management's role be understood.

A Congressional Subcommittee under the Chairmanship of Senator John L. McClellan has for several years been looking into the practices of labor unions. What is nearly a five-foot shelf of volumes of testimony reveals shocking abuses. One striking sample is summarized below.

38 · Abuses of Union Power

KENNETH O. GILMORE

One of the sorriest chapters of self-serving in American history has been unfolding in the last half decade. It is the shameful undermining of our three-billion-dollar-a-year missile and space effort by reckless union leaders and their too willing followers. Even worse is the way our arthritic federal bureaucracy timidly allowed this hijacking of our government through harassments and blackmail to continue. In five years the ballistic-missile bases and test sites have been beset by 330 strikes and walkouts, with a loss of 163,000 priceless man-days—all this at a time when Soviet ability to fire long-range nuclear missiles has launched us on an incredibly expensive crash program to make our ICBM weapons ready for operation. . . .

"Wildcat strikes, work stoppages, slowdowns, featherbedding and a deliberate policy of low productivity on the part of some unions and workers may well be responsible to a substantial degree for whatever lagging behind exists in our space and missile programs. This concerns every man, woman and child in the country who loves freedom. If greed, graft and extortion are to dominate our way of life and our economy, especially in a program vital to our survival, it is time for Americans to wake up."

These were the words of Sen. John L. McClellan after testimony was presented at the recent hearings. . . . For five months the subcommittee's investigators dug into records and fanned out across the land to question hundreds of persons at union and contract offices, missile-assembly plants and ICBM launching centers. Some 40 witnesses from labor, industry and government were brought to the Capitol to testify under oath. . . .

As a reporter I listened to the testimony before that Congressional subcommittee. Then, to measure fully the damage done by the strikes and boycotts, I traveled 7000 miles. . . . At missile sites, on launching pads, deep inside subterranean silos, in blockhouses and construction trailers, I talked with the men shouldering the day-and-night rush assignment of tooling up our space weapons.

One stop was at the missile complex near Lowry Air Force Base at Denver,

---

KENNETH O. GILMORE, "The Scandal of Our Missile Program," *Reader's Digest* (August 1961), copyright, 1961, by The Reader's Digest Association, Inc. Used by permission.

Colo., where . . . 350 craft-union workers put down their tools last April at shelters being built for Titan intercontinental ballistic missiles. A month and a half earlier, construction-union chieftains had issued a stirring pledge not to strike our missile bases until they had exhausted every means for a peaceful settlement. Yet since that pledge, there have been a half dozen craft walkouts on missile bases, with 34 more strikes by other unions.

The Lowry incident began when building-trades workers of all types remained away from the missile complex three days. Why? To press a ridiculous demand that a handful of craft workers be allowed to maintain and operate an intricate subterranean powerhouse where the work had been turned over to employes of the Martin Company, who were represented by another union. . . . It was a blatantly illegal walkout.

Less than two weeks later another walkout occurred at the missile sites. The reason was much the same. This time the walkout spread like a disease to 4000 strikers. Construction on 11 ballistic-missile locations was paralyzed, not only at Lowry but at Atlas pads scattered through northern Colorado. When the union men finally went back to work after five days, our race to offset Russia's awesome missile striking power had been retarded by 64,000 priceless man-hours.

Yet none of these workers was ever penalized or disciplined. On the contrary, they were rewarded. Upon returning to work, many collected generous overtime pay checks because the construction had to go ahead around the clock so as not to fall further behind.

Consider some of the outrageous excuses craft-union members have given for delaying the missile program. Pipefitters, electricians and asbestos workers in Colorado wanted to make their own coffee—so they walked out. Cement finishers in Florida said painters must not fill small holes with the same tool the finishers use, a trowel—so the finishers walked out. Electricians protested elimination of overtime, while ironworkers contended they were too tired to work—so they all walked out. . . .

Why has all this labor sandbagging of our missile effort been tolerated through the years—until the McClellan subcommittee began laying the evidence on the record?

The answer lies in our government's ponderous red tape and in officials cowering before the whim of union demands. It has been their naïve hope that if they bowed to the demands, the problem would disappear. Labor Department bureaucrats have refused to take the decisive action that long ago could have nipped this trouble in the bud. . . .

Nor is management entirely blameless. With taxpayers picking up the bills, some companies have permitted featherbedding, loafing and molasses-like production so as to curry the favor of union bosses and avoid walkouts. Testimony before McClellan revealed how buying of labor peace reached a ridiculous point when company technicians at Cape Canaveral, performing a necessary job, unhooked 1000 wires in a blockhouse. The next day craft-union electricians claimed it was their work and demanded that these same wires be reattached. Once this was done, the craft workers unfastened the wires a second time, at $3.75 an hour.

Step with me into the small blueprint-spattered quarters of a major in charge of three ICBM silo projects at sprawling Vandenberg Air Force Base northwest of Los Angeles. Just yards away sit subterranean launching pads burrowed into the hills overlooking the Pacific. Here, on strict orders from the Pentagon, nothing is officially to be said about the strikes and walkouts which in just one year at Vandenberg alone caused a stoppage one out of every ten days. Yet when the doors close, the conversation voluntarily moves to the labor problem.

"What's happening to our loyalty?" the major asked me. "I don't see any evidence of patriotism here. All the workers are looking for is big money. If I tried to reduce overtime pay by putting these guys on eight-hour shifts, there'd be nobody around in a matter of minutes."

At Vandenberg electricians have averaged $510 a week—$145 more than the combined pay and allowances of the base's missile commander, Maj. Gen. David Wade, a 25-year veteran. Elevator operators have collected as much as $363 a week, truck drivers $324, warehouse clerks $262. . . .

There is reason to worry about the effect this gravy train has on promising young officers who have seen ditchdiggers making more than the total pay and allowances of our astronauts, not to mention the pay scale of their foreman, who exceeds that of the Secretary of the Air Force. "Too often the officers can't stomach it," I was told, "and they quit when their obligated service runs out."

Hand in hand with the absurd pay is shameful featherbedding. When certain factory-made missile assemblies arrived at Vandenberg, union pipefitters insisted that they be allowed to tear this surgically manufactured equipment apart and reassemble it themselves. Rather than permit this damaging process, the Air Force let the pipefitters conduct a "blessing," a bizarre ritual whereby the workers merely watched the equipment for as long as it would have taken them to do the job—the while drawing $4.13 an hour.

. . . . .

The taxpayers have taken a licking in endless ways. The McClellan hearings brought out that local union electricians working at Malmstrom Air Force Base near Great Falls, Mont., rigged their contract last March so that they could receive up to $8.40 a day extra in "hardship" travel pay. They did it by transferring their membership to another local union 100 miles away in Helena, to classify themselves as working in an "isolated area" at Malmstrom.

For unmitigated undermining of our defense effort, however, nothing matches the record of unions at Cape Canaveral, our missile test center. In five years the Cape has been staggered by 110 strikes, but it's not only the strikes that have undercut missile progress. B. G. MacNabb, operations manager for the Atlas testing program at Canaveral, says, "The productivity of trade unions at the Cape is lower than I have seen anywhere in my 25 years of experience in industry."

"Every time we turn around, it seems as if men are walking off or threatening to leave," an Air Force officer told me as we stood at the edge of a concrete-lined 80-foot hole put down into the scrub-covered sand at Canaveral to test the ICBM solid-fuel Minuteman, which in the next three years is supposed to be implanted in more than 700 silos across the nation. The responsibilities of running tests on a missile system such as this, costing the taxpayers at least a million dollars a day, are awesome. Mistakes and delays can be devastating. . . .

One of the major stoppages at Cape Canaveral was touched off by Jimmy Hoffa's Teamsters. As the McClellan testimony revealed, Hoffa's organizer, Joseph W. Morgan, tried to force Canaveral truck drivers into the union, refusing to let the issue be decided by a workers' election. Morgan threw up picket lines and virtually all construction and installation work at the Cape halted. Finally, a court injunction ordered the picketing stopped, ruling it an unfair labor practice. But the damage had been done. The strike had drained away time that could never be regained.

In Washington, Morgan was asked by Senator McClellan: "When you shut down that operation for four weeks, were you serving your country or a foreign country that wants to bury us?" The Teamster ducked behind the Fifth Amendment.

The acknowledged kingpin of labor chieftains at Cape Canaveral, according to witnesses at the Congressional hearing, is Robert Palmer, business manager of Local 756 of the International Brotherhood of Electrical Workers. . . .

Perhaps the most outrageous of Palmer's feats was his battle with the National Aeronautics and Space Administration. Last August a team of its highly trained technicians at the Cape attempted to proceed with high-priority installation of ground-support equipment for the Saturn space rocket. This urgent project now represents America's greatest immediate hope of matching Russia's space achievements. With 1,500,000 pounds of thrust from a cluster of eight improved Jupiter engines, it will be four times more powerful than an Atlas ICBM. Already at the Cape an awesome 30-story service tower has been built for it, the biggest structure on wheels in the free world.

But when the NASA technicians arrived at Pad No. 34 to install the equipment in the blockhouse, Palmer's men staged a protest walkout along with the pipefitters. Immediately, NASA meekly pulled its specialists off the complex, and for more than three months they did not dare go back to the blockhouse except to try to slip in twice for important assignments. Even then the union men threatened to walk out, so the NASA experts left.

Finally, to prevent Saturn's schedule from falling badly behind, NASA had to send its experts back in, last November. Within hours Palmer's electricians again walked out—along with pipefitters, carpenters and laborers, 728 altogether.

Dr. Wernher von Braun and other NASA officials were forced to interrupt their work in order to plead with union representatives behind closed doors in Washington. Only after two weeks could these craft unionists be prevailed upon to return to their jobs, and then only on the promise that a special committee, headed by a Labor Department official, would look into the "dispute."

This official committee, instead of giving Dr. von Braun and his team a full go-ahead, would do no better in its report than offer weak-kneed palliatives such as "continuing re-examination" and an appeal to the unions "to make every effort to work out disputed problems without recourse to work stoppages." This despite the fact that NASA pleaded "it was very necessary" for its experts "to be intimately involved" with certain construction activities so they could "achieve the reliability which is vital to firing success." To do otherwise, NASA warned, "would go to the very heart of its mission and may even render the Saturn project a failure."

To the men who are straining to rush our missile and space programs to completion, union callousness and indifference are more than disheartening. The demoralization in our defense build-up is so serious that in the wake of Senator McClellan's hearings the Kennedy administration hastily promised to prevent stoppages by setting up a Presidential Commission designed to head off and mediate disputes. Yet this commission was given no real authority to enforce its decisions or immediately halt hit-and-run strikes that gnaw away on missile progress. Worse, the President and his Labor Secretary are promoting legislation that would make it legal for union construction bosses to persuade their followers to strike in sympathy with other unions. Throwing open the door to such secondary boycotting, already a cause of scores of missile stoppages, only encourages union bosses to set up picket lines wherever they please to influence other crafts to join in.

The time is long past when lip service to the antistrike cause will suffice. Here is what must be done:

1. The criminal-conspiracy laws that so recently put businessmen in jail should be equally applied to strike-happy workers who conspire to foment walkouts for their own enrichment.

2. Congress must ban strikes at our missile bases, with fair appeal procedures but with severe penalties against those strikers who would endanger the national security. Employers found guilty of certain labor-law violations are blacklisted from all federal contracts for three years. Shouldn't a similar penalty be applied to workers who strike illegally?

. . . . .

3. As a final significant step, the President must inspire a revival of real patriotism, not just as a noble sentiment but as an everyday necessity for survival in the cold war.

. . . . .

For several years thoughtful people inside and outside labor unions have been uneasy about the future role of unions in our economy. (Such concern extends far beyond the worry arising from racketeering and corruption which has been revealed in some unions.) One of the leading professional economists among those working intimately in the labor movement makes positive suggestions in the following selection.

39 · A New Agenda for Labor Unions

SOLOMON BARKIN

No one is happy about the state of industrial relations in the U.S. today. People from other advanced industrial nations who used to come over to study our methods now consider that we have little to teach them. Employers, rank-and-file workers, unions, and the public all feel a sense of mounting frustration. The machinery of industrial relations is stuck at dead center, bogged down in costly and irritating parochial bickering.

SOLOMON BARKIN, "A New Agenda for Labor," TWUA Research Publication No. MU-66, originally published in *Fortune Magazine* (November 1960). Used by permission.

It badly needs pioneering and innovation, and new techniques and new relationships.

The trade-union movement has a major responsibility for doing something about it. The movement itself has lost its dynamism. It has stopped growing. Its outlook is, for the most part, too narrow to meet present challenges. If organized labor is to regenerate itself and better serve American society, it must formulate a new agenda of goals.

Such an agenda would have an abundance of pressing problems to deal with. Stiffer competition from abroad and the decline of certain industries at home threaten American jobs. The economy is carrying too heavy a burden of unemployment, even in boom times. There are gaps in the blanket of social protection and other benefits, leaving too many wage earners exposed to economic risks. Relations between management and labor have degenerated into bitter parochial conflicts incapable of resolving the mutual discontents.

Protection vs. Innovation

The industries threatened by foreign competition and the "sick" industries bypassed by general U.S. economic growth both pose the same problem, so far as organized labor is concerned. In both, jobs are at stake. Since the people whose jobs are in jeopardy belong to some of the most important unions in the movement, the future of trade-unionism in this country is to a considerable extent bound up with what happens in these areas. The unions are hard pressed by their membership to reinforce the security of the dwindling labor force. Employers, on the other hand, are eager to slash their employment rolls. This clash of interests is at the heart of current high tension in industrial relations.

The unions need to lift their heads above the battle and think about some long-term solutions. Protecting present jobholders isn't enough. Ways have to be found to create new job opportunities.

To meet the threat of foreign competition, the unions have been edging more and more into a position of advocating protective trade restrictions. This position is out of harmony with the movement's professed trade-union preference for free trade. A more constructive approach would be to encourage the affected industries to convert to products in which the U.S. enjoys a basic competitive advantage—i.e., those which require high capital concentration and large material consumption. Our international competitors have built upon our past industrial innovations. Now it is our turn to innovate again.

The task of conversion for successful competition is not an easy one. It requires originality, daring, and flexibility. To date little progress has been made. Some companies prefer to stick it out with what they know, rather than venture into new and unknown fields; many simply don't realize the urgency. Where managements have tried to move into more competitive lines, they frequently fail to make their intentions clear to their employees. The unions, with little chance to review the merits of management proposals or to prepare their membership for needed changes, have dug themselves into prepared positions.

Similarly, the "sick" industries can only be brought back to health by a drastic effort to restore their competitive powers. But these industries have insufficient resilience and resourcefulness to find new growth opportunities.

Only a program that is nationwide in scope can bring about needed readjustments in the hard-hit sectors of our economy. The labor movement should advocate a program of industrial redevelopment councils with representatives from management and labor and knowledgeable outside authorities. These councils would mobilize whole industries to find new markets and products and increase their productivity. By participating in the program, the unions would face up to the need for industrial change and do their part to promote, not resist, it. They could then bring home to their members a better understanding of the realities of the economic problems and a reassurance that change, with proper safeguards, would bring more, not fewer, job opportunities. The work of the redevelopment councils would thus lay the foundation for cooperative efforts at the local bargaining table.

Our "Normal" Unemployment

Unions cannot confine themselves to protecting the jobs of their own members. All joblessness is their concern. The level of "normal" unemployment—at the peak of the economic cycle—has been increasing alarmingly since the war. During the past eighteen months of high economic activity, an average of 5.4 per cent of the labor force was out of work. In contrast, European industrial nations have an unemployment rate rarely above 3 per cent and often down between 1 and 2 per cent. Even taking into consideration differing statistical procedures and labor-market characteristics, our rate is at least twice as great as Britain's or West Germany's. These countries are coping with labor shortages while we have a general surplus.

There is also a sharp contrast in national attitudes toward treating pockets of chronic unemployment and underemployment. The British Government, for instance, limits the licenses for industrial expansion in overbuilt areas and makes special grants to enable neglected regions to improve their local facilities and attract new industry. The U.S. has no such national program for its distressed labor markets. [A law passed in 1961 provides Federal loans and other aids to help distressed areas. *Ed.*]

The trade-union movement has been vocal in its protest against unemployment. But its call for federal action and congressional appropriations is not enough. The situation calls for a massive redevelopment effort. Joint councils of the type suggested for "sick" industries should be formed to put new life into distressed areas, both rural and industrial.

The labor movement has a special responsibility to do something about the poverty, income inequality, and underprivilege still evident in our affluent society. Some 14 per cent of production workers in the manufacturing industries still go without paid vacations, 11 per cent with no paid holidays. One-third of all wage and salary employees do not have insurance coverage for death and hospitalization; half are not assured of pay when they are temporarily disabled or sick. Formal severance-pay systems to cover plant closings are rare.

As long as it tolerates such gaps in its structure of workers' benefits, the U.S. will continue to lag badly behind those European nations that afford their people almost universal insurance against economic hazards. The U.S. labor movement has carried on the battle for a higher and more extensively enforced minimum wage, for federal minimum standards in unemployment insurance, and for medical care for the aged through the social-security system. Now it should broaden its goal and demand a national minimum standard of protection benefits and pay for all Americans.

But legislation can eliminate only the grosser inequities. Collective bargaining must do the rest. The trouble is that the workers who are worst off are precisely those who cannot obtain gains by collective bargaining because they have not been unionized. Organizing the unorganized represents one of the largest items of the labor movement's unfinished business. Recent failures and discouragements only indicate that new approaches are needed.

Each group of unorganized workers presents a special challenge. The Negroes, during the late Thirties, were among the most responsive to union appeals. But their enthusiasm has cooled in recent years, largely because of the vestiges of discrimination in a number of older craft unions. This discrimination must be summarily uprooted. Just as unions in the past gave ethnic minorities the leverage for advancing economically, so today unions must give our biggest racial minority the opportunity to enter more confidently into society.

To make headway in organizing white workers in the South, the unions must demonstrate, more persuasively than they have done, how unionization will contribute to the region's growth and bring it up to the levels of the rest of the country. Armed with a good case, the labor movement can then appeal to the American public for legal protection and encouragement of Southerners who want to join unions.

Employees in nonprofit institutions present an especially urgent case for unionization. Here, as the strike in New York hospitals brought to light a year ago, the tradition of low wages and deplorable working conditions is deeply rooted. A strong union would restore the dignity of the jobs and enable the institutions to better serve the community.

Cooperation vs. Conflict

Finally, the labor movement's agenda must include achieving a more constructive relationship with management. Ten and fifteen years ago, the harmony in our industrial relations, born in the war years, was the envy of the free world. Now the emphasis is on conflict. In the plants, collective bargaining has degenerated into haggling over short-term issues. Outside the plant, leaders in labor and management have been able to find no common ground for attacking problems that affect them both.

For instance, organized labor gets a large share of the blame for inflation. But union leaders have been perplexed as to how to proceed responsibly in wage negotiations in order to minimize the possibility of price increases. They have had no guarantee that, if they adopted wage restraint, management would make a parallel commitment for price restraint. Clearly, inflation is one issue where a more cooperative relationship between management and the unions would have benefited both sides and the public too. It is true that management has not been receptive to a joint approach and, in particular, has refused to discuss price and production policy with union representatives. But the labor movement has not stated the case for cooperation effectively enough. It should press for industry-wide and national conferences to bring wage, price, production, and investment policies into harmony with the national interest.

The experience of a few industries shows the value of joint action between employers and unions. The building-trade unions have entered into an agreement with the contractors to settle jurisdictional disputes as well as to promote productivity. The next step would be for the unions to take the lead in a program for revamping local building codes that keep costs high and restrain the introduction of newer functional materials. This would stimulate the expansion of this industry and ultimately of the whole economy.

By taking the lead in removing obstructions to economic growth, the labor movement will restore its reputation as a force for progress, will give its leadership once again a chance for bold initiative, and will generate a new spirit among its rank and file.

What can a union, as a union, constructively do to raise productivity? Here is an example—a successful drive to reduce waste. Note that not just the men as individuals but the group as a whole, the union, played a vital role.

40 · *How a Union Helped Raise Productivity*

KARL DETZER

Some 8000 members of Local 1145, International Brotherhood of Teamsters, work for the Minneapolis-Honeywell company in its huge Minneapolis shops. The union and the firm's management are in the midst of an all-out drive to make the company more prosperous than it already is.

This powerful local is no company stooge. It fights hard for its rights. Nor is the company a soft touch at any bargaining table. It stands up and demands its own rights. But both company and employes are convinced that they are in the same economic boat, and that they must pull together if there are going to be enough profits to give each a worth-while share. Both know that a picket line is never a substitute for a humming production line when it comes to take-home pay or dividends. One result of this realistic viewpoint is that there has not been a strike since 1942, when Local 1145 became the bargaining agent for the workers in the plant. Arguments, to be sure; grievances, complaints; but never a strike.

In the early autumn of 1954, after 12 years of industrial peace, labor and management concluded that an increase in sales of Honeywell products would benefit both, and that a joint effort in that direction should be planned.

More sales, the union recognized, depended in part on keeping the price of Honeywell products competitive and the quality high. Therefore, union and management—everyone from executives, engineers and foremen to truck drivers and clerks—should together declare war on waste, an expensive factor in every industry: waste of materials, motions and minutes, waste of brawn and brains, waste of talent and experience of personnel.

"Many a man down there in the shop," the union pointed out, "is performing jobs that experience and common sense tell him could be done more easily. The fellow on the floor could

---

KARL DETZER, "This Union Found the Best Way to Raise Wages," *Reader's Digest* (February 1957). Copyright, 1957, by The Reader's Digest Association, Inc. Reprinted with permission.

show us how to take short cuts that have not occurred to some of the best engineers."

Men and women from both sides of the bargaining table went to work together on their mutual problem. They drew up a plan they called "POP"—"Planning Our Progress." The plan had hardly passed the blueprint stage, however, when one department began to lay men off.

"I was worried," says . . . the energetic and determined secretary-treasurer of the local . . . "Every layoff worries everyone in both management and labor. But here was a chance to prove that our POP idea would work."

So that the new scheme should be clearly understood by everyone, POP leaders hired the immense civic auditorium, and some 10,000 Minneapolis-Honeywell plant and office employes and their husbands and wives crowded into the building. They ranged from the company president . . . through department heads and foremen, mechanics, and clerks, to the sweepers. The . . . [president and the union leader] outlined the "Planning Our Progress" scheme. . . .

Next day 500 union stewards and committeemen joined management representatives in the campaign. They began by studying each section of each shop, and each individual job.

Union members and management soon were devising schemes to prevent useless effort and wasted materials. They saw to it that no one loafed. They cut carelessness. There was no speed-up but simpler ways were found to do many jobs. Within a few weeks production costs began to show a slow, steady decline. A penny here, a penny there, added up to substantial totals.

After scores of small changes the department that had laid off so many men had cut production costs to a figure low enough to stimulate sales. At the same time, quality improved. Within a few months every one of the idle employes who wanted work was back on the payroll, and the company was putting on extra help.

In another shop it had taken Honeywell 42 different operations to machine a part of an Army ordnance instrument. This not only made production expensive but with so many opportunities for error the percentage of rejections was extremely high. After careful study the union-management team found ways to eliminate half a dozen of the operations.

Then one of the union men made a simple suggestion. "Why don't we transfer the operation on which we are having the most trouble to a different machine?" he asked. "See that fellow over there? He's the best machinist in this shop, never satisfied with anything that's not 100 percent accurate. Yet he turns out a lot of work. Right now he's on a job that doesn't call for such skill." That suggestion really paid off.

Honeywell makes many instruments which, by reacting to heat and cold, turn electric current on and off. Several of these contain a liquid that vaporizes at a certain temperature. The liquid used was expensive. The labor-management team in this shop suggested a new, cheaper liquid. Company chemists began immediate tests, found that the proposed substitute was exactly as efficient as the old liquid. The change was made at a monthly saving of $1000.

. . . . .

A shop employe puts it this way: "We used to talk about a *fair* day's work for a *fair* day's pay. Now we talk about a *good* day's work for a *good* day's pay."

Employe grievances reaching the arbitration table have dropped 25 percent. There are as many grievances as before, but today when an employe feels he has been wronged he and his union steward and his department foreman often settle the matter quickly on the shop floor. Molehills remain molehills.

The workers have cause for satisfaction. For while they help the company increase its profits, they also cash in handsomely on those same profits. In the two years of POP, wages and annual benefits combined rose two million dollars. In individual pay envelopes this means raises of from 14 to 26 cents an hour. The least-skilled production worker now receives $1.51½ an hour, skilled workers as much as $2.91½.

But this is only part of the story. Last winter Local 1145 printed a broadside listing some of the results of its—and the management's—unusual policies. "Through good management relations," the union reported, "members of Local 1145 enjoy the following: arbitration of all disputes; double time for Sundays and holidays; a pension plan; vacations with pay; job protection; fair seniority rules; free paid insurance and free death gratuity to all members; bonuses for night work; good wages; excellent working conditions; guarantees of no racial or religious discrimination." Remember, that's the union—not the company—speaking.

In these days of much talk of "labor bosses," it is refreshing to find Local 1145 completely unbossed. It makes all its important decisions by secret ballot that actually is secret. No one in this union ever tries to push anyone around.

. . . [The union leader] asked if he believes in the guaranteed annual wage, replies: "It can best be achieved through full employment, which management and our union have achieved at Honeywell."

Does he advocate the closed shop?

"It is not necessary when labor and management work together."

He does feel that labor unions should take an active part in worthwhile community projects. No corporation in Minnesota is more deeply involved in public matters than the union he represents. So impressive has been its contribution to good government, to public health and welfare under his leadership that three years ago the Minneapolis Chamber of Commerce and *Time* magazine named him one of the city's 100 most outstanding young men.

Last St. Patrick's Day 500 foremen representing the management and 500 shop stewards and committeemen representing the union sat down together at dinner to plan improvements in the "POP" program. "From now on," they decided, "we will try to eliminate *all* waste. We will not be satisfied so long as there is *any* wasted effort, *any* wasted time."

VIII • PROBLEMS OF AGRICULTURE AND NATURAL RESOURCES

A fundamental approach to the reform of agricultural policy is presented here. The author, a Stanford University professor who has specialized in problems of agricultural economics for many years, was a member of the President's Council of Economic Advisers at the time he presented these proposals.

41 • *Guidelines for a Constructive Revision of Agricultural Policy*

KARL BRANDT

Studies of agricultural policy issues on both sides of the Atlantic stretching over 35 years have taught me that the "agricultural problem" is in all countries a perennial part and parcel of the dynamic process of economic development and of the dislocations and adjustments which are integral elements in it. Under any democratic form of government, farm policy tends to become an increasingly hot political and social issue as the accelerated rise in productivity of manpower in agriculture requires people to shift from rural to urban employment. The ever-changing symptoms of the farm problem can be tackled by an unlimited variety of public policy programs. But the hard core of the farm problem, namely, the structural change involved in a nation's economic growth can never be "solved" in the same sense as one can solve problems of a temporary emergency nature. Being concerned chiefly with the social impact and pains of economic growth, the legislative treatment of the farm problem can diminish the political friction and [the] heat it causes. However, it is well to realize that farm legislation reaches in all countries to the very life of liberty and the core of the values that orient an economic system, the more so the smaller the farm population gets. Farm legislation calls for warm hearts and cool heads.

I.

In the coming decade foreign affairs will outweigh domestic issues far more than in the past because our military security will depend heavily on closest

---

KARL BRANDT, "Guidelines for a Constructive Revision of Agricultural Policy in the Coming Decade," *Journal of Farm Economics* (February 1961), pp. 1–12. Used by permission.

cooperation with our allies. This in turn presupposes more and more economic cooperation within the Atlantic Community, with Latin America and the free parts of Asia. These vital relations reduce the leeway for potential domestic adjustments by any measures of restriction of imports and of foreign exchange controls.

. . . Provided the nation and its statesmen are alert and act with prudence . . . prospects are good that with growing productivity and a rising real output of goods and services per capita, the economy will offer ample opportunities to our people for employment and for the improvement of income while we simultaneously discharge our heavy responsibilities in foreign trade and investment in less developed foreign countries.

However, it must be realized that such growth and performance of the national economy is bound to face a much harder competition in coming years than in the period since the end of World War II.

To assure a continued stable and prosperous development of the Western countries requires that the stability of convertible currencies, recently achieved, be extended, and that foreign trade be liberalized further. This puts a high priority on the maintenance of the integrity of the U. S. dollar as the world's foremost reserve currency. Only if we succeed in containing inflation in the domestic economy will it be possible to hold the balance of trade and the balance of payments in such conditions that the dollar remains a hard, freely convertible currency and that a liberal foreign trade policy prevails.

Due to the strong revival and vigorous expansion of the industrial exports of Western Europe and Japan, there will be less latitude for price increases of U. S. products than during the postwar years in which U. S. industries had a practical monopoly of supply. Increasing competition from Soviet Bloc countries in world trade and in financing of underdeveloped countries will make domestic price stability even more mandatory lest unemployment hit industries that have priced themselves out of their foreign markets.

If these assumptions about the changed impact of the international situation on our national economic policy should be basically correct, it would demand even more than in the past that productive resources be allocated to the uses where they contribute the optimal yield to the social product. In a dynamic economy this calls for a high mobility of resources. Most of all, it calls for the geographic and vocational mobility of the greatest of all resources: manpower.

Within the American economy a universally unique feature of our dynamic progress is the structural improvement and the unprecedented rise in productivity in agriculture. These have yielded a steady flow of labor to the urban economy, and assured for it an abundant and dependable supply of food and fibers at reasonable prices. . . . Sixty years ago 50 percent [of the American population] were in agriculture, and today less than 10 percent.

The farm problem is commonly said to be the result of a sudden revolution or explosion of technology. There is, indeed, a great deal of improvement in machines, tools, plants, animals, feed, and fertilizer. But the essence of the change lies in improved input-output ratios and cost-revenue ratios. The persistence of very powerful price relations between factors and products has forced cumulative shifts in the operations of the firm in agriculture. The much steeper rise of farm wages than of total operating costs of labor-saving machinery has induced the continued substitution of capital for labor. The heavy capital investment in farm machinery and the economies of scale possible in its full utilization have led to acreage enlargement of operational units. The high excess of marginal revenues over marginal costs, still attainable anywhere in the U. S. in the application of more fertilizer and water to crops and pastures, has led to the boosting of yields per acre, or the substitution of purchased inputs for land. In fact, the main increase in the output of crops during the last two decades can be explained by increased input in seed, pesticides, fertilizer (chiefly nitrogen), and water. This increase has contributed a considerable share to the increase of output per man-hour. . . .

As a result of these cost-price relations, which promote intensification and which governmental price supports have accentuated, the aggregate output has exceeded total utilization. This is the part of the farm problem that concerns the 2 million commercial farms and even more the U. S. Treasury.

Despite a large transfer of manpower out of agriculture, there is still a considerable excess of manpower left in agriculture. This is chiefly the problem of low-incomes of many of the people on the other 2 million farms.

II.

Major economic defects of the methods chosen in agricultural legislation are the following:

A price guarantee for a few commodities interferes with the relations between prices of all farm products and all factors, and thereby interferes unintentionally with all supply responses of our agricultural economy.

Price support as the chief method of farm income support, sets each support level above equilibrium and gives powerful incentive to excess production.

The raising of a commodity price above a competitive market level subsidizes non-agricultural producers of substitute products such as man-made fibers and competing farmers abroad, e.g., producers of cotton. Both effects shrink the potential demand in domestic and foreign markets.

Due to excess production, support prices are actually fixed prices.

The guarantee against price changes for a select few commodities puts a premium on the risk-free expansion of their output.

Fixed grain prices vis-a-vis free livestock prices induce farmers to feed less and to sell more to the CCC [Commodity Credit Corporation] as livestock prices fall.

Restrictive acreage allotments establish a premium on intensification and therefore are ineffective as output controls, while they tend to freeze the location of production.

Marketing quotas are more effective [than acreage allotments] in controlling market supply of a commodity, but [such quotas] shift the use of resources and thereby the surplus to other commodities. [Quotas] are applicable and enforceable only for the part of the commodity stocks which are exchanged in the market.

The price-fixing legislation has resulted in truly gigantic stockpiles of unwanted grain and other farm commodities held by the Government, at enormous costs in interest, storage, losses, and transportation. This in itself is a perpetual serious misallocation and waste of scarce resources. It is a waste of a part of the taxpayers' income.

Despite being sealed off from the current market, the excess stocks exert a depressive influence on the markets in the U. S. and the world, particularly in view of the prospect of continued excess production.

So long as this stockpile exists, there

is no possibility of restoring a free market for the commodities concerned.

The price supports, acreage allotments, and marketing quotas have raised land values and land rents and thereby created [both] rigidities in land utilization and vested interests in the perpetuation of such policies. While increased equities benefit operating farmers, the higher land values increase costs for future farmers.[1]

The capitalization of revenues flowing from price support via acreage allotments increases the marginal physical and value productivity of land assets at the expense of returns to labor and capital assets.

The vast expenditures for price stabilization do not correct the regional maladjustment, such as the overproduction of wheat in the Great Plains, or the underemployment of manpower on the low-income farms of the Appalachian and Piedmont area.

As a device for redistributing income to agriculture from within the economy, price supports are an inappropriate and wasteful means.

As a device to redistribute income within agriculture, price supports are even much less effective, because they prorate the increase in income according to the scale of operation. [The larger the output, the greater the benefit from governmental aid. *Ed.*]

Beyond outright donation, the disposal of surplus stocks can be achieved only by heavily subsidized exports. . . . [Such a] policy . . . is counter to the national interest in a maximum liberalization of international trade.

The use of the surpluses under Public Law 480 as aid to underdeveloped countries is a costly *ex-post* method of assistance in which the recipient countries receive less than one-half of the costs to the U. S. Government. . . . [And our government] may perhaps recover no more than 10-15 percent of the costs [and only] after 10 to 20 years.[2]

Price support by the CCC by means of nonrecourse loans and purchases amounts to an open-end commitment of the Treasury, which renders control over the government expenditures ineffective.

III.

In order to have some foundations on which to erect guideposts for a change, I offer a few observations on the essential features of the dynamics of agriculture.

There is no more than a minute grain of truth, if any, in such fundamentalistic assertions by some members of the [economics] profession as that due to physical, biological, and organizational circumstances, agriculture is unable to adjust supply to demand, and that it reacts perversely to prices.

The assertion that agriculture is denied a "just income" by being forced to operate in atomistic competition against monopolistic market power of

---

[1] Cf. Frank H. Maier, James L. Hedrick, and W. L. Gibson, Jr., "The Sale Value of Flue-Cured Tobacco Allotments." USDA ARS Technical Bulletin No. 148, April 1960. This study lists for three North Carolina counties estimates of the sale value of an acre of flue-cured tobacco allotment separate from land and buildings as $1,290 for 1954 and as $2,500 for 1957. The same study found for 203 farm sales in one Virginia county a value for an acre of tobacco allotment in 1957 about 73 times as high as the value of an acre of cropland without the allotment. . . .

[2] Theodore W. Schultz, "Value of U. S. Farm Surpluses to Underdeveloped Countries." The University of Chicago Office of Agricultural Economics Research Paper No. 6005, May 4, 1960. Also paper on the same subject presented at the Annual Meeting of the American Farm Economic Association held at Ames, Iowa, August 10–13, 1960. . . .

industry, commerce, and labor is not supported by any conclusive evidence. To prove such causational relation calls for far more than demonstration of rigidities in "administered" prices or in certain wage rates of 17 million labor union members among a labor force of over 70 million people.

It must not be overlooked that corporate income is an extremely unstable item in our economy and that unions have no control over the volume of employment or the payroll of industries and hence no control over the income of even a fully unionized vocational group. That unions have considerable power in collective bargaining over working conditions for their members is another matter.

The income and financial situation of the commercial farm operators, particularly when due consideration is given to the continual increase in their equity, give no cause for national alarm about an emergency or the urgency of sharply expanding public income support [for farmers], but [the income and financial facts do give] a great deal of cause for pondering a review of the means of policy.

Our agriculture is far from being left to hopeless isolation of millions of atomistically competing farmers who increase production when prices make production unprofitable. On the contrary, it is excellently organized with a farmer-owned and operated up-to-date long-, medium-, and short-term farm credit system, a tax privileged, well-organized vast cooperative system of nearly 10,000 marketing, farm-supply, and service enterprises with $13.5 billion annual turnover and extrardinary bargaining power. Our agriculture is serviced by a government-supported land grant college system with agricultural research stations in every State of the Union and by a Federal-State financed farm advisory system available free of charge to every farmer in every county of the U. S. All farm people, though mostly self-employed, have the same benefits as urban employees under social security legislation.

Agriculture is a system of private overwhelmingly family operated enterprises which in its 2 million commercial units behaves so remarkably businesslike that it gears production in accordance with the effective demand—a demand which for price supported commodities includes the U. S. Government's unlimited commitment to buy any amount offered. The trouble is chiefly one of a lag in effective mobility of resources, particularly manpower, and of adjustments in land values.

Government price-income support policies have reduced the mobility of resources. Allotments and quotas have enhanced the land value. Rational economic adjustment may require use of some land at lower intensity (i.e., less manpower and purchased inputs per acre) in larger operational units. But this involves a certain relative reduction in land value and land taxes. The greatest rigidities that interfere with the mobility of resources are the result of price fixing in combination with allotments.

Arguments on behalf of the gradual restoration of a market economy for agriculture and a less costly, more effective system of farm policy are usually countered with the accusation that this implies laissez-faire and an unfair denial of equal political subsidy treatment of agriculture, and with the absurd assertion that subsidies "built" the railroads, the airlines, and the maritime merchant fleets. Therefore, I want to stress that I do not believe in laissez-faire but [in] a strong government enforcing the rules of competition in a market economy and effectively promoting conditions favorable to economic growth and stability. The question cannot be whether the government should or should not use subsidies in dealing with the farm problem. The question is whether subsidies are being misused to make an economically untenable *status quo* socially bearable, or whether subsidies and intervention are self-liquidating and serve the purpose of keeping the farm economy basically free, self-adjusting, and capable of operating eventually without such aid. Subsidies are justifiable if they assist people in making adjustments and mitigate the hardships involved. The fast tax write-offs on farm equipment and storage facilities, freedom of all farmers from Federal tax on farm-used gasoline and initially subsidized credit for rural electrification are also nonobjectionable forms of subsidies.

However, to have the gross returns from all major farm products fixed and rationed among all farmers in a manner that is just or "fair to both consumers and producers" by the Congress, as some economists propose, appears to me neither compatible with the institutional and legal frame of our economic system, nor feasible.

While it is theoretically not impossible to control the output of 4 million farms by comprehensive control of land and capital inputs, I hold it politically inconceivable that the American people, particularly the farmers, would ever accept the degree of regimentation and law enforcement that would be necessary to execute such control. It is moreover questionable whether the total cost involved for the nation would not by far exceed the exorbitant ones of the present price stabilization. Compulsory supply controls create by definition immediately illegal units of supply, i.e., a black market. To make it effective such control would have to ration all purchased inputs, such as fuel, fertilizer, machinery. It makes no difference whether the "comprehensive supply control" would be exercised by the Government, or by compulsory farmer-operated commodity cartels, or whether quotas would be made negotiable. The assignment to all farmer cartels would be to restrain competition, administer shares in the market, and reduce the mobility of resources. This would lay waste in the realm of food and fiber production the main source of wealth in the American economy.

If supply control should approach effectiveness, it would require extension to the industries which compete with farm production. Beyond that it seems fantastic to believe that in an integrated dynamic economy the conversion of a primary industry like agriculture into a politically directed state monopoly could stop there. Total cartelization of agriculture is only the beginning of total cartelization of . . . [other] industries. The historical precedent of this inescapable sequence under the Weimar Republic in Germany from 1928 to 1933 and its ominous finale under the Nazi regime 1933–1945 should be sufficient deterrent to any repetition by contemporary eclecticists.

Insofar as the results of a decade of extensive research by many of our most competent analysts on the supply function in agriculture are concerned, they have not gone beyond preliminary exploration and in my judgment [they] do not provide any reliable quantitative knowledge with which a supply control system could be operated with any accuracy.

The assumptions by some economists about the possibility of reducing aggregate output to market equilibrium by withdrawing enough crop acreage by expansion of the conservation reserve up to 60 or 80 million acres impress me as unwarranted and extremely expensive illusions. At best the conservation reserve provides additional opportunities for the retirement of elderly farm people chiefly on marginal units.

The unsatisfactory results of the present farm policy are exclusively the result of maladjusted legislation, not of administrative failure in its execution.

The overruling economic argument against a policy change toward effective lifting of farm income beyond the present level by supply restriction lies in the implied substantial jacking up of food and fiber prices to the consumer and the inevitable escalator effect on wages and prices. The cost-push inflation involved in it would tend to cause serious unemployment in export industries and deterioration of the balance of trade. Hence such policy would tend to imperil the exchange rate of the U. S. dollar. The savings in the Federal Budget by reduced CCC stocks would largely be lost in higher export subsidies.

IV.

The foregoing assumptions about the needs of economic policy in general and of agricultural legislation in particular lead me to suggest [certain guidelines] for discussion. . . . [These] guidelines for a possible alternative course in legislation for agricultural adjustment aid . . . go in a different direction from those of fascism or the corporate state. . . .

[The author comments briefly on two other proposals.] . . . I do not believe that the assumed power of the farm bloc is what has kept legislation in the same tracks for 27 years. I believe the causes lie much deeper, namely, in what has so aptly been analyzed by J. S. Davis as agricultural fundamentalism. I would add to it that as an indestructible strand of ontological memory all urban people have a fond affection for the farm, from which they or their forebears all came. It is the paradise lost complex of modern metropolitan electorates that creates the phenomenon of increasing will to grant farm aid as the proportion of farm votes diminishes, a phenomenon typical of all industrial societies under representative forms of government. . . .

I have already mentioned still another plan which envisages the correction of excess aggregate output by . . . [idling] 60 to 80 million acres of cropland by an increase of the conservation reserve. I consider this approach as a dead alley, unless productive acres, not whole farms, were fallowed under tight annual leases.

In view of the crucial need of a constructive alternative I put on the docket of our profession a course of legislation along the following lines:

(a) Since the greatest maladjustment lies in the chronic underemployment of manpower in low-income farms, maximum assistance would be given by all competent Federal and State Government service agencies with particular emphasis on expansion of nonfarm employment.

(b) The excess stocks of grain would be effectively eliminated from the U. S. and world grain market by transferring title to a Grain Conversion Board under the statutory requirement that it cannot dispose of any of its stocks as grain but must convert all of them over a period of 6 to 7 years to staple livestock products. . . . [It would be required to sell these products] exclusively in newly to be developed foreign markets and exclusively on the basis of long term delivery contracts with food dispensing agencies abroad, particularly in underdeveloped countries. These transactions would be carried out by existing private enterprises and business firms. The Board would also be entitled to donate certain quantities to foreign charity.

(c) The Government would gradually (over a period of say four years) and progressively disengage itself from intervention in the commodity markets, thereby assist in the recuperation of their natural buoyancy in the absence of depressive surpluses, and it would simultaneously reprivatize the carrying of all visible stocks in first and second hand.

(d) During this transitional period of disengagement the Government would financially assist producers of chronic surplus commodities in specified regions by buying from farmers, under specified contractual conditions, their allotments and marketing quotas, tapering the installment payments over the four years.[3] One of the conditions would involve the farmer's commitments to fallow a specified percentage of his allotment acreage, with a tapering scale during the four years. Such massive financial aid would amount to indemnification for the abolition of [the present] unworkable means of farm policy adopted basically for war purposes.

(e) In order to get the Federal Budget expenditure for the farm program under control, the Congress would make a total appropriation for each fiscal year covering the expenditures involved in the indemnification, i.e., the purchase of the allotments.

(f) The Government would give maximum support to agricultural exports by diplomatic efforts at removing discriminatory import restrictions abroad and by keeping U. S. markets open to foreign industrial products.

(g) The Food-for-Peace Program would be continued.

This is a set of guidelines for a revision of agricultural legislation which I consider as one of several possible alternatives and which appears to me as an economically, socially, and politically constructive and feasible one. Legislation following these guidelines properly administered would adjust aggregate output via the market mechanism without fettering farm enterprises [and without] cartelization of industries. . . . [It would protect] the economy against more inflation and shield the farmers against decline in their income and equity. Chiefly, such program would create within a period of four years a situation in which the U. S. Treasury would no longer be mortgaged by, and the U. S. Government no longer be tied to, a continuation of anachronistic methods of farm policy.

---

[3] [The purchase by the Government would consist of the farmer's right to produce, *not* of output. Total production would thereby be reduced. The economy would be saved the cost of variable (non-fixed) inputs. *Ed.*]

This selection is one of a group prepared for Congress as part of a broad investigation of problems of America's economic growth. The authors are members of the staff of Resources for the Future, a scholarly, nonprofit research organization specializing in problems of natural resource economics.

42 · *The Adequacy of Resources for Economic Growth in the United States*

JOSEPH L. FISHER
EDWARD BOORSTEIN

Introduction

There is much speculation about the adequacy of natural resources in this country to support an increasing population at higher and higher levels of living. Will we run out of oil, saw timber, fresh water, or some metal? Or, more realistically, will the cost of making them available rise so much that economic growth generally will be checked? Any responsible examination of these questions must be both broad and deep. The look ahead has to encompass new technology, world sources of supply as well as domestic, and changing economic and institutional situations. Especially the interrelations among the various resource materials are important since shortage of one thing usually can be met by substitution of another.

In this paper we can do little more than try to ask the question of the adequacy of resources for economic growth in such a way that historical evidence and future projections of demand can be brought to bear and some of the relevant policy considerations seen.[1] We shall consider, in turn, the historical background for the resource adequacy-economic growth question, some general indicators of adequacy, several important resource materials in particular, and some of the principal trends and problems ahead. Our examination of these matters will be brief and rather highly compressed.

. . . . .

Resources and Growth in the Modern U.S. Economy

Since about the beginning of this century, the resource base has been playing

---

[1] Views expressed in this paper are those of the authors personally. In its preparation, they have drawn on parts of a study now in progress in Resources for the Future, Inc., provisionally called "Resources in the American Future," in which the resource situation and outlook in the United States is surveyed broadly.

JOSEPH L. FISHER and EDWARD BOORSTEIN, "The Adequacy of Recourses for Economic Growth in the United States," prepared for the consideration of the Joint Economic Committee (December 16, 1959).

a noticeably smaller, and in many respects different, role in growth than it did before then. General economic growth has been less closely and clearly tied to abundant resources than it was previously.

But while the resource base may no longer be the dominant dynamic factor it once was, neither has it been exercising any noticeable restraining influence on general growth. There is no longer the same simple superabundance of resources in relation to the size of the population and economy there used to be. However, this seems not to have resulted in any general rise in the cost of resources or pinch on overall growth. The relative costs of some resources have fallen while others have risen depending on a complex of factors, including technologic and general economic development, the possibility of substitutes or of imports, and the significance of the cost of the resource item in the price of the final product into which it enters.

. . . . .

Notwithstanding all this, it is obvious on the face of it that the availability of natural resources to an economy or to a region still has a great deal to do with the level and kind of economic development that can be achieved. Land, water, and minerals of themselves are of no account economically, but with labor and capital applied to them they become of basic importance in satisfying economic demands. This country, as well as most others, cannot expect to continue healthy economic growth except as a bountiful supply of raw materials, and products and services derived from them, are made available from domestic sources, or through imports. . . .

TRENDS IN RESOURCES CONSUMPTION, OUTPUT, EMPLOYMENT, PRICES, AND TRADE. . . . Trends [in absolute and per capita consumption of various raw materials in the United States] during the last 5 or 6 years have been in line with trends in the preceding 50 years.

Taking the period since 1900, it will be noted that per capita consumption of renewable resources, agricultural and timber products together, shows a slight increase; a relatively small increase in the large item, agricultural products, is offset to a considerable extent by a relatively large decrease in the less important item, timber products. Minerals as a whole show a large per capita increase over this period, but with major disparities among the components. Per capita consumption of coal, not unexpectedly, has dropped, while that of oil and gas has increased tremendously. Metal ores have increased considerably, but building and chemical materials, at least since 1900, have increased quite a bit more. Historical statistics on water consumption admittedly are poor, but very recent trends indicate a per capita increase over the first half century somewhere between that of the producible raw materials and the minerals—perhaps an increase of $1\frac{1}{2}$ times in per capita consumption. In absolute terms consumption of nearly all raw materials has increased greatly over the $8\frac{1}{2}$ decades, especially in the minerals category.

. . . Output of all raw materials as a percent of GNP has dropped by about one-half since 1900. Of course, during the same period, GNP per capita has increased more than $2\frac{1}{2}$ times and the population has more than doubled, resulting in a very large increase in total absolute raw materials consumption.

For particular items trends have varied. Still measured in constant prices, the output of such major agricultural commodities as wheat, corn, cotton, and beef and veal has declined greatly as a percent of GNP since 1870. The absolute peak of wood and timber output was reached sometime between

1905 and 1910, so that the decline in the output of this item in relation to GNP has been especially sharp since then. The value of total coal output, both bituminous and anthracite, has generally been declining in relation to GNP since about World War I. On the other hand, the value of petroleum and natural gas output rose greatly in relation to GNP till about 1930, and since then has been moving up at roughly the same rate or slightly higher than GNP.

. . . . .

Finally, it should be noted that the proportion of GNP accounted for by resource output is not a sufficient index of the fundamental importance of resources to the economy. An analogy may illustrate this point: a family's outlay for water is only a small portion of its total expenditures, but without water the family would not last long. Just as the availability of water is a precondition for having a household at all, so the availability of resource materials is a precondition for industrial production.

. . . . .

In the foreign trade of this country in resources, there has been a general tendency for imports to become more important. In timber products the United States first switched to a net import position in 1915; in several later years the country was again a small net exporter, but since 1934, has consistently and increasingly been a net importer.

Net imports of zinc began in 1935, and in 1940 for copper. The United States has been a net importer of iron ore for a long time, but the imports have been significant only since 1953. In crude oil the switch from a net export to a net import position occurred in 1948.

Since the turn of the century there has been a very large increase in imports of agricultural products relative to exports due mainly to increased imports of tropical products such as coffee, cocoa, bananas, and cane sugar. But although there have been fluctuations and interruptions, the United States has remained a substantial exporter of such products as wheat, cotton, and tobacco.

The foreign trade statistics clearly show an increasing dependence of the U.S. economy on resources drawn from other parts of the world. This presents certain problems for military security, but it does not necessarily mean increasing costs of materials since, as compared to domestic sources, foreign sources may yield to American users oil, iron ore, copper, pulpwood and pulp, and other commodities as cheaply or even more cheaply.

Another indicator of the interaction of resource supplies and economic growth is the trend in the amount of employment in extractive industries compared to total employment. The steady and large reduction from 1880 to 1954, from almost 50 percent to about 10 percent, is due mainly to the relative reduction in the agricultural work force and is associated with the diminishing relative importance of farm products in consumers' budgets and with increasing productivity per worker. The economy is getting more resource products and services out of its resource base than it used to, and with fewer workers.

THE FUTURE ECONOMY AND RESOURCES.

. . . . .

Looking ahead to 1975 from 1950, the President's Materials Policy Commission (Paley Commission) projected increases in consumption of raw materials as follows: food products, 41 percent; nonfood agricultural products, 25 percent; minerals taken as a whole, 90 percent; coal, 60 percent; oil and gas taken together, about 150 percent. It was suggested in 1956 that an upward revision averaging about 10 percent might be called for in these estimates of future consumption in view of the more rapid population and GNP increase which ensued in the 5 years following 1950. Furthermore, some internal revisions would have to be made among the specific materials which make up the overall estimates of the Paley Commission, although the larger groupings probably would remain in about the same proportion. Technology has moved forward rapidly during the years following the Paley report so that the underestimate of population and GNP growth made then has been offset to some extent by rapid development of substitute materials for those becoming scarcer and therefore tending to increase in price.

More recent tentative estimates of demand for selected raw materials in 1980 and 2000 are indicated in the following table. Low, medium, and high estimates are derived from a variety of assumptions regarding overall trends in the economy (population, households, labor force and employment, technology and productivity, investment and consumption-Government expenditures, etc.), as well as more specific assumptions about trend in those end product and service categories making large use of resources (construction, heat and power, food, clothing and apparel, hard goods, transportation, etc.).

ESTIMATED DEMAND FOR SELECTED KEY MATERIALS, 1980 and 2000 [1]

	Current	1980 Low	1980 Medium	1980 High	2000 Low	2000 Medium	2000 High
Timber....(billion board feet)....	34.6 (1957)	44	66	103	49	100	215
Wheat.........(million bushels)....	934 (1958)	930	1,120	1,310	1,110	1,480	1,880
Feed grains [2] (billion feed grain units)....	245 (1956)	267	310	410	310	410	660
Cotton...........(million bales)....	13.0 (1959)	11.9	16.7	23.2	12.7	23.2	44.9
Oil................(billion barrels)....	2.97 (1957)	4.65	5.94	7.43	6.92	11.13	17.90
Coal.................(million tons)....	385 (1958)	497	756	1,071	383	978	1,921
Iron ore..........................do........	140 (1957)	132	197	330	125	270	690
Aluminum ....do........	1.9 (1958)	4.1	10.6	23.9	6.7	24.3	77.0
Copper ....do........	1.56 (1958)	2.1	4.1	7.6	2.9	8.9	23.9
Fresh water withdrawals (trillion gallons per year)....	71.8 (1954)	120.5	125.7	149.0	162	178.8	263.6

[1] Estimated export demand is included for wheat, feed grains, and cotton. Export demand for the other items is insignificant, except for coal for which exports in recent years have been around 10 percent of total production.
[2] Includes corn, oats, barley, and grain sorghum. 1 feed grain unit has feed value of 1 pound of corn.
Source: Estimates taken from work in progress by "Resources for the Future" and should be regarded as tentative only.

. . . . .

The adequacy of the domestic resource base to meet these and other demands is mixed. For some such as water it probably is adequate, assuming fairly large investments in developing new supplies, in preventing or abating pollution, in recycling in industrial uses, and in conservation generally. For others domestic sources obviously are inadequate now and will become increasingly so in the future. Many of the metals are in this category. More precise answer to the question of adequacy hinges on technologic and economic events yet to unfold.

The more important question of total adequacy of resources to support economic growth must include foreign sources as well as domestic. As has been pointed out, this country already imports large amounts of crude oil, iron ore, woodpulp, and other basic items. Trends of comparative costs of production in various countries will probably increasingly favor other parts of the world. Whether policy accommodates or resists these trends will be important in terms of supplying the U.S. economy with lower or higher cost new materials. Some restraint on growth, therefore, may arise from this source, but it need not.

In a static sense and making no allowance for technological responses to higher costs of particular materials, increasing shortage would tend to lead to higher costs and prices and ultimately to a reduction of total output of the economy, however slight. Admitting this as an ever-present tendency, one does not find historical evidence that this has happened in any general way. In the dynamic sense incipient shortages by and large have led to new discoveries, improvements in extraction, processing, and use, substitutions that turned out to be as cheap or cheaper, and increased imports.

One of the most notable features of the U.S. economy is the astonishingly numerous ways in which a threatening shortage for any particular material can be met. Substitute materials are usually available and frequently soon prove to be of lower cost. Engineers are very ingenious in figuring out ways to reuse formerly wasted materials and to redesign products and manufacturing processes so as to use less of the scarce material.

Consumers of the end products usually are ready to shift their allegiance to substitutes in response to price advantages. Frequently they do not greatly care which particular raw material is used as long as the resulting performance is satisfactory. For example, a family wants a dry house and will accept a roof made of wood shingles, composition shingles of various kinds, tile, or even aluminum. Or a family will accept oil, natural gas, electricity (produced by coal, oil, gas, water power, or atomic power), or coal used in a modern burner as a source of heat for its home. Beyond all these possibilities for substitution are the incredibly ingenious activities of the chemical industry, or other industries employing chemical engineering, in creating new products altogether by the rearrangement of atoms and molecules. Plastics, synthetic rubber, and new fertilizers may be mentioned.

Substitution in the broadest sense of the term is a pervading characteristic of the modern U.S. technologic economy. It especially characterizes the key raw material stages which lie between the resource base of land, water, and minerals, and the end products and services required by consumers. Distinctions between specific materials are becoming more and more blurred and this is beginning to be true even between whole categories of materials. This means that shortage of particular resource materials is not likely to check general economic growth, at least over any extended period of time. Temporary embarrassment may be acute. A short-run thrust toward inflation may result and for a time a disproportionate share of certain resources and efforts may have to be devoted to overcoming or bypassing the roadblock. Persons tied in some way to the shortage item may gain relatively for a while and then lose as demand turns into other channels. But in a rich and diverse economy such as that of the United States, it is hard to make a case for particular raw material shortage greatly restraining growth. Only when numerous shortages (as seen by relative price increases) occur more or less simultaneously, and continue, can the case be made persuasively. There is little evidence of any such combining at this time or any real prospect of it unless one assumes an extraordinary war or defense situation in which suddenly there would be a sharp and sustained increase in requirements for nearly all raw materials, plus an ability to use them in terms of available labor force, plant, and equipment.

In a basic sense, therefore, the best and perhaps only way to insure that economic growth is not hamstrung by resource shortages is to maintain and increase the flow of research, discovery, and innovation, to improve professional and technical education and the general education on which these rest, to encourage enterprise, ingenuity, and productive work in business, labor, and agriculture, and to improve the efficiency generally of the whole economy, and to organize the international economy more rationally. Policies across the board should favor these objectives. As a part of this, resource discoveries will be made, productivity in resource industries will increase, and substitutions for scarce items will be facilitated.

One is driven back, therefore, to the general indicators of the role of resources in the economy over time if one is to form an opinion as to whether resource scarcity will restrain growth. The upshot of all this seems to be that, despite the prospects for very rapid population increase during the next two or three decades, the outlook for resources supplies at reasonable prices is favorable for this country. Even with this generally optimistic picture, difficult problems of increase cost and shortage for particular resources materials and services undoubtedly will be encountered—for example, ground water in many places, a number of alloy and other metals, high grade saw timber, and desirable outdoor recreation areas. One, of course, cannot peer very far into future technological developments which admittedly would have important effects upon costs and prices of resource products. Nor can one look very far into the future regarding population change with any great degree of confidence, as recent experience has shown. But granting these uncertainties, it is necessary to try to see ahead, and what appears to be there for the next generation or so regarding resources supplies in this country is not alarming. The last 20 or so years of the century can be seen only more dimly: Resource supply problems could cramp economic growth somewhat although with reasonably good foresight in Government and business and among other groups the problems should not be too difficult to handle.

[The authors proceed to a detailed discussion of several important items. *Ed.*]

Having considered in broad terms the question of resources and economic growth, and having found a good chance that resources are not likely to restrain growth in any general way during the next 40 years, we turn now to a more detailed consideration of several important items.[2] . . .

. . . . .

Summary of Trends and Problems Ahead

In casting a fairly long look ahead to 1980 and 2000 and trying to see the future demands the economy may place on resources and the problems that may be involved, several important features stand out.

---

[2] Much of the following material, both the statistical estimates and the analysis, comes from parts of a study already referred to as "Resources in the American Future." It should be emphasized particularly that the estimates of future demand and supply are tentative.

1. The demand for nearly all raw materials may be expected to increase in absolute amounts, for some much more than others, depending on the rate and composition of total economic growth. . . .

2. As a percent of GNP, resource output will probably continue downward, perhaps more slowly than in the past. The same thing will probably be true of employment in resource industries expressed as a percent of total employment. . . .

3. Reliance upon imports of many raw materials can be expected to continue to increase, the extent and nature of which will be greatly influenced by foreign trade policy and international policy generally. . . .

4. Military security problems will obviously have a bearing on the resource segments of the economy; for forecasting and planning purposes the bearing they have will depend on the particular assumptions made about such matters as the nature of any attack on this country, the duration of any war, the rate of recovery from war damage, access to foreign sources of supply, and amount and kind of preparedness activities. . . .

5. The statistical record over the past eight decades does not reveal any general trend up or down in the price of resource products compared to prices generally. A few specific products have tended upward, a few downward, but most have moved sideways, frequently with fairly large but erratic year-to-year fluctuations. While these long-term price trends provide no absolute guarantee against general shortage of raw materials in the future, they are a kind of assurance of a strong likelihood that what has held for seven or eight past decades will continue to hold for a few more.

6. In its technologic and economic evolution this country has passed from a close dependence on basic resources, such as agricultural and forest land and mineral ores, to one geared much more to highly processed and variegated intermediate and final goods and to services. As the range of possible substitutions has broadened and as more has become known about the chemistry of raw materials, dependence on any one material has lessened. Molecules can now be rearranged to produce the specification in an astonishingly large number of instances. Furthermore, techniques for conservation and reuse of materials are improving.

7. Several particular resources have been considered in more detail: Oil, lumber, and water, and more briefly several of the nine widely used metals. These present a somewhat mixed picture, but in each case, assuming appropriate policy and management, shortages should not result in a restraint on economic growth at least over the next few decades. Substitute materials and new sources at home or abroad, frequently at no great increase in cost, furnish ceilings against any tendency for costs of conventional items to rise very much.

8. The cursory examination of historical trends in the resource industries plus the equally cursory look ahead to 1980 and 2000 do not reveal significant danger of general resource shortage in this country, although sharp supply difficulties undoubtedly will appear for particular raw materials at particular times and in particular industries and places. . . .

9. Undoubtedly the price of specific raw materials will rise, perhaps sharply, from time to time as demand increases suddenly. This may be due to any one or combination of factors: rapid inventory buying during upward cyclical movement of business, speculative buying in time of a war scare, a capital goods boom calling for large amounts of metals or other items. Price increases of this nature, one would think, would

normally be followed by price drops, each intensified by the sluggishness of supply adjustments characteristic of the extractive industries. The faster capacity and production can be adjusted, the less extreme such movements will tend to be. Also the more successful are buffer stock and other supply stabilization schemes, the greater chance there will be to hold such price fluctuations within limits.

10. Shorter run price instability of this sort may exert a longer term inflationary influence in certain situations. For example, a large and sudden jump in demand for one, or, more likely, several raw materials (say copper, lead, zinc, iron and steel, and bauxite and aluminum), given the supply inelastic nature of these industries, would undoubtedly lead quickly to relative price increases. Such increases might well be transmitted via higher costs or expected higher costs to the prices of intermediate and final goods, and hence to prices generally. This chain of events would be more likely if managements in the key firms and industries were able and chose to "administer" prices upward, with or without the acquiescence of unions. In a general atmosphere of business upswing and prosperity in which most consumers are sharing by way of wage and salary raises, the "pass through" of price increases of raw materials to finished products ordinarily meets with only feeble opposition. The "cost push" from raw materials can combine with or be closely followed by the "demand pull" of higher consumer incomes and increasing purchases of raw materials by processors in ways that inevitably spell inflation in materials' prices and an impetus to general price inflation.

11. Such inflationary courses may not be reversible as adjustments in raw materials supplies and inventories are reached, or overreached, because of a one-way ratchet underneath prices which permits them to be boosted up but prevents their being hauled down. This ratchet, by now well known, is a part of the structure of many industries and apparently is strong enough to hold against all but the heaviest downward pressures. Part of the strength of the ratchet arises from the power and vigor of unions in many of the materials industries to press wage and related demands especially during periods of expansion, part from the oligopolistic (at least less than fully competitive) nature of some of these industries which permits price advantages to be made fairly promptly following any actual or even expected cost increase and which provides discipline against competitive price adjustments downward, and part from the increasing need for firms in the materials industries (as well as others) to keep increases in the fixed and overhead portions of total costs covered during threatened downswings in business.

12. The result of these shorter run forces, particularly the "price ratchet" effect in raw materials industries, may well be an intermittent but one-way upward pressure on materials' prices and to a less but still significant extent on prices generally. This kind of inflationary pressure does not arise from any underlying and long run tendency for raw materials as a whole, or even any one large category of them, to increase in scarcity, cost, and price. Rather it arises from the more general structural characteristics of modern industry as it responds to the upward and downward tendencies of business and from the special characteristics of the raw materials industries themselves.

. . . . .

Books by professional economists rarely make the best-seller list. An outstanding exception, however, is The Affluent Society. *The author, after a career in government service and some years as an editor of* Fortune, *became Professor of Economics at Harvard. In 1961 he went to New Delhi as U. S. Ambassador to India. The ideas which appear here, and the many more which are contained in the rest of the full book, have stimulated no small amount of debate among economists and among others here and abroad. One should note in any case that since the paragraphs below on "social balance" were originally written, huge outlays have been made on highways, schools, and other governmental facilities and services.*

43 · *The Affluent Society*

JOHN KENNETH GALBRAITH

The Theory of Social Balance

. . . The line which divides our area of wealth from our area of poverty is roughly that which divides privately produced and marketed goods and services from publicly rendered services. Our wealth in the first is not only in startling contrast with the meagerness of the latter, but our wealth in privately produced goods is, to a marked degree, the cause of crisis in the supply of public services. For we have failed to see the importance, indeed the urgent need, of maintaining a balance between the two.

. . . In the years following World War II, the papers of any major city —those of New York were an excellent example—told daily of the shortages and shortcomings in the elementary municipal and metropolitan services. The schools were old and overcrowded. The police force was under strength and underpaid. The parks and playgrounds were insufficient. Streets and empty lots were filthy, and the sanitation staff was underequipped and in need of men. Access to the city by those who work there was uncertain and painful and becoming more so. Internal transportation was overcrowded, unhealthful, and dirty. So was the air. Parking on the streets had to be prohibited, and there was no space elsewhere. These deficiencies were not in new and novel services but in old and established ones. Cities have long swept their streets, helped their people move around, educated them, kept order, and provided horse rails for vehicles which sought to pause. That their residents should have a nontoxic supply of air suggests no revolutionary dalliance with socialism.

The discussion of this public poverty competed, on the whole successfully,

---

JOHN KENNETH GALBRAITH, *The Affluent Society* (Cambridge: The Riverside Press; Boston: Houghton Mifflin Co., 1958). Copyright 1958 by John Kenneth Galbraith. Used by permission.

with the stories of ever-increasing opulence in privately produced goods. The Gross National Product was rising. So were retail sales. So was personal income. Labor productivity had also advanced. The automobiles that could not be parked were being produced at an expanded rate. The children, though without schools, subject in the playgrounds to the affectionate interest of adults with odd tastes, and disposed to increasingly imaginative forms of delinquency, were admirably equipped with television sets. We had difficulty finding storage space for the great surpluses of food despite a national disposition to obesity. Food was grown and packaged under private auspices. The care and refreshment of the mind, in contrast with the stomach, was principally in the public domain. Our colleges and universities were severely overcrowded and underprovided, and the same was true of the mental hospitals.

The contrast was and remains evident not alone to those who read. The family which takes its mauve and cerise, air-conditioned, power-steered, and power-braked automobile out for a tour passes through cities that are badly paved, made hideous by litter, blighted buildings, billboards, and posts for wires that should long since have been put underground. They pass on into a countryside that has been rendered largely invisible by commercial art. (The goods which the latter advertise have an absolute priority in our value system. Such aesthetic considerations as a view of the countryside accordingly come second. On such matters we are consistent.) They picnic on exquisitely packaged food from a portable icebox by a polluted stream and go on to spend the night at a park which is a menace to public health and morals. Just before dozing off on an air mattress, beneath a nylon tent, amid the stench of decaying refuse, they may reflect vaguely on the curious unevenness of their blessings. Is this, indeed, the American genius?

II.

In the production of goods within the private economy it has long been recognized that a tolerably close relationship must be maintained between the production of various kinds of products. The output of steel and oil and machine tools is related to the production of automobiles. Investment in transportation must keep abreast of the output of goods to be transported. The supply of power must be abreast of the growth of industries requiring it. The existence of these relationships—coefficients to the economist—has made possible the construction of the input-output table which shows how changes in the production in one industry will increase or diminish the demands on other industries. . . . If expansion in one part of the economy were not matched by the requisite expansion in other parts—were the need for balance not respected—then bottlenecks and shortages, speculative hoarding of scarce supplies, and sharply increasing costs would ensue. Fortunately in peacetime the market system operates easily and effectively to maintain this balance, and this together with the existence of stocks and some flexibility in the coefficients as a result of substitution, insures that no serious difficulties will arise. . . .

Just as there must be balance in what a community produces, so there must also be balance in what the community consumes. An increase in the use of one product creates, ineluctably, a requirement for others. If we are to consume more automobiles, we must have more gasoline. There must be more insurance as well as more space on which to operate them. Beyond a certain point more and better food appears to mean increased need for medical services. This is the certain result of the increased consumption of tobacco and alcohol. More vacations require more hotels and more fishing rods. And so forth. With rare exceptions—shortages of doctors are an exception which suggests the rule—this balance is also maintained quite effortlessly so far as goods for private sale and consumption are concerned. The price system plus a rounded condition of opulence is again the agency.

However, the relationships we are here discussing are not confined to the private economy. They operate comprehensively over the whole span of private and public services. As surely as an increase in the output of automobiles puts new demands on the steel industry so, also, it places new demands on public services. Similarly, every increase in the consumption of private goods will normally mean some facilitating or protective step by the state. In all cases if these services are not forthcoming, the consequences will be in some degree ill. It will be convenient to have a term which suggests a satisfactory relationship between the supply of privately produced goods and services and those of the state, and we may call it social balance.

The problem of social balance is ubiquitous, and frequently it is obtrusive. As noted, an increase in the consumption of automobiles requires a facilitating supply of streets, highways, traffic control, and parking space. The protective services of the police and the highway patrols must also be available, as must those of the hospitals. Although the need for balance here is extraordinarily clear, our use of privately produced vehicles has, on occasion, got far out of line with the supply of the related public services. The result has been hideous road congestion, an annual massacre of impressive proportions, and chronic colitis in the cities. As on the ground, so also in the air. Planes collide with disquieting consequences for those within when the public provision for air traffic control fails to keep pace with private use of the airways.

But the auto and the airplane, versus the space to use them, are merely an exceptionally visible example of a requirement that is pervasive. The more goods people procure, the more packages they discard and the more trash that must be carried away. If the appropriate sanitation services are not provided, the counterpart of increasing opulence will be deepening filth. . . .

The issue of social balance can be identified in many other current problems. Thus an aspect of increasing private production is the appearance of an extraordinary number of things which lay claim to the interest of the young. Motion pictures, television, automobiles, and the vast opportunities which go with the mobility, together with such less enchanting merchandise as narcotics, comic books, and pornographia, are all included in an advancing gross national product. The child of a less opulent as well as a technologically more primitive age had far fewer such diversions. The red schoolhouse is remembered mainly because it had a paramount position in the lives of those who attended it that no modern school can hope to attain.

In a well-run and well-regulated community, with a sound school system, good recreational opportunities, and a good police force—in short a community where public services have kept pace with private production—the diversionary forces operating on the modern juvenile may do no great damage. Television and the violent mores of Hollywood and Madison Avenue must contend with the intellectual discipline of the school. The social, athletic, dramatic, and like attractions of the school also claim the attention of the child. These, together with the other recreational opportunities of the community, minimize the tendency to delinquency. Experiments with violence and immorality are checked by an effective law enforcement system before they become epidemic.

. . . . .

Residential housing also illustrates the problem of the social balance, although in a somewhat complex form. Few would wish to contend that, in the lower or even the middle income brackets, Americans are munificently supplied with housing. A great many families would like better located or merely more houseroom, and no advertising is necessary to persuade them of their wish. And the provision of housing is in the private domain. At first glance at least, the line we draw between private and public seems not to be preventing a satisfactory allocation of resources to housing.

On closer examination, however, the problem turns out to be not greatly different from that of education. . . . [The] housing industry functions well only in combination with a large, complex, and costly array of public services. These include land purchase and clearance for redevelopment; good neighborhood and city planning, and effective and well-enforced zoning; a variety of financing and other aids to the housebuilder and owner; publicly supported research and architectural services for an industry which, by its nature, is equipped to do little on its own; and a considerable amount of direct or assisted public construction for families in the lowest income brackets. The quality of the housing depends not on the industry, which is given, but on what is invested in these supplements and supports.

III.

. . . By failing to exploit the opportunity to expand public production we are missing opportunities for enjoyment which otherwise we might have had. Presumably a community can be as well rewarded by buying better schools or better parks as by buying bigger automobiles. By concentrating on the latter rather than the former it is failing to maximize its satisfactions. As with schools in the community, so with public services over the country at large. It is scarcely sensible that we should satisfy our wants in private goods with reckless abundance, while in the case of public goods on the evidence of the eye, we practice extreme self-denial. So, far from systematically exploiting the opportunities to derive use and pleasure from these services, we do not supply what would keep us out of trouble.

The conventional wisdom * holds that the community, large or small, makes a decision as to how much it will devote to its public services. This decision is arrived at by democratic process. Subject to the imperfections and uncertainties of democracy, people decide how much of their private income and goods they will surrender in order to have public services of which they are in greater need. Thus there is a balance, however rough, in the enjoyments to be had from private goods and services and those rendered by public authority.

It will be obvious, however, that this view depends on the notion of independently determined consumer wants. In such a world one could with some reason defend the doctrine that the consumer, as a voter, makes an independent choice between public and private goods. But given the dependence effect—given that consumer wants are created by the process by which they are satisfied—the consumer makes no such choice. He is subject to the forces of advertising and emulation by which production creates

---

* Professor Galbraith makes extensive use of this term to mean the opinions widely held by a group, perhaps professional economists, perhaps the great majority of the general public. *Ed.*

its own demand. Advertising operates exclusively, and emulation mainly, on behalf of privately produced goods and services. Since management and emulative effects operate on behalf of private production, public services will have an inherent tendency to lag behind. Automobile demand which is expensively synthesized will inevitably have a much larger claim on income than parks or public health or even roads where no such influence operates. The engines of mass communication, in their highest state of development, assail the eyes and ears of the community on behalf of more beer but not of more schools. Even in the conventional wisdom it will scarcely be contended that this leads to an equal choice between the two.

The competition is especially unequal for new products and services. Every corner of the public psyche is canvassed by some of the nation's most talented citizens to see if the desire for some merchantable product can be cultivated. No similar process operates on behalf of the nonmerchantable services of the state. Indeed, while we take the cultivation of new private wants for granted we would be measurably shocked to see it applied to public services. The scientist or engineer or advertising man who devotes himself to developing a new carburetor, cleanser, or depilatory for which the public recognizes no need and will feel none until an advertising campaign arouses it, is one of the valued members of our society. A politician or a public servant who dreams up a new public service is a wastrel. Few public offenses are more reprehensible.

So much for the influences which operate on the decision between public and private production. The calm decision between public and private consumption pictured by the conventional wisdom is, in fact, a remarkable example of the error which arises from viewing social behavior out of context. The inherent tendency will always be for public services to fall behind private production. We have here the first of the causes of social imbalance.

IV.

Social balance is also the victim of two further features of our society—the truce on inequality and the tendency to inflation. Since these are now part of our context, their effect comes quickly into view.

With rare exceptions such as the post office, public services do not carry a price ticket to be paid for by the individual user. By their nature they must, ordinarily, be available to all. As a result, when they are improved or new services are initiated, there is the ancient and troublesome question of who is to pay. This, in turn, provokes to life the collateral but irrelevant debate over inequality. As with the use of taxation as an instrument of fiscal policy, the truce on inequality is broken. Liberals are obliged to argue that the services be paid for by progressive taxation which will reduce inequality. Committed as they are to the urgency of goods . . . they must oppose sales and excise taxes. Conservatives rally to the defense of inequality—although without ever quite committing themselves in such uncouth terms—and oppose the use of income taxes. They, in effect, oppose the expenditure not on the merits of the service but on the demerits of the tax system. Since the debate over inequality cannot be resolved, the money is frequently not appropriated and the service not performed. It is a casualty of the economic goals of both liberals and conservatives for both of whom the questions of social balance are subordinate to those of production and, when it is evoked, of inequality.

In practice matters are better as well as worse than this statement of the basic forces suggests. Given the tax structure, the revenues of all levels of government grow with the growth of the economy. Services can be maintained and sometimes even improved out of this automatic accretion.

However, this effect is highly unequal. The revenues of the federal government, because of its heavy reliance on income taxes, increase more than proportionately with private economic growth. . . .

Things are made worse, however, by the fact that a large proportion of the federal revenues are pre-empted by defense. The increase in defense costs has also tended to absorb a large share of the normal increase in tax revenues. The position of the federal government for improving the social balance has also been weakened since World War II by the strong, although receding, conviction that its taxes were at artificial wartime levels and that a tacit commitment exists to reduce taxes at the earliest opportunity.

In the states and localities the problem of social balance is much more severe. Here tax revenues—this is especially true of the General Property Tax—increase less than proportionately with increased private production. Budgeting too is far more closely circumscribed than in the case of the federal government. . . . Because of this, increased services for states and localities regularly pose the question of more revenues and more taxes. And here, with great regularity, the question of social balance is lost in the debate over equality and social equity.

Thus we currently find by far the most serious social imbalance in the services performed by local governments. . . .

V.

Finally, social imbalance is the natural offspring of persistent inflation. Inflation by its nature strikes different individuals and groups with highly discriminatory effect. The most nearly unrelieved victims, apart from those living on pensions or other fixed provision for personal security, are those who work for the state. In the private economy the firm which sells goods has, in general, an immediate accommodation to the inflationary movement. Its price increases are the inflation. The incomes of its owners and proprietors are automatically accommodated to the upward movement. To the extent that wage increases are part of the inflationary process, this is also true of organized industrial workers. Even unorganized white collar workers are in a milieu where prices and incomes are moving up. The adaption of their incomes, if less rapid than that of the industrial workers, is still reasonably prompt.

The position of the public employee is at the other extreme. His pay scales are highly formalized, and traditionally they have been subject to revision only at lengthy intervals. In states and localities inflation does not automatically bring added revenues to pay higher salaries and incomes. Pay revision for all public workers is subject to the temptation to wait and see if the inflation isn't coming to an end. There will be some fear—this seems to have been more of a factor in England than in the United States—that advances in public wages will set a bad example for private employers and unions.

Inflation means that employment is pressing on the labor supply and that private wage and salary incomes are rising. Thus the opportunities for moving from public to private employment are especially favorable. Public employment, moreover, once had as a principal attraction a high measure of social security. Industrial workers were subject to the formidable threat of unemployment during depression. Public employees were comparatively secure, and this security was worth an adverse salary differential. But with improving economic security in general this advantage has diminished. Private employment thus has come to provide better protection against inflation and little worse protection against other hazards. Though the dedicated may stay in public posts, the alert go.

The deterioration of the public services in the years of inflation has not gone unremarked. However, there has been a strong tendency to regard it as an adventitious misfortune—something which, like a nasty shower at a picnic, happened to blight a generally good time. Salaries were allowed to lag, which was a pity. This is a very inadequate view. Discrimination against the public services is an organic feature of inflation. Nothing so weakens government as persistent inflation. . . .

VI.

A feature of the years immediately following World War II was a remarkable attack on the notion of expanding and improving public services. During the depression years such services had been elaborated and improved partly in order to fill some small part of the vacuum left by the shrinkage of private production. During the war years the role of government was vastly expanded. After that came the reaction. Much of it, unquestionably, was motivated by a desire to rehabilitate the prestige of private production and therewith of producers. No doubt some who joined the attack hoped, at least tacitly, that it might be possible to sidestep the truce on taxation vis-à-vis equality by having less taxation of all kinds. For a time the notion that our public services had somehow become inflated and excessive was all but axiomatic. Even liberal politicians did not seriously protest. They found it necessary to aver that they were in favor of public economy too.

In this discussion a certain mystique was attributed to the satisfaction of privately supplied wants. A community decision to have a new school means that the individual surrenders the necessary amount, willy-nilly, in his taxes. But if he is left with that income, he is a free man. He can decide between a better car or a television set. This was advanced with some solemnity as an argument for the TV set. The difficulty is that this argument leaves the community with no way of preferring the school. All private wants, where the individual can choose, are inherently superior to all public desires which must be paid for by taxation and with an inevitable component of compulsion.

The cost of public services was also held to be a desolating burden on private production, although this was at a time when the private production was burgeoning. Urgent warnings were issued of the unfavorable effects of taxation on investment. . . . This was at a time when the inflationary effect of a very high level of investment was causing concern. The same individuals who were warning about the inimical effects of taxes were strongly advocating a monetary policy designed to reduce investment. However, an understanding of our economic discourse requires an appreciation of one of its basic rules: men of high position are allowed, by a special act of grace, to accommodate their reasoning to the answer they need. Logic is only required in those of lesser rank.

Finally it was argued, with no little vigor, that expanding government posed a grave threat to individual liberties. . . .

With time this attack on public services has somewhat subsided. The disorder associated with social imbalance has become visible even if the need for balance between private and public services is still imperfectly appreciated.

. . . . .

Sometimes satire is every bit as effective as serious argument—and far more fun. Here we have an example directed at elements of arguments such as those in The Affluent Society *(Galbraith) and* The Waste Makers *(Packard).*

44 · The Sumptuary Manifesto *

SIR EPICURE MAMMON

Consumption . . . is a seamless web. If we ask about the chromium, we must ask about the cars. The questions that are asked about one part can be asked about all parts. The automobiles are too heavy, and they use irreplaceable lead? One can ask with equal cogency if we need to make all the automobiles that we now turn out. . . .

As with automobiles, so with everything else. In an opulent society the marginal urgency of all kinds of goods is low. It is easy to bring our doubts and questions to bear on the automobiles. But the case is not different for (say) that part of our food production which contributes not to nutrition but to obesity, that part of our tobacco which contributes not to comfort but to carcinoma and that part of our clothing which is designed not to cover nakedness but to suggest it. . . .

It is also suggested that uninhibited consumption has something to do with individual liberty. If we begin interfering with consumption, we shall be abridging a basic freedom.

I shan't dwell long on this. That we make such points is part of the desolate modern tendency to turn the discussion of all questions, however simple and forthright, into a search for the violation of some arcane principle, or to evade and suffocate common sense by verbose, incoherent, and irrelevant moralizing. Freedom is not much concerned with tail fins or even with automobiles. Those who argue that it is identified with the greatest possible range of choice of consumers' goods are only confessing their exceedingly simple-minded and mechanical view of man and his liberties.

—OUR PEERLESS LEADER

Accordingly, and with a view to liberating mankind from their insane preoccupation with material comforts of low marginal urgency, the SUMPTUARY SOCIETY (SS) has been formed to DEMAND that this nation immediately and without exception declare it to be a CAPITAL OFFENSE to:

1. Live in a dwelling unit of more than 400 square feet.

2. Own an automobile with wheelbase over 72 inches.

3. Drive an automobile using gasoline of higher octane rating (and lead [1]

---

* [While this article is not a review of any particular publication, readers will not find it difficult to identify the intellectual inspiration of the Sumptuary Society.—*The Editor*.]

[1] Our PEERLESS LEADER has taken a particular interest in preventing waste of the heavy metal.

SIR EPICURE MAMMON [who has been identified as Professor Jack Hirshleifer of the University of California], "The Sumptuary Manifesto," from the *Journal of Law and Economics*, Vol. II (The University of Chicago Law School: October 1959), pp. 120–123. Used by permission.

content) than standard fuel of the year 1923.

4. Drink whiskey aged more than 60 days.[2]

5. Smoke more than ten cigarettes in one day.[3]

6. Possess clothing in excess of, if a male, 1 coat, 2 pairs of shoes, 2 pairs of socks, 2 suits, 4 shirts, 3 handkerchiefs, 1 tie, 1 hat, 1 pair of rubbers, and 1 change of underwear. If a female, the same rules will apply with appropriate modifications (e.g., jackets will button on the left instead of the right).[4]

7. Appear in public clean-shaven (if a male).[5]

Furthermore, it will be declared an exceptionally HEINOUS offense punishable by boiling in oil to:

1. Possess more than two of the following: eye-level kitchen range, refrigerator with across-the-top freezing compartment, combination washer-dryer, two-tone auto paint job, Waring blender, chafing dish, or double-ended egg cup.

2. Be detected reading Orwell's *1984*, a book known to have low marginal usefulness, and whose production consumes irreplaceable timber, ink, glue, and *lead* type.

The following remarks are directed to sympathetic citizens who may not have fully grasped the logic underlying the reconstruction of our greedy wasteful society on sumptuary principles.

The most crucial point to appreciate is that the principles of the SS must be distinguished from a bleak Puritanism which would leave life joyless and empty. Under the false Puritan ideal, the individual was to be restrained from pursuit of the illusory goal of material pleasure by self-discipline. With our deeper knowledge today, of course, we are aware that the internal conflicts thus set up are psychologically damaging.[6] The principles of the SS, in contrast, are to be enforced by a psychologically sound and healthy method, the method of (in the words of our PEERLESS LEADER) "social responsibility." That is to say, through detectives, policemen, judges, and wardens. Furthermore, any residue of frustrations suffered by unreconstructed individuals will be more than compensated by the wholesome (and non-material-consuming) glee in their work which society's guardians may be expected to take.

The second point to realize is that our PEERLESS LEADER has declared certain forms of consumption to be innocuous

---

[2] This may seem an insufficient crime for such a harsh remedy; in fact, few realize the seriousness of this offense. Whiskey in aging evaporates at the rate of 1 per cent per month (!), wasting precious alcohol to pollute our atmosphere. Our PEERLESS LEADER himself quoted with approval criticism of the practice of "blow[ing] thousands of tons of unrecoverable lead into the atmosphere each year from high octane gasoline because we like a quick pickup." How much more objectionable it is to dissipate vast quantities of valuable esters and hydrocarbons merely to gratify effete overrefined palates, especially as no quicker pickup has ever been demonstrated for aged over unaged whiskey.

[3] Executions performed under this section would have the by-product advantage of reducing the lung-cancer death rate, a problem about which our PEERLESS LEADER has expressed concern.

[4] Claims for special treatment on grounds of occupation, place of residence, age, or family status will be ruled on by rationing and allocation boards composed of public-spirited citizens selected from the membership of the SS, many of whom have already contributed to the general welfare by related work in the past.

[5] Revival of the ancient and honorable custom of growing beards will save thousands of tons of irrecoverable high-quality steel now wasted for razor blades. In addition, barbiculturally well-endowed individuals will be able to dispense with scarves in the wintertime.

[6] That asceticism on an individually moralistic basis is erroneous has been demonstrated in the personal life of our PEERLESS LEADER himself. So long as the social system remains corrupt, attempts at personal salvation through individual restraint only befog the true issue.

or even praise-worthy: education, health, good government, clean countryside, and orchestras are specifically commended as having "rather small materials requirements." Of course, under sumptuary principles unaccompanied vocalists are even superior to orchestras, while among orchestras those employing expensive material-consuming mechanical aids like the piano, violin, and French horn should probably be eschewed in favor of those relying on simple instruments like the harmonica, ocarina, and kazoo. We may similarly reason that clean surroundings are best achieved by a man with bag and pointed stick; the tendency toward mechanization of garbage-handling is to be deplored, however creditable the object.

The modern sumptuary philosophy is an outgrowth—the culmination and crowning achievement—of twentieth-century economic science. We place particular importance, therefore, upon matters of economic policy, especially when these are regarded (in the words of our PEERLESS LEADER) as "instruments of social control." Our program includes the following DEMANDS:

1. *Farm price supports at 200 per cent of parity*. Our PEERLESS LEADER (also known as the FEARLESS FRIEND OF THE FARM BLOC) himself refuted those who would have reduced price supports from 90 per cent of parity, showing the enormous contribution these support payments have made to agricultural progress and technological innovation. Still more progress could be anticipated with prices at 200 per cent of parity. This arrangement has the unique sumptuary advantage that improvements of production techniques do not lead to any increase in consumption. Furthermore, the unconsumed produce may be used as fertilizer to restore or even increase the quality of the soil—a vital component of our "resource base" for the future.

2. *Price ceilings on everything not price-supported*. To allow markets to go uncontrolled would be to "ascribe a magical automatism to the price system."

3. *A food excise tax proportioned to calorie content; personal taxes based on avoirdupois or volume displacement*. The anti-corpulence program of the SS is based, of course, upon the concern of our PEERLESS LEADER with the problem of obesity. Our slogan: Fine the fat, stick the stout, and plunder the plump.

4. *A yardage tax on clothing materials*.[7]

5. *A universal protective—nay, prohibitive—tariff*. For, if it is wrong for us to overconsume our own irreplaceable materials, how much worse to use our economic power to rob poorer nations of their limited heritage.

No thinking man today will be swayed by the FAKE FREEDOM ISSUE raised by our enemies, the so-called libertarians or voluntarists. To paraphrase our PEERLESS LEADER, true consumer's freedom gives no one license to buy autos with tail fins—anymore than true freedom of speech gives any misguided person a "right" to propagandize against the views of the SS.

---

[7] Here, however, the position of our PEERLESS LEADER seems anomalous. Perhaps in an unguarded moment, he seemed to argue in favor of clothing covering nakedness rather than suggesting it. However, whether or not clothes should suggest nakedness is after all not a sumptuary issue but "irrelevant moralizing." On the other hand, who can deny that the bikini is exemplary sumptuary garb?

IX • MONEY, BANKING, AND INFLATION

The following brightly written and fecund selection comes from the pen of one of Britain's senior economists.

45 • *The Value of Money: an Introduction*

SIR DENNIS H. ROBERTSON

. . . . .
Once more we can keep on the right lines if we start by remembering that money is only one of many economic things. Its value therefore is primarily determined by exactly the same two factors as determine the value of any other thing, namely the conditions of demand for it, and the quantity of it available. In following out this idea, it is open to us to pursue either of two courses. We can fix our attention either on the *stock* of money in existence at a given *point* of time, or on the *flow* of money being used during a given *period* of time. Each of these procedures has its own advantages, and it will be well to be familiar with both of them before we have done; but since the main purpose of money is to be used, the latter procedure is perhaps that which comes more naturally to the ordinary man. Let us start then by fixing our attention on money on the wing, as opposed to money sitting. And by the value of money let us mean for the present its transaction-value—its value, that is, in terms of all the goods and services which it is used to purchase.

Looking at the matter in this way, we see that the conditions of demand for money consist in the total volume of business transactions of all kinds which has to be performed within a given time with the aid of money. The volume of business transactions to be performed may increase for various reasons. Perhaps the flow of finished goods and services which have to be distributed among the community for final consumption increases. Or perhaps, whether owing to an outburst of speculative activity or to a change in the organization of industry, raw materials such as cotton and wheat come to change hands more often before taking on their final

---

SIR DENNIS H. ROBERTSON, *Money* (Chicago: The University of Chicago Press, 1948), pp. 28–33. Reprinted by permission of the The University of Chicago Press and James Nisbet & Co. Ltd.

form of shirts and loaves of bread. Or perhaps for some reason the exchange of capital goods such as houses and securities becomes more active. In any case, an increase in the volume of transactions means an increase in the demand for money. And similarly a decrease in the volume of transactions means a decrease in the demand for money.

But *given the conditions of demand for money*, its value depends on the quantity of it available. If fewer units were available, there would be more work for each of them to do; each of them would have to exchange for a larger volume of other things—its value, as we have defined it, would be greater than it actually is. If more units of money were available, each of them would have to exchange for a smaller volume of things—its value would be less than it actually is. If we pursue our analysis to the bitter end, we shall be forced to admit that if even *one* unit of money were withdrawn from the quantity actually available, there would be some slight tendency for more work to fall upon the others, and for their value to rise. The value of each unit of money is what it is because there are just so many units, and neither more nor less available: and the value of *every* unit of money is equal to the value of *any* unit among them which we can conceive of as being suddenly abolished.

. . . in this also the value of money resembles that of other things—that *given the conditions of demand*, it depends on the total number of units available, and is equal to the value of any such unit that we choose to conceive of as being suddenly abstracted.

DIFFERENCES BETWEEN MONEY AND OTHER THINGS. We may now pass on to consider two respects in which the value of money is determined differently from the value of other things.

The first respect is very important indeed. The value of bread is not only an expression of the bundle of things in general which can be obtained in exchange for a loaf of bread: it is also in some degree a measure of the usefulness, or enjoyment-yielding power, of a loaf of bread. If one of the available loaves were destroyed, there would be a corresponding loss in real economic welfare. Can we say the same about money?

From one point of view we can. If one unit of money were suddenly abolished, the possessor of the particular unit selected for abolition would clearly be the poorer. Nobody who has ever lost a sixpence through a crack in the floor will dispute this. But it is by no means obvious that the world as a whole would be impoverished in the same degree: for the command over real things surrendered by the loser of the sixpence is not abolished, but passes automatically to the rest of the community whose sixpences will now buy more. If indeed there were a large and simultaneous loss or destruction of money, society might easily find itself hampered in the conduct of its business, and the consequent check to exchange and production might lead to a serious decrease in its real economic welfare. But the fact remains that the value of money is (within limits) a measure of the usefulness of any one unit of money to its possessor, but not to society as a whole; while the value of bread is also a measure (within limits) of the *social* usefulness of any one loaf of bread. And the reason for this peculiarity about money is the fact that nobody generally speaking wants it except for the sake of control which it gives over other things.

The second respect in which money is peculiar as regards the determination of its value is closely allied to the first:

and while it is less important, it has attracted more attention. *Given the conditions of demand for money,* the relation between its value and the quantity of it available is of this peculiar kind: the larger the number of units available, the smaller, in exactly the same proportion, is the value of each unit. A moment's reflection will carry conviction that this must be true. If there is a certain volume of things to be exchanged, and if each of them is to change hands a certain number of times: then, if the quantity of money available were halved, there would be exactly twice as much work for each unit of money to do—each unit would have to pass in exchange for twice as great a volume of things in general. If the quantity of money available were doubled, there would be exactly half as much work for each unit to do—each unit would have to pass in exchange for half as great a volume of things in general. To use the correct arithmetical term, given the conditions of demand for money, its value *varies inversely* as the quantity available, or in other words the "general level of prices" *varies directly* as the quantity of money available.

If, however, we are to avoid drawing false inferences from this interesting peculiarity of money, we must look a little more closely into the phrase "the quantity of money available." We decided, it will be remembered, to fix our attention for the present on the *flow* of money on to the market's during a given period of time—let us say a week. But during that week some of the pieces of money in existence will not be available for work; they may be holiday-making in my pocket, or taking a prolonged rest-cure in the bank, or even being "cooled a long age in the deep-delved earth." On the other hand, some will be available twice or thrice or many times, and will be used in one short week to discharge a number of quite separate transactions. Some pieces of money are very agile, like pieces of scandal, and skip easily from one person to another: others are like an old lady buying a railway ticket—one would think that they had lost the power of locomotion altogether. This truth is often expressed by saying that we must take account not only of the total quantity of money, but also of its average "velocity of circulation." And though we have found it convenient to approach it by a different route, it is precisely analogous to the truth that in estimating the demand for money we must take into account not only the volume of goods to be disposed of within a given time, but also the frequency with which each of them changes hands.

Here is a little story [adapted from Edgeworth] to illustrate this conception of the velocity of circulation of money. On Derby Day two men, Bob and Joe, invested in a barrel of beer, and set off to Epsom with the intention of selling it retail on the racecourse at 6 pence a pint, the proceeds to be shared equally between them. On the way Bob, who had one threepenny-bit left in the world, began to feel a great thirst, and drank a pint of the beer, paying Joe 3 pence as his share of the market price. A little later Joe yielded to the same desire, and drank a pint of beer, returning the 3 pence to Bob. The day was hot, and before long Bob was thirsty again, and so, a little later, was Joe. When they arrived at Epsom, the 3 pence was back in Bob's pocket, and each had discharged in full his debts to the other: but the beer was all gone. One single threepenny-bit had performed a volume of transactions which would have required many shillings if the beer had been sold to the public in accordance with the original intention.

If we are interested, not in the "transaction-value" of money, but in its "income-value"—its value in terms of the goods and services which form part of real income or output—we can adopt the same method of approach. But in this case the velocity of circulation of money will mean, not the average number of times each piece of money is spent for any purpose whatsoever, but the average number of times it is spent in purchase of the goods and services which form part of real income or output, during the week or other period of time in question. This "income-velocity" of circulation of money is naturally much smaller than its "transactions-velocity."

[Prof. Robertson then proceeds to discuss the demand for money or factors affecting velocity. *Ed.*]

. . . . .

What really causes inflation? What are its consequences? How can we prevent this phenomenon? A Harvard professor of economics examines these and related questions.

46 · Inflation: Its Causes and Cures

GOTTFRIED HABERLER

Unless a different meaning is clearly indicated, I shall take inflation to mean a condition of rising prices. . . . [The author discusses other usages of the term "inflation." *Ed.*]

. . . . .

. . . in order to avoid confusion, two factors must be kept well in mind. . . . *First,* when we speak of prices being kept stable . . . and wages being allowed to rise parallel with productivity, we refer to the *average* price level and *average* wage level. Prices of individual commodities (economists speak of "relative prices" as distinguished from the "general price level") must remain flexible in a smoothly working economy and the wage structure ("relative wages") should not be frozen. That is to say, there should be a flexible system of wage differentials as between different skills and localities, and between expanding and contracting industries in order to provide sufficient inducement for the labor force to adjust itself to the changing needs of the economy.

An important corollary is this: Technological progress is never uniform, but affects different industries to an unequal degree. Cost of production is reduced faster in some industries than in others, or expressed differently, output per man-hour rises faster in the more progressive industries. If the average price level is to remain stable, if full employment is

---

GOTTFRIED HABERLER, *Inflation: Its Causes and Cures* (Washington: American Enterprise Association, June 1960), pp. 3-82. Used by permission.

to be maintained, and if the best use is to be made of productive resources, then the industries where costs have fallen more than elsewhere must reduce their prices. (If they produce a better quality product at the same price, this is equivalent to a fall in price but may not find sufficient expression in the indices.) If they fail to reduce their prices, demand for their products will not increase and since output per head has increased, employment will decline. This would also imply the emergence of large profits, and labor unions can be depended on to capture some of these profits in the form of higher wages.

So long as the prices of the cheapened products do not fall, the producers keep the fruits of technological progress in the form of higher wages and higher profits for themselves, instead of passing them on to the community at large, and employment suffers. But since the American economy is rather competitive, the chances are that sooner or later excess profits will be whittled away by competition. Wages, on the other hand, are notoriously sticky in the downward direction. There are then two possibilities. Either wages remain higher in the progressive industries in comparison with wages elsewhere, implying an unjustified and uneconomical discrimination between different groups of workers and a loss of employment; or, and this is the more likely outcome, wages in the less progressive industries will tend to be pushed up to be brought in line with the standard set by the progressive industries. This, of course, necessitates a rise of prices in the less progressive industries which have not experienced the same reduction in cost as the more progressive industries and hence, if they are not to reduce output and employment, must raise their prices when wage costs go up.

. . . . .

The *second* point to remember is this: The postulate that the price level should be kept approximately stable for the long run does not mean that the price level should never be allowed to decline. The reason is very simple. It will hardly be possible, even apart from war and periods of acute international tension requiring large defense expenditure, to avoid periods of rising prices altogether. Business cycle upswings are almost always characterized by price rises. If then the long-term price trend should be horizontal, i.e., if long-run inflation is to be avoided, the price level must be allowed to fall in depressions to make up for the price rise during boom periods. It is well known that this did not happen during the last two depressions (1953–54 and 1957–58). [Nor during the 1960–61 decline. *Ed.*]

. . . . .

Causes of Inflation

Many different factors and policies have been held responsible for inflation. Some say aggregate demand rising faster than aggregate supply "pulls up" prices and wages ("demand-pull inflation"). The rise in demand in turn may be due to a government deficit ("government inflation") or to an expansion of bank credit for private investment ("credit expansion") or rising demand from abroad ("imported inflation") or an increase in gold production ("gold inflation"). Others say prices are being "pushed up" by wage increases forced upon the economy by labor unions under threat of strike ("wage-push inflation"), or costs may be raised by business monopolies ("administered price inflation"). To these positive factors can be added negative ones—for example, the failure of overall output to grow or of savings to stay on their "normal" level—factors for which, in turn, different causes may be found.

It is not difficult to think of conditions under which one or the other of these hypotheses would be valid and for several of these possibilities actual examples can be found in recent economic history.

But let me try to give a somewhat more orderly and systematic analysis of the primary cause. Let us start from the basic fact that there is no record in the economic history of the whole world, anywhere or at any time, of a serious and prolonged inflation which has not been accompanied and made possible, if not directly caused, by a large increase in the quantity of money. This generalization holds for developed as well as underdeveloped countries, for capitalist, pre-capitalist, and even centrally-planned economies. It is true that the velocity of circulation of money changes. . . .

But except in periods of hyperinflation (which could not develop without a sharp and sustained rise in the quantity of money) a rise in velocity by itself has never caused, or substantially intensified, serious inflationary trouble. When judging this statement, it should be remembered that I define inflation as a rise in prices and not as an increase in MV. During depressions V falls and the economy becomes more liquid. Recovery from a depression can, therefore, be financed to some extent by a more intensive utilization of the existing money stocks. The Great Depression and the ensuing war have produced an unusual accumulation of idle funds; hence the postwar expansion could be financed to an unusual extent by a more active use of the existing stock of money. But these facts do not invalidate the statement in question because in such circumstances the increase in velocity is matched by an increase in output. I do not claim that there must be an exact parallelism between the rise in output and the increase in V, so that any rise in prices must be attributed to an increase in M. The increase in V may exceed, or fall short of, the rise in output. What I say is that a prolonged serious inflation (price rise) has never been caused by an increase in velocity.

It follows that in every inflation the quantity of money is a causal factor, either active or permissive, and none of the factors and policies mentioned above can produce serious inflation unless they cause or induce or are accompanied by an increase in that quantity. Sometimes the connection between any one of these factors and the quantity of money is direct and noncontroversial. In other cases it is indirect and subtle. . . .

. . . . .

Let us return to the distinction made between demand-pull and cost-push inflation. Economists both here and elsewhere have been divided into two groups, those who stress demand pull and those who emphasize cost push, with several nuances in each group and quite a few occupying an intermediate position.

There are obviously a number of powerful factors that have operated to keep aggregate demand rising during the postwar period, even after the pent-up demand and piled-up liquidity inherited from the war and the prewar depression —the Great Depression—had been worked off more or less. These factors include: a huge government budget—a multiple of what it was before the Great Depression, not only in absolute terms, but also as percent of GNP—a large part of it for unproductive purposes; a large welfare establishment; a high though fluctuating level of private investment; and above all a profound change in overall economic policy: a firm resolve to maintain full employment and not to tolerate any depression going beyond a mild, temporary drop in output and employment.

This sounds very persuasive and seems quite sufficient to explain postwar inflation, although it must be insisted that it is not enough to point to "pent-up demand," i.e., the urge of governments (national, state, and local) as well as of private producers and consumers to invest in order to make good war and depression-produced deficiencies of the capital stock (including houses and consumer durables) and the wish or necessity to spend for welfare purposes or defense. These forces could not produce inflation but only high interest rates and tight money, unless the quantity of money was continuously increased. Even the piled-up liquidity inherited from war and depression, insofar as it consisted (as it largely did) of Government securities, could be turned into effective demand for goods and services only because the Federal Reserve Banks stood ready to buy those securities at fixed prices, that is, to "monetize the debt" as the phrase goes. Only excess balances consisting of money (currency and bank deposits) can be spent directly without a helping hand from the central bank. But surely this source could not have sustained inflation for long. Moreover, the activation of idle currency and deposits could have been counteracted by central bank policy. . . .

. . . . .

That wages rise in the process of demand inflation is natural and would in fact be inevitable, even if there were no unions and if perfect competition ruled in the labor market. Moreover, unions or none, wages would rise in excess of average productivity, that is to say, faster than average output per head (or per man-hour). That money wages rise faster than average output per head (productivity) is sometimes cited as proof that there is cost-push and not demand-pull inflation. This is not so. Even in a pure demand-pull inflation (unless wages are artificially frozen and labor rationed) wages must rise faster than real average productivity (output in physical terms divided by the number of men- or man-hours). Furthermore, in a progressive economy in which (marginal) productivity of labor gradually increases and consequently real wages go up, money wages must rise faster than prices.

What then, is the nature of cost-push inflation? Can it be distinguished from demand-pull inflation and, if so, what are the criteria that permit us to distinguish one from the other?

One point should be clear. If there were free competition in the labor market, wages would be determined by demand and supply and there could be no such thing as a "wage push." Only if there are monopolistic organizations, i.e., labor unions, can we speak of a wage push.

The argument of the wage-push theorist . . . can be stated as follows: In many countries labor unions have become so powerful that they are able to get periodic wage increases (including fringe benefits) greatly in excess of the overall average increase in output per man-hour. Even if in some industries the wage increase is not greater than the increase in productivity of that particular industry and could possibly be granted without raising the price of the products of that industry, these wage increases, to the extent that they exceed the overall increase in productivity for industry as a whole, must lead to inflation, if the level of employment is to be maintained.

The reason for that is simple enough.

If in the progressive industries output per man rises by, say, 10 percent and wages also go up by 10 percent, the cost and price of the product, as well as the volume of sales, will remain unchanged. Since the same output can now be produced with less labor, some of the workers will be thrown out of work. And in order to reabsorb the unemployed (in this particular industry and elsewhere) demand in general and prices will have to be inflated (or else wages be cut in the nonprogressive sectors). What will probably happen, as was pointed out above, is that the wage increase in the progressive industries will be, to a large extent, generalized over the less progressive sectors which cannot absorb it without a rise in the price of their products. But it should be stressed once more that even if the spread of wage increases from progressive industries to the less progressive sectors did not happen, a failure of the sales prices of the progressive industries to fall (either because wages have gone up in proportion to the increase in productivity or because profit margins have permanently risen) must entail unemployment or inflation.

To sum up, when the wage level rises faster (say, by 5 percent or more per year) than overall productivity (which, on the average of good and bad years, rises probably not more than by 1½ or 2 percent a year), prices must go up *if the level of employment is to be maintained*. If by monetary policy (the same holds for fiscal policy) the price level is kept stable, if, that is to say, the monetary authorities prevent the increase in aggregate demand (MV) that would be necessary to sustain the higher price level (either by refusing to let M go up or by reducing M so as to counteract a possible rise in V) then the inescapable consequence will be unemployment. At some level the pressure of unemployment would presumably become strong enough to prevent a further rise in the wage level.

We thus find ourselves, according to the cost-push theory, facing the dilemma: either let prices rise or permit a certain amount of unemployment. . . .

. . . the mere fact that during a given period of inflation wages have outrun productivity or that wages have outrun prices, is in general not sufficient proof that wage push rather than demand pull has caused the inflation. Only under certain circumstances is the conclusion unquestionably valid—for example, if wages outrun productivity, or in fact if they rise at all, during a period of depression and unemployment when aggregate demand stagnates or contracts. Thus when wages and prices rose during the recession of 1957–58, we had a clear case of wage-push inflation. Moreover, during a period which cannot be regarded as a depression period, because overall output and employment are rising—if wages rise in any particular industry where there still is much unemployment, we would have to speak of wage push; surely under these circumstances a wage rise could not happen in a competitive labor market. Thus the labor contracts in the automobile industry in 1958 and in steel in 1960 would seem to be cases of wage push.

In periods when wages, prices, and aggregate demand all go up more or less parallel . . . it is not easy to diagnose which is the active and which the passive factor. The crucial question to which we should like to have an answer is this: Suppose aggregate demand stops rising or is brought under control by monetary or fiscal measures so as to keep the price level stable; will that bring the wage rise to a halt? If so, we have a case of demand pull. If, on the other hand, wages go on rising and if it requires a sizeable amount of unemployment to bring the wage rise to a halt, we are confronted with a case of wage push.

. . . . .

. . . the fact that . . . when in 1957 demand ceased to grow and wages and prices continued to rise [provides] very strong indication that the wage push had existed for some time. Another indication is supplied by studying the attitude and policies of labor unions. That a scholar of the late Professor Slichter's rank, whose knowledge of the institutions and policies of labor unions and whose insight into the psychology, aspirations, and strategy of labor leaders were unrivaled among economists, said flatly that the unions are responsible for creeping inflation, must carry great weight. . . .

Another clue might be the behavior of profits. A demand inflation, one should think, would result in large profit margins, at least for some time until wages and salaries begin to catch up. A wage-push inflation, on the other hand, would encroach on profits or at least be characterized by unchanged profits. But the difficulty with this test is that profits fluctuate very widely over the cycle. . . .

Disregarding cyclical fluctuations, one can probably say that in the United States profit margins have shown a tendency to decline since the Korean War boom. That boom was clearly a case of demand-pull inflation. But since then wage push seems to have been on the ascendency.

There can be hardly a doubt that wage push, in conjunction with demand pull and full employment policies, has been a powerful factor in the postwar inflation. The wage push is overt during periods of slack, but masked and difficult to evaluate and separate from other factors during periods of prosperity.

Even those who are inclined to discount the wage-boosting power of labor unions will admit that unions make wages rigid in the downward direction. It can be shown that mere wage rigidity combined with full employment policies go a long way to explain chronic though intermittent inflation, that is to say, why the price curve in the postwar period shows the general shape of a rising flight of stairs. During business cycle upswings, wages and prices are pulled up. During the downswing, unions block any reduction of wage rates and anti-depression policies (whether in the form of automatic stabilizers or of *ad hoc* measures of reflation) quickly relieve the contraction. Thus by a sort of "ratchet effect" the price level is pushed up intermittently.

"Cost-push" or "seller's inflation" is often said to stem not only from wage push exerted by labor unions, but also from cost and price increases brought about by business monopolies and oligopolies. This theory usually takes the form of a theory of "mark-up or administered price inflation." A desire to be "impartial" as between different social groups undoubtedly contributes to the widespread habit of blaming business monopolies along with labor unions for inflation.

However, it seems to me that there are basic differences between the operation of "industrial monopolies and oligopolies" on the one hand and of "labor monopolies" on the other hand —differences which make the impact of the two on the price level fundamentally different. But let it be said emphatically that the following analysis of these differences does not imply any ethical or moral discrimination whatsoever between management (business) and labor.

The first difference is connected with the fact that unions make wages rigid downward. We have seen that the rigidity through the "ratchet effect" jacks up the price level in prosperous years and prevents it from falling during recessions. No doubt some prices, too, are rigid downward (especially those subject to public regulations). But wage rigidity is certainly more widespread and enduring than price rigidity.

Secondly, it will hardly be denied that in the United States and many other democratic countries business monopolies are in a much weaker position than labor monopolies. They lack the physical coercive power, rigid discipline, and intense loyalties of their members, which many unions have developed. Moreover, in many countries, especially in the United States, industrial monopolies are subject to special controls from which labor unions are *de jure* or *de facto* exempt.

In addition to these two differences between the operation of labor unions and industrial monopolies, there is another one which can perhaps be best brought out by a mental experiment. Compare two hypothetical situations, one characterized by the existence of many "business monopolies" but with the prevalence of competition (absence of monopolies) in the labor market, the other by the existence of "labor monopolies" but with the prevalence of competition (absence of monopolies or oligopolies) in the commodity market.

Suppose first that there exist no industrial monopolies or oligopolies or that such monopolies or oligopolies are regulated as public utilities actually are, but that labor is organized in powerful unions. It will be agreed, I believe, that this would not essentially change the facts of cost inflation through wage push. It is true that some unions would have to change their strategy. It would no longer be possible for a union to pick out a particular firm and force it by strike to pay higher wages which are later generalized over the rest of the industry. This would not work because a single firm in a competitive industry cannot afford, even for a short period, to pay much higher wages and charge higher prices for its products than the rest. But as unions in competitive industries in this country (e.g., in the textile or coal industries) and abroad have amply demonstrated, competition in the product market is not an insuperable obstacle to the formation of very powerful unions whose bargaining power and ability to strike the whole industry is just as great as that in oligopolistic industries.

Now make the opposite assumption that there is competition and no union monopolies in the labor market, but that there are numerous business monopolies and oligopolies. A brief reflection will show, I believe, that in this case there is no reason to assume that there will be a continuing pressure on the price and cost level resulting from monopoly prices being pushed up higher and higher, confronting the economy with the disagreeable dilemma of either letting prices rise continuously (inflation) or blocking the expansion of demand and stopping the rise of prices by monetary and fiscal measures which would imperil growth and impair the level of employment.

It is true, of course, that business monopolies (to the extent that they in fact exist and are not effectively regulated) keep prices at a higher level than would prevail under competition; but there is no reason to assume that such monopoly prices would be pushed higher and higher. To put it differently, the introduction of *numerous* monopolies where there existed competition before, would lead to higher prices and could be called inflationary. But the existence of monopolies or oligopolies does not lead to continuing pressure on prices. I find it difficult to believe that anybody would seriously want to argue that, unless the government steps in and stops the process, there is a tendency for mark-ups to be continuously increased or of "administered prices" to be continuously raised.

. . . . .

It is perfectly natural, on the other hand, that strong unions should try to force large wage increases every year or every other year and to endeavor to push continuously beyond the level set by the general increase in output per man-hour, especially in industries where productivity rises faster than elsewhere.

Union power is, of course, not unlimited. The main limiting factor, besides restraining influences on the part of the government or of public opinion which come into play only in extreme cases, is the elasticity of the demand for the product of the industry (or firm) in question. The more elastic the demand the greater the threat of shrinking employment when wages are pushed up. In this connection, the fact that in the short run elasticities of demand (for product as well as for labor) are likely to be much lower than in the long run, because it takes time for substitutes to be developed and for demand to shift to substitutes, is of very great importance. It means that employers give in to wage demands more easily and that before the deterrent effect of falling employment has time to restrain union demands for higher wages, wages have been raised elsewhere and aggregate demand and the whole price level have been pushed up. It is inherent in the inflationary process that it makes the earlier wage rises illusory and by the same token tolerable without impairment of employment. Needless to repeat that the process could not develop indefinitely without an expansion of the money supply.

I do not deny that to the extent to which unregulated industrial monopolies exist and to the extent to which it is possible by antitrust policy or otherwise to introduce more competition, such a policy would have an anti-inflationary effect. But such a reform would have only a once-for-all effect and would not remove a continuing pressure for inflation. Moreover, no large once-for-all effects can be expected for the simple reason that the American economy is very competitive except in the area of public utilities (some types of transportation, communication, etc.) where rates are controlled anyway. The most effective method of making sure that there will be a maximum of competition is freer trade. The large free trade area inside the United States is probably a more important factor than antimonopoly legislation, making the United States economy highly competitive compared with most other countries. But the rise of imports and of foreign competition, both in the United States and in foreign markets, in recent years has shown that even for a country of the size of the United States international trade is a strong antidote for inflation. Its anti-inflationary operation is, however, by no means based exclusively on its capacity to counteract monopolies. Competitive industries, too, feel the spur of foreign competition, which stiffens the employer's resistance to inflationary wage demands and promotes progress and efficiency.

There can be no doubt that much more important than private monopolies or oligopolies are a great number of government operated, sponsored, or induced price maintenance and price support schemes ranging from haircuts, "fair price laws," stock piling policies, and import restrictions to the six basic farm products subject to the parity price policy. The last mentioned policy of parity prices for agricultural products is equivalent to a monopoly of gigantic magnitude dwarfing any monopoly that ever existed in the private sector. It not only keeps farm prices high, but involves a tremendous waste of resources in the form of unsaleable surpluses which a private monopoly either could nor would do, and adds substantially to the government budget and deficits.

Like union wage push and unlike business monopolies, the farm price policy (if rigidly adhered to) very likely constitutes a continuing inflationary force. . . .

From basic causes we may distinguish factors accelerating and propagating inflation. If an inflation continues for a long period and is never interrupted by price declines or at least by prolonged periods of stable prices, more and more people will come to expect further price rises. Such expectations, which find their expression in higher interest rates, greater and more frequent wage demands, and eventually adjustments, at shorter and shorter intervals, of "fixed" income, obviously are an accelerating force. Cost of living escalator clauses in wage and salary contracts, and in later stages of inflation also in debts and securities and other contracts, are another accelerating factor. Such arrangements obviously eliminate some, though not all, injustices of the inflationary process, but by the same token tend to bring the process more quickly to a head—accelerating the speed of inflation, if the money supply is elastic, or raising costs and thus slamming on the brakes, if there is no slack in the monetary system. . . .

. . . . .

[The author next examines "conflicting interpretations of the 1955–58 inflation in the United States." *Ed.*]

. . . . .

Some Consequences of Inflation

Discussing the economic and social consequences of inflation, I shall again concentrate in the main on creeping chronic inflation, for two reasons. First, this type rather than rapid inflation is relevant for the United States and most other industrial countries, at least in peacetime, and secondly, it is a more controversial and insidious process than the rapid inflation that is rampant in other parts of the world. But by way of introduction, a few words should perhaps be said about the latter.

I take it for granted that on inflation of, say, 5 percent or more per year continued for more than a few years would become intolerable in a modern industrial country like the United States.

It would bring revolutionary changes in the income distribution, rapidly depreciate hundreds of billions of dollars worth of bonds, life insurances, and other monetary assets, and would be extremely hard on fixed income receivers.

It is true that our capitalist economy has shown tremendous recuperative power. The two war inflations have, in fact, brought about some of the changes I just mentioned, but our productive capacity and social fabric remained undamaged. The war experience does not, however, in the least contradict the statement that a peacetime inflation of 5 percent or more per year would soon become intolerable. Before it brought about radical changes, it surely would accelerate. It would start a flight from monetary assets, raise interest rates, and lead to the introduction of escalator clauses in wages, salaries, and later in debt contracts. We can be sure that before it took on aspects of hyperinflation it would be stopped, if not by financial measures, then by direct controls.

So far, the United States has been spared that type of inflation. The inflations we have had were war inflation, short-run cyclical inflations, and recently chronic, though intermittent, creeping inflation. Rapid, prolonged inflation is, however, rampant in many underdeveloped countries, especially in Latin America. There can be no doubt, I believe, that it retards economic growth. If some of the highly inflationary countries, e.g., Brazil, have experienced economic growth nevertheless, they would have grown even faster with less inflation.

Let me briefly indicate how inflation damages the economies of underdeveloped countries and retards their economic growth. Chronic inflation discourages thrift and makes the development of a capital market well-nigh impossible. It is a constant complaint in underdeveloped countries that they are handicapped by the absence of a well-functioning capital market. But how could it be otherwise? It is true, a poor country cannot hope, even without inflation, to develop a capital market that distributes more capital—or to look at it from the other side, which absorbs more securities—than the meager savings plus the funds that may be attracted from abroad permit. Inflation does not only discourage saving, it also drives savings abroad, i.e., it encourages capital flight and impedes capital imports. Without inflation there is no reason why small and poor countries should not have well-functioning capital markets which efficiently and economically distribute the limited amounts of capital available among competing uses.

Furthermore, inflation not only dries up the sources of capital funds but also misdirects capital funds that become available. It may not discourage global investment, but it encourages the wrong kind of investment—excessive merchandising, building, and inventories.

. . . . .

Even in underdeveloped countries prices are not entirely uncontrolled. The existence side by side of controlled and uncontrolled prices and areas creates very serious distortions. A glaring example is public utility rates. The prices of telephone and telegraph services, railroad fares, and electricity rates are subject to control. These prices then lag far behind in the general rise and the consequence is serious undermaintenance and underinvestment in these vital services. The problem becomes especially acute if these services are provided by foreign companies. Inflation, "planning," and government intervention thus lead to a deficiency in social overhead capital, the importance of which for economic development the advocates of government planning never get tired of emphasizing.

The modern form of repressed inflation and semi-repressed inflation causes or implies a proliferation of controls and interventions—price control, import controls, exchange control, rationing, allocation, etc. This overtaxes and corrupts the administrative apparatus and diverts government energies and know-how from more important functions. This is a serious matter for any country, but especially for underdeveloped countries which are poorly endowed with the precious resource of governmental know-how, administrative efficiency, and political honesty; it involves a great waste of scarce manpower and brainpower which underdeveloped countries can ill afford.

. . . . .

Let me concede freely that situations are thinkable and do arise in which inflation, even rapid inflation, may appear to be the lesser evil—a terrible evil to be sure, but still better than some alternatives.

If a country grows despite inflation, this may be deemed better than no growth at all. And governments sometimes manage to maneuver themselves into a position where this is the only alternative. Let me give two examples, for which it would be easy to cite concrete instances from recent Latin American history. If wage rates of industrial workers are raised exorbitantly by minimum wage legislation—50 or 100 percent jumps of statutory minimum wages are no rarity in Latin America—or by government-coddled labor unions, massive inflation may be the only way to prevent disaster. Or if governments by means of deficit financing continuously try to capture a larger and larger fraction of the national product for unproductive purposes (for the upkeep of an exorbitant military establishment, lavish government buildings, expansion of a huge bureaucracy, overambitious social welfare establishments, etc.) it may well be the lesser evil to top the government inflation by private credit inflation, i.e., to intensify inflation, in order to prevent the government from bidding away too large a portion of available resources from productive investment for its wasteful purposes. But it cannot be emphasized too strongly that such situations where rapid inflation appears to be the lesser evil are always the result of faulty policies. . . .

Let us turn our attention now to the slow creeping type of inflation with which the United States and other industrial countries are confronted.

An annual price rise of 2 to 3 percent is, of course, a lesser evil than one of 5 percent or more. Some people may argue that if the alternative to such inflation is permanent unemployment of, say, 6 or 7 percent of the labor force (on the average over good and bad years) with the corresponding annual loss of output and income, this condition would still be preferable to the injustices and evils of an inflation of 5 percent per year or more; but that they would accept a 2 to 3 percent inflation as the price for reducing unemployment by 3 or 4 percentage points and for avoiding the annual income loss that the unemployment entails. They might add that in the case of a slow inflation it would be easy to eliminate the more glaring injustices by frequent adjustment of fixed incomes and escalator clauses in long-term contracts.

The plausibility and reasonableness of the social preferences ("value judgments") implied by such views are debatable and I shall not discuss them. The crucial fact is that in reality there exists no such choice. A continuous creeping inflation of 2 to 3 percent a year could not go on indefinitely without causing unemployment. After a while the creeping inflation would accelerate, or if it were kept at the creeping pace the unemployment would emerge which the creeping inflation was supposed to forestall. I am speaking now of *continuous* creeping inflation. The case of the *intermittent,* that is, from time to time interrupted or reversed, creeping inflation is not quite so clear. Its course and outcome depend on the frequency and magnitude of the interruptions or reversals.

That the pace of continuous creeping inflation will inevitably tend to quicken, if it is not halted or reversed, follows from the fact that as creeping inflation continues, more and more people will expect a further rise in prices and will take steps to protect themselves. Interest rates will go up because the lender wants protection from the depreciation of the value of money and the borrower thinks he can afford to pay higher rates because the price of his products will go up; labor unions will ask for high wage increases in order to secure real improvement; the frequency of wage and salary adjustments will increase and cost of living escalators will be built into more and more contracts; and eventually "fixed" incomes will be regularly adjusted.

It is, therefore, an illusion to believe that a creeping inflation can remain so indefinitely. How long it takes before it starts to accelerate, and the rate of acceleration, depend on many factors, among them past history. . . .

Intermittent creeping inflation is less serious than continuous inflation, for the lulls in the price rise provide a breathing spell during which confidence in the stability of the value of money can revive. But it seems that since the end of World War II, the intermissions have been too short fully to restore confidence. It takes then only a short period of renewed upcreep of prices to rekindle fears of inflation, which in turn lead to anticipatory actions tending to turn the creep into a trot.

Some proponents of the theory that creeping inflation is no serious menace take the position that the monetary authorities always have it in their power to prevent creeping inflation from accelerating. . . .

It is, of course, true that sufficiently tight money can prevent prices from rising faster than 5 percent annually—or any other preassigned rate. But everything will not be fine if an acceleration of the price rise is prevented by monetary policy. That belief forgets that once a creeping inflation tends to accelerate—because wages, interest, and other cost items are increased in anticipation of rising prices—the policy of keeping the price rise to a creep must have the same results, i.e., unemployment, as would prevention of the price creep in the first place. Creeping inflation is only a temporary stopgap if Professor Slichter were right in saying that labor unions will always insist on, and have the power to obtain, wage increases in excess of the general rise in average productivity. Only under one condition would the distortion be rectified: if unions, and everybody else, could be fooled indefinitely to regard, despite rising prices, exactly balancing increases in money incomes as representing increases in real income.

This obviously is entirely unrealistic, especially during a period of chronic inflation when awareness of changes in the value of money has been greatly sharpened. You cannot fool all the people all the time. If the dilemma of the wage push does in fact exist, inflation cannot avoid but only postpone it.

Moreover, if a wage push did not exist in the first place, that is to say, if demand pull were the original cause of inflation, prolonged inflation is likely to create wage push, because inflation fosters the emergence of labor unions, it gives them prestige and power by offering them unending opportunities for easy (though under those circumstances largely phony) successes in the form of wage increases which would have come anyway, but for which the unions take credit. This will accustom them to annual wage increases, which they then will try to continue when the demand pull has come to a halt.

. . . . .

Business Cycles, Growth, and Inflation

The United States has never before, certainly not during the 19th century, gone through a period of chronic inflation, continuous or intermittent, resembling the inflation of the last twenty years. The same holds true of Western Europe. The inflations that the country experienced before 1940 were war inflations or cyclical inflations which almost always characterize the upward phase of the short-run business cycle, and beyond that the mild undulations of the so-called "long waves," sometimes called "Kondratieff cycles." . . .

However, many prominent economists (not to mention scores of lesser writers and outright cranks) have linked inflation and growth, or pictured inflation in one form or other as a helping or even an indispensable condition of economic growth. Keynes has devoted much space to the discussion of inflation in almost everyone of his economic writings. . . . [The author next quotes from Keynes' writings. *Ed.*]

. . . . .

. . . Keynes' historical examples are taken mostly from the pre-capitalist or early-capitalist era. It may be true that under those circumstances inflation was sometimes an explosive force which served to shake countries loose from feudal bonds and in this way promoted economic progress. But Keynes made it quite clear that he was not speaking of inflations resembling the present creeping type. "It is the teaching of this Treatise," he said, "that the wealth of nations is enriched, not during Income Inflations but during Profit Inflations —at times, that is to say, when prices are running away from costs," i.e., from wages and hence real wages are falling.

The clear implication is that Keynes would have looked with great concern on the present kind of inflation, no matter whether it is of the pure wage-push type in the sense that wages are pushed up and prices follow, or whether prices forge ahead and wages follow without delay, quickly annihilating the profits produced by the price rise. What matters from Keynes' standpoint was that wages (and other nonprofit incomes) should lag substantially behind prices so as to leave a large and long-lasting margin for profits. This is clearly out of the question under present-day conditions. . . . During World War II he became again concerned with the problem of inflation. But he, like many others, underestimated the danger of inflation for the postwar period and was too much preoccupied in his postwar plans with guarding against deflation, thus preparing to fight, like many famous generals, the battles of the last war. There can be no doubt, however, that if Keynes had lived longer he would energetically have taken up the fight against chronic inflation which, in his scheme of things, clearly is in the nature of income rather than of profit inflation.

Schumpeter, too, attributed to inflation an important role for economic growth under the capitalist system, of whose capacity to increase output and to raise the economic welfare of the masses he had the highest opinion. According to him, the capitalist, free enterprise economy necessarily develops and grows in cycles. Mild fluctuations of business activity are an essential part of the capitalist growth mechanism and credit inflation is an essential ingredient of the business cycle upswing. The prosperity phase of the cycle is the time when the innovating entrepreneurs introduce new ventures (new products, new markets, new methods of production, etc.) into the economic system. These innovations require large investments which are partly financed by inflation. Inflation and the forced saving which it entails, are the method by which the innovating entrepreneurs draw resources away from the more stagnant or routine parts of the economy.

Just as Keynes, so Schumpeter regards only profit inflation—inflation which is not too quickly followed by wage rises—as potentially productive. . . .

Another conclusion is also clear, namely, that the current type of chronic inflation in which wage push plays an important role, either as an initiator or as a quick-acting intensifier of a demand-initiated inflation, cannot possibly be justified on Schumpeterian grounds.

Attempts have often been made to shed light on the question whether chronic inflation is likely to help or to hinder economic growth by statistically correlating price changes and growth rates. . . .

Brief reflection should make it clear that a mechanical approach to the growth problem is likely to be grossly misleading or completely worthless. For example, a correlation between *annual* growth rates and *annual* price changes would lead to the conclusion that inflation is highly conducive to economic growth, because as everybody knows business cycle expansions are almost invariably associated with rising prices and business cycle contractions with falling prices. This result is entirely useless for the problem of whether *chronic* inflation is likely to help or to hinder economic growth. Of much importance, however, is the fact revealed by closer study that it is by no means the most vigorous business cycle expansions that are associated with the largest price rises.

. . . . .

... Using Simon Kuznets' data, [Otto Eckstein] gives rates of growth of output per decade and rates of change of price per decade for the U. S., the U. K., and several other advanced countries covering the period of 1870 to 1954. It is highly important that during "the late decades of the 19th century, which saw some of the most rapid growth of Western countries, prices generally were falling." It is, of course, not surprising that there exist periods of falling prices associated with very low growth rates (e.g., in the U. S. in 1929–38) and decades of rapidly rising prices (mainly war inflation) that also were periods of exceptionally slow growth. That destructive wars and deflation retard economic growth is to be expected, but I should like to recall that falling prices, when the price decline is due to rising output (as in the late decades of the 19th century), are radically different from falling prices that are due to the contraction of the monetary demand—deflation of MV. Also recorded are decades of rising prices associated with rapid growth (e.g., in the U. S. in 1904–13 and 1939–48). This checkered statistical picture has induced some investigators to throw up their hands in despair and to conclude that nothing general can be said on whether inflation is good or bad for economic growth. In my opinion, this conclusion is much too defeatist. Surely decadal figures (the only ones available for earlier periods) are too crude, because they overlap cycles and war periods. But it does not follow that a more careful historical-statistical investigation, which pays attention to the cyclical phases and other special conditions of each period and country, would not lead to useful generalization. . . .

Such an investigation ought to keep three points firmly in mind. First, it cannot be denied, I believe, that a moderate inflation can stimulate investment and growth provided (a) that prices keep sufficiently ahead of cost, in particular wage costs, to create the necessary profit incentives for investment; and (b) that strong inflation psychology does not develop. If the latter happens, the chances are that even if profits are still satisfactory, the wrong kind of investments will be stimulated which entail a waste of resources and inevitably come to grief, causing losses and contraction of output and employment.

It seems to me clear that in our times in both respects little margin is left for "creative" inflation *à la* Schumpeter and Keynes. Wages have become very flexible in the *upward* direction (while remaining rigid downward) and inflation psychology has become widespread and is ready to re-emerge quickly even when allayed by a lull in the price rise.

The second point to keep in mind is that the stimulus to investment and growth, which inflation can temporarily afford, can also be provided by non-inflationary policies without the same limitation and detrimental side effects. If it is true (as Schumpeter and Keynes say) that inflation promotes growth by creating profits which serve both as incentives and as financial sources of investment, it is also clear that the same incentives can be provided at stable or even at slightly falling prices, if only the increase in wages (and other costs) is kept in bounds. . . . It should be stressed that under non-inflationary growth *real* wages will rise just as much, and in the long run faster, than under inflationary conditions. That rapid growth is possible with stable or even falling prices is confirmed by the experience of the last decades of the 19th century and during the postwar period by the phenomenal growth of Western Germany and Switzerland. . . .

The third point to remember is that avoidance of chronic inflation is a necessary, though not a sufficient, condition for maximum growth. It is easy, for example, to think of methods of stopping inflation which would make things worse than they are under inflation. Suppose we stop inflation in the face of a strong wage push by monetary or fiscal policy. The consequences will be losses, low investment, and unemployment. If nothing can be done about wage push, the only choice left is one between two evils—the wastes and dangers of inflation or unemployment. Which one is greater depends primarily upon the strength of the wage push and the vulnerability of the economy to inflation. . . . Whatever one's judgment in this matter, one thing is clear: chronic inflation can never be the *best* policy for growth, but only the lesser evil.

. . . . .

It is sometimes said that inflationary wage push is good for growth because it forces entrepreneurs to invest in labor-saving machinery, to cut waste, and improve methods of production in every possible manner in order to protect their profits and not to be squeezed out of business.

This "shock theory" of high wages attributes to wage push and inflation what in reality is the result of the normal forces of competition. The inducement to expand, invent and invest, improve methods, and introduce new products, obviously depends upon profit expectations (including avoidance of losses) and profits as a source of finance (to be ploughed back). Profits (and losses) depend (given technological knowledge and the entrepreneur's abilities) upon the relation between costs and prices. . . .

[Analysis of the relation between "inflation and the deficit in the U. S. balance of payments" leads the author to the conclusion that considerations of international economic affairs must now add to the reasons for which we should avoid inflation. *Ed.*]

. . . . .

Anti-Inflation Policy

. . . . .

One conclusion is certain and cannot be stressed too strongly: In principle, it is always possible, in developed as well as underdeveloped countries, to manage in such a way that chronic inflation is avoided without creating prolonged and serious lapses from full employment and without endangering economic growth. This follows from classical equilibrium theory as well as from Keynesian economics. If inflation seems to become unavoidable or if, compared with practical alternatives, a policy of letting prices rise appears as the lesser evil, it is always due to faulty monetary, fiscal, and wage policies. These include: Excessive government spending; inability to tax sufficiently; impotence or unwillingness to curb labor unions and to prevent them from pressing for wage increases in excess of the average rise in labor productivity; and last but emphatically not least, lack of monetary discipline which either produces demand pull of its own or gives way to cost push and provides inflationary finance for government deficits.

The type of measure used for preventing inflation or stopping it once underway must, of course, to some extent depend on the diagnosis of what kind of inflation it is. Especially relevant is the question of whether demand pull or cost push is responsible, and, if both are involved, their relative strength.

. . . . .

Aggregate demand depends on M and V. We have seen that a prolonged and serious inflation never has developed in the past, and is not likely to develop in the future, without a sharp rise in the quantity of money. But in the short run, changes in V may be disturbing. Velocity of circulation is, however, not subject to direct control, except by means of *comprehensive* price freezing and rationing —a system of regimenation which in the United States is, and let us hope always will be, entirely unacceptable as a peacetime policy.

Aggregate demand can be controlled and, if necessary, cut back and the quantity of money can be regulated, either by monetary or fiscal policy. *Monetary* policy comprises discount rates, open market operations, and changes in reserve requirements of private banks as well as more specialized measures dealing with particular types of credit—such as stock exchange credit, real estate credit, and consumer credit. By *fiscal* policy, we mean variations in government expenditures and government revenues. Through developing a deficit or surplus, the government can add to, or subtract from the expenditure stream and increase or decrease the privately held quantity of money (money held by the government is usually not counted as money in circulation). Care must be taken, of course, that the changes in the public debt, implied by the existence of a deficit or surplus, are managed in such a way as not to counteract, or at least not completely to offset, the direct effects of the deficit or surplus on aggregate expenditure.

. . . . .

Monetary policy has the great advantage that measures can be initiated and changed quickly in case of need, while fiscal policy changes are subject to long delays because they have to go through lengthy parliamentary procedures. Moreover, in countries where the monetary authorities have some political independence—and to some extent this is still the case even in those western countries where the central bank has been formally nationalized— monetary policy is less subject to demagogic political pressures than fiscal policy.

On the other hand, it is probably true that measures of monetary policy (changes in interest rates and availability of credit brought about by discount and open-market policies) unless applied sharply and abruptly in large doses influence expenditure streams and prices slowly, with a lag, while fiscal policy measures, on the expenditure and revenue side, once they are taken, exert their influence more quickly. However, this advantage of quicker effect, of fiscal policy over monetary policy, establishes a superiority of fiscal policy only if the handicap of legislative and administrative delays in taking the respective measures has been overcome—a most serious handicap indeed. Even then this advantage of fiscal policy would be important more from the point of view of counteracting the business cycle rather than from that of the anti-inflation objective. The reason is that, while for the former objective quick decision and rapid action are of paramount importance, persistent application and not quick action counts most in preventing chronic inflation.

If the battle against inflation is to be won, monetary and fiscal policy should be coordinated. At the very least they must not be operated at cross purposes. . . .

This does not exclude the possibility that within limits inflationary pressure generated in one area can be offset, or more than offset, by deflationary policy in the other area. Keeping money tight for private business can mean that a government deficit will not cause a rise in prices. The opposite rarely happens but is equally possible, namely, that a tight fiscal policy (budget surplus) may provide the means for credit expansion without causing inflation.

Such divergent operations, usually of the first kind, are as a rule the result of a lack of coordination, the one arm of government trying to undo the mischief done by the other. But situations may arise in which good reasons could be advanced for consciously operating the two branches of financial policy in a seemingly contradictory manner. If in an emergency the government has to increase its expenditures quickly, it may not be able immediately to raise sufficient revenue. Tightening of credit can then be employed to prevent inflation. But one should not forget that this kind of policy implies the transfer of productive resources from the private sector, that is, from productive private investment, to the government—an indirect concealed method of taxation.

The opposite case, where the inflationary effects of an easy credit policy are offset by a tight budget, is rarely encountered nowadays. . . .

One could discuss endlessly the relative merits of different measures in the field both of monetary and fiscal policy. To what extent should the former rely on the broad measures of discount policy, open-market operations, and regulating reserve requirements of commercial banks, and to what extent on regulating special types of credit (consumer credit, stock market credit, and mortgage credit)? Should non-bank financial intermediaries be subject to regulation? Is the bills-only policy of open-market operations justified or should the Federal Reserve operate over the whole range of maturities? Similarly, innumerable details concerning fiscal policy arise: Which of the many existing taxes and myriad of government expenditures should be changed?

No doubt many of these decisions have their bearing upon the problem of long-run efficiency and growth, short-run stability and social justice—not to mention questions of political expediency, feasibility, and strategy. But it would be self-defeating if endless debates and inability to agree on the optimal package of anti-inflation policy—optimal from the point of view of growth, short-run stability, and social justice—should delay or prevent adoption of any effective policy against inflation, which in the long run is so inimical to these same objectives.

. . . Let us assume now that there are good reasons to believe that wage push, too, is in the picture which, as we have seen, is undoubtedly the case at the present time. Although often asserted, it is wrong to say that monetary policy is of no use against that type of inflation. Monetary policy, fiscal policy, or any combination of the two that prevents expansion of demand will also prevent a price rise resulting from or intensified by wage (or other cost) increases. But it must be admitted that it will do so only at the price of permitting a certain amount of unemployment—how much depending upon the strength of the wage push. It should be observed that in this respect fiscal policy is in precisely the same position as monetary policy, which is often ignored or overlooked by the critics of monetary policy.

. . . . .

. . . The ideal, least painful, and least costly method of stopping a wage-push inflation—or more precisely an inflation which contains an element of wage push—is to remove the wage push at the source or at least to reduce it to innocuous proportions. If there were competition in the labor market, it would be easy to prevent inflation by monetary and fiscal policy, and with a stable price level the wage level would rise roughly in proportion to the gradual rise in average labor productivity. Or if the wage level could somehow be so manipulated as to rise in proportion to the gradual increase in average labor productivity, the price level could be maintained roughly stable without causing unemployment.

I say "roughly," because there is no guarantee that full employment equilibrium may not require slight deviations between the rise in the wage level and the rise in average productivity; in other words, between marginal and average productivity of labor. Suppose average productivity of labor (i.e., output per man-hour) rises largely because of heavy capital investment, then the *share* of labor in total output may have to go down; the equilibrium wage would still go up but not quite in proportion to the rise of output per head.

If, on the other hand, overall output and output per head rise largely in consequence of improvements in labor skills or of "capital saving" inventions and improvements, the *share* of labor in total output would go up and equilibrium wages would have to rise somewhat faster than output per head.

. . . . .

How can the wage level be prevented from outrunning the average productivity of labor? The wage level is, of course, a highly abstract concept. It is not a policy variable, at least not in a free enterprise economy. This does not mean, however, that the problem is in any sense unreal. In practice, it reduces to the question of whether and how the power of the big labor unions can be curbed, because the big labor unions are the spearhead of the wage push. Wages and salaries of non-unionized workers and employees follow the road bulldozed by union pressure. Naturally, there are delays, but in a prolonged inflationary climate these lags tend to become shorter and shorter. . . .

If union pressure on the wages of unionized workers is kept under control, no inflationary wage movements need be expected to emanate from the non-unionized employees. . . .

But how can union power be curbed? Some of the leading experts on labor think it just cannot be done. . . .

We have already taken issue with the idea that it is possible to have a continuing price rise of, say, 2 to 3 percent a year without the creep tending to become a trot, whereupon a monetary or fiscal policy of holding the price rise to 2 or 3 percent a year must lead to unemployment. . . . As soon as the creeping inflation *tends* to accelerate beyond the creeping pace, keeping inflation to a creep by controlling demand without stopping the wage push will produce unemployment and slack.

. . . . .

I find it difficult to believe that our society should be unable to curb union power without resorting to measures so drastic as to be difficult to reconcile with individual freedom and free enterprise. Such drastic measures would be compulsory arbitration, government wage fixing, or splitting or dissolution of unions. At any rate, there are less extreme reforms and changes in policy which have never been tried or at any rate not presistently applied; these should be given a trial before more drastic measures are contemplated.

First, unions have acquired over the years *de jure* or *de facto* numerous immunities and exceptions which go far beyond anything accorded to business and other private associations. It is difficult to believe that legal reforms restoring a more balanced power equilibrium between the parties in wage bargains, and eliminating violence and other abuses, would not have some effect in relieving inflationary wage pressure.

Secondly, and probably more basic and important than legal reform, is a change in the attitude of public opinion and of all branches of the government. It should be possible to arouse public opinion to the dangers of wage inflation and to bring its weight to bear on unions which by force of crippling strike and intimidation impose inflationary wage increases on the economy. Then the aroused public opinion could force the government, in its executive as well as in its legislative branch, to pick up some courage, instead of maintaining a studious neutrality in wage bargaining and issuing platitudinous appeals to everybody to behave, or outrightly capitulating to striking unions and bringing pressure on employers to capitulate. If instead of that unions were told in no uncertain words that their wage demands are inflationary and intolerable, one could expect to observe quickly a marked tendency for moderation in wage bargains.

Is it entirely Utopian to persuade union leaders that wage increases greatly in excess of the rise in over-all productivity must drive up prices and, therefore, are, in the last resort, self-defeating and damaging to labor itself? . . .

It will not be easy to eliminate inflationary wage pressure. But experience in foreign countries, notably in Western Germany and now also in Great Britain and France, shows that it is not a hopeless task to prevent wage inflation without creating much unemployment and checking growth. Though the task is not easy, neither should the magnitude of the problem be exaggerated. If wage inflation is prevented, real wages would increase just as much. In the long run they would rise even faster. For setbacks and interruptions, which are the consequences of inflation, would disappear and cyclical depressions or recessions resulting from other causes than from stopping inflation in the face of wage pressure could be counteracted more quickly and vigorously by monetary and fiscal measures—if the authorities are relieved of the constant fear that by combating a cyclical depression they would give a fresh push to chronic inflation.

Fortunately, it would require only a small decrease in the rate of increase of money wages to eliminate inflationary wage pressure. It is understandable, however, that politicians are reluctant to grasp the nettle of labor-management relations in general and of labor union control in particular, that they seek refuge in side issues and hire experts to write tons of reports on all conceivable aspects and ramifications of the problem and propose minor reforms on hundreds of matters which do not go to the root of the problem, but enable the politician to stay away from the disagreeable fact of wage push. . . .

Clearly, any policy or measure that tends to increase output per head may be thought to that extent to relieve inflationary pressure by creating a larger margin for non-inflationary wage increases. Now there are many ways in which new policies, changes in policies, and last, but emphatically not least, abandonment and discontinuance of established policies can accelerate growth (output per head).

This is not the place to sketch a program for accelerated economic growth. But let me mention a few areas where effective action could be taken. A radical change in agricultural policy would reduce the price level and liberate annually several billion dollars' worth of resources for productive purposes, now wasted in accumulating unwanted surpluses. Large savings could be made in the Veterans' budget and possibly in defense spending. Social Security laws could be changed so as to encourage older workers to stay longer in the labor force by letting them have a part of their pensions even if they continue to work and/or letting them earn higher pensions later. Changes in tax laws to stimulate investment could have a major effect on productivity. There can be no doubt that high marginal tax rates, made more onerous by inflation, encourage waste and check investment. Very substantial tax reductions especially in the higher brackets have greatly contributed to the phenomenal growth of German industrial production since the currency reform in 1948.

However, all these reforms are politically difficult to carry out and even if made, their effect on prices may be slow in coming (except the effect of an elimination of price supports). Suppose it were possible after a few years to raise the annual rate of output growth by 1 or 2 percent, which would be quite an achievement. This would be very desirable on several grounds, but it might not relieve the wage pressure; labor unions may get used to larger wage increases and raise their sights a little bit. If that should happen, and the chances are that it would, the basic problem of wage push would remain.

Control of profits and prices in "monopolistic" or "oligopolistic" industries will be demanded by many as a complement to a policy of curbing union power. Leaving aside questions of political strategy and expediency, nothing useful can be expected from such policies. The reason for this statement was given earlier. Since there does not exist an independent continual cost push emanating from "administered" prices comparable to the wage push exerted by trade unions, there is no room in a rational anti-inflation policy for measures to prevent "mark-up inflation." Any move in that direction would only make things worse by multiplying red tape and diverting attention and effort of business managers away from the pressing problems of increasing efficiency of production and lowering costs.

Some measures in this area which have been proposed by economists as powerful antidotes for inflation and are actively sponsored by influential politicians would have opposite effects from those intended. For example, Senator O'Mahoney's plan starts from the theory that "inflation will be checked if the pricing policies of the [dominant] corporations are publicly reviewed before increased prices may be made effective" and the Senate Bill 215 of April 1959, which embodies some of O'Mahoney's ideas and has received serious consideration in Congress, provides for public hearings and investigations of large corporations whenever they want to raise prices.

Professor Machlup has convincingly demonstrated that a policy which makes price increases difficult and highly embarrassing would provide the strongest possible inducement for the firms concerned to avoid price reduction. The long-run effect would be to freeze prices. In view of the fact that stability of the general price *level* requires, as we have seen, that prices of products of progressive industries and firms be reduced and be flexible downward, any policy that makes precisely these prices rigid is bound to have inflationary effects in the long run whatever may be the short-run effect at the time when the policy is first introduced.

All this does not mean that the substitution of competition for monopoly, wherever the latter exists, would not be desirable. But since the American economy is very competitive anyway, not much can be expected from an intensification of antimonopolistic policies. At best it can be regarded only as a slow-moving reform with uncertain outcome. There does exist, however, a method of antimonopoly policy, which does not involve the use of expensive bureaucratic machinery, red tape, and endless costly litigations—namely, freer trade. The rise in recent years of foreign industries competing with a long list of American industries ("oligopolistic" as well as competitive) has increased healthy competition and further weakened and made obsolete the theory of administered prices and administered price inflation.

Instead of pursuing a policy of harassing business leaders in law courts and before Congressional committees for alleged "profiteering" and monopolistic practices, it would be far better to subject them to still stronger competition from abroad by reducing barriers to imports. Reductions of tariffs and other obstacles to imports could and should be bartered for similar reductions in trade barriers in foreign countries.

Popular judgments of the evils or benefits of inflation and deflation are likely to be based upon the real position of debtors and creditors. Economists, however, as John Maynard (later Baron) Keynes indicates in the following selection, recognize that changes in the value of money also influence the real output of the economy. One reason governments do not use power which they clearly exercise over the supply of money to curb inflation is fear of reducing production because of the reactions Keynes indicates.

47 · Effects of Inflation on Management Efficiency

JOHN MAYNARD KEYNES

· · · · ·

If, for any reason right or wrong, the business world *expects* that prices will fall, the processes of production tend to be inhibited; and if it expects that prices will rise, they tend to be overstimulated. A fluctuation in the measuring rod of value does not alter in the least the wealth of the world, the needs of the world, or the productive capacity of the world. It ought not, therefore, to affect the character of the volume of what is produced. A movement of *relative* prices, that is to say of the comparative prices of different commodities, *ought* to influence the character of production, because it is an indication that various commodities are not being produced in the exactly right proportions. But this is not true of a change, as such, in the *general* price level.

The fact that the expectation of changes in the *general* price level affects the processes of production, is deeply rooted in the peculiarities of the existing economic organization of society. . . . A change in the general level of prices, that is to say a change in the measuring rod, which fixes the obligation of the borrowers of money (who make the decisions which set production in motion) to the lenders (who are inactive once they have lent their money), effects a redistribution of real wealth between the two groups. Furthermore, the active group can, if they foresee such a change, alter their action in advance in such a way as to minimize their losses to the other group or to increase their gains from it, if and when the expected change in the value of money occurs. If they expect a fall, it may pay them, as a group, to

---

JOHN MAYNARD KEYNES, *Essays in Persuasion* (London: Rupert Hart-Davis, Ltd., 1951; New York: Harcourt, Brace & Company, Inc., 1932), pp. 32–39. Used by permission. The essay appeared originally in the early 1920's.

damp production down, although such enforced idleness impoverishes Society as a whole. If they expect a rise, it may pay them to increase their borrowings and to swell production beyond the point where the real return is just sufficient to recompense Society as a whole for the effort made. Sometimes, of course, a change in the measuring rod, especially if it is unforeseen, may benefit one group at the expense of the other disproportionately to any influence it exerts on the volume of production; but the tendency, in so far as the active group anticipate a change, will be as I have described it. This is simply to say that the intensity of production is largely governed in existing conditions by the anticipated real profit of the entrepreneur. Yet this criterion is the right one for the community as a whole only when the delicate adjustment of interests is not upset by fluctuations in the standard of value.

There is also a considerable risk directly arising out of instability in the value of money. During the lengthy process of production the business world is incurring outgoings in terms of *money*—paying out in money for wages and other expenses of production—in the expectation of recouping this outlay by disposing of the product for *money* at a later date. That is to say, the business world as a whole must always be in a position where it stands to gain by a rise of price and to lose by a fall of price.[1] Whether it likes it or not, the technique of production under a regime of money-contract forces the business world always to carry a big speculative position; and if it is reluctant to carry this position, the productive process must be slackened. The argument is not affected by the fact that there is some degree of specialization of function within the business world, in so far as the professional speculator comes to the assistance of the producer proper by taking over from him a part of his risk.

Now it follows from this, not merely that the *actual occurrence* of price change profits some classes and injures others . . . but that a *general fear* of falling prices may inhibit the productive process altogether. For if prices are expected to fall, not enough risk-takers can be found who are willing to carry a speculative "bull" position, and this means that entrepreneurs will be reluctant to embark on lengthy productive processes involving a money outlay long in advance of money recoupment,—whence unemployment. The *fact* of falling prices injures entrepreneurs; consequently the *fear* of falling prices causes them to protect themselves by curtailing their operations; yet it is upon the aggregate of their individual estimations of the risk, and their willingness to run the risk, that the activity of production and of employment mainly depends.

There is a further aggravation of the case, in that an expectation about the course of prices tends, if it is widely held, to be cumulative in its results up to a certain point. If prices are expected to rise and the business world acts on this expectation, that very fact causes them to rise for a time and, by verifying the expectation, reinforces it; and similarly, if it expects them to fall. Thus a comparatively weak initial impetus may be adequate to produce a considerable fluctuation.

The best way to cure this mortal

---

[1] [Under present tax laws Keynes' point here is not always true. The depreciation allowance deductible as an expense in computing taxes is based on original, not replacement, cost. Profit after taxes plus depreciation may be too small to finance replacement of productive capacity at inflated prices. Keynes wrote when tax rates were far below those today and when businesses, especially in England, were much less aware of the realities of depreciation as a cost. *Ed.*]

disease of individualism must be to provide that there shall never exist any confident expectation either that prices generally are going to fall or that they are going to rise; and also that there shall be no serious risk that a movement, if it does occur, will be a big one. If, unexpectedly and accidentally, a moderate movement were to occur, wealth, though it might be redistributed, would not be diminished thereby.

To procure this result by removing all possible influences towards an initial movement would seem to be a hopeless enterprise. The remedy would lie, rather, in so controlling the standard of value that whenever something occurred which, left to itself, would create an expectation of a change in the general level of prices, the controlling authority should take steps to counteract this expectation by setting in motion some factor of a contrary tendency. Even if such a policy were not wholly successful, either in counteracting expectations or in avoiding actual movements, it would be an improvement on the policy of sitting quietly by whilst a standard of value, governed by chance causes and deliberately removed from central control, produces expectations which paralyze or intoxicate the government of production.

We see, therefore, that rising prices and falling prices each have their characteristic disadvantage. The Inflation which causes the former means Injustice to individuals and to classes,—particularly to rentiers; and is therefore unfavorable to saving. The Deflation which causes falling prices means Impoverishment to labor and to enterprise by leading entrepreneurs to restrict production, in their endeavor to avoid loss to themselves. . . . The counterparts are, of course, also true,—namely that Deflation means Injustice to borrowers, and that Inflation leads to overstimulation of industrial activity. . . .

Thus, Inflation is unjust and Deflation is inexpedient . . . It is not necessary that we should weight one evil against the other. . . . The Individualistic Capitalism of today, precisely because it entrusts savings to the individual investor and production to the individual employer, *presumes* a stable measuring rod of value, and cannot be efficient—perhaps cannot survive—without one.

48 · *Hyper-Inflation in Germany*

FRANK D. GRAHAM

The figures in the table on page 286 tell much about one of the great economic cataclysms of modern history. During World War I the German mark lost considerable purchasing power. The drop in value continued unevenly for over two years. Then it speeded up, and in 1923 the stage of true hyper-inflation was reached. This tragic, and to most people incomprehensible, deterioration had a profound effect on the attitudes of financiers, statesmen, and economists—and also on the public of more than one country. Yet World War II and its aftermath witnessed hyper-inflation in several lands.

Treasury Bills Discounted by the Reich, Issues of Paper Currency, Index of Wholesale Prices, and Index of Dollar Exchange Rates against Paper Marks; 1919–1923
(Value figures in millions of marks)

End of Month		Total Amount of Treasury Bills Discounted by the Reich	Total Issues of Paper Currency (Except Emergency Currency)	Index of Wholesale Prices 1913 = 1	Index of Dollar Exchange Rates in Berlin, 1913 = 1
1919	Dec.	86,400	50,065	8.03	11.14
1920	June	113,200	68,154	13.82	9.17
	Dec.	152,800	81,387	14.40	17.48
1921	June	185,100	84,556	13.66	17.90
	Dec.	247,100	122,497	34.87	43.83
1922	June	295,200	180,169	70.30	89.21
	July	308,000	202,626	100.59	159.60
	Aug.	331,600	252,212	192.00	410.91
	Sept.	451,100	331,876	287.00	393.04
	Oct.	603,800	484,685	566.00	1,071.94
	Nov.	839,100	769,500	1,154.00	1,822.30
	Dec.	1,495,200	1,295,228	1,475.00	1,750.83
1923	Jan.	2,081,800	1,999,600	3,286.00	11,672.00
	Feb.	3,588,000	3,536,300	5,257.00	5,407.00
	Mar.	6,601,300	5,542,900	4,827.00	4,996.00
	April	8,442,300	6,581,200	5,738.00	7,099.00
	May	10,275,000	8,609,700	9,034.00	16,556.00
	June	22,019,800	17,340,500	24,618.00	36,803.00
	July	57,848,900	43,813,500	183,510.00	262,030.00
	Aug.	1,196,294,700	668,702,600	1,695,109.00	2,454,000.00
	Sept.	46,716,616,400	28,244,405,800	36,223,771.00	38,113,000.00
	Oct.	6,907,511,102,800	2,504,955,700,000	18,700,000,000.00	17,270,129,000.00
	Nov.	191,580,465,422,100	400,338,326,400,000	1,422,900,000,000.00	1,000,000,000,000.00
	Dec.	1,232,679,853,100	496,585,345,900,000	1,200,400,000,000.00	1,000,000,000,000.00

FRANK D. GRAHAM, *Exchange, Prices and Production in Hyper-Inflation Germany, 1920–1923* (Princeton: Princeton University Press, 1930), p. 13. Used by permission.

The rise in the price level in the 1950's, especially after the end of fighting in Korea, was not a simple matter. Economists were not the only persons debating the relative importance of "demand pull" and "cost push." Here we find an analysis by an economist who draws upon a specialized knowledge of industrial organization and the problems of monopoly.

49 · Steel, Union Power, Administered Prices, and Inflation in the 1950's

M. A. ADELMAN

Introduction

The traditional theory of inflation was that the intended current spending of households, firms, and government exceeded the current value of all goods and services offered. The excess demand was the "inflationary gap." Since higher prices meant also higher incomes and higher spending, the process started by the "gap" was cumulative, self-reinforcing, and continued until something happened, or was made to happen, to aggregate demand—higher taxes, or higher savings, or central bank actions to limit business and consumer spending.

Much or most of current debate on inflation, however, emphasizes not aggregates and economy-wide forces, but rather the policies of unions and business firms. This implies that unions and business concerns have so much discretion or power to raise prices and wages that they can choose to inflate or not to inflate. . . .

. . . It appears that even with aggregate demand not in excess of aggregate supply, somehow prices have a way of rising indefinitely because they are either self-propelled or cost-pushed, chiefly wage-pushed. The reasons why this happens, or is supposed to happen, are not so easily found. . . .

"Administered Prices"

The great bulk of prices are administered. They are not observed in the course of an irregular stream of bids matching offers; the seller (or less often the buyer) announces the price by a deliberate act, sometimes after a good deal of internal bureaucratic effort. Yet this is form, not substance; a description of *how* prices are announced tells us nothing of *why* they are what they are and not other than they are.

It is a meaningless contrast between

M. A. ADELMAN, "Steel, Administered Prices, and Inflation," from *The Quarterly Journal of Economics*, Vol. LXXV, No. 1 (February 1961), Cambridge, Mass.: Harvard University Press, copyright 1961 by the President and Fellows of Harvard College.

agricultural or other raw material markets where prices are determined by current supply and demand, and "imperfect markets" where prices are "administered." For one thing, many agricultural prices are the most clearly monopolistic in the economy, and far above the levels where they would be if determined by competitive supply and demand. Even setting this aside, the more basic confusion remains. All markets, and conspicuously "freely fluctuating" agricultural markets, are governed by imperfect mechanisms run by men with grievously imperfect knowledge of supply and demand. Hence they generate prices which do *not* equate current supply and demand, and which must therefore be changed up or down, no matter how and by whom. . . .

. . . . .

. . . "Administered prices" are not a theory, but an evasion of the need for a theory. If prices rise or fall or are as some level *because* they are administered, then the plays of Shakespeare were written by his pen. The theory of "administered prices" is appealing because it provides a phrase that seems to explain everything. Thereby it liberates us from the need to work at explaining the forces of supply and demand in a given instance, and from the dismal compulsions of supply and demand themselves. . . .

. . . . .

A theory will always be popular if it presents specific visible individuals as authors of our misfortunes. A well-fed man in a gray flannel suit squinting into a flash bulb is infinitely superior as a hate-object to the intersection of marginal curves. . . .

. . . . .

Almost all versions of the administered price theory reduce to this: prices do not rise, prices are raised. Therefore the way to keep businessmen from raising prices is either (1) to exhort and inspire and admonish and uplift them; or (2) to denounce them, hold public hearings on whether increases are "justified" by "costs," and so forth. The choice between these two views is ideological and political. Their economic content is the same.

The Problem in Steel

No attempt will be made here to discuss any more respectable (but less influential) theories of cost-push inflation; we propose only to examine the most striking case. . . . Steel is the home of Big Business and Big Labor, and in the 1950's it pushed up prices and wages in fair weather and foul, apparently regardless of demand. We need some theory to explain this behavior and also the turnabout of 1959, when management decided to stand and fight rather than raise wages and prices.

Not only is steel a striking example of the phenomenon, it is a very large part of it. In an important recent paper, Eckstein and Fromm have used the input-output technique to make full allowance for the secondary price-raising effects of the steel increases. They show that 52 per cent of the 1953–58 rise in the wholesale price index is accounted for by steel. . . .[1]

Eckstein and Fromm cannot explain the steel price increases—to their satisfaction, or mine—by the pressure of excess demand. . . . The steel labor force has actually shrunk, and the principal steel-producing centers have seldom or never been labor-shortage areas, yet wages have steadily advanced.

. . . . .

Interdependence of Costs and Prices

The payments to any factor, including labor, are not necessarily to be con-

---

[1] Otto Eckstein and Gary Fromm, "Steel and the Postwar Inflation," Study Paper No. 2, Joint Economic Committee, 86th Congress, 1st Session (Washington, 1959), p. 12.

sidered as costs in economics because they are "costs" for purposes of accounting. A union can act as a monopolist of labor, setting the price to get the best return available in view of the derived elasticity of demand, i.e., derived from the demand for the product. If that elasticity is high, because of easy product substitution, non-union firms, etc., the union's monopoly power is negligible; if elasticity is low, it may be considerable. The nature and interdependence of product markets and labor markets is the strategic factor. Lest this sound too abstruse, one might point to a recent milestone, Mr. John L. Lewis' retirement from the presidency of the United Mine Workers. Since the end of World War II, at least, Mr. Lewis has worn two hats. As the grand co-ordinator of the coal industry he has done for it what it cannot do for itself, because of the antitrust laws or even without them. By controlling the input of labor he has controlled the output of bituminous coal (other than strip-mined) in such a way as to maximize the revenues of the industry. But then Mr. Lewis has turned around to claim for his inner constituents, the mine workers, the maximum slice of the total revenue which he can get without provoking a showdown with the mine owners, who must get their share if they are to go along.

Obviously coal wages are far more than a cost; they also include a share of monopoly profits. Now, coal has never figured prominently as an example of cost-push inflation. For one thing, little of coal is the Big Business stereotype; furthermore, the price of coal has in fact not risen much since about 1950. In fact, it declined during 1953–1955, then rose again. The most simple explanation would be that a monopoly price is by no means a rising price. A monopoly price is higher than a competitive, so that if the industry is gradually monopolized the price should, *ceteris paribus*, gradually rise; but the increase ends when monopoly is accomplished. This was the case in coal, though we cannot tell the year when it was accomplished. But years before his resignation, the chorus of management disapproval of Mr. Lewis had died away, and also the jibes at how he was the best of oil and gas salesmen. The coal industry considered as a whole—i.e., as a monopoly —was simply better off selling less at a higher price than more at a lower price. But the better-offness was only within a limit; when that price was reached, the industry settled down to a period where prices were affected only by general business conditions.[2] It is worth exploring the differences and similarities between coal and steel.

Price Determination in Steel

The steel industry may best be viewed as a set of separate but highly interdependent markets, such that the most meaningful grouping for our purposes is the whole industry. Concentration has always been high, though it has persistently declined, as would be expected if prices were usually maintained above long-run marginal cost and sometimes far above short-run marginal cost, providing an incentive, strong or weak, depending on the point in the business cycle, for smaller producers to grow at the expense of larger. Entry is expensive and relatively difficult. The pattern of uniform price behavior and of highly developed industry consciousness is quite familiar. Since the war, wage bargaining has in effect been on an industry-wide basis, though nominally it was not before last year.

---

[2] The reader should be warned that formidable objections can be raised against our sketch of coal wage and price determination. . . . My hypothesis is far from being proved, and is submitted not for any substantive importance but only to set off, by likeness and contrast, the main thesis of the paper.

The process of price increase has been a striking spectacle, especially for the last few years. Between March and July, the industry has staged a yearly ritual—one might call it the rites of spring, only it is far more sedate than anything Igor Stravinsky ever thought of orchestrating. First, a steel company issues a statement that the price of steel "should" by rights be raised. For one thing, wages are expected to go up; but even without this, a higher price is "justified" because since some convenient base year prices have not gone up as fast as "costs," and because only by raising prices can the industry raise enough money to provide investment in the new steel capacity so urgently needed for both peaceful use and national defense. . . . One company after another publicly announces agreement, sometimes spicing it with resentment at U. S. Steel if they have not yet spoken up. By midsummer the Corporation has been heard from, as have the late returns from outlying precincts; opinion is unanimous, and the price goes up. . . . A drop-off in demand for steel is only no obstacle, but actually a help, since it raises unit "costs" and thereby makes a price increase all the more "justified."

. . . . .

. . . Even the mildest propensity to compete would have generated some bidding for more volume and would have put the price under downward pressure. For the price to hold and then actually to increase provides a laboratory demonstration that the steel firms could disregard individual interests and move as one toward the group interest, just as would a single monopolist, who *is* the group all by himself. Some degree of monopoly, then, must be part of the explanation for steel price changes—not "administered prices" or "modern-day markets," etc., but control of supply by a group of firms acting as a group. But monopoly is not sufficient. Other things being equal, a group of rational monopolists would not keep raising the price year after year; they would rather set the price at the monopoly level in the first place. We need a modification of the general monopoly model to account for this.

For any given period, long or short run, there exists a demand function for steel as a product. Under competition the price gravitates toward somewhere around industry marginal cost;[3] under

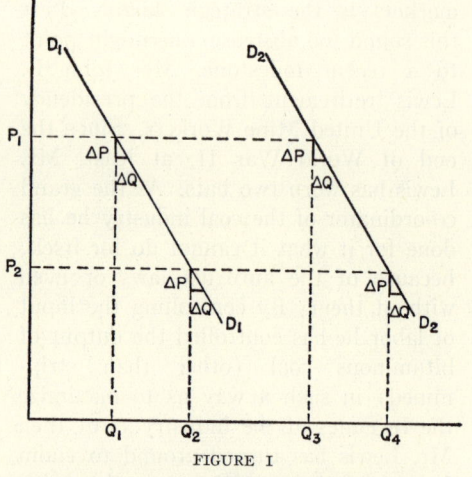

FIGURE I

The two demand curves are linear, so that to any given $\triangle Q$ there corresponds the same $\triangle P$, and all four triangles are identical. At the intersection of P_2 and Q_2 the *relative* change in P is much greater and the *relative* change in Q is much less than at the intersection of P_1 and Q_1; i.e., demand elasticity is much greater at P_1. Similarly, the *relative* change in Q at the two intersections on D_2D_2 are much less than at the corresponding intersections on D_1D_1. Hence, for any given point, demand is more elastic for the product depicted in D_1D_1.

monopoly it will be set where industry marginal cost equals industry marginal

---
[3] Marginal cost may be higher or lower than, or equal to, average cost. Marginal cost less than average registers a condition of excess capacity. The statement that a price in the neighborhood of marginal cost is insufficient to cover fixed costs is either sheer misconception or else implicitly assumes excess capacity.

revenue, at a lower level of output and a higher price. Demand is much more elastic at the point of monopoly price than where it would be under competition, and the more inelastic is the demand curve taken as a whole, the greater the difference of elasticity between the competitive and the monopoly price. (See Figure I.) [4]

This is a point perhaps unduly neglected. We are replete with statements to the effect that wage or other cost increases can be passed on to steel customers because the demand is inelastic, and there is enough truth in this idea to disguise the even more basic truth that elasticity only exists at some price. As a price is raised, we enter a region of increasing elasticity because substitutes for the product grow increasingly more attractive. The monopoly price will be set in theory at the point, or in practice in the zone,[5] where demand for the product as a whole is so elastic as to make a further increase unprofitable. This is the ceiling. The difference between the competitive and the monopoly price defines the possible range of the industry's price control; the degree of monopoly may be roughly equated to the per cent of the distance between the two extremes which the industry has managed to traverse. (In the diagram, the difference between P_1 and P_2.)

Outside of this range, i.e., above monopoly price or below competitive price, the market is in violent disequilibrium —there are powerful forces pushing the price back into it. Inside this range, there may be (and usually is) disequilibrium, but of a much milder sort. With price anywhere above the competitive level, it is above marginal cost, and there is a temptation for individual firms to shade price for the sake of profitable additional volume. Contrariwise, if the price is anywhere below the point of crucial elasticity (i.e., if marginal revenue is less than marginal cost), there is a temptation for the firms to get together to do something to raise the price. And our theory of industrial markets, such as it is, consists mainly in ways of recognizing where on the scale a firm or industry is, and whether they are likely to move in either or neither direction.

Both business management and the outside student want to know the real determinants of cost and of demand which determine this scale between the polar extremes. . . . The basic determinants of cost can often be reduced to engineering data or rules of thumb; the basic determinants of demand—why and how much customers will substitute at what price—can only rarely be so analyzed. Most managements could estimate within a reasonable margin of error the effect on unit cost of increasing or decreasing the level or the scale of output by 10 or 20 or 50 per cent; they could make no such estimate on price. Experience with price is too entwined with particular circumstance to afford much of a basis for prediction.

An intelligent monopolist would, therefore, usually have some difficulty knowing when he was getting into the zone of increasing elasticity. If so, there is a good chance that he would unknowingly overreach himself and get past it, and be forced to beat a retreat. And increasing the risk would be the possi-

---

[4] The diagram is a translation, not an explanation. The linear demand curves merely register the assumption of increasing elasticity of demand at the higher price and lower quantity; but this must be supported by economic reasoning, as in the text.

[5] The boundaries of the zone will in any case be vague because of imperfect knowledge, as discussed two paragraphs below. Compounding the uncertainty is the variation in costs, such that the most profitable price for one firm is not the most profitable for others. Unless a compensation scheme can be worked out—which is very unlikely—there must be a compromise, with greater instability of the price.

bility of the demand curve shifting to the left gradually or suddenly, so that a guess correct at one time would become falsified at another. The closer one gets to the top, i.e., to monopoly equilibrium, the more vulnerable one is to a shift in the demand curve. This would make for caution, for a step-by-step approach to the summit.

One obvious point—the zone of increasing elasticity is encountered long before "the average customer" of the industry begins to substitute in major amounts. The average customer never reacts in the short run to anything— that is why he is average. Movement always begins with marginal customers and peripheral uses. And, of course, a given customer may have a dozen or a thousand uses for a given product, with a different ease or difficulty of substitution for each one. The term "customer," not "consumer," is used advisedly. Most markets are producer markets, where sales are by one business concern to another concern, and where elasticity of demand is determined not by the vagaries of consumer psychology but by relative profitability to the buying firm. The problem is—for how many needs, out of the thousands filled by the product, will other products be substituted at the higher price? And this usually permits only the roughest sort of answers.

The structure of demand for coal is much simpler than for steel because it is derived from a general need for fuel, and faces only a few readily identifiable substitutes—oil, gas, and strip-mined coal. Control of output was entrusted by both sides to Mr. Lewis. With fair though not complete success he penetrated the fog of uncertainty about what the traffic would bear, and what the co-operating parties would accept. Price quickly went to the monopoly level; there was no annual saturnalia of price increases, no "inflation," no "adminis-tered prices," no menace to social peace, no Congressional hearings, no big-business big-union "danger"—just the charm of a quiet life.

But in steel the demand curve was less well defined, industry-labor co-operation less complete, and the pursuit of equilibrium more difficult and protracted. The elastic section of the demand curve was not easily found. The industry, limited by the antitrust laws to a somewhat awkward and inefficient "fall-in-and-be-counted" kind of collusion, had to be sure of the ground at each step. Hence the need for the yearly ritual. The price would be raised, and so long as the market did not react unfavorably, the next year would see a repetition.

The problem was made even more difficult by the great expansion of capacity that took place after 1949. The industry was faced with a constantly outward-shifting demand curve, and it may well be that its response was essentially in two steps—expanding capacity where it seemed profitable on the basis of the average price expected, and then feeling its way along toward that price or past it. . . .

The Crisis of 1959

A respectable theory of cost-push inflation (other than the verbal magic of "administered prices") might explain the price rise in steel through 1958 about as well as our theory of imperfect management-labor collusion. I think the latter is preferable because it is simpler, in that it includes only the traditional theory of monopoly plus one additional assumption, that of very imperfect knowledge of demand. . . .

The events of 1958–59, however, may provide a good crucial test. Our theory of a noninflationary price increase is that the price would cease to rise when it became unprofitable for the industry as a whole to raise it. This would in turn be due to the possibility of substitution by steel customers. . . .

One type of substitution would be of products other than steel to do essentially the same work, such as aluminum for "tin" cans or for aircraft, prestressed concrete for construction, etc. Individual examples are easy to find, but a general assessment is difficult, and beyond the scope of this paper. For our purposes we must disregard this type of substitution.

The second type of substitution would be by steel customers themselves integrating backward to perform some of the functions previously performed, and charged for, by the steel industry. In general, a wide margin over expected minimum average cost offers a great temptation for customers to integrate backward. If steel customers began doing for themselves what the industry had previously done for them, they would doubtless have to pay the same wages. But they would gain the wide margin over cost which the steel industry was getting in 1958, and would not suffer from a low per cent of capacity utilized, since they could always expect to be making at least enough of their own product to make full use of their own steel capacity. This has, of course, been a traditional motive for vertical integration in the face of a monopolized supplying industry, except where the latter controlled an essential factor (e.g., iron ore).

We have not been able to explore this type of substitution adequately either, with one . . . exception. In November 1958 the largest can manufacturing company decided to begin fabrication at an earlier stage in the production process, doing operations previously done by the steelmakers. Curiously enough, the company had been forced to revise its own price structure because some of its own customers had begun making their own cans. Demand for tin plate may also have been made more elastic by what seems to have been a successful trial of aluminum cans for lubricating oils.

A more general evidence of substitution would be a selective pattern of price increases. Increasing elasticity of demand for steel would not affect the various products equally; hence some could be raised more than others, and still others could not be increased at all. An approach to a summit, and increasing difficulty in raising the price (i.e., much greater competitive pressure at the higher price), is suggested in the way the 1958 price increases took about four months to accomplish, product by product, in contrast with the almost overnight change of previous years. A confirmation in one direction, but making appraisal of the evidence more difficult in another, is that the 1958 price increases were rather small. Stainless steel was not raised at all, either as plates or bars. Otherwise, an unweighted frequency distribution shows increases to range from 2.7 to 4.8 per cent, with a median of 3.6 per cent, and quartiles of 3.2 and 4.1 per cent respectively.

The last and most important substitution the industry had to face was the impact of foreign competition in reduced exports and increased imports. As a per cent of total domestic output, foreign trade was very small, but to leave the matter there—as the union was painfully anxious to leave it—makes no sense. What matters is not the per cent represented by imports and lost exports as of 1958, but the per cent that one should expect to be lost as foreign steel companies put new facilities into operation and established channels of communication with steel users and distributors, a notoriously time-consuming and risky process.

From 1953 through 1957 United States imports and exports of steel moved generally in harmony with domestic production. But during the 1957–58 recession, in contrast with 1954 and 1949, steel imports actually increased, while steel exports dropped. As business revived in early 1958, imports regained and then exceeded the 1957 peak, before soaring in the pre-strike inventory build-up. But exports fell throughout the first half of 1958, then leveled off iregularly. The net foreign trade balance therefore dropped by more than three-fourths, from 4,023 million tons in 1957 to 984 million tons in 1958. Since late 1958, imports have actually exceeded exports.

The pattern of foreign trade, in time and by-products, suggests that imports and exports were responding to an influence other than the fluctuations of the steel market generally. . . .

. . . . .

The most reasonable expectation as of the end of 1958 was that U. S. steel imports would continue to grow. It is difficult to say whether this ought to be considered as the elastic section of the original demand curve or as a shifting to the left (as from D_2D_2 to D_1D_1 in Figure I), so that the elastic section would be encountered at a lower price than previously; and even more difficult to say how much imports would grow. The facts are obviously few and imprecise. The industry might have been, and may now be, in the position of someone walking in apparent safety on a barrier reef who belatedly notices the water starting to come up around his ankles, and dry land a way off. If at existing price levels there was a danger of increasing foreign competition as trade channels were established, then to increase prices further would be reckless. Even the danger of imports taking over any large per cent of the market is less than the danger of wrecking the price structure which the industry has successfully maintained, but which is vulnerable to the impact of even small increments of uncontrolled capacity; for as one seller and then another shades a price to hold a customer, there is lost that unquestioning mutual trust, group mentality, and the ignoring of marginal cost, which is the indispensable condition for group existence.

This brings us to 1959, which seems difficult to explain by any theory of cost-push inflation, unless one assumes a sudden and simultaneous spasm of civic virtue and horror of "inflation" (and disregard of stockholders) among steel executives. At any rate, the steel companies no longer predicted further wage and price increases in the spring of 1959. They elected instead to take a strike lasting nearly half a year, which lends some support to the suggestion that they really believed they could not raise prices, and knew that higher wages would come out of profits.

Why could they not convince the union that prices could no longer rise? Apparently they never tried. True, Mr. McDonald [the President of the United Steelworkers and its chief bargainer. *Ed.*] might have been hard to convince, for he was in some difficulty in his own union, where an unknown had rolled up about a third of the total vote in the last election, and he needed a success or a struggle to rebuild solidarity. But it does not appear that the union was ever approached quietly and privately with the suggestion that both sides were in trouble and had to hold the cost line in order to keep what they had. Instead, management only brought up the work rules-productivity issue very late in the day, and publicly, in an obvious effort to put the union in the wrong. And perhaps the union was protecting inefficiency. Mr. McDonald seems to think so, for he said the companies' suggestions would save vast sums of money and eliminate a hundred thousand jobs.

If even half true this would prove the companies' case handsomely. . . . One cannot be sure. For similar reasons it is hard to appraise the companies' case that great economies could be achieved by work-rule changes. . . .

Perhaps the union could not have been convinced anyway, since it was one layer of responsibility away from the brute facts of the marketplace, and had heard steel cost-push inflation so long treated as gospel that it had come to accept it as such. . . .

The strike ended with an agreement for further wage increases and other benfits. . . . As for prices, there was some talk of "a general price rise expected in two to three months" just after the agreement with the union, but it lacked the confident tone of the last observances of the ritual. . . . [Through 1960 and the first half of 1961, a period when the steel industry operated at far below capacity levels, steel prices did not rise. *Ed.*] I would expect . . . that steel prices have ceased to be independent of the general price level. Henceforth only the increase in productivity will be available for appropriation by the joint decisions of industry and labor. If this increase is substantial in the near future, there may be a fresh bone of contention.

If this analysis is correct, what happened in steel had nothing to do with [causing] inflation; it was a purely sectoral phenomenon of joint labor-management monopoly approaching the point of maximum return. Once having attained it, the ceiling was reached, and no further increases were possible. Because the two parties were in a posture of both co-operation and conflict in sharing the fruits, communication between them was necessary but difficult, and broke down in 1959. This theory is submitted as simpler than cost-push inflation, and a better fit to the facts.

. . . This paper has not proved that there cannot be such a thing as cost-push inflation; it is only that when the strongest example of the phenomenon, which also accounts for half the 1953–58 ["post-Korean" period] increase in the wholesale price index, is seen upon examination to be something else, we may doubt whether the thing existed and operated at all in the fifties. . . . The real problem in steel and similar industries is that of resources badly allocated, and of the conflict that is endemic under monopoly, when contending factions strive to get the lion's share.

. . . . .

[The author then discusses possible types of public policy, concluding "Perhaps the only useful suggestion with any chance of acceptance is simply not to make things worse." Presidential or other governmental intervention may only make things worse over the years by re-enforcing monopoly elements. *Ed.*]

X • THE NATIONAL ECONOMY: CYCLES AND STABILITY

In the 1961 hearings of the Joint Economic Committee, Representative Thomas B. Curtis asked the Council of Economic Advisors several questions about GNP. Some of the replies follow.

50 • Uses and Limitations of Gross National Product Figures

WALTER W. HELLER
KERMIT GORDON
JAMES TOBIN

QUESTION: Do you recognize any limitations to the Gross National Product as a meaningful series of statistics in measuring economic potential? If so, please set forth what these limitations are and what we must guard against in relying upon GNP in obtaining a meaningful picture of our economy.

ANSWER: Gross National Product, like any aggregative index of economic activity, is an imperfect measuring-rod. Most of its limitations are inherent in trying to describe a complex economic system by a single number. Inevitably much that is important and interesting is left out. Other difficulties and limitations stem from:

1. The very concept of production (e.g. the omission of leisure), the exclusion of many non-market activities (e.g. the services of housewives), and the necessity of imputing values to other goods and services that do not pass through the market (e.g. the services of owner-occupied homes).

2. The often tenuous distinction between final and intermediate output (in particular the treatment of government expenditures, the replacement of plant and equipment, and research and development expenditures).

3. Questions of valuation and price-correction, and the related problems posed by product changes.

Despite these difficulties, we believe, in common with the overwhelming majority of economists, that GNP corrected for price change is the best overall measure of economic activity that we possess.

QUESTION: Specifically, do you believe that GNP is valuable primarily as a long range measure of economic growth and economic capabilities?

WALTER W. HELLER, KERMIT GORDON, and JAMES TOBIN, *Replies of the Council of Economic Advisers to Questions Submitted by The Honorable Thomas B. Curtis,* Joint Economic Committee Hearings (April 10, 1961).

ANSWER: Each of the difficulties mentioned above becomes more substantial as the time scale of comparisons is lengthened. For this reason GNP, like any summary measure, is a safer guide to short-range comparisons than to very long-range ones.

QUESTION: How do you take account of economic mistakes which become just as much a part of the GNP of a particular year as economic activities that prove to be fundamentally sound.

ANSWER: A basic principle underlying GNP computations is that goods and services are valued at market prices. The economist does not presume to substitute his judgments about the relative worth of things for the market's judgments. Expenditures which, with the advantage of hindsight, may be seen to be misdirected are nevertheless included in the National Product. So are expenditures which yield greater benefits than are foreseen on the market. This problem does not seem to us to be a serious one to the user of GNP data—first, because we do not believe "mistakes" of valuation to be quantitatively large, and second, because, unless their magnitude changes markedly from year to year, comparisons over time will not be affected.

QUESTION: Do you recognize a difference in an economy based upon war and one based upon peace, particularly as measured in terms of GNP?

ANSWER: There are several differences between wartime and peacetime economies with respect to GNP measurement:

1. Military goods are not always priced on a free market, and price control and rationing may be introduced even for civilian goods. For this reason the problem of appropriate valuation may be especially severe in wartime.

2. Military commodities are essentially destructive or defensive and do not contribute to social welfare in the same way as ordinary peacetime goods and services. They should not therefore be omitted from GNP. After all, economic output is not all there is to social welfare, and GNP purports only to measure economic output. Moreover, even in peacetime we count regrettable necessities, like police departments, as contributions to national output.

3. In normal peacetime conditions a strong case can be made that Net National Product, which makes proper allowance for wear and tear of durable equipment [depreciation], is a more appropriate measure of aggregate output than GNP. It is not often used because of the unreliability of estimates of capital consumption. But in wartime, when the short sprint is of prime importance, it may be desirable to consume capital in order to maximize military potential. In this case GNP is the appropriate measure.

4. In the second World War, one source of the rapid rise in GNP was the extraordinary increase in the labor force and in hours worked, in response to the national emergency.

QUESTION: Do you recognize a difference between an economy that is becoming industrialized and one that has been industrialized for some time in using GNP as a method of measuring the further advancements of both economies?

ANSWER: The two most important distinctions between industrializing and already industrialized economies with respect to the use of GNP are these:

1. The relation between NNP and GNP will differ. The larger and older capital stock of an industrialized country makes it necessary to charge a larger share of GNP to capital consumption.

2. A country becoming industrialized will normally experience a transfer of many productive activities from the non-market to the market sector of the

economy, and this will distort GNP comparisons over time. For already advanced economies this source of difficulty does not seem to be very large.

QUESTION: Do you recognize a difference between an industrialized economy that has had its industrial plant largely destroyed by war and is rebuilding [e.g., Germany] with an industrialized economy that has not had this experience in using GNP as a method of measuring the further advancements of the two different kinds of economy?

ANSWER: War destruction and reconstruction offer no fundamental problems to the user of GNP statistics. They have, of course, important economic effects, but these are reflected in the size, composition and rate of growth of GNP and could be analyzed in normal ways.

QUESTION: (a) Do you believe that as an industrial economy develops and advances technologically that there is a shift from manufacturing to service and distribution?

(b) Do you believe that the United States economy is experiencing a noticeable shift in economic emphasis from manufacturing to service and distribution?

ANSWER: It is often claimed that, as an industrial economy develops, there is a shift from manufacturing to service and distribution. The facts in the U. S. since 1929 are far from clear. It is certain that during that period the part of the population engaged in agriculture declined and the part engaged in government and government enterprises increased sharply. Eliminating these two sectors from the total, one can roughly divide the remaining industries into a commodity-producing group and a distribution-and-service group. Between 1929 and 1953 the first group increased while the second decreased (in terms of fraction of persons engaged), and between 1953 and 1959 the reverse was true. Between 1929 and 1959 there is almost no difference in the distribution of the working population between the two groups. The shift to services since 1953 may represent a new long-run trend, or it may simply reflect the development of general slack in the economy. [The latter point refers to efforts of men (or their wives) who can not get jobs in manufacturing to seek work in service activities. *Ed.*]

QUESTION: Do you recognize a limitation in the use of GNP as a measurement of economic development to reflect [a shift from manufacturing to service jobs]?

ANSWER: The great merit of GNP as a measure of over-all economic activity is that it is *not* affected by a shift of final demand from one kind of output to another. Equal market values are counted equally in all sectors of the economy. This is not true of other production indicators, which emphasize particular sectors—e.g. the industrial production index. To the extent that there is a shift to services, the major problem with respect to GNP arises from the public sector, which is increasing in importance. Since the services of government are not generally sold at a market price, the convention has been adopted of measuring their value by their cost. Any increase in the productivity of general government is thus underestimated. It follows that the rate of growth of an economy in which general government is growing relative to market output is somewhat understated by the rate of growth of GNP [assuming a growth in productivity, e.g., quality of service per dollar of wage or salary, in the government sector].

In addition, as already noted, it is sometimes argued that much of government expenditures on goods and services consist of intermediate rather than final uses. The standard examples are the commercial use of roads and the provision of police protection for business property.

If it were true that the advance of productivity is inherently slower in services than in manufacturing, the shift [from manufacturing] to private services since 1953 might account in part for the indicated slowdown in growth. The facts are difficult to disentangle. The staff of this Committee has produced figures which show that between 1947 and 1953 productivity increased in the service sector at an average annual rate of 1.8 percent and in trade at 2.4 percent. Between 1953 and 1958 (1957 for trade) these rates fell to 1.5 percent and 1.4 percent; and between 1955 and 1958 to 0.8 percent and 0.1 percent respectively.

Before we leap to any interpretation of these facts we should note that there was a parallel reduction in the rate of productivity increase within manufacturing. Between 1947 and 1953 manufacturing productivity rose by 3.3 percent per year and from 1953 to 1957 the rate of improvement fell to 1.9 percent per year. Moreover, it is possible that the poor performance of the service and trade sectors after 1955 does not reflect an inherent sluggishness in productivity. Instead it may be that general weakness in the economy released workers from relatively high-productivity employment in all sectors and left them to be absorbed in low-productivity and low-wage employment in services and trade.

Since the shift in resources to services after 1953 was small, and since the productivity growth differential was also small in those years, this factor cannot account for more than a very small fraction of the slowdown in over-all growth of GNP.

QUESTION: Do you believe that money spent in research and development and in education is measured with the same weighting that money spent on capital expansion such as more steel capacity by the GNP statistical series?

ANSWER: There is indeed an anomaly in the treatment both of education and of research and development in the national accounts. Both types of expenditures are in large part a kind of capital formation, indeed an important kind of capital formation; yet both are treated as current expenditures. Public education, as noted, enters into the measured GNP simply at cost. Private research and development expenditures, except for buildings and equipment, are treated as current expenses by business firms. They enter into GNP only indirectly as they are reflected in the value of final goods and services, but do not themselves appear as final product. Since the volume of research and development expenditures is growing more rapidly than GNP, the result is to underestimate somewhat the rate of growth of national product. But since the absolute volume of such outlays is small relative to GNP, the amount of the underestimate cannot be great.

QUESTION: Do you agree that the Consumer Price Index has an upward bias resulting from the difficulties in measuring increases in quality and choice of goods and services? If so, do you not believe that the adjustment of GNP in 1960 or the current year prices will reflect this bias and so not give us as accurate a picture of real GNP for the particular year as GNP unadjusted?

ANSWER: [We] said in [our] March 6th statement: ". . . as noted in the Report of the Price Statistics Review Committee, which the Joint Economic Committee has just published, many experts believe that the price indexes, by failing to take full account of quality improvement, contain a systematic upward bias."

Unless the extent of the bias varies widely from year to year, it will not seriously distort comparisons of rates of growth. The Consumer Price Index is not used to "deflate" [adjust] GNP for price change. This "deflation" is done by special price indexes with appropriate weights, one for each major GNP component. These indexes are subject to the same sources of upward bias as the CPI. But it is certain that this bias cannot be so large or so erratic that *undeflated* GNP [a figure with no adjustment for price level changes—*Ed.*] would be a better measure of changes in real output. Genuine changes in the general price level are often very substantial and vary widely from year to year. In common with nearly all economists, we believe that deflated GNP gives a more accurate picture of real output and its changes than current-price GNP [i.e., the GNP figure in prices of the year being measured—*Ed.*].

The author of the following selection, Professor of Economics at Columbia University, is one of America's leading students of business cycles. His active participation in the exhaustive study of cycles at the National Bureau of Economic Research began in the 1920's and has continued since. He has, however, also engaged in a wide variety of other activities which have added to his impressive qualifications for interpreting our economy. From 1953 to 1956 he was Chairman of the Council of Economic Advisers.

51 · *Progress Towards Economic Stability*

ARTHUR F. BURNS

The American people have of late been more conscious of the business cycle, more sensitive to every wrinkle of economic curves, more alert to the possible need for contracyclical action on the part of government, than ever before in our history. Minor changes of employment or of productivity or of the price level, which in an earlier generation would have gone unnoticed, are nowadays followed closely by laymen as well as experts. This sensitivity to the phenomena of recession and inflation is a symptom of an increased public awareness of both the need for and the attainability of economic progress. It is precisely because so much of current industrial and governmental practice can be better in the future that our meetings this year are focused on the broad problem of improving the performance of the American economy. However, as we go about the task of appraisal and criticism, it will be well to discipline our impatience for reform. In the measure that we avoid ex-

ARTHUR F. BURNS, "Progress Towards Economic Stability," *American Economic Review*, Vol. L. No. 1 (March 1960). Used by permission.

aggerating our nation's failures or understating its successes, we shall make it easier for ourselves as well as for economists in other countries to see current needs and developments in a just perspective.

It is a fact of the highest importance, I think, that although our economy continues to be swayed by the business cycle, its impact on the lives and fortunes of individuals has been substantially reduced in our generation. More than twenty-five years have elapsed since we last experienced a financial panic or a deep depression of production and employment. Over twenty years have elapsed since we last had a severe business recession. Between the end of the second world war and the present [1959], we have experienced four recessions, but each was a relatively mild setback. Since 1937 we have had five recessions, the longest of which lasted only 13 months. There is no parallel for such a sequence of mild—or such a sequence of brief—contractions, at least during the past hundred years in our own country.

Nor is this all. The character of the business cycle itself appears to have changed, apart from the intensity of its over-all movement. We usually think of the business cycle as a sustained advance of production, employment, incomes, consumption, and prices, followed by a sustained contraction, which in time gives way to a renewed advance of aggregate activity beyond the highest levels previously reached. We realize that changes in the price level occasionally outrun changes in production, that employment is apt to fluctuate less than production, and that consumption will fluctuate still less; but we nevertheless think of their movements as being roughly parallel. This concept of the business cycle has always been something of a simplification. For example, during the early decades of the nineteenth century, when agriculture dominated our national economy, occasional declines in the physical volume of production, whether large or small, had little effect on the number of jobs and sometimes had slight influence even on the flow of money incomes. As agriculture diminished in importance, the nation's production, employment, personal income, consumption, and price level fell more closely into step with one another and thus justified our thinking of them as moving in a rough parallelism. In recent years, however, and especially since the second world war, the relations among these movements have become much looser.

The structure of an economy inevitably leaves its stamp on the character of its fluctuations. In our generation the structure of the American economy has changed profoundly, partly as a result of deliberate economic policies, partly as a result of unplanned developments. In considering problems of the future, we can proceed more surely by recognizing the changes in economic organization which already appear to have done much to blunt the impact of business cycles.

I.

In the early decades of the nineteenth cenutry the typical American worker operated his own farm or found scope for his energy on the family farm. Governmental activities were very limited. What there was of industry and commerce was largely conducted through small firms run by capitalist-employers. Corporations were rare and virtually confined to banking and transportation. As the population grew and capital became more abundant, individual enterprise expanded vigorously but corporate enterprise expanded still more. An increasing part of the nation's business therefore came under the rule of corporations. By

1929, the output of corporate businesses was already almost twice as large as the output of individual proprietorships and partnerships. The gap has widened appreciably since then. Corporate profits have therefore tended to increase faster than the incomes earned by proprietors, who still remain very numerous in farming, retail trade, and the professions. Fifty years ago the total income of proprietors was perhaps two and a half times as large as the combined sum of corporate profits and the compensation of the corporate officers. By 1957 this corporate aggregate exceeded by a fourth the income of all proprietors and by two-thirds the income of proprietors outside of farming.

The great growth of corporations in recent decades has occurred preponderantly in industries where the firm must operate on a large scale to be efficient and therefore must assemble capital from many sources. But a corporation whose stock is held publicly and widely has a life of its own, apart from that of its owners, and will rarely distribute profits at the same rate as they are being earned. While profits normally respond quickly and sharply to a change in sales and production, the behavior of dividends is tempered by business judgment. In practice, dividends tend to move sluggishly and over a much narrower range than profits. Corporations have therefore come to function increasingly as a buffer between the fluctuations of production and the flow of income to individuals. In earlier times the lag of dividends was largely a result of the time-consuming character of corporate procedures. More recently, the advantages of a stable dividend—especially its bearing on a firm's financial reputation—have gained increasing recognition from business managers. Meanwhile, modern trends of taxation have stimulated corporations to rely more heavily on retained profits and less on new stock issues for their equity funds, and this development in turn has facilitated the pursuit of stable dividend policies. Thus the evolution of corporate practice, as well as the growth of corporate enterprise itself, has served to reduce the influence of a cyclical decline of production and profits on the flow of income to individuals.

The expansion and the means of financing of governmental enterprise, especially since the 1930's, have had a similar effect. The increasing complexity of modern life, a larger concept of the proper function of government, and the mounting requirements of national defense have resulted in sharp increases of governmental spending. Fifty years ago the combined expenditure of federal, state, and local governments was about 7 per cent of the dollar volume of the nation's total output. Governmental expenditures rose to 10 per cent of total output in 1929 and to 26 per cent in 1957. This huge expansion of governmental enterprise naturally led to increases in tax rates and to an energetic search for new sources of revenue. In time, taxes came to be imposed on estates, gifts, employment, sales, and—most important of all—on the incomes of both corporations and individuals. Fifty years ago customs duties still yielded about half of the total revenue of the federal government, and none of our governmental units as yet collected any tax on incomes. Twenty years later, personal and corporate income taxes were already the mainstay of federal finance. Subsequently, the activities of the federal government increased much faster than local activities and taxes followed suit. By 1957 the income tax accounted for nearly 70 per cent of federal revenue, 8 per cent of state and local revenue, and a little over half of the combined revenue of our various governmental units.

This dominance of the income tax in current governmental finance, together with the recent shift of tax collection toward a pay-as-you-go basis, has measurably enlarged the government's participation in the shifting fortunes of the private economy. During the nineteenth century, taxes were not only a much smaller factor in the economy, but such short-run elasticity as there was in tax revenues derived almost entirely from customs duties. Hence, when production fell off and private incomes diminished, the accompanying change in governmental revenues was usually small. In recent years, however, governmental revenues have become very sensitive to fluctuations of business conditions. When corporate profits decline by, say, a billion dollars, the federal government will collect under existing law about a half billion less from corporations. When individual incomes decline by a billion, the federal government may be expected to collect about $150 million less from individuals. State income taxes accentuate these effects. In short, when a recession occurs, our current tax system requires the government to reduce rather promptly and substantially the amount of money that it withdraws from the private economy for its own use. The result is that the income from production which corporations and individuals have at their disposal declines much less than does the national income.

Moreover, the operations of government are now so organized that the flow of personal income from production is bolstered during a recession by increased payments of unemployment insurance benefits. Unemployment insurance was established on a national basis in 1935, and the protection of workers against the hazards of unemployment has increased since then. Not all employees are as yet covered by unemployment insurance and the benefits, besides, are often inadequate to provide for essentials. Nevertheless, there has been a gradual improvement in the ability of families to get along decently even when the main breadwinner is temporarily unemployed. At present, over 80 per cent of those who work for a wage or salary are covered by unemployment insurance in contrast to 70 per cent in 1940. The period over which benefits can be paid to an unemployed worker has become longer and the typical weekly benefits has risen in greater proportion than the cost of living. Furthermore, arrangements have recently been concluded in several major industries whereby benefits to the unemployed are supplemented from private sources.

Other parts of the vast system of social security that we have devised since the 1930's have also served to support the flow of personal income at times when business activity is declining. Payments made to retired workers kept iscreasing during each recession of the postwar period. The reason is partly that workers handicapped by old age or physical disability experience greater difficulty at such times in keeping their jobs or finding new ones and therefore apply for pensions in somewhat larger numbers. Another factor has been the intermittent liberalization of statutory benefits. But the most important reason for the steady increase of old-age pensions is the maturing of the social security system. In 1940, only 7 per cent of people of age 65 and over were eligible for benefits from the old-age insurance trust fund, in contrast to 23 per cent in 1948 and 69 per cent in 1958. The trend of other public pension programs and the various public assistance programs has also been upward. Between 1929 and 1957 the social security and related benefits paid out by our various governmental units rose from 1 per cent of total personal income to 6 per cent. In 1933, with the economy at a catastrophically low level, these benefit payments were merely $548 million larger than in 1929. On the other hand, in 1958—when business activity was only slightly depressed—they were $4.4 billion above the level of 1957. Even these figures understate the difference between current conditions and those of a quarter century ago, for they leave out of account the private pensions which are beginning to supplement public pensions on a significant scale.

As a result of these several major developments in our national life, the movement of aggregate personal income is no longer closely linked to the movement of aggregate production. During the postwar period we have had several brief but sizable setbacks in production. For example, in the course of the recession of 1957–58, the physical output of factories and mines fell 14 per cent, the physical output of commodities and services in the aggregate fell 5.4 per cent, and the dollar volume of total output fell 4.3 per cent. In earlier times personal incomes would have responded decisively to such a decline in production. This time the government absorbed a substantial part of the drop in the dollar volume of production by putting up with a sharp decline of its revenues despite the need to raise expenditures. Corporations absorbed another part of the decline by maintaining dividends while their undistributed profits slumped. In the end, the aggregate of personal incomes, after taxes, declined less than 1 per cent and the decline was over before the recession ended.

Although the details have varied from one case to the next, a marked divergence between the movements of personal income and production has occured in each of the postwar recessions. Indeed, during 1953–54 the total income at the disposal of individuals defied the recession by continuing to increase. This unique achievement was due to the tax reduction that became effective soon after the onset of recession as well as to the structural changes that have reduced the dependence of personal income on the short-run movements of production.

II.

When we turn from personal income to employment, we find that the imprint of the business cycle is still strong. During each recession since 1948, unemployment reached a level which, while decidedly low in comparison with the experience of the 'thirties, was sufficient to cause serious concern. But although the fluctuations of employment have continued to synchronize closely with the movements of production, the relation between the two has been changing in ways which favor greater stability of employment in the future.

As the industrialization of our economy proceeded during the nineteenth century, an increasing part of the population became exposed to the hazards of the business cycle. Manufacturing, mining, construction, freight transportation —these are the strategic industries of a developing economy and they are also the industries in which both production and jobs have been notoriously unstable. Shortly after the Civil War, the employees attached to this cyclical group of industries already constituted 23 per cent of the labor force. Employees of industries that have remained relatively free from cyclical unemployment—that is, agriculture, merchandising, public utilities, financial enterprises, the personal service trades, and the government —accounted for another 32 per cent. The self-employed in farming, business, and the professions, whose jobs are especially steady, made up the rest of 45 per cent of the work force. This was the situation in 1869. Fifty years later, the proportion of workers engaged in farming, whether as operators or hired hands, had shrunk drastically, and this shrinkage was offset only in part by the relative gain of other stable sources of employment. Consequently, the proportion of employees in the cyclical industries kept rising, decade after decade, and reached 36 per cent in 1919.

Clearly, the broad effect of economic evolution until about 1920 was to increase the concentration of jobs in the cyclically volatile industries, and this was a major force tending to intensify declines of employment during business contractions. Since then, the continued progress of technology, the very factor which originally was mainly responsible for the concentration in the cyclical industries, has served to arrest this tendency. The upward trend of production in manufacturing and the other highly cyclical industries has remained rapid in recent decades. However, advances of technology have come so swiftly in these industries as well as in agriculture that an increasing part of the nation's labor could turn to the multitude of tasks in which the effectiveness of human effort improves only slowly, where it improves at all. Thus the employees of "service" industries constituted 24 per cent of the labor force in 1919, but as much as 44 per cent in 1957. The proportion of self-employed workers in business and the professions, which was 9.4 per cent in the earlier year, became 10.6 per cent in the later year. True, these gains in types of employment that are relatively stable during business cycles were largely canceled by the countervailing trend in agriculture. Nevertheless, the proportion of employees attached to the cyclically volatile industries has not risen since 1919. Or to express this entire development in another way, the proportion of workers having rather steady jobs, either because they work for themselves or because they are employed in industries that are relatively free from the influence of business cycles, kept declining from the beginning of our industrial revolution until about 1920, and since then has moved slightly but irregularly upward.

Thus, the changing structure of industry, which previously had exercised a powerful destabilizing influence on employment and output, particularly the former, has ceased to do so. The new stabilizing tendency is as yet weak, but it is being gradually reinforced by the spread of "white-collar" occupations throughout the range of industry. For many years now, the proportion of people who work as managers, engineers, scientists, draftsmen, accountants, clerks, secretaries, salesmen, or in kindred occupations has been increasing. The white-collar group, which constituted only 28 per cent of the labor force outside of agriculture in 1900, rose to 38 per cent in 1940 and to 44 per cent in 1957. Workers of this category are commonly said to hold a "position" rather than a "job" and to be paid a "salary" rather than a "wage." Hence, they are often sheltered by a professional code which frowns upon frequent firing and hiring. Moreover, much of this type of employment is by its nature of an overhead character and therefore less responsive to the business cycle than are the jobs of machine operators, craftsmen, assembly-line workers, truck drivers, laborers, and others in the "blue-collar" category. For example, during the recession of 1957–58, the number of "production workers" employed in manufacturing, who approximate the blue-collar group, declined 12 per cent, while the employment of "nonproduction workers," who approximate the white-collar group, declined only 3 per cent. This sort of difference has been characteristic of recessions generally, not only the most recent episode, and on a smaller scale it has also been characteristic of industry generally, not only of manufacturing.

It appears, therefore, that changes in the occupational structure of the labor force, if not also in the industrial structure, have been tending of late to loosen the links which, over a considerable part of our economic history, tied the short-run movement of total employment rather firmly to the cyclical movement of total production, and especially to the cyclical movement of its most unstable parts—that is, the activities of manufacturing, mining, construction, and freight transportation. This stabilizing tendency promises well for the future, although up to the present it has not left a mark on records of aggregate employment that is comparable with the imprint that the stabilizing influences we discussed previously have left on personal income. In the postwar period, as over a longer past, the number of men and women at work, and even more the aggregate of hours worked by them, has continued to move in fairly close sympathy with the fluctuations of production.

We can no longer justifiably suppose, however, when employment falls 2 million during a recession, as it did between July 1957 and July 1958, that the number of people who receive an income has declined by any such figure. In fact, the number of workers drawing unemployment insurance under the several regular plans rose about 1.3 million during these twelve months, while the number of retired workers on public pensions rose another million. Hence, it may be conservatively estimated that the number of income recipients increased over 300 thousand despite the recession. In the other postwar recessions our experience was fairly similar. In other words, as a result of some of the structural changes on which I dwelt earlier, the size of the income-receiving population has grown steadily and escaped cyclical fluctuations entirely.[1]

III.

Turning next to consumer spending, we must try once again to see recent developments in historical perspective. The fact that stands out is that the impact of business cycles on consumption has recently diminished, while the effects of consumption on the business cycle have become more decisive.

In the classical business cycle, as we came to know it in this country, once business investment began declining appreciably, a reduction of consumer spending soon followed. Sometimes the expansion of investment culminated because the firms of one or more key industries, finding that their markets were growing less rapidly than had been anticipated, made an effort to bring their productive capacity or inventories into better adjustment with sales. Sometimes the expansion culminated because the belief grew that construction and financing costs had been pushed to unduly high levels by the advance of prosperity. Sometimes it culminated for all these or still other reasons. But whatever the cause or causes of the decline in investment, it made its influence felt over an increasing area of the economy. For a while consumer spending was maintained at a peak level or even kept rising. But since businessmen were now buying on a smaller scale from one an-

---

[1] This upward trend would appear steeper than I have suggested if recipients of property income and of public assistance were included in the count. In the present context, however, it has seemed best to restrict the income-receiving population to the working class, or more precisely, to members of the labor force or those recently in the labor force who receive an income as a matter of right and on some regular basis.

other, more and more workers lost their jobs or their overtime pay, financial embarrassments and business failures became more frequent, and uncertainty about the business outlook spread to parts of the economy in which sales and profits were still flourishing. If some consumers reacted to these developments by curtailing their spending in the interest of caution, others did so as a matter of necessity. Before long, these curtailments proved sufficient to bring on some decline in the aggregate spending of consumers. The impulses for reducing business investments therefore quickened and the entire round of events was repeated, with both investment and consumption declining in a cumulative process.

As the contraction continued, it tried men's patience, yet in time worked its own cure. Driven by hard necessity, business firms moved with energy to reduce costs and increase efficiency. Consumers whose incomes were declining often saved less or dissaved in order not to disrupt their customary living standards. Hence, even if sales and prices were still falling, profit margins improved here and there. In the meantime, bank credit became more readily available, costs of building and terms of borrowing became more favorable, the bond market revived, business failures diminished, and the investment plans of innovators and others began expanding again. When recovery finally came, it was likely to be led by a reduced rate of disinvestment in inventories or by a new rush to make investments in fixed capital. At this stage of the business cycle, consumer spending was at its very lowest level, if not still declining.

Many of these features of earlier business cycles have carried over to the present. However, the behavior of consumers in the postwar recessions has departed from the traditional pattern in two respects. In the first place, consumers maintained their spending at a high level even after business activity had been declining for some months, so that the tendency of recessions to cumulate was severely checked. During the recession of 1945 consumer spending actually kept increasing. In each of the later recessions it fell somewhat; but the decline at no time exceeded one per cent and lasted only a quarter or two. In the second place, instead of lagging at the recovery stage of the business cycle, as it had in earlier times, consumer spending turned upward before production or employment resumed its expansion. This shift in cyclical behavior appears clearly in department store sales, which have been recorded on a substantially uniform basis for several decades and are widely accepted as a tolerably good indicator of consumer spending. In the recoveries of 1921, 1924, 1927, and 1938, these sales lagged by intervals ranging from two to four months. In 1933 their upturn came at the same time as in production and employment. It thus appears that, during the 1920's and 1930's, consumer spending in no instance led the economy out of a slump. In the postwar period, on the other hand, department store sales have led successive recoveries by intervals stretching from two to five months. Of course, department store sales cover only a small fraction of consumer expenditure, and correction for price changes would alter their historical record somewhat. But the main features of the cyclical behavior of dollar sales by department stores are broadly confirmed by other evidence on consumer spending, which is extensive for recent years. We may therefore conclude with considerable assurance that consumer spending has played a more dynamic role in recent times. Not only have consumers managed their spending during recessions so that the cumulative process of deflation has been curbed, but consumer spending has emerged as one of the active factors in arresting recession and hastening recovery.

This new role of the consumer in the business cycle reflects some of the developments of the postwar period that we considered earlier, particularly the greatly enhanced stability in the flow of personal income, the steady expansion in the number of income recipients, and the relative increase in the number of steady jobs. It reflects also the improvements of financial organization and other structural changes which have strengthened the confidence of people, whether acting as consumers or investors, in their own and the nation's economic future. Whatever may have been true of the past, it can no longer be held that consumers are passive creatures who lack the power or the habit of initiating changes in economic activities. There is no harm in thinking of consumer spending as being largely "determined" by past and current incomes, provided we also recognize that the level of current incomes is itself shaped to a significant degree by the willingness of people to work hard to earn what they need to live as they feel they should. The evidence of rising expectations and increased initiative on the part of consumers is all around us. It appears directly in the rapidly rising proportion of women in the labor force, in the sizable and increasing proportion of men who hold down more than one job, in the slackening of the long-term decline of the average work week in manufacturing despite the increased power of trade unions, as well as indirectly in the improvement of living standards and the great upsurge of population. Indeed, the expansive forces on the side of consumption have been so powerful that we must not be misled by the cyclical responses of consumer spending, small though they were, to which I referred earlier. There are no continuous records of inventories in the hands of consumers; but if such statistics were available, we would almost certainly find that consumption proper, in contrast to consumer spending, did not decline at all during any of the postwar recessions.

In view of these developments in the realm of the consumer, it is evident that the force of any cyclical decline of production has in recent years been reduced or broken as its influence spread through the economy. Production has remained unstable, but the structure of our economy has changed in ways which have limited the effects of recessions on the lives of individuals—on the numbers who receive an income, the aggregate of personal incomes, consumer spending, actual consumption, and to some degree even the numbers employed. It is, therefore, hardly an exaggeration to assert that a good part of the personal security which in an earlier age derived from living on farms and in closely knit family units, after having been disrupted by the onrush of industrialization and urbanization, has of late been restored through the new institutions that have developed in both the private and public branches of our economy.

IV.

In concentrating, as I have thus far, on the changes of economic organization which have lately served to reduce the impact of business cycles on the lives of individuals, I have provisionally taken the cyclical movement of production for granted. Of course, if the fluctuations of production had been larger, the impact on people would have been greater. On the other hand, the stabilized tendency of personal income and consumption has itself been a major reason why recent recessions of production have been brief and of only moderate intensity. Many other factors have contributed to this development. Among them are the deliberate efforts made in our generation to control the business cycle, of which I have as yet said little.

In earlier generations there was a tendency for the focus of business thinking to shift from the pursuit of profits to the maintenance of financial solvency whenever confidence in the continuance of prosperity began to wane. At such times experienced businessmen were prone to reason that it would shortly become more difficult to collect from their customers or to raise funds by borrowing, while they in turn were being pressed by their creditors. Under the circumstances it seemed only prudent to conserve cash on hand, if not also to reduce inventories or accounts receivable. Such efforts by some led to similar efforts by others, in a widening circle. As pressure on commodity markets, security markets, and on the banking system mounted, the decline of business activity was speeded and the readjustment of interest rates, particularly on the longer maturities, was delayed. More often than not the scramble for liquidity ran its course without reaching crisis proportions. Sometimes, however, as in 1873, 1893, and 1907, events took a sinister turn. Financial pressures then became so acute that doubts arose about the ability of banks to meet their outstanding obligations and, as people rushed to convert their deposits into currency, even the soundest banks were forced to restrict the outflow of cash. With the nation's system for making monetary payments disrupted, panic ruled for a time over the economy and production inevitably slumped badly.

It was this dramatic phase of the business cycle that first attracted wide notice and stimulated students of public affairs to seek ways and means of improving our financial organization. The Federal Reserve Act, which became law under the shadow of the crisis of 1907, required the pooling of bank reserves and established facilities for temporary borrowing by banks. The hope that this financial reform would ease the transition from the expanding to the contracting phase of business cycles has been amply justified by experience. But the Federal Reserve System could not prevent the cumulation of financial trouble during business expansions. Nor could it prevent runs on banks or massive bank failures, as the Great Depression demonstrated. The need to overhaul and strengthen the financial system became increasingly clear during the 'thirties and led to numerous reforms, among them the insurance of mortgages, the creation of a secondary market for mortgages, the insurance of savings and loan accounts, and—most important of all—the insurance of bank deposits. These financial reforms have served powerfully to limit the propagation of fear, which in the past had been a major factor in intensifying slumps of production.

But more basic than the financial innovations or any other specific measures of policy has been the change in economic and political attitudes which took root during the 'thirties. The economic theory that depressions promote industrial efficiency and economic progress lost adherents as evidence accumulated of the wreckage caused by unemployment and business failures. The political belief that it was best to leave business storms to blow themselves out lost its grip on men's minds as the depression stretched out. In increasing numbers citizens in all walks of life came around to the view that mass unemployment was intolerable under modern conditions and that the federal government has a continuing responsibility to foster competitive enterprise, to prevent or moderate general economic declines, and to promote a high and rising level of employment and production. This new philosophy of intervention was articulated by the Congress in the Employment Act of 1946, which solemnly expressed what had by then become a national consensus.

In recent times, therefore, the business cycle has no longer run a free course and this fact has figured prominently in the plans of businessmen as well as consumers. During the 1930's, when the objectives of social reform and economic recovery were sometimes badly confused, many investors suspected that contracyclical policies would result in narrowing the scope of private enterprise and reducing the profitability of investment. These fears diminished after the war as the government showed more understanding of the need to foster a mood of confidence so that enterprise, innovation, and investment may flourish. In investing circles, as elsewhere, the general expectation of the postwar period has been that the government would move with some vigor to check any recession that developed, that its actions would by and large contribute to this objective, and that they would do so in a manner that is broadly consistent with our national traditions. This expectation gradually became stronger and it has played a significant role in extending the horizons of business thinking about the markets and opportunities of the future. The upsurge of population, the eagerness of consumers to live better, the resurgence of Western Europe, the revolutionary discoveries of science, and the steady flow of new products, new materials, and new processes have added impetus to the willingness of investors to expend huge sums of capital on research and on the improvement and expansion of industrial plant and equipment. Some of these influences have also been effective in augmenting public investment. The fundamental trend of investment has therefore been decidedly upward. The private part of investment has continued to move cyclically; but it is now a smaller fraction of total national output and it has displayed a capacity to rebound energetically from the setbacks that come during recessions.

The specific measures adopted by the government in dealing with the recessions of the postwar period have varied from one case to the next. In all of them, monetary, fiscal, and housekeeping policies played some part, with agricultural price-support programs assuming special prominence in one recession, tax reductions in another, and increases of public expenditures in still another. Taking a long view, the most nearly consistent part of contracyclical policy [by government] has been in the monetary sphere. Since the early 1920's, when the Federal Reserve authorities first learned how to influence credit conditions through open-market operations, long-term interest rates have tended to move down as soon as the cyclical peak of economic activity was reached, in contrast to the long lags that were characteristic of earlier times. Since 1948 the decline of long-term interest rates in the early stages of a recession has also become more rapid. This change in the cyclical behavior of capital markets reflects the increased vigor and effectiveness of recent monetary policies. Inasmuch as optimism, as a rule, is still widespread during the initial stages of an economic decline, a substantial easing of credit, provided it comes early enough, can appreciably hasten economic recovery. This influence is exerted only in part through lower interest rates. Of greater consequence is the fact that credit becomes more readily available, that the money supply is increased or kept from falling, that the liquidity of financial assets is improved, and that financial markets are generally stimulated. The effects of easier credit are apt to be felt most promptly by smaller businesses and the home-building industry, but they tend to work their way through the entire economy. There can be little doubt that the rather prompt easing of credit conditions, which occurred during recent setbacks of production, was of some significance in keeping their duration so short.

Business firms have also been paying closer attention to the business cycle, and not a few of them have even tried to do something about it. These efforts have been expressed in a variety of ways —through the adoption of long-range capital budgets, closer control of inventories, and more energetic selling or some relaxation of credit standards in times of recession. I do not know enough to assess either the extent or the success of some of these business policies. Surely, business investment in fixed capital has remained a highly volatile activity—a fact that is sometimes overlooked by concentrating attention on years instead of months and on actual expenditures instead of new commitments. There is, however, strong evidence that the businessmen of our generation manage inventories better than did their predecessors. The inventory-sales ratio of manufacturing firms has lately averaged about a fourth less than during the 1920's, despite the increased importance of the durable goods sector where inventories are especially heavy. The trend of the inventory-sales ratio has also moved down substantially in the case of distributive firms. This success in economizing on inventories has tended to reduce the fluctuations of inventory investment relative to the scale of business operations and this in turn has helped to moderate the cyclical swings in production. Not only that, but it appears that the cyclical downturns of both inventories and inventory investment have tended to come at an earlier stage of the business cycle in the postwar period than they did previously, so that any imbalance between inventories and sales could be corrected sooner. Since consumer outlays—and often also other expenditures—were well maintained during the recent recessions of production, the rising phase of inventory disinvestment ceased rather early and this naturally favored a fairly prompt recovery of production.

Thus, numerous changes in the structure of our economy have combined to stimulate over-all expansion during the postwar period and to keep within moderate limits the cyclical declines that occurred in production. Indeed, there are cogent grounds for believing that these declines were even more moderate than our familiar statistical records suggest. The line of division between production for sale and production for direct use does not stand still in a dynamic economy. In the early decades of the industrial revolution an increasing part of our production was, in effect, transferred from the home to the shop and factory. This trend has continued in the preparation of foods, but in other activities it appears on balance to have been reversed. The great expansion of home ownership, the invention of all sorts of mechanical contrivances for the home, longer vacations, the general eagerness for improvement, if not also the income tax, have stimulated many people to do more and more things for themselves. Consumers have become equipped to an increasing degree with the capital goods they need for transportation, for the refrigeration of food, for the laundering of clothes, as well as for entertainment and instruction. They have also been doing, on an increasing scale, much of the carpentry, painting, plumbing, and landscaping around their homes. Such activities of production are less subject to the business cycle than the commercial activities which enter statistical reports. Yet these domestic activities have undoubtedly been expanding rapidly, and perhaps expanding even more during the declining than during the rising phase of the business cycle. Hence, it is entirely probable that the cyclical swings of production have of late been smaller, while the average rate of growth of production has been higher, than is commonly supposed.

V.

It is in the nature of an economic vocabulary to change slowly, when it changes at all. We keep speaking of the price system, the business cycle, capitalism, socialism, communism, and sometimes we even refer to the "inherent instability" of capitalism or of communism; but the reality that these terms and phases are intended to denote or sum up does not remain fixed. I have tried to show how a conjuncture of structural changes in our economy has served to modify the business cycle of our times. Some of these changes were planned while others were unplanned. Some resulted from efforts to control the business cycle while others originated in policies aimed at different ends. Some arose from private and others from public activities. Some are of very recent origin and others of long standing. The net result has been that the intensity of cyclical swings of production has become smaller. The links that previously tied together the cyclical movements of production, employment, personal income, and consumption have become looser. And, as everyone knows, the once familiar parallelism of the short-term movements in the physical volume of total production, on the one hand, and the average level of wholesale or consumer prices, on the other, has become somewhat elusive.

To be sure, special fatcors of an episodic character played their part in recent business cycles, as they always have. For example, a pent-up demand for civilian goods was highly significant in checking the recession of 1945. The tax reduction legislated in April 1948 helped to moderate the recession which began towards the end of that year. The tax cuts announced soon after business activity began receding in 1953 merely required executive acquiescence in legislation that had been passed before any recession was in sight. Again, the sputniks spurred the government's response to the recession of 1957–58. Special circumstances such as these undoubtedly weakened the forces of economic contraction at certain times; but they also strengthened them at other times. In particular, governmental purchases from private firms have not infrequently been an unsettling influence rather than a stabilizing force. We need only recall the drop of federal expenditure on commodities and services from an annual rate of $91 billion in the early months of 1945 to $16 billion two years later, or the fall from $59 billion to $44 billion soon after the Korean hostilities came to a close. The ability of our economy to adjust to such major disturbances without experiencing a severe or protracted slump testifies not only to our good luck; it testifies also to the stabilizing power of the structural changes that I have emphasized.

It seems reasonable to expect that the structural changes in our economy, which have recently served to moderate and humanize the business cycle, will continue to do so. The growth of corporations is not likely to be checked, nor is the tendency to pay fairly stable dividends likely to be modified. The scale of governmental activities will remain very extensive, and so it would be even if the communist threat to our national security were somehow banished. Our methods of taxation might change materially, but the income tax will remain a major source of governmental revenue. Governmental expenditures might fluctuate sharply, but they are not likely to decline during a recession merely because governmental revenues are then declining. The social security system is more likely to grow than to remain stationary or contract. Private pension arrangements will multiply and so also may private supplements to unemployment insurance. Our population will continue to grow. The restlessness and eagerness of consumers to live better is likely to remain a dynamic force. Research and development activities will continue to enlarge opportunities for investment. Governmental efforts to promote a high and expanding level of economic activity are not likely to weaken. Private businesses will continue to seek ways to economize on inventories and otherwise minimize the risk of cyclical fluctuations in their operations. Employment in agriculture is already so low that its further decline can no longer offset future gains of the service industries on the scale experienced in the past. The spread of white-collar occupations throughout the range of industry will continue and may even accelerate. For all these reasons, the business cycle is unlikely to be as disturbing or troublesome to our children as it once was to us or our fathers.

This is surely a reasonable expectation as we look to the future. Yet, it is well to remember that projections of human experience remain descriptions of a limited past no matter how alluringly they are expressed in language of the future. A lesson of history, which keeps resounding through the ages, is that the most reasonable of expectations sometimes lead nations astray. If my analysis is sound, it supports the judgment that the recessions or depressions of the future are likely to be appreciably milder on the average than they were before the 1940's. It supports no more than this. In view of the inherent variability of business cycles and our still somewhat haphazard ways of dealing with them, there can be no assurance that episodic factors will not make a future recession both longer and deeper than any we experienced in the postwar period.

Nor can there be any assurance that the conjuncture of structural changes on which I have dwelt will not be succeeded by another which will prove less favorable to economic stability. For example, although the stabilizing influence of the rising trend of white-collar employment in manufacturing has been more than sufficient to offset the cyclically intensifying influence of a greater concentration of employment in the durable goods sector, the balance of forces might be tipped the other way in the future. This could happen all the more readily if, as white-collar work continues to grow, the need to cut costs during a recession should make this type of employment less stable than it has been. Again, our exports in recent decades have tended to intensify the business cycle somewhat, and this factor may become of larger significance. Also, it still remains to be seen whether the rising trend of prices—to say nothing of the rapidly growing consumer and mortgage debt—may not serve to complicate future recessions.

A generation ago many economists, having become persuaded that our economy had reached maturity, spoke grimly of a future of secular stagnation. Parts of their analysis were faulty and their predictions have proved wrong; yet their warning helped to mobilize thought and energy to avert the danger of chronic unemployment. Of late, many economists have been speaking just as persuasively, though not always as grimly, of a future of secular inflation. The warning is timely. During the postwar recessions the average level of prices in wholesale and consumer markets has declined little or not at all. The advances in prices that customarily occur during periods of business expansion have therefore become cumulative. It is true that in the last few years the federal government has made some progress in dealing with inflation. Nevertheless, wages and prices rose appreciably even during the recession. The general public has been speculating on a larger scale in common stocks, long-term interest rates have risen very sharply since mid-1958, and the yield on stocks relative to bonds has become abnormally low. All these appear to be symptoms of a continuation of inflationary expectations or pressures.

Such developments have often led to economic trouble. They could do so again even if our balance of payments on international account remained favorable. That, however, has not been the case for some time. The "dollar shortage" which influenced much of our economic thinking and practice during the past generation seems to have ended. The economies of many areas of the Free World, especially of Western Europe and Japan, have lately been rebuilt and their competitive power has been restored. This re-establishment of competitive and monetary links between our country and others may cause us some inconvenience, but it is basically a promising development for the future. It should stimulate our economic growth as well as contribute to the economic progress and political stability of other nations of the Free World. Our financial policies, however, will gradually need to be adjusted to the changed international environment. Although our gold stocks are still abundant and the dollar is still the strongest currency in the world, we can no longer conduct our economic affairs without being mindful of gold, or of the short-term balances that foreign governments and citizens have accumulated here, or of the levels of labor costs, interest rates, and prices in our country relative to those in other nations. Unless the deficit in our balance of payments is soon brought under better control, our nation's ability to pursue contracyclical policies during a business recession may be seriously hampered.

We are living in extraordinarily creative but also deeply troubled times. One of the triumphs of this generation is the progress that our nation has made in reducing economic instability. In the years ahead, no matter what we do as a people, our economy will continue to undergo changes, many of which were neither planned nor anticipated. However, the course of events, both domestic and international, will also depend—and to a large degree—on our resourcefulness and courage in deliberately modifying the structure of our economy so as to strengthen the forces of growth and yet restrain instability.

Great opportunities as well as difficult problems face our nation. Monopoly power, which is still being freely exercised despite all the exhortation of recent years, can be curbed by moving toward price and wage controls or, as many economists still hope, by regenerating competition. Higher protective tariffs, import quotas, and "Buy American" schemes can be embraced or, as many economists hope, avoided. A tax structure that inhibits private investment and directs people's energy into activities that contribute little to the nation's economic strength can be retained or reformed. Costly farm surpluses can be further encouraged by government or discontinued. The problems posed by the slums and the inefficient transportation of many of our cities can be neglected or attacked with some zeal. The inadequacy of our unemployment insurance system can be ignored until the next recession or corrected while there is opportunity for a judicious overhauling. In general, our governmental authorities can deal with recessions by trusting to improvisations of public spending, which often will not become effective until economic recovery is already under way, or by providing in advance of any recession for fairly prompt and automatic adjustment of income tax rates to a temporarily lower level of economic activity. The coordination of governmental policies, which may make the difference between success and failure in promoting our national objectives, can be left largely to accidents of personal force and ingenuity or it can be made systematic through an economic policy board under the chairmanship of the President. These and other choices will have to be made by the people of the United States; and economists—far more than any other group—will in the end help to make them.

Can Keynes' epoch-making theory really be summarized in a few pages? Not perfectly, of course. Yet Professor Dillard of the University of Maryland has arranged the crucial elements so systematically that study—very careful study—of this selection will give a good general impression of the theory that has had profound influence on economics and politics.

52 · Keynes' General Theory of Employment: A Summary

DUDLEY DILLARD

... There are several alternative ways of expressing the essence of the general theory of employment. An over-all summary may be stated in the form of the following propositions:

1. Total income depends on the volume of total employment.
2. According to the propensity to consume, the amount of expenditure for consumption depends on the level of income, and therefore on total employment (from No. 1 above).
3. Total employment depends on total effective demand (D), which is made up of two parts: (a) consumption expenditure (D_1) and (b) investment expenditure (D_2).

$$(D = D_1 + D_2)$$

4. In equilibrium, the aggregate demand (D) is equal to the aggregate supply (Z). Therefore, aggregate supply exceeds the effective demand for consumption by the amount of the effective demand for investment.

($D = D_1 + D_2$, or $D_2 = D - D_1$. Since $D = Z$, therefore $D_2 = Z - D_1$.)

DUDLEY DILLARD, *The Economics of John Maynard Keynes* (Englewood Cliffs, N. J.: Prentice-Hall, Inc., 1948), pp. 48–50. Used by permission.

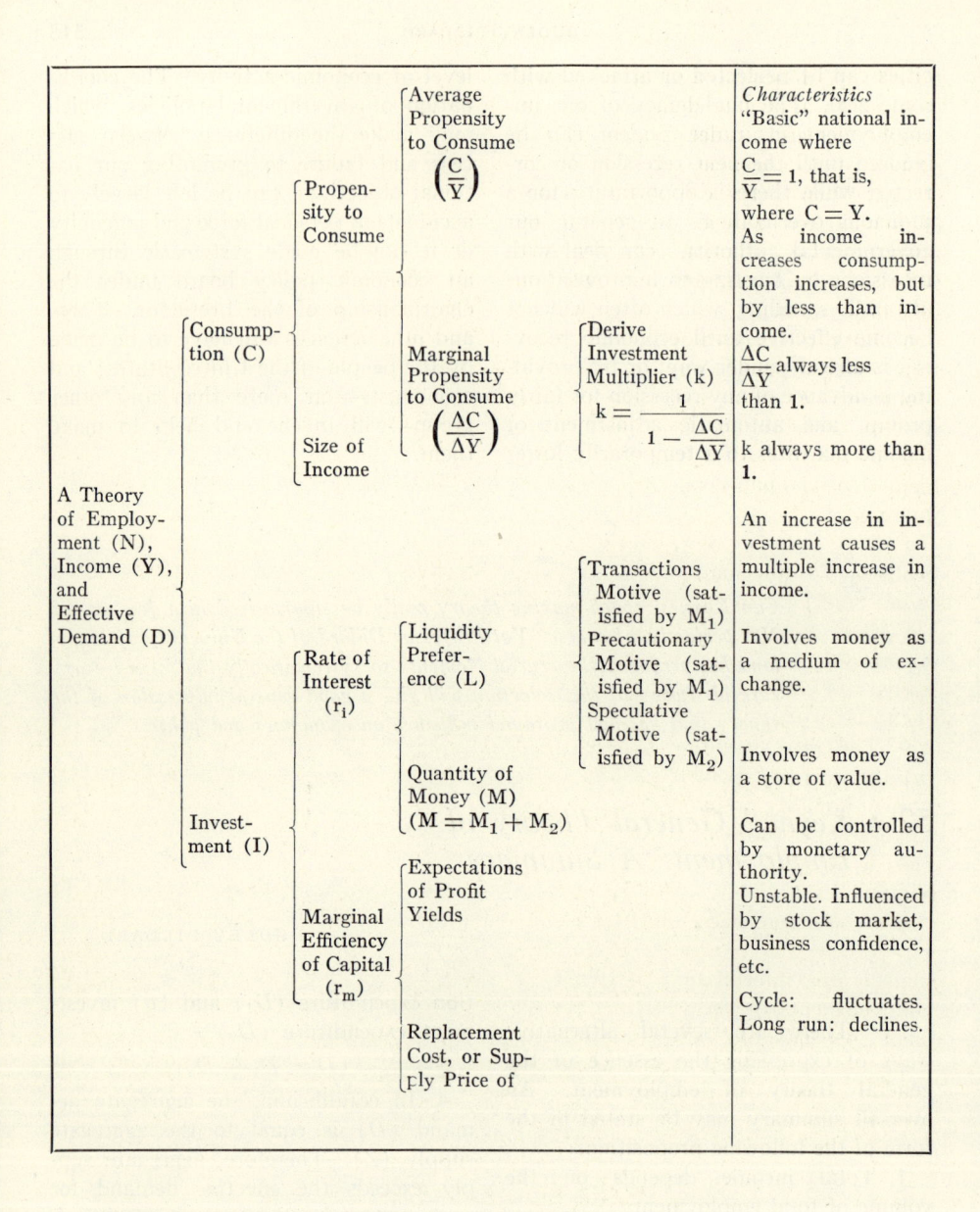

					Characteristics
A Theory of Employment (N), Income (Y), and Effective Demand (D)	Consumption (C)	Propensity to Consume	Average Propensity to Consume $\left(\dfrac{C}{Y}\right)$		"Basic" national income where $\dfrac{C}{Y}=1$, that is, where $C=Y$. As income increases consumption increases, but by less than income. $\dfrac{\Delta C}{\Delta Y}$ always less than 1.
			Marginal Propensity to Consume $\left(\dfrac{\Delta C}{\Delta Y}\right)$	Derive Investment Multiplier (k) $k = \dfrac{1}{1-\dfrac{\Delta C}{\Delta Y}}$	k always more than 1. An increase in investment causes a multiple increase in income.
		Size of Income			
	Investment (I)	Rate of Interest (r_i)	Liquidity Preference (L)	Transactions Motive (satisfied by M_1)	Involves money as a medium of exchange.
				Precautionary Motive (satisfied by M_1)	
				Speculative Motive (satisfied by M_2)	Involves money as a store of value.
			Quantity of Money (M) ($M = M_1 + M_2$)		Can be controlled by monetary authority.
		Marginal Efficiency of Capital (r_m)	Expectations of Profit Yields		Unstable. Influenced by stock market, business confidence, etc. Cycle: fluctuates. Long run: declines.
			Replacement Cost, or Supply Price of		

1. Employment (and income) depend on effective demand.
2. Effective demand is determined by the propensity to consume and the volume of investment.
3. The propensity to consume is relatively stable.
4. Employment depends on the volume of investment if the propensity to consume is unchanged.
5. Investment depends on the rate of interest and the marginal efficiency of capital.
6. The rate of interest depends on the quantity of money and liquidity preference.
7. The marginal efficiency of capital depends on the expectations of profit yields and the replacement cost of capital assets.

5. In equilibrium, aggregate supply is equal to aggregate demand, and aggregate demand is determined by the propensity to consume and the volume of investment. Therefore, the volume of employment depends on (*a*) the aggregate supply function, (*b*) the propensity to consume, and (*c*) the volume of investment.

6. Both the aggregate supply function, which depends mainly on physical conditions of supply, and the propensity to consume are relatively stable, and therefore fluctuations in employment depend mainly on the volume of investment.

7. The volume of investment depends on (*a*) the marginal efficiency of capital and (*b*) the rate of interest.

8. The marginal efficiency of capital depends on (*a*) the expectations of profit yields and (*b*) the replacement cost of capital assets.

9. The rate of interest depends on (*a*) the quantity of money and (*b*) the state of liquidity preference.

These propositions contain the essentials of the general theory of employment. . . .

We may now carry our provisional survey one step further and indicate some of the interrelations among these main elements of the theory. Employment depends on effective demand, which is determined by the propensity to consume and the inducement to invest. If the propensity to consume remains unchanged, employment will vary in the same direction as the volume of investment. Investment tends to increase either with a fall in the rate of interest or a rise in the marginal efficiency of capital, or both. But the tendency for investment to increase through a fall in the rate of interest may be offset by a simultaneous fall in the marginal efficiency of capital. An increase in the general level of economic activity will increase the demand for money as a medium of exchange and, by draining the fund of money available as a store of value, will increase the rate of interest unless the monetary authority and banking system act to increase the total supply of money. And even though the quantity of money may be increasing, the rate of interest may nevertheless rise as a result of an unfavorable shift in the attitude of wealth-holders toward liquidity. Expectations of rising future yields from capital assets will tend to raise the marginal efficiency of capital and thus raise investment and employment. This favorable effect may be offset by a simultaneous rise in the current supply price (cost of production) of capital assets.

Officials of the Federal Reserve are expected to explain to Congress and thus to the public what their monetary policy has been. (In foreign lands, as a rule, central bankers live under no such obligation to account to the public.) An early 1961 statement by the Chairman of the Board of Governors of the Federal Reserve System is more than usually interesting. After briefly summarizing (in paragraphs not included here) the actions taken in 1960, the statement sketches important background developments which began in World War II. The Chairman describes the "peg" of prices of long-term bonds and the "accord" of 1951. The nature and reasons for a much-criticized policy—"bills usually"—is followed by an explanation of why the policy was abandoned, at least temporarily, in 1961. Finally, there are references to a kind of unemployment which monetary policy cannot be expected to do much to help solve and to a variety of problems faced by monetary authorities over the world. (The side-headings have been added by the editor.)

53 · *Monetary Policy in Practice: Background and Problems*

WILLIAM MCCHESNEY MARTIN, JR.

Actions During 1960

Taking the year 1960 as a whole, the change in bank reserve positions was dramatic. From net borrowings from the Federal Reserve of $425 million in December 1959, member banks as a whole moved by December 1960 to a surplus reserve of $650 million. The total turnaround exceeded a billion dollars.

Nevertheless, the money supply showed a stubborn downtrend until mid-1960. In the spring, bank credit seemed to respond less promptly to easier reserve conditions than in comparable periods in the past. After May, however, the seasonally adjusted money supply did begin to reflect our actions. In the second half of the year, the money supply rose at an annual rate of about 1.5 per cent. By year end, it had risen to $140.5 billion, just below the end-of-1959 peak. The money supply has expanded further in January and February of this year. Indeed, the annual rate of increase calculated from the performance of these two months was in the neighborhood of 4 per cent and the total money supply is now above year-ago levels.

The savings and time deposits of banks continued to grow in 1960 and after midyear the pace of growth was unusually rapid. This increase in time deposits permitted an increase of total

WILLIAM MCCHESNEY MARTIN, JR., Chairman, Board of Governors of the Federal Reserve System, a statement delivered before the Joint Economic Committee, March 7, 1961. Used by permission.

bank loans and investments for the year as a whole by $8.4 billion. That was twice as much as the year before.

Total credit [debt] in the economy in 1960 expanded by some $37 billion. That figure was about two-fifths less than the record expansion of $61.5 billion in 1959, on which I reported to you a year ago, and more nearly in line with total credit extensions of other recent years. The smaller growth in 1960 was attributable to reduced pressure of borrowing demand, especially on the part of the Federal Government.

Flexibility in Monetary Policy

The most significant thing about the Federal Reserve's operations in 1960 is not that they were extraordinary but, instead, that they were typical of Federal Reserve operations under the flexible monetary policy that has been in effect now for a full decade.

That policy, as I have capsuled it before in the shortest and simplest description I have been able to devise, is one of leaning against the winds of inflation and deflation alike—and with equal vigor.

It is, in my opinion, the policy that the Federal Reserve must continue to follow if it is to contribute to the provision of conditions conducive to a productive, actively employed, growing economy with relatively stable prices.

Yet, while the necessity for adhering to that policy remains as great as ever, the difficulty of executing it has become vastly greater. This is so because of economic and financial cross-winds that have been developing for years and, since mid-1960, have been gaining in force.

The problem, it now appears, and it is by no means a problem for monetary policy alone, is to lean against cross-winds—simultaneously. I do not know how effectively this can be done. I do know, however, that it will not be easy —just as the problems of monetary policy and of other financial policy have never been easy.

To put in perspective the problems that the Federal Reserve faces today— and how it is adapting to this problem— let me briefly review monetary policy over the past 20 years.

World War II Financing

Immediately upon the United States' entry into World War II in December 1941, the Board of Governors announced that the Federal Reserve was prepared—

1. To use its powers to assure that an ample supply of funds is available at all times for the war effort, and
2. To exert its influence toward maintaining conditions in the United States Government security market that are satisfactory from the standpoint of the Government's requirements.

Making good on its words, the Federal Reserve saw to it that the banking system was supplied with ample lendable reserves to provide the Government with all the war-financing funds that it could not raise through taxation and through borrowing people's savings.

It did so by buying outstanding Government securities on a huge scale. The Federal Reserve's payments for these securities wound up in bank reserves. In turn, the banking system used these additional reserves to purchase new securities that the Treasury was issuing to obtain further funds to finance the war effort.

To keep the process going, the Federal Reserve in effect maintained a standing offer to buy Government securities in unlimited amount at relatively fixed prices, set high enough to assure that their interest rates or yields would be pegged at pre-determined low levels. When no one else would accept those yields and pay those prices, the

Federal Reserve did so. And in so doing, it helped to finance the war.

The process was successful for its emergency purpose. But the procedure of pegging Government securities at high prices and low yields entailed a price of its own that the economy—the people and the Government alike—would later have to pay. The results were two-fold:

1. During wartime, money was created rapidly and continually, in effect setting a time bomb for an ultimate inflationary explosion—even though the immediate inflationary consequences were held more or less in check by a system of direct controls over prices, wages, materials, manpower, and consumer goods.

2. The market for Government securities became artificial. The price risks normally borne by participants in that market were eliminated: bonds not payable for 20 years or more became the equivalent of interest-bearing cash since they could be turned into cash immediately at par value or better—at the option of the owners, at any time.

The pegging of yields and prices of Government securities was continued for some time after the war to provide a gradual transition to a market freely responsive to the changing demand for and supply of securities. A gradual transition was especially important because capital values generally had become moored to the artificial yields and prices in the pegged market for Government securities.

Korean Hostilities and the Accord of 1951

By 1950, however, the need to end the dependence of the Treasury and the Government securities market upon money creation by the Federal Reserve, and to halt the inevitable inflationary consequences, had become clear to many observers. The outbreak of hostilities in Korea and the inflationary crisis that accompanied it brought the matter to a head.

Understanding of the problem was enhanced by an exhaustive investigation conducted by a Special Subcommittee of the Joint Congressional Committee on the Economic Report, under the chairmanship of Senator Paul Douglas. In its report in January 1950, the Congressional Subcommittee said means must be found for discontinuing the pegging of the Government securities market—if financial stability and effective control over the creation of new money were to become possible in the decade of the 1950's.

After considerable negotiation, the Treasury and the Federal Reserve System reached an Accord, jointly announced by them on March 4, 1951, that served to recognize and reaffirm that:

1. To serve the public welfare, Federal Reserve policy must be directed toward maintaining monetary conditions appropriate for the economy as a whole, rather than toward special treatment for the Treasury and the Government as if their interests could differ properly from those of the people as a whole.

2. Likewise to serve the public welfare, the Treasury's borrowing operations in management of the Government's debt must be reasonably calculated to induce loans to the Government in an economic system where no one can be compelled to lend his money at interest rates that he would be unwilling to accept voluntarily.

Thus, the Accord re-established the complementary operation of monetary and debt management policies: by the Federal Reserve, to regulate the availability, supply, and cost of money with a view to its economic consequences; by the Treasury, to finance the Government's needs in the traditional context of a competitive market.

To provide for the gradual withdrawal of the pegs that had fixed market prices and yields, several procedures were instituted immediately and carried out over the next weeks and months.

That's much easier to say now than it was to do then. . . .

. . . . .

. . . [A special refinancing] paved the way for discontinuance of Federal Reserve purchases of Government bonds in support of their prices.

In May and June [1951], net purchases by the Federal Reserve of long-term bonds dropped off to $250 million, but that was enough to assure against development of disorderly conditions in the market. After that, the Federal Reserve ceased buying almost altogether: purchases during the entire last half of 1951 totaled only $20 million. And prices, which had been supported around 100¾ at the start of the year, fluctuated around 97 during the last half of the year when the bond market was on its own.

As the years 1951 and 1952 progressed, however, market developments demonstrated a disturbing skepticism among investors that the Federal Reserve was in fact abstaining (or would continue to abstain) from attempting to maintain certain predetermined interest rates, regardless of the over-all state of the demand for and the supply of savings. This skepticism was fed by market observation that the System engaged in purchases of securities involved in Treasury financings around the periods of such financings.

Development of "Bills Usually"

After very careful study of the functioning of the Government securities market and of the relation of Federal Reserve monetary operations to the market, the System decided that it would limit its open market transactions to short-term securities, usually those of the very shortest term: Treasury bills. It also decided to refrain from operations in securities involved in Treasury financings. In taking these steps, the Federal Reserve objective was to convince the market that it was not undertaking to peg interest rates—and most certainly not those on intermediate- and long-term securities.

Accordingly, to minimize market uncertainty as to possible Federal Reserve operations affecting market rates, and thereby to aid the effective competitive functioning of the market, the System announced in April 1953 that until further notice, unless disorderly conditions arose in the market, it would operate only in the short-term area, where its operations would have the least market impact.

I think I should point out here, in fairness to my colleagues on the Federal Open Market Committee, that in this decision to limit our open market operations to the short end of the market, we were not unanimous—neither then, nor since then.

Indeed, the divergence of views in the System on this question has been more marked and more continuous than on any other that I can recall in my ten years in the Federal Reserve. That, I think, is readily understandable because the question relates to the *techniques* of open market operations—a highly technical and involved subject—rather than to general credit policy itself.

In my opinion, it is and always will be easier to achieve full agreement on what to do than on how to do it. To me, that explains why the uninterrupted character of the divergence in the System over operating techniques contrasts sharply with the rather high degree of agreement we have had, most of the time, over questions of general credit policy—whether and when to ease or restrain, and how much. Also, why it contrasts completely with the undeviating firmness of our opposition, at all times, to returning to a pegged market.

These matters, however, are too well known to members of this Committee for me to labor them further at this point: the records of your past hearings, as well as our Annual Reports, contain the views on that score of several members of the Open Market Committee. . . .

In any event, following the 1953 decision I have described—the decision to confine our open market transactions to the short-term sector of the market—the emphasis in Federal Reserve operations continued to be placed upon providing bank reserves to meet the economy's needs rather than to set particular rates of interest. Inevitably, however, interest rate movements, since they reflected basic demand and supply conditions, continued to be one of many factors considered by the Federal Reserve in making judgments about the need for changes in the reserve base. Conversely, Federal Reserve operations in the market continued, inevitably, to be an important influence affecting the general level of market interest rates.

Despite confinement of its operations ordinarily to the short-term area, the Federal Reserve stood prepared to buy securities other than Treasury bills should unusual developments create disorderly conditions in the Government securities market and thus in credit markets as a whole. When disorderly conditions seriously threatened as in late November of 1955 or actually developed as in the summer of 1958, the Federal Reserve bought longer term securities to maintain or re-establish orderly trading. Apart from these exceptional and infrequent circumstances, however, the Federal Reserve maintained its reliance upon operations in Treasury bills without interruption until 1960. With the introduction of the 6-month Treasury bill in 1958 and the 12-month Treasury bill in 1959, the System extended the maturity range of its operations within the short-term area.

New Problems of 1960

Toward the close of 1959 there were increasing indications, signaled by rapid rises in market interest rates accompanying a mounting intensity of borrowing demands, that conditions bordering on the disorderly might be encountered increasingly in the future and that there might be more occasions than in the past for corrective operations by the Federal Reserve in maturities beyond the range of Treasury bills.

After the middle of 1960, another consideration pointing to a possible need for Federal Reserve operations in longer term securities arose from the convergence of two important developments.

1. On the domestic front, a decline in key sectors of business activity, accompanied by gradual rise in unemployment, suggested that the economy might be moving downward on a broad pattern of recession.

2. In the area of international financial accounts, a big deficit in the U. S. balance of payments was made larger by a substantial outflow of short-term funds from the United States to foreign money centers, partly in response to higher interest rates abroad.

As I stated earlier, the Federal Reserve had been making bank reserves available to ease the credit situation since the winter of 1960. Thus, it had been a contributing influence in the decline in market interest rates to mid-1960. In the light of the domestic business and employment situation and the balance of international payments deficit, this decline presented us with a dilemma in the latter part of 1960.

If the Federal Reserve continued to supply reserves by buying only Treasury bills, the direct impact of its purchases might drive the rate on those securities so low as to encourage a further outflow of funds to foreign markets and thus aggravate the already serious balance of payments deficit.

If, on the other hand, the Federal Reserve refrained from further action to supply funds for bank reserves because of the balance-of-payments situation, it would be unable to make its maximum contribution toward counteracting decline in domestic economic activity through the stimulative influence of credit ease.

Thus, in an effort to expand reserves and yet to minimize the repercussions on the balance of payments, the Federal Reserve began, in late October 1960, to provide some of the additonal reserves needed by buying certificates, notes, and bonds maturing within 15 months. Since that time, the System has bought and sold such securities, in addition to bills, on a number of occasions, duly reporting these portfolio changes in a public statement issued every Thursday.

Now here let me note something about the decline in interest rates that took place in 1960. During the first eight months, market rates on Treasury bills and intermediate-term issues fell much more sharply than on bonds, as is usual in a period of declining rates.

After late summer, however, the differential between short- and long-term rates ceased to widen, and the average level of rates itself remained relatively unchanged. The increased net outflow of domestic and foreign capital from the United States in the second half of the year, in response partly to the attraction of higher interest rates and potential capital gains abroad, was itself a factor in keeping interest rates in the United States from declining, because it reduced the supply of funds available here.

It was in the latter part of 1960, as I have noted, that Federal Reserve operations were directed more and more toward reducing the direct impact on Treasury bill yields of Federal Reserve purchases. Thus, when the System was providing for the large seasonal expansion in credit needs that occurs in the fall and pre-Christmas seasons, it did not rely solely on further open market purchases but took actions that made vault cash holdings of banks fully available for meeting reserve requirements. And on the occasions when the System did engage in open market operations, it often conducted these operations in short-term Government securities other than Treasury bills.

Open Market Operations in Longer Term Securities

With the domestic economy and the balance of payments continuing to pose conflicting problems, open market transactions in securities other than Treasury bills are continuing. Beginning on February 20 . . . the Federal Reserve has engaged in purchases of securities having maturities beyond the short-term area, putting to practical test some matters on which it has been possible in recent years only to theorize.

There is still a question as to the possibility of bringing about a meaningful decline in longer term rates through purchases of longer term securities without, at the same time, causing a shift in market demand toward short-term securities that would also press down levels of short-term rates.

On the other hand, it seems to me, few could question the desirability of the result, if it can be attained, as a means of keeping financial incentives attuned to the current needs of our domestic economy and our international financial position.

We will want to observe closely, of course, the effect of this change in operating techniques on the market and its capacity to fulfill its role in transferring a large volume of securities among our various financial institutions to facilitate their responses to shifts in the supply of savings and the demands of borrowers.

In our country, the Government cannot force anyone to lend his money at rates he is unwilling to accept—any more than it can force him to spend his money at prices he is unwilling to pay. In the securities market, investors always have the alternative of investing their funds in short-term securities if they feel that yields in the longer-term area are unfavorable. Therefore, in the outcome of this test much will depend on the reactions of investors.

. . . I am in favor of interest rates being as low as possible without stimulating inflation, because low rates can help to foster capital expenditures that, in turn, promote economic growth.

Yet, as I assume we can all agree, interest rates cannot go to and long remain below the point at which they will attract a sufficient volume of voluntary saving to finance current investment at a relatively stable price level. At least we can agree, I think, that interest rates cannot be driven and long held below that point without resort to outright creation of money on such a scale as to invite inflation, serious social inequity, severe economic setback, and, under present conditions, an outflow of funds to other countries and consequent drains on this country's gold reserves.

I do not believe anyone expects the Federal Reserve to engage in operations that will promote a resurgence of inflation in the future. In combating inflation in the past, undue reliance has perhaps been placed on monetary policy.

I can readily agree with those who would have fiscal policy, with all of its powerful force, carry a greater responsibility for combating inflation, and I am encouraged to think that this may be likely in the future. If we do this, we should more nearly achieve our over-all stabilization goals, along with some reduction in the range of interest rate fluctuation.

Unemployment: Cyclical and Structural

That, however, is a matter for another day. Today, we have in this country a serious problem to contend with in the erratic but persistent rise in unemployment that has taken place since mid-1960. In January, the seasonally adjusted rate of unemployment was 6.6 per cent of the labor force, the highest percentage since 1958; the actual number of persons unemployed was 5.4 million, the highest number since the days before World War II.

The contracyclical operations that the Federal Reserve is and has been conducting, despite the handicaps imposed by the balance of international payments difficulties that we hope will be overcome, should be helpful, as they have been in the past, in combating that part of unemployment caused by general economic decline. Certainly we mean them to be.

While the unemployment that arises from cyclical causes should prove only temporary, there are, however, forces at work that have produced another, structural type of unemployment that is worse, in that it already has proved to be indefinitely persistent—even in periods of unprecedented general prosperity.

The problem of structural unemployment is manifest in the higher total of those left unemployed after each wave of the three most recent business cycles, and in the idleness of many West Virginia coal miners, Eastern and Midwestern steel and auto workers, West Coast aircraft workers, and like groups, in good times as well as bad.

To have important effect, attempts to reduce structural unemployment by massive monetary and fiscal stimulation of over-all demands likely would have to be carried to such lengths as to create serious new problems of inflationary character—at a time when consumer prices already are at a record high.

Actions effective against structural unemployment and free of harmful side effects therefore need to be specific actions that take into account the who, the where, and the why of unemployment and, accordingly, go to the core of the particular problem.

Analysis of current unemployment shows that, in brief:

1. The lines of work in which job opportunities have been declining most pronouncedly for some years are farming, mining, transportation, and the blue collar crafts and trades in manufacturing industries.

2. The workers hardest hit have been the semi-skilled and the unskilled (along with inexperienced youths newly entering the labor market). These workers have accounted for a significant part of the increase in the level and duration of unemployment. Among white collar groups, employment has continued to increase and unemployment has shown little change even in times of cyclical downturn.

3. The areas hardest hit have been, primarily, individual areas dependent upon a single industry, and cities in which such industries as autos, steel, and electrical equipment were heavily concentrated.

Actions best suited to helping these groups would appear to include more training and re-training to develop skills needed in expanding industries; provision of more and better information about job opportunities for various skills in various local labor markets; tax programs to stimulate investment that will expand work opportunities; revision of pension and benefit plans to eliminate penalties on employees moving to new jobs; reduction of impediments to entry into jobs, and so on. Measures to alleviate distress and hardship are, of course, imperative at all times.

In some of the instances cited, the primary obligation of the Govvernment will be leadership, rather than action, for obviously a major responsibility and role in efforts to overcome unemployment, both cyclical and structural, rests upon management and labor.

For our part, we in the Federal Reserve intend to do our share in combating the cyclical causes of unemployment, as effectively as we can, and in fostering the financial conditions favorable to growth in new job opportunities.

International Economic Relations and Problems

Meanwhile there is, I think, need on the part of all of us to recognize that the world in which we live today is not only a world that has changed greatly in recent years, but also a world that even now is in a period of further transition.

In economics and finance, no less than in other relationships, the lives of nations and peoples throughout the earth have been made more closely interlinked by developments that have progressed since the beginning of World War II—inter-linked at such speed, in fact, as to outstrip recognition.

Today, the condition of our export trade, from which a very large number of Americans derive their livelihood, depends not only upon keeping competitive the costs and prices of the goods we produce for sale abroad, but also upon the prosperity or lack of it in the countries that want to buy our goods.

Whether our Government's budget is balanced or not, a factor that greatly affects our economic and financial condition, depends not only upon our own decisions respecting expenditures and taxes, but also upon decisions by governments abroad as to how far they will share the costs of mutual defense and of programs to aid underdeveloped nations of the world. The decisions those governments make affect, in turn, their budget positions and, through them, economic and financial conditions in their own countries.

Every country, of course, will always have problems of its own that differ from the current problems of other lands. Communist Russia, for example, gives some signs of worry over a problem old and familiar to us and to them: The danger of economically destructive inflation. The New York Times of January 30 reported that Premier Khrushchev, in a recent public speech, had pointed to precisely that danger, noting that "the purchasing power in the hands of the Soviet people might exceed the value of the goods available for them to buy."

In Brazil, a new administration is seeking means to cope with an inflation that already has exacted an enormous price in suffering inflicted upon her people by soaring increases in the cost of living.

In Belgium, a program of austerity, to bring about adjustments made necessary by the loss of the Congo, provoked riots that recently made headlines across the United States.

In the Free World, the United States has not been alone in finding that its domestic situation and balance-of-payments position seemed to call for conflicting actions, thus presenting monetary and fiscal policy makers some complicating cross-currents.

On January 19, for example, the German Federal Bank reduced its equivalent of our discount rate and made known at the time that it was doing so, despite the high level of activity in the German economy, for the purpose of reducing a heavy and troublesome inflow of funds from other countries. A month earlier the Bank of England had reduced its bank rate also, to curb a short-term capital inflow.

Over the last weekend, Germany and the Netherlands up-valued their currencies by nearly 5 per cent; these actions should help them to reduce the inflow of volatile capital.

The truth of it is that the major countries of the Western world, after a long and painful struggle in the wake of World War II to restore convertibility of their currencies, and thus to lay the necessary basis for interchanges that can enhance the prosperity of all, have succeeded—only to find that success, too, brings its problems.

Today, though currency convertibility does in fact make possible an expanding volume of mutually profitable interchanges among nations, it also makes possible dangerously large flows of volatile funds among the nations concerned —flows on a scale that could shake confidence in even the strongest currencies, and cause internal difficulties in even the strongest economies.

To the causes of these flows—differences in interest rates, conditions of monetary ease or tightness, budgetary conditions, and developments of any kind that raise questions and doubts about determination to preserve the value of a country's currency—we must remain alert and ready, willing and able to meet whatever challenge arises.

I, for one, am confident that we will meet such challenges as may come. Our opportunities for the future are more important than the problems they bring with them. Let us seize these opportunities, firmly and without fear.

Young people today may find difficulty in sympathizing with their parents' horror of depression. Yet anyone who was subject to the economic misery of the 1930's will be desperately anxious to help prevent a recurrence of anything of the sort. Perhaps, however, nothing more need be done. In the selection below a leading economic theorist and monetary expert gives his reasons for believing that changes in the structure of our economy have removed the danger of depressions. Recessions are to be expected, but they will not, he believes, grow into serious depressions as on the occasions in the past which he describes briefly.

54 · *No More Depressions?*

MILTON FRIEDMAN

. . . One of the few things that has been firmly established by past research on business cycles is that we do not yet know how to predict the detailed course of business activity. We can describe, as business analysts are wont to do, the detailed movements in inventories, employment, retail sales, interest rates, stock prices, and the like. But we do not know how to use these signs as a sure guide to the precise severity of a particular cyclical movement or to the precise date when it will be reversed.

In this instance, as in so many others in economics, a roundabout method promises to be more productive. Though we cannot get a detailed answer by the direct path of predicting the immediate future, I submit that we can get a meaningful general answer by examining the institutional environment within which the current [1954] recession is proceeding and interpreting it in the light of the known past. For there have been fundamental changes in institutions and attitudes in the United States since the Great Depression. Changes in the banking structure and in the fiscal structure have basically altered the inherent cyclical responses of the American economy. Changes in general psychological attitudes toward inflation and deflation have basically altered the likely political responses toward economic change. In my view, the combined effect of these alterations in institutions and in attitudes has been to render a major depression in the United States almost inconceivable at the present time. . . . Let me turn first to the changes that have occurred in the banking structure of the United States.

Changes in Banking Structure

As you know, the American banking structure is very different from that which exists in most other countries. It is composed of some 15,000 independent banks, about a third chartered by the Federal government, the rest by the forty-eight states. About half the banks,

---

MILTON FRIEDMAN, "Why the American Economy is Depression-Proof," *Nationalekonomiska Föreningens Förhandlingar* (Stockholm: April 28, 1954), pp. 57–77. Used by permission.

including almost all the large ones, are members of the Federal Reserve System, which performs the functions of a central bank. This unit banking system has had great advantages in flexibility, competition, and enterprise. But it has also lent itself to banking panics and widespread bank failures, most recently, of course, in the early 1930's.

Three major changes have occurred in this system since the great depression: first, the establishment in 1934 of the Federal Deposit Insurance Corporation; second, a growth in the importance of government obligations among bank assets; third, a loosening of the links between gold and domestic monetary conditions. . . .

ESTABLISHMENT OF FEDERAL DEPOSIT INSURANCE CORPORATION. In my view, the federal insurance of deposits is by all odds the most important of these changes in its effects on the cyclical characteristics of the American economy. Indeed, I venture to suggest that it produced a more basic change in American banking institutions than did the much more widely heralded establishment of the Federal Reserve System in 1913. Federal deposit insurance has made bank failures almost a thing of the past. . . . The statistical record of yearly bank failures requires three to four digits up to 1934; one digit suffices for recent years. The result has been that depositors in insured banks have suffered negligible losses. . . . The Federal Reserve System was never more than a "lender of last resort"; it gave depositors no protection against bad banking, and, partly as a consequence, was unable even to perform its proper function of protecting them against bad central banking. The F.D.I.C. has in effect converted all deposit liabilities of private banks into a Federal liability. It has thus eliminated the basic cause for runs on banks of the kind that occurred in 1931 to 1933, as well as at earlier periods. Such runs represented attempts by bank depositors to convert liabilities of private banks—deposits—into liabilities of the Federal government—currency. . . .

CHANGE IN STRUCTURE OF ASSETS. Federal deposit insurance was deliberately enacted to protect bank depositors. Without intention or design, a change has occurred in the structure of bank assets that has in part duplicated the effect of deposit insurance. The change I refer to is the increased importance of government obligations among bank assets. . . . In 1929, commercial and savings banks owned government obligations equal in value to around 15 per cent of their deposit liabilities to the public; today they own government obligations equal in value to more than half of their deposit liabilities to the public. More than half of the deposits of the public are thus government liabilities at one remove, in the sense that the bank assets corresponding to them are government liabilities. . . . The high ratio of government obligations has the further consequence that it greatly reduces the potential effects of changes in private demand and supply for credit on the quantity of money. . . .

. . . . .

CHANGED ROLE OF GOLD. The third change in the banking structure that I want to call to your attention is the role played by gold. The removal of gold from public circulation in 1934 was the first step in a successive loosening of the links between gold and the internal supply of money. The monetary role of gold in the United States today is largely nominal. The Federal Reserve has almost twice as large a gold reserve as it legally requires; and even this understates its leeway for there can be little doubt that if the reserve ratio were ever to approach the legal minimum, the maximum would be lowered. The fixed U. S. buying price for gold, rather than being the kingpin of its monetary structure, is in the same class as the fixed buying price for domestically produced wheat: gold is a storable commodity for which there is a rigid support price. The only difference is that the support price is offered to foreign as well as domestic producers, so that the gold program is also part of our foreign economic aid.

SIGNIFICANCE OF THE CHANGES. The combined effect of Federal Deposit Insurance, the higher ratio of government obligations to other assets of banks, and the dethroning of gold, is to eliminate as a practical possibility anything approaching a collapse of the American banking structure. Insurance rules out an internal drain or banking panic; the importance of government obligations reduces the sensitivity of the stock of money to internal private credit changes; the dethroning of gold reduces its sensitivity to changes in external conditions. It is hard to see how under these circumstances any sharp *decline* in the stock of money could occur except through deliberate action by the monetary authorities to bring one about. . . .

Importance of Changes in the Banking Structure

Granted that a substantial change has occurred in the American banking structure, how important is this change for the avoidance of a major depression? From the 1930's until almost the present, economists tended to deprecate the role of monetary factors and of the banking system. . . . Post war experience has forced a considerable revival in the attention paid to monetary factors. Easy money policies were adopted in most countries after the war. And every country that adopted an easy money policy also experienced inflationary pressure and did so whether its governmental budget was yielding a surplus or deficit. On the other hand, the adoption of a tighter monetary policy accompanied every successful attempt to stop inflation.

These events produced a healthy reaction against the view that money doesn't matter. But this reaction has not yet gone far enough. The fashionable view at the moment is to grant that monetary measures are vitally important in preventing inflation but to argue that they are of minor importance in preventing depression. Monetary policy, it is said, is like a string. You can pull it but you can't push on it.

This view is based in large measure on the belief that monetary measures were tried in the great depression and found wanting. And this belief—which seems to me completely mistaken—in turn derives partly from accepting the protestations of monetary authorities at their face value rather than looking at what they in fact did; partly from looking at the effect of policy on the liabilities of the central bank rather than on the total stock of money. In the United States—and the experience of the United States is not atypical—the total stock of money in the hands of the public declined by more than a quarter from 1929 to 1933. The subsequent expansion in the stock of money was not out of proportion to the expansion in money income. Far from being testimony to the irrelevance of monetary factors in preventing depression, the early 1930's are a tragic testimony to their importance in producing depression. . . .

I do not myself believe that the string-analogy is valid. If it were, one would expect to find that major depressions had occurred despite favorable monetary conditions. Yet so far as I know, there is no such example on record. Certainly, in the United States

... there has been no major depression that has not been associated with and accompanied by a monetary collapse. Let me run briefly over the record; it is most instructive.

Perhaps the best starting point is the major depression that began in the late 1830's and continued through the early 1840's. Statistical records are too meagre for this period to permit detailed comparisons with later depressions. Such records as there are, together with qualitative and descriptive evidence, suggest that it was comparable in severity and duration with the great depression that came not quite a century later—though of course the lesser importance of industry and of the market made its social and human consequences quite different. This depression followed hard on the political battle over the Second Bank of the United States which ended in the spectacular demise of the bank. The initial effect of the battle was to produce widespread inflation of the currency and a speculative boom. The ultimate result was a drastic deflation of the currency, disorganization of the banking system, and numerous bank failures.

The next depression of comparable magnitude was the long-drawn out period of hard times during the 1870's. This was the period when vigorous efforts were being made to return to the gold standard at the former parity after the greenback inflation of the Civil War. The effort was crowned with success when specie payments were resumed in 1879, but at the cost of a decade of more or less steady deflationary pressure, and of the longest continuous contraction in the recorded annals of American business cycles. Resumption, which meant the cessation of the deflationary pressure, ushered in a period of expansion.

The 1890's produced an even more pronounced depression than the 1870's; it was probably less severe than the 1930's but this is by no means unambiguously clear. It was a period of great monetary agitation when the burning political issue was whether silver or gold should be the monetary standard, agitation that reached its highest emotional peak with Bryan's famous "cross of gold" speech. The United States almost went off gold; J. P. Morgan and associates were called upon by the Treasury to help and were widely given the credit for keeping the dollar on gold, though it seems clear that Dame Fortune, who produced good harvest in the United States and poor harvest abroad, deserves much of the credit. A banking panic was a striking feature of the depression and bank failures were numerous.

The stream of gold from South Africa undermined the economic basis for the political agitation and ushered in a period of monetary expansion, which produced a rise of over a third in the American price level from 1898 to the outbreak of World War I. This period was punctuated by a banking panic in 1907, but the accompanying depression was nothing like so severe as those of the 1870's or 1890's. It did however produce renewed pressure for banking reform, pressure which eventuated in the establishment of the Federal Reserve System in 1913.

The Reserve System was established just in time to serve as the channel for war time inflation. Doubtless there would have been inflation in any event during World War I. However, without the newly established central banking system, the inflation probably would have been less severe during the war than it was and almost certainly would have come to an end by early 1919. As it was, the Reserve System, more by default than by design, continued to add fuel to the inflationary fire on a large scale for more than a year after the government ceased calling on it to do so to finance its expenditures. When the System woke up to what it was doing in 1920, it put on the brakes sharply, producing a contraction in the supply of money and the sharp if brief depression of 1921, so adding yet another to our list of depressions accompanied or occasioned by monetary contraction.

The final exhibit in this chamber of horrors that I shall discuss is the 1929-33 depression, which is also in many ways the most interesting and instructive. From 1929 to 1931, the Reserve system was largely passive. It allowed the stock of money to decline by about 10 per cent and banks to fail in a steady if not spectacular stream. Yet by summer 1931, there were signs of revival: if one examines the statistical records of that year and closes one's eyes to what followed, they bear all the earmarks of the typical turning point of a cycle. Had the decline come to an end in 1931, it would have been entered in statistical annals as a severe recession but certainly not a major depression comparable to the depressions of the 1840's, 1870's, and 1890's. But the decline did not come to an end. In the autumn of 1931, England went off the gold standard. The Reserve authorities became frightened that there would be a drain of gold from the United States. Although their gold reserves greatly exceeded legal requirements and were extremely high by any absolute standards, they succumbed to something approaching panic and proceeded to take strong deflationary measures, putting up the bank rate more sharply and suddenly than at any previous time in their history—and this after two years of economic contraction. The result in my view was to nip a putative revival in the bud and to initiate a new and sharper contraction. Up to this point, deposits in commercial banks had fallen by about 10 per cent. In the next year and a half they fell by over a third.

Bank failures increased at an alarming pace and the sorry tale was not completely told until the official closing of all banks in the banking holiday of March, 1933. True, the Reserve system reversed its policy in early 1932 and undertook moderately expansionary measures; but by then it was too late. Measures of this magnitude might easily have saved the day in 1931; by 1932 they were utterly inadequate to stem the raging flood of deflation that the Reserve System had unleashed.

A major motive in establishing the Reserve System was to prevent banking panics of the kind that had been recurrently experienced. The system completely failed to do so. The panic of 1933, when it came, was of the same company as the panics of 1837, 1873, 1893, and 1907. The existence of the Reserve System did make one difference. It postponed the panic until after a shamefully large fraction of the banks had failed, whereas in the bad old days, a panic occurred before any large number of banks failed and was indeed the device for preventing the failure of a few banks from spreading to the rest of the system. It was this experience, as I have already noted, that brought the Federal Deposit Insurance Corporation and an effective end to banking panics.

There is no gainsaying the fact illustrated by these episodes: major depressions and monetary contraction or collapse go hand in hand. But, it will be asked, which is the hen and which the egg? May not the monetary collapse be the inevitable result of severe depression rather than a cause thereof? And if this is so, may not the only effect of the change in the American monetary structure be to remove a manifestation of severe depression rather than to prevent the severe depressions themselves? The episodes I have outlined give, I believe, a reasonably clear answer to these questions. Many of the events that produced monetary contraction or collapse were clearly independent of the particular state of business when they occurred. If they did not produce the severe depression, they were certainly not produced by it, and their simultaneous occurrence would have to be explained by sheer coincidence. . . .

The conclusion seems inescapable: monetary contraction or collapse is an essential conditioning factor for the occurrence of a major depression. To avoid misunderstanding, let me say explicitly that I do not mean to assert that all cyclical fluctuations are monetary in origin. Far from it. The usual run of cyclical fluctuations have occurred under a wide variety of monetary institutions and conditions, and have been accompanied by no standard behavior of the stock of money or other monetary indexes. Monetary factors doubtless play a role in such fluctuations but I believe that we do not yet know what role. Nor do we as yet in my view have any alternative explanation of such fluctuations: we are here in an area where we simply do not know the answers. My proposition is much more limited. It is that we must distinguish between minor recessions and major depressions and that it takes a monetary contraction or collapse—a monetary mistake—to convert a minor recession into a major depression. Though not directly connected with my present theme, a similar proposition seems to me valid for expansions: it takes monetary measures to convert minor expansions into inflationary booms.

If this conclusion is valid, it means that the structural change in the American banking system is alone enough to rule out a major American depression. But it is not the only institutional change that works in this direction. It is strongly reinforced by changes in the American fiscal structure, to which I now turn.

The Fiscal Structure

During the last few decades, the size of governmental activity has grown sharply relative to the economy as a whole. In the 1920's, government expenditures, both national and local, amounted to less than one-eighth of the national income; they now amount to more than one-quarter.

This increase in the role of government is fundamental for the long run trend of the American economy and for the prospects of political freedom. It is not fundamental for its cyclical behavior. From the cyclical point of view, the change in the character of both expenditures and receipts is more important than the change in their size.

On the expenditure side, the two most important changes have been the introduction first of a broad program of social security benefits, in particular, of unemployment insurance, and second of a farm program designed to support the prices of agricultural products. The effect of these and similar programs is that a decline in general business automatically raises government expenditures: people become unemployed and start drawing unemployment expenditures; agricultural prices tend to fall—though this link is much looser than the unemployment link thanks to the importance of variations in weather at home and in production abroad—and so support payments to increase. Conversely, an expansion of business in general reduces these expenditures. These programs thus make for high expenditures in depression; low expenditures in prosperity. Let me hasten to emphasize that here as with the banking changes discussed earlier I am simply describing the effects of these changes on the cyclical prospects of the economy, not evaluating or approving them in general. . . .

On the income side, the important changes have been mostly in the personal and corporation income tax: these have come to account for a much larger share of total tax receipts, the personal income tax has been made much more progressive, and methods of collecting the tax have been radically reformed. The reason these developments are important for cyclical purposes is that they have greatly increased the sensitivity of tax payments to changes in economic conditions. Let national income rise and liabilities for some taxes, like property taxes, will be affected little if at all; for other taxes, like property taxes, they will rise with income but generally by a smaller percentage. Income tax liabilities, on the other hand, are almost sure to rise with income and to rise by a larger percentage. Similarly, when national income falls, income tax liabilities fall even more sharply. And the more progressive the income tax, the sharper the rise or fall in tax liabilities for a given rise or fall in income. Increased reliance on income taxes and their greater progressiveness have therefore combined to make *tax liabilities* more responsive to changes in business conditions than at an earlier date. But there is a slip between *tax liabilities* and *tax payments,* and it is here that the third change mentioned, in methods of collection, has been important. Prior to World War II, the income tax for any year was collected entirely after the end of the year. There was a lag of over a year on the average between the receipt of income and the payment of taxes on that income. During World War II, collection at source was introduced for wages and salaries, and prepayment for other personal income. And more recently, corresponding changes have been made for corporations. The result has been to reduce to very small proportions indeed any lag between the receipts of income and the payment of tax on that income.

Under the existing fiscal system any decrease in national income is accompanied, or followed with only a brief lag, by a sharper decrease in tax receipts and by a rise in expenditures on unemployment benefits, farm price supports, and the like. The changes in taxes and in expenditures reinforce one another and together are by no means negligible in size. Roughly speaking, a decline of, say, $10 billion in the national income means a combined effect on the government budget of some $3-to-$4 billion. This is the amount by which any budget surplus is reduced or a budget deficit increased. And this occurs without any legislative or executive action whatever. The strictly automatic changes in the government budget in this way offset directly from 30 to 40 per cent of any change that would otherwise take place in national income.

. . . . .

Psychological Climate of Opinion

The structure of institutions is important, but so also are the ideas and attitudes of the men who run them. The golden mean is universally sought but seldom attained. Men tend to overdo things; to react from having gone too far in one direction by going too far in the opposite direction. So it has been in attitudes toward inflation and deflation.

Before the Great Depression, the men who guided our economic institutions, and the responsible body of public opinion, were much more concerned about the dangers of inflation than of deflation. The origins of this attitude go back to the birth of the nation. Monetary experience during the American Revolution gave the nation at its outset a horror of unrestrained inflation that led to the inclusion of provisions in the American Constitution to prevent—or so it was thought—the issuance of fiduciary money by the Federal government. . . .

The War of 1812, with the doubling of prices, confirmed and strengthened the fears engendered by the hyperinflation of the Revolution. Whatever weakening was produced by the great depression of the 1840's—and it was little because so much of the blame was rightly attributed to the preceding inflationary frenzies—was more than reversed by the Civil War inflation. The rest of the nineteenth century, with its generally downward pressure on prices and its several really severe depressions worked strongly in the opposite direction, as is evidenced by the political strength that the free silver and greenback parties attained. The effect was less than might have been expected, however, thanks partly to the near-self-sufficiency of much of the society, partly to the flexibility of the economy that enabled the deep depressions to manifest themselves mainly in monetary magnitudes. In any event, this change in attitudes was in turn reversed, and the earlier biases reinforced, by the fifteen years of generally rising prices that preceded World War I, the sharp inflation during and immediately after the War, and the ten years of prosperity that followed the sharp but brief slump of 1921. By 1928, more than three decades had passed since a really deep and long-continued depression; these decades had seen generally rising prices and had been punctuated by the wartime episode in which prices more than doubled in a few years. [Is it] any wonder that men viewed inflation as the chief threat to their prosperity?

This attitude, with its emphasis on "hard-money" at all costs, was surely a major factor explaining the actions of the Federal Reserve authorities that I have already discussed as well as other governmental actions during the recession and depression. Being more afraid of inflation than of deflation, men overdid their reactions to any events that seemed to them to threaten inflation, and in the process produced a serious deflation.

The deflation changed all that. It took place in an economy in which agriculture had become of minor importance, and in which rigidities had greatly increased. Widespread unemployment and human misery understandably pushed depression into the front rank of the evils to be avoided at all costs. Even today, despite 20 years of nearly continuous price rise, despite widespread political agitation about rises in the cost of living and the dangers of inflation, the real fear of the public at large is of depression. Even the objections to inflation are indirect evidence: again and again one finds that the chief criticism of inflation is the assumption that what goes up must come down, so inflation now must produce a depression later.

We have swung from the one extreme to the other. And just as deflation resulted from going too far in trying to avoid inflation; so now inflation is likely to result from going too far in trying to avoid depression. The reaction to the current [1954] recession is striking evidence for this view. The recession is to date exceedingly mild, yet it has been watched over and reported about with the care and in the tones of an anxious mother whose child has been given only a 50–50 chance to live. Never in its history has the Federal Reserve system shifted so rapidly and completely from a tight money policy to an easy money policy. Pressure for tax cuts and for public works to stimulate purchasing power came hard and fast on the first slight faltering in the pace of economic advance and have multiplied since, even though purchasing power is still near an all time peak. . . .

. . . . .
... the President and his Council of Economic Advisors deserve unreserved tribute for political courage and economic wisdom. The easy and politically attractive path is to take precipitate and drastic action. This would steal the opponents' thunder and be applauded by the bulk of economic and business opinion. The claim that the Republicans had avoided a serious depression by their action would be one of those claims that could never be shown to be wrong. When their actions produced subsequent inflation, that could always be explained by special circumstances of the morrow. They have instead chosen the much harder course of trying to restrain vigorous actions designed to forestall the depression that is not yet here; of trying to reconcile the public to a minor recession that still has some time to run.

Prospects for the Future

I can perhaps best summarize the implications of my argument by outlining what seem to me the prospects for the American economy for the next few decades.

Our present monetary and fiscal institutions are so constructed that anything more than a minor economic recession is extremely unlikely, even if, or especially if, no explicit action is taken by Congress or the Administration. But unless the recession is *exceedingly* minor, explicit action will be taken. The widespread general fear of depression would lead Congress to force such action on any Administration and whatever its own political complexion. ... If my basic premise is sound, such additional action will be unnecessary. Even more, it will be positively harmful. Contractions in the United States have averaged about 20 months in length over the past century or so, and this average includes the long contractions that were produced by monetary mistakes. Judging by this record, the present recession is probably more than half over, so that any actions that are taken are not likely to have much effect until after recovery has already begun. But even if they should, their effects are almost certain to last well beyond the onset of recovery. It is one thing to reduce taxes; it is another thing to raise them again. Public works once undertaken will turn out to have lives of their own not closely linked to the life of cyclical movements. Other public activities entered into in an atmosphere of approval for any kind of government spending will not rapidly be reversed. The result is that measures taken to stem a supposed depression will serve to stimulate the succeeding recovery and to convert it into another round of inflation.

This inflation will not get out of hand; the same built-in stabilizers that would prevent a depression from getting out of hand, will also prevent a runaway inflation. Sooner or later another recession will come along. After all we have been having such recessions for hundreds of years and we doubtless shall continue to for some time. When it does, the same process is likely to be repeated.

The prospect is therefore a period of recurrent bouts of inflation produced by over-reaction to the temporary recessions that punctuate it. How long will this period last? How serious will the inflation be? Will overreaction to recession and a spurt of inflation begin with the present recession? These questions seem to me to admit of no easy answer. Much depends on accidents of timing and politics, both internal and external.

Economists have known—at least intermittently—for over a century and a half two propositions: first, that by printing enough money you can produce any desired degree of activity; second, that the ultimate result is destruction of the currency. The American public has learned the first proposition. It once knew, but has now forgotten, the second. Only experience is likely to teach it once again.

. . . . .

One of the AFL-CIO's regular publications is a bulletin on problems and developments in the sphere of collective bargaining. The following selection comes from an early 1961 issue. (There have been no deletions. The original has nothing to say about the source of money to pay wage increases.)

55 · *Value of Wage Increases for Nation's Economy: A Union View*

AFL-CIO

Some industry spokesmen have tried to spread the notion that, for the good of the economy, wage increases should be extremely small or eliminated altogether. Unfortunately, there is a tendency for some union members to be misled by their propaganda and to believe that restraints on wage increases are in the national interest.

In fact, however, rising wages are beneficial for the economy and indeed are desperately needed by the nation to build up consumer demand so that idle men and machines will be put back to work.

The United States has been in an economic recession in 1960. Production has been cut back, unemployment has increased severely, and as much as a fifth of the nation's productive facilities remain unused.

The major reason for this falling off of economic activity is fundamentally a lack of sufficient markets for industry's output. Production has been reduced and workers laid off because there is not enough buying. Buying is inadequate largely because of an inadequate and slowing rate of increase in consumer buying power in recent years.

Who Buys Nation's Output

Who buys the nation's output? Where do wages fit in—how important are they in deciding the amount of buying power and effective demand?

A brief examination of these basic questions points up why rising wages are so necessary to help reverse the re-

---

AFL-CIO, "Value of Wage Increases for Nation's Economy," *Collective Bargaining Report,* Vol. 6, Nos. 1–3 (January–March 1961), a publication of the AFL-CIO. Used by permission.

cession and to bolster and expand our economic growth.

Most of America's goods and services are bought by consumers (individuals), with government the second largest customer and business the third. The proportions they buy of all the nation's output are:

Consumers	65 per cent
Government	20 per cent
Business	15 per cent

Consumers buy food, clothing, appliances and a wide range of other consumer products, plus various services such as laundry, repairs, transportation, etc.

Government buying (the federal government buys 11 percent and state and local governments 9 percent of all output) is, for the federal government, mainly for defense, construction of public facilities, and operation of the various services provided by the different departments. State and local government buying is largely for education, road, and police and fire services.

Business buys mainly materials, equipment and construction. (Actually much of this is materials for homebuilding, which account for 4 to 5 percent of national production, and which are included in this "business purchases" category, although they also are rooted in consumer buying.)

Foreign purchases, which account for 3 to 4 percent of American output, do not affect this overall picture, because they are offset by almost as much American purchases of foreign production.

Sources of Consumer Income

The great bulk of consumer buying power comes from wages and salaries. Specifically, wages and salaries account for about 70 percent of consumer income. A breakdown of the sources of consumer income shows:

Wages and salaries	70 per cent
Business and professional income	9 "
Interest	6 "
Farm income	3 "
Dividends	3 "
Rent	3 "
Transfer payments [1]	7 "

What happens to wages and salaries therefore clearly influences heavily the level of national production. If wages and salaries decline or merely hold steady, there is little incentive for industry to increase production. If wages rise, then they permit increased consumer spending, with a corresponding incentive for expansion of production.

Increases in wages and salaries are particularly valuable in a recession period, when it is necessary to offset the loss in total wage income stemming from rising unemployment and reduction in hours worked.

This is why substantial wage increases are in the national interest. With consumer income and buying power coming mainly from wages and salaries, increases in wages and salaries are the key means of expanding consumer markets and, in turn, national production and employment.

---

[1] These are principally social security benefits and private pensions and other benefits.

XI • GOVERNMENT FINANCE

If people want something badly enough to pay for it, will not private producers make it available? Is there a valid economic reason for any other method of economic organization than the business (market) system plus philanthropy? The following three selections deal with some aspects of these questions. Professor Brownlee is at the University of Minnesota, and Professor Allen taught at Iowa State University. John Stuart Mill was one of the outstanding British economists of the nineteenth century, and the paragraphs presented here are some of the ones for which he is best known. Professor Maxwell heads the economics department at Clark University.

56 • *Government Functions: Economic Aspects of Government Spending*

O. H. BROWNLEE
E. D. ALLEN

. . . . .

It is with the public economy—with the effects of governmental money-spending and money-raising activities upon the allocation of resources, the distribution of incomes, and the general level of economic activity within the economy—that . . . our analysis will be concerned.

Differences Between Government and Private Economic Units

Although governments are economic units similar in many respects to businesses or consuming units, their operations differ in many ways from the operations of other units. Of these differences, four stand out as important in explaining how and why governments should not and do not conduct their operations as private businesses.

(1) Governments try to achieve objectives which are different from objectives sought by most private businesses.

(2) The terms under which services and contributions are exchanged between the public economy and individuals differ from the terms under which the goods and services of the private economy are exchanged. Participation in much of the

---

O. H. BROWNLEE and E. D. ALLEN, *Economics of Public Finance*, 2nd ed. (Englewood Cliffs, N. J.: Prentice-Hall, Inc., 1954), pp. 9–10, 157–168. Used by permission.

public economy is compulsory, whereas participation in any given sector of the private economy is voluntary.

(3) Government is able to undertake projects which are not feasible—because of the risk involved and the consequent danger of impairment of liquidity—as private projects.

(4) The Federal government could, if desired, make payments from money it has issued rather than from receipts obtained from other economic units.

The objective of governmental operations is primarily that of maximizing social welfare, whereas the private business usually tries to maximize the welfare of its operators. Consequently, government must take into consideration benefits and losses which are indirect in character. A business usually recognizes only benefits and losses direct enough to affect its receipts and costs. . . . The absence of a market which will register participants' preferences, however, makes it difficult to determine whether the public sector of the economy is undertaking too little or too much.

The fact that the national government can, if desired, make payments from money issue rather than out of its receipts from taxes or the sale of goods, services, or securities, means that the government has at its disposal an additional means for injecting money into the economy. Private businesses cannot pay their bills indefinitely by circulating their own I.O.U.'s. . . .

How Much, and for What Purposes, Should Government Spend Money?

One of the most controversial questions of fiscal policy is, "How much should government spend?" There are genuine differences in the values—the weights assigned to the various objectives of social policy—held by the participants in the argument. In addition, there is disagreement over how a particular set of objectives should be reached. This latter disagreement probably could be narrowed considerably by more rigorous analysis of the effectiveness of the various techniques being proposed.

. . . an expansion in government expenditure for goods and services—unless it is accompanied by an equal or greater reduction in private expenditure —will increase the equilibrium level of gross national product. Either employment or the general level of prices or both will be expanded. Increased government expenditure for goods and services—government purchases of privately produced goods or additional employment of labor by government—represents a way by which the equilibrium level of employment or the price level could be raised or kept from falling.

However, when government uses resources or directs the allocation of resources in the private sector of the economy through its purchases, these resources are not available to be used in producing other goods and services. And the level of employment can be raised by increasing (through tax reduction or increased government transfer payments) the amount of disposable income that businesses and consumers have available to spend for goods and services. Consequently, except in instances where additional government expenditure for goods and services is the only feasible method for increasing total money . . . [outlay] in the economy, such expenditures should be evaluated according to criteria other than what they do to the level of employment or the price level.

Their effects upon the distribution of income are also unlikely to be important in judging the worthiness of government expenditures for goods and services. It is not necessary that government buy something from an individual in order to make him richer. His disposable income can be raised if government gives him money or takes less money away from him through taxes . . .

Thus the principal criterion by which we might evaluate government expenditures for goods and services is the effect of such expenditures upon the allocation of resources—the amounts of each of the various goods and services produced in the economy as a whole.

The Best Allocation of Resources

Much of economics has been concerned with merely defining the best allocation of an individual's, a nation's, or the world's resources. . . . It is usually assumed that the prices which buyers are willing to pay for a given number of units of a product are reasonable measures of what buyers are willing to give up for the marginal units. The price is a measure of the amounts of other goods and services that buyers are willing to sacrifice for the marginal unit of the commodity under consideration.

Most services rendered by government, however, are not priced, in that they are not bought and sold in the same manner as wheat or clothing or autos. Many of these services would be produced in smaller quantities if they were sold. The benefits from any person's taking advantage of these services go not only to this person but to others as well. For example, the student attending a state university receives training that increases his earning power, but his education may improve the general welfare as well as his own welfare. He should have gained a wider understanding of social problems and be able to act more intelligently in their solution. If he makes a technological discovery, the benefits of this advance are likely to be widely spread throughout society. Similarly, the benefits from public parks, public fire protection, public housing, and public health may accrue not only to the people who use the parks or the housing or who call upon the fire department or the health service, but to others as well. Crime, widespread fires, and disease epidemics may be kept at a lower level as a result of such public activities.

. . . the market demand for a good or service may underestimate the total social benefits provided by this commodity. The price at which the commodity would sell in the market cannot be taken as the sole guide in estimating the benefits provided by that commodity.

Just as the demand schedule for a commodity represents an estimate of what people are willing to give up for various quantities of that commodity, the costs of various amounts of the commodity represent estimates of what has to be given up. The resources that are used to produce one commodity could, in most instances, be used to produce other goods and services. . . .

Since various users of resources bid against each other for these resources, the sacrifices that have to be made of one commodity in order to obtain a given amount of another enter as costs of producing the commodity under consideration. However, just as there are benefits that may be overlooked when one considers only the price that people are willing to pay for a product . . . similarly there are certain costs that may not be included in determining the social cost of a product. An example, frequently cited, relates to the cost of products produced by the use of high-volatile coal; consider the added costs of keeping houses and clothing clean in the area near the factory or railway using coal—costs that are not typically taken into account by the coal user. An accounting of costs based solely on outlays ... for resources needed to produce a product may underestimate the total social costs of getting this commodity produced.

It is generally agreed that resources are best allocated when the marginal social benefit from each good or service is equal to the marginal social cost; that is, when what society is willing to give up for the marginal unit of a particular good or service is equal to what society has to give up. For goods and services where all benefits are represented in the market-demand schedules and all costs must be paid by producers, the price of each product must be equal to the marginal cost of getting each good produced in order for the best allocation to prevail. For other goods and services, the benefits omitted from market-demand schedules and costs omitted from producers' cost schedules must also be considered. The criterion of equality between price and marginal cost is not adequate for such commodities.

Government—through regulation of prices, taxation, or subsidization—may induce private businesses to produce that output at which price is equal to marginal cost. It may also force producers to consider all costs—make compensation for smoke, stream pollution, or other nuisances. But this achievement might still leave a considerable area in which resources were not best allocated. Government might be more efficient—have certain technological advantages—in producing or distributing some goods and services. And those goods and services, use of which yields benefits to persons other than the immediate users, would be under-produced. These are areas in which government should use resources or should direct resource allocation in order to achieve the best production pattern.

Government Can Produce Some Services More Efficiently

Government may be able to produce some services more efficiently than private producers because government may be able to eliminate some steps in getting the product to consumers.

Fiscally, it is not necessary for government to collect from the users of its services in the same way as private producers collect. Government may (and does) make some services available to all who wish to use them without reducing the incomes of each user by an amount necessary to cover production costs for the services. This is the net effect of general taxation to finance government services.

Imagine a situation in which all highways were privately operated and funds were collected on the basis of the amount of services used—the number of ton miles, for example. A large administrative staff would be required to see that consumers paid to use the roads and that they paid according to amount of service received. ... The administrative costs might not be excessive for a particular highway but would become absurdly high if the highway system as a whole was operated on this basis.

. . . . .

Relative Demand Prices Not Always an Accurate Index of Relative Social Benefits

. . . . .

A sizable proportion of services produced by government is of the kind which provides benefits to persons other than the immediate users. Public education, national defense, public health, police and fire protection are among the many examples. The widespread benefits from public education are particularly evident. Although total productivity is increased as a result of education, the additional product is not always entirely captured by persons who learned and now possess the skills. Part of the benefits of the skills acquired are passed on to the members of the economy as a whole. Education which consists of transmitting knowledge of the way in which our social and economic system functions is likely to result in improved economic and social institutions benefiting others in addition to those receiving the training. In areas where the range of these extra-buyer benefits is large—as in education—there is a case for government either producing these services or altering relative incentives to encourage additional production and use of them in the private economy. The latter procedure, however, is likely to be rather cumbersome. It would involve subsidies to producers to encourage production and discriminatory subsidies to consumers to encourage more widespread use of these goods and services which provide extra-buyer benefits. Consequently, governmental production and dissemination of a portion of such services appears desirable.

Extra-Buyer Benefits Do Not Necessarily Justify a Large Program of Public Expenditure

Although the principle of extra-buyer benefits justifies a good deal of government expenditure for resources, expansion in some fields of expenditure which superficially appears justifiable by this principle appears uneconomic when subjected to more rigorous examination. Even our present expenditures for public education may be too large.

First of all, it is our belief that a good deal of the clamor for additional government production of goods and services—of housing and steel, for example—is based on the erroneous assumption that it is possible, simply by having government enter the field, to produce more of some goods without reducing the production of others. Such a possibility exists only if there are strong elements of monopsony present in the economy or if inferior technology is being used. . . .

That there are goods and services which would be produced in insufficient quantities if they were not produced or purchased by government and sold to consumers at less than cost is obvious. However, if the principle of extra-buyer benefits is invoked in order to determine which services in the list produced by government should be expanded or contracted, some interesting cases arise. Education is one which will be examined in further detail.

The case for publicly provided education—instruction sold to students at a price less than marginal cost—is rightly based on the assumption that giving students certain kinds of training benefits persons other than those receiving the training and that these extra-buyer benefits are proportionately greater than those resulting from some forms of training in a factory or on a farm. Training which will permit more intelligent appraisals of social policies might be expected to result in the election of more competent legislators and in the formulation of better social policy. Such training would fit appropriately into the category which should be publicly supported, according to our criteria.

However, not all forms of training provided by publicly supposed educational institutions yield substantial extra-buyer benefits. Although the quantities of vocational and professional training which would be provided in the absence of public support probably would be smaller than those which are economically desirable, such underproduction could be explained by the inability of individuals generally to borrow on the basis of their prospective future earnings from the sale of their services. . . .

Rather than subscribe funds to support business schools, law schools, medical schools, and the like, government might act as the lender to individuals who wished to borrow in order to purchase vocational and professional training, and agencies supplying such services might sell them at cost. Individuals would then pay for the benefits which they receive. . . .

Relative Supply Prices Not Always an Accurate Index of Relative Social Costs

A second kind of divergence between private and social interests is presented on the supply side of the market picture. Not only may demand prices underestimate social benefits, but supply prices may underestimate social costs.
. . . The problem posed in this situation where supply prices do not include all of the costs is one which has been given considerable attention by economists. Finding solutions to these problems entails either discovering ways to force private producers to include all costs or having government take over production in these areas. Subsidies to producers conditional upon their reducing the smoke nuisance, conserving the soil, and the like may be one solution. However, this may prove an extremely cumbersome procedure. Governmental operation in these areas where these external diseconomies are relatively large may be desirable.

Expenditure for Transfer Payments Should Be Directed Primarily toward Modification of the Income Distribution

Consumption of only a relatively few goods may provide benefits to persons other than the consumers themselves. For example, the cigarettes you smoke, the clothing you wear, the music to which you listen, or the pattern of the rug upon your floor is of relatively little concern to anyone other than you. Consequently, it is not in the interest of society to try to encourage you to consume either more or less of these commodities. Nevertheless, society may consider your income too small to provide you with an adequate standard of living—enough of whatever goods and services you might choose to consume —and may be willing to supplement this income through payments made by government.

Relief payments of various kinds grow out of a belief that the incomes of certain groups are too small to provide the recipients with enough goods and services to maintain minimum health. Also, problems of social stability— higher crime rates and potential or actual revolution—may mount in importance as the incomes of a sizable group of the population are depressed.

The impacts of income distribution upon the size of the product to be distributed or the stability of the political and social framework, provide objective criteria by which one can judge whether one income distribution is better or worse than another. Otherwise, about all that can be said is that the income distribution should conform as closely as possible to society's notions of what this distribution ought to be. For example, the payment of bonuses to war veterans can hardly be justified on grounds that such bonuses will increase the total product or that veterans are poor and hence should have their incomes supplemented. Some veterans may be poor, but so are some nonveterans. And not all veterans would fit into the category of income receivers generally considered as in need of additional income in order to attain minimum living standards. Yet veterans' bonuses can be adequately justified on grounds that society believes veterans ought to have additional income because they are veterans. . . .

Efficiency in Government

The principles we have tried to set forth as guides to government spending are (1) that government should spend for goods and services (including resources) only if the resulting resource allocation is superior to that which would otherwise prevail and (2) that expenditures to change the distribution of income should be transfer payments. Resource allocation will be improved by government expenditure for goods and services if government can produce a given amount of product more efficiently than can private producers or if the goods purchased or produced by government provide substantial benefits to others besides those who use them.

JOHN STUART MILL

1. One of the most disputed questions both in political science and in practical statesmanship at this particular period relates to the proper limits of the functions and agency of governments. . . . On the one hand, impatient reformers, thinking it easier and shorter

---

JOHN STUART MILL, *Principles of Political Economy*, Book V, Ch. I, ed. Ashley (London: Longmans, Green & Co. Limited, 1909). Used by permission.

to get possession of the government than of the intellects and dispositions of the public, are under a constant temptation to stretch the province of government beyond due bounds: while, on the other, mankind have been so much accustomed by their rulers to interference for purposes other than the public good, or under an erroneous conception of what that good requires, and so many rash proposals are made by sincere lovers of improvement, for attempting, by compulsory regulation, the attainment of objects which can only be effectually or only usefully compassed by opinion and discussion, that there has grown up a spirit of resistance *in limine* to the interference of government, merely as such, and a disposition to restrict its sphere of action within the narrowest bounds. . . .

. . . there must be a specification of the functions which are either inseparable from the idea of a government, or are exercised habitually and without objection by all governments; as distinguished from those respecting which it has been considered questionable whether governments should exercise them or not. The former may be termed the *necessary*, the latter the *optional*, functions of government. . . .

2. In attempting to enumerate the necessary functions of government, we find them to be considerably more multifarious than most people are at first aware of, and not capable of being circumscribed by those very definite lines of demarcation, which, in the inconsiderateness of popular discussion, it is often attempted to draw round them. We sometimes, for example, hear it said that governments ought to confine themselves to affording protection against force and fraud: that, these two things apart, people should be free agents, able to take care of themselves, and that so long as a person practices

no violence or deception, to the injury of others in person or property, legislatures and governments are in no way called on to concern themselves about him. But why should people be protected by their government, that is, their own collective strength, against violence and fraud, and not against other evils, except that the expediency is more obvious? If nothing but what people cannot possibly do for themselves, can be fit to be done for them by government, people might be required to protect themselves by their skill and courage even against force, or to beg or buy protection against it, as they actually do where the government is not capable of protecting them: and against fraud every one has the protection of his own wits. . . .

Under which of these heads, the repression of force or of fraud, are we to place the operation, for example, of the laws of inheritance? Some such laws must exist in all societies. It may be said, perhaps, that in this matter government has merely to give effect to the disposition which an individual makes of his own property by will. . . . And suppose the very common case of there being no will: does not the law, that, is, the government, decide on principles of general expediency, who shall take the succession? and in case the successor is in any manner incompetent, does it not appoint persons, frequently officers of its own, to collect the property and apply it to his benefit? There are many other cases in which the government undertakes the administration of property, because the public interest, or perhaps only that of the particular persons concerned, is thought to require it. This is often done in cases of litigated property; and in cases of judicially declared insolvency. It has never been contended that, in doing these things, a government exceeds its province.

Nor is the function of the law in defining property itself so simple a thing as may be supposed. It may be imagined, perhaps, that the law has only to declare and protect the right of every one to what he has himself produced, or acquired by the voluntary consent, fairly obtained, of those who produced it. But is there nothing recognized as property except what has been produced? Is there not the earth itself, its forests and waters, and all other natural riches, above and below the surface? These are the inheritance of the human race, and there must be regulations for the common enjoyment of it. What rights, and under what conditions, a person shall be allowed to exercise over any portion of this common inheritance cannot be left undecided. No function of government is less optional than the regulation of these things, or more completely involved in the idea of civilized society.

Again, the legitimacy is conceded of repressing violence or treachery; but under which of these heads are we to place the obligation imposed on people to perform their contracts? Non-performance does not necessarily imply fraud; the persons who entered into the contract may have sincerely intended to fulfil it: and the term fraud, which can scarcely admit of being extended even to the case of voluntary breach of contract when no deception was practised, is certainly not applicable when the omission to perform is a case of negligence. Is it no part of the duty of governments to enforce contracts? Here the doctrine of non-interference would no doubt be stretched a little, and it would be said that enforcing contracts is not regulating the affairs of individuals at the pleasure of government, but giving effect to their own expressed desire. . . . But governments do not limit their concern with contracts to a simple enforcement. They take upon themselves to determine what contracts are fit to be enforced. It is not enough that one person, not being either cheated or compelled, makes a promise to another. There are promises by which it is not for the public good that persons should have the power of binding themselves. To say nothing of engagements to do something contrary to law, there are engagements which the law refuses to enforce, for reasons connected with the interest of the promiser, or with the general policy of the state. A contract by which a person sells himself to another as a slave would be declared void by the tribunals of this and of most other European countries. There are few nations whose laws enforce a contract for what is looked upon as prostitution, or any matrimonial engagement of which the conditions vary in any respect from those which the law has thought fit to prescribe. But when once it is admitted that there are any engagements which for reasons of expediency the law ought not to enforce, the same question is necessarily opened with respect to all engagements. Whether, for example, the law should enforce a contract to labour when the wages are too low or the hours of work too severe: whether it should enforce a contract by which a person binds himself to remain, for more than a very limited period, in the service of a given individual: whether a contract of marriage, entered into for life, should continue to be enforced against the deliberate will of the persons, or of either of the persons, who entered into it. Every question which can possibly arise as to the policy of contracts, and of the relations which they establish among human beings, is a question for the legislator; and one which he cannot escape from considering, and in some way or other deciding.

Again, the prevention and suppression of force and fraud afford appropriate employment for soldiers, policemen, and criminal judges; but there are also civil tribunals. The punishment of wrong is one business of an administration of justice, but the decision of disputes is another. Innumerable disputes arise between persons, without *mala fides* on either side, through misconception of their legal rights, or from not being agreed about the facts, on the proof of which those rights are legally dependent. Is it not for the general interest that the State should appoint persons to clear up these uncertainties and terminate these disputes? It can not be said to be a case of absolute necessity. . . . Still, it is universally thought right that the State should establish civil tribunals. . . .

Not only does the State undertake to decide disputes, it takes precautions beforehand that disputes may not arise. The laws of most countries lay down rules for determining many things, not because it is of much consequence in what way they are determined, but in order that they may be determined somehow, and there may be no question on the subject. The law prescribes forms of words for many kinds of contract, in order that no dispute or misunderstanding may arise about their meaning: it makes provision that, if a dispute does arise, evidence shall be procurable for deciding it, by requiring that the document be attested by witnesses and executed with certain formalities. The law preserves authentic evidence of facts to which legal consequences are attached, by keeping a registry of such facts; as of births, deaths, and marriages, of wills and contracts, and of judicial proceedings. In doing these things, it has never been alleged that government oversteps the proper limits of its functions.

Again, however wide a scope we may allow to the doctrine that individuals are the proper guardians of their own interests, and that government owes nothing to them but to save them from being interfered with by other people, the doctrine can never be applicable to any persons but those who are capable of acting in their own behalf. The individual may be an infant, or a lunatic, or fallen into imbecility. The law surely must look after the interest of such persons. . . .

There is a multitude of cases in which governments, with general approbation, assume powers and execute functions for which no reason can be assigned except the simple one, that they conduce to general convenience. We may take as an example, the function (which is a monopoly too) of coining money. This is assumed for no more recondite purpose than that of saving to individuals the trouble, delay, and expense of weighing and assaying. No one, however, even of those most jealous of state interference, has objected to this as an improper exercise of the powers of government. Prescribing a set of standard weights and measures is another instance. Paving, lighting, and cleansing the streets and thoroughfares is another; whether done by the general government, or, as is more usual, and generally more advisable, by a municipal authority. Making or improving harbours, building lighthouses, making surveys in order to have accurate maps and charts, raising dykes to keep the sea out, and embankments to keep rivers in, are cases in point.

. . . enough has been said to show that the admitted functions of government embrace a much wider field than can easily be included within the ringfence of any restrictive definition, and that it is hardly possible to find any ground of justification common to them all, except the comprehensive one of general expediency; nor to limit the interference of government by any universal rule, save the simple and vague one, that it should never be admitted but when the case of expediency is strong.

JAMES A. MAXWELL

. . . . .

What, then, today should be the agenda of government, and particularly, what should be its fiscal program? Admitting that government may be able by taxes to take some money from the pockets of the people and spend it more advantageously than private persons, what limit should be set to the process? For what services has government a relative advantage over private enterprise?

Collective vs. Noncollective Services

A distinction can be drawn between services which render collective benefits and those which do not. Collective services are rendered to citizens as a whole, rather than to individual citizens. Defense is the clearest example, and decisions concerning its provision must be governmental. A wide range of other services—education, welfare, construction of highways—are largely collective, although particular benefits are rendered cutting across the collective benefits. The justification for governmental, rather than private, action

---

JAMES A. MAXWELL, *Fiscal Policy: Its Techniques and Institutional Setting* (New York: Holt, Rinehart and Winston, Inc., 1955), pp. 5–8. Copyright 1955 by Holt, Rinehart and Winston, Inc. Used by permission.

is always that a large element of collective benefit inheres in the services. Where it does not, services can be rendered privately by citizens to other citizens. Inevitably, of course, the division between the public and the private sphere is a penumbra within which the actual line of demarcation will shift because of shifts in public opinion concerning the admixture of collective and particular benefits in certain services.

Contrasts Between Private and Public Economy

RESOURCE ALLOCATION BY THE MARKET IN PRIVATE ECONOMY. In bold outline the contrast between the private and the public economy is clear. In the former, individual citizens as consumers in possession of dollars try to maximize their satisfactions and as producers try to maximize their net incomes. Labor and capital are allocated in response to these dollar demands. In the private economy individual citizens buy goods and services from private businesses (and also sell to private businesses) taking as much or as little as they choose. The price paid is uniform for each buyer and seller, and must in the long term cover the firm's cost of production. The balancing of satisfaction received and given is a matter for individual decision.

RESOURCE ALLOCATION BY COMPULSION IN PUBLIC ECONOMY. In the public economy provision of collective services and allocation of costs is through compulsion. An individual is not allowed to specify the amount of defense he will take or the price he will voluntarily pay for it. Not only is the decision concerning the proper amount of defense collective, but the government distributes the cost among citizens through taxes; that is, through compulsory payments assessed by general rules rather than by prices which are voluntary payments not assessed at all.

These characteristics outline in the broadest terms the boundary between the public and the private economy. The crucial debate arises when the boundary is made precise. For instance, does the collective interest in economic security justify governmental provision of health insurance? What is the collective interest in provision of the supply of electrical energy?

POLITICAL BASIS FOR ALLOCATION IN PUBLIC SPHERE. The basis upon which decisions are taken to allocate resources of labor and capital to the public sphere is political. In a country like the United States, citizens—the majority of them—are responsible for the amount and the direction of governmental expenditure. The process is indirect and haphazard, since it operates through a system of representative government, and is in contrast with the process by which decisions concerning the allocation of resources operate in the private economy. Over the long run the limit of expenditure for an individual is set by his current income; unless he can earn more, he cannot spend more. But because government has the power of compulsion, it is limited in its spending only by its ability to raise money from all the citizens. With respect to the direction of expenditure, the individual citizen tries to use his dollars so that the satisfaction secured by him from each of them is equal. This feat is performed with indifferent success by most of us, even after long experience. But the decisions of government concerning the direction of its expenditure—whether it shall expand or contract present expenditures or begin new expenditures—rest on the precarious basis of a collective judgment. The people as citizens must decide upon the appropriate allocation of resources between the public and private spheres, and within the public sphere.

THE RESPONSIBILITY OF CONGRESS. The immediate responsibility for collective decisions concerning governmental expenditures rests upon Congress. By voting appropriations it decides both the amount and the direction of public expenditure. And since most of these will be financed by taxation, Congress has the related task of deciding how and in what amount resources will be taken out of the pockets of citizens and put into the public purse. Congress will, of course, not have to re-examine yearly every detail of the budget, since it will assume that the broad pattern set by the past is a present guide. But a limit must be determined for expenditures as a whole and for each avenue of expenditure. Congress will attempt to make its decisions with the opinions of the majority of the citizens in mind, and these opinions are not constant over time. What one generation of voters rejects, another will embrace, sometimes because of changed conditions and sometimes because of a shift in social philosophy.

Socialist vs. Free-Enterprise Economies

In the exposition above a distinction was drawn between the collective and the noncollective functions of government and this distinction offers a nebulous boundary between a free-enterprise and a socialist economy. In the latter government would not only provide collective services, but also would own and operate the major industries which supply particular services to citizens. In the former private enterprise operating on the basis of profit-seeking would provide many particular services for citizens. . . .

A great economist, Lord Keynes, who was not a socialist and yet was not inhibited by "capitalist" conventions, has offered a realistic test for the agenda of government in a free-enterprise economy. It is that government should not attempt to do any job which is being done, or can be done, reasonably well by private enterprise. What government should handle are those tasks which, unless done by it, will not be done at all. . . . prominent among them stands the function of fiscal policy; i.e., *the use of government expenditure and revenue as balancing factors to secure economic stabilization.*

With government spending—and taxes—amounting to more than one-fourth of the gross national product, and with so many things denied us because spending is already so high and funds short—better schools, more police, larger parks—getting the most for each dollar spent is tremendously important. Business has a great advantage in being able to value both inputs and outputs in dollars and then to measure one alternative against another. Government, however, can rarely get a reliable measure of the worth of ouputs. The selection below, taken from one of the most thorough studies ever made of government management, discusses six kinds of "economy."

57 · "Economy" in Government

THE CITY OF NEW YORK

Six Kinds of "Economy"

It is easy to get confused about the word "economy" when we are considering how to get it in governmental affairs. "Economy" seems to mean different things at different times and to different people. From this study . . . it appears that there are six kinds of "economy."

(1) "GET ALONG WITHOUT IT" ECONOMY. This is the result of doing without some activity or service. If you go without a welfare center, a public retail market, a playground, a branch library, a bridge, or a proposed reservoir, you save money in a very visible form. If you decide not to increase a certain staff, you save money. . . .

This type of economy appears also if an old activity is discontinued. If the Police Department stops furnishing free guards for baseball parks or for payroll messengers, you save the money involved. If you decide not to fill a vacancy in some office, you save a salary. . . . If you consolidate fire or police stations and do without the extra station, you save money. . . . Even if you close a hopsital or a school instead of repairing the leaky roof, you "save" the cost of the new roof.

(2) "CHEAPER SERVICE" ECONOMY. This is the economy which comes from lowering your standards. If you clean streets once a week instead of three times a week in a given area, you save money, but your streets will not be so clean. If you have three nurses in a given hospital ward instead of five, you save money, but the patients are given less attention. If you have 50 building inspectors instead of 100 doing the same work in the same way, you have less thorough work done, but you save money in the budget. . . . If you increase class sizes in the schools, you cut salary costs per child, but you may lessen the quality of the education offered. If you cut the cost of hospital meals from 93 cents to 83 cents per patient-day, you save

From *Modern Management for the City of New York,* the Mayor's Committee on Management Survey, Vol. 1 (New York: 1953), pp. 32–37.

money, but you reduce the nutritional standards.

(3) "BETTER METHODS" ECONOMY. This is the economy which comes from doing the same job in a better or quicker way. This is what is generally meant by efficiency. Labor-saving machinery and good tools enter into this, and the application of machine power instead of human power. This is where the efficiency engineer does his stuff. . . .

Another aspect of better methods is found in work simplification, where unnecessary forms or motions are eliminated, one process is made to do the work of two, and the flow of work is revised to make it easier and faster.

The quest for better methods carries us also over into standard management techniques in organization, budgeting, personnel administration, planning, accounting and reporting.

Some economies from better methods are immediately visible in reduced needs for manpower and materials. But many important better-methods economies cost money to install. The first step increases the budget before the economies begin to be realized. This is especially true when new organizations or new labor saving machinery are involved in the improvements.

(4) "PENNY WISE AND POUND FOOLISH" ECONOMY. This is the "saving" in the current budget that produces greater expenditures in the long run. The whole sad story of lack of maintenance of City schools, hospitals, and the transit system . . . is a case in point.

Unfortunately, in this case, the foolish economy can be measured in dollars "saved" and shows immediately as a reduction of departmental requests in the City budget, while the "pound" lost thereby will not show up until later.

(5) "TAKE A LOOK AHEAD" ECONOMY. Some of the greatest sheer waste in government comes from "compulsory, inescapable, emergency expenditures" which could have been avoided by just a little clearheaded advance planning, analysis, and courage. Population settlement that is permitted without proper streets and sewers creates nothing but trouble and unnecessary costs, both for the householders and for the City. Big projects that are started with a small commitment can lead into the millions. Even bad designs in schools, hospitals, incinerators, disposal plants, or subway stations can produce a long crop of damage suits, most of which could have been avoided by good designs. Unique and meaningless specifications for fire apparatus bring needlessly high costs for the City. The failure to acquire school lands and play fields in advance of housing and other developments can make the cost for needed properties much larger in the end.

In this category, also, must be placed the economies which come from deciding not to build an institution if the City cannot afford to operate that institution later on. Once the building is built, the City is virtually forced to find the money to operate it. . . .

Unfortunately the economy which comes from taking a look ahead never can be measured in dramatic budget reductions. This economy is the money the City would have been forced to spend if it had not taken action in time to avoid the need. While this is iffy money, it is extremely real to those who understand the situation and frequently it involves very large sums of money. . . .

(6) FINALLY, WE HAVE "BLUE SKY" ECONOMY. This is pure conversation. It is like the economy of window shopping, with its noble decision not to buy something which there was never any chance of buying anyway.

. . . . .

ONE-TIME VERSUS RECURRING SAVINGS. Whenever an "economy" is recommended, it is important to note whether the "saving" is a one-time gain or one that will repeat itself from year to year. If, for example, an idle piece of laundry equipment is transferred and installed instead of buying a new piece, there is a saving in one budget year of the price of the new machine. But if the heating system of a housing development is designed economically . . . there will be an annual saving as long as the building stands. Both types of economy are desirable, but the second is many times more important.

PUBLIC "SAVINGS" AND PRIVATE LOSS. What government does for the citizens may cost him in taxes a great deal less than it would cost him if he did it for himself. This is true of street lighting and waste collection, for example. The costs of private street lighting, which we used to have before the Civil War, were prohibitive and the service was very poor. When small cities change from private scavengers to public waste collection, the cost drops at least to half. This general situation is true of many other public activities, to say nothing of those, such as public health and general crime protection, which the individual is powerless to furnish for himself even if he were a millionaire.

It follows that some City budget savings can actually cost the taxpayers a great deal more out of their private pockets than the budget saving is worth. If, for example, the City saves money by cutting out all traffic lights, the cost to the citizens in congested streets and accidents would be many times the appropriation saved. Or if the City decided not to chlorinate the City water, typhoid would return and hundreds of people would die each year.

Thus public savings which involve the abandonment or curtailment of services, or the noninitiation of needed activities, must always be looked at in relation to their connection with the private sector of the economy.

Pressures for Efficiency in Government and Business

There are apparently four things that keep any large, organized, human activity efficient. These are economic competition, the pride of craft, intelligent and human supervision and organization, the continuous application of scientific advances.

These four forces play an important part in modern big business. . . .

But in government we start without competition, which is the mainspring of business efficiency, because governments are by definition monopolies and go on regardless of their efficiency. There is "pride of craft" in government, but this is harder to discover and maintain than in most businesses. And very little has been done in government to develop intelligent human supervision, or to keep up with and install the results of scientific research. Thought has been given to organization in government, and progress has been made with such matters and with budgeting, personnel, procurement, and other procedures. . . .

A handicap making the drive for efficiency in government harder to maintain than in private business is the nature of the work performed and the test of "success" which is imposed in government as compared with private business.

Business makes and sells a product or performs a service at a competitive price. There is a continuous effort to bring the costs down, because lower prices generally increase the market and push up the profit. The whole enterprise is run for the profit and cannot be continued once the profit disappears. Careful accounts are maintained, which show the profit and loss picture from period to period, the status of the capital accounts, and also, in great detail, what each process contributes toward the total end result.

Government deals not so much in products as in services and in controls. It is seldom possible to put comparative price tags on the services, because of differences in quality required. The controls are, of course, unique with government and cannot be subjected to pricing. . . . However, government almost never keeps its books to give a true picture of costs or of capital status. The end purpose of government not being "profit," the accounts are not set up to show costs in comparison with returns. Moreover, in government these returns are in most services not susceptible of statement in accounting terms; while in business, in most cases, no return is of significance unless it can be put into financial terms and entered on the books.

For those reasons the measure of "success" differs in government and business. In business the test is a continuous record of profits and dividends, with a maintenance of the capital structure, a preservation of status in the industry, with a prospect of continued existence and future development. Such an enterprise is in a position to give its employees and officers satisfying and worthwhile participation, to maintain its community responsibilities, and to justify its place in the social and economic system. These are the tests of private business success.

In our governments the short-run test of success is the re-election of the officials and the continuation of the party in power. The long-run test is still in the elections, but the "general opinions of qualified observers" enter the picture to a greater degree and may even diverge at times from individual election results. In the ballot box test, "efficiency and economy" may or may not be important. The human factors involved in services and controls are much more likely to capture public attention and support. However, the tax rates are always significant.

Some agencies of the Federal government make detailed studies of the expected costs and expected benefits of public works projects. Then, of course, final judgment on the economic wisdom of going ahead with investment in the project requires the use of an interest rate. But what rate? A professor of the University of Chicago gives an answer to this important question.

58 · *Investment in Public Works: Use of the Interest Rate*

ARNOLD C. HARBERGER

It would be hard to overstate the importance of the interest rate used in the discounting of benefits and costs to judge the worthwhileness of proposed long-term Federal investment. Suppose a project were expected to yield benefits of $1 million a year beginning 5 years from the initiation of construction and extending indefinitely into the future. Using an interest rate of 2½ percent, we would evaluate this stream of expected benefits at $35.36 million as of the date of initiation of the project. But if we were to use a 6-percent rate, our evaluation would be no more than $12.45 million. The choice of interest rate becomes more critical, the longer the duration of the project in question, and the longer the lag between the beginning of construction and the time when benefits begin to accrue. Clearly major mistakes can be made if the wrong interest rate is used in evaluation. If the cost of the above project were $20 million, it would be a fine investment if 2½ percent were the right rate and a terrible mistake if 6 percent were the right rate. I propose to argue in this paper that a rate of 6 percent or better is the proper rate to use in evaluating Federal projects. This compares with a rate of 2½ percent most commonly used by the Government agencies which undertake cost-benefit analyses.

The justification most commonly given for the use of the 2½ percent rate is that that is the rate at which the Government can borrow. This, of course, is no longer true; perhaps a 3½ percent rate would accord better with the present state of the money market. Be that as it may, my argument for a rate of 6 percent or better does not depend critically on the state of the money market. It holds equally well for the easy-money days immediately following the second World War and for the hard-money period through which we are now passing.

The essence of my argument is that there exist and have existed ever since the war widespread opportunities for investments yielding 6 and 8 percent and higher. So long as such opportunities are available, our society does itself a disservice by investing at yields of merely

---

ARNOLD C. HARBERGER, *Federal Expenditure Policy for Economic Growth and Stability,* Papers submitted before the subcommittee on Fiscal Policy, Joint Economic Committee Hearings (November 5, 1961).

2½ or 3½ percent. The opportunities I speak of are those at the margins of industrial and agricultural investment, and I suspect it is also true that investment in residential construction might yield close to 6 percent.

Let us consider a typical industrial investment. Let it be financed half out of equity (or retained earnings) and half out of borrowings. What must it yield in order that it be a successful investment in the market sense? Presumably, the total yield should be sufficient to pay the interest on the borrowings and provide a rate of return on the newly invested equity equal to the market rate of return on equity. Taking figures which are reasonably representative of the period since the war, let us assume the interest charge on borrowings to be 4 percent, and the earnings yield of equities to be 10 percent. This earnings yield is, of course, after taxes; the before-tax yield of equity capital has typically been in the order of 20 percent. Thus our typical successful investment yields 4 percent on half the invested funds and 20 percent on the other half, making the rate of return on the whole equal to 12 percent. It may be objected that the 10 percent figure for earnings yield, while representative of the whole postwar period, has been rendered obsolete by the great rise in stock prices that has occurred. For recent years a figure of 7 percent might be better for the after-tax yield of equities. This means 14 percent before tax, and together with a 4 percent borrowing rate applied to half the total capital implies an overall yield on capital of 9 percent, rather than the 12-percent figure obtained earlier.

Another approach to estimating the rate of return on capital in the United States is to compare total income received on account of capital with the total value of the capital itself. Neither of these components is easy to estimate, but much work has been done in recent years to improve our knowledge of both.[1] In spite of the lack of absolute precision in the presently available estimates, one may feel quite confident that the stock of capital in the United States is somewhere between 3 and 4 times the national income, and that the income accruing to capital amounts to somewhere between one-third and one-fourth of the national income. Our estimate of the rate of return on capital in the overall economy lies, then, in the range between 6¼ percent (income of one-fourth divided by capital of 4) and 11.1 percent (income of one-third divided by capital of 3), and probably closer to the middle than to the extremes of the range.

In the case of agriculture we have a reasonably good measure of the return on capital in the ratio of the gross rent paid to the value of rented farms. For 12 Corn Belt States this rent/value ratio ranged from an average of 5½ percent in Ohio to an average of 8½ percent in Wisconsin, with most States averaging between 6 and 7 percent. The figures are for 1954–57, and apply to farms rented wholly for cash.[2]

It is clear that there do exist many alternative investments yielding 6 percent and more per year. One might ask, however, whether these differ substantially from typical government projects in their degree of riskiness, so as to warrant a substantially different rate of return. I cannot help but feel that Federal projects are highly similar in their degree of riskiness to many private projects. Both power and irrigation facilities are provided by the private market side by side with Federal installa-

---

[1] Cf. Raymond Goldsmith, *A Study of Saving in the United States.* (Princeton: 1956.) Moses Abramovitz, "Resource and Output Trends in the United States Since 1870," *American Economic Review,* May 1956, pp. 5–23, and the sources cited therein.
[2] U. S. Department of Agriculture, *The Farm Cost Situation,* May 1957, p. 19, table 8.

tions, as are, from time to time, river and harbor improvements, flood-control facilities, etc. These rank, to the best of my judgment, neither as especially safe nor especially risky investments. It therefore seems reasonable to expect that Federal investments in these activities should pay off at least at 6 percent, which, as we have seen, appears to be somewhat below the average return on investments in the private sector of the economy. The purpose of Federal investment is, I believe, to improve our level of living and that of our children. The measure of this improvement is provided in dollar terms through the estimation of benefits. There seems little or no justification for the Government's withdrawing resources from the private sector unless these will yield as much improvement in levels of living as ordinary private investments.

My recommending the use of a substantially higher interest rate in cost-benefit analysis does not imply any prejudgment that serious mistakes were made because a lower rate was used. [The author reports on investigations applying the principle he advances. Many, but by no means all, of the sample of Bureau of Reclamation projects and Department of Agriculture watershed projects would not meet the test. *Ed.*]

President Kennedy proposed in 1961 that businesses be offered an "investment credit." The proposal was highly complicated. Yet in essence it provided that a firm get a reduction in its tax bill when it invested varying amounts above those it was deducting for depreciation. The business world strongly opposed the proposal. In the hearings before the Committee on Ways and Means, Mr. C. R. Sligh, Jr. presented the arguments of the National Association of Manufacturers. Most of his discussion is more technical than is suitable here. However, some of the major points and, what is more important, the alternatives proposed are summarized below. The NAM has for many years pressed for gradual, systematic, and substantial reduction of tax rates.

59 · *A Business Program for Federal Tax Reform*

NATIONAL ASSOCIATION OF MANUFACTURERS

For full economic growth, and adequate job opportunities, our economy must have more capital. The key to a tax program for increasing human well-being at home and enhancing our national security is the release of capital. The more capital released, the greater will be the nation's progress. Legislation which starts the quickest and provides the most thorough reform of tax rates and

---

"A Tax Climate for Economic Growth," NATIONAL ASSOCIATION OF MANUFACTURERS, testimony presented before the Committee on Ways and Means (1961). Used by permission.

methods, will best serve the interest of America.

Giving and Taking

As significant a development as is the President's [Mr. Kennedy's] recognition that the present tax system restrains capital formation and economic growth, we must recognize that his program as a whole would do more harm than good, in its immediate impact, and in its precedent for future legislation. It would take away with one hand what it gives with the other. And what it would give is wrong in concept because the private economy does not need giving. It needs release from a harassing structure of tax rates and methods which defeats the public interest.

. . . . .

Basic Fallacy of an Investment Credit

The concept of an investment credit implies something that isn't so, namely, that a free economy has to be encouraged or stimulated by government to function at full effectiveness. To suggest that there is such a weakness is to downgrade the system, and to mislead the American public and the world. The only reason to offer an investment credit is the existence of discriminatory tax rates and methods which keep the economy from performing at full efficiency. In obscuring this fact, the credit proposal avoids the real problem and implies the giving of a special privilege.

The situation conjures the picture of the government strangling the taxpayer with one hand and offering him artificial resuscitation with the other.

The Administration has placed great emphasis on the incentive or stimulating effect to be expected from an investment credit.

. . . . .

The publicized thinking of the academicians who first advised President Kennedy on introduction of an investment credit goes much further than such a credit in the use of the tax system for government direction, manipulation and control of the economy. Their theorizing reflects belief that government is wise enough to pull the strings and make the economy perform like a puppet.

The institution of an investment credit would add a new element of uncertainty to the basically punitive nature of the present tax structure. Business is quite sensitive to the fact that, once any kind of a tax break for doing what the government wants done at a particular time is accepted, the right of the government to exact a tax penalty for inconsistent or contrary action could be readily asserted. *The power to favor is but the opposite of the power to penalize.* . . .

There is no safety for a free people or for a free enterprise in any tax system except one in which the purpose is raising necessary revenue, and not the achievement of economic or social objectives according to government whim or judgment at a particular time.

It is clear that instead of stimulating, an investment credit would have less incentive-releasing effects than would result from an equivalent amount of tax reduction which carried no overtones of government manipulation.

. . . . .

Inefficiency of Investment Credit

THE GOODNESS OF PROFITS. The Administration at one point asserts that an investment credit is preferable to depreciation reform because the booking of more depreciation reform would provide corporations the excuse for raising prices in order to maintain the pre-existing level of reported profits. The implication here is hard to pin down, since the Administration seems to have no objection to increased profitability if it were induced by use of an investment credit. But it seems not to accept the importance of profits per se.

The prospect for profit is the only motivation for entering into or expanding a business enterprise. Profits are a major source of capital for expansion. Hence, just as capital is inherently good, so are profits. Adequate business profits are an end reflection of economic health and vitality. They provide the key to adequate employment opportunity. The volume of capital derived from profits and other sources determines the rate of economic growth. The increasing productivity which accompanies growth is the source of better jobs and higher standards of living. Government attitudes should not cast official disfavor on any of the processes involved in achieving the highest possible level of economic growth.

For these reasons, it should be apparent to all that the current inadequacy of profits is a limiting factor on investment, job creation and economic growth. In 1960 total corporate profits after taxes amounted to only 23 billion dollars, practically unchanged from the 22.8 billion dollars reported ten years earlier. In this period, corporate profits have fallen from 8.0 per cent to 4.6 per cent of gross national product. At the same time, there has developed a nagging problem of increasing unemployment.

. . . . .

STIMULATION OF INEFFICIENCY. At one point, the Secretary [of the Treasury], stated that "The purpose of the investment credit is not to provide general tax reduction for recipients of private income," but "Rather, it is to stimulate investment in the most efficient manner." This is the equivalent of saying that a business decision based on the incidence of taxation, in this case a tax favor, is a more efficient one than if based on business judgment under a nondiscriminatory tax policy. This view repudiates the experience that the market place is the best determinant of business decisions. As proven in the agricultural area, interference with free markets results in distortions and maladjustments, including the uneconomic allocation of capital. The next step inevitably is more government regulation.

. . . . .

Good and Bad Economic Action

. . . . .

. . . whether to invest or not to invest at a particular time is a matter of business judgment, which should not be second-guessed by government. If the right of the government to second-guess business decisions is granted, then we may soon hear that the government also has the responsibility to validate its second-guessing. Validating could come through guaranteeing profits, or limiting markets, or perhaps even through a commodity credit operation for all who take advantage of an investment credit, and get stuck with surplus production.

. . . the inadequacy of investment for expansion and modernization in the past is not the fault of enterprise nor of economic areas which have lagged behind. The free market allocates capital, just as it allocates other resources. The capital which has been generated in the past under existing tax rates has been used. There hasn't been any more capital available. *Contrary to general impression, there is never any significant amount of surplus capital in a free economy. All enterprises together can use only the aggregate of capital which is available. If more capital becomes available, it will be used.*

The way to get greater and more consistent economic growth which the nation needs is not to grant tax favors to what might be considered the good firms of industry at a particular time, but to release the tax restraints on capital and to moderate the tax destruction of capital once accumulated. When this is done there will be more investment, there will be greater expansion, there will be faster modernization, there will be more jobs, and we will enhance our strength relative to the rest of the world.

The greater the release of capital from unfair and unsound taxation, the greater will be our progress.

A Tax Climate for Growth

In his testimony, Secretary of the Treasury Dillon stated "Our purpose is to stimulate new investment, not to give general tax reduction." And he added that the idea of a general cut in the rate of the corporate tax is therefore rejected.

To release the potential for growth and good for people inherent in our free system, the purpose of tax action should be neither to "stimulate" nor "to give," but *"to relieve."*

What this nation needs is abandonment of the tax philosophy which places limits on growth, human well-being and national strength. It needs dedication to a new philosophy opposite in concept.

Beginning with the depression of the 1930s, the advocates of steep graduation had a field day at the expense of American progress. On the false assumption that graduation is inherently good, they created a climate for tax action which, in effect, said if some graduation is good, why is not more graduation better. This climate was extended all across the board in regard to federal taxation which limits capital accumulation, preservation and use.

That the advocates of steep graduation and of capital confiscation were wrong, should be evident to all. It is past time for establishing a new tax climate, namely, that if less taxation of capital is good, then still less taxation of capital would be better.

This new climate can be initiated without any thought that an unfair advantage will ever be provided to the businesses and high-income people as against the average citizen. As long as exemptions and dependency credits are retained in the individual tax, there will be substantial protection from payment of tax in the lower income ranges, and substantial effective graduation up the income scale.

. . . . .

Delay and Jobs

. . . . .

In the era of easy money, during the first 6 years after World War II, the process of inflation obscured some of the effects of tax restraints on capital accumulation. As the money supply was inflated, significant amounts were channelled into facilities for the production of goods and services. In March 1951, under President Truman, the policy of easy money was brought to an end by an accord between the Treasury and the Federal Reserve Board. From then on, it was inevitable that the federal tax structure would become more and more of a strait-jacket on capital formation. Over the following 10 years, the problem of a capital-destroying tax structure has been compounded by uneconomic wage increases, which on first impact have been inflationary, but on second impact deflationary under the necessary stringency of a stable money policy. Overall wage increases beyond the bounds of national productivity increases which could not be recovered in price have first reduced profits, then production and employment.

In the second year of the 1960s, the

federal government has not yet faced up to a problem which should have been resolved in the mid-1950s. In the dynamics of progress, and in our position of relative strength and leadership in the world, we have slipped, seriously so. We are still way ahead of the rest of the world in accumulated strength, and in the average of citizen well-being. But it is dangerous to take comfort in what we have achieved, at the expense of facing the issue of what we must achieve from here on. Past records don't win future Olympics.

. . . . .

Growth in Government Versus Growth in the Private Economy

There should be no misunderstanding of the contest involved in the reforging of tax policy to serve the nation's need for greater economic growth and job creation. This contest is over the revenue gain from economic growth, a gain which amounts to approximately $1 billion for each 1 per cent increase in gross national product. As the latter gets bigger, the former will do likewise.

If this revenue gain is used for increased spending, it cannot be used to release capital by comprehensive reform of tax rates and methods. There is no question where the general public interest lies in this contest. As members of the general public, there is no basic difference in interest between people who are part of the spending blocs and groups and those who are not. The only question is whether the narrow interests in spending on old and new programs will continue to rule supreme over the general public interest.

To the present, the contest has been an unfair one, with the general public as the loser. Congress is organized so as to provide repetitive annual forums for increased or new spending. Often, opposing witnesses are given little attention.

. . . . .

There have not been enough leaders in either political party pointing out that the sum total of this trend is to defeat the general public interest in reform of tax rates and methods.

. . . . .

It has become more difficult to initiate a program of thorough reform because of unwise spending increases, and commitments for greater spending in the future, enacted over the past few years. Consistently, every increase in current spending, and every commitment for future spending, enacted at this time, will make it more difficult to initiate a tax policy for growth next year or later.

All contemporary American experience is that time serves the narrow interests represented by increased spending, and defeats the general public interest in releasing the tax restraints on economic progress.

The best time to act has already passed. The next best time is the present. Further delay will only make thorough reform of tax rates and methods more difficult to accomplish.

. . . . .

We Can't Overwin

In his testimony, Secretary Dillon stated:

As we look back over the past century we see that our record of economic growth has been unmatched anywhere in the world. But of late we have fallen behind. From an historic growth rate of 3 per cent per annum in gross national product (1909–1956, in constant prices), we have fallen to 2 per cent in the latter part of the 50's. In the last five years Western Europe has grown at double or triple our recent rate and Japan has grown even faster. While there is some debate as to the precise annual growth rate of the Soviet economy, CIA estimates that their GNP grew at a rate of 7 per cent in the 50's. Clearly, we must improve our performance. Otherwise, we cannot maintain our national security, we cannot maintain our position of leadership in the eyes of the world and we cannot achieve our national aspirations. The pressing task before us, then, is to restore the vigor of our economy and to return to our traditionally high rate of economic expansion and growth.

To this, we can all say amen, *with one exception.* We should realize that there is no reason why our growth of the future should be limited to our growth of the past. A high income, high standard of living economy has the capacity to save and invest more than a low income, low standard of living economy. The rapid advances of technology, and of the managerial arts, have resulted in an increasing efficiency in the use of capital, i.e., dollars returned in value of production for dollars invested. We should not tolerate the idea that limitation of capital by immoderate rates of tax and unsound tax methods should be allowed to continue to put a ceiling over our growth potential.

We know that we are engaged in a contest with the Russians which we can't "overwin."

We know that we should release the tax restraints on capital accumulation and use in our own interest even if we had never seen a Communist.

America has a rich heritage to live up to, and to improve upon. Here was the first civilization to prove that the free economic system, given its head, would provide a steady increase in the economic well-being of its citizens. Even greater progress can be achieved hereafter—if our economy is freed from an uneconomic tax system.

The greatest and most durable progress is made when men are free to move upward on the income scale, without pulling down those who have led the way.

Men are motivated by self-interest. In a free society, it is the accumulation and interbalance of the various expressions of self-interest which spell progress and greater well-being for all citizens. Businessmen have a self-interest in paying lower taxes but the businessman serves a larger interest when he urges moderate tax rates compatible with the character of a free economy.

More capital would mean the relatively greatest uplift to the weaker sectors of the economy—the people who need jobs, and then better jobs . . . the enterprises which don't get started and can't keep going or growing because of lack of adequate financing . . . the areas of the country in which incomes and living standards are on the lower side of the scale . . . the states which cannot hold their well-trained young people because of greater opportunity elsewhere.

What is good for people is good for America.

Tax Blocks to Progress and Jobs

There are five major tax blocks to progress and job creation:
- Steeply graduated individual tax rates.
- Excessive top rate of corporate tax.
- Unrealistic length of lives and classification of depreciable property.
- Taxing of gains on transfers from one investment to another.
- Destructive rates of estate and gift taxes.

Reform of these rates and methods is the purpose of the legislation, H. R. 2030 and H. R. 2031, sponsored by Representatives A. S. Herlong, Jr., and Howard H. Baker, of this committee, and which has such widespread support throughout the nation.

Reform of Tax Rates and Methods

The manner in which H. R. 2030 and H. R. 2031 would deal with our tax problems at source may be briefly summarized:

PERSONAL INCOME TAX

The Problem

The ruthless graduation chokes off venture capital at its source, discourages risk-taking, smothers incentives, curtails business starts and expansions—all of which prevents job creation. It is the scourge of small business and the man on the ladder. . . . By exacting stiff penalties on hard work and long hours, graduation is in direct conflict with the universally accepted principle of reward for extra effort and achievement. Rates top out at 91%, and hit 50% at $16,000 of taxable income from a start of 20%.

The Solution

Over a 5-year period the rates would be stringently compressed with the top rate reduced to 47% and the other graduated rates lowered in a consistent pattern. . . . Every personal taxpayer would get a minimum reduction of 25%, with the first rate reduced to 15%.

On the principal that no unincorporated business, professional person, or other individual taxpayer should pay a higher tax rate than a corporation, the new top of 47% would be the same as that on corporate income.

CORPORATE INCOME TAX AND DEPRECIATION

The Problem

The excessive top rate severely limits retained earnings, a major source of business expansion and job creation. The tax takes 30% of profits up to $25,000 and 52% above that. More of current business income, incorporated and unincorporated, is subject to excessive tax rates because of continued requirement of depreciation allowances based on length of property lives which are unrealistically long in this period of rapid technological change.

The Solution

Five annual reductions of one-percentage point each would be made, bringing the top rate down to 47% and the first rate to 27%. For depreciation purposes—over the 5-year period—the required time for writing off new property would be reduced by 25%, on the average. On top of the double declining balance and sum-of-the-years digits method established by the 1954 Code revision this would mean a 33% increase in the rate of property write-off. The legislation also substitutes broad property groupings for present detailed classifications, providing greatest depreciation relief where taxpayers are most unfairly treated.

CAPITAL GAINS—ESTATE AND GIFT TAXES

The Problem

The tax on capital gains converts capital into current government spending whenever an asset is sold at a gain. Estate and gift taxes also result in conversion of accumulated capital to government use. Capital taxed away must be replaced by new savings out of current income before there is any net addition to capital supply.

In penalizing the movement of capital, the capital gains tax also discriminates against new, risky, job-creating enterprises.

The effective top rate on long-term capital gains is 25%; the rates on estates go from 3% to 77%; those on gifts from 2.25% to 57.75%.

The Solution

Following the roll-over principle applied on the sale and re-purchase of homes, the tax on long-term capital gains for individuals would be deferred until the taxpayer fails to reinvest the proceeds from the sale of affected property. To qualify for deferral, transfers between investments would have to take place within a taxable year.

The top rate of the estate tax would be

reduced to 47%; the top gift tax rates to 35.25% and all lower rates of both taxes . . . would be reduced in proportion.

Growth and Revenue

Under H. R. 2030 and H. R. 2031, the needed reform of tax rates and methods would be achieved out of the revenue gain from economic growth, with an increasing margin of revenue for other purposes as the economy achieves faster growth.

By enacting H. R. 2030 and 2031, Congress would provide to the public each year the opportunity to weigh the value to the nation of the scheduled tax reductions against competitive spending proposals.

When the economy grows, federal tax revenues grow more rapidly. This is because the base (taxable income) of the personal income tax increases, under present exemptions and deductions, at a rate roughly 50 per cent faster than the increase in total personal income. The personal tax provides more than half of the total revenues. *The addition to federal revenue from all sources is now about $1 billion for each 1 per cent annual increase in gross national product—the total of all economic activity.*

The revenue cost of H. R. 2030 and H. R. 2031 would average about $3.5 billion annually over 5 years. . . . This cost would be offset by the revenue increase from a rate of economic growth of no more than 3.5 per cent annually, as compared with a recent growth rate of somewhat less than 3 per cent under present restrictive tax rates.

. . . . .

Capital for Growth and Jobs!

Representatives Herlong and Baker have estimated the annual tax savings under their legislation at the end of five years as follows:

	(Millions)
Individual tax	$11,000
Corporate tax	2,000
Depreciation	3,000
Capital Gains	500
Estate and Gift	500
	$17,000

The greater part of the total inevitably would become new capital. . . .

. . . . .

Under the intense pressure of wage-cost and domestic and foreign competition, it is safe to say that most of the capital now available to industry and business goes into replacement and modernization of facilities, in order to increase productivity as well as total production.

Much of the tax savings released by H. R. 2030 and 2031 would become new, mobile, venture capital for use in the expansion of production of goods and services and the creation of new jobs—in new and old enterprises.

The Capital-Minded World

The world is capital-minded as never before. Everywhere the demand is for more capital for faster economic progress and advance in living standards. Since World War II, American policy has been to recognize the need for more capital everywhere but at home.

H. R. 2030 and H. R. 2031 would reinstate the United States as the most dynamic economy of the world, providing new opportunity to prove that capital in a free society is more productive of good for more people than under any other system.

In this dangerous age we cannot afford a lesser program.

We cannot afford further delay in enactment of this program.

Americans are not unaccustomed to see their country at the top of the list in economic comparisons. One example appears in income tax rates. Comparisons of income tax burdens from one country to another are exceptionally difficult. The following article deals with top rates of tax on personal and corporation income in several lands. There are also proposals for reform of our system.

60 · *Income Tax Rates: International Comparisons*

FIRST NATIONAL CITY BANK OF NEW YORK

Both political parties, during the course of the election campaign, gave attention to the need for tax reform. The Republican platform emphasized changes to stimulate individual incentive and encourage business investment in order to spur national growth. The Democratic platform similarly urged tax reform to "increase legitimate incentives for growth" and also emphasized the desirability of closing "loopholes" in the tax laws. Senator Kennedy, now President-elect, in a statement issued on October 18, advocated tax reform to "broaden the tax base and lower the extremely high rates that cut down business and personal incentives."

There is widespread agreement that the present federal tax system is urgently in need of reform. The Ways and Means Committee of the House of Representatives, which originates all revenue legislation, has had the question under close study for years, gathering data, soliciting expert opinion, and taking thousands of pages of testimony. During . . . 1959-60, the Committee published 3,685 pages on the subject of broadening the tax base for the purpose of achieving lower income tax rates. Many well thought out proposals . . . have been offered for consideration. Business groups, such as Chambers of Commerce, the National Association of Manufacturers, and the Committee for Economic Development, have dealt with the subject, giving earnest attention to the revenue requirements of an expensive government machinery as well as to the need to lower tax impediments to economic progress. But nothing has been done save piecemeal revision, usually with the effects of making the tax laws even more bewilderingly complicated and increasing the backlog of tax cases awaiting court interpretations.

The federal tax system is open to the following general criticisms:
1. It is too complicated.
2. Taxes are concentrated too much

FIRST NATIONAL CITY BANK OF NEW YORK, *Monthly Letter* (January 1961), a publication of the First National City Bank. Used by permission.

on employment, the development of taxable income, and capital accumulation.

3. The progressive rates ascend to such heights as to defeat their purpose of raising revenue.

4. The income tax base is so narrowed by exemptions, allowances, and deductions that rates must be high.

These points are interrelated. For example, tax laws must be complicated—and exemptions, allowances, and deductions must be numerous—because the economy could not otherwise function under such a stiff rate structure.

Competitive Handicaps

In a day when we are concerned with a balance-of-payments problem, and the ability of American business to compete in world markets, it is vital to consider the disadvantages under which U.S. business operates. One disadvantage, widely publicized, is the element of higher wage costs. A second disadvantage—much less widely understood—is the severity of our taxation on employment, income, and capital accumulation. Individual and corporate income taxes, estate and gift taxes, and employment taxes are relied on for 82 per cent of the total revenues of the Federal Government.

The core of the problem is the income tax rate structure. In fact, our corporate rates are often effectively higher than the nominal rate schedule, because of the inadequacy of capital consumption allowances. Bipartisan support has developed in favor of revision of depreciation rules. President-elect Kennedy, in his October 30 statement addressed to the balance-of-payments situation, said:

> . . . we must stimulate plant modernization programs which are vital both to increased production and to building industrial facilities which can compete successfully with the modern plants of Europe and the Soviet Union. Wherever we are certain that tax revision—including accelerated depreciation—will stimulate investment in new plant and equipment, without damage to our principles of equity, we will proceed with such revision.

In this age of rapid technological change mixed with inflation, growing amounts of capital must be continuously poured into any business that wants to expand. Over the 13 years, 1947–59, the massive sum of $300 billion was expended by U.S. corporations on plant and equipment and a further $168 billion was needed to cover increased working capital requirements.

If we are to speed our rate of progress, and put in place expensive plant and machinery to make efficient use of the growing labor force, even bigger sums will be needed in the years ahead. More flexible depreciation is one way of tackling this problem.

As was documented in our September 1960 *Letter,* governments in Western Europe allow faster write-off of new investment in tax accounting. Some European countries have permitted revaluation of asset values—and hence depreciation allowances—in recognition of the higher replacement costs resulting from inflation. Others grant investment allowances over and above original costs, thus permitting total deductions greater than the historical cost of a machine. More broadly, the acceleration of depreciation by special allowance is common practice. In some cases, these special provisions have permitted deductions in the year of investment approaching half the cost.

It is worthy of comment that even socialist governments have pursued liberal policies in the matter of depreciation charges. This was true, for example, under the former Labor Government of England, which introduced special allowances. Sweden has set some examples of the ultimate in liberality in depreciation allowances.

Corporate Tax Rates

Reform in depreciation allowances which affects only the timing of tax liabilities is no substitute for income tax reform. Our highest rates of tax are on corporate profits paid out in dividends, as the chart shows. The compounding of corporate and personal taxation, for example, gives a 62.6 per cent effective rate of tax for a person in the $4,000 to $6,000 tax bracket, and the top rate goes all the way up to 93.8 per cent. These calculations are after allowance for the limited 4 per cent dividends-received credit. Other nations go much further in crediting to shareholders taxes paid by corporations.

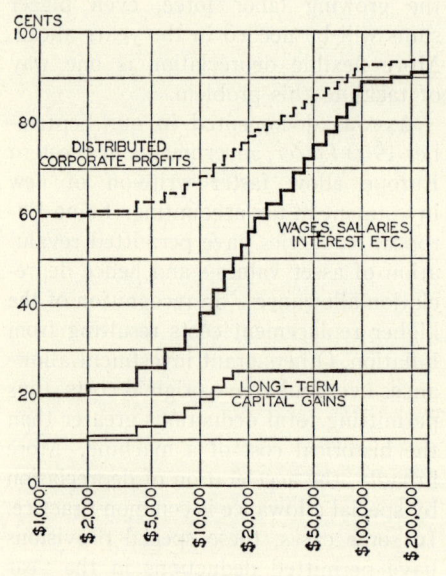

U.S. TAXATION OF ONE ADDITIONAL DOLLAR OF INCOME AS RELATED TO TAX BRACKET OF RECIPIENT
(Logarithmic scale for personal income brackets)

Methods of taxing corporations and their shareholders vary radically from one country to another. It is a pity that greater attention has not been given to foreign tax systems for there is a great deal that we could learn from the experience abroad. So far as corporate net income distributed in dividends is concerned, some degree of double taxation is common. As the table shows, where the tax paid by the corporation is comparatively high, a large part is construed more or less as a tax on the shareholder withheld by the corporation. In other words, while the individual, on his personal income tax return, may be required to report a sum larger than he actually received, he gets a substantial credit for the corporate tax paid.

TAXATION BY CENTRAL GOVERNMENTS OF CORPORATE PROFITS DISTRIBUTED AS DIVIDENDS [1]

	Maximum rate paid and withheld by corporation	Credit allowed individual shareholder
France	62%	24%*†
Netherlands	54.95	15†
United States	52	4
United Kingdom	51.25	38.75‡
Canada	50	20
Belgium	45.31	30†
Germany	42.58§	25†
Sweden	40	0
Australia	40	0
Switzerland	35.60	27†
Japan	35.20	17.5-25
Norway	30	0
Union of South Africa	25	33.33-100
Italy	20	8

* Credit is 8% against taxable income and 16% against personal tax liability. † Deducted at source and credited to individual shareholder. ‡ The individual, if subject to surtax rates on his personal income tax return, must, however, pay the surtax on the gross dividend actually declared rather than the net dividend actually received. § Ignoring the variable effect on the tax base of property tax on net worth.

In light of the more liberal adjustments which other nations make to mitigate double taxation of corporate income distributed as dividends, it is ironical that our 4 per cent dividend received credit has been under sharp

---

[1] [From the April 1961 issue of the same publication. An error in the original is corrected. The later article also deals with taxes imposed by state or provincial and local governments. *Ed.*]

attack as "an unjust loophole." In contrast to our 4 per cent, a 20 per cent credit is given in Canada while dividend recipients in the United Kingdom are credited with the 38¾ per cent standard tax rate already paid by the corporation. A minimum dividend credit of 33⅓ per cent is granted in the Union of South Africa to taxpayers with incomes beyond £2,300 ($6,440), scaled upward to 100 per cent credit for those with incomes below £1,300 ($3,640).

Undistributed Profits

The U.S. Government is a majority shareholder in the profits of every substantial American corporation. On taxation of undistributed corporate profits, the general U.S. rate of 52 per cent applies. This is higher than in any other leading industrial nation, as the accompanying table shows. The top rate in many countries abroad is well below 50 per cent, and, in the case of Belgium and Switzerland, the effective burden is even lighter than the stated rate indicates since taxes paid in one year are deductible from taxable income in the next.

Our 52 per cent general rate of corporate tax is supposed to come down to 47 per cent on June 30, 1961. This was the rate prior to the Korean War but the 52 per cent temporary emergency rate has been extended from year to year ever since. If the Congress wishes to energize the U.S. economy it can do so by letting the corporate rate come down and thus increasing the opportunities of business to absorb rising cost pressures from other directions, shave prices to the benefit of everyone, or enlarge the plowback of profits to help build the equity capital base for a growing economy.

The Personal Income Tax Progression

The most widely condemned feature of our federal tax system is the steepness of our progressive tax rates on personal income. An individual with taxable income of $16,000 finds that the Federal Government becomes an equal partner in any earnings beyond that amount. Beyond $50,000, the tax collector demands three quarters. Beyond $200,000 the taxpayer is called upon to pay 91 per cent. On top of the punishing federal rates, many states (and some cities) levy income taxes which further cut the value of earning additional money.

The progressiveness of personal income taxation can be most simply measured by the top rate. Here, as the table shows, we can lay claim to the highest rate in the world. The United Kingdom, former holder of this distinction, has been gradually shaving its rates and two years ago bequeathed us leadership in this department. [British rates were lowered again in 1961. *Ed.*] (Denmark

MAXIMUM TAX RATES IMPOSED BY CENTRAL GOVERNMENTS ON UNDISTRIBUTED CORPORATE PROFITS

United States	52%
United Kingdom	51.25
Germany	51
France	50.98*
Canada	50†
Netherlands	47
Belgium	40§
Australia	40
Sweden	40
Japan	38‡
Norway	34
Union of South Africa	25‖
Italy	20¶
Switzerland	8§

* Includes tax levied on reserves of accumulated profits. † Inclues 3% tax for old age security contribution. ‡ There is an additional 10% tax on retained profits of closely held corporations. § Taxes paid in previous year are deductible in determining taxable income, thus lowering the effective burden. ‖ An extra 25% tax is levied on profits (beyond certain limits) not distributed. ¶ In addition, there is a 15% tax on profits in excess of 6% of capital and reserves.

has a 110 per cent top rate but this is ineffective since income tax paid in one year is deductible from taxable income in the next.) It is no coincidence that the two countries at the top of the list in income tax progression are laggards in real progress.

MAXIMUM (MARGINAL) RATES OF PERSONAL INCOME TAXATION IMPOSED BY CENTRAL GOVERNMENTS

United States	91%
United Kingdom	88.75
Puerto Rico	82.95
Canada	80
Ireland	77.50
France	73*
Netherlands	72.50
Japan	70
Australia	66.67
Belgium	65
Sweden	65
Greece	63†
Austria	59.34
Italy	58
Mexico	33-55‡
Norway	55
Germany	53
Denmark	52.38§
Union of South Africa	47.50
Switzerland	8

* Includes an 8% complementary tax on nonwage income. † Includes a 3% tax on investment income. ‡ Tax rate applicable depends upon source of income. § Effective maximum, allowing for deductibility of previous year's tax, where income is stable.

Practically every plan for tax reform includes topping off the personal income tax progression at 50, 60, or 70 per cent as opposed to 91 per cent. The revenue loss would not be significant, particularly since the main effect of present rates is to impel the taxpayer to seek income which is tax-exempt, or income on which the tax liability can be deferred or converted into the form of capital gains. The final escape, of course, is emigration of persons and income to friendlier tax climates abroad.

The Congress has attempted to take the curse off excessive rates by adding to the list of special relief provisions. The present situation was described by Mr. Seidman as follows:

What are called "loopholes" are often Congress' way of apologizing for the high tax rates. There are special provisions to afford some taxpayers relief. For example the average taxpayer gets sick-pay tax-free. Married people are taxed more lightly through split income. Executives get a break through stock options, and investors have the cushion of capital gains. In effect, Congress sets high rates and then tears down some of the rate structure by allowing special benefits for some taxpayers. The trouble is that other taxpayers, who feel that they are likewise entitled to relief, then start helping themselves with all sorts of gimmicks.

This short-sighted approach has drawn us into a vicious circle in which excessive rates lead to a shrinking tax base, while the smaller tax base requires preservation of high rates to produce the needed revenue. Yet, we could achieve our revenue objectives at more reasonable rates if we broadened out the base. Chairman Wilbur D. Mills of the House Ways and Means Committee has calculated that:

If all the exceptional provisions now in the law were eliminated, if a uniform tax base were provided, while maintaining the present system of personal exemptions, we could collect the same revenue we now get from the individual income tax with a rate schedule in which the first bracket was nine per cent and the top bracket was 41 per cent.

Unless this self-defeating circle is broken through tax rate reform, further erosion of the tax base must be expected.

Overdose of Progressivism

When the Constitution was amended in 1913 to permit income taxation no limit was set on tax rates. The initial top rate of tax was set at 7 per cent and the idea was ridiculed that "confiscatory" rates like 25 or 50 per cent might at some time be adopted. Nevertheless, we had rates as high as 77 per cent adopted in World War I and again as high as 94 per cent during World War II. But it is fair to say that confiscatory rates like these were never designed to be kept outside war emergencies. So far as people exposed substantial income to taxation at such rates, it was out of a spirit of patriotism.

Failures of the American economy to function more effectively can be attributed to an overdose of the "heavy progressive or graduated income tax" that Karl Marx in the Communist Manifesto suggested as a means of making "despotic inroads on the rights of property, and on the conditions of bourgeois production." For all his errors, Marx assessed correctly what this kind of taxation could do to a capitalistic country.

Meanwhile, Khrushchev's Russia plans to do away with income taxation entirely.

Our type of society is seriously vulnerable to taxation on capital because we rely on private capital formation for progress. The steeply progressive personal income tax is a levy on capital accumulation. We also have heavy taxes on accumulated capital—gift and inheritance taxes—which require people to sell capital assets to raise money which government proceeds to spend. Unlike most other countries we also tax capital gains which are not income at all in the economic sense of the word.

A clear starting point for tax reform in the coming session of Congress is a scaling down of excessive rates which lead to pressures for special relief. If this is done boldly, consistent with revenue requirements, everyone can raise his estimate of the future of the U.S. economy.

What is the justification for taking, through taxation, a larger percentage of a bigger than a smaller income or inheritance? Professor Taussig gives his answer.

61 · *Progressive Taxation: A Justification*

F. W. TAUSSIG

The courageous advocates of progression base their views precisely on the ground that the existing social order is not perfect and that taxation should be one of the instruments for amending it. Even though it be an open question whether all inequality in wealth and income be unjust, such great degrees of inequality as the modern world shows are regarded as not consonant with canons of justice. Very rich persons should be called to pay taxes not only in proportion to their incomes but more than in proportion. This proposal has been called "socialistic," and it is, if all measures looking to mitigation of inequality be so called. Those who hold it place progressive taxation in the same class with free education, factory legislation, regulation of monopolies, extension of government management,—measures all of which are based on a desire to improve the social order in the direction of less inequality. The extent to which they are willing to go with progression no doubt depends on the degree of their fervor for social reform in general; nor are they themselves able to give a precise answer to the question often asked, how far is progression to go? Their opponents have urged, to use a much-quoted phrase of McCulloch's, that when once you diverge from the rule of proportion you are at sea without rudder or compass. The same difficulty might be urged against all sorts of movements for reform. Few except the rigid and extreme socialists have clear notions as to their ultimate goal. It suffices for the average man to know in what direction he is moving. Most unsophisticated persons in the advanced countries of modern times, though they have very hazy ideas about taxation and socialism and economics in general, will instinctively declare it "right" that the rich should contribute to the public burdens, as compared with the poor, not only in proportion to their incomes, but more than in proportion. In so saying, they show that influence of the spirit of the time from which none of us can escape.

F. W. TAUSSIG, *Principles of Economics*, 4th ed. (New York: The Macmillan Company, 1939), pp. 539–540. Used by permission.

The following passage presents the views of another professional economist, one who condemns progressive taxation.

A Criticism

HARLEY L. LUTZ

Progression in taxation means that method of adjusting the tax rates whereby the rate becomes greater as the size of the tax base increases. Its principal use in this country is for the taxation of incomes and estates. As applied in the case of the income tax, it means the taxation of the first installment or section of an income at a certain rate, taxation of the second section of the income at a higher rate, of the third section at a still higher rate, and so on. . . .

The advocates of progressive taxation fall into two major groups. One group consists of those who see in this method of taxation a means of providing public revenue according to some standard which they regard as equitable. In the other group are those who regard it as an excellent device for the destruction of the private enterprise system and the inauguration of a socialist regime. Unfortunately, the effects of progressive taxation are not dependent upon, nor determined by, the motives of those who believe in its use. In consequence, the first group becomes, unwittingly, a collaborator with the second group, although its members would indignantly deny any affiliation or sympathy of purpose.

Those who regard progressive taxation as a proper and suitable method of determining the respective contributions of the citizens toward the support of government usually base their case upon the ability-to-pay doctrine. They interpret this doctrine to mean that the person who has a large income is better able to pay tax than the person who has a small income. This ability, it is assumed, increases faster than the size of the income; hence it is concluded that the tax rate must likewise increase with the size of the income in order to keep pace with the growth in ability as income expands.

The difficulty with this theory is that there is no standard by which to distinguish a good progressive tax rate scale from a bad one. That is, there is no way of deciding upon the particular scale of rates and the particular size of income brackets to which these rates apply, in order to achieve the most equitable relation of tax burden to ability. It is impossible to ascertain just how much faster ability increases than income, and there can be no certainty whatever that the relation between ability and income is the same in the case of all individuals or in the case of different kinds of income. On the contrary, it is extremely likely that the ability-income ratio varies greatly among indi-

---

HARLEY L. LUTZ, *Guideposts to a Free Economy* (New York: McGraw-Hill Book Company, Inc., 1945), Ch. 9. Used by permission.

viduals having the same income, and that it varies greatly among different kinds of income.

. . . . .

Since there is no standard whereby a choice can be made among progressive rate scales, it follows that one scale is just as good as any other as an application of the principle. A progression that rises to a tax rate of 100 per cent on all income in excess of $25,000, or even in excess of $5,000, is quite as defensible in terms of the vague and half-baked theory on which the entire system rests as one that imposes a top rate of 5 per cent on all income in excess of $1,000,000.

Advocates of progression as a revenue device will contest the preceding statement on two grounds. First, it will be said that the revenue needs should determine the precise scale used and that a perfect adjustment to ability at all times is not necessary. On the hypothesis that some progression is always better than none, this view would provide for the tax to approach as near to some highly theoretical standard of ability as the budget requirements might demand. Presumably also, it would allow for relaxation of the tax rate scale in periods of budgetary surplus. That is, the scale actually used at any time would be entirely a matter of revenue expediency.

But, there is a long-range view as well as a short-range view of the revenue aspect. Temporarily, it is always possible to squeeze a little more revenue out of the larger incomes, a process limited only by the amount to be realized through their complete confiscation. . . . In the long run, an excessive progression of tax rates is quite capable of destroying the revenue productivity of any tax base to which it is applied.

Second, it will be said that the progressive rate scale should always be reasonable. But, what is a reasonable progression? To those who have less than $5,000, it may seem entirely reasonable that no one should be permitted to have more than that amount after taxes.

The obvious fact is that, viewed simply as a revenue device, progressive taxation is an extremely dangerous fiscal instrument for the reason that there are no natural or self-operative checks to guard against abuse. The American experience reveals that there is no degree of progression beyond which those not affected by the progressive rates would be moved to protest on the general ground of inequity. There is no convincing basis for such protest under any scale of rates, since no one knows anything about the relation of so-called ability to income. The only logical stopping place, according to the current ability theory, is at the complete equalization of incomes by a confiscation of all incomes in excess of the lowest amount received by any one. As long as any inequality of income remains, it can be as plausibly argued that these larger incomes, however small their absolute amount, indicate some excess of ability to be levied upon, as it can be that existing inequalities of income indicate differences in ability.

. . . . .

Because there is no sure definition of the limits to progression, no firm basis of its "reasonable" use, no protection against its unconscionable abuse, those who uphold the system as a revenue device are playing into the hands of the group that would use progressive taxation as the means of destroying private capitalism and ushering in the collectivist state. Here, at any rate, is a clear case for tax progression, the only clear case for it that can be made. In this view, the more drastic the tax rate scale, the more quickly and certainly will the desired result be accomplished.

For progressive taxation can and will produce these results, and the arguments of those who wish to apply it to this end make far better sense than do those used by the Pollyanna tax theorists who seem to believe that it is possible to eat the seed corn and also, at the same time, to plant it.

The destructive effects of severe progressive taxation should be apparent to all who are capable of even a slight understanding of the nature and the operation of the present economic system. It is of little avail to plead that this method of taxation should never be carried to such an extreme, for experience has demonstrated that it inevitably will be so extended, since those who presumably benefit vastly outnumber those who are most affected by it. As one writer has put it, the popularity of progressive taxation is traceable in no small part to the opportunity that it affords to place added burdens on the group which, while economically strong, is often politically weak.[1]

In order to assure the requisite flow of funds into the creation of new capital and the maintenance of existing capital, it is necessary that those who successfully weather the risks involved should be permitted to keep such profits as are received as a result of that success.

Progressive taxation can be, and usually is, pushed to a point at which these conditions for the maintenance of private enterprise in a vigorous and flourishing condition can no longer be met. The virtual confiscation of all income above a moderate level robs the capital fund of its principal source of supply, and at the same time it destroys the incentive to take the risks of new or hazardous investment. Having thus paralyzed the process of private saving, investment, and initiative, it becomes an easy matter for the government to assume, first, control, then ownership and direction of the economic factors of production. The most elementary principle of aggression in any sphere is to soften the opponent before engaging him in conflict. Progressive taxation is the most effective possible way of softening the enterprise system before moving in to take it over into a collective regime.

At this point a curious lapse in logic suffered by the ability theorists is of definite value to the collectivist cause. It is frequently said, in justification of steep progression, that the person with a large income will still have enough left, after paying the tax, to provide for his personal needs. Hence, the conclusion that even very heavy tax progression can involve neither injustice nor harm to the economic system.

If it were true that there is no other important use for income than to minister to the personal gratification of its recipient, then the case for government expropriation of it would be on better ground. But, there is another highly important use for income in the support and enlargement of the capital fund. This use is so vital to the maintenance of production and to the advance of the general well-being as to be superior to any use that government is likely to make, in ordinary times, of the funds so taken. Public expenditure of the proceeds of progressive taxation is for ordinary current operating purposes, and the proportion of the tax revenues spent to create self-sustaining public enterprises is negligible. Private investment of these funds adds to the nation's productive capacity. The effects of the public current-purpose spending quickly wear off, while the effects of private-investment spending endure while the capital goods thereby provided remain in use.

---

[1] R. M. Haig, article on "Taxation" in *Encyclopedia of the Social Sciences* (1934), XIV, 539–540.

. . . . .

. . . . There is excellent ground for believing that with a restoration of the incentives that motivate and energize the private enterprise system, jobs can and will be provided for all who are willing and able to work. True, this will mean that some will have larger incomes than others, but the most important thing is that everyone will have more income, and will be able to enjoy a higher standard of living in terms of real income, than will be possible while enterprise languishes in the straitjacket of repressive and burdensome taxation. It is impossible to conceive of a program that would more effectively vitalize and energize the productive forces in this country than the announcement of a firm and definite public policy of eliminating the excesses and abuses of progressive taxation. . . .

It would seem a fair and reasonable statement that the remarkable advance of the American scale of living in the past generation has been made possible by the rise of a long list of large industries—concerns large enough to develop and apply the methods of mass production. The history of American business makes it clear that the typical and characteristic way of creating large business units is by the "plowing back" of earnings, the reinvestment of profits. It is true that in this process some persons may eventually amass substantial, even large, fortunes; but the continual growth of a business through the process of reinvestment of earnings has resulted, over and over again, in a large volume of employment, a huge total of wages, and a steadily lower price for some article that contributes to the comfort, the pleasure, and the well-being of millions of consumers.

One way to visualize the paralyzing and destructive effects of progressive taxation is to assume that this kind of tax system, even with rates such as were levied in 1938 and 1939 (i.e., prior to the war tax acts), had been in effect since 1900. Then, on the basis of this assumption, one should ask, How many automobiles would this country have today and at what price would they sell?

In this writer's opinion, the answer is clear. There would be only a few, and the price would be high. Certainly, there could have been no such growth and development of the automobile industry as actually did occur. The record of Henry Ford should provide convincing proof. The manner of the growth of the Ford Motor Company is well known. It was created entirely by "plowing back" the earnings. A tax system that would have taken a large part of these earnings for the current and, possibly, the foolish expenditure purposes of government since 1900 would have effectively stunted the growth of this company. Such a result would have had the approval of those who set the equalization of wealth and income above every other consideration, but it would have been a great tragedy for the millions who have had their living standards expanded by the incomes created by Henry Ford and by the pleasure and convenience of the sturdy, inexpensive, highly practical automobile that this great pioneer in a great industry was able to produce.

The world of the future has many other potential products that can and should be made available for all. While the people are so shortsighted as to retain a tax system that so effectively and completely destroys both the source of the capital funds and the incentive to search out the best and cheapest form of these products as does progressive taxation, they can no more materialize than could the automobile, if Henry Ford had been obliged from the beginning, to give over to the government 88 per cent of all income in excess of $200,000 a year.

The American people face a serious choice here, one that involves their destiny as certainly as any foreign battlefield or postwar peace conference. Concretely and in terms of an historical parallel, it is the choice between the Ford fortune and the Ford automobile. If they should decide that there shall be no more fortunes, they will also thereby decide that there shall be no commodities of mass comfort and enjoyment other than those now known. A few large fortunes would appear to be a small price to pay to gain the full benefit for all the creative and productive capacity that can be stimulated most effectively and most certainly by allowing those who succeed to keep the fruits of their success.

Jonathan Swift

One of the world's great satirists deals with a problem of public finance in an unusual way.

I heard a very warm debate between two professors, about the most commodious and effectual ways and means of raising money without grieving the subject. The first affirmed the justest method would be to lay a certain tax upon vices and folly, and the sum fixed upon every man, to be rated after the fairest manner by a jury of his neighbors. The second was of an opinion directly contrary, to tax those qualities of body and mind for which men chiefly value themselves, the rate to be more or less according to the degrees of excelling, the decision whereof should be left entirely to their own breast. The highest tax was upon men who are the greatest favorites of the other sex, and the assessments according to the number and natures of the favors they received; for which they are allowed to be their own vouchers. Wit, valor, and politeness, were likewise proposed to be largely taxed, and collected in the same manner, by every person's giving his own word for the quantum of what he possessed. But as to honor, justice, wisdom, and learning, they should not be taxed at all, because they are qualifications of so singular a kind, that no man will either allow them in his neighbor, or value them in himself.

The women were proposed to be taxed according to their beauty and skill in dressing, wherein, they had the same privilege with the men, to be determined by their own judgment. But constancy, chastity, good sense, and good nature were not rated, because they would not bear the charge of collecting.

. . . . .

JONATHAN SWIFT, from *Gulliver's Travels*, "Voyage to Laputa," Part III, Chap. VI.

The following statement summarizes a striking approach to public finance.

62 · Functional Finance

ABBA P. LERNER

The purpose of taxation is never to raise money but to leave less in the hands of the taxpayer.

The second great prejudice shows itself in the inability to see that taxation should never be imposed merely as a means of raising money for the government on the grounds that the government needs the money. The government can raise all the money it needs by printing it if the raising of the money is the only consideration.

This device is illegal for the private citizen and so it is usually regarded as somehow illegitimate for the government, by the same identification of the government with a private business that makes the government's debt look dangerous and which treats the government's revenue from taxes as equivalent to business earnings and therefore the only really proper source of money for the government to spend. Of course, there are definite limits to the extent to which a government should pay out money (or indeed do anything whatever), but these limits must be defined in terms of the actual effects on the well-being of society and not derived from cloudy analogies with what is prudent and legal for a businessman.

The rational procedure is to judge all actions only by their effect and not by any vague notions of their propriety or impropriety. *"By their fruits ye shall know them."* The effects of a tax are twofold. It increases the money in the hands of the government and, by decreasing the money left in the taxpayer's hands, it makes him spend less. The first effect is unimportant for the government, however important it could be to any citizen to be able to acquire money in this way, because the government can much more easily get the money it wants to have by printing it, without any fear of the police. The important effect is the second, and the question of taxing or not taxing should be governed entirely by whether this effect on spending by the individual taxpayer is desired or not. The effect, which is not easily obtained in any other way, is the basis on which a rational government uses the instrument of taxation. It will tax individuals, or a certain class of individuals, when it believes it to be socially desirable that they should not be so rich or should not spend so much. It will tax particular forms of spending (*i.e.*, on whiskey) as a means of decreasing them. It will tax more generally as a means of cutting down total spending when this is necessary to prevent excessive total demand and inflation. Taxation is important *not* as a means of raising money but as a means of cutting down private spending.

ABBA P. LERNER, *The Economics of Control* (New York: The Macmillan Company, 1944), pp. 307–308. Used by permission.

An extensive study of the country's financial system was completed in 1961, the first of such scope in half a century. A commission of distinguished citizens from banking, labor, business, agriculture, and universities, aided by a staff of specialists, devoted more than two years to the project. The work was financed by three private foundations. Many government agencies, however, supplied information. The final report represents much thought, and doubtless much compromise. It deals with all major aspects of our system of money and credit. The selection here presents only highlights of one of the more important topics. Several dissents by Commission members to statements included here have been omitted.

63 · Fiscal Policy for Economic Stabilization

COMMISSION ON MONEY
AND CREDIT

The contribution which fiscal policy can make toward the achievement of the three major national economic goals [1] is examined in this chapter. In its most general sense, fiscal policy deals with the effects of changes in the level of government receipts and expenditures and with the effects of changes in the budget deficit or surplus on economic activity. . . .

The role of fiscal policy in economic stabilization is far better understood now than it was during the depression of the thirties, and it is now likely that the fiscal adjustments undertaken in major inflations or depressions will be appropriate in direction though perhaps not in magnitude. However, the challenge of the future is to improve the use of fiscal measures to level out lesser fluctuations of prices, output, and employment, and to promote growth.

The federal budget has served as a useful stabilizing force in the economy. In part this force is exerted through automatic changes in tax receipts and transfer payments as incomes rise and fall. In part it is the result of deliberate changes in tax and expenditure programs. The combination of automatic and discretionary budget forces has generated surpluses in prosperity and deficits in recession. The surpluses were helpful in restraining inflation and the deficits in cushioning recession and aid-

---

[1] [The three goals which the Commission endorses in an earlier chapter are reasonable price stability, low levels of unemployment, and economic growth. The discussion of the relation of fiscal policy to economic growth is not included here because of space limitations. *Ed.*]

COMMISSION ON MONEY AND CREDIT, *Money and Credit: Their Influence on Jobs, Prices, and Growth* (Englewood Cliffs, N.J.: Prentice-Hall, Inc., 1961). Reprinted by permission.

ing recovery. But neither the size nor the timing of fiscal policy changes has been appropriate to the movement of the business cycle. The Commission therefore examined what changes could be made in fiscal policy to further improve this record.

During the postwar period most changes in taxes and in transfer payments, such as unemployment compensation or other social security payments, were not undertaken by themselves for stabilization reasons. Except during the early part of the Korean War, any stabilizing increases in tax rates were offset by equal or greater increases in government expenditures, and tax rate decreases were offset by declines in expenditures. Also with the same exception, discretionary changes in tax or transfer rates, either taken or recommended, were tardy and inadequate. And high tax rates were generally retained during recessions.

Wide fluctuations in the level of government purchases have been a major factor in the fluctuations in economic activity in the postwar period. Some were stabilizing and some disrupting. Usually even the stabilizing changes could be called discretionary in only the loosest sense, for they were dictated by major shifts in social priorities. . . .

An examination of the postwar record reveals that discretionary fiscal policy, correctly timed, was hardly ever used independently as a stabilizer. Thus automatic fiscal stabilizers had to shoulder the major share of the stabilization burden appropriate for fiscal measures, and they were very helpful.

Automatic Stabilizers

With a given tax and expenditure structure, changes in total output and income result in automatic changes in tax yields and in certain outlays, the first changing in the same direction as income and the latter in the opposite direction. For example, as personal incomes fall, the yield of the personal income tax falls along with them, while payments for unemployment compensation rise. Consequently, the absolute decline in income available for personal spending is less than the absolute decline in national income. As personal incomes increase, tax yields rise, and unemployment compensation payments decline. These and other similar cushioning effects on fluctuations in the amount of income available to the private sector of the economy occur without legislative or administrative changes in tax and expenditure programs and are thus called *automatic stabilizers*.

The higher the tax rates, the more progressive the rate structure, and the more sensitive the tax base to swings in the cycle, the more will changing tax yields absorb variations in national income, and the smaller will be the remaining change in income available for private spending. The more closely unemployment compensation payments approximate the wage the employee loses, the less will unemployment reduce disposable income. But because tax rates are much less than 100 percent at the margin, and because unemployment compensation is less than the lost wages, changes in national income are only partially offset by the tax and transfer-payment changes. Nevertheless automatic fiscal stabilizers do cushion the fall in income. As a result, private expenditures fall less than they would otherwise. Thus, automatic stabilizers aid recovery by reducing the cumulative deterioration in economic outlook that would otherwise take place and facilitate the forces of recovery contributing to an early upswing. Although the built-in stabilizers are very useful when the economy contracts, they are a mixed blessing when it expands. When business conditions recover from a recession, the federal tax system automatically cuts the growth in private spendable incomes, and hence the expansion tends to proceed more slowly. If the recovery is strong, the automatic stabilizers provide an important and desirable curb to the inflationary pressures that may ensue.

The very size of government expenditures and tax receipts relative to gross national product today, compared with the period before the thirties, greatly increases the potential cushioning effect of the automatic stabilizers. Whatever the merits or demerits of large government expenditures and tax receipts may be on other grounds, it is clear that the larger they are in relation to the total level of economic activity, the stronger is the impact of the automatic stabilizers. . . .

The effectiveness of the automatic stabilizers does not, however, depend exclusively on the relative size of government expenditures and the level of tax rates. It also depends on the degree to which the tax base (the particular incomes or expenditures subject to tax) fluctuates with changes in the national income and on how tax yields vary with changes in the tax base. Broadly speaking, corporate income taxes are most sensitive to changes in national income because of the great sensitivity of corporate profits before taxes (the tax base) to changes in national income. The remaining major taxes can be ranked in order of sensitivity as follows: the personal income tax; sales and excise taxes (with the degree of their sensitivity depending on the commodity or service taxed and on whether the tax is specific or *ad valorem* in nature); payroll taxes; and, finally, the property tax.

The major portion of federal revenues is derived from the corporation and personal income taxes, both of which (especially the former) are highly sensitive to change in national income. In contrast, local tax receipts, primarily from property taxes, vary little with income. State governments have a wide variety of revenue sources, a large proportion representing general sales taxes or sales and excise taxes levied on particular commodities or services. State tax revenues are therefore much less sensitive to changes in national income than are federal revenues but more so than local revenues.

. . . . .

In this eventuality the strength of the automatic stabilizers could be partially maintained by modifications which would permit a substitution of the more flexible components of the federal revenue system for the less flexible components of the state and local systems. One means would be to expand the use of federal grants to state and local governments, thereby enabling taxes to be collected at the federal level and spent at the state and local level.

It is impossible to estimate precisely the effectiveness of existing automatic stabilizers. The best available evidence indicates that during the postwar period the built-in flexibility of the federal budget offset between one-third to two-fifths of the fall (or increase) in the gross national product. This is a sizable fraction, far greater than that prevailing before World War II. Recent experience with recurrent and moderately severe recessions raises the question whether the automatic stabilizers can and should be strengthened to play a greater role in reducing the amplitude of cyclical fluctuations.

The discussion, therefore, turns next to possible means of increasing the strength of the automatic stabilizers at given over-all tax and expenditure levels. . . .

CHANGES IN THE TAX STRUCTURE. The Commission examined a variety of changes in the existing tax structure aimed at increasing its strength as an automatic stabilizer and came to the conclusion that no changes in the tax structure that would result in substantial gains for automatic stabilization are feasible.

. . . . .

REVISION OF UNEMPLOYMENT INSURANCE. Changing the present structure of unemployment compensation offers one of the more promising approaches to a strengthening of the existing automatic stabilizers, though once again only moderate improvements can be hoped for by action in this area. A primary reason for the attractiveness of a strong system of unemployment compensation as an automatic stabilizer is that such payments are related directly to employment rather than to income. Among the measures that may be taken to increase the countercyclical action of the system, the most important is an increase in the benefit level. The upper limit of benefits is set by the need to maintain adequate work incentives, but there is wide agreement that the present level is too low because the ratio of benefit payments to current wage rates has declined in recent years. An increase in benefit levels would thus be consistent with stabilization objectives and with social policy. However, the basic principle that insurance benefits should be materially less than the net money earned at full employment must be observed. Next, the practice of lengthening eligibility periods during the recession phase of the cycle should be regularized and might be rendered automatic. If this is done, however, the regulations should be reviewed and tightened to prevent abuses.

. . . . .

FORMULA FLEXIBILITY. The limited possibilities of strengthening the automatic stabilizers of the conventional type led the Commission to explore the possibility of strengthening automatic stabilization through the device of formula flexibility. The introduction of some type of formula flexibility is probably the only feasible automatic method of substantially strengthening the built-in stabilizers. Indeed, if the principle of formula flexibility were adopted, the automatic stabilizers could be strengthened to almost any desired degree.

Formula flexibility implies provision for automatic changes in the level of certain tax rates whenever prescribed economic indicators change by specified amounts. If such flexibility were to be introduced, the most attractive possibility would be to provide that the first-bracket rate of the personal income tax should be reduced by a specified number of percentage points whenever these economic indicators suggested deficient demand, and conversely that the tax rate would automatically be raised to its old level when the indicators revealed the restoration of adequate demand. In a similar fashion the first-bracket rate of the personal income tax could be increased by a specified number of percentage points whenever the indicators suggested excess demands; conversely, the tax rate would be lowered automatically to its original level as excess demand was eliminated.

. . . . .

If a formula approach is taken, it is of critical importance that the tax adjustment should be as simple and straightforward as possible. For this reason a change in the first-bracket tax rate is to be preferred to alternatives such as an across-the-board cut in rates or changes in exemptions.

The formula approach has much to recommend it. It would ensure that changes in tax rates, by their very nature, would work both ways. If rates were cut in a recession because of the formula adopted, the same formula arrangement would ensure that they would be raised again in the upswing. Thus, the formula approach would avoid any bias that might result from discretionary action. In making discretionary changes, the decision-making authority, either legislative or executive, might well be subject to heavier pressure to reduce tax rates in recession than to raise them back to normal during the subsequent recovery and to above normal in booms.

. . . . .

A possible disadvantage of the approach is its unconventional nature, which may retard ready acceptance. Another criticism might be that it would be difficult to choose appropriate indexes to which changes in tax rates should be related. These considerations carry weight, but they are hardly decisive. More important is the question of whether greatly increased reliance upon automatic stabilizers is desirable. If the built-in effect is too strong, it may overshoot the mark and become destabilizing. Moreover, the nature of successive business cycles may well differ, and a formula suited to deal with one particular situation may not be suited to deal with another. Finally, formula flexibility can deal with changes in aggregate demand only, and cannot deal with changes in employment and the price level due to structural factors. For these reasons, destabilizing effects may arise if reliance on built-in stabilizers is carried too far, and the need for discretionary action is neglected.

. . . . .

Discretionary Fiscal Measures

Even if the automatic stabilizers can be improved, discretionary fiscal measures will remain an important instrument of stabilization policy. Consequently, the advantages and disadvantages of possible discretionary actions must be considered. Two major objections are commonly raised against discretionary fiscal measures.

The first is that economic forecasts are necessarily so inaccurate that there is always the possibility that discretionary action taken on the basis of such forecasts may do more harm than good. However this objection is applicable to all discretionary stabilization policies, monetary or fiscal. It is a serious objection, for much is yet to be learned before we can assess the economic outlook as well as we need to. Nevertheless, the Commission is convinced that judicious use of discretionary measures, including fiscal policy, cannot be dispensed with.

Secondly, it is frequently alleged that the time required by Congress to enact discretionary measures and by the executive to put them into effect may rule them out. . . .

The alleged inability of Congress to act promptly is usually based on the fact that the passage of major revenue legislation has been typically an extended process. This was true in the case of the Revenue Act of 1942, the Revenue Act of 1951, and the Internal Revenue Code of 1954, all of which took the major part of a year to enact into final form. These measures, however, dealt with complicated long-run structural reforms rather than with short-run problems of economic stabilization. In certain instances, when emergency conditions dictated a need for speed, even complicated reforms were put through in a shorter time. For example, the Revenue Act of 1950 was halted halfway through its passage as a tax reform measure and sped to enactment as a substantial tax increase in only 60 days. The Excess Profits Tax of 1950 was passed within 49 days of a special presidential message despite enormous complexities.

Of more relevance as a measure of congressional legislative speed are the simple tax extension measures, such as those in the postwar period covering the excise and corporate income tax rates. They have generally consumed less than a month's time from the initial action by the Ways and Means Committee. . . .

In sum, when Congress has had straightforward changes before it which it wished to enact, ways have been found to accelerate the legislative process. Fear that action will be delayed by legislative lags, therefore, provides no valid excuse for executive failure to recommend action. These precedents indicate that there is no technical or institutional barrier to a discretionary fiscal policy designed to promote economic stabilization and growth *provided* that the need for such policy is recognized by Congress and the executive and that appropriate discretionary measures are proposed. This conclusion, however, rests on the acceptance of the following basic proposition.

Discretionary fiscal policy requires speed of decision and effect and can only be successful if temporary and reversible fiscal changes for stabilization purposes are dissociated from permanent and structural changes. Techniques should be developed by which taxation and expenditure policies can be applied more flexibly, and the first step in this direction lies in a sharp demarcation between short-run cyclical changes and long-run structural changes.

. . . . .

TAX POLICY CHANGES. What component of private demand should bear the brunt of fiscal adjustments to promote short-run stability? Should it be consumption or investment, and what kind of expenditures within these broad groups? It would be helpful if investment outlays could be pushed up in recessions and pulled down in booms, since they are the primary short-run destabilizer. Such a result would provide a more steady level of capital formation and more sustainable rate of growth. Yet this sector is probably more difficult to affect than any other. Consequently, it would appear that at present the best policy is to consider both investment and consumption as potential candidates for stabilization adjustments.

To be able to alter taxes or transfers for this purpose, they must meet certain criteria. Changes must be easy to make without creating uncertainty in the administration of, and compliance with, the tax law. They must be promptly effective and easily reversible. And they must not create uncertainty in business output, planning, and efficiency.

The personal income tax ranks high in satisfying these criteria, with cyclical varying of the starting rate preferable to varying personal exemptions. The tax is not a major factor in business planning; it is broadly based; and the rate can be easily varied and changes can take effect promptly through withholding. Variation in personal exemptions might create uncertainty from year to year for many taxpayers about whether they needed to file.

Excise taxes can be easily raised or lowered, but their initial effect on demand is perverse. Advance notice of changes must be given. Therefore, if rates are to be raised because demand is excessive, taxpayers are put on notice that their purchases will shortly cost them more. This encourages them to speed up purchases and increases demand. Similarly, if demand is deficient, a coming reduction in excise tax rates can lead to the postponement of purchases, further weakening demand. This perverse effect on demand would not be significant for all excises; for example, those on some of the nondurable goods and services—gasoline, admissions, telephone service. But for a large group of other taxed commodities, such as liquor, tobacco, and the durable goods, it might be substantial. . . .

Temporary changes in social security contributions have some of the same advantages as changes in the starting rate of the personal income tax, but the employer contribution is a cost item and changes in it may disturb costs and prices. Furthermore, countercyclical variation in contributions may not be readily compatible with the nature of the old age insurance system; the government tries to maintain a schedule of contribution rates that matches actuarial estimates of costs in the long run. . . .

Countercyclical adjustments in the corporation income tax rate, the remaining important tax to be considered, would almost surely create the most uncertainty for business. This holds for changes in the tax rate, as well as for changes in depreciation allowances or in investment credits.

As in the proposal for formula flexibility, the most appropriate choice for short-run discretionary changes in taxes is the first-bracket rate of the personal income tax. They are least likely to open up controversial questions of income tax structure. The legislative and administrative problems in making such changes would be relatively simple. No uncertainty would be encountered in complying with such changes. They could be made effective with very short notice to taxpayers through the withholding mechanism. They would be easily reversible. They would have a minimum of adverse side-effects such as causing uncertainty in business planning or speculation in commodities. Moreover, small changes in the tax rate would provide large amounts of additional spendable funds to consumers. A 1 percentage point reduction in the tax rate would provide consumers with additional disposable income at an annual rate of well over $1 billion.

If this proposal were enacted, the 20 percent rate applicable to all taxpayers on their first $2,000 of income could be increased or reduced, but all other bracket rates would remain unchanged. . . .

If this rate reduction were expected to continue in effect for some time, the best evidence indicates that consumer expenditures would rise by a very large fraction of the increase in disposable income, probably by upwards of 80 cents on the dollar within a year of the date of tax reduction. In fact, more than half this response would probably occur in the first quarter following the tax reduction. . . .

. . . . .

A change of this sort is also flexible and reversible. Withholding changes can be made promptly, regardless of their size. Congress and the administration have had experience with intra-year changes in withholding rates, for example in 1948, 1950, and 1951. The technique is readily and easily applicable. Declarations of estimated tax can also be promptly modified in line with the new tax liabilities.

The Commission therefore concludes that when discretionary tax adjustments are used to promote short-run economic stabilization, they should consist of variations in the first-bracket rate of personal income tax.

. . . . .

The main point to emphasize here is that short-run stabilization adjustments are not the place to make basic changes in the tax structure. The permanent rate structure should be governed by such considerations as tax equity, investment incentives, and economic growth. Full consideration of all these factors is not really relevant to this section on short-run stabilization policy.

Because of the vicissitudes attending the consideration of ordinary legislation, the President's responsibilities for prompt and decisive action under the Employment Act . . . warrant a limited delegation of power to initiate a tax rate change as an instrument of countercyclical fiscal policy. Any proposal to vest the President with stand-by power to alter tax rates for any reason under any circumstances runs counter to the long-established tradition, jealously guarded, that gives the House Ways and Means Committee exclusive jurisdiction to originate revenue measures. . . .

The delegation should specify the particular rate to be changed and limit the maximum amount and duration of the changes, as well as the conditions under which it is to be made. Finally, the delegation should be accompanied by an opportunity for a congressional veto of its application in particular cases, along lines currently employed when executive reorganization plans are authorized. . . .

EXPENDITURE CHANGES. Discretionary expenditure policy can also be used to promote economic stabilization, though its potential is more limited than that of discretionary tax policy. The opportunities for expenditure variations for stabilization purposes may be greater for state and local governments than for the federal government. Limitations on the use of expenditure policy are imposed by two considerations. Only a portion of expenditure programs are sufficiently flexible to permit countercyclical timing, especially where the phases of the cycle are relatively short and not easily recognizable at an early stage. Beyond this, care must be taken so that countercyclical use of expenditure programs does not interfere with their long-run objectives and efficiency.

The immediate difficulties of countercyclical timing are technological as well as well as administrative. Certain projects, once started, must be carried through even if the projects extend into the high-employment phase. For example, buildings, once started, must be completed. Not all projects, however, are in this category. Some, such as highway programs, can be carried out in steps. Much the same division governs the administrative processes. Although it takes considerable time from the initial planning of a project, through the placing of orders, to the beginning of actual construction, this process may be speeded up if advance preparations have been made. Also some projects already authorized and scheduled for later starts can be accelerated. Those projects already under way can be speeded up or retarded.

A more basic objection to expenditure variation as a vehicle for short-run stabilization is the view that the government should shape programs according to the economy's long-run requirements for public services independent of short-run stabilization considerations. Moreover, some believe that the use of changes in expenditures for short-run stabilization will result in an undesirable increase in the level of government purchases of goods and services because programs instituted in recessions will not be stopped in prosperity.

Appraisal of this position cannot be well documented, because there has been little or no postwar alteration of expenditures for short-run stabilization. Further study of this purported inflexibility is urgently needed. . . .

For countercyclical decisions, projects and programs should be ranked both according to the social priority of the expenditures and the length of time necessary to complete the project, as well as according to its time pattern. The social priority test ensures that only the most useful expenditures will be made; it would be foolish to undertake low-priority expenditures simply to stimulate the economy when the same result can be achieved through tax reductions or other means. Subject to the social priority test, the most desirable expenditures from the standpoint of combating a recession are those in which a high ratio of spending will take place within a brief time span when it can safely be assumed that the expenditures undertaken will be cyclically stabilizing.

Changes in planning and budgeting techniques would also help to make expenditure policy more flexible. The possibility of advance appropriations for public expenditure programs should be considered. If Congress approved a capital expenditure budget for a number of years in advance, the program of the government might be seen in better perspective, and the executive might be given more flexibility in timing particular projects. Congress might require the executive to show cause whenever the conduct of the program exceeded or fell short of what would be a constant annual rate. Capital budgeting of this nature, involving the planning of capital outlays over a relatively long period, would be highly desirable. It should be noted, though, that such capital budgeting carries no necessary implication that capital outlays should be financed differently from current outlays.

The distribution of expenditure functions between levels of government is such that state and local expenditures should play a crucial role in any countercyclical expenditure policy. Efforts should be made to provide incentives for state and local governments to modify their expenditures in a countercyclical direction. A program of emergency short-run grants or loans, which would expire if not used within a specified time, could be used to accomplish this objective. New grants or loans or increases in existing ones could be initiated in a recession and terminated or decreased in boom periods. Such a program would also contribute to the stability of state and local finances.

. . . . .

XII • INTERNATIONAL TRADE AND FINANCE

Here is a classic. Though written long ago by a French economist, its major argument—seen easily through the satire—is never out of date.

64 • Petition of the Candlemakers

FREDERIC BASTIAT

Petition from the manufacturers of candles, wax lights, lamps, chandeliers, reflectors, snuffers, extinguishers; and from the producers of tallow, oil, resin, alcohol, and generally of everything used for lights.

To the Honorable the Members of the Chamber of Deputies:

GENTLEMEN—You are in the right way: you reject abstract theories; abundance, cheapness, concerns you little. You are entirely occupied with the interest of the producer, whom you are anxious to free from foreign competition. In a word, you wish to secure the *national market* to *national labor.*

We come now to offer you an admirable opportunity for the application of your—what shall we say? your theory? no, nothing is more deceiving than theory—your doctrine? your system? your principle? But you do not like doctrines; you hold systems in horror; and, as for principles, you declare that there are no such things in political economy. We will say, then, your practice; your practice without theory, and without principle.

We are subjected to the intolerable competition of a foreign rival, who enjoys, it would seem, such superior facilities for the production of light, that he is enabled to *inundate* our *national market* at so exceedingly reduced a price, that, the moment he makes his appearance, he draws off all custom for us; and thus an important branch of French industry, with all its innumerable ramifications, is suddenly reduced to a state of complete stagnation. This rival, who is no other than the sun, carries on so bitter a war against us, that we have every reason to believe that he has been excited to this course by our perfidious neighbor England. (Good diplomacy this, for the present time!) In this belief we are confirmed by the

---

FREDERIC BASTIAT, "Petition From the Manufacturers of Candles, Wax Lights, Lamps, Chandeliers, Reflectors, Snuffers, Extinguishers; and From the Producers of Tallow, Oil, Resin, Alcohol, and Generally of Everything Used for Lights," *Economic Sophisms* (New York: George P. Putnam & Sons, 1882).

fact that in all his transactions with that proud island, he is much more moderate and careful than with us.

Our petition is, that it would please your honorable body to pass a law whereby shall be directed the shutting up of windows, dormers, skylights, shutters, curtains, *vasistas, oeil-de-boeufs,* in a word, all openings, holes, chinks, and fissures through which the light of the sun is used to penetrate into our dwellings, to the prejudice of the profitable manufactures which we flatter ourselves we have been enabled to bestow upon the country; which country cannot, therefore, without ingratitude, leave us now to struggle unprotected through so unequal a contest.

We pray your honorable body not to mistake our petition for a satire, nor to repulse us without at least hearing the reasons which we have to advance in its favor.

And first, if, by shutting out as much as possible all access to natural light, you thus create the necessity for artificial light, is there in France an industrial pursuit which will not, through some connection with this important object, be benefited by it?

If more tallow be consumed, there will arise a necessity for an increase of cattle and sheep. Thus artificial meadows must be in greater demand; and meat, wool, leather, and above all, manure, this basis of agricultural riches, must become more abundant.

If more oil be consumed, it will cause an increase in the cultivation of the olive tree. This plant, luxuriant and exhausting to the soil, will come in good time to profit by the increased fertility which the raising of cattle will have communicated to our fields.

Our heaths will become covered with resinous trees. Numerous swarms of bees will gather upon our mountains the perfumed treasures which are now cast upon the winds, useless as the blossoms from which they emanate. There is, in short, no branch of agriculture which would not be greatly developed by the granting of our petitions.

Navigation would equally profit. Thousands of vessels would soon be employed in the whale fisheries, and hence would arise a navy capable of sustaining the honor of France, and of responding to the patriotic sentiments of the undersigned petitioners, candle merchants, etc.

But what words can express the magnificence which Paris will then exhibit! Cast an eye upon the future and behold the gildings, the bronzes, the magnificent crystal chandeliers, lamps, reflectors, and candelabra, which will glitter in the spacious stores, compared with which the splendor of the present day will appear trifling and insignificant.

There is none, not even the poor manufacturer of resin in the midst of his pine forest, nor the miserable miner in his dark dwelling, but who would enjoy an increase of salary and of comforts.

Gentlemen, if you will be pleased to reflect, you cannot fail to be convinced that there is perhaps not one Frenchman, from the opulent stockholder of Anzin down to the poorest vender of matches, who is not interested in the success of our petition.

We foresee your objections, gentlemen; but there is not one that you can oppose to us which you will not be obliged to gather from the works of the partisans of free trade. We dare challenge you to pronounce one word against our petition, which is not equally opposed to your own practice and the principle which guides your policy.

Do you tell us, that if we gain by this protection, France will not gain, because the consumer must pay the price of it?

We answer you:

You have no longer any right to cite

the interest of the consumer. For whenever this has been found to compete with that of the producer, you have invariably sacrificed the first. You have done this to *encourage labor,* to *increase the demand for labor.* The same reason should now induce you to act in the same manner.

You have yourselves already answered the objection. When you were told, The consumer is interested in the free introduction of coal, iron, corn, wheat, cloths, etc., your answer was, Yes, but the producer is interested in their exclusion. Thus, also if the consumer is interested in the admission of light, we, the producers, pray for its interdiction.

You have also said, the producer and the consumer are one. If the manufacturer gains by protection, he will cause the agriculturist to gain also; if agriculture prospers, it opens a market for manufactured goods. Thus we, if you confer upon us the monopoly of furnishing light during the day, will as a first consequence buy large quantities of tallow, coals, oil, resin, wax, alcohol, silver, iron, bronze, crystal, for the supply of our business; and then we and our numerous contractors having become rich, our consumption will be great, and will become a means of contributing to the comfort and competency of the workers in every branch of national labor.

Will you say that the light of the sun is a gratuitous gift, and that to repulse gratuitous gifts is to repulse riches under pretense of encouraging the means of obtaining them?

Take care—you carry the death blow to your own policy. Remember that hitherto you have always repulsed foreign produce *because* it was an approach to a gratuitous gift, and *the more in proportion* as this approach was more close. You have, in obeying the wishes of other monopolists, acted only from a *half-motive;* to grant our petition there is a much *fuller inducement.* To repulse us, precisely for the reason that our case is a more complete one than any which have preceded it, would be to lay down the following equation: $+ \times + = -$; in other words, it would be to accumulate absurdity upon absurdity.

Labor and nature concur in different proportions, according to country and climate, in every article of production. The portion of nature is always gratuitous; that of labor alone regulates the price. If a Lisbon orange can be sold at half the price of a Parisian one, it is because a natural and gratuitous heat does for the one what the other only obtains from an artificial and consequently expensive one.

When, therefore, we purchase a Portuguese orange, we may say that we obtain it half gratuitously and half by the right of labor; in other words, at *half-price* compared with those of Paris.

Now it is precisely on account of this *demi-gratuity* (excuse the word) that you argue in favor of exclusion. How, you say, could national labor sustain the competition of foreign labor, when the first has everything to do, and the last is rid of half the trouble, the sun taking the rest of the business upon himself? If then the *demi-gratuity* can determine you to check competition, on what principle can the *entire gratuity* be alleged as a reason for admitting it? You are no logicians if, refusing the demi-gratuity as hurtful to human labor, you do not *a fortiori,* and with double zeal, reject the full gratuity.

Again, when any article, as coal, iron, cheese, or cloth, comes to us from foreign countries with less labor than if we produced it ourselves, the difference in price is a *gratuitous gift* conferred upon us; and the gift is more or less considerable, according as the difference is greater or less. It is the quarter, the half, or the three quarters of the value of the produce, in proportion as the foreign merchant requires the three quarters, the half, or the quarter of the price. It is as complete as possible when the producer offers, as the sun does with light, the whole in free gift. The question is, and we put it formally, whether you wish for France the benefit of gratuitous consumption, or the supposed advantages of laborious production. Choose, but be consistent. And does it not argue the greatest inconsistency to check as you do the importation of coal, iron, cheese, and goods of foreign manufacture, merely because and even in proportion as their price approaches *zero*, while at the same time you freely admit, and without limitation, the light of the sun, whose price is during the whole day at *zero*?

For many years after World War II the ability of foreigners to buy what they wanted in the United States was restricted by their inability to get the dollars needed. In the future, however, we may find our ability to import restricted by difficulties in getting enough foreign currency by exporting. What factors will influence our ability to export? Professor Hirschman of Columbia University discusses a part of the problem.

65 · Forces Changing the U.S. Export Outlook

ALBERT O. HIRSCHMAN

The emergence of a sizeable deficit in the United States balance of payments during 1958/59 seems to have definitely settled the great debate of the last fifteen years about the existence of a "chronic" dollar shortage. In the light of our present payments position it is tempting to ridicule those who endeavored to explain the postwar dollar crisis by appealing to deep-seated structural maladjustments rather than to disturbances of a purely temporary and monetary character.

But the evidence before us permits a different interpretation. It could be argued that the end of the dollar shortage and the emergence of the new dollar problem, far from proving the dollar shortage theorists wrong, can largely be traced to their analytical efforts, to the alert they sounded, and to the soul-searching that they caused. It will surely be granted that the postwar outburst of economic vitality in Western Europe is intimately bound up with advances in productivity and in regional economic cooperation and integration. But these advances arose precisely from the conviction that fundamental changes in the functioning of the European economy were required if international equilibrium was to be restored on a satisfactory basis—a conviction which was derived from the writings of the dollar shortage theorists.

In this sense, then, those who were skeptical about the existence and ade-

---

ALBERT O. HIRSCHMAN, "Invitation to Theorizing about the Dollar Glut," *The Review of Economics and Statistics*, Vol. XLII, No. 1 (February 1960). Copyright 1960 by the Presidents and Fellows of Harvard College. Used by permission.

quacy of the traditional adjustment mechanism actually seconded the return to equilibrium by pointing to causes and cures of international imbalance which traditional theory had left out of account. To consider the dollar shortage theories entirely refuted simply because the dollar shortage is no more, reminds one of the patient who after submitting to a variety of fairly radical treatments finally recovers his health and then exclaims: "I told you that there was nothing wrong with me."

If theories of structural disequilibrium thus appear to perform a useful role in providing the international adjustment mechanism with an additional dimension, we need not feel shamefaced about exploring possible types of "dollar glut" theories. In the following I shall try to offer some purely experimental thoughts on this topic.

I.

A hypothesis about structural change that could account for our balance-of-payments difficulties has to do with the speed of industrial migration. Looking at the time-span it took the textile industry to spread out from the United Kingdom and comparing it with corresponding periods for the chemical and automobile industries and then for such new products as antibiotics and transistors, one has a distinct impression of a *continuous shortening* of the time needed for a new industry to become "footloose." Such a development has important implications for the pioneering industrial countries. As long as the innovating country could count on retaining a lead in the industries it developed for at least some twenty or thirty years, it made sense to think of a pattern of international division of labor which, while far from static, evolved in a most orderly fashion. On the one hand, we had a few innovating countries who made a specialty out of this very innovation, and on the other there were the imitators who could slowly acquire industries that had passed through the period of rapid technological transformation. These imitators would then displace the innovators not only at home, but could also encroach upon their international markets in "old-line" manufactures. The general impression that arose from this situation and which was strengthened by some important statistical findings amounted to a new view of the international division of labor: Instead of dividing the world into manufacturing countries and primary producers we have a division of countries into the talented innovators, on the one hand, and, on the other, the imitators who were expected to proceed at a respectful distance and with well-adjusted speed to occupy positions of comparative advantage which the innovators were more or less ready to yield.

While somewhat overdrawn, this is essentially the image we have had of the nature of United States participation in world trade, particularly with respect to manufactures. Unlike some European countries we have never opposed industrialization abroad; we were always convinced that, given our unlimited ability to invent new, universally desirable, and therefore highly exportable products, our ability to "take" world-wide industrialization was assured.

The conclusion is still sound, but the reasoning behind it may have to be revised. We may have to look for a role in world trade that is not wholly based on our ability to innovate; for as a result of the enhanced transferability of productive processes, the innovating countries may increasingly find that they cannot necessarily count on a prolonged period during which they will enjoy a comparative advantage in the product or process in which they have innovated. Apart from the question of transferability there is no reason why an innovating country should develop only those commodities in whose production it has a marked comparative advantage.

Some of the recent difficulties of U.S. exports may derive from the fact that we can no longer rely on innovation to throw off a continuous flow of exportables, while encroachment of foreign producers on the older-line goods we used to sell proceeds unabated. It may well be, therefore, that we need to rethink the basis on which we participate in world-trade. For instance, we may have to work directly at having something to sell that foreigners want, instead of taking it for granted that anything we turn out will immediately be a worldwide success. In the latter respect, we have taken the succession to the British who, in the nineteenth century, assumed that the whole world would be thrilled to wear tweeds and who, at the turn of the century, thought it exceedingly vulgar on the part of the Germans to design goods specifically for foreign lands and to learn their language to boot. We have similarly—and quite correctly for a long time—taken it for granted that the American way of life could be exported without any account being taken of the characteristics of foreign climate, terrain, tastes, and stages of development.

If exports no longer take care of themselves in an automatic fashion, a look at the administration of the export function in the U.S. corporation might also be in order. There are at least two reasons for thinking that managerial quality is lower in the export area than in the domestic division of U.S. business: first, the principal avenue to central power in the typical corporation is definitely not via the export branch and therefore the most aggressive talent is not attracted into the foreign field. Second, performance is not easily checked in the export business: it is hard to explain away a setback on the home market, but a falling off of sales abroad can always be blamed on local factors, foreign competition, or on other uncontrollable forces. It is therefore easy for the export managers to find excuses, and since the top management has only limited knowledge of, or interest in, the export business, the excuses are likely to be accepted. All of this was not serious so long as the United States was facing an international sellers' market. But these factors may bear some watching now.

. . . . .

[The following concrete example is taken from the audited figures of an American corporation which manufactures three identical items in its United States and in its European plants. *Ed.*]

Manufacturing Costs *
(Five-Year Period)

	1953	1958	Percent of Increase or Decrease
Small Size Centrifugal Pump			
U.S.A.	$ 244.96	$ 348.55	+42.3%
Europe	148.96	140.57	— 5.6%
Large Size Centrifugal Pump			
U.S.A.	$ 719.11	$1,072.19	+49.1%
Europe	384.90	376.32	— 2.2%
Medium Size Air Compressor			
U.S.A.	$4,178.88	$5,649.32	+35.2%
Europe	2,230.99	2,166.56	— 2.9%

Note the contrast. The manufacturing cost of these products has been lower in Europe all along. But the gap has been growing wider. Unit costs actually declined in the European plants between 1953 and 1958, whereas they increased substantially in the U.S. plants of the same company.

---

* [Reproduced by permission from National Association of Manufacturers, *Foreign Competition—a Challenge for America* (New York: 1960), p. 27. The complete report, too long to include in a volume like this, is a valuable study of the problem indicated by its title. *Ed.*]

Gold has been in the news in recent years. It will probably appear again and again. The article here helps explain the role of gold in world affairs today. The author has for many years specialized on this range of problems.

66 · *Gold in World Monetary Affairs Today*

MIROSLAV A. KRIZ

Gold remains supremely important in world monetary affairs. This is so partly because the United States, the British Commonwealth of Nations, and France, as well as Russia, have a vital stake in gold, partly because the entire community of nations makes essential uses of it.

To help appraise the rôle of gold in the new era of the 1960's, this article reviews the place of gold in our present currency systems, domestically as well as internationally, and takes yet another look at the world gold picture—output, international flows, and official monetary stocks, with particular reference to the United States and the United Kingdom, the two reserve centers in whose currencies most other nations are holding a part of their reserves. It ends with the pragmatic conclusion that the problems of international liquidity are continuing ones; as some are dealt with, others arise. At this time, however, there is no need for any drastic innovations in our institutional arrangements and practices to provide more man-made reserves. Our international monetary system works after a fashion and, accordingly, it needs no drastic overhaul but rather a continuous, sensible adaptation to meet changing circumstances.

I.

In the world today, central banks do not issue gold coins at a fixed statutory price in exchange for bank notes, as they did prior to 1914 in most countries and prior to 1933 in the United States. Nor do they redeem their note and deposit liabilities in gold bullion, as in the mid-1920's. Several nations, including the United States, the United Kingdom, the Netherlands and the Scandinavian countries, do not allow their citizens to hold or trade in gold. A gold market exists in London, but British and other sterling-area residents are not allowed to buy gold there, except for licensed uses in the arts and industry; only residents of nonsterling countries can buy gold in London—against U. S. dollars and other convertible currencies. Most other countries allow domestic holding of gold and some also permit free gold markets; very few countries—Germany and Switzerland, for example—allow

---

MIROSLAV A. KRIZ, "Gold in World Monetary Affairs Today," *Political Science Quarterly*, Volume LXXV, No. 4 (December 1960), Columbia University, New York. Used by permission.

their nationals to export gold freely. In France, the authorities intervene in the gold market to smooth out day-to-day fluctuations. But nowhere do central banks deliver gold to their nationals at a fixed price for domestic holding.

Yet, gold has retained an essential rôle in our domestic financial affairs. In the United States and in some other countries, the central bank is legally required to hold a gold cover against its currency and deposit liabilities; in the United States, the required proportion is 25 per cent. In many countries, specified foreign exchange is eligible along with gold for currency backing. In the United Kingdom, Canada and certain other countries, on the other hand, the counterpart of the currency issue consists almost entirely of government securities; the domestic money supply is thus isolated from gold and foreign exchange flows.

Whether or not the note and deposit liabilities of the central bank are subject to statutory reserve requirements, however, no nation can frame its economic and financial plans and policies without regard either to the external influences to which it is subject or to the external repercussions of its own domestic economic and financial conditions. To be sure, the state of the country's gold (and foreign exchange) reserves is only one criterion for monetary and fiscal policies, and the importance of this guidepost varies from country to country and from time to time; but it is of greatest concern to countries that are heavily dependent on foreign trade or that have to operate on a narrow margin of reserves.

The idea that domestic monetary conditions could be divorced from the country's international reserve position —and money thus made more abundant and cheaper—was put forward a generation ago by a British iconoclast, the late J. M. Keynes, who resented the link between domestic currency and gold as taking the control of money supply out of a country's own hands. He dismissed gold as a "barbarous relic" and advocated "scientific" monetary management. He applied his ideas principally to the United Kingdom and the United States, countries for which balance-of-payments "complications" could, at the time, be discarded. He paid little attention to countries that could not afford to neglect their international reserve position; nor was his theory worked out for the United Kingdom or the United States on the assumption that these countries would find themselves with inadequate reserves.

But postwar experience has taught us otherwise. Most Continental Western European nations began to reaccept the link between domestic financial affairs and the country's gold (and foreign exchange) reserve position as far back as the early postwar years; the United Kingdom did so during the sterling crises of the 1950's; and Latin American and other countries during their economic stabilization efforts in the late 1950's. In 1959, the United States itself took very much the same measures as other countries to reduce a gold and dollar outflow that persisted throughout most of the 1950's but was greatly accentuated toward the end of the decade. It balanced the budget, restricted credit, and endeavored to improve the structure of the public debt and resist inflationary wage spiraling.

In the world of the 1960's in which the currencies of the principal trading nations have become convertible for most practical purposes and may well become convertible fully, the need for monetary discipline is being reinforced by competitive pressures from other nations for improved productivity, lower costs, attractive prices, and interest rates in proper relationship to those in other principal markets. These competitive pressures turn inflation into an immediate threat to profits and employment. Therefore, no country can with impunity allow its domestic monetary conditions, and hence its over-all demand for goods and services as well as its costs, to get out of line with those of other nations.

Domestic gold convertibility is gone, probably forever. But if a country restrains credit and lets interest rates rise in order to correct a balance-of-payments deficit, is it not following the rules of the gold standard?

II.

In the community of nations, there is also much more similarity in substance than is sometimes believed between the traditional gold standard and our present gold arrangements. Indeed, if we define the gold standard as a system in which the value of currency is fixed in terms of gold, or in terms of another currency that itself is fixed in terms of gold; as a system where gold is the ultimate means of international settlements; and as a system where monetary reserves of the principal trading nations are held wholly or mainly in gold, then the similarity in substance stands out quite clearly.

(1) Gold serves as the common denominator of currencies. The United States dollar and certain other currencies like the Belgian, French and Swiss francs, or the Dutch guilder, are defined by monetary legislation in terms of gold. Currencies that are not so defined—among which the pound sterling is the most prominent—are linked to gold through par values established in agreement with the International Monetary Fund, which are expressed in terms of gold or in terms of the United States dollar of the present weight and fineness, and are binding for all gold and foreign exchange operations of Fund members (unless the Fund otherwise approves, as it has done in the case of certain multiple rate practices in Latin America, etc.). This makes the United States dollar an anchor for the world's currencies.

(2) Gold remains the ultimate means of settling balances among the principal trading nations. To be sure, the bulk of international transactions is, as it has always been, "cleared" in the exchange markets, and the balances remaining after transactions have been set off against one another are settled, to an extent varying according to the country, by the use of United States dollars and pounds sterling, currencies in which many central banks and treasuries keep a part of their monetary reserves. But monetary authorities of the leading trading nations buy and sell gold bullion, at fixed prices or within prescribed margins on each side of a fixed par value, to settle international balances—hence the name "international gold bullion standard."

The U. S. Treasury thus sells gold to foreign governments and central banks, at the official price of $35 per troy ounce, to settle international balances; these foreign monetary authorities can exchange dollars for gold virtually automatically for such normal purposes. On the other hand, the U. S. Treasury stands ready to buy gold from foreign governments and central banks, without limitation in amount, at the official price.

The U. S. Treasury has, however, no commitment to buy or sell gold. The present practice could, therefore, be changed without notice. But if the U. S. Treasury were to stop selling gold to foreign monetary authorities or buying gold from them, the whole system of trade and payments of the western world would be thrown into confusion.

The Secretaries of the Treasury have repeatedly stated that the assured interchangeability of dollars and gold at $35 per ounce is a basic element of strength in the international financial structure.

In the United Kingdom, the institutional arrangements are quite different from those in the United States. The London gold market was reopened in 1954 after a closure of sixteen years. As already noted, only residents of countries outside the sterling area may purchase gold there—against United States dollars and other convertible currencies; the demand stems mostly from central banks On the other hand, the supply originates mostly from new mining, but official sales, including Russia's, are also important. The chief differences between the London market and the gold arrangements in force in the United States are that private interests can purchase gold in London but not from the U. S. Treasury and that there is no fixed statutory gold price in the United Kingdom.

(3) Gold is the principal form in which central banks and governments hold their country's international reserves. The preference for gold is only in part a matter of legislation; it also reflects consideration of prestige and tradition, and the desire to protect the country's reserves against the hazards of depreciation.

The United States keeps its reserves exclusively in gold. Some countries hold the bulk of their reserves in gold (Belgium, the Netherlands, Switzerland, and the United Kingdom). Some others have, in recent years, been increasing the proportion of gold in their reserves (Austria, the Federal Republic of Germany, Italy, and Japan). The remainder of Western Europe's and Japan's reserves are held mainly in dollars sterling. Elsewhere in the world, most countries hold much smaller total reserves—and, out of these smaller reserves, much lower proportions in gold—than Western Europe.

With regard to the side directly related to balances of payments, reserve movements, and exchange rates, therefore, the main difference between the traditional gold standard and our present institutional arrangements is that a certain leeway has been built into the world monetary system by the International Monetary Fund. Under the old gold standard the limit to the balance-of-payments deficit that a country could run on current account was determined by the size of its disposable gold (and foreign exchange) reserves plus the amount that it (or rather its nationals) might borrow abroad. Today, the function of equilibrating the balance of payments is performed not only by gold and foreign exchange, and by borrowing in world financial markets, but also by credits extended by the International Monetary Fund.

Furthermore, the Fund, while standing for stability in exchange rates, also makes possible orderly changes in exchange rates. The Fund thus aims to provide a pattern of exchange rates sufficiently rigid to enable traders and investors to count on reasonable exchange stability, and yet supple enough to permit such orderly adjustments of exchange rates as might be required to deal with a fundamental balance-of-payments disequilibrium.

III.

If gold is to fulfill its essential functions in our monetary system, its supply must, of course, be just about "right." If there were not enough gold, it might be difficult to ensure a proper growth of international trade and investment in an environment of economic freedom. On the other hand, if there were too much gold, its usefulness for the world's monetary system might well be impaired. This, indeed, has happened to silver, and if a lesson for gold may be drawn from the history of silver, it is that gold can retain its usefulness as a monetary metal only if it remains abundant enough to permit a steady increase in monetary reserves and yet scarce enough to be sought and absorbed.

Let us look for the moment at the world gold supply. World gold production, excluding Russia,[1] has been rising by 5 per cent a year since the end of 1953, when the current phase of expansion began; in 1959, the rise was 7 per cent. . . . [1959] gold production was worth approximately $1,150 million. . . . The postwar rise in output has been due basically to an increase in South African production which now accounts for two thirds of world gold output. . . .

In addition to its current gold output, the western world, year after year, gets a sizable amount of gold from Russia, which sells it to cover deficits in its international payments. Considering the rôle of gold in the Soviet economy—a war chest and a means of paying for imports—it appears probable that Russia will consistently sell some, but not all, of its newly-mined gold. According to western sources, such sales have been about $150–$250 million annually during recent years. Russia's output and reserves remain a closely guarded secret; but Russia is generally believed to be the second largest world gold producer —after South Africa—and the second largest gold holder—after the United States.

Apart from current output and Russian sales, there is, potentially, a third source of gold supply: release of privately-held gold, which added greatly to gold supplies in the 1930's. Some gold may well have been released by Frenchmen during the past two years; for the world as a whole, however, dishoarding has been conspicuous by its absence.

Altogether, therefore, the additions to the Free World's gold supply in 1959 can be estimated at some $1,400 million —$1,150 million from annual gold output in the western world and $250 million from Russia. . . . since the mid-1950's, the trend has been decidedly up.

Of the current gold supply, some is consumed in the arts and industry or absorbed in private hoards, and some finds its way into official monetary stocks. . . . In 1959, an estimated $800 million was added to reserves while close to $600 million was consumed in arts and industry or "disappeared" in private hoards.

In the Middle and Far East, gold hoarding is a normal form of saving. In Europe and in the Americas, on the other hand, it appears to be essentially a means of minimizing losses that are expected to result from political, economic, and social upheavals and the concomitant inflationary pressures and currency depreciations. Monetary stability and confidence in the leading currencies, including the United States dollar, must unquestionably be maintained if gold is to flow into official monetary stock in adequate amounts.

As a matter of fact, from the end of 1948 through 1952, official gold stocks increased by $400 million a year; during the following four years, by $600 million a year; and during the subsequent three years ended 1959, by about $700 million a year. The increase in 1959 alone was, as just noted, $800 million. More and more gold has thus gone into monetary reserves to buttress international liquidity.

In spite of growing accretions, world

---

[1] Unless specifically stated, gold data given in this article exclude the U.S.S.R., Mainland China, and countries in their orbit.

gold reserves have been increasing during recent years at an annual rate of only 2 per cent while international trade, even at constant prices, has been expanding at a rate two or three times as great. In 1937, total official gold reserves were almost as large as total world imports; in 1959, they equaled only two fifths of imports. It is this discrepancy, more than anything else, that has given rise to fear that there might not be enough gold to go around.

These statistical findings are, of course, most interesting but as G. K. Chesterton once said, statistics should be used "as a drunkard uses a lamppost, for support rather than illumination." For one thing, there is, in the complex real world, no scientific proof of any direct causal relationships between gold, commodity prices, and world trade. And for another, arithmetical comparisons of international reserves and world trade over time are inconclusive.

There are, at least, two reasons for doubts concerning such causal relationships. First, the booming present-day world is very different from that of the depression of the 1930's; and second, a mechanistic calculation of ratios between trade and reserves neglects the essential fact that trade is financed by reverse trade and capital flows. More trade may mean more interdependence, but not necessarily more instability and hence greater need for larger reserves.

This, indeed, has been the experience of the past decade. World trade has grown by leaps and bounds but it is undoubtedly balanced much better today than ten years ago. A given volume of monetary reserves can thus support a larger volume of trade than was possible in the early postwar years. Furthermore, trade and other current payments are much freer, more orderly, and more multilateral than ten years ago; capital also moves more freely in response to rewards, which greatly helps balance international payments. Also, in a world where currencies are increasingly convertible, a country can offset deficits vis-a-vis some of its trading partners with surplus elsewhere. Finally, private credits may be obtained to finance imports and exports; the "float" of such credits, which is very large, is an essential element of international liquidity.

IV.

To present a realistic and meaningful picture of the world gold position today, it is necessary, above all, to take into account the distribution of reserves among various countries and the position of the United States and the United Kingdom as centers in which other countries hold reserves.

Today, the economically and financially developed countries of Western Europe other than the United Kingdom —as well as Japan—have reserves that may well be regarded as adequate. Western European countries as well as Japan have restored currency convertibility, at least for nonresidents; European countries have freed a substantial part of their imports from discriminatory restrictions directed against United States goods while Japan has begun to liberalize its imports step by step.

It is the less developed nations of Latin America, Asia, and Africa that are short of reserves. But this is in no way a sign of a faulty international monetary standard. It merely shows that less developed countries have been unable to earn reserves or unwilling to put into reserves some of their exchange earnings. Like an individual, a nation can build up its cash reserves only the hard way—by living within its means and saving part of its income. In fact, for the less developed countries, the shortage of reserves is, basically, a shortage of long-term capital for development. Recently, even countries that wish, more than anything, to speed up the rate of economic growth have begun to realize that investment in monetary reserves may, within a short period, prove more productive than some of the real investment they must thus forego. By building up reserves, countries are able to avoid exchange crises and the accompanying restrictions on economic growth. It may well be that in the years to come countries in Latin America, Asia and Africa will wish to keep higher reserves than today.

Another crucial aspect of the world gold position is the adequacy of reserves of the United States and the United Kingdom relative to their short-term liabilities to other nations and thus their ability to fulfill effectively the rôle of international bankers.

The improvement during the past decade in the reserve positions of other countries has been made possible principally by an enormous transfer of gold and dollars from the United States to the rest of the world. In June, 1960, monetary gold reserves held outside the United States (that is, those of foreign countries and international financial institutions) stood at some $21 billion—over $11 billion more than in December, 1949, three months after the devaluation of sterling and many other currencies as a result of which the world exchange rate structure became much more realistic than in earlier postwar years. Of this increase in gold stocks, $5 billion came from the United States and the remainder mainly from new gold output and Russian sales. At the same time, foreign countries added over $12 billion to their liquid dollar assets. Altogether, therefore, gold outside the United States and foreign dollar holdings, at some $40 billion in June, 1960, increased by $23 billion in the past decade, of which $17 billion came from the United States.

Redistribution of reserves is a good thing insofar as it measures the success of Europe, where most of the gold has gone, in stabilizing its currencies and increasing its industrial power. This was a long-sought objective of the postwar international economic and financial policies of the United States, beginning with the Marshall Plan in 1948.

As now redistributed, with the United States gold stock slightly less than one half of the world total, the gold held in monetary reserves can be more actively employed in international settlements than ten years ago when the United States held two thirds of the world's stock. In 1928, it should be recalled, the United States held approximately two fifths of the world monetary gold stock, and in 1913 one fifth. Even now, after substantial transfers of gold to other countries and to the International Monetary Fund, the gold reserves of the United States . . . are far larger than those of any other country.

The United States needs a comfortable gold reserve. As Secretary of the Treasury Robert B. Anderson pointed out . . . our reserve "should be large in order to provide a cushion against various contingencies and to secure our short-term liabilities. It seems to me that substantial changes in that reserve can be viewed with equanimity only if they are likely to be of relatively short duration and not persistently in one direction."

Far-reaching deductions are sometimes drawn from the fact that, out of a gold stock of $18.5 billion, gold required as cover for currency stood in October, 1960 at about $11.5 billion and only $7 billion was thus left "free." On the other hand, our short-term liabilities to foreigners amounted to $17.4 billion in July, 1960. With short-term liabilities to foreigners of over $17 billion and "free" gold of only $7 billion, so runs the argument, the United States will have to restrict gold convertibility and devalue the dollar.

Nothing of the sort is, of course, inevitable. The international standing of the dollar is affected not only by the size of the gold stock relative to short-term liabilities abroad but also by the intrinsic strength of the United States economy and by our monetary, fiscal, and other policies.

. . . . .

So long as the United States manages its affairs properly, other countries will be satisfied with a gold backing of less than 100 per cent for their short-term dollar claims. If they were to lose confidence in the dollar, they would, of course, seek to transfer funds into more desirable currencies or into gold. Even more important, however, if the idea gained ground that conditions were developing under which a rise in the price of gold would be inevitable, Americans themselves would seek gold. Americans and foreigners, it must be hoped, will not take fright at shadows. More than anything else, however, their willingness to hold dollars is directly and immediately influenced by the monetary, fiscal, and other policies that our Government and the Federal Reserve decide to pursue.

. . . . .

. . . although we are not confronted with an emergency, we must not take our balance-of-payments deficit lightly. For it could not be sustained for many years, nor will it be corrected by the mere passage of time without conscious effort.

The position of the United Kingdom as a reserve center also shows light as well as shade. The very fact that the pound sterling has become, for foreign holders, increasingly convertible into dollars or gold is, in itself, a substantial contribution to international liquidity. Furthermore, the rehabilitation of exchange, gold, and money markets has greatly enhanced the position of London as an international center. These are developments of great import that have far-reaching implications for the financing of world trade, the international movements of funds, and the functioning of the international currency system.

Holdings of sterling by foreigners totalled in mid-1960 the equivalent of some $10 billion; of this amount, however, $2.4 billion was held by British colonies and $5 billion by other countries that have special political or financial ties with the United Kingdom. Furthermore, these balances, which look big on paper, are in part earmarked as backing for domestic currencies. Of the remaining $2.6 billion, Continental Western European countries held about $1.4 billion, and the United States and Canada only $250 million.

On the other hand, the United Kingdom held in mid-1960 some $2.5 billion in gold. External sterling liabilities to others than colonies are thus roughly three times as large as Britain's gold holdings; liabilities to countries outside the sterling area are approximately equal to Britain's gold holdings.

Admittedly, British reserves are not as large as might be desirable for an international center. Furthermore, as the British authorities have repeatedly stressed, sterling cannot continue to be used as an international trading and reserve currency unless it remains strong. On several occasions during the past decade, Britain was compelled to resort to drastic monetary and fiscal restraints to preserve reasonable monetary stability and counter the withdrawal of sterling balances.

Our present international monetary standard thus operates with two reserve centers. In periods of calm, a two-center world can function as well as a one-center world, but in periods of stress, wide and sweeping movements of funds create strains in the international financial structure. As the International Monetary Fund's report on *International Reserves and Liquidity* states: "There is always the possibility—slight though it may be—that there may be a run to convert dollars into gold and sterling and sterling into dollars or gold." Clearly, the reserve centers must remain strong if our monetary system is to function well.

V.

To help strengthen the United States' gold position and at the same time provide more reserves for an expanding world economy, several ideas have recently captured the imagination of some students of international banking and have received considerable publicity here as well as in Europe.

One suggestion is that Congress abolish the 25 per cent legal gold requirement against Federal Reserve note and deposit liabilities. Another is that the United States Government guarantee against devaluation all dollar balances in the hands of foreign treasuries and central banks so that dollars held by foreign monetary authorities would become as good as gold.

Still another proposal is that dollars held as reserves by foreign treasuries and central banks be transferred to a reformed International Monetary Fund —an arrangement that would remove once and for all the threat of a run on our gold. Another variant seeks to ease the access to the resources of the International Monetary Fund as presently constituted; this would enable members, including the United States, to regard at least a part of their drawing rights on the Fund as an addition to their own reserves.

The proponents of these ideas are, of course, fully aware of the overwhelming need for monetary stability in the United States. For my part, however, I strongly doubt whether the policies necessary to maintain monetary stability would be implemented more promptly, more courageously, and more effectively if we were to eliminate our legal gold reserve requirement or dispense with the use of the dollar as an international reserve currency.

To deal with our external deficit effectively and responsibly, we must concern ourselves with the substance of difficult and delicate problems. There is, I think, genuine danger that changes in our present institutional arrangements and practices might mistakenly be regarded as substitutes for substantive policies. The fundamental task we face is to secure as much economic growth, and as high a standard of living, as are attainable with reasonable monetary stability. We would deceive ourselves by thinking that mere changes in our institutional arrangements and practices would solve these fundamental problems for us.

VI.

Having discarded radical innovations, I am bound to conclude that the problems of international liquidity can best be met within the framework of the existing international monetary system. Surely, international liquidity is a legitimate object of concern. But it is not pressing at this time, and—considering everything—our currency standard is capable of providing the reserves required to ensure a growing flow of international trade and investment.

The first source of world monetary reserves is, of course, gold itself. Given the arrangements that have been made for economizing on the use of gold, the annual accretions to reserves from new output should go far toward satisfying the world's needs for reserves. Over the next decade, the addition to reserves from current gold production at the present price of gold is likely to amount to at least $7 billion, and perhaps considerably more, even after allowing for continuing gold "disappearance" into private hoards.

Man-made reserves are, however, also important. As already noted, the largest single factor in the growth of foreign monetary reserves during the past decade has been the balance-of-payments deficit of the United States. As our balance of payments is righted, as it must be, this source of reserves will dry up. But the reserve position of foreign nations has by now improved so much that a reduction in the United States payments deficit to manageable levels would not leave them pinched. Clearly, gold and dollars that foreign nations have acquired through transactions with the United States will remain outside this country so long as the rest of the world does not incur deficits with us, as in the earlier postwar years; there are currently no signs of this. Therefore, even after the United States has succeeded in reducing its external deficit, the rest of the world will be reasonably well off, at least for some time, with regard to its dollar holdings.

Furthermore, the convertible pound sterling is an essential aid to world commerce. Its usefulness and standing have recently been greatly enhanced. With the present output and productivity in Britain, and with present British economic and financial policies, the pound is able to do a much better job than ten or fifteen years ago.

Liquidity is a relative thing. A country usually meets a deficit in its balance of payments first out of its own monetary reserves. A credit-worthy country is, however, increasingly able to supplement its reserves by borrowing, whether from the United States or from some countries of Western Europe. Private credits may be obtained to finance imports or exports, and public credits may be obtained by one country from banks in, or governments of, other countries as well as from international institutions. Besides, movements of short-term capital in response to interest-rate differentials among the money markets within Europe, and between the various European centers and the United States, are once again becoming more frequent. Such movements were a primary equilibrating factor before 1914; and although they can worsen rather than relieve payments imbalances (as in the 1930's and, in the case of sterling, on certain occasions during the past decade) this is not necessarily so since matters like these very much depend on policies.

Finally, the International Monetary Fund has proved itself to be a responsible custodian of international reserves for emergencies. The Fund's resources, though small when compared with total gold and foreign exchange reserves, are nevertheless substantial. For example, the Fund's holdings of gold and of the eight currencies which have thus far been drawn amount to about $9 billion. While these resources can be drawn by members only within the context of the Fund's policies on the use of its resources, they can be and have been used in ways which have a wider and deeper effect than the actual amounts would seem to warrant. . . .

Indeed, the recent increase in the Fund's resources seems adequate to meet such reserve needs as are likely to arise as far ahead as one can see. In an extraordinary contingency—whether a run on a major currency, prolonged weakness of primary commodities, or a deep business recession in industrial countries—the Fund might be endowed with the additional resources required by the circumstances. These could then be put to use where they would be most needed to prevent a crack in the international monetary structure.

VII.

Our present arrangements come as near as may be practicable today to providing a single worldwide currency system. But is it still a gold standard?

Before 1914, when gold coins in active circulation were used as a means of payments, a rise in prices led to a greater demand by the public for gold coins, and hence to a drain on central bank reserves, in addition to whatever external drain might arise. On the other hand, if prices fell, reserves increased. Price changes thus brought certain corrective forces almost automatically into play. Gradually, as paper money became more and more important, central banks began to counter an outflow of gold by increasing the discount rate and by other restrictive measures; in fact, it was frequently sufficient to call a halt to domestic credit expansion to stop the gold outflow. . . .

The pre-1914 gold standard provided a basis on which output and living standards had been increasing at a rate beyond anything known up to that time. After the First World War, practically all nations that had suspended gold payments returned to gold, but in the early 1930's the re-established gold standard broke down. In the perspective of history it is fairly clear that the gold standard of the 1920's proved unworkable not because of any inherent institutional defects but because of conflicting policies. No international monetary system, whether or not based on gold, could have stood the strain of such mutually inconsistent policies as those followed with regard to German reparations, trade, money and credit, and foreign exchange in France, the United Kingdom, and the United States, the three pillars of the financial order of the 1920's. The idea thus spread that the gold standard could no longer work, and nations began to practice "monetary management."

As the world has learned through bitter experience, "management" has not always shown itself as vigilant, skillful, and courageous as is necessary to safeguard reasonable price stability at home and enable the international monetary system to function properly.

The consequences for the international monetary system of faulty domestic policies are direct and immediate. Indeed, whenever a country loses reserves in large amounts, there is reason to believe that it has faulty policies. It may tolerate inflation, which brings about excessive spending on imports or draws exportable goods into domestic uses; it may fail to check cost increases and thus price its exports out of world markets and make imports unduly cheap; and, because of expectations of further monetary and fiscal disorders, it may suffer from loss of confidence in its currency. When, on the other hand, a country restricts domestic demand and prevents or moderates the rise in domestic costs—and thus expands exports, holds down imports, and maintains confidence in its currency—the result is an improvement in its balance of payments.

To be sure, the balance-of-payments problem of a given country is not necessarily a mere by-product of inflation; it may also stem from structural problems of production, productivity, and foreign trade. But even though these structural problems are important, they cannot be dealt with realistically without checking inflation, which greatly aggravates such problems.

Postwar currency experience in Western Europe and elsewhere offers many striking examples of these ineluctable relationships between domestic economic and financial conditions and policies and the balance of payments. At the same time, the insulation of the United States from the influence of forces at work through the balance of payments may well have come to an end. Among other things, the United States must pay greater attention than it has done until quite recently to the effects of wage settlements upon its ability to compete with other industrial nations. Countering inflationary pressures in a buoyant American economy is, of course, necessary for overwhelming domestic reasons; but injury to the international standing of the dollar clinches the case.

Thus, although we are far from the "few plain rules" of the old gold standard, the need for monetary discpline is as real, and penalties for its disregard as direct, as before. But our problems are much more complex.

It has now been realized in many countries that, to safeguard monetary stability and thus provide for sustained economic growth, monetary policy must be flexible: There is a time for cheap money, and another for dear money, and it all depends on the circumstances.

It has not yet been fully realized, however, that in "managing" our financial affairs fiscal policies are as important as monetary policies. . . .

Finally, in economies that are always close to a position of practically full employment, price and cost structures have become quite rigid. In none of the postwar business recessions did costs and consumer prices show any appreciable downward trend. It should be noted, however, that in many European countries whose prosperity depends on exports, labor is, as a rule, more alive to the need for avoiding excessive cost increases than in the United States. In a world in which currencies are convertible for most practical purposes, comparative costs and prices have become once again vitally important.

The need for monetary discipline does not, of course, imply that a country can-not take reasonable measures, including easier credit conditions, to help counter a business recession. In the case of a key country like the United States, other nations would expect it to take expansionary steps in such circumstances; they themselves have a large stake in the maintenance of business activity in the United States, which provides the biggest import market in the world. But even the United States may well need to exercise more discretion in the use of economic stimulants than at some time in the past. Specifically, it can no longer afford to carry cheap money to extremes or loosen the reins on government spending. It needs to find fiscal policies, such as tax reforms, that can check recessions and stimulate production effort and economic growth without opening the floodgates to inflation.

Amidst the many uncertainties in the world today, there can be no assured hope that nations will submit to monetary discipline. Optimist though I am, I feel unable, therefore, to conclude in a wholly reassuring way. But if there is any hope at all of succeeding in our endeavors to safeguard domestic monetary stability, which is the foundation of any stable international monetary system, success will have to come the hard way. We cannot rely on such formal attributes of the gold standard as gold-coin convertbility. On the contrary, we must deal with our problems in their very substance. Above all, we must recreate conditions, in each country and in the world at large, in which free dynamic economies will learn how to maintain a rapid economic growth and high living standards without at the same time allowing the purchasing power of their currencies to be whittled away bit-by-bit and without indulging in chronic balance-of-payments deficits. This, indeed, is the hard core of the problem of international equilibrium in the twentieth century.

Harmony in Canadian–United States relations is eminently desirable. Unfortunately, however, strains have appeared in recent years. Some of the economic issues are examined here by the President of the Royal Bank of Canada, Mr. McLaughlin, and by Professor Stykolt of the University of Toronto.

67 · Canadian–United States Economic Relations

W. EARLE MCLAUGHLIN

. . . . .

It is sometimes argued that Canada is a victim of her own geography: that her loosely integrated regions from the Atlantic Provinces to the Pacific coast must in all areas respond so completely to the massive economic power of the United States that she can hope for little or no autonomy in the realm of monetary or fiscal policy.

It would be idle of course to deny the enormous economic impact of the United States. It is not sheer coincidence, for example, that the United States and Canada had roughly the same recession-recovery-recession pattern in the 1957–60 period. The response of the monetary authorities in both countries has, naturally enough, been in the general direction of monetary ease. . . .

. . . . .

. . . similarity in the type and timing of monetary, and possibly fiscal, measures to meet similar conditions in Canada and the United States does not mean that Canadian policy cannot be independent in a meaningful sense. I would suggest that the similarity of the conditions to which Canadian and U.S. monetary and fiscal policy must respond is not entirely a matter of transmission from the United States to Canada: the United States is not the only source of instability in the Canadian business picture. In fact, there are forces affecting the North American economy as a whole that do not originate uniquely in either the United States or Canada.

It is nothing new of course for Canada to find that she has to take account of forces beyond her control, which affect adversely the prosperity and growth of her economy, and of repercussions from abroad to any policies she may adopt to counteract those forces. But it is something new in recent history for the United States to find itself in this position. The recent overflow of

---

W. EARLE MCLAUGHLIN, "*Maintaining Canada's Economic Independence,*" an address given at the annual meeting of shareholders of the Royal Bank of Canada (Montreal: January 1961). Used by permission.

gold has dramatized a fact that has always been true in some degree: that the United States, in spite of its enormous economic strength, is, like other countries, an interdependent part of the world economy.

Moreover, there is another aspect to the recent loss of gold by the United States that may have direct repercussions in Canada. Briefly, the U.S. gold loss arises, not from a true deficit on trade in goods and services but from generous American economic aid compounded by large outflows of *private* capital to Canada and Western Europe. In other words, the United States has a current-account surplus which is more than offset by a capital outflow while Canada, in contrast, has a current-account deficit that is more than offset by a long-term capital inflow. Those Canadians who have recently given public expression to their fears regarding the inflow of foreign capital may well have their "problem" solved for them, regardless of any change of Canadian policy, through some kind of U.S. restriction on the export of private capital to Canada and other foreign countries.

The External Conditions of Monetary Independence

I turn now to what might be called "the external conditions of Canada's monetary independence." And in this category there is one special feature of our economy that increases to a marked degree the freedom of action of our monetary and fiscal authorities in spite of the fact that our borders are open to the free movement, both ways, of goods, services and capital. I refer to the free or "floating" exchange rate on the Canadian dollar.

Before considering some of the recent criticisms of our free exchange-rate policy, and some of the measures offered as alternatives, I would like first to state what I consider to be its overwhelming advantage. It is the same advantage that recommended it to our monetary and fiscal authorities when the policy was adopted in September, 1950: namely, that it automatically neutralizes and renders inert the potentially explosive effect of international "hot money" flows.

It is sometimes argued that "times have changed," we "face new problems," and hot money of the 1950 variety is no longer one of them. But hot money is no longer a problem for Canada precisely because we *have* the free exchange rate. Hot money today is an embarrassment to West Germany and Switzerland, now on the receiving end; the outflow of hot money has become far more than a minor annoyance, even to the United States with its enormous gold reserves, and is inhibiting its freedom of monetary and fiscal action to fight recession; and unpredictable inflows and outflows of hot money have plagued the British Treasury almost continuously since the end of the Second World War.

The U.S. dollar and the pound sterling are the world's leading reserve currencies. As such they are depended upon by the many countries that hold a large part of their exchange reserves in pounds sterling or U.S. dollars to maintain a fixed rate of exchange. This is the burden of leadership in the exchange markets of the world, and it exposes these reserve-currency countries to large and unpredictable swings in their exchange reserves as hot money in the slipstream of rumour, fear, optimism or greed, sweeps at far greater than jet speed from one exchange market to another. Were we to revert to a fixed rate of exchange, we too would be faced with hot money swings of this magnitude. Under such conditions Canada might as well renounce all pretence to independence in monetary and fiscal policy.

There are those who argue that, whatever its past virtues, Canada's floating exchange rate has behaved very badly in recent years because it has been at what is called a "premium" over the U.S. dollar, even though we have been running a large current-account deficit in international trade and payments. Canada's exchange rate is actually determined by the forces of demand and supply in world exchange markets. Nevertheless, it is even argued that this rate is an "artificial" rate, and that it should be reduced forthwith, presumably to whatever these advisers on public policy define to be its "natural" level! In fact, of course, such a rate could only be a set, or artificial, rate—the *true* natural rate, whether high or low, is the current floating rate.

But, to say that the floating rate is natural does not mean that, when it is high, it wreaks no hardship on exporters and on domestic producers facing import competition. Nor does it mean that we must necessarily sit back and let nature take its course. But the proposals heard most often in recent months with regard to exchange-rate policy do not attack the fundamental causes of our discontents. Instead, they would launch a massive assault on the obvious, the innocent, or the merely symptomatic; and when the rate is high, they would call for monetary manipulation to reduce the exchange "premium" directly or, in a more sophisticated version, to reduce interest rates and through them the exchange "premium" indirectly.

Unfortunately for the success of such operations, both the exchange rate and the interest rate are merely indicators of real forces in their respective markets. They will respond only temporarily to monetary manipulation. We can change them, if we wish, but only by an appropriate change in the real forces that determine them.

It is time we stopped talking dangerous nonsense about using fiscal and monetary policy, not for their legitimate purposes, but as an allegedly "easy" way of bringing down the exchange rate or the interest rate, or both. We are blaming the steam gauge for the lack of pressure in the boiler. Instead of stoking the fire we are pushing the needle to the right, while the pressure continues to fall. There is no easy way to bring down our exchange rate or our long-term interest rates or to achieve an excess of exports over imports or to cut down on foreign borrowing, if we think any or all of these things desirable; and the sooner we recognize the facts of life as they relate to economic policy, the sooner we will achieve the goals we seek.

I would suggest that our immediate goals at this time should be increased employment and balanced economic growth without inflation. And I would suggest further that these goals can be attained through appropriate monetary and fiscal measures buttressed by positive measures in a broader range of economic policy. They cannot be attained —indeed our problem can only be made worse—by concentrating on and trying, through monetary policy, to manipulate the exchange rate, or long-term interest-rate differentials between Canada and the United States.

The Internal Conditions of Monetary Independence

Independence in monetary and fiscal policy depends not only on freedom from undue interference from outside forces, which has been the burden of my remarks so far; it depends equally on effective domestic machinery through which policy may operate, and a healthy financial structure to implement that policy.

From what I have said so far you will probably have inferred, quite correctly in fact, that I do not share the critical attitude towards the Bank of Canada and its management that has found recent, and in some cases extreme, expression in the nation's press and elsewhere. I am opposed to the use of the Exchange Fund Account as an allegedly easy way to bring down the exchange value of the Canadian dollar and thereby presumably to solve the problems of exporters and domestic manufacturers, and increase employment. I am also opposed to increasing the money supply as an allegedly easy way to bring down long-term interest rates and thereby presumably to cut down our dependence on foreign sources of saving for investment in Canada.

I am not opposed to an increase in the money supply under appropriate conditions, but the decision to increase the money supply should be taken for the right reasons and not for its presumed effect on the rate of exchange or on long-term interest differentials between Canada and the United States. I would include among the right reasons the existence of slack in the economy due to a general failure of effective demand—that is, the kind of slack, the kind of unemployment and overcapacity, that can be overcome through the brute force of monetary and fiscal policy.

. . . In so far as unemployment in Canada is due, not to a failure of effective demand, but to structural faults in the economy, we shall still have too high a level of unemployment in spite of an increased money supply geared to an expansive fiscal policy.

Once this hard core of unemployment is reached, monetary and fiscal policy cannot help. We shall be forced to abandon the comparatively easy devices of monetary and fiscal policy and face the hard facts. We shall have to face up to the failure of labour mobility to keep pace, through retraining and through movement to appropriate areas and industries with our rapid rate of technological change. We shall have to face up to our inflated costs and slow growth in productivity which together account for the greater part of all the ills that are currently blamed either on the exchange rate or on the monetary policy of the Bank of Canada. These real, and apparently chronic, problems are the true cause of abnormally high levels of unemployment in good times and bad and of the general malaise which has been accurately labelled "high-level stagnation."

In taking measures to meet these problems, which are beyond the power of fiscal and monetary policy to solve, we must avoid, except as purely temporary measures, all forms of cost-inflating "make work" or "share the work" schemes: and I would include in this category any increases in tariff or other protection prompted merely by calculations (which may be wrong) of their direct effect on employment. Such measures could result in immediate retaliation at the expense of our exporters.

It is often said in defence of make-work schemes that our export industries, especially in the resource field, though highly efficient, are not large employers of labour. The implication is that we should encourage those branches of industry making products with a high labour content, even at the expense of our exporters. But this argument ignores almost every major contribution to the storehouse of economic wisdom made in the last thirty years.

Our export industries relative to their size may not be large *direct* employers of labour, but the income generated by our big, efficient, highly productive export industries has a multiple effect as it flows through our economy, and *indirectly* is a major, if not the greatest single source of demand for labour in Canada.

We should do everything in our power to strengthen the competitive position of our domestic manufacturing industry, beset as it is with tough import competition aggravated at times by the high exchange value of our dollar; but if in the process we should harm our export industries, the multiplier effect of a decline of income generated in that sector will work in reverse and the adverse *indirect* effect on employment in Canada may more than offset any direct gain to employment in manufacturing. Eventually, we shall have to face up to what is perhaps the most vital of all requirements for our long-run economic survival: that our so-called "domestic manufacturers" and not merely our traditional exporters, get out and sell at world prices in the world market.

I agree with the general aim and direction of our exchange-rate policy and our monetary policy; and, in what I have said so far, I have stated what I believe to be their impressive claim to our confidence. I shall now proceed to what I consider to be legitimate points of criticism.

The Governor of the Bank of Canada, in the course of his duties, has on appropriate occasions taken a strong and courageous stand against mounting pressure, and I include here pressure from the private sector of the economy. The soundest ground for the critics of exchange-rate and monetary policy lies, not in second guessing the monetary authorities in the performance of their often unpopular public duty, but in urging that, if their operations were smoother, and especially if the direction of policy were made clear to the banks, the money market, and the public, a number of intermittent crises, and a host of relatively minor upsets in the market, would disappear.

Under the present system, with a floating bank rate* completely useless as a signal, the banks are in the position of having to forecast not only the course of the eocnomy—that's our job—but also the course of monetary policy—and that I maintain is *not* our job. I realize that the same uncertainties regarding the coarse of economic events and changes in public policy have to be taken into account by the Governor of the Bank of Canada. For this reason all that the banks can realistically hope for is that they may be told, not what monetary policy will be in the future, but what it actually is at the moment. They must be content with "spot" not "futures," so far as monetary policy is concerned. The trouble today is simply that they do not get even this.

What is needed is a clear and unmistakeable sign of central-bank policy. This could take the form of a return to a "fixed" but periodically adjusted bank rate. Or, perhaps a return to a bank rate periodically adjusted by the Bank of Canada is not the best answer. There is no special reason for a rigid adherence to the British, or the American system. In fact there may be room here for a genuine innovation in monetary policy to suit Canadian conditions. But, whatever measure is adopted, the objective should be kept clearly in view: namely, to achieve, by innovation or otherwise, some clear and unmistakeable sign of central-bank policy that can be easily interpreted, not only by the chartered banks but by the rest of the money

---

* [In Canada the rate which the central bank charges commercial banks when they borrow varies with the market rate. Each week it is set at $\frac{1}{4}$ per cent above the average yield of Treasury bills. *Ed.*]

market and, especially perhaps, by the general public.

The Bogy of Foreign Investment

. . . . .

. . . there is a growing doubt in the minds of many, not only concerning our independence in monetary and fiscal policy, but concerning the future of our whole economy on some dread day of reckoning when, it is alleged, Canada will have to pay back an enormous debt largely contracted in the United States. This of course is an over-simplification of the issue and I know of no authority who has stated it in precisely this way; and yet this, I believe, is a fair statement of a widely held impression in the public mind. I should like now to attempt to define just what the problem is, and, more important still, what it is not.

It has been estimated that our "net international indebtedness," excluding offsetting investment by Canadians in foreign countries, was $17 billions by the end of 1960. But of this net figure at least two-thirds is not true debt but net "direct investment," largely in Canadian subsidiaries of U.S. corporations, which will never have to be "paid back." The remainder only, or probably less than one-third of the total, is net deadweight debt. This, of course, is a very much smaller burden of true debt than the statistics of our so-called "balance of international indebtedness" seem at first to indicate, and the imminence of the dread day of reckoning, the alleged inevitability of national bankruptcy, must be correspondingly discounted.

Nevertheless, five or six billions of dollars is still a lot of debt and, as a number of authorities have correctly pointed out, the sum is growing. There will come a time when Canada will rank as a "mature debtor," that is, she will find that in-payments, including long-term capital flows, will be exceeded by out-payments, including interest, amortization and dividend payments. But the problem some observers see of "providing foreign exchange" to meet this contingency is a spurious one—provided always that we keep our free exchange rate. Except under conditions of uncontrolled inflation, such as that experienced by Germany after the First World War, there can be no shortage of foreign exchange with a floating rate which automatically equates the demand for, and supply of, foreign exchange in the market.

When we become a "mature debtor" in the sense that I have defined the term, all we have to do is to let nature take its course. Our excess demand for U.S. dollars and other foreign currencies will result in an automatic fall in the Canadian dollar, a stimulation of exports and a discouragement of imports. In other words, when we *need* a surplus on merchandise and service account, because long-term capital inflow is exceeded by miscellaneous foreign payments, we shall undoubtedly get one! The lower exchange value on our dollar, through which this will be brought about, will undoubtedly please our exporters as well as domestic manufacturers subject to import competition. But there will also be sacrifices to be made. Debtors will find that the real burden of their interest and principal payments will rise if payable in foreign currency. But we must assume either that these debtors have accepted a long-term exchange risk with their eyes open —and deserve no sympathy, or have adequately reserved against the risk—and need none. Consumers, too, will be forced to pay higher prices for imports and other commodities, all of which means only that, as in any "mature debtor" economy, real resources have to be devoted to the servicing and repayment of debt. Nevertheless, in retrospect, I believe that we shall find these costs amply offset by the immense contribution of foreign capital over the years to Canada's economic growth.

It is in the light of these homely truths that I would like to comment on the recent wave of sentiment, amounting almost to hysteria, against the import of foreign capital. Tremendous pressure has been brought on the government to discourage a further inflow, and thus presumably to bring down our exchange rate, reduce foreign indebtedness, and in general to solve in one easy stroke of economic nationalism all the problems of trade, employment and debt that currently beset us. Apparently the Government has resisted this pressure, as concessions made in the "baby budget" of last December were relatively mild.

What this pressure group advocates in effect is not to delay or avoid but actually to *hasten* the arrival of the Day of Judgement which they profess to fear. All the burdens of debt repayment, overestimated as they are, would be on us immediately and without the benefit we could have derived from a continuing flow of long-term foreign capital. Moreover, if the value of the Canadian dollar is reduced through scaring off foreign capital, the supply of lendable funds available to Canadians is also reduced, and demand for funds in the Canadian market, by those formerly financing abroad, is correspondingly increased. As a result the capital market will be tighter and interest rates higher than they would be without the restrictions on foreign capital inflow.

To the extent that the higher than normal interest rates [which would then result] attract hot money, or even some long-term capital, the price of the Canadian dollar in the exchange market will be restored and the hoped-for effect on employment nullified. To the extent that higher than normal interest rates fail to attract capital, the effect of the lower exchange rate will be offset by continued tightness in the capital market and continued high interest rates, and again the hoped-for effect of employment may be nullified. In either case, the falling off in the supply of productive long-term capital will ensure that the final result will almost certainly be an actual *rise* in the level of unemployment in Canada.

The easy way out of this dilemma, according to some, is simply to increase the money supply and reduce the embarrassing interest differential between Canada and the United States. In fact, the inflationary potential of the increase in the money supply required for even temporary success in such an endeavour would so upset the Canadian bond market that the supply of lendable funds based on savings would be drastically reduced and the appropriate rate of interest even higher than at the beginning of the experiment.

The differential in interest rates between Canada and the United States is of long standing and it is no accident. It results from a difference in institutional factors, in the broadest sense of that term, including the power and the will to save and invest and, interdependent with these, the demand for and supply of lendable funds in the two countries. The differential is moderated, but not erased, by capital inflow; it is bound to become wider to the extent that capital inflow is inhibited; and it certainly cannot, in the long run, be erased by monetary policy.

Moreover, if the vote of non-confidence in the Canadian dollar, attendant on crippling legislation against foreign capital, has sufficient impact on investors abroad who are now investing in Canada's future, our dollar may indeed fall—further and more disastrously than was ever intended. Under these conditions, no practical level of interest rates or profits in Canada will be sufficient to overcome the *risk barrier* thus erected against the foreign capital we so urgently need if we are to achieve high employment and balanced economic growth without inflation.

The Real Problem

There *is* a real problem associated with the large capital inflow of recent years, but it is not that of finding the means of repayment. The real problem is simply that Canadians are becoming increasingly concerned about the growing foreign control over their industry. This is basically a political problem; a problem of maintaining national sovereignty, of being master in our own house.

Because foreign capital is necessarily tied up, sometimes in a rather complicated way, with the trade balance and the exchange rate, capital inflow has become a victim of "guilt by association" and has had to bear the brunt of much obscure criticism, most of which completely misses the point.

Once we have cast out the fear of some imminent Day of Judgement when all our massive (and overstated) debt will become due and payable, the nature of the problem is not only changed but made vastly simpler. The solution is clearly not to "do something" about the trade balance or to frighten foreign capital away, or to hobble it in some manner. In part, of course, the solution is to encourage Canadian saving, and *especially* Canadian investment in the kind of risk enterprise that is so dependent on foreign capital.

But, at least as important, if we are concerned about the behaviour of foreign-owned subsidiaries—now or in the future—let us secure, through *moral* suasion or appropriate legislation, the kind of behaviour we want. The foreign parents as well as their Canadian children would probably welcome a clarification of their position and a removal of the uncertainty which now arises from much Canadian grumbling but no clear-cut definition of where they stand and where we stand.

The problem of reconciling Canadian independence with the economic advantages of foreign invemstment is, like that of independence and economic strength through monetary policy, basically one of opening lines of clear and unambiguous communication.

Foreign owned subsidiaries are corporate Canadian citizens, subject to Canadian law. The government has the power to protect Canadian sovereignty by direct action. As in monetary policy, so in its policy towards international capital, the government, in ensuring a high degree of Canadian economic independence, need not resort to any tinkering with exchange rates, trade balances or capital flows which, even if it achieved its immediate objective in the short run (an extremely doubtful possibility), would do so only at the risk of incidental disaster to Canada's long-run economic development.

Such a failure to maintain, through right policy, both high-level employment and balanced growth will mean the end of all our hopes that Canada might, in this century, achieve her rightful stature as a prosperous *and* independent member of the family of free nations throughout the world.

STEFAN STYKOLT

The Canadian "Baby Budget" . . . was brought down by Conservative Finance Minister Donald Fleming on

---

STEFAN STYKOLT, "Anti-U.S. Trends in Canadian Economics Policy," *Monthly Business Letter* (March 1961) of the New England Merchants National Bank, prepared by the Institute for Business Science, Cambridge, Mass. Used by permission.

December 20, 1960. The ostensible reason for the "Baby Budget," and for the special session of Parliament called to receive it, is the high current level of unemployment in Canada, which amounted to 8.2% of the labor force in mid-December. But, the Baby Budget is likely to be remembered less for any contribution which it makes to the solution of unemployment than for its hostility towards foreign investors—which, though mild in fact, was over-dramatized in the press.

United States Investment in Canada

Canada's net borrowing from foreign countries and especially the U. S. has increased greatly in recent years during which the Canadian economy was experiencing a period of rapid growth. (See Table I)

TABLE I

CANADA'S NET INTERNATIONAL DEBT

Year	Canada $ billions (in 1960 prices)	Share of debt held in U.S.	in U.K.
1926	5.1	52%	48%
1945	3.9		
1950	4.0		
1958	13.0	87%	13%

In 1958 total U. S. [debt and equity] investment in Canada amounted to $14.6 billion and constituted 77% of all foreign investment in Canada. About two thirds of long term U. S. foreign investment in Canada is direct investment, the remainder being portfolio investment. U. S. investment in Canada is highly concentrated in two types of enterprises: those which supply the United States markets with raw or semi-processed materials, and those which supply the Canadian market with a variety of goods, often consumer durables or semi-durables, which the U. S. parent companies decide to manufacture in Canada because of the Canadian tariff and other obstacles to free trade. (See Table II)

TABLE II

PERCENTAGE OF INVESTMENT IN CANADIAN INDUSTRIES CONTROLLED OR OWNED BY U.S. INVESTORS, 1958

Mining and smelting	52%
Petroleum and natural gas production	71%
All manufacturing	43%
Automobiles and parts	95%
Rubber products	89%
Electrical apparatus and supplies	64%
Chemicals	50%
Pulp and Paper	43%
Agricultural machinery	41%

The rapid increase in foreign, particularly United States, ownership and control of considerable sectors of Canadian industry has led in the past five years to expressions of anxiety about its consequences for various facets of economic, social and political life in Canada. The Preliminary Report of the Royal Commission on Canada's Economic Prospects (published in December 1956) . . . recognized that growth of the Canadian economy requires "a 'package' of substantial capital, technology, skill and markets" which foreign investors do provide frequently. Nevertheless, it recommended measures intended to reduce the extent of foreign ownership, on the grounds that "many Canadians are worried about such a large measure of decision-making being in the hands of non-residents or in the hands of Canadian companies controlled by nonresidents."

The somewhat insubtantial fear was used to justify [a variety of proposals]. . . .

. . . . .

These recommendations, which one reviewer of the Report described as "another attempt to blackmail successful alien risk-takers into paying tribute to unenterprising but powerful local capitalists as the price for controlling the mob," have not been implemented. However, fretting over the foreign ownership question has been constant ever since the Report appeared. Motives for this anxiety range from selfless and genuine, though sometimes uninformed, concern for the preservation of *Canadian national entity* to a narrower preoccupation which maintains that what is good for Canadian underwriters is good for Canada.

Some of the discussion of the undesirable side-effects of foreign investment is based on sensible analysis, for instance the assertions that issues of Canadian securities payable in U. S. dollars may exert undesirable pressure on Canada's *terms of trade;* and that Canada's exports are restricted because U. S. corporations forbid their subsidiaries to "trade with the enemy."

Some is based on shoddy thinking, for instance the presumed effect of United States subsidiaries on monopolistic concentration in Canadian manufacturing, on plant location and expansion and the growth of research and development. Some is conducted without any attempt to measure the numbers involved, for instance the contention that dividend payments to foreign investors are likely to cause a drain on the economy's resources at some future time—which ignores the fact that the ratio of new payments for servicing the foreign debt to Canada's Gross National Product was only 1.3% in 1958, as against 3.9% in 1926, 4.4% in 1939, and 2.0% in 1946, before the great recent inflow of foreign capital started. Finally, some discussion of the social behavior of "foreign corporate citizens," especially discussion of their policies and attitudes on philanthropy and public information, merely expresses irritation with the not always tactful behavior of business corporations, some of them United States owned.

The New Isolationism

Preoccupations with the effects of United States investment in Canada have been intensified by recent events. In 1957 and again in 1958 the Conservative Government of Mr. John Diefenbaker won the general elections in which Mr. Diefenbaker's "vision" is alleged to have played a vital part. *The safeguarding of Canada as a separate national entity* is somehow believed to be a part of the vision, and so is the method of safeguarding this entity, which is to insulate Canada from some of the influence exerted on her economic, social, cultural and political life by the activities of citizens as well as the government of the United States.

Parallel to Mr. Diefenbaker's vision runs the vision of Mr. James E. Coyne, the Governor of the Bank of Canada, the central bank. Although Mr. Coyne was appointed by the Liberal Government in 1955, he has in the recent past become a very outspoken defender of Canada's *national identity* against the threat which he imagines is raised by the penetration of capital and goods from the United States. In his view, national independence requires economic independence, which he thinks consists of independence from U. S. imports.

Mr. Coyne's prescription, epitomized by his well-known call to Canadians to live within their means, requires that many of the most important economic decisions be surrendered to those who can take them solely with a view to securing an *economically self-contained Canada*, and whose judgment is not beclouded by unpatriotic market considerations of profit and loss or narrow political considerations of social cost and benefit.

In Mr. Coyne's view it may become necessary for the good of the country to impose a *variety of restrictions* on the inflow of foreign capital, to the entry of goods from abroad, and directives to the capital market so that the flow of domestic savings stimulated by high interest rates will be directed into channels considered productive and diverted from such apparently unproductive uses as the financing of consumers' purchases or the financing of social capital by borrowing on the part of provincial and municipal governments.

Monetary Policy and National Destiny

Canada's monetary policy, managed by the Bank of Canada, has been consistent with Mr. Coyne's views of the needs of national destiny. Despite the very high and rising level of unemployment, Canada's *interest rates rose steadily* from the beginning of September 1960 until the end of the year when the climb was halted. Associated with high interest rates has been the *high premium* on the Canadian dollar resulting in part from inflows of foreign capital. Part of the capital inflow was the result of foreign borrowing by Canadian corporations, provinces, and municipalities, which in 1960 sold between 20% and 40% of their new bonds outside Canada, in the effort to escape high interest rates.

Since it is Mr. Coyne's view that interest rates in Canada cannot be lowered without discouraging the flow of domestic savings and incurring the danger of inflation, the only way of reducing the premium on the Canadian dollar, undesirable at a time of severe unemployment, is to deter foreigners from lending to Canada. Thus, the short run need to cure unemployment is to deter foreigners from lending to Canada. Thus, too, the short run need to cure unemployment and the long run need to gain economic independence are made to coincide by the economic policy of Mr. Coyne.

Foreign Investment and the Baby Budget

Neglecting the indirect effects on Canada's borrowing from abroad of the protectionist provisions of the Baby Budget, the budget contains three provisions intended to restrict the flow of capital into Canada. First, there is the application of *a 15% withholding tax* to dividends [interest] on federal, provincial, municipal and corporate bond issues when these issues are payable in a *foreign* currency.

Previously, no such tax was levied. Since some institutional bond buyers in the United States are not subject to United States taxes, they are unable to offset this new Canadian tax against their United States tax liabilities. Therefore, it is estimated that Canadian bond issuers may now have to offer a *higher yield* than before, the estimates ranging between $1/2\%$ to $3/4\%$ on a typical issue by the Province of Ontario.

Second, the raising of the withholding tax from *5% to 15%* on issues payable in Canadian dollars, has an analagous, though smaller, effect in raising the yield that may have to be offered to lenders in the United States. Third, the requirement that all Canadian mutual funds must derive 75% of their dividend income from *Canadian* stocks is likely to provide foreign investors with some bargains in Canadian bonds and stocks that do not pay dividends, such as Alberta Gas Truck or Trans Canada pipelines, and to deter foreign investors from purchasing Canadian stocks which do pay dividends, because the prices of these are likely to rise.

Summary and Conclusion

Anti-U. S. trends in Canadian economic policy date back to 1955 and are related to the rapid rise since 1950 in

United States ownership and control of some sectors of Canadian industry. The Baby Budget of December 1960 is the first translation of such sentiments into policy. However, since the Budget merely imposes a tariff on imports of foreign capital, the main burden of the measures falls *not on the foreign investor* to whom a higher yield must now be offered, but on the Canadian borrower for whom the cost of borrowing abroad goes up. Thus, in so far as the budget has any unfavorable implications for foreign investors, they are first, a reduction of the opportunities to lend to Canadians, and, secondly, a change in the attractiveness of Canadian investment projects, this due more to uncertainty about future intentions of Canadian authorities rather than to anything the authorities have actually done to date.

The number of politically sovereign nations in the world, substantially increased in recent years, continues to grow as new nations are born. It is characteristic of these new states that their governments participate directly and extensively in forming and conducting the national economy. Governments of older nations, too, tend now to direct and control more actively the courses of national economies than they did before World War II; and there are some groups, including those who consider themselves socialists, who advocate still more active and extensive government participation in the conduct of national economic policy. Professor Viner of Princeton University, a leading expert on international affairs, gives his reasons for believing that an effect of governmental direction of economic life will be to increase political frictions between nations.

68 · State-Controlled Economies and International Quarrels

JACOB VINER

This paper deals with some aspects, primarily some "politico-economic" aspects, of the probable pattern of international relations in a world of sovereign nation-states in which all or most of the national economies are "state controlled." By a state-controlled economy, I mean one in which the major decisions of what is to be produced, exported, imported, lent abroad, borrowed abroad, etc., are exercised by the state (or agencies thereof), as distinguished from a "free enterprise" economy, where the decisions are predominantly in private hands and are made on the basis primarily of calculations of private profit. State control may take the form of merely bureau-

---

JACOB VINER, "International Relations Between State-Controlled National Economics," *The American Economic Review, Supplement* (March, 1944), pp. 315–329. Used by permission.

cratic control, or of direct operation of business activities, or of intermediate types of governmental intervention. . . .

. . . It is essential for my argument that by a state-controlled economy be understood one in which the extent of state control goes much farther than it did, say, in the United States, England, France, Sweden, or Canada, in the twenties or even in the thirties, although what I have to say has implications for any substantial degree of substitution of decisions of state for decisions of (small or moderate-scale) private enterprisers. . . .

1. Private enterprise, as such, is normally nonpatriotic, while government is automatically patriotic. The only important exceptions to this rule are to be found in the behavior of certain hermaphroditic corporations, which in form are more or less routine instances of profit-seeking private business, but in mode of operation are only with some difficulty distinguishable from governmental agencies . . . Such was the British East Africa Company, which, set up as a corporation to earn dividends for its shareholders, sank much of its proprietors' capital in the extension of territory for the British flag to fly over. Giant private corporations in general tend to acquire institutional objectives other than their proper ones of maximizing their shareholders' profits. These objectives occasionally have or seem to have a patriotic character, but it may generally be safely assumed that they have not been adopted by the corporations on their own initiative or of their own free will but have been accepted under government coercion, real or imagined or anticipated. Perhaps I should explain that for present purposes I will take "patriotic" activity to mean the deliberate utilization of privately owned resources by the owners, at financial cost to themselves, to serve national ends of power, prestige, prosperity.

If follows that the pattern of international economic relations will be much less influenced by the operation of national power and national prestige considerations in a world of free-enterprise economies than in a world of state-operated national economies. . . . Under Mercantilism, there were important branches of industry and commerce where the state held a tight rein, or even established state monopolies. But there was also a residual area, even in the international field, in which the legally recognized and protected freedom from state interference went further than anything we are now familiar with. Even as far back as Magna Carta the effects of foreign merchants were protected against seizure or confiscation in case of war against their state. As I read the evolution of international law under modern capitalism, as revealed from before 1600 to 1914 in the detailed provisions of international treaties, one of its outstanding characteristics was its attempt to build a legal protection for property and for private enterprise from the power activities of foreign states both in times of peace and in times of war. This protection was even extended to the property interests of nationals of one's own state which served enemy states and to the property interests of nationals of enemy states, sometimes with what, from a patriotic point of view, would seem to be fantastic results, as, for instance, when in the eighteenth century British insurance companies were free to insure the French owners of French merchant vessels against the risk of loss from capture by British naval vessels, or when during the Crimean War the British foreign minister lamented the absence of legal barriers against the London money market financing Russia's military activities against Britain.

2. If international business is conducted by private enterprise it will for

the most part be conducted on a substantially competitive basis. The difficulty of organizing monopoly is ordinarily too great to make its achievement on a durable basis and with a high degree of monopoly power possible except by virtue of governmental aid in the form of special franchises, concessions, legal sanctions against breach of monopoly agreements, or biases, deliberate or fortuitous, in the tax system against small-scale enterprise. Even when business achieves a high degree of monopoly power in the domestic field, competition from foreign sources and protective measures by foreign governments will often prevent it from attaining an appreciable degree of monopoly power, whether as buyer or as seller, in the foreign trade field. A government engaged in economic activity, on the other hand, even if it is only moderately centralized and administers its affairs with only moderate efficiency, will achieve monopoly power almost effortlessly and automatically within at least the range of operations subject to its jurisdiction. Even if government is itself loose and decentralized, or disinclined to engage directly in commercial enterprise, it can delegate to specially chartered companies, as in the Mercantilist period, the task of exploiting its potential monopoly power. . . .

3. The process of competition . . . will in the normal course of events give rise to a constant stream of allegations of chicanery, misrepresentation, gouging, unfair discrimination, and others of the less attractive manifestations of the Mercantile art. If the alleged perpetrators of such practices in the international field, as also those who feel themselves injured thereby, are private individuals or firms, the resultant ill-feeling may put a strain on the maintenance of friendly relations, and if the individual or groups concerned are influential may find expression in diplomatic complaints by the government of the aggrieved individuals. Where either perpetrators or victims are governments, however, and even more so if both parties are governments, the sense of grievance will result much more directly in an issue between governments, and the fact that a government, or governments, is involved will give the incident a much greater potency in inflaming public opinion in the countries concerned. The process of substitution of government business for private business is in the international field, therefore, also a process of transformation of private quarrels into intergovernmental quarrels.

This transformation of private quarrels into governmental quarrels is dangerous for peace. This is not only because resort to force is an immediately available instrument of persuasion for governments, and not only because the boiling point of patriotic public opinion is lower where governments are immediately involved in controversies than where either they are not formally involved at all or are involved only because of their intercession on behalf of individual nationals. There have been developed, in the course of centuries, detailed and elaborate codes and routine judicial procedures whereby disputes on commercial matters between nationals of different states can obtain adjudication in the courts of one or the other of the states upon the initiative of the complainant and on precisely the same terms as if both parties to the dispute were nationals of that state. These codes and procedures are, of course, incomplete in their coverage, and full enjoyment of the national standard of justice of the defendant's country may often leave the complainant with the feeling that all that he got thereby was the addition of insult and legal expense to the original injury. The situation in the private field is nevertheless incomparably better in this respect than in the field of intergovernmental relations. Here there is no code—except for the code of war. Except for mutual agreements, of very limited scope and effectiveness, for resort to arbitration or impartial adjudication, the only available procedures are diplomatic process, which in such cases is liable to be little more than a mechanism whereby threats and mutual recriminations can be transmitted in the most polite language; resort to political or economic reprisals; and, in extreme cases, or in cases where the aggrieved country appears to itself to be clearly the stronger, resort to force. . . . In the private economic field the instability of equilibrium is of itself of no large consequence. . . . In the international field where the monopolists are governments, however, the impossibility of reaching stable economic equilibrium has grave significance, for it involves as a corollary the persistence of economic factors working powerfully against the attainment of stable political equilibrium. Transfer of international business from private to governmental hands thus involves not only the economic costs of substitution of monopolistic for competitive procedures, but also the grave political disadvantage of the absence of any code or of any agency to enforce a code if one existed. . . .

To sum up the argument so far, I have tried to establish the propositions that the substitution of state control for private enterprise in the field of international economic relations would, with a certain degree of inevitability, have a series of undesirable consequences, to wit: the injection of a political element into all major international economic transactions; the conversion of international trade from a predominantly competitive to a predominantly monopolistic basis; a marked increase in the potentiality of business disputes to generate international friction; the transfer of trade transactions from a status under which settlement of disputes by routine judicial process is readily feasible and in fact is already well-established to a status where such procedure is not now routine, where a logical, administrable, and generally acceptable code does not seem to be available, where, therefore, *ad hoc* diplomacy is the best substitute available for the nonexistent law or mores, where diplomacy will by inherent necessity be such that the possibility of resort to force in case of an unsatisfactory outcome of the diplomatic negotiations will be a trump card of the powerful countries, and where weak countries will have to rely for their economic security primarily on their ability to acquire powerful friends, who will probably be acquirable, if at all, only at a heavy political or economic price.

. . . Socialists . . . , who have been brought up in or converted to the belief that a world of socialist states would be a world in which international relations, in the political as well as in the economic field, would be relatively frictionless as compared to anything we have known in the past, and that peace, harmony of interests, and mutual collaboration would come almost automatically in a socialist world, will be moved to strong protest. I am not able myself, however, to find any logical basis for confidence that if only state-controlled economies were equalitarian and democratic—which, I take it, would make them "socialist"—that would of itself take the curse off state control. . . .

. . . . .

It is—or was until the rise of Hitler —orthodox socialist doctrine that war arises out of the conflict of economic interests between the ruling classes of different countries. Under capitalism, in particular, the workers, as a class, have no fatherland, have nothing to gain from victorious war. Wars are fought by them, but never for them. . . . As samples of conventional formulations of the doctrine, I cite, from the very many available, two statements, one [1906] by an English "liberal," J. A. Hobson . . . and the other [1943] from an authoritative Soviet source, so as to include both poles of socialist belief:

> The apparent oppositions of interest between nations, I repeat, are not oppositions between the interests of the people conceived as a whole; they are expositions of class interests within the nation. The interests of American and Great Britain and France and Germany are common. The interests between certain groups of manufacturers or traders or politicians or financiers may be antagonistic at certain times within these groups, and those antagonisms, usurping the names of national interest, impose themselves as directors of the course of history; that is the actual difficulty with which we are confronted.[1]
>
> The capitalistic structure of the various States and their competition on the world market, the chase after profits and super-profits are creating among them irreconcilable contradictions which unavoidably will lead to international conflicts—so long as capitalism exists.[2]

This doctrine of the purely economic causation of war and of its special affinity with capitalism and its associated class structure was not confined to socialists. After the last war, in fact, it was the prevailing doctrine taught in American colleges, especially in the history and political science departments. As I know to my cost, to question its validity before the properly indoctrinated undergraduate "Liberal Clubs" of the time was to disclose oneself as either incurably naïve or a hireling of the capitalists. It is my impression that economists for the most part escaped the contagion. . . . Even when expounded by historians, the doctrine was in no case that I am aware of the product of genuine and reasonably objective historical research. For the most part, no research of any kind or quality was involved. . . .

. . . The doctrine was basically *a priori*, but it was often dressed up in alleged facts. . . . I am particularly fond of a statement [1933] of the doctrine in historical terms by Harold Laski, because in a single paragraph he cites almost every one of the stock episodes in the repertoire:

> No one now denies that the British occupation of Egypt was undertaken in order to secure the investments of British bondholders; and that the South African War was simply a sordid struggle for the domination of its gold-mines. The French invasion of Mexico under Napoleon III was an effort to protect the interest of French investors in that ill-fated state. Nicaragua, Haiti, San Domingo, to take only the most notable cases, have all been reduced to the position of American provinces in the interest of American capitalists. The Russo-Japanese war was, in the last analysis, the outcome of an endeavor by a corrupt Government to defend the immense timber-concessions in Manchuria of a little band of dubious courtiers. The savage cruelties of the Congo; the struggle between British and American financiers for the control of Mexican oil; the fight between Germany and the Entente for the domination of pre-war Turkey; the reduction of Tunis to the position of a French dependency; the Japanese strangulation of Korean nationalism; all these are merely variations upon an identical theme. Men have sought a specially profitable source of investment. They have been able to utilize their Government to protect their interest; and, in the last analysis, the Government becomes so identified with the investor, that an at-

---

[1] Hobson, J. A., "The Ethics of Internationalism," *International Journal of Ethics,* XVII (1906–07), p. 28.
[2] Communist Academy, Moscow, *Encyclopedia of State and Law,* 1925/1926, p. 749. i, as cited in *International Conciliation,* No. 386, January 1943, p. 24.

tack on his profit is equated with a threat to the national honour. In those circumstances the armed forces of the state are, in fact, the weapon he employs to guarantee his privilege.[3]

Of all this long series of positive assertions as to historical fact, there is not one which would withstand even the most cursory inspection. Historical episodes always seem to grow more complex as one learns more about them, and I am sure that no one simple pattern of interpretation will fit any two of these episodes. But of almost all of these episodes this at least is true, that if you exactly reverse the role of the capitalist *vis-à-vis* his government assigned to him by Laski, you will be much closer to the truth than he is. In almost all of these cases, the capitalist, instead of pushing his government into an imperialistic enterprise in pursuit of his own financial gain, was pushed, or dragged, or cajoled, or lured into it by his government, in order that, in its relations with the outside world and with his own people, this government might be able to point to an apparently real and legitimate economic stake in the territory involved which required military protection against unfair treatment or general misgovernment by the local authorities or against encroachment by other powers. In perhaps two or three of these cases, illegitimate profits of investors, even in terms of bourgeois morality, were notoriously involved. But seekers of illegitimate profits are likely to try to find a foothold in any large-scale operation, and will sometimes succeed. I know of only one case, of these cases, in which there is even plausible evidence that the act of imperialist aggression originated in a desire to promote the special financial interests of a small number of wealthy men. The one exceptional case was the case of the Congo. Here private profit was clearly the major, if not the sole, objective. But the profiteer and the imperialist statesman were here the identical person, King Leopold of Belgium, and the moral to be drawn from this case would seem to be the general moral I am trying to expound; namely, that it is dangerous to peace for governments as governments to engage in international business transactions.

. . . . .

. . . The neo-Marxians have developed, alongside and conflicting with the scandal theory, another more sophisticated theory of imperialism and war which seems to my meager acquaintance with the Marxian system of thought to be much more in harmony with its inner logic. This other doctrine, instead of imputing imperialism to the profit-seeking machinations of a few unscrupulous capitalists, explains it as a natural and inevitable product of the *modus operandi* of the capitalist system as a whole. This theory has been expounded in terms of the famous three "surpluses"—of capital, of population, and of goods—held to arise inevitably out of the capitalist process, and to be susceptible of liquidation only by the acquisition by force or threat of force of industrially backward areas, which can supply hitherto unexploited fields for the employment of surplus capital, new markets for goods, and opportunities for settlement of the redundant workers of the older countries.

This theory, which, like the scandal theory, is accepted by many who are not, as far as they are aware, socialists, is certainly not without plausibility. There is no *a priori* reason why war should *not* arise from the search for more profitable fields than are available

---

[3] Laski, H. J., "The Economic Foundations of Peace," in Leonard Woolf, *The Intelligent Man's Way to Prevent War* (London, 1933), pp. 507-508.

at home for the employment of capital, or from the desire for settlement colonies as a relief from population pressure at home, or from rivalry in obtaining privileged access to undeveloped export markets. Considerations of this character have, in fact, undoubtedly played a considerable role in the history of modern imperialism. These considerations, of themselves, fall far short, however, of accounting adequately for the prevalence of imperialism and war, either today or in any past period. Debtor countries alike with creditor countries, countries with declining population trends alike with countries conscious of acute population pressure, countries without commercial interests alike with actively trading countries, have engaged in imperialist ventures. Moreover, there is nothing in this theory, except perhaps its assumption of an embarassing abundance of capital in the aggressive countries, which justifies any special association of the three surpluses as causes of war with modern capitalism or any diasssociation of them from the socialist state, or from any other form of nation-state.

In the socialist state, moreover, such considerations should be expected to be given more weight, and to exercise more direct and more forceful influence on policy, than in a capitalist society where free enterprise prevails. In the first place, the socialist state, with its unified and centralized administration, would be technically better equipped to harness the national resources to national policy than would a loosely organized capitalist democracy. In the second place, the equalitarian element in the socialist doctrine, while it might create an ideological barrier against making demands on poorer countries, would provide a moral basis not available to capitalist countries for aggression against richer countries reluctant to share their riches with other countries.

The equalitarian logic of socialism has no natural stopping place at national boundaries. Third, in the full-fledged socialist state an aggressive foreign policy directed toward economic objectives could not be checked at home by an opposition believing or asserting that the profits of the aggression would go exclusively to a small privileged class. One of the disadvantages of the socialist state in this connection, as compared to the capitalist state, would be the absence of an antipatriotic socialist opposition. Fourth there would not be in the socialist state a powerful middle class with property interests to protect against risks of all kinds, including the risks of war.

. . . . .

. . . Even if under capitalism socialists tended to be internationalist and pacifist, that provides no assurance that in a world of socialist states socialists would not be unqualified national patriots.

. . . . .

I have stated my reasons for believing that the extension of state control over national economies would, of itself, not be conducive to peaceful relations between nations, but, on the contrary, would make international economic intercourse, and national restrictions on such intercourse, a breeding ground for deep and dangerous international friction. I have argued that, insofar as, in the past, war has resulted from economic causes, it has been to a very large extent the intervention of the national state into economic process which has made the pattern of international economic relationships a pattern conducive to war. I have given reasons for expecting that socialism on a national basis would not in any way be free from this ominous defect. It may seem, therefore, that I have argued, in effect, that economic factors can be prevented from breeding war if, and only if, private enterprise is freed from extensive state control other than state control intended to keep enterprise private and competitive. This is my conviction, *for a world of autonomous nation-states*.

War, I believe, is essentially a political, not an economic, phenomenon. It arises out of the organization of the world on the basis of sovereign nation-states. Sovereign states will find occasion for friction and for war with other states in all the types of contact, and of state-suppression of contact, across national boundaries, economic and noneconomic. This will be true for a world of socialist states as for a world of capitalist states, and the more embracing the states are in their range of activities the more likely will be serious friction between states. If states reduce to a minimum their involvement in economic matters, the role of economic factors in contributing to war will be likewise reduced. Only, however, if mankind shall establish, or evolve, or have imposed on it, a world political order in which some form of world-authority will have the power and the will to restrain the activities of nation-states, whether economic or not, when they are such as to threaten the maintenance of peace, and perhaps also to enforce upon the nation-states positive action conducive to international collaboration, will mankind have any reasonable prospect of freedom from the recurrent threat of war. The greater the movement toward state control of economies, whether on a socialist basis or not, the more will this be true.

The emergence in recent years of nation-states which were certainly not free-enterprise states, which assumed the socialist label, and which conformed in their economic, if not in their political, organization much more to the orthodox socalist than to the bourgeois capitalist pattern, but which were avowedly and unashamedly advocates and practitioners of the use of national economic and military power for aggressive purposes, has brought even some socialists to the same conclusion. . . . I will quote from an English socialist, Barbara Wootton: "the notion that you must get socialism first, after which all things international will be added unto you, is a notion which ignores the lessons of experience." [4]

---

[4] Wootton, Barbara, "Socialism and Federation," *Federal Tracts No. 6* (London, 1941), p. 13.

XIII • ECONOMIC GROWTH: THE UNITED STATES

"Growth" is perhaps the aspect of economics of greatest concern today. What is it? How much have we had in the past? What conditions are necessary for growth? What will help, or hinder, growth? How does the United States compare with other lands? Ten economists with different backgrounds examined such questions at one of the regular forums of the National Industrial Conference Board. The Board, for almost half a century, has been one of the world's leading private, nonprofit, fact-finding organizations. Although it is financed by contributions from business, the Board seeks to provide facts which will help the public as a whole, as well as private enterprise, to solve economic problems. Discussions sponsored by the NICB deal with important subjects about which opinions differ. The excerpts which follow include less than one third of the complete discussion. The economists whose views are presented—but in no case is the entire contribution of the speaker reproduced—are: Solomon Fabricant (Chairman), Jules Backman, Martin R. Gainsbrugh, Edwin B. George, Raymond W. Goldsmith, George P. Hitchings, Donald Paarlberg, Lloyd G. Reynolds, O. Glenn Saxon, and Woodlief Thomas.

69 • Economic Growth: A Discussion by Economists

A SYMPOSIUM

CHAIRMAN FABRICANT: . . . Economic growth may be defined as *increase in national product per capita,* which is, at any rate, an important ingredient in every definition of economic growth. And economic growth in itself is important not only because it is the major way out of the poverty that afflicts the mass of mankind, but also because it is inextricably interwoven with most of the serious political and other world problems that are troubling us.

In this day of jet travel, it does not take long to see the dire poverty in

---

NATIONAL INDUSTRIAL CONFERENCE BOARD, "Prerequisites for Economic Growth," A Discussion by the Conference Board Economic Forum and Guests (New York: September 24, 1959). *Studies in Business Economics,* No. 66, National Industrial Conference Board, New York. Excerpts used by permission.

which most of the people on this earth live. But even in Western Europe, levels of living are substantially below ours. . . .

Today in Western Europe, the average level of national income per capita or its nearest measurable equivalent (which is usually gross national product) is about half that of the United States. . . . Even on optimistic assumptions, the level they might expect to reach in 1975 is 20% below the *present* average level in the United States. Now these Western European countries are among the most prosperous countries of the world. The comparison then only serves to highlight the degree to which the bulk of mankind still needs goods and services.

. . . . .

Martin Gainsbrugh has pointed out that it would be useful to have a capsule summary of some of the basic facts on economic growth. Perhaps the best way to do that is to present some of the figures that we have for the United States. We know from the studies that have been made—at the National Bureau of Economic Research, the National Industrial Conference Board, the National Income Division in Washington, and elsewhere—that national product per capita in this country has been rising at an average of something like 20% a decade over the past century or so. This is a very substantial rate of increase. Sustained over so long a period—and our record is remarkable in that respect—it means the sixfold increase I mentioned earlier.

It is rather interesting also to observe that there has been no significant sign of any diminution—or acceleration—in the rate of growth in national product per capita.

MR. BACKMAN: That is an important point, because there have been so many statements, made on the basis of selected statistics, that it's accelerating.

MR. SAXON: This rate, as I understand it, is the real per capita growth, regardless of price changes.

CHAIRMAN FABRICANT: That's right; these are deflated figures. It is interesting, and important to keep in mind, that this rather persistent rise of about 20% a decade in real income per capita has taken place with the population going up—with man-hours of work per person in the labor force falling, not rising—with the distribution of income among the families of this country less, not more, concentrated, at least for the period for which we have reasonably adequate records; and I might say that the same seems to be the case for the distribution of wealth.

Now, if hours of work per capita have fallen, it is clear that national product per man-hour of labor has increased more rapidly than national product per capita. Indeed, the rate of increase in real product per man-hour for the United States over the past ninety years or so has been about 25% a decade.

Gain in Output Per Man-Hour

MR. GAINSBRUGH: Let's have that again slowly. Output per man-hour for the nation as a whole has increased at about 25% per decade.

CHAIRMAN FABRICANT: That is correct —a 25% increase every ten years, on the average, in real national product per man-hour of work done. . . .

The facts point to an increase in the rate of growth in recent decades. I can illustrate that by pointing out that during the period preceding World War I, the average rate of increase in national product per man-hour was around 22% per decade. Between World War I and the present, it has averaged about 29% per decade. During the most recent period, that is, since World War II, national product per man-hour has been going up at an even greater rate—in the neighborhood of 35% or so per decade.

Just to highlight the magnitude of this increase in national product per man-hour, let me observe that in a ten-year period we in the United States have *added* to output per man-hour of American labor an amount that is well in excess of the *total* output obtained per hour of work in most parts of the earth. . . .

. . . I don't know that the rate of savings of the United States is unusually high in relation to what it has been in other countries at one time or another. This is one of the blind spots in our statistics. But we've had this rate of savings decade after decade after decade, with hardly a letup. It's been persistent and of the order of 10%, or perhaps 12%, of national product—that is, the savings going into investment of a tangible sort.

MR. GEORGE: This would, of course, include corporations . . .

CHAIRMAN FABRICANT: . . . and also governmental savings. . . . To judge from the figures, . . . [saving] is not *the* factor that accounts for economic growth. It is an essential and necessary factor. Let us be clear about what I'm saying. I'm talking about the volume of tangible capital. I am not, at the moment, talking about the quality of tangible capital, which is better treated under technological change. Nor am I talking now about intangible capital—which is so important: intangible capital in the form of education of human beings, or intangible capital in the form of new ways of doing business. . . .

What the economists have learned over the years about the causes of increase in real income per capita points to the fact that, while investment in tangible capital is necessary, it alone is not sufficient to account for the rate of growth that we have had. . . .

. . . Let me underscore the words *necessary and important:* investment of tangible capital, and the savings that make that investment possible, are *necessary and important for growth.* The United States would be an utterly different country in terms of level of production if it were not for the vast amount of factory, plant and equipment we have, our enormous investments in railroads and public utilities, our business inventories that bulk larger than many major categories of plant and equipment, our housing. This latter, incidentally, is something many underdeveloped countries fail to appreciate: if they are to raise productivity as well as their standard of living, it is important for them to invest in things like housing. Some people also ignore the fact that our vast volume of consumer durable goods likewise plays a very important role in producing the standard of living that we have. . . .

The same can be said for the kind of investment that goes on in new ideas, scientific work, research generally, and in the development of new products, new methods and new materials. The fact that our books of account fail to include this investment does not mean that these are not truly inputs as much as tangible capital, as much as man-hours of labor. . . .

One of the big questions that confronts us is what will be our future rate of growth in national product per man-hour or per capita as compared with that of other countries? . . . The figures clearly show that the more recent rates of increase of real product per man-hour in the United States—on the average—has been in excess of those of earlier generations. This, however, does not provide a solid basis for assuming a further increase in the rate. All we can say at the moment, is that we have been doing better in this generation than our fathers or grandfathers did in theirs.

Available figures would also suggest that in some countries the rate of increase in real income per man-hour or per capita not only has been greater than that of the United States but will continue to be greater. . . .

. . . This brings me to the last point that I want to make. . . . Far too much emphasis has been placed on increasing input. That takes the form . . . of an undue emphasis on capital investment; and it often takes the particular form of an undue emphasis on capital investment by government.

Need for Some Clear Answers

I think a reasonable interpretation of the records of the United States and other countries would suggest that other factors are also important, particularly the economic policies that determine the environment within which individual decisions are made about efficiency and investment. The questions that arise here are of the following sort:

To what degree can we ascribe the rate of increase in our national income per capita to the degree of competition we have had in the past? to an environment favorable to savings and investment? to an environment favorable to the mobility of labor and mobility of capital?

To what extent can we expect an unfavorable impact upon our rate of growth if the kind of competition we have in this country is lessened through institutional and other changes?

If some of the efficiency that we have had in this country is lessened through a continuation or expansion of subsidies of a wasteful sort, to what extent will that affect the incentives that move men to improve, to invest for the future?

Have these incentives already been hurt or will they be hurt sooner or later by improper kinds or unduly high rates of taxation?

[In 1959] there appeared a translation of . . . a paper by a Russian economist. . . .

Let me quote just three sentences:

The many years of experience in the organization of social labor under socialism have shown that equalitarianism is incompatible with the interests of the development of socialist production . . . The Communist Party of the Soviet Union has always conducted a consistent struggle against all efforts to 'replace' distribution in accordance with labor by petty-bourgeois equalitarianism in the payment of labor . . . It is necessary more completely to utilize the . . . principle of personal material incentive for a further upsurge of socialist production and the hiring standards of the people.

MR. GAINSBRUGH: Very shortly, I suppose we'll be reading about their discovery (or rediscovery) of the incentives of capitalism?

CHAIRMAN FABRICANT: Martin, some people put your point as follows: Is it that the Russians are moving toward an enterprise economy, while perhaps the United States and other countries of Europe are moving away from an enterprise economy?

. . . . .

MR. THOMAS: . . . We are learning that we can use scarce resources more efficiently and do a lot of things for welfare by means other than just purely physical resources, but we still have to consider that one reason why certain of these countries have lower standards of living than we have is that they simply have more people relative to their basic physical resources than we have. It is indigenous to the situation—and there is not much that you can do about it—that they will have to do a tremendous amount of adjusting before they can get to our levels of living—a great deal more than needs to be done in other richer countries.

. . . I would say that there are three

essentials. One is a high level of utilization of available resources. The second, already discused here, is improvement in processes and methods so as to increase the productivity of resources. The third, which is necessary for the second, is maintenance of a balanced economy with reference to consumption, savings, and investment and with respect to price and income relationships. This latter is the principal point I should like to emphasize: that a prime requisite for economic growth is the persistence of balance in economic development.

We cannot rely simply on increasing consumer incomes by arbitrary action. It is essential to have growth in production as well as growth in demand. To get growth in production we must have proper utilization of our available resources; for that, the proper combination of investment and savings is necessary.

. . . In the end, we cannot increase capital resources unless we save. We cannot increase even the expenditures on education or these other things that add to welfare unless we decrease some other elements of personal consumption. There has to be saving by government or a diverting of personal resources from consumption into other channels, either by voluntary action or by the action of government, in order to provide for increases in productive capacity or increases in welfare or whatever it is that government provides. . . .

. . . so many of the programs and exhortations that we get these days for growth are expressed in terms of increasing demand, not in terms of allocating our resources in a manner that may contribute to growth. We can certainly increase consumption: I mean we can increase the consumption of an individual by increasing his income.

But can we increase consumption for the economy as a whole unless a certain portion of that income is allocated to investment and expenditure for capital equipment?

MR. BACKMAN: By "demand," do you mean in this case consumer demand or the total demand for all types of goods?

MR. THOMAS: I would say total demand. But you have to be sure that some part of the toal demand goes into investment.

MR. BACKMAN: Those who advocate that we can increase growth by increasing demand really emphasize consumer demand rather than other types of demand.

MR. THOMAS: Yes. They generally emphasize consumer demand or governmental activities, one or the other; and they emphasize government spending without taxation. . . .

I don't rule out grants for the development of underdeveloped countries. All I say is, if we give grants we have to curtail our own consumption accordingly in order to develop the other country. This is just a general proposition. . . .

. . . We can get increased savings without necessarily getting increased productivity. That's one of the characteristics of recent developments.

A large proportion of our savings currently goes into credit, for consumption and for government; and less into producers' capital. Federal Government expenditures are now 9% of the gross national product instead of 1% as in the 1920's, and deficits are larger and more frequent. Much of our savings are siphoned off by federal, state and local governments.

Our savings also have been heavily invested in home mortgages. Homes are capital, but to what extent do they contribute to increasing the productivity of the economy? Their contribution is indirect; it's more intangible. A tremendous lot of recent credit expansion has been in the consumer field, including mortgages and consumer indebtedness for durable goods, and now even for all sorts of other types of consumption—travel and so forth. That type of credit absorbs the savings of our people—the financial savings of certain individuals are going to other individuals for these purposes rather than into producers' goods. . . .

. . . Since the war, the rate of credit expansion has been much larger for state and local governments and consumer credit and mortgages than it has been for business capital. I suspect that would be true even if you put in retained corporate earnings. . . .

I don't want to imply that these proportions are necessarily harmful. It may be that we did not need any more capital expenditure to provide the proper rate of growth. It may be that we needed more consumption and less saving. But it is nevertheless a characteristic of our economy that a great deal of our savings are now going through consumption channels. That may be one of the reasons why we have high interest rates. It may be one of the reasons why our prices are less attractive than foreign prices.

If we had allocated more resources to expand our productive capacity, we might have had more competition and more price reductions. We might not have had all, or nearly all, the benefits of increased productivity going to wages. We might have had more of it going to consumers. We might, therefore, have had a stimulus to increased consumption through those channels rather than the channels of government and credit sources that have been used. . . .

MR. BACKMAN: How do you reconcile the suggestion that we might have invested these savings in productive capacity with what appears to be an over-expansion of capacity in many industries, including railroads, steel and aluminum? I gather that the automobile industry can turn out more than six million or seven million cars a year if it has to. Would there really have been an outlet for these funds in the form of productive equipment as you mentioned?

MR. THOMAS: In answer to your . . . question as to whether we would have overcapitalization, or overcapacity, there is of course that possibility. But I am not sure that that is true. That leads to my second point, about what is essential for the maintenance of a balanced economy; that is essentially a question of price and income relationships. Both consumption and investment demands can be influenced by pricing policies. It may be we could have sold more automobiles if the automobile people had produced cheaper cars instead of the more expensive ones. It may have been that we would have sold more steel if the steel industry had lowered the price for steel. . . .

. . . there are other policies and factors that are far more important than monetary policy in the determination of growth. So much of recent economic thinking and talk places too much emphasis on aggregates—aggregate consumption, aggregate demand, aggregate investment and so forth.

. . . Wesley Mitchell felt that the heart of the problem in the business cycle lay in the question "how an economic system of inter-related parts develops internal stresses during expansions, stresses that bring on recessions, and how the uneven contractions of its varied parts ultimately pave the way for revivals."

Mitchell placed great emphasis upon pricing, price policies, and price relationships. Now we have a whole system of economic theory in which pricing plays no part at all. Most economic forecasts are based on aggregate demand, investment, and so forth, with little if any consideration given to the pricing policies that may be followed by business and by labor. There is something wrong with an economic theory which assumes that any producer or seller can demand any price for his product that he wants to and expect to get it; and that it is the task of government to see that it is possible for him to get it and not have to curtail production if he cannot sell his products. This is fundamentally incorrect as a body of economic theory. And yet that is the assumption of so much of economic thinking today. . . .

. . . the effects of incorrect pricing policies cannot be overcome by inflating the currency. . . . You cannot have growth if you have inflation. Inflation brings about its own correctives. Eventually it will create speculative and unhealthy situations.

So there is a conflict between inflation and growth. They are not alternatives. . . . Riefler summarized his main points briefly as follows:

Inflation is the enemy of growth, particularly when there is public expectation that the purhasing power of money will continue to decline. Inflation impairs growth:

1. *Because it increases instability—high level of activity cannot be sustained for long when inflation is expected to prevail;*

2. *Because it fosters the misallocation of capital and impairs the quality of the managerial and investment decisions on which growth is based;*

3. *Because it distorts the saving-investment process and encourages overspeculation; and*

4. *Because it undermines the country's position in international trade.*

MR. GAINSBRUGH: Would it be a correct summary of what you have said, . . . that monetary policy has only a secondary rather than primary role to play?

MR. THOMAS: Decidedly, a very secondary role. The task of the monetary policy is to provide for adequate cash balances that the public wants to hold, or provide for the temporary credit needs that will supply the cash balances the public wants to hold. If you want a broad concept of savings, it's the amount of savings that people want to hold in cash. That is all that monetary policy is supposed to provide.

When monetary policy provides more cash than people want and more credit than people want to hold in the form of cash, then we're going to have an inflationary influence. I explained the role of monetary policy with respect to growth in a paper. . . .

At that time I said:

. . . . .

It is most important that bank credit not be employed as a substitute for saving at a time when investment demands exceed the supply of savings available for lending and when there is relatively full utilization of resources. In a broad sense, bank credit changes should correspond to changes in savings that are held in cash form, if economic balance is to be maintained.

Monetary policies should be conducted so as not to contribute to instability by forcing credit liquidation or stimulating unsustainable credit expansion. Monetary policies, however, cannot be expected to offset instability arising from other factors. To attempt to do so would be likely to accentuate rather than prevent instability in prices and employment in the long run. There is no case—at least since the establishment of the Federal Reserve System—in which a downturn has been brought on by tight money. Downturns have usually developed because of pricing policies and income distortions or unsustainable speculative developments that were often aided by excessive credit expansion.

In summary, I would include among the prerequisites for growth the following:

1. *Adequate saving so as to make available the resources for investment and the funds for their financing*

2. Investment of types that add to productive capacity
3. Pricing policies (including wages) that encourage the movement of additional goods produced into consumption or investment. This would require a cessation of the wage-price spiral and preferably decreases in prices in reflection of increases in productivity
4. Avoidance of inflationary fiscal and monetary policies that would encourage excessive commitments of a speculative or otherwise unsustainable nature

CHAIRMAN FABRICANT: We are very grateful to you, Woody, for raising this question about inflexible prices, and I presume you would include inflexible wage rates. Your comments raise some very real questions about competition, markets for goods, and markets for labor. Perhaps they would be something, Lloyd Reynolds, about which you might want to direct some attention. May I call on you now?

Some Notes from a Traveler from Russia

MR. REYNOLDS: . . . I can't present a very glowing report on the state of economics in Russia, I'm sorry to say. It's a technocratic society where the engineer is king and the cream of the talent goes into engineering and science. Those who go into economics are apt to be the also-rans.

One suspects that there must be some good economists, but they are mainly in government and operating positions rather than teaching. The Russian university economists seem even more ivory-tower than many of our American economists, spinning the prayer wheel and writing footnotes to Marx.

CHAIRMAN FABRICANT: Are you implying that the Russian economists will do even more damage to the economy than American economists do?

. . . . .

MR. REYNOLDS: Oh, yes, I think they have probably done considerable damage to the Russian economy and would do more if they were given more influence; but they do not seem to have much influence. . . .

I pushed the factory managers quite hard on labor questions. Their setup in this respect is, in a way, very-early-capitalistic. To find anything comparable in this country you would have to go back to 1900, to the early days of scientific management, with not much union organization or worker control over what the engineers were doing. This was quite striking.

The position of the Russian factory director also seems to be quite similar in many respects to that of a capitalist manager. It seemed to me that those fellows were working for about the same reasons that an American corporation executive would work. If they do well, they get promoted to a bigger enterprise, and get a good bonus at the end of the year. Conversely, if they do not do well, presumably they will be demoted, have less interesting work, and make less money.

Despite all the talk about working for the joy of socialist labor, and so on, it seemed to me that these fellows were quite like American business executives in their outlook on their job. They are almost all engineers. In fact, they cannot understand how we allow people to become business executives without engineering training. This they regard as the standard way of getting into an executive position. Not only the plant director, but the deputy director and a good many people lower down are engineers.

. . . . .

MR. PAARLBERG: It seems to me that government planning in the United

States and government planning in the Soviet Union are two very different things. Some of the obvious inefficiencies that we associate with government planning here can't be carried over and interpreted as being inherent in the Soviet system. In our planning in this country, we properly take very careful account of the wishes of the individual. In the Soviet Union they can make plans which deny people current consumption, in favor of substantial investment which would yield greater return at a later date. We may make an error when we simply infer that the inefficiencies which we see in central planning with our system are inherent in the central planning that the Soviet Union has.

MR. GAINSBRUGH: But there may be other inefficiencies in their type.

MR. PAARLBERG: They may in some respects be very great and in some respects greater than ours. Certainly they downgrade the cause of human freedom, which to us is most important. But I think we must reexamine the prevailing thought in this country; namely, that government is by nature inefficient and that you cannot get a very rapid rate of economic growth with an authoritarian system.

MR. HITCHING: Growth in total output is essential for a prosperous economy. Productivity advances are not enough to provide more leisure time. Total output must grow to take care of increased population and desires for a higher standard of living per capita. Growth in total output and in productivity does not just happen automatically. Action by individuals and groups of individuals is required. Our present standard of living has evolved from continued additions to the stock of human knowledge and capital.

We have developed new and improved products, together with new and improved techniques of production. A major driving force in these developments has been individual striving for financial reward in a competitive, free-choice society. Allocation of resources has been based largely upon degree of success in competing for the customer's dollars. This allocation and income flow through the free market has been increasingly modified by government and by organization of labor and business on a larger scale. . . .

Some of the more vocal exponents of growth call for (1) increased government spending; (2) higher pay rates; and (3) arbitrary total growth rates without regard to the kind of growth or how it is obtained. Some types of government spending—national defense, highways, basic education, police and fire protection, etc.—must be made available on a social group basis. To the extent that this spending is financed by drawing upon funds which would otherwise be spent for other goods and services, there is no net addition to total output. To the extent that credit or otherwise idle funds are tapped, the total economy may be stimulated—beneficially or otherwise.

If there is already excess demand relative to supply, such government spending adds to inflation, with consequent danger of subsequent interruptions to economic growth. In this respect, there is no special "multiplier" effect of government spending in itself that does not apply to private spending under the same circumstances. We should neither praise nor condemn government spending as such. Each type of expenditure should be assessed in terms of its desirability relative to other goods and services or to providing the particular item on a private basis. The government share of the total economy can become so large, however, that the benefits of a competitive, free-choice society are largely dissipated.

The second proposal—to promote economic growth through higher pay rates—puts the cart before the horse. . . .

Higher pay rates can provide more real buying power for the total economy only if they reflect an increase in output per man-hour. It is this that makes possible economic growth. Benefits of increased productivity must then flow to owners, employees and customers in such a way as to stimulate markets and provide incentive for future productive efforts. Higher pay rates are not the causal factor, except where a redistribution of the income flow from one group to another stimulates total buying and output. Each proposal to expand the economy by taking from one group to give to another must be carefully examined as to the impact on buying of the group whose share is reduced.

Many of the more vocal supporters of the third point—growth for the sake of growth—look upon growth in the abstract rather than on the kind of growth or how it is achieved. To them, the important objective is to have, for example, 5% growth a year regardless of the kind of output.

. . . the test is whether this kind of output is what we want. We might, for example, go out and put $50 billion into something that isn't particularly desired by the people. Even though this might increase our total output figure, it is not accomplishing what we want in a free-choice society in terms of growth. . . .

As the determinant of what we want, the only adequate test that I know of is the market place. It might be a very proper goal, for example, to have more money diverted to education; but we have to rely upon the people as a whole to, in effect, cast their votes as to what they want. . . .

. . . My viewpoint on government types of expenditures is that there you have to rely upon the majority vote of the people. The individuals are bound, in effect, by the majority vote of the people. This is one disadvantage of most types of government spending. You have no choice; it can be done adequately only on a collective basis. The disadvantage of government spending versus private spending is that the individual cannot exercise any choice as to whether he wants it. He is forced to pay the tax so that the service can be provided on a collective basis. This does not mean that the spending shouldn't be done. It just means that it faces a different kind of test than that of the market place.

Incentive Suffers from Straitened Choice

When you get to the point where you are diverting such a large share of output into an area where there is not freedom of choice, the impact on incentives to growth comes into question. Take the tax rate. Suppose you raised it to 70% in the case of corporations. What effect would this have on incentives? Or in the case of individuals, take the marginal rate in the higher income brackets. It's way up there now, but suppose you raised the rates all along the line. What effect would this have on incentives, even though the expenditures to be made were very desirable?

. . . Other countries starting from a lower base have the advantage of looking to this country for the methods that we have used to achieve our growth. It takes time to build up the knowledge and the capital to do the job. We had to do it over a long period of time. Nations can shorten that time if they are intelligent enough to draw upon the cumulative knowledge and the accumulated capital of other countries. Russia has gained, for example, because it has the advantage of this accumulated knowledge. The Russians have built on it, but they had the advantage of our accumulated knowledge to draw upon in order to shorten the time. . . .

MR. PAARLBERG: I was reading a review of a series of lectures given by Professor Rostow of Cambridge, recorded in part in a couple of recent issues of *The Economist*, of London. . . . He divided the nations of the world into five groups, based on their relative stages of economic development. There are, he says, the traditional societies in which modern science is still inaccessible. They are mostly at a subsistence level; food production takes about 75% or more of their effort. Their income above the subsistence level is chiefly spent nonproductively. Their social structure is quite archaic, and there is no vertical mobility within the social structure. We still find such societies in various parts of the world.

And then, says he, there is another group of countries, the transitional societies, such as those in parts of Southeast Asia. Here where there has been the emergence of a new elite and an increase in investment, transition has begun from the traditional to an advanced form of organization.

Then, he says, there is another group at what he calls the take-off stage in which the rate of investment exceeds 10% of the national product. One or more substantial areas of industrialization have become stabilized or established, and there is a high rate of growth. The political, the social and the institutional frameworks have become developed, and a degree of self-generated progress has come about. In this group he places such countries as China, India, Pakistan, Egypt, and Indonesia. In these nations, the take-off toward economic improvement has begun.

Another group comprises those countries with a maturing society. He says, for example, that Mexico is entering this stage. In the maturing society, new methods and new outlooks are beginning to spread throughout the entire society. The form of economic and political organization has become rather well established. There is no serious challenge to those who are in control of capital, and technology is making progress. Industrialization is accelerated.

Finally, there is, he says, a stage which is called maturity, which, he says, was reached in Great Britain around one hundred years ago; in the United States around the turn of the century; in France and Germany, before the outbreak of the First World War; in Japan, before the outbreak of the second war; and in the Soviet Union, about ten years ago.

CHAIRMAN FABRICANT: These are interesting speculations, but it is important to emphasize that that is what they are —speculations.

MR. GOLDSMITH: Rostow, like other stage theorists, apparently claims that all countries run through these same stages. Maybe they do so at different speed, but there is some implication that there are limits to the extent to which you can compress stages. I think the essential point, as in all such theories, is that all countries are supposed to go through the same stages. . . .

. . . This is an essential part of his theory, it seems to me. There are certain stages of economic development and therefore all countries will go through them with certain deviations in the rate of speed. Basically, these are stages of development similar to, well, the development of an animal, or a human being, or a plant, through which they all go; if it weren't for that, the theory would lose its point and become purely an exercise in classification.

MR. PAARLBERG: . . . Everett Hagen, from MIT, has done some work on how economic development gets started in these traditional societies, what it is that kicks it off. He has many ideas about this. Obviously, it is important to have some notion as to how it gets generated, whether by education, supplying certain public facilities like roads, or whatever it might be. Hagen says, if I understand him correctly, that the thing starting it is some new force, sometimes a very great disturbance such as forced migration, which brings to these people the fact that they are capable of making changes. When this occurs, their minds, closed to change for generations, accept the idea they have this power to make change, and the process begins.

He further says, every interestingly, that this sort of idea does not come from the top classes in the society, who generally haven't much motivation for change, they already having economic position and social status. It doesn't come either from the people at the bottom of the economic scale because, being so near the subsistence level, they have no latitude for experimentation and thus are not inclined to make changes. It comes from some group in between, and a group that in some of these societies is not very numerous.

. . . . .

MR. GEORGE: . . . There are many valuable government services that sooner or later I think we must have; in order to prevent the temperature in the room from rising too high, I won't bother to identify them here.

The reason we can't have them is not merely the threat of inflation from new spending, but the lack of political self-control with respect to the good things we already have. Badly needed public services are denied to the country because of the excesses of farm politics, public works, aid to veterans that has nothing to do with their services as veterans, etc. I could mention several more but will stop here because these matters are only on the fringe of our subject. You drew me into them. The point that matters is that with fiscal resources strained, it is difficult to get, except through elimination of political wastes in existing services, the contribution that several useful new public services can make to growth. In short, we can't get the latter by ignoring wastes and trying to pay for new services through deficits.

. . . efforts to strengthen the economy would be the most prudent and soundest course we could follow. . . .

. . . I would expect good results from allocation of more resources to basic and applied research. I would expect the same from greater tax stimulus to investment; for example, there should be greater integration of individual and corporate income taxes, greater latitude in computing depreciation, amendments to make losses fully deductible and to extend the carry-back and have it include unused exemptions in justice to low-income taxpayers and those with fluctuating incomes. I would also strengthen other cyclical snubbers, (i.e., automatic stabilizers), but only in a limited way, as by modernizing the duration and size of unemployment benefits. I think that we need more intensive development of the skills of the young through means that I am not competent to develop, except that the need for it has impressed me strongly. Lastly, perhaps there is need for the better education of scientists and administrators.

MR. GAINSBRUGH: And more research funds for them, too.

MR. GEORGE: It is also important and not trite that federal activities, even though the scope I leave for them is not narrow, be confined to essential jobs that cannot be handled well by the lower governments and the private economy.

. . . I suspect that, vital as it is, we don't reason closely enough what we want from growth. If domestic welfare is what we have in mind, small differences in rate of growth will not be vital to its beneficiaries, damage to deeper values could be considerable, and by forced draft we might conceivably get less, over time, out of anxiety to get more. Much depends on the means adopted to get it. We might find a steep climb unsustainable, if we did get it, unstabilizing in that case, and of poorer composition from pulling and hauling the economy in a sort of intoxicated chase after one idea.

If we are primarily thinking of ourselves as in a race with Russia, statistical victories won't mean much; we would really have to take control over resources and specialize to predetermined ends as she does. The distribution of additional increments over new shades of toothpaste, more Western gun toters, and new accordion sinks won't add noticeably to our rocket power which may still drag in the face of general growth.

Certainly, the difference between a historical rate of growth, of which we were once proud, and a forced rate, the costs of which we do not yet know, is not a malady like depression and shocking unemployment, or gross concentration of wealth and income such as still keeps many countries of the world in misery. It more nearly involves manipulation for the aggrandizement of one value at disproportionate risk to others.

. . . . .

MR. BACKMAN: . . . You started this discussion by saying economic growth is the most important problem we face. I would just like to modify that and say it is an important economic problem. There are many others. This is a problem that, if you want to call it such, has been with us from the beginning of time. I see nothing which makes it "the" problem today. It's "a" problem, not "the" problem.

In your discussion, Sol, you de-emphasized the importance of saving and investment as the most important factor in economic growth. Now many people in the past have emphasized that new investment decisions—and I'm using the term broadly to include technology, because technology finds its expression through new investment—and output per man-hour have been closely related to economic growth. You have de-emphasized the importance of this factor. You said it is a factor but you gave it somewhat less importance than many people have in the past given it.

CHAIRMAN FABRICANT: I would give it the kind of importance that you give to each of the legs of a three-legged stool. I don't know that you could just choose one leg and say it is the most important.

MR. BACKMAN: I don't think it belongs in that category. On the basis of observable past experience, saving and investment must be treated as the prime factor in economic growth. The other basic factors you talked about, whether it's education or anything else, finally must have an expression in some set of numbers that must take the form investment.

MR. GAINSBRUGH: But, Jules, aren't you broadening the definition of "investment" sharply beyond the current treatment in national and even business accounting? Isn't that exactly what Sol has been telling us; namely, that our definitions of "investment" in the past were sharply limited to brick and mortar and equipment—that was the area of primary emphasis. Sol then talked about other types of investment that are not ordinarily viewed as "capital formation." Now are you saying all this adds up to investment—whether we account for it under consumers' durable goods (*e.g.*, cars or homes) or under the heading of government capital expenditures, including outlays for education?

MR. BACKMAN: Let's take the concrete case of education, since it was mentioned as an illustration. Education is not something existing in a vacuum. As people are educated, certain other things happen. The efficiency of labor is increased, and therefore presumably is reflected not as a separate force but as "efficiency of labor." There was some reference made to the fact that education will, in turn, increase investment. Perhaps we shall see relationships better and this will help us in whatever we want to do. We shall be better trained to discover or participate in a new industry's inception. But, when we participate, how do we do it? We participate by the brick and mortar to which reference has been made; and we participate by the machines, by new processes. In other words, education does not exist independently of these new forces. If it finally is effective it is reflected either through the labor factor or the capital equipment factor.

MR. PAARLBERG: But in either case, it's a saving, of a form. It represents some denial in current consumption; it represents time spent in receiving this education. It's an investment, it's a "saving," in that sense.

MR. BACKMAN: But let's look at it in terms of growth, which we are measuring as deflated national product or income. Simply because I go to school and get an education, that doesn't help the nation until I do something with it.

MR. PAARLBERG: But this might well be a basis for reexamining our national accounts to see if we shouldn't show some of these items in GNP as investments—such an item as "outlays for education."

MR. GOLDSMITH: In other words, whether we shouldn't shift certain expenditures, like education, to the investment category.

MR. BACKMAN: This is part of it, Don; but I would say it goes one step further. What we have been talking about here is how we allocate savings in the broad sense. It may, in part, be allocated to something called education, part to something called government, part to something called business investment. But until we do something with that education, so that it will ultimately come into business investment or labor efficiency, it hasn't affected growth. . . .

. . . There is one school of thought that asserts that "an inescapable cost" of a desirable rate of growth is creeping inflation, higher prices. It holds that there are only two alternatives: "creeping inflation and economic growth" or "price stability and unemployment." A second school of thought holds that not only can we have both a desirable rate of growth and stable prices, but also that we can maintain this growth only by keeping prices stable. . . .

Creeping inflation refers to a price rise of 2% or 3% a year. The late Professor Sumner Slichter, one of the exponents of the first school, stated that this type of "slow inflation must be expected to continue more or less indefinitely." While it does not seem to be very large, an annual rise of 2% would wipe out half the purchasing power of the dollar in thirty-five years, and one of 3% would result in a similar reduction in less than twenty-five years.

. . . Some say that we must step up our rate to about 5% as compared with our long-term record of about 3% a year. While the difference between 3% and 5% appears to be small, it becomes enormous with the passage of time. With a growth rate of 3%, total output of goods and services in our economy increases fourfold in about fifty years. With a 5% rate of increase, total output in a half century would be more than ten times as large as it is at present.

Everyone is in favor of the highest possible rate of economic growth. But there are practical limits to expansion that must be faced. When we exceed these limits, the pressures for inflation become intensified. President Eisenhower properly has pointed out that a stable price level is "an indispensable condition" for achieving the maximum growth rate in the long run.

Impact of Rising Prices

History does not support the assumption that economic growth must be accompanied by rising prices. Economic growth has occurred in many periods of stable or declining prices. Two such major periods in the nineteenth century —1820's and 1830's and the last third of the century—were periods of declining prices. During the 1920's, when prices remained relatively stable, national output rose about 4% a year. On the other hand, from 1955 to 1957, when prices crept upward almost 3% a year, national output rose less than 2% annually. The relation of price changes and economic growth is not an easy one to depict. The selection of terminal dates can very significantly influence the results derived. In the report of the Cabinet Committee on Price Stability for Economic Growth dealing with the record of prices, an effort was made to portray in very broad strokes what has happened to price trends. After considering four designated periods, it concluded that "whether these long tidal movements in prices were rising or falling had no consistent relation to economic growth."

An examination of the periods discussed by the committee suggests to me that they are not too meaningful. The committee attempted to distinguish between what happened in war years and what happened in peacetime years. However, its comparisons seem seriously distorted by the inclusion of immediate postwar years as peacetime years.

Let me illustrate by the experience recorded for the period from 1933 to date. The committee says that "from 1933 until now consumers' prices have risen in years of peace (omitting war years) at an average rate of 3% per year." Here is official support for the assumption that we have had a "creeping inflation" of 3% annually in the "peacetime" years of the past quarter of a century. An examination of the underlying data reveals that this 3% average was largely the result of deferred wartime inflation that developed between 1945 and 1948. . . .

Now, this 3% figure seems to reflect the creeping inflation about which much public discussion has centered. Actually, it is a distorted figure. What really happened, excluding the first three postwar years, was a rate of increase of about 1.3% or perhaps 1.4%. This is a somewhat different dimension: A 3% rate of increase over a period of twenty-four years would double the price level. The 1⅓% rate would result in a doubling of the price level in about fifty-three years. It should be emphasized that this rate is measured from 1933, which was the low point of a deep depression. This starting date also acts to exaggerate the magnitude of the "peacetime" increase in the years reviewed. . . .

What factors contribute to growth and how do price changes fit into the picture? If we look at the raw numbers, the approximately 3.5% a year rate of growth divides into nearly 1.5% for population (man-hours or labor input) and 2% roughly for output per man-hour. A larger part of the gain came from increases in output per man-hour than from added labor input. It was the more important figure over the period of years. At any rate, the key factor is what happens to output per man-hour and productivity in the broader sense. . . .

. . . Output per man-hour is affected by many factors, but the most important has been the investment in new machines and new equipment—largely the results of new technology. The magnitude of such investments depends upon the level of savings—although for some periods bank credit may be used to finance new investment. But savings will tend to be discouraged by creeping inflation and thus long-term economic growth will be stultified.

Now, how do rising price levels or changes in the price levels affect this particular variable? During the early postwar years, many persons just didn't believe that prices would continue to rise. The reaction of the average person to rising prices is more one of what he anticipates for the future than whether he acted or did not act in a certain way in the preceding twenty or thirty years. What seems to have happened in the last few years is that there has been a greater consciousness, a greater awareness, of the erosive effects of rising prices than people were willing to recognize before. What brought this about? Almost any number of factors. It could be that when the average person found the purchasing power of his series-E bonds had gone down sharply, he became aware of it. It could be that the cumulative impact of higher prices year after year finally made him aware of it. It could be that the failure of prices to experience a sharp postwar decline was a factor. The point is that there appears to have come a moment in time when people became aware of the erosive effects of rising prices.

CHAIRMAN FABRICANT: On what . . .

MR. BACKMAN: . . . on the value of savings . . .

. . . It's rather interesting to note that we have failed to increase the rate of savings, despite the large increase in our incomes. As incomes rise we should be able to save a larger proportion of our incomes.

MR. THOMAS: The saving ratio in the period 1951–1958 was smaller than it was in 1922–1929.

SAVING AS A PER CENT OF INCOME*
1922–1929   12.8
1930–1939   3.5
1951–1958   9.4

* [This table has been condensed from the original. *Ed.*]

MR. SAXON: It's the fear of inflation.

MR. GOLDSMITH: It cannot be that simple. There are so many other changes that have taken place that deserve consideration.

. . . . .

MR. PAARLBERG: Another important difference is what the expectation of the people was and what their expectation is presently, not just the movement of the prices related to the future course of prices.

MR. SAXON: It's quite clear in an economy which is being rapidly inflated that the fear of inflation itself prevents savings or investment of those savings in favor of hoarding and widespread speculation in commodities, land, and equities.

MR. BACKMAN: There is another factor which has not been mentioned that is extremely important—the anticipations of price collapse. After the end of World War II, there was frequent publication of charts going back to 1800 to show that prices declined sharply after each war. . . .

We did not have that type of collapse [after World War II], and we have gotten to the point now where people are becoming convinced that we now have a one-way street upward. . . .

. . . Confronted by creeping inflation, savers become more interested in speculating—to protect themselves against losses in purchasing power—than in providing capital for industry. There is ample evidence of this tendency in the rampant speculation which appears to have taken place in stocks. . . . Creeping inflation also interferes with business planning. When protection against price rises becomes a dominant factor, businessmen are not likely to plan boldly for expansion. One result is an adverse impact on job creation.

To stimulate economic growth it is necessary to create an environment in which savings will be encouraged and business will be willing to convert those savings into new plant and equipment. Price stability encourages savings, while tax incentives could be used to induce new investments. This is the road to greater economic growth.

One important caution must be noted. There is no magic in a stable price level. Stability of prices during the 1920's did not prevent the most catastrophic depression in modern history. Stability of prices from 1952 to early 1956 did not prevent the 1957 boom or the subsequent recession. General price stability may conceal important disparities in price relationships or in cost-price relationships that, in turn, upset the effective functioning of the economy. In other words, general price stability is not a cure-all for the problem of the business cycle. . . .

. . . . .

The Central Themes

MR. GAINSBRUGH: I shall try to put together under five or six central themes what it is we have said about economic growth during our discussion. . . .

✔ *The first major point* that we made is that our rate of growth, judged over the long term, is as high as, if not higher than, any other country in the world. Despite all of the impatience that we may have with our economic system at times, the work that Goldsmith, Fabricant, Kuznets, and others have done in the way of measurement fully supports that conclusion. No other system in world history can lay claim to so rapid a rate of growth as ours over the past century or more.

✔ *Our second major point* is perhaps just as disconcerting as was the comfort we found in our secular or long-term rate of growth. This was the conclusion, voiced by several authorities here, that in the short run, as we enter the Sixties, we are almost low man on the totem pole in terms of the rate of economic growth. . . .

✔ *Our third and most important point* involved the purpose of economic growth in this country and some of the vital distinctions between the market-determined rate of economic growth in this country and government-determined or "forced" growth achieved in others.

. . . our fundamental purpose is to raise and improve the economic welfare of the individual. The purpose of other societies may not necessarily be the same. It may be their ultimate target or perhaps a by-product. But I think in some instances their primary current purpose can be viewed as either militaristic, or the aggrandizement of the state today, with the promise of a better life for the individual at some future tomorrow—but not today.

. . . Can we continue to center our economic growth around the satisfaction of individual desires, catering to the individual, to his desire for more and more leisure as well as for higher material standards? Can we safely do this in a world in which different growth targets are being sought by other nations, and not necessarily the same peaceful targets as our own?

. . . we have continued to preserve

or expand the leisure of the individual as well as to improve his economic welfare. Our preference for more leisure may be among the factors contributing toward a lower rate of economic growth in this country than in others during the past decade. . . .

Certainly, if we believed we were in a state of economic war at the moment, and one that was not going well for us, we as a people could do much to raise the rate of economic growth in this country. We could, conceivably, place a higher priority upon output than upon leisure. . . .

✔ *Our fourth major area of discussion* moved us from examination of our postwar position to speculation about the prospects of the future rate of economic growth here and elsewhere. Raymond Goldsmith was of the belief that the pattern of growth of the past decade may for the major nations well be continued in the next decade. . . .

. . . such careful observers as Sol Fabricant and Raymond Goldsmith and Lloyd Reynolds found substance in the thesis that it is possible that economic growth may well continue to be more rapid among the other world powers. They left us with no grounds for complacency about our current or future performance so far as relative economic growth is concerned.

I did detect, however, this implicit belief in some of our presentations: just let time work upon these other systems; let them, too, mature; let their consumers begin to plump for steadily higher levels of living, particularly as compared with ours! With that proviso, perhaps we needn't be too concerned about their rates of economic growth surpassing ours in the interim.

How much can we rely upon this reservation? It is quite conceivable that slow but steady progress in the level of personal consumption may be satisfactory to their masses, viewed relative to the subsistence levels of living that still prevail. And the improvement can be coupled with the maximizations of two appeals other than the economic status of the individual—greater liberty, say, than he has had, and more personal dignity.

✔ *The fifth area* that we talked about at considerable length is what makes for economic growth. . . . I know it will come as a shock to some of our readers to see that, while we put capital investment high on the roster of factors contributing toward economic growth, we had some reservations about giving it top billing or to endorsing it as the sole prerequisite or essential in the achievement of more rapid economic growth.

Among the other factors . . . were education and an environment conducive to risk taking and to individual incentive; I was particularly struck with Woody Thomas's emphasis on the contribution to economic growth made by the vigorous types of competition that have prevailed in this country in the past and how such competition, at least in the past, has in turn affected our wage-cost-price calculus. We certainly were not inclined to endorse rising prices as a prerequisite or essential for growth.

CHAIRMAN FABRICANT: It should be made clear, Martin, that while rising prices were not viewed by any, or hardly any of us, as essential to economic growth, we would all agree, thinking back to Eddie George's goals, that inflation is disastrous to many individual sectors of the economy and very disruptive of the standards of living of those sectors. That point is extremely important to our summary.

MR. GAINSBRUGH: But that assumes that slowly rising prices will necessarily lead to all-out inflation.

MR. THOMAS: I don't think that was discussed at all. There wasn't any indication that rising prices might help to speed up economic growth.

MR. BACKMAN: Woody, Glenn, and I said they probably wouldn't.

MR. GOLDMSITH: You could put it the other way around and say that there is some doubt whether price stability is an essential requirement of economic growth.

MR. SAXON: Decidedly no—we mentioned several periods of declining prices in which our real growth and real production gains were fully maintained . . .

MR. GAINSBRUGH: Perhaps it is more accurate by way of summary to say that the emphasis was placed upon increased productivity as being far more conducive to economic growth. And, to repeat Jules' record of history: we've had economic growth in periods of stable and declining prices as well as in years of rising prices.

The sixth and last point of major emphasis involves the question: could we grow faster if we wanted to? Eddie George, responding to that question, said we could over the short run. But he found it difficult to prescribe for the longer term. Conceivably, intensified research would help; so would resort to more effective tax stimuli and incentives, as would more intensive development of the skills of the young. Still another point that I think warrants considerable emphasis; any substantial lowering of cyclical instability—reducing the amplitudes of recession—would contribute significantly to a rise in our secular rate.

. . . If we want to grow faster, if we want to have more for all to share, if we want more leisure but not at the expense of national security, the secret again seems to be to raise productivity. In raising productivity we find the ultimate answer to increasing our rate of economic growth.

Finally, it was noteworthy that, despite all of the sobering conclusions, disconcerting at times, that were voiced here tonight, no one really seemed to be too alarmed about our rate of economic growth . . .

CHAIRMAN FABRICANT: We don't want to leave the impression that we are complacent . . .

MR. GAINSBRUGH: . . . not complacent, yes; but not overly alarmed as yet. . . .

I believe it was Toynbee who said that every great civilization is faced with a challenge to which it either responds or disappears. One of the greatest challenges that we as a people face now and in the years ahead is a test of our ability to maintain a competitive rate of growth. Can we do this in our society and still enhance the life, liberty and the pursuit of happiness of the individual while elsewhere in the world those purposes are subordinated to nationalism and military might?

. . . . .

As noted in the introduction to selection 71, Congress has sought the views of businessmen on the vast subject of automation. The facts and interpretations of 20 men required about 350 printed pages. No selection such as is possible here can fully represent this wealth of material. The three excerpts used, however, do come from men with differing experience. The first speaker is the president of a "small" business but also, at the time he spoke, the president of the National Association of Manufacturers. The second is an official of one of the largest manufacturing companies in the country, one whose employees belong largely to the union headed by Mr. Reuther. (See selection 71.) The third summarizes some of the experience and policies of a corporation which for over 40 years has been dealing with the problems of automation.

70 · *Automation—As Seen by Business Leaders*

RUDOLPH F. BANNOW

. . . . .

No one can deny the desire of our population for the products and services which automation can produce. The production of more, better, and cheaper consumer items will raise American living standards to undreamed of levels. Automation is capable of achieving such goals. Aside from producing such desirable effects, automation is sorely needed by the U.S. economy if we are to maintain our competitive position. Both our allies and the Russian bloc have had considerable success in automating their present industrial structure and they are continuously working toward the introduction of more automated processes. In the case of the Russian bloc we must automate for security reasons and in the case of our allies, we must automate to maintain a competitive position. If the United States does not provide the proper economic climate for the development and innovation of automated processes, other nations will.

. . . . .

Although it has already been stated that some form of automation has been going on continuously since the dawn of history, automation as currently envisioned by experts in the field is only in an infancy stage. The complex problems that individual firms face in introducing automation eliminates an overnight arrival of automated processes on

RUDOLPH F. BANNOW, D. J. DAVIS, and PAUL A. GORMAN, "New Views on Automation," papers submitted to the Subcommittee on Automation and Energy Resources, Joint Economic Committee, Washington, 1960.

the industrial scene. The nature of the product or service to be automated will determine the timetable for the introduction of automation in specific instances. First, a product must be in large demand which necessitates a continuous production schedule. Next, the product cannot be subject to frequent fundamental design changes which would make the present automated machine obsolete in a short time. To automate a productive process is a costly venture and there must be sufficient useful life to the machine to pay off the original cost. For example, the preparation, canning, labeling and carton packing of food products is highly automated already. By the very nature of this operation it is a natural for automation. Within the food-processing industry a great variety of products such as soup, vegetables, meats, etc., are the products of highly automated plants. More and more supply plants for the automobile industry are introducing automated machinery. The production of engine blocks is currently referred to as an example of automated plant. At the same time no one is likely to plan on automating the production of hulls for large racing yachts.

There have been various estimates as to just how much of American industry is suited for automation. Diebold estimates that only 20 percent of manufacturing industry is now well suited for automation. In addition, completely new industries producing completely new products will be highly automated in their initial construction. However, at present the most serious concern does not arise from this type of situation, but from the transition of existing productive facilities to automated production. The transition will not occur overnight to disrupt the employment picture. The changeover will be an evolution, rather than a revolution—a glacier, rather than a flood.

No automated process simply arrives on the scene. Various steps, machines and groups of machines are constantly improved over the years. These steps alone are often slow and usually costly. Once the separate steps of the productive process are developed to a stage where automation of the entire production line is a possibility, then the real job of integrating these separate steps can begin. It is a time-consuming, costly and not always a successful process. The over-all integration of the automated individual steps in the productive process often requires a complete rebuilding of the individual machines which independently were considered to be fully automated. Much as we anticipate the advantages which will flow from automation, its development and installation will require time. We are fortunate that we have the time to prepare for the adjustments which must accompany the arrival of automation.

Impact of Automation

. . . Often the displacement of workers by machines is referred to as "technological unemployment." This is a misnomer for it conotes the general idea that technological improvements are accompanied by increases in unemployment. The economic history of the United States disproves that theory. The long-term transition of our economy from one of agriculture to one of industry, the shift of employment from goods-producing industries to service industries, and the shift in the occupational makeup of the labor force between blue collar and white collar workers are examples of the displacement of workers due to technological changes. Yet, as these fundamental transformations were occurring, employment expanded and the only serious unemployment problems encountered were associated with general economic recessions.

Therefore, the term technological displacement is more descriptive of the particular situations where machines have displaced manpower on specific jobs. The impact of technology is on the allocation of our labor force to specific occupations and industries, and not on the level of employment generally.

At present, studies are available which show how this problem of displacement has been handled in plants where automation has been introduced. Admittedly, the results of these studies are not necessarily indicative of any body of hard and set rules as to what will happen to that portion of the labor force which may be subject to displacement as a result of automation. . . .

These case histories were prepared by the Division of Productivity and Technological Developments, Bureau of Labor Statistics, U.S. Department of Labor. . . .

INSURANCE COMPANY. This particular insurance company decided to install electronic computers in its classification section, which employed 800 people. Of this number, 198 worked in areas directly affected by the introduction of the electronic computer. Installation required 2 years and during this period the personnel department interviewed and screened the 198 people whose jobs would be affected by the installation. Aptitude and screening tests showed that nine employees from this group had the ability to operate the new equipment. They were retrained and assigned to operate the computers. There were 133 employees in the section transferred to jobs within the same division or in other divisions. The remaining 56 employees were retained in the classification section of the same division performing noncomputer duties.

To staff the automated classification section, 20 additional employees were brought in to complement the 65 employees who remained in the classification section. The end result of this innovation was that 85 employees (at an average salary of $4,200) operate 21 machines and manage work which under the old system required 198 employees (at an average salary of $3,700) to operate 125 older machines.

In the entire transition not one employee was laid off and no employee was required to accept a salary cut. On the contrary, many were promoted to positions requiring more skill and received appropriate pay increases.

[A second case involved automatic reservation systems for airlines. Total employment rose—this industry was expanding—79 percent. There were no layoffs. *Ed.*]

MECHANIZED BAKERY. Unlike the insurance company computer and the airline reservation system, both of which dealt with the programing and processing of informational data, the case history of the automated bakery involves an industry that produces a material product. In addition, the bakery workers affected by the introduction of automated machinery were members of a trade union and worked under conditions set in a contract. Finally, this particular baking plant was not in the dynamic business expansion category that prevailed in the insurance and airline industry. As a result, the employees displaced by innovations were not immediately placed in positions created by expanded business activity.

This history of the Z Co. bakery showed that it had a good size business but it was not able to fulfill the demand for its output. Most of its machinery was a pre-World War II vintage and its unit costs were high. After a 2-year survey, the company decided to change its whole operation over to the latest automated machinery. To house this new operation it was necessary to construct an entire new plant. There was a 2-year span between the time of the decision to automate and the completion of the new operating unit. The union was informed immediately after the decision to automate was made and negotiations to iron out the matters affecting workers were begun. Where jobs were eliminated or the nature of specific jobs changed, workers were shifted to other jobs whenever possible. If the new jobs were lower graded, as far as skill requirements, the shifted worker was paid at the scale of his former job. Where new and/or higher skilled positions were created, every effort was made to fill these jobs from the existing work force. News of the company's attitude toward the displacement problem eliminated the natural anxiety which occurred with the news of the new plant. Furthermore, the company's pledge to maintain the pay scale of any downgraded employee was incorporated in a contract negotiated before the new plant opened. In the process of screening displaced employees, many talents were uncovered which could be used to fill openings created by the more highly technical nature of the new machinery. Some workers were laid off as they could not be fitted into the employment scheme of the new plant. Employment dropped 4.4 percent in the first year of operation of the new plant as a result of layoffs and normal attrition. In the following year employment rose 3.6 percent and by 1955, 3 years later, employment had surpassed the preautomated high year by 6 percent. During the same period 1952–56, the average wage rate increased by almost 60 cents an hour and fringe benefits were expanded.

[Two other case studies included a modern petroleum refinery and 20 offices where electric data processing replaced older methods.]

. . . . .

SUMMARY. In the five case histories reviewed above, these important facts are worth noting:
1. Out of a total of 3,906 jobs affected by automated innovations, layoffs and discharges were negligible.
2. Installation time allowed plenty of time to plan and prepare reassignments for employees affected by new equipment.
3. Management and labor, in cases where union representation prevailed, cooperated to minimize the impact of dislocation. In addition, retraining was provided by the employer.
4. Downgrading was kept to a minimum and pay rates were kept at the old scale in most instances. In a substantial number of cases employees were upgraded with resulting pay increases.
5. Wage rates were increased during the period.
6. Management was satisfied with the increased efficiency and the employees adjusted to the technological skills associated with their new job ratings.

. . . . .

The introduction of technological improvements will place an obligation on the labor force but at the same time it will help solve some of the problems associated with efficient utilization of our manpower. The most serious need will be for technical and skilled personnel to develop, produce, and operate the new equipment. This will require expanded educational and training facilities. Thus far our labor force has shown it has the flexibility to adjust to this upgrading in technology and skills. Concurrently automation, by eliminating manual jobs, can release manpower for use in the more skilled jobs. The chain reaction can proceed all the way up the scale of technical skills. Actually, this process has been going on with our technological development. The accelerated rate of future development of manpower skills requires only that we proceed with this upgrading in labor skills so as to minimize the hardship of any employment displacement that might possibly ensue. In this development process it is in the older age group where problems may arise. The ability of this group to adapt themselves to new jobs is restricted by human nature. Understanding this problem and skillful utilization or redirection of their present skills will require expert personnel administration on the part of management.

The prediction of a very material increase in workers under 25 years of age is a distinct advantage to the economy as we progress further with automation. These young workers will be better educated than their predecessors and, hence, will be more flexible. These younger workers will understand that the development of technological improvements requires changing skills and that the development of one particular skill is only one step up the ladder and not the establishment of a lifelong job niche.

. . . . .

Automation and Investment

While there is available a whole host of information about automation and future employment, there is not much information available on the amount of capital that will be needed to finance the development and installation of automated processes. Actually, no one knows how much capital will be needed. We do know that the sum will be quite large, as the expenditures already made stagger the imagination. . . .

. . . . .

The individual decisions by firms to automate either all or part of their plant and/or office will be based on business judgment and not on whims resulting from a fascination with automated machines. The huge cost of automation must be balanced by the soundest estimates of the possible return.* Machines should pay for themselves over their useful life, and produce a profit, without which there is little reason to make such investment. In addition to paying for itself, machines must generate new capital for expansion. This is the system upon which the private enterprise system was built and expanded, and which must be maintained if the economy is to grow and prosper.

The availability of capital will affect the rate at which automation is introduced. In the final analysis the availability of capital is dependent upon the savings of individuals and corporations.

One of the most important factors affecting the availability of capital is the tax system. Under present laws, the excessive rates applied to the sources of investment capital are a serious deterrent to growth in two ways. In the first place, the present high rates reduce the actual amount of money that is available for investment. Secondly, and equally important, the realization that any gains earned through investments will be subject to the very high tax rates

---

* [The Chairman of the Council of Economic Advisers during part of President Truman's administration, Dr. E. G. Nourse, made the following point in his testimony—*Ed.*]: "[A] point which I think could properly be kept active in the thinking of the committee relates to the rate at which automatic systems can profitably or should, in terms of economic policy, be introduced into our industrial life. This is a point which I discussed with Vannevar Bush, and found that he as an engineer was in agreement with my thinking as an economist, that the craze for automation might prove a pitfall to some managements. Impressed by the pressure of rising wage rates, they may adopt automation as a way of saving labor and raising unit efficiency, not fully mindful of the burden of overhead cost under conditions of less than full-scale operation."

seriously reduces the incentive to invest. The retention of present tax rates is completely incompatible with the principles of the free market system upon which our economy is built.

Challenges Associated with Automation

While automation can bring us new, more, better, and cheaper goods plus an easier way of life, the innovation of automation is not automated. Adjustments to promote a systematic inculcation of automation into our economy presents a challenge to American labor, management, and government.

In the case studies reviewed earlier in this statement, we had some fine examples of labor's cooperation in ironing out displacement problems arising out of automation. The forward-looking approach exemplified by these labor leaders made for an orderly transsition to the automated machines and plants. . . .

Unfortunately, the record of union cooperation evidenced in the case histories mentioned earlier in this statement is not reflected in the speeches and actions of many national labor leaders. While paying lipservice to the desire and need for automation many of these labor leaders have thrown or threaten to throw up roadblocks against automation. The great technological advances of the past, electricity, oil, automotive power, and radio, increased employment in this country rather than unemployment. There is nothing on the horizon to indicate that new technologies will have vastly different effects on employment and the economy than those of the past.

There is one type of situation in which this optimistic conclusion may not apply. That is the case where labor costs are pushed up so rapidly that, in order to survive, the industry must automate "under forced draft." This is what happened in the bituminous coal industry. In order to offset the rapid rise in wage and fringe-benefit levels, the industry was forced to change its technology at a rate which has left the bituminous coal mining areas with considerable unemployment. Had it not been for the monopolistic power of the union to force wages up in this industry, automation might have been achieved at a more normal pace, with a much less severe impact on employment.

(In such cases, union pressure does not really accelerate technological progress in the economy as a whole. A larger part of the supply of capital available to society is allocated to the industry which is under such pressure. The result is that less capital is available for other industries, and hence their opportunities for technological progress are reduced.)

On the other side of the picture, labor can halt or seriously deter the orderly process of technological change by appropriating the benefits of automation. The west coast longshoremen's union and some meatpacker unions have obtained contracts providing for royalty payments, from savings due to automation, to a fund. In less than a year from the contract date the longshoremen have proposed that the annual payments into the fund be doubled. Both funds are in addition to contractual wages, pensions, welfare and vacation provisions. A continuation of this trend to siphon off part of the savings from automation —even before they are known—or to load special costs on those who adopt improvement is the surest way to bring technological change to a halt.

. . . . .

. . . With this paucity [of manpower in the 35–44 age group] facing us, it behooves American management to work for the best utilization of the existing labor force in this age group. In addition, the development of the skills of the entire labor force needed to man our automation processes will need the wholehearted cooperation of management.

Management will face challenges on the social plane also. In the case studies reviewed earlier, management, through advanced planning, eliminated hardships created by employee displacement by retraining and/or reassigning displaced employees. Such programs are not always practical, but management must be aware of their advantage wherever such policies are applicable.

. . . . .

Government, which today is so enmeshed in our economic life, also faces challenges associated with automation. Taxation and monetary policies will directly affect the availability of capital. In the legislative field, successful automation will require sensible and just labor policies. On the State and local level, automation will require an educational program capable of adequately training our young people in the skills which automation demands. Fundamentally, Government must permit an economic climate that fosters national growth. Without that, minor adjustment problems are magnified and management, labor, and the consumer all suffer.

. . . . .

D. J. DAVIS

. . . . .

We can expect no sudden revolution in automobile manufacturing techniques on an industrywide scale.

Accordingly, the effect of automation on employment should follow the trend of the recent past. The gradual shift to job opportunities into maintenance and other types of work should continue on a small and localized scale.

The committee is undoubtedly concerned with the effect of automation on employment. There is danger in overgeneralization in this area. The effects can differ greatly in various industries, between different companies in the same industry, and between different applications within the same company.

The situation at Ford was described . . . in November 1959 [as follows]:

Our experience also has a bearing on the notion apparently prevailing in some quarters that people displaced by automation or other technological change constitute an identifiable group with respect to whom separate governmental policies can be formulated and applied. We have found it impossible to identify any group of laid-off Ford employees whose unemployment is attributable to automation as such. The fact is that changes in processes and technology occur simultaneously with changes in demand, product design, product mix and sourcing, with normal attrition in our work force, and with other factors.

Some displacement of employees does occur from time to time, and the reasons for this displacement are less important than the remedial action taken. At Ford, we meet the problems of retraining and re-employment in several ways wherever and whenever they occur.

It has been pointed out many times in the past that where older production machines are replaced by more efficient facilities, there is usually a need for additional skilled maintenance help. This is particularly true in the area of electrical maintenance, because of the tremendously complex control systems required for automated facilities.

In recent years, Ford training programs have included the retraining of employees to meet the needs for maintaining new equipment. In this respect, we have instituted special courses, especially in the areas of hydraulics maintenance, electrical maintenance, electronic maintenance, lubrication, and welding. Each individual has received from 5 to 200 hours of company-paid instruction.

In those cases where another job is not available within the plant, a displaced employee is given hiring preference in another company plant in the same labor market area.

Furthermore, under the company's retirement plans, an employee who is 60 or more years old with 10 or more years of service who is retired at the option of the company or under mutually satisfactory conditions may be eligible for a special early retirement benefit equal to twice the normal retirement benefit. This special benefit continues until he reaches the normal retirement age of 65 (or until social security becomes payable), at which time his benefit continues at the normal retirement level.

In addition, provision has been made under the company's supplemental unemployment benefit plan for separation payments to eligible laid-off employees who have not been reassigned to another job within a specified period of time.

. . . . .

Taking the overall view, it is increasingly evident today that the net result of the introduction of more productive machinery and other efficiencies in our production processes has been to increase, rather than decrease, total employment in Ford Motor Co.—despite the fact that Ford's hourly labor rates (including the cost of fringe benefits) for each hour worked have more than doubled since 1946. We are convinced that without the increased efficiency made possible by technological development to partially offset this rising labor cost, Ford Motor Co. could not have prospered and grown in one of the most highly competitive industries in the economy. Rather than providing more jobs, we would have had fewer jobs, and possibly none at all.

The need for further technological development in the automobile industry will become increasingly acute because of one factor in particular. Since 1955, sales of foreign-made cars in this country have had a tremendous impact on the American automobile market [and]. . . . exports of American passenger cars dropped from 254,000 in 1955 to 116,000 in 1959.

In comparing the years 1955 and 1959, the net shift in the export-import relationship amounted to 749,000 units. If we assume that all of this change was a loss to the American auto industry, it represents enough production to employ a large number of workers.

Of course, the lower labor rates paid by foreign manufacturers are a major factor in their ability to compete pricewise in our domestic market. Less well understood, however, is the contribution of technological progress in reducing their manufacturing costs.

In 1957, I saw firsthand evidence of the improvements that European automobile companies are making in production techniques. Because of their advancing technology, some English, French, German, and Italian plants are more highly automated than many American automobile plants.

It is particularly significant to note that despite the lower wage rates prevailing in Europe, European auto manufacturers are developing and using automatic equipment in two areas of manufacturing which have seen little application of technological progress in the American industry. I refer to low-volume parts manufacturing operations, which, in the United States, often will not pay for the high investment costs in automated equipment, and to component assembly operations, which are still largely manual in our plants.

Europeans have begun to overcome the risk involved in low-volume jobs by designing more versatility into their automatic machines, so that the equipment can be used to machine several different parts, rather than just one, thus reducing piece costs. They are also assembling more components by automatic methods than we are. In fact, at the Renault assembly plant at Flins, France, the entire unitized body is assembled almost completely without manual effort through the use of automated handling, fixturing and welding devices.

. . . . .

To meet the challenge of foreign automobile manufacturers, we in this country must use every possible means to encourage development and application of more efficient production facilities.

Some progress has been made in reducing the risk of obsolescence involved in a facilities investment decision. American builders of automated machinery and presses are standardizing many of their dimensions so that these facilities will accommodate a greater degree of product design change than previously. These improvements also tend to reduce initial investment costs.

However, application of automation principles is not feasible in some automobile production operations, because our yearly model changes continue to impose a major limitation on the rate of such development.

. . . . .

Looking toward the future, it is perhaps ironic, but nevertheless true, that the same technological progress which was considered by some to be a threat to the automobile worker may prove to be his greatest security in the 1960's.

. . . Professor Seymour Melman of Columbia University [in an April 1960 report to the Industrial Union Department, AFL-CIO, Machine Tool Industry Committee]

. . . asserted [according to the news dispatch] that increased efficiency for the U.S. machine tool industry would not result in fewer jobs or in job downgrading in the industry. Unless such greater efficiency is achieved, he pointed out, the U.S. industry may lose present markets. He noted that "on the other hand, a more efficient industry will mean broader markets at home, and the best hope for successful competition in world markets." In this industry, efficiency is the key to job protection.

The news dispatch went on to say that:

Melman's report was corroborated by a lengthy study made by the industrial union department's own researchers.

I would add to this that the economic laws which operate in the machine tool industry operate also in the automobile industry.

Automation offers the best defense we can see at this time against the challenge of a foreign industry which is strong principally because it is fully utilizing the fruits of technological progress.

. . . . .

PAUL A. GORMAN

Since 1920 the Bell System has been building the world's largest computer—the nationwide dial telephone system. About 96 percent of the 59 million Bell System telephones are now dial operated, compared to 85 percent in 1955.

This is therefore an appropriate time for a progress report on Bell System automation.

. . . . .

... before we began installing dial switching equipment in 1920, we worked out carefully a program dealing with the human factors involved. We knew the importance of a job to an individual. The program worked well in practice.

Whenever technological changes are made in the business our long-term objectives are kept in mind; to improve our service and meet the communications needs of the country at reasonable cost. We are certain that these objectives are in the best interests of our customers, our employees and the investors in our business.

Before going into detail on automation in the Bell System, it might be well to summarize briefly what has been accomplished to date, with the system now virtually all dial.

The 730,000 men and women now working for the Bell System companies are more than 2½ times the number employed in 1920, when dial conversion began.

Investment in our business, less than $1.4 billion in 1920, has grown to over $21 billion. Our shareowners total more than 1,850,000, as compared with 140,000 in 1920.

Another measure of our growth is as a taxpayer. Last year we paid $1.7 billion in Federal, State, and local taxes. In addition, in 1959 our telephone users paid directly about $600 million in Federal excise tax. In 1920 we paid $27.5 million in taxes and there was no excise tax imposed on our customers.

Western Electric, the manufacturing and supply arm of the Bell System, last year purchased more than 1 billion dollars' worth of materials from more than 35,000 suppliers for use by the Bell System telephone companies.

Service has improved tremendously. For example, a long-distance call to anywhere in the country goes through in less than a minute on the average, with some calls which are dialed directly going through in as little as 15 seconds. Back in the early 1920's it took about 10 minutes to complete a long-distance call. A 3-minute cross-country call costs $2.25 today. In 1920 the price was $16.50.

Today it takes the wage earner only half as long to earn enough to have a telephone in his home as it did 20 years ago. This goes far toward exlaining why we now have more than 38 million customers.

Because of automation we have the finest communications system anywhere. But the effects of telephone automation have reached far beyond the telephone business. The general economy and the Nation's defense have also benefited greatly.

Many businesses have been created or transformed by Bell System research and automation. The creation of the half-billion dollar semi-conductor industry is a case in point. . . .

[Mr. Gorman gives examples of improvements in service, the growth of new businesses on the basis of Bell System research, and the investment outlays made in expanding and improving telephone facilities. *Ed.*]

. . . . .

THE EFFECT OF BELL SYSTEM AUTOMATION ON TELEPHONE EMPLOYMENT AND ON EMPLOYMENT IN OTHER INDUSTRIES. Notwithstanding the high degree of automation in the Bell System, the backbone of the telephone business continues to be people. All our central offices and equipment are fully effective only when properly staffed by competent people. Automation has meant more employees and higher rated jobs.

... During the latest 5-year period, 1955 through 1959, there was a small increase in the number of employees in the telephone companies. For the Bell System as a whole, including Western and the laboratories, the increase in the number of employees was over 40,000. ...

The Bell System gives employment to such a large number of people because automation has made it possible to hold the line on costs and to furnish telephone service at a price which virtually every American household can afford. Without automation, telephone service long ago would have been priced out of the reach of a large portion of present subscribers. It is also a fact that, had automation not taken place, it would not now be possible to get enough qualified people to provide the volume and scope of telephone service which the public, industry, and Government need and have today.

In addition to creating more jobs, automation has greatly increased the number of Bell System people in higher graded jobs. Men and women receive much higher pay than the telephone men and women of the past.

The 5-year period 1955 through 1959 illustrates the kind of changes in work force which are brought about through automation. The number of plant craftsmen in the telephone companies increased from 120,000 to 142,000, or 18 percent. Supervisory employees in these companies grew from 88,000 to 103,000, or 17 percent. Business office and sales employees grew from 28,700 to 33,000, or 15 percent. Other instances of increases in the number of people in higher graded jobs could be given. While there was a reduction in the number of operators during the period, this was more than offset by the additions to the work force.

In the past 5 years annual wages and salaries and other payments to employees increased by $997 million, or over 34 percent. This reflects not only higher wage rates and increased benefits but the fact that there are now more people in better jobs.

The changeover from manual to dial. When technological changes occur, they are integrated into our business only after much research, experimentation, and testing. Thus time is assured for adequate planning and consideration of the human as well as the technical problems involved.

With careful planning, normal force turnover can solve most of the personnel problems. This is particularly true in the case of operators, where high force turnover is normal. For example, last year it was necessary for us to hire more than 50,000 operators.

When conversions of manually operated offices to dial have been scheduled, replacements for operators resigning or retiring have been largely from persons seeking temporary jobs. Often these are former operators who gave up their jobs when they married, and are now happy to come back on a temporary basis. As the conversion proceeds, regular employees are offered jobs in other types of work at the same location or in other offices in the same or other communities.

The observation made in 1934 by Frances Perkins, then Secretary of Labor, properly describes the regard for employees which has characterized the Bell System planning.

Of the hundreds of occupations in which women are listed in the Census of Occupations, only about a dozen employ more women than do the telephone companies. The human problem of the displaced worker when the cutover was made from the manual to the dial system telephone exchanges is an almost perfect example of technological change made with a minimum of disaster. It was accomplished through human as well as technical planning.

Bell System employee training. The Bell System takes the responsibility for retraining employees who are given new assignments because of automation. However, they are but a small part of the employees who change from one job to another for various reasons—to fill a vacancy created by a promotion or a retirement, to balance the force with the workload, to handle growth in the business, or to stimulate the individual's own growth and development. In all of these situations the Bell System provides the training needed to handle the new job well.

Moreover, training of employees going into other positions is only part of the overall training programs enabling employees to carry out their assignments better, and giving them more satisfaction from their jobs. This applies to all levels—to clerks, to skilled craftsmen and on up to top levels of management.

Training is of two kinds: on-the-job, carried out by the individual's supervisor, and off-the-job, carried out in a classroom by an instructor. On-the-job training helps an employee achieve his maximum potential in his present job. Off-the-job training provides a firm foundation for the development of a more highly skilled craftsman or manager.

One department alone, the plant department, has more than 200 schools throughout the country providing classroom facilities for off-the-job training of installers, linemen, repairmen, and other craftsmen who construct, install, and maintain the many different kinds of telephone plant. Courses range from basic subjects such as electricity and electronics, through station installation and maintenance, all the way to crossbar central office maintenance. The periods covered by the courses are as long as 20 weeks or more.

This plant school program is the equivalent of a trade school with a full-time enrollment of 5,000 students.

Since classroom training is usually followed by on-the-job training by the individual's immediate supervisor, it is exceedingly important that the supervisor be well qualified to give maximum assistance. For this purpose, training is given supervisors in new methods and on new tools and new equipment as they are introduced. In addition, last year over 335,000 supervisory man-days were spent in courses dealing with the general subject of human relationships, including employee problems.

. . . . .

The Bell System expects to continue its program of research and automation as a necessary means of further improving the speed, accuracy, and convenience of telephone service, increasing its usefulness and broadening its scope. Our aim has been and will continue to be to give to the public, to industry, and to our defense forces the best possible communications service.

As we look to the future we see that it will continue to be necessary to attract very large amounts of money into the business. The American people will continue to be called upon, through their savings, to finance construction needed for the communications service the Nation demands and must have.

Automation will undoubtedly continue to change the nature of some telephone jobs. As in the past, we expect these changes to be of an evolutionary nature. We will, of course, continue to minimize any adverse effect of these changes on our personnel.

. . . . .

Definitions of "automation" differ. Whatever the definition, however, profound technological changes are taking place. In 1955 the Joint Economic Committee of Congress heard testimony on the subject from dozens of men from business, labor, government, and universities. New hearings were held in 1960. Major elements of the recent testimony of two outstanding leaders of the labor union movement are included here. (See the previous selection for the views of three representatives of business.) George Meany is President of the AFL-CIO and Walter Reuther is President of the United Automobile, Aircraft and Agricultural Implement Workers of America.

Following the views of Mr. Meany and Mr. Reuther is a statement on automation which appeared, in the spring of 1961, as an advertisement paid for by a labor union—the Amalgamated Lithographers of America. The questions are asked by writer-commentator Henry Cassidy. The replies are those of Edward Swayduck, President of Local 1 of the union.

71 · Automation—Views of Labor Leaders

GEORGE MEANY

. . . .

Rapid and radical changes in technology are creating vast changes in machines, production methods, workflow, office procedures, manpower requirements, labor skills, and industry location. They are also creating great changes in products. . . .

. . . .

Organized labor welcomes technological change, as providing the basis for potential benefits for the Nation and all Americans. In the past, American trade unions made technological progress possible. The present advanced stage of technology in the United States stands as testimony to the acceptance of technological advances by the American people and to the cooperative efforts of organized labor.

But organized labor insists that the burdens of rapid technological change must be cushioned, that Government and business must assume their responsibilities to minimize social dislocations and to provide adequate cushions that will protect workers, their families and communities against the hazards of radical technological advances.

In our sense of values, as Americans and as trade unionists, human beings and human welfare are more important than machines and technology. In considering the costs of technological ad-

---

GEORGE MEANY and WALTER P. REUTHER, "New Views on Automation," papers submitted to the Subcommittee on Automation and Energy Resources, Joint Economic Committee, Washington, 1960.

vances, one must include more than the cost of buildings and machines alone. The costs of assisting human beings and communities to adjust to changing technology should be included as an important part of the total investment costs in the new technology.

* * * * *

As technological progress increases production, with less manpower, standard working hours should be reduced, without any cut of weekly earnings. In addition, labor-management cooperation and collective bargaining procedures are required, as well as Government programs, to assist displaced workers, their families and communities in the transition to the new technology.

Examples of Employment Effects

* * * * *

The effects of technological change can be seen . . . by briefly examining the record of a few industries.

Neither the food nor textile industries are leaders in recent technological changes. Nevertheless, there are continuing improvements in technology in these industries. Between April 1953 and April 1960, production rose about one-fifth, while production and maintenance jobs in the food and beverage industry fell 82,000 or 8 percent. In that same period, with a similar rise in output production and maintenance jobs in textile mills dropped 246,000 or 22 percent. . . .

In the rapidly growing chemical industry, which is experiencing radical changes in technology, production rose almost 80 percent in these past 7 years, while the number of production and maintenance jobs declined slightly, by 13,000. In this industry, however, there was, at the same time, a rapid expansion of white-collar jobs. . . .

* * * * *

In the basic steel industry, technological changes, at present, are moving ahead rapidly. Steel production was declining last April and was only moderately greater than in 1953, but production and maintenance jobs were down 52,600. . . .

The electrical machinery industry, which includes the production of automation equipment, is likewise in the midst of radical technological change. Production and maintenance jobs dropped 89,000 between April 1953 and last April, while white-collar, nonproduction jobs rose 136,000. There is no indication from this record that the production of automation equipment is providing alternative job opportunities for workers displaced from other industries. . . .

* * * * *

Important Role of Collective Bargaining and Labor-Management Cooperation

A faster rate of economic growth would not be, in itself, a panacea for all problems connected with radical and rapid technological change. It would narrow down these problems to more manageable size. In the workplace, however, there would remain a vast number of specific problems to be solved.

Even in periods of high and rising employment, the widespread introduction of automatic and semiautomatic machines means that some workers may be displaced and others would be affected by changes in jobs and skill requirements.

The new technology usually means the elimination of some jobs, downgrading some skill requirements and upgrading others. For many skilled and semi-skilled workers, automation results in making their skills obsolete. The group of workers that has been most directly hit by rapid technological change in recent years has been semiskilled employees—the machine tenders and machine operators of the older technology, which is now passing from most parts of the economy.

... Helpful precedents are developing, however, as unions and management grapple with these problems, and these precedents can be general guides toward workable solutions.

Advanced notice to the union of the company's intention to install new equipment is essential to permit joint labor-management planning to schedule the introduction of automation in periods of high employment, to permit attrition to reduce the size of the work force, and to allow time for the retraining of employees. Since expensive equipment is ordered long before its installation, advanced notice can provide the union and management with as much as 2, 3, or more years to plan jointly for the changeover. Such a period of time is of value, however, only if it is used wisely to plan the introduction of the new equipment with a minimum of dislocations and hardship.

Collective bargaining and labor-management cooperation can and should provide safeguards for employees during the transition period—such as fair and orderly procedures governing layoffs, rehiring, transfers, promotions, retraining opportunities, changes of job classifications, and wage rates.

Financial cushions can and should be provided employees who are laid off—such as supplemental unemployment benefits (SUB) and severance pay.

Adequate seniority provisions should assure workers an opportunity to qualify for higher skilled jobs. Fair procedures should be developed to permit and assist employees in retraining for new jobs with changed skill requirements.

Many workers, particularly semi-skilled employees, are downgraded in the changeover period, as a result of being transferred from one department to another. Such downgrading may also occur when employees are unable to adjust to new jobs and are shifted to lower rated jobs or when the new equipment makes old skills and job classifications obsolete. Job and wage protections should be developed for employees whose job classifications and skill requirements may be downgraded.

Consideration should be given to methods for permitting and aiding workers whose plants or departments move to new locations—provisions to give workers the opportunity, on the basis of seniority, to change to the new location and financial assistance to aid their families to move to the new area.

Special procedures have to be developed to assist older workers. Many older workers are too young to retire under present pension plans but find it difficult to adjust to the new machines. Efforts to find special jobs may be required for some older workers. Pension plans may have to be changed, through the collective bargaining process, to permit early retirement.

Pension plans may also have to be changed to permit the transfer of pension rights from one plant or company to another within an industry or area, so that displaced workers may receive some protection against the loss of accrued pension rights.

The new technology requires changes in wage structures, as the new machines change production methods, job contents, and responsibilities. New job titles may have to be created. With rapidly rising production and increases in job responsibilities, rising output, and much more expensive equipment, wage rates have to be revised upward. Existing wage incentive systems and job evaluation plans require careful review for possible changes, since radical technological change usually eliminates the basis of old incentive pay systems and job evaluation plans.

Automation increases output per man-hour. Substantial improvements in wages and fringe benefits are needed to spread the gains of the new technology to the great mass of American families. Growing mass consumer markets are required in an economy whose productive ability is increasing rapidly.

. . . . .

. . . One recent example of a collectively bargained procedure to develop plans for future adjustments to technological change was contained in the new contract, signed last August, by Armour & Co. with the United Packinghouse Workers and the Amalgamated Meatcutters and Butcher Workmen. The contract, which had already provided for severance pay and other provisions for technological adjustment, now provides for an automation fund committee to study and propose additional and improved methods to assist workers in the adjustment to technological change and shifts in plant location.

. . . . .

Behind the creation of the fund [paid for by the employer] lay a recognition, which was expressed in the unions' agreement with Armour, that—

. . . Mechanization and new methods to promote operating and distributing efficiencies affect the number of employees required and the manner in which they perform their work. Technological improvement may result in the need for developing new skills and the acquiring of new knowledge by the employees. In addition, problems are created for employees affected by these changes that require the joint consideration of the company and the unions.

Prof. Robben Flemming, of the University of Illinois, in accepting the directorship of this fund, states:

Our objective is to set up methods and procedures which will work toward security of employment as the company continues its modernization program. Automation and mechanization will be a problem for a long time and we want to establish some understandings as to what will be done in a given situation. Training programs, transfer possibilities, employer experience, and job opportunities will be studied by the committee.

In many other cases, significant agreements have already been reached on supplemental unemployment benefits, severance pay provisions, retraining procedures, transfer rights to new plants and numerous adjustments of wage structures, job titles, and wage rates. Collective bargaining reports in recent years reveal a wide variety of procedures that are being developed to provide concrete aid for workers and their families during this period of technological changeover.

. . . . .

Community Programs Are Needed

With the spreading tendency of companies to shut down old plants and to build others in new areas, a comprehensive program of Federal Government assistance for economically distressed communities is essential—to aid businesses in such localities to change their production lines, to help attract businesses into such area, and to retrain workers in new skills. Such a national effort is needed to prevent the large-scale waste of private and public investment in homes, schools, community facilities, shops, factory structures, and old family ties.

Relocation allowances, under law, as well as collective bargaining, may be necessary to assist workers and their families to move, if they wish, to locations of new job opportunities.

The new technology frequently makes it less costly for a company to build a new automated plant in a new area than to automate an old plant. In addition, changes in costs that are related to the new technology may convince many companies to move their plants closer to consumer markets or central geographical locations, rather than to remain close to raw material supplies or supplies of semiskilled manpower. Furthermore, radical and rapid changes in technology speed up the decline of some industries and the growth of others, with direct effects on one-industry towns.

. . . For many cities and towns, the removal of several departments from the major industry or the shutdown of old plants, mines, or railroad repair shops result in distress for the entire community.

. . . . .

. . . rapid technological change will inevitably leave some declining industries and communities.

This problem requires Federal Government action and assistance, since very few, if any, economically distressed communities can possibly revive their economies adequately, without a Federal program of grants and long-term loans at low interest rates. The communities, themselves, however, require planned local community efforts to maintain their economic health and growth.

Such needed community efforts require much more than committees to attract new industries. Joint labor-management-public community committees are needed to prevent community distress before it occurs, as well as to revive declining communities. Economic studies of the communities are needed to indicate the state of the community's economic health and to point to its future needs—which existing industries in the community are likely to decline and to which growing industries can possibly be attracted. In this effort, plant structures and private investment are important, but hardly enough.

It is essential for industrial communities to recognize that their educational, cultural, recreational, and community facilities must be maintained on an adequate level for economic growth. Such community facilities are needed in an attempt to prevent skilled manpower and managerial talent from leaving for other areas. Such facilities are needed, too, to maintain and attract skilled manpower and management and to retrain workers in new skills. This is particularly true in this age of radical and rapid technological change, with its emphasis on education and new skills, on engineers and technicians, on research and development.

. . . . .

America needs the added production that automation makes possible—to provide an adequate national defense; to improve living conditions, particularly of low-income families; to provide adequate public services; to provide financial and technical assistance for the peoples of the less developed regions of the world. Our national and international requirements could well use the additional output of an automated economy.

But the mere existence of automatic and semiautomatic machines provides no assurances that the new technology will be used fully and wisely. America needs government and private policies that will encourage full employment and the maximum use of productive equipment.

The pace of economic growth should be increased substantially above the rate of the past several years. Assistance should be provided to minimize and cushion the hazards of rapid and radical technological change on workers, their families and communities.

. . . . .

WALTER P. REUTHER

. . . . .

In its day-to-day activities the UAW has had to face up to these questions of job displacement, not as academic issues, but as stern realities which vitally affect the lives of hundreds of thousands of its members. I should like to say something of what the union has done at the collective bargaining table and in the plants to help solve these problems, of further steps that have been planned for the future, and of those areas in which legislative action also is required.

. . . . .

Since [1955] . . . further investigation and analysis have strikingly confirmed the fact of acceleration in the trend of productivity advance. . . .

In 1956 John Kendrick of the National Bureau of Economic Research, a pioneer in the field of productivity measurement, wrote:

> . . . one striking fact stands out: there has been a significant acceleration of productivity advance since the end of World War I as compared with the prior two decades.

Even more specific evidence of a continuing trend to acceleration was provided by Solomon Fabricant, research director of the National Bureau of Economic Research. In the Bureau's 1959 annual report he wrote:

> Also—a fact of great importance—the long-term pace of advance in output per man-hour has been speeded up. It was 22 percent per decade during the quarter century preceding World War I. It has averaged 29 percent since. During the most recent period—after World War II—national product per man-hour has been rising at an even greater rate, 35 to 40 percent per decade. This means, in absolute terms, that a 10-year period sees added to the output of each man-hour of American labor an amount well in excess of the *total* output obtained from an hour of work in most parts of the earth.

. . . . .

Automation and technological progress generally provide the physical and technical means by which these needs can and should be met. These means to progress are increasing, not at a linear rate of advance, but at an accelerating rate.

Faulty Economic Policies Add to Automation Problems

In referring to the economic troubles which have beset our country in the past 7 years, I do not want to suggest that automation can be held responsible for them. The cause of our troubles has been that those who have been placed in positions of responsibility have been trying to live and to force our country to live by the economic theories of the 19th century. They have been obsessed with the idea that a balanced budget is more important than a balanced economy. They have clung stubbornly to the belief that the general prosperity can best be served by a system of incentives to the wealthy, by helping the rich to grow still richer so that some of their surplus riches may trickle down to those below. They have rejected entirely the alternative view of modern economists that the only way to assure a prosperous industry is to insure that the demand for goods and services keeps pace with industry's growing ability to produce. They have failed to recognize the true cause of inflation in today's economy, the abuse of the power which is held by a relatively small group of corporations to administer prices without effective competitive checks, and in consequence they have persisted in applying monetary policies which have not stopped inflation but have very seriously checked our economic growth and have been among the major causes of our economic difficulties.

It is perfectly true that automation has helped to accelerate the rate of productivity advance, and to that extent has made it more necessary than ever before that we adopt vigorous and imaginative policies designed to insure the full utilization of our growing productive capacity. But for the most part it is our failure to adopt economic polices suited to our needs that has aggravated the problems caused by automation, rather than automation's having been responsible for our economic difficulties.

We still know too little about what the consequences of automation have been, to what extent workers have been directly or indirectly displaced, what problems they have had in finding new employment, or what special help in the way of retraining or other assistance would have enabled them to find jobs more quickly. It is quite true that the Department of Labor has done a few studies of the impact of automation in specific instances, but the employers who have been willing to cooperate in making such studies possible appear to be those for whom automation has presented no serious problems of worker displacement.

. . . . .

Let me make our position clear. We welcome automation as a major force for growth in our economy, holding forth the promise of increasing abundance for all if we use it wisely and well. But it is necessary to look facts in the face if we ever hope to enjoy the benefits of automation without the cost of unnecessary hardship for those whose lives it dislocates. And when the combination of national policies which hamper economic growth and new technologies which accelerate man-hour productivity results in employment declines and displacement of hundreds of thousands of workers in major industries, it is clear that there is going to be hardship and suffering unless active measures are taken to prevent it. In fact, during the past 5 years there has been a tremendous amount of hardship and suffering affecting millions of American families which could have been prevented and was not because necessary measures were not taken.

. . . . .

Worker Protection Has Been Improved

What can be done and what has been done to protect workers against either temporary or permanent severance from their jobs, or to cushion the impact of unemployment when it does occur? As I said above, our union has long maintained the principle that protection of workers against such catastrophes should be considered one of the costs of doing business. Industry as a whole profits from technological advance and from the general dynamism of our economy, and one of the first charges against those profits should be the cost of reasonable protection for those workers to whom the change brings only loss of a job.

. . . . .

One of the major forms of protection which was pioneered by the UAW, not only against the opposition of the auto manufacturers but against all the propaganda weapons of the NAM and the U.S. Chamber of Commerce, is the supplemental unemployment benefit plan. This plan, as amended in 1958, provides our members with amounts which, when added to unemployment compensation, assure most laid-off workers of income equal to 65 percent of their take-home pay for periods up to 39 weeks. . . .

Perhaps the greatest benefit derived by workers from SUB plans . . . is their effect in stimulating management to provide increased stability of employment by making unemployment costly to the employer. For many years one of the bugbears of work in the auto industry has been its uncertainty. Workers laid off for model changes might be unemployed for a few weeks, or for months. There were sharp alternations between full employment and overtime in one month and reduced workweeks and layoffs in another. The danger that whole plants might be closed as a consequence of modernization programs added to the instability. That instability has by no means disappeared, but we believe it has to some extent been curbed. . . .

. . . . .

. . . Every company policymaker knows that decisions which result in layoffs of employees will result in payments from SUB funds which must subsequently be replaced at a rate of 5 cents per man-hour in added labor costs. . . .

. . . . .

Over the years we have been able to negotiate numerous provisions in our collective bargaining agreements which protect our members against dismissal in the event of job displacement. These provisions are the worker's frontline of defense against the threat which automation poses to him as an individual. Even the employers who fought most stubbornly against them when we first proposed them now point with pride to the measures they have taken under these provisions as evidence of their concern to cushion the impact of automation on their employees.

For the most part now employees who are permanently displaced from their jobs can exercise plantwide seniority in transferring to other jobs they can do. This eliminates the evil of older workers being dismissed because job requirements in one department of a plant have changed, while another department might be hiring new men off the street.

In areas such as Detroit, where one company may have several plants, our major agreements now provide that a plant which is hiring must give preference to seniority employees of the company laid off from other plants. These employees can now carry with them to the new job the rights to such benefits as insurance, pensions, and supplemental unemployment benefits which they may have built up at another plant.

When jobs are transferred to a new plant, many of our agreements protect the right of workers to transfer with the job if they wish, carrying with them their seniority rights. In addition, some agreements provide that when a new plant is hiring it will give preference to laid-off employees from any other of the company's plants.

Willingness of employers to make such arrangements has been affected by the negotiation in 1958 of amendments to our SUB plans which provide for separation payments, graduated in accordance with length of service up to 30 weeks' full pay, to workers who are permanently displaced from their jobs. Once again, by making loss of employment a cost item on the employer's books, we have been able to increase greatly the employer's concern to maintain employment.

In a period of rapidly advancing technology many problems revolve around the acquisition or updating of workers' skills. Our major agreements have been broadened to help workers meet these problems. Apprenticeship programs, for example, have traditionally provided an upper age limit, typically in the midtwenties, after which an applicant would not be accepted for skilled trades training. We have been able to negotiate the elimination or very substantial raising of this age limit for employees already on company payrolls, so that workers beyond the normal apprenticeable age have an opportunity of training themselves in new skills.

An important protection for the older worker who may find it impossible to adjust to the demands imposed by automation has been the negotiation of flexible pension programs permitting retirement before the normal age. Typical provisions permit workers to retire of their own volition at any time after age 60 with a pension which is actuarially reduced in accordance with the added years of payment, or to retire at company request or by mutual agreement with a pension which until age 65 is double the normal amount, to compensate for the fact that the retiree is not yet eligible for OASI. The latter provision, for retirement by mutual agreement, is commonly applied to meet the problems of workers over 60 in such situations as plant closing or large-scale job displacement due to automation.

In addition, the vesting of pension rights, although not yet complete, affords workers who are displaced with substantial protection of the pension rights they may have earned through many years of service.

Further Progress Planned

The substantial progress we have made in negotiating the protection workers need in the age of automation has not blinded us to the fact that many improvements in the present programs are still required. We anticipate that such improvements will be opposed by employers just as the present programs were when we first proposed them. We anticipate also that their opposition will be overcome, and that in future hearings management representatives will be claiming full credit for the advances they now oppose, just as they now claim credit for those they opposed in the past.

Among those features of our proposed collective bargaining program which relate closely to the needs created by automation, strengthening and extension of workers' transfer rights when jobs or plants are moved rank high. Workers displaced by a change in plant location should have the right to transfer to the new location whether or not the same job as they have been doing will be available, provided there is work at the new plant which they can do or can learn to do. . . .

Workers transferring to new locations because a company decision has displaced them from former jobs should be reimbursed by the employer for the costs involved in effecting such transfer, including allowances to defray the workers' unusual expenses connected with the move. Many corporations already recognize this principle as it applies to their executives. The principle behind this demand is the familiar one that the company will not make such a move unless it expects to profit by it, that the worker's moving and relocation costs are in fact part of the total cost of the company's decision, that the worker should not have to make a financial sacrifice in consequence of a decision from which his employer will profit, and that by reflecting such costs on the company's books, moves which in fact are not economically sound will be discouraged.

Workers who elect not to transfer should receive adequate separation pay without loss of seniority status. . . .

In multiplant corporations, we have made a start at broadening areawide preferential hiring agreements into areawide seniority agreements. Broadening of many seniority agreements within plants is also progressing.

Areawide preferential hiring agreements should also be broadened to cover not merely plants of the same corporation, but other companies in the same industry and area. . . .

The age of automation requires the establishment of programs under joint union-management control and direction, to train or retrain workers without loss of wages for jobs which will enable them to meet the requirements of technological change. Agreements should also protect against threatened dilution of skills and encroachments on standards of workmanship.

. . . . .

Collective Bargaining Cannot Answer All Problems

While collective bargaining has an essential role to play in meeting the problems raised by automation, it cannot provide all the answers. Negotiated programs must function side by side with public programs. Negotiated retraining programs, for example, cannot meet the needs of all workers who require retraining, nor can negotiated relocation programs help the employees of a firm which has gone out of business. In addition, programs similar to those negotiated through collective bargaining will have to be provided for the millions of workers still unorganized. . . .

. . . . .

One of the most distressing features of the advance of automation is the spread of areas of chronic unemployment, where industries have either moved out or have sharply declined as a result of technological change. Communities can become blighted for reasons not closely related to technological change, and the distinction matters little if their problems are the same, but in a high proportion of cases the advance of technology can be accorded a large measure of responsibility—whether it be an automobile center such as Detroit, a Pennsylvania railroad town hit by the replacement of steam by diesel locomotives, a West Virginia mining community affected by technological advances in mining plus the change from coal to other power sources, or a New England textile town abandoned by runaway employers when the need to modernize plants gave them the excuse to relocate elsewhere.

[Mr. Reuther then suggests policies for governmental action to help deal with problems of automation: a commission to gather facts on what has, and is, happening and on industry plans; higher minimum wages; shorter working hours without reduction in weekly pay; plans and money for area and industrial redevelopment; larger unemployment benefits and improved services for letting workers know of job opportunities; training and other special aids, including funds for moving, for displaced workers; strengthening the process of collective bargaining; general improvement of educational opportunities and facilities; more vigorous actions to maintain full employment and speed economic growth. *Ed.*]

EDWARD SWAYDUCK

Q. *Eddie, it has been my understanding that unions are opposed to automation on the grounds that it reduces jobs for workers. What is your view?*

A. Well, for 79 years now the Amalgamated Lithographers of America has vigorously fostered technological development. We have found over these four generations that if the lithographic industry brings down product costs to the customer, more jobs are created for our members.

EDWARD SWAYDUCK, President, Local 1, Amalgamated Lithographers of America, "Automation? Absolutely!" an advertisement appearing in *U.S. News and World Report* (May 15, 1961), published at Washington, D.C., p. 118. Used by permission of J. S. Fullerton, Inc.

Q. *Can you give me some figures on that?*

A. Certainly. In 1906, three men ran a hand-fed stone press that produced 800 sheets per hour. If I had gone into that plant 55 years ago and told the members that in 1961 there would be a lithographic press that would produce 11,000 sheets per hour in ten colors on both sides, do you know what they would have told me? They would have said there would be only a handful of workers left—there'd be nobody in the industry! But what are the facts? As we progressed through that revolution of automation and technological development our industry has grown by leaps and bounds. Lithography has become the fastest growing method of reproduction in the graphic arts. Does that answer your question?

Q. *It does—as far as the industry is concerned. But how has all this worked out for the union and its members?*

A. About three years ago the Wall Street Journal was checking facts for a front-page story based on a proposal I made before our international convention for a joint union-management automation research fund. The newspaper interviewed people from all over the industry. One New York plant owner told them that because we had automated his unit costs were identical with those of 1914. But in this same period the benefits to our members have increased tremendously. In addition to higher wages we have a 35-hour week, three weeks vacation, ten paid holidays and the finest welfare and pension programs in the nation. And during those years our membership has increased 1,000% while the population of the country has gone up only 80%.

Q. *So automation has worked, and worked well, for both the industry and the union?*

A. The facts speak for themselves. How could an industry absorb all those extra costs and stay in business competitively if the Amalgamated Lithographers of America had not worked with them for automation and technological development? In this way we made the product less expensive and more attractive, and everyone is benefiting.

Q. *But it seems to me, Eddie, there are still a number of labor leaders who haven't come around to this viewpoint.*

A. They haven't, but they're going to have to sooner or later. In the past, labor officials lacked the political courage to tell their members "This is good for you," because they had to live with it for two, three, four or five years before they showed results. They didn't have the courage to stand up to that kind of a barrage. But in industries where they did, the members have reaped the benefits. These are the facts of life.

Q. *Then to wrap it up, Eddie, you are for automation and you think other unions should be for it, too?*

A. Not only am I for automation—it's the history of our organization to be for it—but I'm convinced that other unions that are not for it are actually and literally underestimating their country. People might be momentarily displaced, but for that brief period the economy would be able to take care of them. Then, as soon as the products were brought down in cost, the general business picture would be enhanced and the various industries would absorb everyone who was displaced. As I see it, it's the story of America.

. . . . .

The Economic Editor of Business Week *deals here with one of the great changes taking place in our economy.*

72 · Why Research Spending Soars

LEONARD S. SILK

The great thing the United States will have going for it in the years ahead will be the swift scientific and technological progress of our time—and a rising tide of investment resulting from American industry's new principle and practice of programed innovation, creating a multiple flow of planned new products out of research in a new and powerful extension of capitalism's growth process.

How important this force is you can see by looking at the past impact of improving technology on output. Robert Solow of M.I.T. has estimated that, of the total increase in United States output per man-hour from 1909 to 1949, only 12.5 per cent was due to increase in capital equipment, while 87.5 per cent was due to technological progress. In a second study, Solomon Fabricant of the National Bureau of Economic Research has found that, during the period 1871 to 1951, technological advance accounted for 90 per cent of the rise in output per man-hour, as against 10 per cent for capital formation. And Benton F. Massell, in still a third independent study, done at the Cowles Foundation for Research in Economics, likewise has found that, during the period 1919 to 1955, technological change accounted for approximately 90 per cent of the rise in output per man-hour.

In other words, it was not primarily more machinery in back of every worker, but an unknown combination of better machinery and technology, better organization, better management and greater skills on the part of workers, that sent United States output soaring in the past half-century.

The implications of these findings are of outstanding importance for policy makers and economists. They mean that the overwhelming emphasis of any program for growth must come to focus on technological progress—and the factors that promote it or obstruct it.

Once said, this may seem to be an obvious conclusion, one that "we have always known." . . . But the idea was never really built into the corpus of economic analysis or policy. Like many "new ideas" in economics, this new stress on the role of technology and research represents simply a shift of emphasis, perhaps a somewhat different way of looking at old knowledge—but a way that can be of crucial importance

---

LEONARD S. SILK, "Why Research Spending Soars," from *The Research Revolution,* by Leonard S. Silk, Copyright 1960, McGraw-Hill Book Company, Inc., reprinted from *Challenge,* The Magazine of Foreign Affairs (January 1961). Used by permission of the editors of *Challenge* and McGraw-Hill.

in reconstructing the economics of growth. . . .

Investment Process

To stress the role of technological advance is, of course, not to deny that its impact upon the economy is largely communicated through the investment process. By and large, technological progress does not become "real" until it is embodied in new investment: knowing how to plough a field faster does nothing until tractors replace horses. To be sure, changes in organization, techniques and skills requiring little or no capital investment can also be important; and such new knowledge, similarly, means nothing until it is put to work. . . .

Generally speaking, however, an economy which is rapidly increasing its capital stock is also likely to be accelerating the process of technical advance. And that proposition has its converse: the rate of capital investment will be greatest when innovational change comes fastest—because the rate of profit will then also be high.

Technological advance should therefore help to keep an economy not only growing but also more stable. The reason is twofold: (1) technological advance will be an underlying force for profit, for capital investment and for expansion—and an economy, like a bicycle, is more stable when it is rolling forward than when it is standing still; and (2) in periods of recession, the opportunities created by technological advance for profit-conserving investment, aimed at modernizing and replacing obsolescent equipment, will place a fairly high floor under capital investment —whose downswings have in the past been the main cause of recessions and depressions.

But, in order to get the steady flow of investment in plant and equipment that results from technological progress, there must be regular and sustained efforts in research and development.

To speed up technological progress, the curve of research and development expenditures in the United States keeps rising. In 1928 American industry spent less than $100 million on R&D. By 1953–54, over-all research spending had jumped to more than $5 billion a year. In 1959 the total was $12 billion. . . .

Since *research* has become an "okay" word, applied to operations which produce no new knowledge, one certainly must try to distinguish the real rise from the phony. But one needs only one's naked eyes, regardless of what the imperfect data show, to reveal how the research revolution has transfigured the American scene. . . . All around the country, sleepy old college towns have turned into boom towns where you are lucky to find a parking space or a table at the best restaurants —let alone a good house near the campus—because of the competition of the scientific and engineering elite that has engulfed those towns. In places like Cambridge, Princeton and Palo Alto, the elite has become a mob.

And the research spending curve, which has done all this, will continue to rise. By 1969, according to a new McGraw-Hill study, the R&D total will be more than $22 billion. Some observers put the future level of research spending still higher. . . .

At some point, clearly, R&D spending must taper off—or else, as Guy Suits, Vice President and Research Director of General Electric, says, ". . . it would eventually constitute the entire economy —an anomaly that even the most partisan supporters of R&D would view with dismay." United States business is already trying to determine the proper balance between research and development and other industrial functions, including capital investment, manufacturing and marketing. The optimum combination of these interdependent activities, as Suits suggests, isn't a constant, but a variable that reflects changes in each industry and in the over-all economy brought about by growth and by growing complexity.

. . . . .

The most obvious (and doubtless the most fundamental) cause of the rise of research spending lies in the nature of scientific research itself. Research feeds upon itself: discovery breeds discovery; innovation breeds innovation; and with each new discovery or innovation, the total body of scientific and technological knowledge increases.

Of course, this has always been so. But in our time the process has been accelerating.

Inventive Genius

The world has always had scientific and inventive geniuses. But frequently they were, as the common phrase has it, "ahead of their time." William Ogburn observed:

"Leonardo da Vinci couldn't invent an airplane, although his brain was probably as good as those of the two bicycle repairmen who did invent it. But the materials for the airplane did not exist in da Vinci's day. The light gas engine was not invented until several centuries later. In the same way all scientific discoveries are built upon preceding scientific discoveries and are not something that comes full created from the researcher's mind, as a result of only wishes and will power."

The thing that seems to be happening in our time is that all the once widely separated avenues of scientific and technological knowledge are converging, like the roads that lead into a city—a city where ideas are then swiftly exchanged, where civilization then swiftly grows.

"Building Blocks"

Unlike the situation that confronted Leonardo, vast numbers of elements needed for further scientific and technological progress are now at hand, waiting for scientists and engineers to put them together. Miller B. Spangler has categorized these elements—which he calls "building blocks"—in this way:

1. Process materials—metals (including "new" metals like uranium, titanium, beryllium), alloys, plastics, laminates, fuels, chemicals, fibers, clay, etc. New or improved process materials frequently lead to technological changes in many industries where cost saving is involved.

2. Process equipment—turret lathes, boring mills, planers, milling machines, gear cutters, grinders, welding machines, forges, deep-drawing presses, centrifuges, agitators, ball mills, boilers, condensers, compressors, jet-molding machines, glass-blowing machines, extrusion dies, rolling mills, billeting machines, cyclotrons, etc. New models of these machines are capable of greater speeds and precision than those of only a decade ago. Automatic or semiautomatic operation of these machines has led to large cost reductions. New process equipment may result from new process materials —for instance, metallurgical advances may permit the construction of machinery of greater durability, or permit its operation under greater ranges of temperature and pressure.

3. Tools of measurement and observation—chronometers, compasses, sextants, telescopes, microscopes, pressure gages, thermometers, calorimeters, micrometer calipers, protractors, planimeters, levels, plumbs, transits, spring scales, analytical balances, volumeters, ammeters, wattmeters. . . . These have importance in many industrial applications, such as exploration or quality control or automatic operations, but their most significant use is in scientific and

industrial research itself. New and better instruments lead to new experiments—and whole series of scientific discoveries and industrial innovations.

4. Calculating devices—adding machines, electronic computers, mathematical tables such as trigonometrical functions, random numbers, Poisson distributions. . . . The greatest importance of these devices probably is that they astronomically expand the productivity of scientific investigators.

5. Recording devices—photographic equipment, sound-recording equipment, microfilm, memory tapes, geophones, time recorders, temperature recorders, pressure recorders, volume-of-production recorders, etc. These improve production control and facilitate automation. Improved handling of statistical and engineering information accelerates research and development.

6. Instruments of communication—telegraph, telephone, radio, television, intercom systems, teletype, radar, photoelectric cells, dictaphones, signaling devices, sirens, limit switches, alarms, moving pictures, etc. These permit the swift interchange of ideas and information from human to human—and from machine to machine. . . .

7. Inventories of standardized items—wrenches and repair tools, nuts and bolts, chemicals, batteries, condensers, transistors, valves, motors, pumps, fork lifts, etc. These minimize delay in fabrication and repair, and reduce the costs of industrial processes and of research and development work.

8. Reference literature—encyclopedias, dictionaries, bibiliographies, indexes, technical books, handbooks, periodicals, trade journals, etc. These stores of information are of enormous importance to the scientist and engineer. . . . In fact, the enormous difficulties of keeping up with the work in one's own field (which requires the assistance of growing numbers of exceptionally well-qualified librarians, and editors and teachers), together with the essentiality of having access to the enormous apparatus required for scientific and technological research in so many areas today, is the basic force behind the shift from the individual investigator to the research team, from the bicycle shop to the large industrial, or government or university research center. This shift need not mean debasement of the individual intelligences and imaginations required—but it does imply greater specialization, and more emphasis upon communication and cooperation among the specialists.

Reactionary Move?

Although some outsiders (including many economists, and sociologists and social critics) seem to feel that the move toward the team approach in research is somehow a reactionary move—an instance, perhaps, of George Orwell's "group-think"—the more gifted investigators appear to be drawn to large institutions where they can find skills and talents complementary to their own, and where the resources will be adequate to permit the researcher to tackle critical problems with some hope of success. Studies which emphasize the great contributions made in the past by individual inventors as proof of the individual's superiority over the team would appear to have limited application to the present or the future. This is of course not to say that, in all fields, the day of the individual researcher or inventor is gone; there doubtless are still many opportunities for the lone thinker to make tremendous contributions in mathematics, theoretical physics, symbolic logic, economics, etc., as well as in the area of practical gadgetry. In any case, the argument about the merits of the individual researcher versus the research team is somewhat meaningless—for individuals in the sciences are simply not "alone"; they depend upon the enormous heritage of Western science, language and civilization—and they are fools if they do not keep up and benefit from what colleagues in their own field or related disciplines are doing. . . .

In any event, the enormous expansion of scientific and technical endeavor, utilizing the building blocks of new materials, new tools of measurement and observation, new calculating devices, recording devices, instruments of communication, standardized parts, and catalogued stores of ancient and recent information and ideas, makes it virtually certain that we are still in the *early* phase of our research revolution. . . .

Industry is becoming more and more aware of the necessity of that shift to basic research. Before World War II, very little fundamental research originated in industrial laboratories; scientists in the universities were in fact constantly astonished to learn that any "pure" research was done in any industrial laboratory. And most university men thought that a concern with the practical usefulness of fundamental research was rather vulgar or even sinful; and that notion persists in some quarters, though it is changing, as the urgent importance of science for industry, government and economic development becomes more widely understood by scientists.

"Inner Logic"

Of course, one cannot be sure [what is] . . . a fair division of the fundamental research burden among industry, government and the universities. One might even argue that industry should be *less directly* involved in basic research (while spending more on basic research via grants to universities and other research institutions), should not be seducing fundamental researchers from the campuses, where they can choose their tasks more freely, without any commercial direction. It is at least possible that science and technology expand optimally when they grow by their own "inner logic," without any concern about proximate or ultimate goals. That old argument still goes round and round inconclusively; it is a general "philosophical" argument that doubtless can only be settled by detailed examination of the particulars in many fields. . . .

The United States government is, by far, the major source of funds for research and development work. In 1959 the government put up $7.2 billion—or 60 per cent of total R&D outlays. (Private industry provided $4.6 billion, or 37 per cent of the total; colleges and other institutions provided $300 million, or only three per cent of the total.) Most of the funds the government put up went to finance R&D work by private industry and research institutions; of the $7.2-billion total provided by government, $4.6 billion went to industry, $1 billion to colleges and other institutions—and only $1.6 billion was spent in government laboratories. And of the $7 billion the government provided, $6 billion went for research in defense and defense-oriented industries.

. . . . .

Costs Big Money

Basic research, especially in some of the newer fields of physical science—solid-state physics, cryogenics (cold-temperature research), plasma research, electronics, hypersonics, and so forth—costs big money. Except for the very largest companies, few individual corporate budgets are big enough to support this highly risky research investment; the probability of success in cases of individual projects . . . is pretty low. But the results of successful gambles may be so tremendously valuable not just to industry but to the nation and its security that the risks of investment in research should be socially borne.

It would, however, be a serious mistake to exaggerate the degree to which the continuing rise in research spending depends on government support. Of the $9.1 billion in R&D work performed by industry in 1959, industry itself did, after all, provide half the financing. And that $4.5 billion spent by industry on R&D in 1959 was more than twice as much as industry put into research in 1953, more than four times as much as it invested in research in 1946. The chief reason for this trend is simple but dramatic: much of United States industry has caught on, with a bang, to the proposition that research produces innovations and innovations produce profits—either by creating or expanding markets, or by cutting costs.

Since World War II, the most profitable industries and companies, and the ones with the best growth records, have been those that had an outstanding performance in research and innovation. The importance of the research-profit-growth nexus has been sharply pointed up by a study of 50 large industrial companies by A.T.&T. This study clearly showed that, as between different industries or between companies within the same industry, the research-minded companies tended to be the most profitable. One cannot, of course, lay out a simple cause-effect (or chronological) sequence leading from research to profit to growth. Some would make profit the initiating factor. Some would put far more emphasis on good management. Some would give more weight to shifts of demand upon particular companies or industries from outside political, demographic or technological forces. The causes of company profit and growth are obviously highly complex. Nevertheless, some of A.T.&T.'s case histories reveal that research can in fact frequently be isolated as the critical cause of a company's profits and growth.

For instance, the A.T.&T. study contrasts the performance of International Business Machines Corp. with two other, unnamed companies—both of which had larger sales than IBM just before World War II. All three companies prospered

RESEARCH AND DEVELOPMENT ESTIMATES:
MAJOR SOURCES OF FUNDS
(In billions of $)

Year	Total	Industry	Govt.	Nonprofit*
1945	1.8	0.9	0.8	.1
1946	2.1	1.0	1.0	.1
1947	2.7	1.3	1.3	.1
1948	3.1	1.4	1.6	.1
1949	3.1	1.4	1.6	.1
1950	3.4	1.5	1.8	.1
1951	4.0	1.8	2.0	.2
1952	4.5	2.0	2.3	.2
1953	4.9	2.2	2.5	.2
1954	5.5	2.4	2.8	.3
1955	6.3	2.5	3.5	.3
1956	8.4	2.9	5.2	.3
1957	10.0	3.5	6.2	.3
1958	11.0	4.0	6.7	.3
1959	12.0	4.5	7.2	.3
1969 (est.)	22.2	9.0	12.4	.8

* Colleges and institutions.

through the war and the period of high postwar demand immediately after the war. But, in 1951, IBM saw tougher competition ahead and decided to boost its already substantial research expenditures, though this meant lower profits in the short run. IBM's heavy investment in research led to new and improved products, more rapid growth and higher profits in the long run.

Meanwhile, the other two companies tried to grow by buying other companies, rather than by finding and making better products. As the 1950s wore on, they fell farther and farther behind. Finally, one started a crash program, pouring back into research a larger part of each sales dollar than any other company in the industry, hoping to get back in the running; the other company, the A.T.&T. study said, ". . . is now so poor it cannot devote much money to research." . . .

Such cases—and they can be found in other industries—are what lie behind the change in management thinking about the importance of R&D. More and more companies have come to regard expenditures for research not as a luxury but as a necessity to meet both domestic and foreign competition; many executives have come to refer to research as the lifeblood of successful business operation. Wall Street has learned to keep a close watch on a company's research activities; that a company has a strong and productive research program has come to be one sure way of judging management's competence and the company's growth prospects.

. . . . .

XIV • GROWTH OF UNDERDEVELOPED ECONOMIES

In this selection, Professor Wright of McGill University discusses the requirements for economic growth. An economist, he does so with a heavy emphasis on social factors, an approach sometimes neglected by economists in their writings.

73 • Basic Factors Affecting Economic Development

DAVID MCCORD WRIGHT

Our task . . . will be a twofold one, first to give a systematic account of the essentials of economic growth, and second to make our theory of growth so broad that it will apply to all types of developing human society. . . .

(1) Natural Resources, Labor, and Knowledge

Not many people, no matter what their political opinions, will dispute the statement that increased output requires some labor, some natural resources, and a great deal of knowledge. We hardly need, for example, to go to college to find out that a moron turned loose in a desert without food, water, or knowledge would die. There is a danger, however, that in concentrating upon economic problems and technological achievements or the discovery of *new* knowledge, education as such will be overlooked. Yet each generation is a "new invasion of barbarians." Human knowledge and human cultures do not perpetuate themselves. Books do not simply walk out of a library and force people to read them. The ideas they contain must be taught. Hence any civilization that fails to pass the key ideas of its society on to its younger members will fall. And no matter what economic system may have been adopted, or what momentary success such a society may have had in increasing the output of turbines or stepping up production of atomic power, if its main social ideas are not passed on to succeeding generations, that society will collapse.

(2) Saving

Yet in speaking of knowledge and education we are still dealing with

---

DAVID MCCORD WRIGHT, *A Key to Modern Economics* (New York: The Macmillan Company, 1954), pp. 10–25. Used by permission.

things which, in principle at least, are universally conceded. Really fundamental misunderstandings and disputes do not begin until we come to the next requirement . . . saving. . . .

Mankind has been described as a "tool-using" animal. Suppose we took a group of the strongest, most intelligent, most vigorous, and most highly educated young women and men in our society. Suppose we took away all their equipment and dropped them into a primeval forest or on a desert island. What good would all their knowledge or their strength do them? They would barely survive, or they would die—*unless* they used their knowledge and their strength to begin to make for themselves some approximations of the tools, the shelters, the weapons, and the equipment they once knew. And it is easy to see that the eventual level of comfort they would reach would be set very largely by the stock of equipment they could create.

Next, let us split the group into two. One group, we may suppose, goes in for playing games and admiring sunsets. It is willing to make out on such bits of foods as it can get by picking berries or by casual hand-to-mouth hunting without weapons of any sort. A second group, however, is more industrious, more vigorous, more energetic, and more anxious for eventual food and comfort. The members of this second group are willing to spend less time playing, and to eat fewer berries for a while, in order that they may use the time and energy thus left available to make, let us say, bows and arrows, or other crude weapons to help in their hunting. Or perhaps they may make plows to help in farming. Such people would be the first savers and the first investors. They have saved because they have gone without some of the *immediate* enjoyment and some of the *immediate* food which they *might* have had, had they not spent their time trying to make tools or weapons. They are investors because they use the energy thus set free in order to make lasting items of equipment or "means of production" which will ultimately give them a higher living standard.

. . . No country, be it capitalist, socialist, or Communist, can hope for economic growth unless it is willing to forego part of its potential present consumption and enjoyment in order to accumulate more skills, more machinery, and more equipment. Furthermore, once a society, however crude, has accumulated a stock of equipment upon which its standard of living depends, it not only cannot grow without some saving, but also it cannot even hope to stay at the level it has already reached unless it is willing to spend some of its energy to replace its stock of equipment as it wears out.

(a) UNSUCCESSFUL SAVING. . . . Now saving is sometimes *un*successful, and on this point depends a great part of the disputes in a modern economy. Among the institutions which make saving easier, and at the same time can help most to keep it from being successful, is the use of money. Speaking very crudely, each bit of money may be thought of as a "ticket" or "vote" controlling a certain tiny portion of the stock of labor and resources which a society has available. When, therefore, we spend our money on clothes, or food, or other immediate satisfactions, we are voting to keep resources busy producing the things which satisfy our personal wants.

In the same way if we save money and use it to build a house for ourselves, or to buy a share of stock in a company which wishes to expand, we are voting to keep people busy in the production of more equipment for society—in other words, more saving and more investing. But if we get money and neither spend it nor invest it, but simply leave it under the mattress or in the bank (at a time when the bank cannot or will not make an offsetting loan) then, in the first instance anyhow, we are voting to keep certain men and resources *idle*. This process of saving without either spending or investing is called "hoarding," and unless our hoarding happens to be offset by someone *else's* spending or investing (for example the bank's), we are, by hoarding, helping to force our society into a state of unemployment or dislocation.

. . . the simple fact that some saving will always be needed for growth does not mean, as some writers sometimes say, that every bit of money *actually* saved will *actually* be used for growth. Such a conclusion can sometimes be quite misleading. In the world which we know, the impulse to save under certain circumstances may not only fail to benefit the individual doing the saving, but also actually serve to cause unemployment and dislocation for other people. . . .

(3) Enterprise and Pressure Groups

One of the most popular and most mistaken ideas in modern thought is the notion that scientific discoveries somehow introduce themselves. It seems often supposed that, once an idea has taken shape in the brain of a scientist or been discovered in his laboratory, that idea will automatically be put to practical use without anything more than routine action being necessary. This belief that science somehow puts *itself* to work is entirely mistaken, no matter what sort of social system we are dealing with. For, just as books left to themselves have no power to get themselves read unless some human being comes along to read them, so also scientific ideas and scientific discoveries require special effort before they are given practical use. In the first place, the scientist or man of ideas may not be the type of person most likely to put across a new way of going about things. There are many obstacles to be overcome, and the contemplative lover of pure wisdom, having made his discovery, may be content to stop at that point. Let us run over some of the main types of obstacles which may discourage him or make his job difficult even if he is not discouraged. First of all there is always simple stupidity or ignorance, but that is only a small part of the trouble. Far more important is the ingrained dislike which a large proportion of the human race seems to have for new ideas, or for ideas which disturb the regular habits of their lives. Men's minds have a tendency to become "set," and the man who tries to disturb the favorite ideas of others will often receive little mercy from the people he wants to stimulate. You would think that in the case of a scientific discovery all that would be needed would be an opportunity to perform the experiment that would test your idea. But frequently on one pretext or another even the chance to *show* that one is right is denied. The history of science is full of cases of this sort. . . . In such instances it may usually be said that the opponent has already become worried that the new notion is probably correct, and is unwilling to allow an experiment because he is consciously or unconsciously afraid that it will succeed and thus deprive him of "face" and hurt his ego.

Obstacles to change, however, are not only of so subtle and psychological a type. A man's direct financial interests may be involved. . . .

The trouble is that the process of raising *total* output always involves change. There are two reasons why change is always involved. First of all, on the production side, if we want to make a plant twice as big as it was before, to give it twice as big an output, we can't just take a drawing of the old plant, multiply every dimension by two, and expect an efficient result. No indeed. The whole plant must be *redesigned*. ... In technical economic language what we are saying is that we do not live in a world of "constant returns to scale." Increases in mere size induce important changes in *relative* force and efficiency. Unless these changes are allowed for we cannot get a satisfactory result. If you merely doubled the size of every part of a boat, that boat would have a good chance of turning over when it was launched. Thus the relation of the *parts* of a factory to the plan as a whole changes as its size increases. But in addition to the type of redesigning needed in any case and without new inventions, it is an observed fact that without *new* discovery, and *new* advances in technique, the process of growth will become progressively more difficult. Thus we see that, even if we are thinking of the production side alone, growth both *comes through* change and *causes* change.

But the same thing is also true when a rise in consumption is involved. If people become better off, they do not simply continue to buy more of the same things. The youth who used to buy one chocoloate soda a day doesn't just buy twenty chocolate sodas a day. He may soon change his wants entirely. The man who has lived in one small house will not simply try to live in two small houses. He is apt to buy or build an entirely different house— one which seems to him more beautiful or more convenient. Thus, as total output rises, the pattern of wants shifts. Many "luxuries" become "necessities," and former necessities disappear altogether. ... with wants constantly changing and production methods constantly changing—as must occur if there is to be growth—the process of total expansion *must* involve a constant reorganization and redirection of industry. Old towns making old products must modernize themselves or give way to new towns making new products. People with obsolete skills, if they wish to try to maintain their incomes, must retrain themselves, or be retrained; or they must move themselves, or be moved, to new locations; and so it goes. ...

. . . . .

Any realistic social psychology forces us to realize that, even under a socialist state with equal income, many men would come to have a special fondness for certain jobs, certain towns, certain scenery, certain teams of workmates, certain friends, and that they would resent a disturbance of all these habits and ways of living. Yet the industrial reorganization we have seen to be necessary for growing output involves precisely such disturbances. Worse yet, the *power* and *prestige* of particular individuals will be linked to the social demand for their skills. And if the need for a particular skill changes, the power and prestige of the man who possesses it will change. If a man is commissar of coal production, and oil supersedes coal, he will probably not enjoy the loss of personal power and importance involved in the decline of his industry. Furthermore, it will be easy for him to find excuses for trying to stop the transfer. "Coal is better than oil," he will say, or "Military necessity requires us to keep up the mines," and so on.

But when we consider that pressure-group problems of the sort we have sketched are universal, and add to this the unwillingness of many people to be jarred out of their usual ideas, we can easily see why it is that under any society a special amount of force, energy, and insight will be required to put across a new social or technological combination. Sometimes (for instance in the case of the Pullman car) the inventor is also the man who puts across the new idea. But . . . in a number of cases, the man who is interested in pure research is psychologically unfitted for the rough-and-tumble that may be necessary to get his idea used. He either will let his discoveries languish or will willingly turn them over to someone else before they are ever introduced. Economists have found, therefore, that a special name is needed for that type of man who is willing to make the special effort and undergo the frequent social onus and difficulties involved (under any system) in putting across a new social or technological idea. Such men economists call "enterprisers" or "entrepreneurs," though the word "promote" in ordinary language comes close to meaning the same thing. . . . *Anyone* in *any* type of society who gets put into practice a new technical, artistic, or social program we will call an enterpriser. Viewed by this definition, Stalin and Lenin are enterprisers; and indeed Josef Stalin, no less than Henry Ford, becomes one of the most remarkable entrepreneurs of social history. Furthermore, just as all enterprisers do not have to be business men, so also all business men are not necessarily enterprisers. . . . Schumpeter draws a sharp distinction between "managers" on the one hand and "enterprisers" on the other. A manager, to him, is an official or leader, in any society, who makes his decisions on routine lines, and operates within the limits of established ideas and technology. Such a man may have a great deal of power, for the distinction is not one concerning his legal rights or official position. The only things a manager cannot do, and still be called a manager under our terminology, is to explore *new* paths or to revise the general framework of ideas and policies within which he is operating. When he does that we call him an enterpriser; and unless a social system, whatever its name, manages to contain within itself a certain number of these enterprisers, it cannot hope for the continued introduction of new ideas.

Yet we have already seen that, without new ideas and inventions, social growth becomes more and more difficult. Thus not only do men need to save a certain amount in order to create new machinery, new equipment, and so on, but in addition men must be constantly varying and improving the type of machinery and equipment which they are trying to install. If you doubt this, think what sort of standard of living the United States would be enjoying today if we were forced to go back to the kinds of equipment which were used, say, in 1870, and if we had limited ourselves during all the past half century simply to repeating over and over the same methods that were used at that time. Progress comes through change, and change is not automatic. Unless, therefore, there are individuals who are able to see the possibilities around them and willing to put them across, the ideas of the scientist and the philosopher will remain forever sterile. . . .

(4) Ideology

. . . just as saving in the long run is likely to become useless or even harmful unless there are enterprisers who can put it to work, so also enterprisers by themselves will be helpless if they find themselves in a society which does not allow them to exercise their peculiar gifts. Not only, therefore, do we need resources, labor, knowledge, saving, and enterprise—also we need an "ideology," or set of social ideas, which will permit all these factors to operate together. Thus one of the most important and most usually overlooked requirements for economic growth is the general acceptance of a set of ideas which will allow growth to continue.

Fish, someone has said, are not likely to be the first people to discover the existence of water. The individual who moves in given surroundings is apt to take the ideas around him so much for granted that he will not be able to appreciate either the way they are actually related or which are the most important. Yet these social ideas are absolutely fundamental. Nations, cultures, and societies are held together by basic sets of ideas or "symbols"—ideas concerning what men think is fair, what is the right way to live, what is polite, what sort of behavior shows a good citizen, and so on. These fundamental notions run all the way from the fact that the people may all be learning a single alphabet to the fact that they all believe in a special kind of government. Every tribe, whether it be the dwellers on the island of Madagascar or of the island of Manhattan, has such a set of social ideas. . . .

Perhaps the most important thing to remember is that the social ideas of an economy which wants to grow cannot be too one-sided. We don't want to insist too much upon order and quiet, for then enterprisers will not be allowed to introduce the new ideas without which growth cannot continue. On the other hand we don't want things so completely upset that no one can make plans. For enterprises would not then be able to act either. In the same way there must always be rulers of some sort, but too much power is likely to create a narrow, self-perpetuating group, and that is also not likely to be a good thing for growth over the long pull. Again, if everyone is consumed with ambition and never stops to play, the people are likely to become grimly neurotic and there will be many nervous crack-ups. But on the other hand if nobody is ambitious and nobody tries to enjoy working, not very much will get done and living standards will not rise. What we mean to stress is that the ideas of a successfully growing society must show a very special *balance* of social qualities. . . .

HARMONY AND CONFLICT. Economists have expressed one of the important sides of this problem of balance in terms of two opposing principles: the principle of social harmony and the principle of social conflict. It is easy to give an example of the principle of social harmony. Suppose a man desiring to make money (for example Henry Ford) invents or introduces a new kind of automobile which is much cheaper and much more efficient than any existing car. As a result the general standard of living may be raised, more people will have cars, and so on. Thus in getting rich himself he has made many others better off too. Again, a commissar by introducing a new idea may raise output and also obtain prominence and power for himself. We can list behavior like this among examples of the harmony of individual and social good.

But there is a principle of conflict too. Many of the makers of more expensive cars, many people who bred horses or made carriages, and so on, were ruined by the rise of Henry Ford's new cheap car. Nor were the railroads helped by it. In the same way we have already seen that the commissar who introduces a productive new idea may nevertheless destroy the value of many people's skill, upset their cherished habits, and also oust various established government officials from power. Here we have the principle of conflict. Both sides are important in describing social life. For it would seem fair to say that any expansion or change in any society is likely to be good only on *balance*. Some individuals are always likely to be disturbed. So if our social ideas say that no one is ever to feel any insecurity whether as to money, ideas, or way of life, then we will not be able to have either change or growth. On the other hand, if everything is kept always entirely mixed up, there won't be growth either.

(5) Stability

What is true of ideology is also true of economic policy. We have therefore listed . . . some degree of stability. We have just argued that perfect security and perfect stability, and great emphasis upon them, cannot be combined with continued growth. Yet on the other hand we have seen that sometimes an expanding society may run into trouble; also that saving may sometimes run to waste and cause unemployment . . . failure to keep economic upheaval within tolerable limits may result in a terrific waste of social energy and a needless wrecking of millions of lives. In fact, one can see that under some circumstances, the whole gain of an expansion could be lost in an unnecessary resulting unemployment. Thus, if rapid growth is really to be a continued gain, some policy of stabilization will be necessary from time to time.

(6) Criticism

One last, most important requirement for successful social growth should be mentioned, though it is unfortunately the one concerning which the economist is least qualified to speak. This requirement is criticism. By criticism is meant insistence upon standards of quality in social development. Although it is convenient to define progress or growth as the mere rise in the size of output per head, any honest economist must admit the incompleteness of such a standard. Mere change as such can just as well be change toward evil as change toward good. Mere increase in output can mean increased garbage as well as increased sources of better living.

. . . . .

(7) Summary

. . . It must be stressed again that this list is not limited merely to capitalism, but applies to any form of economic order. We may explain the way the different headings fit together as follows: Natural resources, labor, and knowledge are generally admitted to be needed for social growth. But we pointed out that there were further requirements—for example saving. By saving was meant only a failure to use all of one's productive potential to satisfy immediate personal wants. . . . But while some degree of saving is a necessary condition for social growth, it is not sufficient by itself. For although we have seen that *some* saving must be done in order to produce any investment, we cannot jump to the conclusion that every dollar actually saved will actually lead to increased production of machinery and equipment. . . .

. . . Now the most important factor needed to employ saving is the one which we have called enterprise. Enterprisers we define as those men who, besides seeing the values in, or discovering new technical or social ideas, also have the energy and determination to put such ideas into action. . . .

The hope for improvement of the conditions of the masses throughout the underdeveloped areas of the world lies, to a greater or lesser extent, with capacities to draw capital from wealthier areas. The late Professor Nurkse, who taught at Columbia University, draws upon nineteenth-century history to study the prospects. In doing so, he gives many insights into different aspects of the economic process.

74 · International Investment and the Growth of Underdeveloped Areas

RAGNAR NURKSE

... Ever since the last world war great expectations have been placed on the export of private American capital as a means of bridging the dollar gap as well as financing world economic development.... We suspect that the export of capital from Great Britain was one reason why the international economy of the Victorian era did not know of a chronic sterling shortage. We recognize, above all, that foreign investment was associated during that era with a tremendous spurt in world production and trade. There is in America a feeling of nostalgia for the nineteenth-century environment that made this flow of capital possible. The question is: why can we not recreate that environment?

The answer, I submit, must start from the fact that the circumstances in which overseas investment ... went on in the nineteenth century (which I take to have ended in 1914) were in some ways quite exceptional. ...

... Over the fifty years that preceded the outbreak of the First World War, ... Great Britain invested overseas about 4 per cent of her national income. In the later part of the period (1905–13) the ratio was as high as 7 per cent. If the United States to-day were to devote similar percentage portions of her national income to the same purposes, she would be exporting funds to the tune of $12 billion or, if we apply the higher percentage, some $20 billion each year. These figures are almost absurdly large and tend to confirm the view that there was something unique about Britain's foreign investment.

It was unique in that the greater part of it—roughly two-thirds—went to the so-called "regions of recent settlement": the spacious, fertile and virtually empty plains of Canada, the United States, Argentina, Australia and other "new" countries in the world's temperate latitudes. It was unique in that it went

---

RAGNAR NURKSE, "International Investment To-Day in the Light of Nineteenth-Century Experience," *The Economic Journal* (December 1954), pp. 744–758. Used by permission. Some footnotes have been omitted.

to these places together with a great migration of about 60 million people, including many trained and enterprising persons, from the British Isles as well as Continental Europe. . . .

It was in the newly settled regions, which received two-thirds of the capital exports and practically all the emigrants, that nineteenth-century international investment scored its greatest triumphs. The remaining . . . British capital exported . . . was employed in a different type of area, where its achievements were much more dubious: tropical or sub-tropical regions inhabited, often densely, by native populations endowed in some cases with ancient civilizations of their own. The areas that formed a minor field for overseas investment before 1914 are the major problems to-day: the truly backward economies, containing now about two-thirds of the world's population. The empty and newly settled regions, from which international investment derived its brilliant general record and reputation, are to-day, in *per capita* income, among the most prosperous countries in the world.

Labour and capital are complementary factors of production, and exert a profound attraction on each other. The movement of labour to the new regions attracted capital to the same places at the same time. And the other way round: the flow of capital stimulated the migration of people to these places. . . . Any barrier to the transfer of one would have reduced the flow of the other. Labour and capital moved along side by side, supporting each other.

In the twentieth century the situation is totally different. The capital exports from the United States can be viewed rather as a *substitute* for the movement of people. Capital and labour are still complementary, and still basically attract one another. But as things now are, restricting the movement of labour in one direction increases the need, if not the incentive, for capital to move in the opposite direction. Cheap labour, instead of being allowed to come to the United States to work with American capital there, is to some extent supplied with American capital abroad. . . . The underlying pressure—not necessarily the profit motive, but what we might call the global social pressure—is very strong for more capital to move out from the United States to work with the cheap labour in the world's backward economies. But notice that in this situation, in sharp contrast to the predominant nineteenth-century pattern, capital is being urged to go out to work with people that have not grown up in a capital-minded milieu, and may not be culturally prepared for the use of western equipment, methods and techniques.

With this situation in mind, we can perceive what I think is the basic rationale of the present American emphasis on direct business investment as a means of financing economic development. The advantages rightly attributed to it are, first, that it goes out with American enterprise, tied up with American "know-how," and, secondly, that it is likely to be productively used, not swallowed up—directly or indirectly—by immediate consumption in the receiving country.[1] Since, however, in

---

[1] [In July, 1957, Eldridge Haynes, publisher of *Business International,* a weekly publication, testified in an advisory capacity to the Senate Committee on Agriculture and Forestry. He put the point this way—*Ed.*]:

. . . . .

". . . in the economic struggle between the free and communist worlds we have one—and I believe just one—instrument for economic development which the communists do not have and can never duplicate. We can enter a friendly foreign country and build a plant, stay there, own it, and operate it. The communists cannot do this. They are

the low-income areas the domestic market is small, this type of investment tends inevitably in such areas to concentrate on extractive industries—mines, plantations, oil wells—producing raw materials for export mainly to the advanced countries. This is, in effect, the so-called "colonial" pattern of foreign investment, of which American oil operations abroad are now an outstanding example. . . .

In the aggregate flow of capital in the nineteenth century, the "colonial" type of venture played a minor role. Looking at Britain's foreign investment portfolio in 1913, we find that . . . thirty per cent was in loans to governments, as much as 40 per cent in railway securities and some 5 per cent in other public utilities, so that no less than three-quarters of the total was in public or public-utility investments. The rest includes banking, insurance and manufacturing companies, as well as investments directly in raw-material extraction. . . . It is therefore far from correct to assume, as is sometimes done, that the "colonial" form of enterprise in the extraction of mineral and plantation products for the creditor country was the typical pattern of foreign investment. . . .

To the new countries . . . capital moved chiefly through the medium of securities carrying a fixed return (*i.e.,* bonds and preference shares) issued by public authorities and public-utility undertakings. To these countries, it appears, capital could safely be sent in the form of relatively untied funds, with a good chance that it would remain capital there, because the people in these places, having come from Europe themselves, knew what to do with capital and how to handle it. Cultural adaptation was no problem.

These countries . . . were offshoots of European civilisation. For Britain, or at any rate for Europe as a whole, investment in these areas was essentially a process of capital widening rather than deepening. Indeed, when Britain sent capital out to work with Swedes, Poles, Germans and Italians emigrating overseas, she may have done so at the expense of the deepening which her own economy is said to have needed in the period just before the First World War. But international investment in the nineteenth century was, of course, unplanned, and was determined by private rather than national advantages. French and German activities in Eastern Europe and the Near East were an exception in this respect. . . .

Great Britain's national advantage, apart from the return flow of interest and dividends, seemed to be handsomely served through cheaper food and

---

permitted in a few rare cases (notably India), to enter a foreign country in the capacity of a contractor and to build a plant —and then turn it over to the host government. But they are not permitted to remain in any foreign country as the owners and operators of a plant. This we do. This is the unique role of private enterprise in economic development. Hundreds of U.S. firms have built and now own and operate several thousand manufacturing and assembly plants in scores of foreign countries.

"Now, when a manufacturing plant is erected any place, but particularly in an underdeveloped nation, that plant contributes measurably to the economic progress and development of the host country. Jobs are created—permanent jobs; technical and managerial skills are developed; more goods are made available to more people; the local government has a new source of revenue from the taxes paid by that plant; other industries are stimulated by purchases of raw materials, components, fuels and services from other industries; foreign exchange formerly spent to import the product is saved—sometimes foreign exchange is earned by exports of the product made in the plant. And this economic development is constant. It goes on day after day—indefinitely or permanently. This form of economic development does not require the appropriation of one cent of U.S. taxpayers' money."

raw materials, though this benefit was shared by other importing countries that had made no corresponding investments. . . .

Production of primary commodities for export to the industrial creditor countries is characteristic of the "colonial" pattern of direct investment in economically backward areas. In the regions of recent settlement foreign investment can also be said to have been induced essentially by the raw-material needs of the industrial centres—especially by Great Britain's demand for the wheat, wool, meat and dairy products, which she decided not to try to produce for herself, and which these temperate regions were particularly well suited to produce. The capital that came into these regions did not, however, enter into primary production itself, but was employed above all in building up the costly framework of public services, including especially transport, which laid the basis for domestic industrial development, as well as for the production of raw commodities for export. . . .

Nineteenth-century foreign investment centered on the railway—that "great instrument of improvement," in Lord Dalhousie's phrase. If account is taken not only of railway securities but also of the use to which many government loans were put, it seems that well over half of Britain's external investment before 1914 went into railway construction. The great bulk of this was in the newly settled countries. . . . The great pioneer lines—first in the United States, later in the Argentine and elsewhere—were deliberately planned and built *in advance* of current traffic needs; they themselves created the settlement and economic growth that eventually led to a full demand for their services.

Although individual promoters sometimes played the most conspicuous part, the railways in the new countries were built, as a rule, if not directly by governments, at any rate with extensive government assistance in the form of land grants, subsidies and guaranteed returns to the investors. In view of this fact, one can safely say that the bulk of international investment in the nineteenth century depended on government action in the borrowing countries. In French and German capital exports, some of which also went to the new world, the proportion of government loans and other public investments was even higher than in the British case.

. . . . .

It is clear that the main flow of capital in the nineteenth century was not to the neediest countries with their "teeming millions," which were indeed neglected, but to sparsely peopled areas where conditions for rapid growth along familiar western lines were exceptionally favourable. If we were to look round for similar opportunities in the twentieth century, I do not know where we should find them if not in the further development of the same regions of recent settlement; or else perhaps in Siberia—a vast area reputedly rich in natural resources, which may be longing for an injection of skilled labour from Europe and capital from the United States.

Once the main facts about the nineteenth-century capital flow are set out in something like their true proportions, it is curious to see how little they fit in with some pre-conceived notions that have been widely current. . . . Consider . . . the summary which Mrs. Joan Robinson gives (in *The Rate of Interest and Other Essays*, 1952, pp. 157–8) of the views of Rosa Luxemburg:

> The capitalist nations are surrounded by primitive economies, such insulated from the others like a nut within its shell, waiting to be cracked. The capitalists break open a primitive economy and enter into

trade with it, whether by enticing its inhabitants with commodities they have never seen before, by political cunning or by brute force. Now exports to the primitives provide an outlet for the product of the last batch of capital goods created at home. After a little while another nut is broken, a use for more capital is thereby found, and so on, as long as the supply of untouched primitive economies lasts. . . . When the stock of unbroken nuts is exhausted, the capitalist system collapses for want of markets.

This is one variant of neo-Marxist doctrine and, like others, it neglects some crucial facts. No pre-existing markets were conquered in the new countries. Markets were *created* there by labour, enterprise and capital all drawn from Europe. In the industrially primitive countries markets were and have remained unattractive because of mass poverty. Why is it, for example, that in the 1920s Canada, Australia and New Zealand, with already quite highly developed industries of their own and with a combined population of only 17.4 millions, imported twice as much manufactured goods as India with her 340 million people?

The American public also, perhaps because it lives in one of the new countries itself, does not always appreciate the peculiar nature of the nineteenth-century investment experience. . . . Keynes in 1922 made a remark that is worth recalling: "The practice of foreign investment, as we know it now, is a very modern contrivance, a very unstable one, and only suited to peculiar circumstances."[2] He cautioned against extending it by simple analogy to a different set of circumstances. . . .

Will [private foreign lending] . . . work, and if so, how will it work, in the "under-developed" areas of which we hear so much to-day? The preceding remarks have all been leading up to this question. My purpose here is to present the question, against the background of past experience. . . . I will only hazard a few brief comments on three general topics: direct business investment, public-utility investment and governmental grants.

. . . . .

For reasons mentioned earlier, direct investments by American business firms —usually financed from corporate reserves rather than security issues on the capital market—are thought to be particularly well suited to the economically backward countries. But they have their shortcomings also. In the life of an industrially primitive community they are apt to create not only a dual economy but also a dual society, in which conditions for the diffusion of western technology may actually be the reverse of favourable. Foreign business investment is not always a happy form of encounter between different civilisations. Besides, if techniques are to be of wide and permanent use, they must be adapted to local conditions. The methods of giant corporations, whose foreign operations are sometimes only a side-show, are often too standardised to favour such adaptation. And so the local economy may not get much help from the example they give; the example is often inapplicable. Let us remember that the Japanese acquired industrial techniques very effectively before they began to receive any substantial foreign business investments. Also the technical assistance programmes now in operation remind us that there are other ways of spreading technical knowledge.

As a rule, when foreign business enterprise is attracted to economically backward areas, it is mainly for the production of raw materials for export markets, for the simple reason that the

---

[2] J. M. Keynes, *A Revision of the Treaty* (New York: Harcourt, Brace and Company, 1922), p. 161.

domestic market in such areas, even if protected by import restrictions, is generally too poor to afford any strong inducement to invest. The natural result is a "colonial" investment pattern, open to the familiar criticisms that it tends to promote lopsided rather than "balanced" growth, and that it makes for instability due to high dependence on foreign demand for one or two staple products. If this type of direct investment is to take place in any considerable volume, it presupposes a long-run prospect of rapidly expanding demand in the industrial centres for the raw materials which it seeks to provide. . . . there is no firm assurance of such an expansion except for certain minerals. Governmental purchase agreements alone cannot give this assurance in the absence of favourable basic demand conditions. . . .

In the last few years one of the chief economic obstacles to a greater flow of business funds to low-income countries has been the high level of business profits obtainable at home, from developing American natural resources and catering to the American mass market. Conditions may change. It is not inconceivable that business investment abroad might greatly increase in the future, and that it might bring substantial benefits to the poorer countries. Yet, on the whole, it seems unlikely that direct investment alone can become anything like an adequate source of international finance for economic development. . . .

What is most urgently needed to-day is a revival of the public or public-utility type of international investment that used to dominate the scene. The International Bank has hardly begun to fill the gap left by the disappearance of this type of private foreign lending. If the past cannot be reproduced, it is all the more imperative to devise a new pattern suited to present needs and conditions. . . . The Bank, being dependent on the private capital market for most of its loanable funds, inevitably reflects to some extent the attitudes of the private investor. And the private American investor is still waiting for a change in the weather, and remains unimpressed by statistics showing that only 15 per cent of the dollar bonds (not counting direct investments) floated in the 1920s by underdeveloped countries—that is, aside from Central Europe—have proved a permanent loss.

It is said that there are not enough productive projects in the low-income countries to absorb much more money than is now going out. It is pointed out that the Marshall Plan, which accustomed the world to the sight of a large dollar outflow, was not a plan of new development so much as one of reconstruction, in an area where a solid industrial foundation and the "know-how" of a skilled population already existed.

No doubt this point has considerable force. But if there are not enough projects, can we not ask for international technical assistance to design them and to draw up the blueprints? Lack of basic services, such as transport, power and water supply, is a particularly serious bottleneck in the poor countries. Because of this the *physical* environment—quite apart from the obvious difficulties arising from the political or social climate—is unfavourable to private investment. A large foreign firm producing raw materials for export may find it profitable to set up incidental facilities such as roads or waterworks, of which the local economy, too, can make some use. But the general utility of such things often depends in haphazard fashion on the technical features of the firm's main activity. It may be fairly high in the case of a railway built by a mining company from the interior of Peru to the sea-coast. It is virtually zero in the case of the pipe-line in which Arabian oil is pumped to the Mediterranean.

In the United States a hundred years ago public authorities, as well as private promoters, played a leading role in the drive for "internal improvements," financed in part by foreign capital. There is no question that ample scope exists for international financing of public improvements in the poor countries to-day. Until these countries have acquired a skeleton framework of such facilities, conditions will not be particularly attractive for the more varied and smaller-scale business investments there. Even with such basic improvements, of course, the individual business investments, domestic as well as foreign, may fail to materialise, because of other obstacles. It is conceivable, therefore, that some of these public works would turn out to be white elephants. But the risk has to be taken; any form of capital investment is, in the last analysis, an act of faith. However hard it may be for the pioneering spirit that opened up the new countries to apply itself to the low-income areas to-day, not much can be achieved without that spirit, and no international organisation concerned with development can remain untouched by it.

Apart from the distribution of the promoter-function, there still remains the question of finance. If the profitability of American business at home has kept down direct investments abroad, a simple comparison of bond yields does not explain why "portfolio" lending cannot get started again. However, while the private investor has been standing on the side-lines, we may have witnessed the beginnings of a system of international grants-in-aid and low-interest loans from government funds. . . . The man who gave his name to the Marshall Plan, in accepting the Nobel peace prize . . . said that it was "of basic importance to any successful effort towards an enduring peace that the more favoured nations should lend assistance in bettering the lot of the poorer." [3]

. . . . .

Even if we hesitate to accept the assumption that world peace can be bought or that material progress makes for contentment, the fact of growing pressures for international income transfers must nevertheless be recognised. It may be precisely because the problem of international investment is now, unlike what it was in the Victorian era, concerned in the main with the backward economies that the need for such transfers is felt to arise.

. . . . .

The idea of international grants-in-aid is essentially a consequence of the increased gaps in living standards and of the closeness of contact that is creating at the same time an increasingly acute awareness of these gaps—a situation without historical precedent. This awareness is perhaps the most fundamental obstacle to the resumption of private international lending. In contrast to the position of the backward economies to-day, income per head in the principal debtor countries of the nineteenth century—the newly settled regions—can never have been far below European levels. Interest payments from poor to rich are now, it seems, not only basically unwanted by the rich countries but indeed are felt to be somehow contrary to the spirit of the age. And although public grants (for "social overhead capital") and private foreign lending (for more specific investments) can ideally be looked upon as complementary rather than conflicting sources of finance, it is easy to see why in practice the two do not mix at all well. This applies not only

---

[3] *The New York Times* (December 12, 1953).

to grants but also in some degree to international loans from government sources.

Persistent attempts in the United Nations organization to set up a system of international grants under U.N. auspices . . . have foundered on the rocks of American opposition. Yet American practices and pronouncements alike have kept world expectations alive. . . .

It must be recognised that international unilateral transfers have no necessary connection with the subject of foreign *investment*. They may be for current consumption or for military use. Even if they are intended for, or tied to, particular capital projects, a net increase in the overall rate of accumulation is not always assured. If they are to make an effective contribution to economic development, they call for domestic action in the receiving countries—fiscal, monetary and other policies designed to withhold resources from immediate consumption and to direct them into capital formation.

But once the receiving countries are capable of devising the necessary controls for the productive use of outside aid, they should be equally capable of using such policies for the mobilisation of potential *domestic* sources of capital (*e.g.*, skimming off resources now absorbed by luxury consumption, making use of labour set free from the land through better farm methods or recruiting any surplus labour already existing on the land). It is far from my intention to suggest that in these circumstances foreign aid becomes unnecessary. Yet this consideration does shift the emphasis upon the need for domestic policies to ensure that in the overall use of resources, domestic as well as external, investment is given top priority. . . .

. . . . .

Professor Villard of the College of the City of New York analyzes a problem whose seriousness is widely recognized but whose nature is imperfectly understood.

75 · *Population Growth and Per Capita Income in Underdeveloped Areas*

HENRY H. VILLARD

It is today rather generally accepted that the gloomy future which Malthus predicted as a result of the application of an increasing population to a fixed quantity of resources can be warded off by increases in the quantity of capital and improvements in the techniques of production. This will undoubtedly be true for a century or so; but it cannot be true for periods which are, after all, fairly short in terms of human history. Specifically, at the present time world population is probably increas-

HENRY H. VILLARD, "Some Notes on Population and Living Levels," *The Review of Economics and Statistics* (Cambridge, Mass.: Harvard University Press, May 1955), pp. 189–195. Copyright 1955 by the President and Fellows of Harvard College. Reprinted by permission of the publishers.

ing at an annual rate of about one and one-half per cent, which means that population is doubling every fifty years. If this rate of increase were to be maintained until 4250 A.D., the population of the world would weigh six sextillion, six hundred quintillion short tons, which is also the estimated weight of the world. Given the law of conservation of matter, it follows that there is nothing that science will be able to do even in an atomic age to increase output sufficiently to maintain the present rate of population growth until 4250 A.D.; sometime well before that date the increase must come to an end. . . .

I.

The practical problem is, of course, far closer. At the present time there is available for each living person an average of perhaps 650,000 square feet of land, including deserts, Antarctica, and the like. The per capita total for the United States is over 500,000 square feet, contrasted with 100,000 square feet for the average Indian and 50,000 square feet for the average Japanese. But only perhaps 15 per cent of Japan is arable, so that (apart from fish and imported food) the Japanese diet is raised on 7,500 square feet of land per capita by what is probably the most intensive agriculture prevailing anywhere (for a comparable land area). Let us assume that science can make the whole world—Greenland, Antarctica, and the Sahara desert included—50 per cent more productive than the arable area of Japan, so that every 5,000 square feet of land would be able to support a person. This would involve a population density for the entire world about seven and a half times the present density of England and one quarter the present density of New York City. Maintenance of the present rate of population increase would reduce the square feet available per person to 5,000 by 2300 A.D. . . . Note that the time to 2300 is the same as has elapsed since the first permanent settlement of the American continent. . . .

II.

What is far more important than the mere fact of the inevitable cessation of population growth is whether cessation takes place *with population or living levels at a maximum.* But the interrelationship between increases in population and real income is complex and little understood. Given the supply of the other factors and the state of the techniques of production, the principle of diminishing returns tells us that there is a quantity of labor which will maximize average output and a larger quantity which will maximize total output. The under-employment characteristic of many underdeveloped countries probably indicates that they are in the vicinity of the point of maximum total output under prevailing conditions, so that a smaller population might well increase per capita income if capital and technology did not change. But development will both increase the quantity of capital and improve technology. Thus in practice it is hard to demonstrate that any given present population is excessive, as the demonstration must be made with reference to the conditions which will prevail in an uncertain future as a result of development itself. . . .

. . . How do increases in population contribute to increases in total income? Short of the point of maximum total output, the principle of diminishing returns suggests that as population (and labor) increases, so will output (and income). But population growth may have *adverse* effects on saving and capital formation and even on the rapidity of technological change. For in an economy interested in general welfare, rapid population growth may keep average income and therefore average saving low, and there are many types of technological improvements that are not easily developed by a man uncertain as to the whereabouts of his family's next meal. . . .

In any event until we know more about the interelationship of increases in population and total income, it seems appropriate to consider the two as independent variables. If this is correct, it follows that the rise in living levels is a function of the excess of the rate of increase in income over the rate of increase in population. The effects of various excesses on living levels in the year 2000 for a country such as India with a 1950 average income of $50 are set forth in the following table.

INCOME IN 2000 GIVEN VARIOUS EXCESSES OF INCOME INCREASES OVER POPULATION INCREASES *

Percentage Excess	Resulting Income
0	$50
½	64
1½	82
1	105
2	135
2½	172
3	219
3½	279
4	355
4½	452
5	574

* Starting with 1950 average of $50.

These figures indicate that, if it is desired to raise the Indian income level to $135 in the year 2000, it can be done by a 2 per cent annual increase in income if population is stationary, a 3½ per cent annual increase in income if population continues to increase at the present rate of 1½ per cent, and a 5 per cent annual increase in income if population were to increase at a 3 per cent rate. Note that the annual increase in American real income since the Civil War has been about 3½ per cent. Some of the possible combinations are:

INCOME IN 2000 UNDER VARIOUS CONDITIONS *

Annual Percentage Increase in Population	Annual Percentage Increase in Real Income				
	2	3	3½	4	5
0	$135	$219	$279	$355	$574
1	82	135	172	219	355
1½	64	105	135	172	279
2	50	82	105	135	219
3	31	50	64	82	135

* Starting with 1950 average income of $50.

Always assuming that income and population can, at least for the range under discussion, be taken as independent variables, the purely economic problem in the *short run* would appear to be whether (say) a one per cent reduction in the rate of population increase can be achieved at less cost than a one per cent increase in income. Remarkably little is known *either* about the cost of making birth control available *or* the cost of maintaining any given increase in income. . . . [yet] I do not see how an economist can justify the use of resources to increase output without considering the possibility that such resources would do more to raise incomes if they were used to make birth control available.

. . . For if the present rate of Indian population increase were to continue, the land area available per Indian would be reduced to 5,000 square feet in 215 years, at which time the Indian population would number seven billion. Hence, assuming that a living level above the subsistence level is desired and that adequate population limitation is not achieved by war, it follows that the cost of introducing birth control is a cost which will have to be met in the case of India within a century or so *in any event*. Thus the long-run comparison is between the *inevitably necessary* annual cost of making birth control devices effectively available and the annual cost, not to raise living levels but merely to offset population growth, of a *continuous* increase in income.

Thirdly, the present high birth and death rates typical of underdeveloped countries involve a vast waste of resources through investment in children who do not live to become productive. In the case of India it has been estimated that 22.5 per cent of the national income is devoted to maintaining those who die before reaching the age of 15, contrasted with 6.5 per cent in the case of England. If the 16 per cent of the national income which is thus in effect allocated to unproductive investment, over and above that allocated in England, could instead be added to productive investment, the percentage of Indian income devoted to saving and capital formation would rise from perhaps 5 to more than 20 per cent—a level higher than that prevailing in the United States!

Finally, and most important of all, there is a real possibility that no progress whatsoever will be made in raising Indian living levels without birth control. Given the fact that less than a third as much of the Indian national product is devoted to net capital formation as in the United States—and the fact that in practice the amount of foreign aid is likely to be relatively small—it will be no mean feat to bring about a 2½ or 3 per cent annual increase in the Indian national income for the next fifty years. For underdeveloped areas as a whole the United Nations Report on "Measures for the Economic Development of Underdeveloped Countries" suggested that an annual increase in real income of 2½ per cent would be possible only if vast quantities of foreign capital were forthcoming. But even if a 2½ or 3 per cent rate of increase in Indian income could be maintained, the level of living would nonetheless remain stationary if the population were to increase at the same rate.

III.

. . . . .

It would be hard to overemphasize the danger that slow development . . . may merely increase population without raising living levels. But it is perhaps equally important to stress that, in the absence of population restraints, the speed of development (size of displacement) may have to be very large to be successful. Thus one of the assumptions utilized by Prof. Leibenstein is that development can be expected, at least temporarily, to raise the rate of population growth to its biological maximum—say, 3 per cent or more per year. But if this is so, increases in income as rapid as the 3½ per cent realized in the United States since the Civil War would be needed if much of an increase in average income was to be achieved. As the income-increasing effects of additional capital in underedeveloped areas may well be low because of the small amount of non-capital resources per capita, the achievement of adequate displacement by increases in production may be extremely difficult; it may well be that the only effective displacement— as well as the most economical—would be the introduction of birth control.

There seems to be a widespread belief . . . that the mere effort to raise living levels will in some rather mystical fashion immediately reduce the rate of population increase. But if there is any connection between living levels and birth rates, it must predominantly be with levels which have *actually risen*. There has been a vast development of agricultural production in India and China since 1700—perhaps a fourfold increase. Yet the per capita calory intake remains but little above the starvation level. Further, quite apart from the recent upsurge of births in developed countries, living levels may have to rise immensely before birth rates are affected. For example, Puerto Rico, with a present standard of living far higher than India has any reasonable hope of attaining for many years, has an annual rate of population increase of almost 3 per cent, which is about double that of India. The higher Puerto Rican rate is the result of sanitary and health measures which have left the birth rate unaffected but have brought the death rate down to about the American general level of 10 per thousand. As the Indian death rate is perhaps twice as high, enthusiastic application of DDT and penicillin and the provision of enough food to eliminate dietary deficiency diseases should easily be able to bring about a 2½ per cent, or perhaps even a 3 per cent, rate of increase of Indian population if the birth rate is unchanged.

Moreover, there is every reason to believe that it is not the mere rise in living levels which reduces birth rates but the fact that birth control devices become available as a part of higher living levels. It is, of course, true that the availability of birth control devices is by no means the sole factor affecting birth rates, but with the possible exception of Ireland, I am not aware of any case in which birth rates have fallen appreciably without birth control devices being available. . . .

To summarize: if any realistic estimate is to be made of the *probability* that efforts to increase output will raise living levels, a comparison between probable increases in population and income is required. Obviously *present* rates of population increase are not necessarily relevant, as development may well bring about a higher rate of population increase. . . . Equally no purpose is served by stressing the increase in output that might be achieved if unlimited amounts of capital were available. In fact, nothing here said should be construed as denying the *possibility* that large enough gifts of capital to an area such as India might succeed in increasing output fast enough to outrun the likely expansion of population for a few decades. But if the *probability* that living levels will be raised is to be demonstrated, it must be shown that the capital likely to be available during the period, from both domestic and foreign sources, will be sufficient to offset the likely expansion of population, including any higher rate of increase that may be induced by development itself. . . .

Note that examples from history are not particularly encouraging. Japan, which is frequently cited as a country which succeeded in raising its level of living without restricting population growth, had a death rate during most of the period of her modernization *above* the present Indian rate. In addition, a considerable amount of abortion and infanticide appears to have persisted, so that the increase of the Japanese population was in fact restricted to a rate substantially below that which can be achieved under modern conditions.

IV.

Is there any case to be made for economic development in the absence of a reasonable probability that living levels will be raised? To the extent that one wishes to maximize living levels rather than numbers of people, the answer depends on the relationship between present and optimum population. Clearly a full definition of "optimum" is going to be difficult even in economic terms, so that much additional work on this matter is urgently needed. To cast some quite preliminary light on the subject, a very crude estimate of what is involved in providing the present Indian population with the current American diet seems worth making.

The comparison is, of course, not undertaken to suggest that the particular components of the American diet should be inflicted upon Indians, but rather is made because there seems no reason why Indians should not ultimately aspire to a diet of *equal variety and complexity,* however different the particular ingredients may be. . . . Over-all the average American consumes over four pounds of food (or drink) each day, containing perhaps 3,200 calories, while the average Indian consumes one pound with perhaps 2,000 calories. To provide this quantity of food there is under cultivation in the United States 100,000 square feet of land per capita, with an additional 215,000 square feet in farms but not under cultivation. In contrast, the total land area works out at 100,000 square feet per capita in India, with about 40,000 square feet under cultivation. . . . [Assuming certain ideal conditions,] it follows that Indian agriculture could provide the *present* Indian population with an approximate equivalent of the American diet by achieving average yields three times those prevailing in the United States. In time this is perhaps not an impossible achievement, but if population growth continues at its present rate, then to provide the Indian population with the American diet in 2050 would involve growing on 15,000 square feet what we now grow on the equivalent of 180,000 square feet, which seems likely to be rather more difficult.

V.

In any determination of optimum population the increasing drain of larger populations on wasting resources will certainly have to receive attention. . . . Suppose it became our objective to raise the level of living of the whole world to two-thirds of the American level by 2100. Assume that this would involve world-wide resource consumption at two-thirds our present rate. As world population is fifteen times ours, it follows that world-wide consumption of resources would be ten times the present American rate *even if* no interim increase in population took place. But if population over the next 150 years were to continue to increase at 1½ per cent anually, then in 2100 world resource consumption would, *ceteris paribus,* be at 80 times our present rate.

[Estimates of resource use with various populations are given. *Ed.*]

. . . In actual practice, ruling out catastrophic developments, it is certainly possible that significant efforts at world-wide industrialization will seriously deplete available supplies of everything except coal in the course of the next 150 years; the longer restraints on population increase are postponed the more certain does this conclusion appear to be. Thus any serious effort to raise world living levels to anything approaching those of the West may well involve an undertaking to supplant economies based on steel and fossil fuels with economies based either on atomic or solar energy and perhaps aluminum or magnesium. The more population increases, the more necessary does this change become. It follows that the more population increases, the more will the inventive efforts and the capital formation of mankind have to be devoted to offsetting resource depletion and the less will they be available to bring about a rise in living levels.

VI.

I believe that the implications . . . are quite broad. Within a time which seems to me remarkably short, man is going to have to determine the sort of world he wants to live in. There is for example, nothing sacred about the figure of 5,000 square feet which we have used as the amount of land that might be necessary to support a person. It may be that much less will be needed if we are prepared to live in cells like hens in a hen bank and be fed protein gruel piped in from the roof. On the other hand, inasmuch as the ultimate maintenance of any level of living above the subsistence level is going to involve conscious limitation of population, it may well be that we will strive for something closer to the optimum level defined as that which maximizes the average level of living.

To the extent that this is accepted as an ultimate objective, it may mean that immediate action is required for underdeveloped countries such as India. For it seems to me that the analysis previously presented suggests the possibility that the Indian population may well already be as large—or perhaps larger—than the number which will maximize living levels even with the resources and technology likely to be available a century hence. Moreover, if we go beyond agriculture, I still see no reason to believe that economies of scale elsewhere will require a market of more than 350 million in view of our own achievements with a market less than half as large. Hence it may well be that further growth of Indian population will merely serve to reduce living levels more or less permanently below the optimum level. Even the *possibility* that this conclusion may be correct indicates the urgency of further work on the meaning and implications of optimum population.

A second reason for immediate concern is the real possibility that increases in population will prevent living levels from rising and so frustrate all our present efforts to develop underdeveloped countries, leaving such countries just as good targets for communism as they are today. On the other hand, if we bring about in the near future the restriction on population increase which must inevitably come within a century or so if living levels are to remain above bare subsistence, we have for the first time in history a real chance of raising the living level of the whole of the free world by an appreciable amount. . . .

This note, of course, has made no effort to explore the noneconomic problems that are involved, including religious opposition to providing technical assistance in regard to birth control. But it would certainly be an outstanding irony of history if Catholic opposition to birth control were to insure, by making development programs ineffective, ultimate communist domination of underdeveloped areas, and hence the suppression of Catholicism in such areas.

. . . . .

Since World War II total production in Latin America has grown by about 4.5 per cent a year. Per capita income has increased almost 2 per cent a year. Averages like these, of course, conceal great disparities. Nevertheless, such a record is impressive. Why, then, did Mr. Kennedy as one of his first acts after inauguration urge Congress to adopt new programs for aiding growth in Latin America? Some of the answer is found below. The selection is taken from The Economist, *a weekly published in London but concerned with economic, business, and political developments all over the world. Most of the basic material for special studies such as this (and for the valuable regular feature, "American Survey") is gathered by regular and special correspondents on the spot.*

76 · Latin America's Economic Problems and Outlook

THE ECONOMIST

Today Latin America is involved in a real revolution, the "revolution of rising expectations." . . . Its leaders are faced with problems that would frighten the rulers of older nations. They are problems that are the legacy of Latin America's history, a history that shows how unreal it is to judge the Latin Americans, their problems, or the solutions they attempt, by Anglo-Saxon standards.

The Growing Awareness of Inequality

Inquisitive vistors to any Latin American capital will, sooner or later, find themselves leaning across a desk while their host traces a worried finger along the curves on a couple of charts. The first of these charts shows the birth rate; the second, the gross national product. Latin America now has approaching 200 million people; in another 25 years or so, the expectation is that it will have twice as many. Mostly, the rise in production is creeping ahead of the rise in population but only just. Those republics that are running as fast as they believe to be within their power, only succeed in holding their positions. And those that are failing to spurt, drop further and further behind.

Latin America's economic frustrations might be less dismaying if the relative lightening of the political sky did not show them up so bleakly. So long as most of the people were in the dark about what they were missing, it mattered less, from the governments' point of view, that there was not enough money to go round. But the popular revulsion against the hegemony of small groups that has succeeded, indirectly,

---

THE ECONOMIST, "From Monroe to Castro," published in *The Economist* (London: April 22, 1961). Used by permission.

in sweeping the political dictators from the scene, has begun to range itself as a force against the economic oligarchy as well. Already it has become an anachronism to think of Latin American politics in terms of tin-pot dictators and palace revolutions. The next entrenched line to crack may be the deadening rigidity of the economic and social structure.

The pressure of a fast growing population is by itself less of a threat to the existing order than the improvements in education and communications that are happening at the same time. The mass movement from the country to the towns has had two immediate and significant consequences. The first is that evidence of the existence of a large unemployed section of the population has been thrust upon the governments' notice. The peasants may have come to town only because they had no work on hand, or not enough. But their rural unemployment could be hidden under the blanket of archaic agricultural systems, and was in any case less pressing because more remote; whereas once in the towns, and irrefutably workless, they begin to figure in the statistics, and even more in the minds of politicians. Their presence is a discomfort that cannot, like the agricultural problem, be tucked away into a back file for action later. The second consequence is the effect on the peasants themselves. As they come into closer contact with other ways of living, they are bound to be stirred by the crude social contrasts of city life. At the same time, through the radio, press and some politicians, they become aware that excessive social equilibrium is not necessarily part of the natural order.

For the most part, the new Latin American leaders who have followed on the heels of the dictators are sensible and enlightened politicians, fully aware of the dangers inherent in the gross inequality of wealth that tilts the continent's social and economic stability. But nowhere, except in Cuba, has the redistribution of income yet been seriously thought about as a primary means to avert this danger. Instead, the governments tend to pin their hopes to projects for increasing the total wealth of their countries, in the belief that, according to the simple arithmetic of the two charts, all the people will eventually have more.

This, however, is not an automatic development. The mathematical division of export earnings stops short long before it reaches the people most urgently in need of relief. The bulk of the profits are divided between the producing companies, often owned by foreign interests, and the governments, which need most of the money they can collect from taxation on exports to keep their civil services and their armies in being. What is left percolates through to industry, to commerce, and to the local labour employed by the export industries. But the vast disparity in the wages earned by workers in the main export industries and by the ordinary urban worker is in itself a disrupting social factor: a Chilean copper miner, for instance, earns the equivalent of $90 a week compared with an average industrial wage of $14 a week.

All the Latin American governments are now setting their sights on more diversified economies. But will industrial development, if allowed to run its own course, necessarily result in a more equitable division? Probably not, for two reasons. Trade union organisation in Latin America is sitll very weak, and as a rule is unable to make its voice effectively heard above the din of conflicting interests. The pressure groups that, between them, wield the most power include the armies, the church, the foreign companies, property owners and industrialists; only in Argentina, with its vestigial traces of *peronismo*, and to a lesser extent in Chile, do the labour organisations compete to any effect. In Brazil, the weakness of the trade unions is recognised as an important contribution to the speed and impulsiveness of the state's economic development.

The slow expansion, in some countries the actual contraction, of agricultural production is another reason why an increase in national income is unlikely to be distributed evenly over the population. The poorer a man, the bigger the part played by food in his personal budget: growth in the manufacturing industries may mean very little to him. But in most of the Latin American republics it is easier, more agreeable and politically safer to compose blueprints for assembling, or even producing, a domestic motor car than to come to grips with the obstinate problems of an old-fashioned and inefficient land tenure system. It is less hazardous to plan a new industrial city than to venture into the tropical belts where the agricultural frontiers lie. . . .

Possibly it is only Brazil, with its large market and its powerful momentum of development, that can afford to dismiss the dangers of disequilibrium. Brazilian planners, during Sr Kubitschek's presidency [1956 to 1961], tended to regard any deliberate attempt to narrow the gap between rich and poor as a luxurious diversion, an ill-timed distraction from the main road to development. They may still get away with it; the other republics may not.

What Directions Offer the Best Prospects for Growth?

. . . . .

In the early nineteen-fifties, when the Korean war was turning commodities to gold, the Latin American republics had money to spend, but not the plans for investing it. Today plans are plentiful but money is scarce. The wealth that slid into the republics during the good years slid out again just as fast, without much to show for its passing. In Brazil, Mexico, Colombia, and one or two other countries a fair quantity of it got caught on the way and was spent sensibly on capital equipment, but in general only a fraction of the export earnings that came to Latin America after the second world war, and during the Korean boom, was used in ways that would provide for the leaner years ahead.

The Latin American governments have reacted in two ways to the worsening in their terms of trade. First, they have exerted themselves to organise and to propagate trading agreements for their main export commodities; and, in particular, they have been trying to convert the United States to the principle of fixed prices. Secondly, they have plunged themselves into a great bustle of economic planning. Studies of investment goals, projections of the balance of payments, analyses of the past; . . . while nothing much may yet be on the ground, all this and a great deal more is in the air. With the encouragement, and in some cases, the direction, of the United Nations Economic Commission for Latin America (ECLA), the republics are attempting to impose order on the haphazard process of their economic growth. The targets they set are not, by and large, extravagant; in Chile and Colombia, for instance, the projected increase in production is only barely ahead of the estimated increase in population. But even to get as far as this, the plans have to assume that the republics are going to be able to lay their hands on substantially more money than they can get.

Most of the Latin American republics are already largely self-sufficient for their supply of durable consumer goods. There are exceptions, particularly on the

Caribbean littoral, where exports, foreign interests, the proximity of the United States and the smallness of the consumer markets have damped down the enthusiasm for domestic manufacturing. But in general, the difficulty they had in obtaining the goods they needed from abroad during the war combined with periodic shortages of foreign exchange, has encouraged the republics to substitute home-produced goods for their imports of, say, clothes, shoes or cigarettes, and to do their own food processing and brewing. A vast number of goods are manufactured under licence; they appear, and indeed are, precisely the same as the parent companies turn out in the United States, Europe or Japan, but their labels proclaim them homemade.

Until such time as a radical change in the social structure extracts the money from a few pockets and spreads it among a great many more, the growth of light industry will be kept within the tight limits of consumer markets that are always far less than the population figures suggest, and, in the smaller republics, are meagre in the extreme. Mostly, these limits have already been touched. At least half, and probably nearer two-thirds, of Latin America's population do not rank in the statistics as consumers at all. These are the people who, in the country, live on what they can grow; in the towns, on what they can pick up.

Since the consumer industries cannot now, or indeed in the foreseeable future, expand, the Latin Americans believe themselves to be presented with a choice between economic stagnation and the expansion of heavy industry. They are therefore, with varying degrees of enthusiasm, preparing for their venture into the second and far more expensive and committing stage of industrialisation. Thus, all the economic plans follow basically one pattern in which power, steel and communications are the dominant themes. Most of the major regional projects . . . turn on enormous schemes for hydroelectric power. . . . But whether dreams or facts, the direction in which most of the larger republics are making their separate plans is towards the expansion of their energy supplies (whether from water, oil or coal), the improvement of their road networks or railways, and the building of steel mills, petro-chemical plants and other heavy industries. All of which demand formidable capital expenditures now, and will demand formidably large markets later on. The Latin American free trade area may provide bigger markets than the republics on their own can look for; on the other hand, the fact that neighbouring countries are developing on parallel lines is bound to be awkwardly at odds with prospects for a common market.

The treaty setting up the free trade association was signed at Montevideo last year by the governments of Brazil, Argentina, Chile, Uruguay, Mexico, Peru and Paraguay. As it stands, the treaty which is supposed to come into full operation within twelve years is a weak instrument dotted generously with escape clauses. Clearly it will only work as well as its members want it to, and several of them, notably Brazil, have little interest in its working at all. But the logic in favour of trade between the republics (at present confined to the exchange of primary products) increasing and becoming more liberal is so glaringly evident for countries that have miniscule markets and ambitious plans, that economic necessity may in the end overcome the formidable obstacles.

To finance their plans, the governments are turning first to private investment, and then, where this is not forthcoming, to international loans and credit. . . . But the reliance on foreign capital illustrates one of the basic shortcomings of nearly all the plans: the fact that they do not probe deeply into Latin America's failure to raise more of its own money for development. True, several of the schemes, notably in Colombia, provide for a switch in government spending from services to investment, but nowhere is there a radical attempt to divert the money that flows into salaries, defence and food imports.

So the problem twists back, as do most economic and social problems in Latin America, to the weary tangle of under-employed land and a weak and discriminating tax system. . . .

The Role of Government

Exhortations from Washington lustily call upon the Latin American leaders to root up their social disorders. But only a few years ago, the same men, or their predecessors, were being admonished from the same quarter to lay no hand on the ownership of land, and to put their trust in the seminal virtues of private enterprise. The requests for government-to-government aid that the Latin Americans regularly advanced at the inter-American economic conferences were as regularly brushed aside with the brisk rejoinder that an economic project worth its salt should be able to find a private backer. But the perplexity . . . is that the projects that are eminently desirable from a social and political point of view are not always those that are likely to be profitable to a private investor.

Washington's torpidity towards its southern neighbours has been whipped into life by the anxieties that *fidelismo* [attraction of Fidel Castro] has aroused. But it is still not at all clear what encroachments upon private enterprise the United States government is prepared to accept with equanimity, and even less whether North American and European business men in Latin America are prepared to accept government officials as their active partners. Moreover, it would be utterly misleading to suggest that the Latin Americans themselves are automatically responsive to the idea that the state should play a more important part in planning and controlling their economies. True, in many of the republics there is a stubborn and, in some cases, a passionate belief that it is safer, more profitable and even more patriotic for the state to control, or at least to check, the exploitation of mineral resources, but this feeling is shot through with a profound scepticism about the state's ability to act as entrepreneur. Classical examples of official incapacity, red tape or corruption abound. In every republic there are countless tales to illustrate the incompetence of a civil service in which all the major appointments, and many of the minor ones, are political; this cynicism and lack of confidence has been summed up in the Brazilian proverb: "Our country grows by night, when the politicians sleep."

But private enterprise, too, has left its wreckage. As Latin American politicians and economists pick their way through the shambles of misdirected and misused capital investment, they are more inclined to listen to the arguments that the United Nations Economic Commission for Latin America, in particular, is trying to get across: that economic analysis and planning by the state are required if priorities are to be established for the investment of domestic resources and international contributions. The economic development of the republics is bound to be spasmodic, and may turn out sterile, unless their growth is bedded in sound appreciation of the order in which things are to be done. ECLA itself, sensitive to the charge that it follows marxist lines in opposition to private enterprise, is inclined to present its advocacy for state control over investment as a defence against waste and unpreparedness; the point that the commission, and its executive director, Dr. Raúl Prebisch, continually drum home is that state planning must come first if private enterprise is to fulfill its own dynamic task. But, beyond this argument, there is a stronger reason why some of the Latin American governments are feeling compelled to take so decided a hand in their country's economic development. Many of the things that urgently need to be done now would not, in the ordinary way, attract private finance.

The line that divides the public and private investment provided for in the various plans, or coming into the republics without benefit of a master plan, is only patchily consistent. So far as there is any guiding principle at all it is that the governments should be responsible for laying the foundation of power supply, roads, railways, irrigation and education, and that private initiative should take over from there. But this principle is criss-crossed by innumerable exceptions having their birth in the special circumstances of the country, in national pride or prejudice, or merely in historical accident and tradition.

A comparison of the present policies of the Chilean and Argentinian governments illustrates some of the paradoxical elements at work. Chile has a right-wing government led by a business man. . . . Recovering from one of the severest bouts of inflation that any of the republics has ever known, Chile has followed most of the injunctions of the International Monetary Fund. But now in its preparations for launching the country towards a further stage of industrialisation, Chile's conservative government is relying almost exclusively on state enterprise. The government is getting, or hoping to get, money from the World Bank for its development of hydro-electric power and for the modernisation of its coal industry, a loan from the Export-Import Bank for its railways, and substantial long-term credit from the west German government. The only considerable private investments in the air are the plans for expansion being made by the copper companies.

The explanation is that Chile, with its seven million people, many of them too poor to rank as consumers, is not an appealing proposition to the private investor; in order to participate in this second stage of economic development, he would have to risk large capital sums for, possibly, very little return. The situation would be vastly changed if the Latin American common market knocked down the trade barriers between Chile and its neighbours. But this is a tenuous hope for the future; as things stand, the government must invest because it can find nobody else who will. . . .

In Argentina the situation is reversed. The country is run by a radical government under a president, Dr. Frondizi, whose views before his election were very far to the left. But private investment is flowing faster into Argentina than into any of the other republics, except Brazil, and the government possibly boasts of the fact that it is spending the minimum possible on economic development. The Argentinian government's control over the country's oil, hydro-electric resources and infant steel industry is established by law and strengthened by national pride. But Dr. Frondizi has been backpedalling vigorously since his election. . . .

Politically he undertook his most dangerous exercise in extrication when he put an end to the state monopoly for oil production by fixing a series of contracts with foreign companies. From a political, rather than from an economic, point of view, this was an astute compromise. The country urgently needed to cut down its oil imports, and while the state oil company, YPF, had done a great deal of the groundwork for an increase in domestic production, it had run out of money before it could complete the job. The contractual arrangements could be presented at home as less of a surrender than an outright concession would have been. . . . His next step has been to persuade congress to modify the laws that govern the state's share in power and steel production, and so open the way to private investment. Only the state railway system baffles the president's ingenuity; there is presumably no way of persuading the British to take back this expensive white elephant.

. . . private foreign capital is coming in fast, but the utility of some of its investments at this moment from a national point of view can be questioned. A large slice of the inflow of private foreign money has been going into automobile plants; but automobiles built in Argentina still require such a high proportion of imported parts that the starting up of these plants involves the country in a heavy new foreign exchange burden. . . .

President Frondizi's staunch antisocialism has gone a long way towards resurrecting Argentina's reputation in the United States. During General Perón's ascendancy, Argentina was often the odd man out at neighbourly inter-American meetings; now, Argentina is one of the few Latin American countries in which United States private investment actually showed an increase last year. Whatever line Washington may take in advising the republics for their own good, North American business men still look first for a government that avowedly supports a free economy. Traditions die hard, and the tradition that the safe countries to put one's money in are those that make a show of welcoming private foreign investment is no exception. . . .

The alarm with which foreign investors recoil from any hint of government intervention is illustrated by the steep decline last year in North American investment in Mexico and Venezuela. In both republics, the governments in their different, and hesitant, ways are taking steps to safeguard their countries' natural resources, to appease left-wing pressure groups and, finally, to promote certain social reforms, which, to anybody not on the qui-vive against creeping socialism, appear modest indeed.

[In 1960] . . . the Mexican government, for a number of practical reasons, and on generous terms, took over the electric light industry. It also took power to take over the foreign-owned mines, should it want to, at some unspecified future date. Less intelligibly, it has nationalised film renting. These and similar measures, many of them only precautionary, have created a great outcry among foreign companies, and particularly among North American business men, that they are being "squeezed" out of Mexico.

The Venezuelan government, politically much less secure than Mexico's semi-autocracy, has had to weave a path between right-wing and left-wing extremists. [In Venezuela] President Betancourt's concessions to the left have been moderate; nevertheless, they have been badly received. Much less welcome are the measures now being taken by . . . the minister of petroleum and mines. The minister was bound to come into conflict with the oil companies by his stance over profits and prices; what is sadder is the complete lack of sympathy for his efforts to conserve Venezuela's oil resources by persuading the international companies to make fuller use of the concessions they already hold rather than spread their nets wider afield. . . .

. . . the foreign companies who interpret government action as an unwarrantable incursion into their private preserves are spitting into the Latin American wind. Brazilians, more prone to exaggeration than most, happily make the point that Brazil, with its markets, its resources and its freedom from a single oligarchy, may be the one Latin American country still able to develop successfully under a capitalist system. The argument need only be carried as far as this if the private investors whom Latin America so urgently needs persist in seeing a marxist, or Cuban, bogy behind every effort that the governments make to direct or stimulate their economic growth. Many people, and many interests, share responsibility for the direction that Latin America decides to take.

Inflation

Self-denigration, once a characteristic Latin American approach, has now been largely superseded by the more normal habit of finding fault with others. But Latin Americans are still apt to exaggerate their past failures and misfortunes: their claim, for instance, that they have suffered under the world's cruellest dictators falls oddly on European ears. However, in describing the inflation that plagues, or has plagued, their economies, superlatives are in order. During the past ten years . . . Argentina, Brazil, Chile, Bolivia, Uruguay and Paraguay—have been weakened by uncontrolled inflation. To take the two extreme cases, the Chilean cost-of-living index has risen tenfold since 1953; in Bolivia, over the same period, the index rose three times as fast.

So high a fever is bound to be debilitating. It plants the germs of a number of disorders, some of which live on when the inflation itself has subsided. The gross distortion in the price pattern has hampered economic development (except in Brazil), and it has plunged the invalids into debt. It has also widened the gap between social classes, since wages in Latin America are seldom able to mountaineer as high as prices. Only in Argentina, under General Perón, were wage increases steep enough and prompt enough to compensate for the rise in costs; usually, there is a long lag in time before wages begin to catch up, and since any such adjustment immediately sets off a fresh price reaction, they are soon left far behind again.

Thus, in several of the republics, spiralling prices have had the effect of an additional and penalising tax on the urban masses. The better-off, with practice, can usually ride an inflation, helped by rates of interest that take into account the fact that the value of money is liable to be halved; speculators, if they are sharp enough, may thrive on the crazy price patterns. But if there is one lesson inflation has taught the rich, it is that saving is foolish. One of the legends told about Sao Paulo is that it contains more men with a million dollars in their pockets than any other city in the world. The description is meant to be taken literally. A wealthy Brazilian, insisting on a quick return for his unreliable money, will vastly prefer a cash property deal to a long-term investment. Brazil is one of the few countries where, at least until the change of government at the beginning of the year [1961], inflation has been allowed to range unchecked. But even in those republics that now manage to keep their currency stable, the hangover from the inflationary days remains. The rich have not got the habit of saving, and nothing their governments have been able to do has persuaded them that it is now safe, wise, or patriotic to invest in their country's development.

Unable to lay their hands on much domestic money, and with their export earnings painfully down, the Latin American governments turned their attention, urgently, to the pursuit of foreign capital and credit. Substantial investment, both private and public, is the basic equipment for their safaris towards economic growth and industrialisation. But here came the rub. Foreign banks or international lending agencies are disinclined to hand over money to countries in the throes of excessive inflation. Before they could borrow or attract capital from the industrialised countries, and in particular from the United States, several Latin governments found that it was up to them to put their own economies in order first. Thus the ideal of economic growth, which had dominated the early postwar years, gave way, through necessity and external pressure, to the dimmer aspirations of price stability and balanced payments.

Cheered on from outside, several of the republics adopted stabilisation policies, based on credit restriction, limited wage increases, simplifying the exchange rates, the removal of some import controls and, above all, efforts to balance their budgets. Brazil alone pursued its unrepentant way, refusing to give priority to anything except its development programme, which it managed to pay for with private foreign capital—and by printing money when need be. Now President Quadros is having to consider a number of concessions in order to find a way of meeting the vast foreign debts that Sr Kubitschek's government accumulated. Brazil has formidable problems, but it has one overwhelming advantage; because of Sr Kubitschek's obstinacy and single-mindedness, its economic momentum has not yet been halted.

The stabilisation policies of the other republics have been reasonably successful. Although in most cases the budgets are still imperfectly balanced, the currencies have been steadied and the price distortions corrected. In Argentina, Chile and Peru, the rise in the cost of living last year was kept at a respectably low rate; the governments have passed their test with colours flying fairly high and they have qualified for their loans. The price they have had to pay is a continued postponement of their economic growth. By reducing consumption and discouraging investment, stabilisation inevitably lowers the level of economic activity.

This is a situation that the governments have been forced to accept and which they rationalise by saying, in effect, that first things had to come first. Now that their bank balances are reasonably in order, and the way clear for foreign loans, they can move on to the next stage which was, after all, the ultimate object of the disinflationary exercise. The question of timing has become important. The economic plans are waiting on the desks, but, in general, there is a feeling of timelessness about their execution. The interval of economic stagnation has accentuated the social tensions that, in many cases, existed already. . . .

A second, and more serious, question is how to find ways and means of starting the momentum of development rolling again without the same inflationary troubles recurring. The distortion of prices was arrested by the measures that arrested economic growth; if the one is resumed, why not the other, too? In discussing this problem, Latin Americans are apt to criticise the part played by the International Monetary Fund in its efforts to engineer the stabilisation programmes. The fund is criticised on two levels. The first, but in the long run less important, cause for resentment seems to result from a failure in communication. The missions that were dispatched by the fund to preach economic restraint into ears that were very probably unreceptive did not have enviable tasks; on the other hand, complaints of tactlessness and bossiness are drummed in from all sides. . . . There is little sense of shared purpose between the fund and the governments it is helping; instead, Latin American economists see the strict orthodoxy of the fund's tenets as a challenge to them to find ways of outwitting the lawgiver.

The second reason for criticising the fund, and the policies it sponsors, comes from the belief, held by many economists, that the stabilisation programmes should have included positive measures for relieving some of the most urgent shortages. As it is, the bottlenecks of agriculture, energy and transport are mostly as jammed as ever; the fact that the obstacles to economic growth have not been budged gives substance to the fear that when the dynamo of economic development is recharged, it will once again explode into inflation. Again, it is feared that if restrictive monetary policies are adopted without social safeguards, the countries run the risk of serious social eruption.

The argument, put forward with vigour by the United Nations Economic Commission for Latin America, is that it is self-defeating for an underdeveloped country to try to cure its inflation by monetary and financial measures alone. The commission does not quarrel with the principle that the inflation had become excessive and had urgently to be checked. What it disputes is that the financial tourniquet should, necessarily, have brought economic activity to a stop. The critical question is not whether a republic can balance its budget this year or next, but whether it can find a balance between economic growth and financial stability that will carry it through the years.

New Directions and U.S. Policy

Latin America is one big part of the world where the poor still grow poorer. As the numbers multiply and the cost of living jerkily soars, more people have less to share. This is not necessarily related to economic growth; to the people at the bottom it makes very little difference whether their country's economy is running, jumping or standing still. Even in those republics where economic growth has pushed ahead of the birth rate, the additional wealth does not seem to get shaken up. In Mexico, for instance, after ten years of economic expansion, only a tenth of the population were substantially better off; 70 per cent remained much as they had been, and the fifth at the bottom were worse off than ever. President Kennedy summed up the situation when he presented to the United States Congress the principles of his "alliance for progress" to assist the Latin republics in their social development:

> Economic growth without social progress lets the great majority of the people remain in poverty while a privileged few reap the benefits of rising abundance.

. . . President Kennedy stressed the fact that the Latin republics were expected to meet the United States halfway. He emphasised that the United States would be prepared to lend or give money only to countries whose ruling classes had shown themselves ready to give up some of their wealth and privileges. The countries that would be helped first would not necessarily be those whose need was greatest, but those where the governments had demonstrated their readiness to "make the institutional improvements which promise lasting social progress."

Mr. Kennedy has struck to the heart of Latin America's troubles. But two questions are still to be answered. Is the United States administration prepared to accept the consequences of its advice if the consequences extend to, say, expropriating certain American properties? . . . Second, have the Latin American governments any intention of responding seriously? Or do they hope to bluff their way through?

Since the inter-American economic meeting at Bogotá in [1960] when Washington began to prepare the ground for its new assistance programme, most of the Latin American governments seem to have been working on the assumption that so long as they are able to show plans for houses, schools, hospitals and the like, they qualify for economic aid. Since several of the governments are already including a large slice of the "Bogotá money" in their estimates of available capital, the promised $500 million has been spent many times in advance. Land reform programmes are much in evidence; . . . some are more serious than others. No government appears yet to have digested the fact that if the United States Administration sticks to what Mr Dillion hinted at Bogotá, and to what Mr Kennedy said in plain terms in Washington, they will have to drive the knife deep into their tax systems.

But even over the much less painful business of providing more houses and more schools, no Latin American government is able to give its plans for social improvement the same urgency as its plans for, say power, steel, roads or heavy industry. Brazil is an extreme example of this attitude. The fashion during Sr Kubitschek's presidency was to deplore the wrong-minded extravagance of the social reforms undertaken during the nineteen-thirties and nineteen-forties when President Vargas had his first long session at the top. The argument put forward by the young Brazilian planners of today is that if they press forward regardless with their schemes for economic development and industrialisation, the Brazilian income per head will be doubled in thirteen years. But . . . there is no convincing reason for believing that the money would be any less unevenly distributed than it is today.

Argentina, for its part, is going to considerable lengths to give the appearance of public economy on all fronts. . . . Except for its house building programme, the government has expressed itself determined not to spend any additional money on health or on education. This economy might be more impressive if it were not that so much else seems extravagant—such as supporting a host of 30,000 officers (some active, some retired on full pay) which includes as many generals as there are in the United States.

Brazil and Argentina, for very different reasons, have shown reluctance to spend money on social reform. Most of the other republics have compromised by producing modest, and often highly theoretical, programmes for public spending on education, health and housing. More often than not, the acknowledged target of these programmes is to prevent things from getting worse; not to narrow the gap between numbers and services, but only to stop it widening. Some governments are more ambitious —at least in their plans. Colombia's four-year plan for public investment allows for an increase in the proportion allotted to "social and cultural services" from 13 per cent of total investment in 1960 to 22 per cent in 1964. If this increase is continued, the Colombians estimate that they will have elementary schools for all by 1970.

. . . the Latin governments have got tremendous distances to cover before the education that they are able to provide is anywhere near adequate. At present at least half the population cannot read or write. The elementary schools are over-crowded, they operate on a shift basis, and, even so, parents often wait all night in the streets in order to place their children. The position over secondary education is worse. To generalise, there are very few secondary or technical schools, and those that exist are not good. The Latin American republics, like other countries that are short on development and long in numbers, have to face the difficult choice of deciding whether to try to teach as many as possible to read and write, or whether to push a smaller group rather further. In both cases, the starting point for improvement is low.

The republics are prepared, and in most cases anxious, for this kind of improvement. What about the changes that hurt? ... President Kennedy listed "archaic tax and land tenure structures" among the obstacles to social progress. The question is whether the Latin politicians are in any mood to bring these structures up to date.

There are two basic faults with the taxation system in most of the republics: taxes are not progressive, and they are easy to evade. In Mexico, for instance, a man may be taxed on his salary and on his private income, but the two sources of income are not added together. Tax evasion is flagrant everywhere. Salaried workers cannot avoid paying income tax, and public companies are stung for company tax. But farmers, self-employed people and professional workers more often than not get by with the minimum of discomfort. Most of them are taxed on a presumed minimum income, but the system is patchy, the underpaid tax officials are susceptible to bribes, and often at least half the people who should by rights be paying taxes get away scot free.

Even in times of national emergency the Latin American parliaments have been remarkably reluctant to tighten the tax system. ...

It is unfair, but not grossly so, to suppose that landowners, businessmen and politicians are all one and the same in Latin America. In some countries, and Peru is a good example, the oligarchy is a closely knit unit; in others, such as Brazil, there is no single dominating group. But, in general, it is true to say about Latin American legislators, though not necessarily the [cabinet] ministers, that they share the interests of the better-off communities, and that those are the interests they do their best to promote. Consequently, they are prepared to obstruct legislation that appears to discriminate against the well-to-do. ...

Bureaucracy Luxuriant

One of the things often said about Latin Americans is that they have inherited an Iberian scale of ethical values which places so much emphasis on personal *dignidad* that it leaves social responsibility dangling weightless in the air. Certainly the average Latin American, with his belief in both his personal honour and the sanctity of his family, has less sense of responsibility towards the community than can be found in most economically advanced countries and in some very primitive ones. ...

The liberalism of the industrial labour codes and the ambition of the social security schemes [however] are well beyond anything being attempted in other parts of the world that are roughly at the same economic level. They are certainly far ahead of anything that Europe burdened itself with during the early years of industrialisation. ... Generally speaking, it is impossible to sack an industrial or white collar worker without giving him the kind of compensation that would be considered generous anywhere; several of the republics have extended the compensation laws to civil servants and to domestic servants. The one big class of workers whom such laws invariably pass by are the peasants. ... The principle if not the practice of free education and a free health service is taken for granted. Several of the republics have schemes for insuring against industrial accidents; others are experimenting with ambitious pension schemes. In Argentina, for instance, it is theoretically possible for railway employees to retire at 50 and to go on getting three-quarters of their . . . [prior wages]. Unemployment pay is beyond the capacity of the republics; any attempt at it would be bound to collapse under the surge of under-employed labour from the country. For a short time President Betancourt of Venezuela was forced to give what amounted to dole to the vast corps of labourers who were thrown out of work when his government slammed down on its predecessor's construction programme. But more often unemployment in the towns is disguised by over-staffing or by the thousands of made-up jobs—the men selling lottery tickets or toys at every traffic light, the families sorting the less rotten tomatoes from the more rotten —that are the sad entrails of an underdeveloped economy.

The ambition of the social security schemes is evidence of radical thinking; the more pity, therefore, that this very ambition is also their undoing. At their worst the institutions that are supposed to hand out the sickness or pension benefits have swollen so monstrously that they can support themselves and that is all; the workers' or employers' contributions go to pay the salaries of the institution's staff and nothing, or nothing much, is left over for the payment of benefits. People die before they get their pensions; cure themselves, or die before medical help reaches them —and the institutions barrenly prosper.

In Brazil, a country where two-thirds of the population lives at subsistence level and where one child in five dies before it is a year old, an ambitious scheme for social benefits is run by a number of semi-official organisations. The money is supposed to be contributed by the government, the employers and the employees, and, in theory at least, the organisations have a total budget that is larger than the national budget. But only those employees who have their pay packets docked are paid up; many employers are badly in arrears, and the government even more so. The organisations have developed into unwieldy bureaucratic giants unable to carry out their tasks effectively or quickly.

Chile has no less than 48 separate social security funds covering different categories of industrial and white collar workers. In some cases the contributions from employer and employee combined add up to as much as half the worker's wage. But the efficiency of the organisation varies enormously and there has been no attempt at co-ordination. The Socialist party . . . calculates that, on the whole, it would be less wasteful if the system were abolished, and if those who needed medical care received it free without having to pay contributions—and without having to support the bureaucracy of social insurance.

. . . . .

The Brazilian civil service is swollen out of all proportion to the work that gets done. . . . The fault lies partly in a system under which a departing government rewards its friends with civil service sinecures from which they cannot be dislodged, partly in the fact, true in several of the republics, that since a single government job does not provide a living wage, many people try to do two or even three. Sr Quadros, the new president, has already cut government spending by 30 per cent by insisting that all civil servants stay at the one job from morning till evening. Argentina, with a population of 20 million, has 1.3 million civil servants, about a fifth of whom work on the preposterously uneconomic state railways. Venezuela, on the other hand, is planning to prune its bureaucracy. . . .

On a continent where social improvement is so evident a need, it seems illogical to conclude that in some directions too much is being attempted. But this conclusion seems unavoidable: if the paper scope of some of the social security schemes were less ambitious, more might be achieved.

Land Reform

. . . . .

. . . it is not altogether unfair to make the generalisation that the agricultural worker in Latin America, whether he is hired labourer, sharecropper, tenant farmer or smallholder, is underprivileged, underpaid and usually underfed.

. . . It has been estimated that as little as five per cent of the continent's eight million square miles is suitable for arable cultivation. Even so, this five per cent allows one and a half acres a head, which, according to a similar calculation, is three times as much cultivable land a head as is available in Asia.

. . . three adverse factors combine to create a situation that is socially threatening and economically crippling. The bulk of the most fertile land has been absorbed into huge diffuse estates where much of it is often underemployed. Many of the independent farms are too small and too unproductive to yield more than a bare livelihood for their owners; there is nothing left over to sell to anybody else. And, thirdly, most of the areas that are still uncultivated, but potentially rich, are remote from the centres of population. Projects for opening them up are bound to involve vast capital expenditure and all the social hazards attached to transplanting groups of people.

During the last half century a few preliminary steps have been taken towards some kind of land reform. The fact that (except in Mexico, Bolivia and Cuba) these steps have led virtually nowhere is due to lack of money, lack of administrative ability and, probably most important, lack of interest. . . . In most of the Latin American countries there is no reserve of industrial wealth to ease the load of new commitments. . . .

Now under the influence of the hot winds blowing from Cuba—and salutary words from Washington—several of the republics are again picking a stumbling way in the direction of land reform. In Venezuela a land reform law passed in March, 1960, is already showing good results, particularly in the opening up of new land and the growing of new crops. In Peru and Colombia land reform laws will be coming before the national congresses before the end of the year. Probably both will be passed; but if the obstructionist elements have their way, they will be so whittled down that their usefulness may be marginal. . . . In Brazil a pressure group needles away at the government on behalf of the grindingly poor farm workers in the north-eastern states. In a rush of good intentions, the governments of Latin America are showing their awareness that agricultural problems cannot for ever be pushed into the background; what in most cases is still lacking is a national awareness that the problems cannot be solved without sacrifice.

There is no easy and no cheap answer to any of the land problems. The over-large and under-used estates can be cut down to economic size in two ways: either by expropriation by the state, or by increasing the land tax so that it becomes unprofitable to leave good land idle. Several of the republics already have laws that give their governments the power, under certain circumstances, to expropriate land. But the technical and administrative difficulties in deciding whether these circumstances apply to a particular case are endless, and leave ample loopholes for any astute landowner to slip through. A Colombian law, passed in 1936, allows for the expropriation of unproductive land, but nobody was ever able to determine what "unproductive" meant. In 1957, another law was passed that divided all agricultural land into four categories, but nobody can decide which category is which.

Then there is the question how the dispossessed owners are to be compensated. If the law lays down that the owners are to be paid at least partly in cash for their land, the project is at once limited by the government's shortage of ready money. Possibly only a revolutionary government, bold in its convictions and strong in popular support, will have the resolution to take land and give no more in return than bonds and an IOU.

An increase in the land tax might seem a more painless, and less politically hazardous, way of persuading the estate owners to rid themselves of their surplus land. But there are two difficulties. The landowners would, naturally enough, sell their worst land first. Then, the parliamentarians who jib at voting for a workable method of expropriation are no less chary when it comes to taxes. . . .

The first problem is to get hold of the land for redistribution: the second is to help the new owners to farm it. Since most of the republics have not yet managed the first operation, the question of after-care is more talked about than acted upon. Few of the republics have tried experimenting with schemes for their existing smallholders, whose need for generous credit and for co-operative effort is sometimes as pressing as that of any new farmer. Clearly, it is foolishly short-sighted to give a peasant farmer a piece of virgin land and tell him to get on with it as best he can without money, equipment or knowledge. On the other hand, it is hard to avoid the suspicion that the complications of the second stage of land reform are sometimes used as a pretext for maintaining the *status quo*.

Bolivia, Mexico and Venezuela provide examples of three different ways of doing, very roughly, the same thing. The Bolivian revolutionary government in 1952 turned the peasants into landowners. But beyond this it could not go; the government had neither the money nor the men to help the new owners farm their land. The result nine years later is probably a slight decrease in agricultural production. . . . The Bolivian farmer is still desperately poor; on the other hand he is a better-off and more contented man than his pre-revolutionary peasant self.

Mexican land reform is based on the agricultural code in the 1917 constitution. But for many years the redistribution of land went slowly and clumsily; it was only when President Cárdenas took office in 1934 that land began being handed out right and left. The president's aim was to return to the old Indian system of land tenure, and this formed the basis of the *ejido* system, under which each village was made responsible for the cultivation of its land, although farming was not necessarily on a communal basis. But whether *ejido* or small property, most of the individual holdings were too small to be profitable, the new farmers ran into difficulties, and . . . from 1946 to 1952 there was a tendency for the former landowners to reassert, by various discreet means, their control over large acreages. Only in the last decade has the Mexican government begun turning its attention to ways of helping the small farmer; now, with much talk of irrigation, technical assistance, roads, marketing and schools, there is the grand aim of converting a rural community, living mainly at subsistence level, into a middle class of producers and consumers.

Venezuela, richer and much less impetuous than Bolivia or Mexico under their revolutionary governments, is taking time and money to help its landless population. Venezuela's land reform project is run jointly by the institute of land reform, which allocates the new land, the ministry of agriculture, which helps the new farmer with technical advice, and the agricultural bank, which supplies the credit. The first year of the scheme was in many ways experimental; nevertheless during this year the agricultural bank gave credit to 90,000 families owning close on a million acres. The agricultural bank provides the farmer with seeds on credit, and buys his crop when it is ripe; since the bank also controls the import of competitive foodstuffs, it is able to find markets for domestic products. It thus gets round the great obstacle to agricultural development in Venezuela—the fact that in the past it has been cheaper, and the foreign exchange has been available, to fly a lettuce from Holland rather than grow it at home. Even if some lettuces still come the same way, no maize, rice or cotton has been imported since the scheme began showing results.

Venezuela has a small population and a fair amount of cultivable but unused land in relatively accessible areas. It has therefore, with some exceptions, been able to avoid breaking into the large estates, and has not been faced with too impossible a bill for opening up new lands. In other Latin American countries, and particularly in the Andean republics, the colonisation of virgin land is a tremendous undertaking. Yet it is probably the only long-term answer to land-hunger. . . . But the overwhelming problem [today] in the Andean republics, Peru, Bolivia and Ecuador, is that too many people, the bulk of them Indian, are trying to support themselves on land that, however treated, will always be meagre and unyielding.

[A discussion of colonization plans and problems follows. *Ed.*]

Problems Arising from Castro's Changes in Cuba

. . . .

[One problem is U. S. willingness to support land reform which involves continuing governmental participation in operation.]

The second problem for the United States is to grasp that the raising of capital for rapid economic growth is a stern—even harsh—business in backward countries. Unless Mr Kennedy persuades the purse-holders in Congress to be more lavish with foreign aid than anyone expects, the Latin Americans will look to expedients far removed from the quiet accumulation of private capital preferred by the United States. State investment, the manipulation of price levels, the expropriation of private industry's handsome profits—these are the directions in which they will be tempted to turn. In short, they will experiment with marxism if the processes of capitalism strike them as too sluggish. For North American business men the result will be, at the least, the loss of some of their special advantages in Latin America and, at the worst, the seizure of their property. The . . . [problem] is not whether [the United States] can stop this happening altogether, but whether . . . [it can be held] within acceptable limits. It might help if . . . [President Kennedy] invited his southern neighbours to discuss the ground rules for government intervention in the economy.

The third unanswered question is how far the United States will agree to let the Latin Americans expand their trade with the communist countries. . . . It is clearly a mistake for a nation to let its economy become so dependent on any one trading partner that the latter is in a position to break it. (This is precisely what most Latin Americans complain about in their economic relations with the United States.) But it is equally a mistake to define one set of possible trading partners as "alien" and therefore beyond the commercial pale. The sensible compromise is to let business relations be governed by economic considerations rather than by political ones—to let trade flow where the price and the service are best rather than along channels marked out by regional or ideological loyalties. In the case of most Latin American countries this would almost certainly lead to more trade with the communist world than there is at the moment. . . .

. . . the Latin Americans. . . . are tempted to imitate many of the measures of the Cuban revolution. They suspect that some of its less desirable characteristics have resulted partly from the failure of the United States to deal with it sympathetically enough at the beginning. . . . They cannot discover in what respects the United States will acquiesce in their using Cuba as a model, and in what respects it will not. . . .

. . . . .

The elected leaders, who now run all the major republics . . . are, for the most part, serious and honourable men, not obsessed with the ends of personal acquisition and perpetuated authority that dominated many former autocrats. Their thoughts are on social and industrial development, on bringing their economies up to date with the rest of the western world, on the projection of their country's personality, not their own. Their failure is that in the pursuit of these aims they seldom penetrate the thick skin of tradition and privilege that protects the Latin American republics from self-generated change. Until these politicians, whose good intentions are unquestioned, can bring themselves to contemplate bulldozing a way through the economic and social structure of their countries, they give the impression, at least to an outsider, of coasting their way towards less peaceful revolution.

. . . impatience with the timelessness of the ticking over of evolutionary processes in so many of the republics drives . . . [many Latin Americans] to look for a revolutionary answer. Grossly simplified, their argument is that unless the social system is stood on its head, nothing serious will happen. The Establishment . . . (the entrenched groups of landowners, industrialists and some politicians) sits heavily in the path of any project aimed at fundamentals; if the governments dare not, or will not, shift this deadweight of privilege, its violent dislodgement becomes the more probable.

Fidelismo is an image with many faces. At its simplest, it means to millions of Latin Americans that in a remote, but still a sister, country, a man as glamorous as any film star has given land to the poor, rooked the rich, and put the *gringos* in their place. This, although it has almost no relevance to the grind of their own lives, is a concept that pleases them. . . .

The left-wing intellectuals, professional men and politicians from other parts of Latin America who have actually visited Cuba, or have access to reliable information, single out three achievements of the revolution for praise. First comes the system of land redistribution, managing to combine a certain amount of individual small-holding with exacting and conscientious state supervision; second, the industrialisation effort which, if the Cuban production figures are to be believed, is producing encouraging first results; finally, the nationalisation of all large concerns (most of them owned in the United States). . . .

. . . . .

The immediate circumstances that made the Cuban revolution possible, and relatively quick, were the compactness of the country, a weak and grotesquely corrupt army, a magnetic revolutionary leader and a people sickened by an unusually harsh dictatorship. Beyond this is the fact that Cuba more than any of the other republics was dependent on a single crop, mostly produced by foreign absentee landlords. Nowhere in Latin America does this combination of circumstances now apply. All the signs are that revolution, if it comes, will be a painful, obstinate struggle, leaving deep scars. . . .

. . . . .

The resentment felt by Latin Americans against what they regard as the bossiness, parsimony and insensitivity of the United States has been given a very good airing in the last two or three years. So also has the built-in conviction of most of the republics that it is the responsibility, if not the privilege, of the United States to pay for the lion's share of their development programmes. What surprises a visitor a little is the condescension, even patronage, in the attitude of many Latin Americans towards their northern neighbour. Washington's obsession with the dangers of international communism is treated by many (not by all) Latin Americans as a harmless if tiresome foible to which they must courteously defer, while going their own way so far as possible. . . .

. . . . .

As the situation is now, any attempt by the Soviet Union, or less probably by China, seriously to penetrate the Latin American mainland would be blunted by Latin American disinterest, caution and determination to get North American money. Revolution, erupting from indigenous cancers, would still, probably, be suppressed before it spread. But these assurances are too faint and too conditional for much comfort. As the clock ticks on, it seems to be time for the Latin American governments to stop coasting on the surface. No less, it is surely high time for the West to come to terms with the character and the aspirations of a continent. . . .

This selection tells a small part of a big and hopeful story. The big story concerns the activities in lesser developed economies of U.S., British, Canadian, and other business firms. The case summarized here is that of one large U.S. corporation in one Latin American country. The study is the ninth in a series, "United States Business Performance Abroad," being prepared by the National Planning Association. The NPA is an "independent, nonpolitical, nonprofit organization. . . . where leaders of agriculture, business, labor, and the professions join in programs to maintain and strengthen private initiative and enterprise." The other studies deal with widely varying types of businesses and economies. They constitute a large and growing volume of literature on the problems and accomplishments of direct business activity in stimulating growth in poorer lands. The corporations studied have cooperated with the NPA but have not financed the inquiries. The findings and conclusions are those of trained and independent investigators working under the direction of a small advisory committee consisting primarily of professors from such universities as the University of California, Columbia, Harvard, and Massachusetts Institute of Technology.

77 · United States Business Performance Abroad: A Case Study

THEODORE GEIGER
and LIESEL GOODE

[The authors open with a description of Brazil's natural resources, its people, and its government. Then follows a discussion of the general development of manufacturing. Ed.]

GE's Activities in Brazil

The industrial innovator in an agrarian, raw-material exporting economy has a particularly difficult set of problems to solve. What product should he start to make and when is the most proptitious time? What must he do to develop the potential market? Will he automatically attract the necessary skilled and unskilled workers, or will he have to recruit them? Must he conduct extensive labor training programs? Will he be able to buy locally the raw materials and components he needs, or must they be imported? Can he meet the competition of imported products? These and many other problems must be overcome by the pioneering firm if it is to become a successful operation.

THEODORE GEIGER and Liesel Goode, *The General Electric Company in Brazil*, Copyright 1961, The National Planning Association, Chapters III, IV, and V. Used by permission.

The history of the General Electric Company * in Brazil is the story of how one of the country's first and largest innovators met and overcame these problems. In essence, it consists of the gradual evolution of an originally simple importing operation into a set of highly complex and interdependent engineering, manufacturing, marketing, servicing, financial, training, and managerial activities. As each new activity was developed, and as the products made in Brazil increased in variety and quantity, the Company became more deeply integrated into the Brazilian economy and its contributions to Brazilian advancement became progressively more significant.

. . . Through trial and error, and with the help of the parent organization in the United States, GE has surmounted most of the obstacles to industrial innovation in Brazil. In the course of its evolution . . . the Company has worked out certain policies and practices which have provided helpful guides for other foreign-owned corporations and Brazilian-owned firms as well. . . .

. . . . .

GROWTH OF GE'S BRAZILIAN OPERATIONS. Ever since the 1880s, the variety and complexity of the electrical products sold in Brazil have enormously increased.

Whether as an importer or as a local manufacturer, GE has usually been both the first and the largest company contributing to the evolution in Brazil of an industrial economy based on electricity. In each of the three main types of electrical goods—lamps and illumination equipment, producer goods, and consumer products—GE has attained an impressive list of "firsts." After providing the first lamps [1881], the first dynamos and generators [1883], and the first street railway equipment, GE continued to be Brazil's major supplier of electrical goods through the decades from 1920 to the present. . . .

The Company first became interested in the possibilities of manufacturing in Brazil during World War I, which demonstrated the vulnerability of any country dependent upon imports of manufactured goods. By then, the growth of the Brazilian market for manufactured products had reached the point where domestic demand was likely to be sufficient to sustain some types of local industry.

At the end of the war, there was at least one General Electric product in this category—incandescent lamps. It was then, and still is, the Company product sold in the largest number of units in Brazil. Despite the wide variety of voltages in the country (even today voltages for lamps range from 6 to 250), lamps are a standard product and the adjustments required in the machinery to make the different sizes are comparatively minor. Hence, the economies of scale operated in favor of lamps becoming the first product to be made by GE in Brazil.

. . . . .

. . . By 1929, there were enough new users of electricity each year to warrant the capital investment required to manufacture watt-hour meters in Brazil. In the same year, production started at the factory in Rio.

In 1930, the factory added another new department for the manufacture of transformers for power distribution. Thereafter, the great depression of the 1930s put a stop to further industrial growth until 1936. In that year, the

---

* Unless otherwise specified, the abbreviation "GE" will be used to refer to the Brazilian subsidiary, while the term "General Electric" will denote both the parent company in the United States and its wholly-owned subsidiary, the International General Electric Company, through which it controls its foreign operations.

first power transformers were produced in the Rio factory, the assembling of radio receivers was begun in a newly-purchased building in Sao Paulo, and a technical laboratory for testing and development was also inaugurated in Rio.

With the economic revival at the end of the 1930s and the approach of World War II, GE's manufacturing activities in Brazil expanded rapidly. . . .

. . . World War II greatly increased Brazilian demand for all GE products. . . . It was not until 1948 [however] that additional General Electric products could be manufactured in Brazil. . . .

The initial postwar expansion of GE's manufacturing activities reached a high point in 1951 with the starting at the new Santo André factory of an assembly line for domestic refrigerators. The production of some X-ray apparatus began in 1952. More recent additions to the lines of local manufacture have included: at the Rio factory—large high-voltage power transformers, a plant for the metallurgical reduction of Brazilian tungsten-bearing ores and the production of metallic tungsten in ductile form for the drawing of lamp filaments; 15-KV oil circuit breakers and 600-volt automatic air circuit breakers; and at the Santo André factory—vertical and special application squirrel-cage induction motors, including horizontal types up to 300 hp, oscillating fans, hermetically-sealed motor compressors for domestic refrigerators and their controls, and a wide variety of other producer and consumer electrical goods. The Sao Paulo factory, which began during the 1930s with the assembly of radio sets, and added television receivers in 1954, has since expanded its production to include portable transistor radios; standard, hi-fi, and stereophonic electric phonographs and radio-phonograph combinations; automatic flatirons; automatic waffle irons; and other appliances.

GE's local manufacturing activities will experience a major expansion in the next few years when a large new factory . . . is completed. . . . [It will] be devoted to manufacturing . . . increased quantities of the types of transformers, circuit breakers, switches, motors, and generators already being made in its other factories as well as to add many new and larger sizes and varieties of these and other producer goods, which have hitherto had to be imported. . . .

Today, General Electric's Brazilian subsidiary is the Company's largest manufacturing unit outside the United States and Canada. . . .

EXPANSION AND SPECIALIZATION OF GE'S OPERATIONS. It has been as a local manufacturer rather than as an importer that GE has made the deepest impact on the Brazilian economy. Any U.S. business firm that starts to manufacture its products in a foreign country inevitably becomes more concerned about the state of the market demand in its new location than it was before, when only a small fraction of its U.S. output may have been exported there. Manufacturing—particularly in the electrical and electronics industry—requires a sizable capital investment, which can be preserved and made remunerative only if the market can be developed for its output. In addition, a firm's production costs and methods must be sufficiently economical to enable it to sell its products at a price which the market can afford and which can meet the competition of imports. Hence, an enterprise that undertakes to manufacture its products abroad immediately becomes concerned with, and must actively engage in, a much greater and more specialized range of functions and relationships than does an importing firm.

It is by means of such a progressive

diversification of activities involved in manufacturing that a foreign company has the most pervasive and profound impact on the economic growth of a developing country. . . .

Incandescent lamps—an example. Perhaps the best way to convey a picture of this increasingly complex diversification of activities is by means of an example. . . .

- The materials and components required to make incandescent lamps are comparatively few and simple: glass bulbs and stems, brass bases, tungsten filaments and supports. At the beginning, the Rio factory carried on an assembly operation using imported components; indeed, it was jokingly said that the only Brazilian product in these original lamps was the vacuum. But, as early as 1923, glass lamp bulbs were being blown in a new department of the Rio factory and brass lamp bases were being made, using imported brass or copper, by Brazilian suppliers, whom GE had helped to initiate this production. Thereafter, only tungsten wire for filaments, lead-in wires, brass for bases, and soda ash for glass-making continued to be imported.
- In 1948, machines were imported for drawing tungsten wire to the various sizes needed for filaments of incandescent lamps, although the wire itself was still purchased abroad. Finally, in 1954, production of ductile metallic tungsten wire made from Brazilian ore began at the Rio factory. In 1959, limited production of aluminum lamp bases was started to substitute Brazilian material for imported brass.
- Except for the tungsten wire, the skills needed to make and assemble the components of a finished lamp, though specialized, are not very difficult. But their acquisition was necessary and a logical first step toward the local manufacture of more complicated electrical and electronic material.

The groundwork laid and the lessons learned by producing lamps at the Rio factory helped make possible the subsequent introduction by GE of the manufacture of parts, components, and subassemblies for watthour meters, radios, and television sets, all of which required considerably higher engineering skills, more complex production equipment, and more difficult assembly and testing techniques. This advance has been especially important because, in the case of radios and television sets, many of these components are not produced in GE's Brazilian factories but are made by independent Brazilian manufacturers helped by the Company to learn how to make, and maintain the quality of, the products it needs. . . .

Of no less importance to Brazil has been the development of the marketing and promotional activities needed to sell GE's incandescent lamps after production started at the new Rio factory in 1921. Until the early 1920s, the Company had been content if its sales increased more or less directly with the growth of the Brazilian economy, and particularly with the expansion of electric power facilities. Thereafter, it was faced with the necessity of actively and imaginatively promoting its products if its investment in manufacturing was to be justified.

This necessity was made all the more pressing by the nature of consumer tastes in Brazil. As in most underdeveloped countries dependent upon imported manufacturers, goods produced by domestic industries were generally regarded by consumers as of inferior quality—and, therefore, as less desirable—than imports from Western Europe and the United States. Though the lamps made in the Rio factory were identical with those produced in GE's factories in the United States, sales of the former lagged seriously wherever the latter were still available. Not only were retailers reluctant to stock the national product, but even GE's Brazilian salesmen made only half-hearted efforts to sell the output of the Rio factory so long as they could still take orders for imported GE lamps. . . .

An accident in 1923 gave the decisive impetus to the sale of lamps produced by GE in Brazil. Fire destroyed the Rio warehouse in which virtually all the available inventory of imported GE lamps was stored. GE's salesmen had to sell the national product or do no business at all. Thus, necessity produced the needed conviction and initiative. By the mid-1920s, lamps made at the Rio factory were widely accepted throughout Brazil as equal to the imported product.

. . . Outside the already familiar field of textiles, this was the first national product manufactured on a substantial scale to supersede imported goods. And this achievement was all the more noteworthy because it was accomplished without tariff protection, direct or indirect governmental subsidies, or any other type of special competitive advantage.

Nonetheless, so firmly rooted has been the Brazilian consumer's conviction of the greater desirability of imported goods that the battle for acceptance of national products has had to be fought over again each time GE has introduced a new product line in its Brazilian factories. Of considerable assistance to the Company in these efforts has been the growing prestige throughout Brazil of the GE brand mark. Brazilian consumers generally have tended more and more to regard it as a guaranty of high quality. . . .

. . . Unlike its marketing practices in the United States, GE maintains direct contact with most Brazilian retailers as well as with the wholesalers. This situation reflects not only the fact that the network of wholesalers does not yet cover the entire country but also the inability of most wholesalers to provide the required sales guidance and assistance to their retail outlets. Consequently, GE has had to fill these gaps with its own personnel, who serve as zone sales promoters. . . .

Wholesale distributors are a comparatively recent development in Brazil—and one to which GE has made a significant contribution. Originally, like all importers of manufactured goods, GE dealt directly with retailers, usually helping them to start their businesses and often opening its own retail outlets until a Brazilian entrepreneur could be found to take over the operation. . . . The great majority of Brazilian firms now engaged in wholesale distribution of GE products were actively encouraged and helped to go into business by the Company.

. . . . .

The main regions where GE's salesmen sell directly to retailers—and often to individual consumers—are the vast but sparsely populated states of Pará and Amazonas in the Amazon basin and the highlands of Mato Grosso. Salesmen in these zones have specially equipped jeeps which carry about one month's supply of lamps. In this wild country, the rare dirt road is the equivalent of a superhighway; most roads are only pairs of wheel tracks meandering through the bush. Yet, there are enough electrical installations powered by small steam and internal combustion engines, windmills, or waterwheels to warrant the expense of maintaining this sales force. . . .

. . . . .

Other GE products. In general, the manufacturing and marketing of other GE products in Brazil have presented similar problems, which have been overcome by similar methods. But there have been some significant differences. For example, the development of the Brazilian market for electrical appliances has been a slower and more difficult process than for lamps not only because of the former's substantially higher cost but also because of the consumer's relatively greater unfamiliarity with the benefits to be derived from most of the products involved. . . .

. . . In contrast to lamps, a demand for which exists even in low-income homes, most appliances can be afforded only by consumers with incomes large enough for them to be considered good credit risks.

Consumer credit has been one of the most important factors in the booming sales of appliances in Brazil since World War II. In accordance with government policy, Brazil has no consumer financing facilities available to the buying public through banks or other credit financing institutions. Hence, it has been necessary for the selling organizations—the retailers, wholesale distributors, and producers—to provide consumer credit to facilitate purchases on extended time terms. Cash sales to customers are less than 5 percent of the total because the incomes of the buying public (except for a comparatively small group . . .) are too low to permit purchases other than on an installment basis.

. . . . .

Depending on the availability of commercial bank credit, GE's terms on appliance sales to wholesale and retail distributors may vary from as much as one year to as little as 30 days. . . . the necessity of maintaining sales above the "break-even" point, of minimizing the dealers' hardships, and of meeting the growing competition in the appliance market operates to lengthen GE's credit terms beyond the desirable minimum whenever government policy restricts the banks' credit facilities. GE's credit terms also vary with the cost of the appliance involved. The more expensive the product, the longer the consumer will take to pay for it; hence, the longer the chain of credit originating from the manufacturer.

Credit terms also vary somewhat with the size of the dealer. GE's five largest retail distributors in Sao Paulo account for nearly a third of its total sales in this territory. These large outlets, as well as the Mesbla firm in Rio, which is one of GE's biggest wholesale distributors, receive the longest credit terms when they need them to sell on long terms to consumers. However, these big organizations are generally also eligible for their own lines of credit at the commercial terms. The fact that a substantial portion of GE's appliance sales is made through a relatively small number of large dealers enables the Company to be somewhat more liberal in its credit terms to the many small distributors.

Development by GE's Producer Goods Department of its local manufacturing and marketing operations has not entailed the creation of a distribution network as large or elaborate as in the cases of lamps and consumer appliances. . . . Large transformers, large motors, switchgear, unit substations, and similar heavy electrical capital equipment are usually custom-made products, designed to meet specific application needs, and therefore are sold by GE direct to central station, industrial, and railway customers.

. . . Formerly, such large, especially-designed electrical equipments produced as single items or in small lots were imported from GE's plants in the United States. In the last few years, GE's Brazilian engineers and skilled workers have been acquiring the experience and developing the competence necessary to design this special equipment and to produce it efficiently. . . . production from GE's Brazilian factories—rather than imports from the United States—now fills an ever-growing proportion of orders awarded to the Company for large, high-voltage transformers, power circuit breakers, motors, and other electrical equipment for new power stations and industrial enterprises.

RECENT DEVELOPMENTS AFFECTING GE'S POSITION IN BRAZIL. In the three main fields of electrical products—lamps and illumination equipment, consumer appliances, and producer goods—GE has been mainly responsible for initially developing the market and inaugurating the manufacture in Brazil of many of the constituent commodities. At the same time, the growth of the Brazilian economy and the example of the success of GE's efforts have opened the way for local manufacturing competitors, both foreign and Brazilian. . . .

GE dominated the market for producer goods until the early 1950s. Since then, a number of leading European electrical equipment firms have started, or substantially increased, production in Brazil, and the Westinghouse Electric Corporation has licensed some of its smaller products for manufacture by Brazilian firms. . . . [The author cites several examples. Ed.]

. . . . .

Until the post-World War II period, GE's only lamp competitors were firms in the United States, Europe, and Japan, who exported their products to Brazil. In consequence of the prestige of GE's brand name, this competition was not serious. However, in the past decade, two European firms and one Brazilian company have begun to manufacture lamps in Brazil. . . .

- A little more than half of the lamps sold in Brazil are made by GE.
- The well-known N.V. Philips Gloeilampenfabrieken of the Netherlands has captured over one third of the market by vigorous and expensive selling efforts which—among other activities—involve supplying more than 12,000 retail outlets directly by means of its own fleet of jeeps.
- The German firm of Osram enjoys around a sixth of total sales.
- The remaining few percent of the lamps sold are made by Marcicano, a Brazilian company.

Despite the fact that the local manufacturing activities of these three firms have meant more competition for GE, the Company has nevertheless helped them get produtcion started. In the beginning, both Philips and Osram bought all lamp components from GE and merely assembled them into finished products, which bore their own brand names. Osram still buys all of its components from GE, but Philips has been reducing its purchases as its own component production lines have gotten under way. Marcicano has a special arrangement with GE under which the latter supplies it with components for assembly by this Brazilian firm into the many special sizes and types of lamps not made by the three other producers.

GE's early efforts to acquaint Brazilians with the respective labor-saving, sanitary, and entertainment advantages of electric irons, refrigerators, fans, radios, television sets, and other appliances have borne ample fruit in the past decade, not only for the Company itself but also for other appliance manufacturers, both foreign- and Brazilian-owned. Until the 1950s, GE's main competition was from imported appliances. . . . However, once the growth of consumer incomes and GE's promotional work had created a substantial and rapidly increasing demand for consumer durable goods, other manufacturers began to enter this attractive new market. So enterprising have some of these newcomers been that in the case of refrigerators their sales now exceed those of G.E. For example:

- By 1959, about 30 percent of the market for refrigerators had been captured by a Brazilian firm called Climax, which makes a very low-priced product selling for one half the price of GE's quality models. Six other smaller Brazilian firms together accounted for another 15 percent of the market. The remaining 55 percent of the Brazilian market for refrigerators is shared among GE, Frigidaire (General Motors), and Brastemp, a Brazilian firm in which the Whirlpool Corporation owns a one third interest. . . .
- More than 60 firms, mostly small Brazilian companies, assemble television sets, but the five biggest manufacturers account for 85 percent of the total. In 1959, GE was the largest. The quality market for TV receivers is shared among GE, Philco, and the Netherlands firm of Philips. Invictus, a Brazilian manufacturer of low-priced sets, was second in 1959 in volume of production.

The Company's attitude toward loss of its pre-eminent market position in some lines is significant. On the one hand, GE welcomed the advent of other manufacturers, particularly Brazilians, because of the greater security for private enterprise which results from a larger number of entrepreneurs. On the other hand, some of the new competitive facories, with the most up-to-date production equipment and techniques, were more efficient than GE's older plants. This situation led the Company to adopt and implement a more aggressive policy toward modernization and expansion of facilities and new marketing methods. . . .

. . . . .

It is sometimes said that the pioneering firm in industrial and technological innovation finds that the enterprises which later follow its lead take over the cream of the market it has developed. Despite the increasingly competitive situation that has emerged in Brazil in recent years, GE has maintained the industrial leadership it has held for over half a century. . . .

GE's Policies and Practices

. . . . .

. . . Judged by its activities in Brazil, GE is an outstanding example of a company which has successfully adapted U.S. business policies and industrial techniques to the particular needs and capabilities of a different environment. In the United States, General Electric is well-known for having a distinctive management philosophy and set of basic policies. These lay great stress upon raising productivity and profitability by means of large-scale development and research, continuous improvement of management methods, fostering employee welfare, and very extensive employee training. But there are limits within which such policies and practices can be followed in an economically less developed country. . . .

GE'S ORGANIZATION AND MANAGEMENT POLICIES. Unlike the foreign subsidiaries of some U.S. companies, GE's Brazilian organization has from its beginning been entrusted with a great deal of autonomy. The parent corporation recognized that its managers in Brazil must have the flexibility and freedom required to cope effectively with Brazilian conditions. . . .

Major policy questions have, of course, normally been referred to the appropriate top management personnel of the International General Electric Company in New York. These questions generally relate to financial matters—the profitability of the Brazilian operation, the remittance of earnings to the United States, the export of additional capital to Brazil, plant and product expansion in Brazil, and so forth. Also, International General Electric actively supervises the career development of GE's managerial and professional personnel, Brazilian and foreign, and selects or passes upon all officers and top-level managers of the Brazilian subsidiary.

In addition, there are close and continuous working relationships between the Company's U.S. and Brazilian organizations regarding the export to Brazil of General Electric's U.S.-made products; the solution of engineering, design, and production problems in the Brazilian factories; the provision of specialized technical and managerial assistance to the Brazilian organization; training in the United States of personnel from Brazil; and many other operating matters. The U.S. organization is also responsible for hiring, or assigning from its own staff, the small number of U.S. citizens employed in the Brazilian operation to fill specific needs.

. . . . .

GE's decentralized structure enables it to cope more effectively with the growing competitiveness of the Brazilian market. It should also make possible greater initiative and inventiveness in the expansion of manufacturing operations and in the development of new lines of related commodities not hitherto produced, since each department concentrates on its particular market potentialities. . . .

LABOR-MANAGEMENT RELATIONS. If the present organization of GE in Brazil is an example of borrowing almost entirely the policies of the parent Company, the same cannot be said of GE's labor-management relations. Because of the special character of organized labor in Brazil, . . . GE has had to devise wholly different policies from those followed by its U.S. parent. . . .

. . . direct relationships between companies and local unions are much less important in Brazil than in the United States. Hence, the major decisions affecting GE's labor-management relations are generally made at the industry-wide or national level, with the formal or unofficial participation of the government. And, even the Company's relations with the local *sindicato* are more often conducted through the Labor Court than they are in direct dealings with the union's officials.

Most of GE's workers are members of the Sindicato dos Metalurgicos e de Material Elétrico. This is one of the unions that informed and objective Brazilians believe has been penetrated by crypto-Communists and fellow travelers in recent years. It is impossible for an outside observer to determine if, and which of, the Sindicato's officers are in this category and the extent to which their commitment to communism is ideological rather than merely opportunistic in nature. Nevertheless, some indication of the Sindicato's present orientation may be seen in the fact that it has recently voted to maintain close contacts with the international metal workers affiliate of the Communist-dominated World Federation of Trade Unions (WFTU), though it has not yet joined the latter organization.

. . . At the time this study was completed, GE had no problems of major magnitude in its relations with the Sindicato, and there appeared to be widespread good will toward the Company among all grades of employees regardless of whether they were members of the Sindicato or not.

. . . the only problem in dispute between the Company and the Sindicato arose from the fact that GE had recently raised the price of the subsidized meals served in its cafeterias and had instituted a small charge for fresh milk, which had hitherto been provided free. The Company continued to pay half the cost of the meals and maintained that, owing to Brazil's persistent inflation, it was justified in increasing slightly the price charged employees for the other half. . . .

This absence of labor-management difficulties has not, however, protected the Company from criticism from the *Voz do Metalúrgico,* an unaffiliated labor newspaper published for workers in the metal-working industries. Written, to judge from its content, by crypto-Communists and fellow travelers, *Voz* periodically makes sensational charges against GE, as well as against many other large employers, in an effort to discredit the Company in particular and to whip up anti-U.S. sentiment in general. Its stories, which are highly distorted and exaggerated misinterpretations of usually innocuous facts, seem so far to have had no discernible impact on the Company's employees or on Brazilians generally.

. . . the future problems that GE may have with the Sindicato are likely to arise less because of the Company's specific policies and actions than from the current general leftward drift of the Brazilian labor movement and the increasing seriousness of Communist penetration of the trade unions.

BRAZILIANIZATION. General Electric Sociedade Anônima is a Brazilian company not only in name but also in the people who compose it. At all levels, the Company is staffed overwhelmingly by Brazilians. . . .

. . . GE was among the first in Brazil to initiate a program of deliberately encouraging and training Brazilians to qualify for all positions within its organization. At present, GE's managerial, supervisory, and technical personnel total about 500. Of these, nearly 90 percent are Brazilians; about 7 percent are U.S. citizens; and the remainder are of other Latin American and European nationalities. Of the 51 highest managerial positions in the Company, 35 are held by Brazilian nationals, 15 by U.S. citizens, and the remaining position by an Argentine citizen.

Among the engineering and other specialized professional personnel, the proportion of Brazilians is equally striking. Of 19 engineers in the Consumer Goods Department, only one is a U.S. citizen; in the Producer Goods and the Lamp and Illumination Departments, all the engineers are Brazilians. In the Corporate Finance Operation, which handles such functions as negotiating for bank credits and auditing the accounts of the operating departments, half of the responsible supervisory and technical positions are held by Brazilians. The Employee Relations Division has only one non-Brazilian in its total of 36 managerial and technical employees. All of the supervisory positions in the Legal Operation are held by Brazilians.

. . . . .

An interesting indication of the success of Brazilianization is the fact that managerial and technical personnel serve in their assigned jobs without regard to the nationality of their supervisors. Thus, many of the comparatively small number of U.S. citizens and all of the Europeans employed by the Company serve under Brazilian supervisors. . . .

One consequence of the effectiveness of GE's Brazilianization policy has been that qualified Brazilian managerial and technical personnel, who received their initial training and experience in a GE factory or sales office, have been in great demand throughout Brazil. While most of GE's Brazilian personnel have made their careers with the Company, many of those who have left now fill important positions in other industrial and commercial enterprises. But whether they leave the Company for other posts or stay on, the prominence of GE-trained Brazilians at top management levels and in technical and specialized positions testifies to the Company's forward-looking policies and to the intelligence and capacity for personal development of the people of Brazil. . . .

EMPLOYEE TRAINING AND EDUCATION. A major precondition for the Brazilianization of GE's staff has been the extensive employee training and educational programs which the Company conducts. . . . GE in Brazil has not only been conforming to general Company policy but it has also been overcoming the deficiencies in training and education which are inevitable characteristics of lesser developed countries. . . .

GE's training and educational programs in Brazil are of several kinds, each designed to fit the needs of a particular group of employees:

- Most newly employed factory workers have no technical skills or previous industrial experience and hence are given a basic orientation course and on-the-job training in the particular tasks they are to perform. In cases where special knowledge or a semiskill is also required, workers are given supplementary courses by their supervisors.
- Owing to the great shortage of experienced skilled workers who can be obtained outside the Company, GE makes a practice of providing opportunities to its semiskilled workers for upgrading themselves through special training courses in more advanced skills. These courses, conducted from time to time by experienced supervisors, are open to all qualified GE employees, who contribute half of the required time, while the Company pays them for the other half and meets all expenses of the courses.
- In addition to training in skills and semi-skills, GE also provides a basic literacy and arithmetic course for all employees on the same 50-50 basis.
- Once they have learned reading, writing, and arithmetic with a fair degree of proficiency, GE's factory employees are then eligible to take a series of more advanced technical courses which are offered from time to time in such subjects as mathematics, blueprint reading, elementary chemistry and physics, general mechanics, metallurgy, and electricity. All of these courses are voluntary, the workers contributing half of the time involved and GE paying them for half time and meeting all the other expenses.
- For its clerical and other office employees, GE has a parallel series of more advanced training and educational courses. In addition to the required basic orientation courses and on-the-job training in their specific tasks, office employees are offered voluntary courses in English, shorthand and typing, business correspondence, and other clerical skills. These are financed on a similar basis.

. . . . .

Educational opportunities are provided for engineers and technicians at an early stage of their development. In contrast to many lesser developed countries, Brazil today has good educational institutions and facilities for training many types of engineers. . . . GE continues to work closely with the engineering schools to encourage improvement in the quality of their electrical and electronic engineering curricula, instruction, and laboratory work.

Since the 1930s, GE has provided financial assistance and special opportunities for applied training to a selected number of electrical engineering students. At regular intervals, the Company interviews likely candidates in the third year of their electrical engineering course. Those who meet GE's standards are hired to work part-time for the Company during the fourth and fifth years of engineering school. Thus, these students obtain good practical experience in electrical engineering work along with their academic studies. Upon graduation, many of these young men are offered—and many accept—full-time, permanent positions with the Company.

Virtually all Brazilian engineers who are permanent employees of GE are from time to time offered opportunities to take advanced courses at the parent company's training facilities in the United States. . . . GE pays its engineers' salaries and expenses while they attend these advanced courses in the United States.

Extensive opportunities for further training and educational improvement are also provided for GE's managerial and supervisory employees regardless of nationality. These follow the pattern of the management training programs established by General Electric in the United States. Supervisory personnel can take courses in indoctrination and job-instruction methods, employee relations, job-safety training, and production methods improvement. For higher managerial personnel, GE provides courses in management methods improvement, leadership, and other areas of advanced management. Each year, the Company sends a number of its managerial employees to the United States to take advanced courses in business management. . . .

Upon their return to Brazil, these employees are expected to conduct identical courses for their colleagues. Thus, many of the benefits of advanced management training are widely disseminated in the Company. . . .

GE is justifiably proud of its extensive training and educational programs. They provide opportunities for economic and cultural advancement for every category of the Company's employees, from the lowest-paid unskilled laborers to the general managers of its departments and even to the president of the corporation himself. The Company is more than satisfied that the comparatively modest costs of these programs are far outweighed by their benefits in improving productivity, both directly through the increase of skills and indirectly by stimulating higher employee morale.

For their part, GE's employees are equally enthusiastic about the Company's training and educational facilities. In surveying the attitudes of Brazilian employees, there were no queries which evoked more positive and strongly felt responses than those pertaining to the worth of GE's educational activities. . . .

EMPLOYEE POLICIES AND BENEFITS. While GE continues clearly to be the leader in Brazil in employee education and training, the extensive social welfare programs of the Brazilian government and the rapid advances of Brazilian enterprises have been closing the gap between Brazilian practices and GE's standards in other aspects of employee relations. . . . In the provision of health and medical care, employee housing, paid vacations, bonuses, and other "fringe benefits," . . . [some] Brazilian firms are second to none, not only in Latin America, but in the United States as well.

However, many of GE's employee welfare policies were innovations in normal Brazilian practices when the Company first introduced them many years ago, and they have served as standards for other business firms and employers to emulate. . . . Brazil—in common with many Latin American countries—has in recent years adopted an elaborate system of labor and social welfare legislation. Minimum wages, sickness benefits, pension retirement arrangements, and accident compensation are required by law and, in some cases, are administered by governmental institutions. All business enterprises must conform to the minimum standards established under these legislative and administrative arrangements. . . .

GE follows a policy of conscientiously complying with all the requirements of the country's labor and social welfare regulations. In most areas, the Company voluntarily exceeds minimum legal requirements because it believes that its employees are entitled to greater or more secure benefits, which in turn may contribute to improving labor productivity. . . .

After negotiations with the employers' and workers' *sindicatos,* the Brazilian government establishes the minimum monthly wage rates for all types of employees. Owing to the post-World War II inflation, the minimum monthly wage rates have been periodically revised upward as the purchasing power of the currency has declined. However, even for unskilled workers GE generally pays in excess of the minimum monthly rates. Also, it has on occasion increased its wage rates (owing to the inflationary situations) well before a change in the mandatory minimum was decreed. . . .

One reason for GE's forehandedness is the abnormally high rate of turnover, particularly among unskilled workers, which is a feature not only of Brazilian industrialization but of most lesser developed countries in the throes of their revolutions. Wherever and whenever rural populations are experiencing for the first time the unaccustomed disciplines of modern production systems and the novel opportunities of urban living, there is generally a high rate of turnover among unskilled workers. At GE's factories in Brazil, the rate may average as much as 30 percent a year.

In addition to keeping ahead of the legal minimum wage, GE has endeavored to minimize its turnover problem by devising tests and screening interviews which aim at enabling its personnel sections to select applicants who seem least likely to change their residences and jobs frequently during their initial years in or near the big city.

In the successively higher grades of semiskilled and skilled workers, the rate of turnover becomes progressively lower. However, workers in the skilled categories are in great demand in the booming industrial centers of Brazil. This, too, has had its effect on GE's pay scales. From time to time, the Company must unilaterally raise its pay for particular types of semiskilled and skilled labor to hold its own in the competition.

Absenteeism is another problem that is markedly more important in a lesser developed country than it is in the United States, and which requires special action on GE's part. . . . Often ill-health is offered as an excuse, despite the care provided by GE's medical staff. Employees can usually obtain from lenient individuals in the government's medical institutes written excuses for such absences which the Company must honor.

To combat absenteeism, GE offers its factory and office workers an extra day's pay for every week in which they have a perfect attendance record and are not more than 15 minutes late for the job. While this is a measure of how seriously GE regards absenteeism, neither this problem nor that of turnover are more critical at GE than among other industrial employers, Brazilian or foreign. In no sense do these problems reflect specific employee dissatisfaction with working conditions at GE's plants, but rather they stem from the much more profound sociological and psychological difficulties of the transition from agrarianism to industrialism.

The Company maintains elaborate employee welfare programs for its workers which have also helped to enhance

GE's good reputation in Brazil. Some are required by the laws of the country:

- From 12 to 15 paid holidays are common each year depending upon government proclamation.
- Except in cases of excessive absenteeism, all employees receive paid annual vacations of 20 working days (excluding paid holidays).
- All employees are legally entitled to 15 days of sick leave each year. While on sick leave, the worker is paid one third of his regular wage by a governmental institute, to whose support all employers must contribute 2 percent of their gross payrolls.
- Accident insurance premiums must also be paid by the employer.
- A governmental institute established for each industry administers the retirement system. The pension benefit is 80 percent of the average of the employee's last three years' salary for retirement at age 55, and 100 percent for retirement at age 60, up to a maximum retirement benefit of three times the highest minimum salary established by law. This retirement system is supported by a levy of 8 percent each on employers' gross payrolls and on employees' wages. The government is supposed to contribute a similar amount.

However, in the case of most of these legally-required benefits, GE substantially exceeds the minimum standards fixed by legislation. . . .

. . . substantial medical benefits are made available by GE to its employees in excess of those required by law. At GE's factories, where the largest concentrations of employees exist, there are clinics and conveniently-located subsidiary dispensaries at which all employees and their families get the free services of doctors, X-ray technicians, dentists, oculists, and trained nurses. . . . Prescriptions are provided free and common proprietary drugs are sold to the employees at cost. Medical care is available to employees and their wives or husbands, children, parents, and minor brothers and sisters. . . .

Retirement benefits is another area in which GE's practice goes beyond legal minimums. Owing to inflation, the purchasing power or the fixed pension benefits of older retired employees has drastically declined. Unfortunately, under the law, it is practically impossible for an employer to supplement the inadequacy of the official retirement system with a voluntary pension plan of his own. Hence, in hardship cases involving meritorious employees due for retirement, GE resorts to the morally justified procedure of continuing to employ them at purely nominal jobs in order to ensure that they have an adequate income in their old age.

Other employee benefits voluntarily provided by the Company are:

- A production incentive plan, whose rate of extra compensation depends upon the type of work done by each worker.
- GE's Christmas bonus plan. . . .
- A voluntary program of providing term life insurance for all employees after one year of service. . . .
- The privilege of purchasing GE products at discounts of from 30 to 50 percent of the retail price. In consequence, most employees' homes are well-stocked with GE appliances, a not inconsiderable addition to their standard of living.

Because of the suburban location of its factories and the advisability of ensuring workers a well-balanced, high-energy meal, the Company maintains cafeteria-style restaurants open to all factory and office employees at the Rio and Santo André factories. Both lunch and dinner are served in these restaurants. The employee pays only about half the actual cost of the meal. In addition, coffee—strong and sweet, as the Brazilians like it—is served free twice a day to all employees.

Social clubs, organized and run by the employees, are helped in various ways by the Company. It provides free club rooms and maintains football (soccer) fields and other recreational facilities for the use of club members. In addition, GE sponsors the operation of Holiday House—a mountain resort hotel accessible from both Rio and Sao Paulo—where club members may spend their vacations at very reasonable rates.

GE's Contributions to Brazil

DEVELOPMENT OF MANUFACTURING INDUSTRY. GE has contributed to the economic development of Brazil in a variety of ways. Perhaps the most obvious is the extent to which the country's stock of capital equipment includes producer goods either manufactured in GE's Brazilian factories or imported from General Electric's plants in the United States and Canada. For example, close to 40 percent of Brazil's combined hydroelectric and thermoelectric generating capacity has been manufactured by the Company. Almost half of the electric locomotives and nearly two thirds of the diesel-electric locomotives on Brazil's railroads have been built in whole or in substantial part with General Electric equipment. . . .

Equally important have been the indirect effects of the Company's increasingly diversified activities. . . .

An example from each decade since GE began to manufacture in Brazil will give some indication of the variety of activities stimulated and of the nature of the assistance provided:

- In the early 1920s, when GE first began to manufacture lamps, it required containers in which to wrap these fragile products for shipment. At that time, there was no producer of paperboard containers in Brazil. Accordingly, the Company found a small Brazilian paper-products manufacturer who was willing to venture into a new field. GE lent him the funds to purchase the necessary machines and received reimbursement in the form of containers. Today, this Brazilian-owned firm of Costa Ribeiro is one of the largest manufacturers of paper products and paperboard containers in Brazil.

- In the late 1930s, GE needed a variety of small metal parts for the new appliances and producer goods it was starting to manufacture. The Company found a small Brazilian-owned metal-working firm whose management was willing to expand. GE's engineers taught Delta's personnel how to design and make the parts required and how to ensure the output of large quantities within very small tolerance limits. Delta was informed of the quantities that GE was prepared to buy for a considerable period of time so that the Brazilian firm could make plans, on the basis of assured sales, to increase its production in accordance with the prospective growth of GE's needs. In more recent years, GE's requirements for these small metal parts have grown so much more rapidly than it or Delta had anticipated that the Company has had to develop additional production of such components by other Brazilian suppliers.

- In 1949, when GE began to manufacture electric motors, it needed cast-iron frames in large quantities. Sofunge, a very small Brazilian-owned iron foundry, was approached to see if it would be interested in expanding to meet this new demand. GE brought one of its engineers from the United States to show Sofunge how to make the patterns for the castings, and the Company supplied technical assistance in many other ways as well. Sofunge proved to be an enterprising firm and, with the help of GE's orders and technical advice, soon became the largest cast-iron foundry in Brazil. In the last few years, it has begun to make castings for Brazil's new automobile industry and has no longer been able to meet all of GE's needs. In consequence, the Company has begun to develop other small Brazilian-owned cast-iron foundries as supplementary suppliers.

- In 1958, GE needed top quality porcelain bushings for high voltage transformers. A Brazilian manufacturer of porcelain products, Cerámica Santana, was asked whether he wished to expand into a new field. When he replied in the affirmative, GE arranged for him to obtain a patent license and the technical "know-how" for producing the same kind of high quality porcelain bushings that General Electric makes in the United States. Today, the Brazilian firm is also manufacturing these porcelain bushings for other electrical goods producers in Brazil.

In each of these cases—and there are many more—GE has actively searched for Brazilian firms who might already be undertaking, or could be encouraged to start, the production of needed materials, components, and subassemblies. The Company's policy has enabled Brazilians to acquire the technological and managerial skills needed to develop their own manufacturing activities. At the same time, GE has helped Brazilian entrepreneurs to accumulate productive capital.

GE has helped local producers and suppliers in the following ways:

- Its patents have been licensed to Brazilian firms.
- It has financed the purchase by some of its Brazilian suppliers of the necessary capital equipment and its engineers have helped many of them select the most suitable machinery and set up efficient production processes.
- It has provided technical and managerial "know-how" through "trouble-shooting" services; by testing the quality of the products produced; by bringing new scientific and technological advances to the attention of Brazilian producers; and in other ways. A metallurgist on GE's permanent staff works continuously with the Company's Brazilian copper and brass suppliers to improve their productive efficiency and the quality of the materials and parts they make for GE. Inevitably, the benefits to productivity arising from these technical assistance activities affect other products and operations of these Brazilian firms.
- It has given its Brazilian suppliers considerable financial help. The Company has often contracted on a long-term basis for all, or a large part, of the prospective output of new enterprises, thereby ensuring them of markets during their most difficult early years. GE has been willing to make advance payments to its Brazilian suppliers—sometimes as much as 40 percent upon placing the order—so as to provide them with the operating capital needed to fulfill their contracts.

In the 1920s and 1930s, when Brazilian manufacturers were comparatively few and inexperienced, GE usually had to take the initiative in seeking out a prospective supplier. Today, with Brazilian entrepreneurs multiplying rapidly, the Company has the satisfaction of being approached with increasing frequency by new or expanding Brazilian firms desirous of supplying it with materials, components, and subassemblies. Each producer soliciting GE's business is visited by the appropriate Company personnel, who inspect his plant, assess his capabilities, and investigate his record. If their report is favorable, the Company asks the prospective supplier to make samples of the products it needs. After testing the quality of these samples, GE determines whether or not to develop a continuing relationship with the Brazilian firm.

The Company is interested not only in helping new suppliers to get started, but also in keeping old suppliers abreast of technological and competitive developments. For example, a Brazilian firm in Sao Paulo has for many years supplied GE with screw-threaded and other machined hardware for watthour meters. A competitor installed a new thread-rolling process, which substantially reduced his costs and enabled him to undersell GE's supplier. The latter approached the Company to ask for assistance in meeting this serious competition. GE engineers helped him prepare the designs for a new plant, select the most efficient equipment, iron out the initial production "bugs," and solve other technical problems. Today, GE's supplier is able to meet any competition in price, quality, quantity, or delivery. . . .

GE has, of course, considerable self-interest in the productive efficiency of its suppliers and the quality of the products it buys from them. If one of its suppliers lags too far behind in these respects, the Company must in self-protection avail itself of the alternatives of purchasing from a more efficient competitor or of helping a new firm get started. However, unlike the usual practice elsewhere, GE in Brazil adopts one or the other of these alternatives only after it has tried to help its regular supplier keep abreast of the latest technological advances or meet price and quality competition in other ways.

Thus, one of GE's most significant contributions to the development of Brazilian industry has been its efforts from the beginning to produce itself, or to stimulate the production of, the many components and subassemblies needed for its increasingly complex finished products. In consequence, a considerable proportion of the numerous commodities produced by GE in Brazil are now truly national products. The table [below] shows the percentage by value of the raw materials, components, and subassemblies produced in Brazil and used in the manufacture of some leading GE commodities.

In the case of refrigerators, only 76 percent of the value of materials and parts is of Brazilian origin owing primarily to the fact that the Brazilian steel industry cannot supply all of the needed sheet steel for cabinets. . . . When radio and television picture tube production starts in Brazil—expected very shortly—the imported portion of these products will fall to less than 5

Produced in Brazil	Percent (by value of raw material)
Electric lamps	95
Electric irons	90
Electric motors	84
Watthour meters	80
Radios	80
Refrigerators	76
Transformer (depending on size)	60–70
Television receivers	60

percent. For most GE commodities, there is apparently an irreducible minimum of necessary imports—mostly raw materials, such as copper and nickel, and semi-processed materials, such as special alloy steels, cold-rolled silicon sheet steel, and certain chemicals—which have so far not been produced or are unlikely soon to be made in Brazil. A similar dependence upon certain indispensable imports exists in the United States, as in all industrialized countries.

The Brazilianization of television receiver production is an especially good example of GE's efforts to stimulate development of component manufacture by Brazilian firms. Television receivers contain numerous small but highly intricate resistors, capacitors, potentiometers, and many other electrical and electronic components which require high-quality workmanship to ensure that they will meet the strict tolerances and other standards necessary for the higher-grade products made by GE. At first, all of these components had to be imported from the United States or Europe. But the Company worked diligently to help new and existing Brazilian firms meet its standards and supply the quantities it requires. Today, only 40 percent by value of the materials and parts necessary to make television receivers must still be imported. This will soon decline to less than 5 percent when the production of electronic tubes (including picture tubes) by Brazilian firms is achieved. The creation of an electrical and electronic components industry in Brazil is one of the most significant economic advances that country has made in recent years.

GE provides a prominent example of another important aspect of the growing maturity of Brazilian industry. When an economy is able to make its own technological innovations, as distinct from adopting or adapting those developed in more highly industrialized socities, it can be considered well on the way to self-sustained economic growth. GE's engineers and technicians have not only been adapting the Company's discoveries and advances in the United States to the needs and capabilities of Brazil; they have also developed on their own some entirely new processes and products. One example is a new white inside coating for the tubes of fluorescent lamps. This was developed by GE's Brazilian engineers, who also designed the special equipment needed to make and apply it. This new white coating is now used not only at the Rio factory but also in General Electric plants in other parts of the world.

Another GE activity potentially significant for the general economic advancement of Brazil has been the Company's contribution to the creation of a capital goods industry in the country. Mention has already been made of the fact that GE has been manufacturing in Brazil more and more of the electrical producer goods which the country requires for its development—large power transformers, motors, distribution transformers and equipment, electric control and switchgear devices, and similar items. In addition, it has been helping many Brazilian manufacturers design manufacturing equipment of all types for which the Company has supplied the electrical components. . . .

. . . . .

Finally . . . GE has fostered the development of wholesale and retail distribution in Brazil. Originally, the Company carried on the wholesaling function itself and in some localities the retailing function as well. Even today, GE provides the retail distribution system for its products throughout much of the vast wilderness of the Amazon valley and the interior highlands of Goiás and Mato Grosso. But, in the more populous and advanced states of eastern Brazil, the Company has always ceased its retailing and wholesaling activities just as soon as other organizations were able and willing to take them over. Again, its usual practice has been to help Brazilian firms assume these functions and to provide them with continuing assistance in carrying them on more effectively.

. . . . .

THE DEVELOPMENT OF STANDARDS AND PEOPLE. . . . GE has had a very substantial impact in Brazil on consumer tastes and standards; it has had singular success in inculating high standards both in the design and manufacture of its products and in business management; and, through its Brazilianization policy, it has done much to make modern manufacturing and marketing, with all their many ramifications, respectable careers in the eyes of the population at large. Each of these contributions will be examined in turn.

Consumer standards. In the field of consumer attitudes and expectations, GE's contribution has been both unique and arduous. In the 1920s, the Company was one of the leaders in the struggle against Brazilian consumers' strong preference for imported goods. . . .

. . . in many cases the problem faced

by GE was not only to make the national product competitive with the imported one; it was to interest Brazilian consumers in the commodity itself, regardless of where it was made. . . .

It might be assumed that in a largely tropical underdeveloped country the main, if not the sole, obstacle to the purchase of household refrigerators would be a financial one—the inability of the people to afford them. This is not always the case. In the early 1930s, GE decided to make a vigorous effort to interest the Brazilian public in domestic refrigerators. . . . The Company opened its own retail outlets in Rio and Sao Paulo, but sales lagged badly despite favorable prices and generous credit terms. Upon investigation, GE found that the resistance of consumers financially able to afford refrigerators was owed in the main to the widespread notion that there was a grave danger of catching pneumonia from the cold air released whenever the refrigerator door was opened.

The Company determined to prove the falsity of this fear by a mass demonstration both of the harmlessness of refrigerators and of their practical utility. Trucks loaded with refrigerators toured the residential suburbs of Rio and Sao Paulo, stopping at likely homes and offering to install the machines for a free trial period. At the same time, a U.S.-type advertising campaign through the press, radio, and other channels explained to the Brazilian public that, far from making people ill, refrigerators promoted better health by preventing food spoilage and, by so doing, saved them money as well. . . .

. . . For years, the mistaken fear of pneumonia and other respiratory diseases blocked the introduction of air conditioning not only to private homes but, more importantly, into offices, shops, theatres, public buildings, and even hospitals. In 1938, GE held a national conference in Rio of doctors, hospital administrators, sanitary engineers, and public health officials to explain and demonstrate the benefits of air conditioning in hospitals, clinics, and other health installations. The results of the conference were widely publicized in Brazil. In consequence, many Brazilian hospitals introduced air conditioning in their operating rooms and later in their wards. Their example was soon followed by business firms, theatres, retail establishments, banks, and, finally, apartment dwellers and home owners.

. . . the Company's practice of training service and repairmen for its electrical equipment and appliances was an important aspect in stimulating sales. But, at the same time, it has enabled large numbers of Brazilians to acquire skills that would otherwise have been beyond their means and to get higher paying jobs with retail firms or to start their own businesses, many of which have prospered and grown substantially. Here, as in the case of GE's aid to Brazilian manufacturers, what is significant is not that the Company acted in its own interest, but that it interpreted its interest broadly so that its market development activities could also be of benefit to others.

Standards of business performance. Hardly less important than its impact on consumer attitudes has been GE's effort to acquaint Brazilians with the fact that industrial growth requires high performance standards in the factory and in the office. . . .

A modern industrial system depends for its efficiency on the economies of scale made possible by the extensive use of automatic machinery, by long production runs, and by the rapid assembly of finished products from ready-made, standardized materials and parts.

The more complex and advanced the industry, the more it becomes dependent upon the availability of increasingly intricate and carefully made standardized materials, components, and subassemblies. As each industry progresses, the relevant qualities (size, shape, durability, speed, weight, etc.) of each type of part are permitted to vary from an established standard by smaller and smaller tolerances. To make increasing quantities of such parts with finer and finer limits of tolerance requires greater skills and closer attention to the quality of the production methods and of the products made by them.

One of the most difficult obstacles to overcome during the early stages of industrialization is the unwillingness or inability of newly-established manufacturers to appreciate the essentiality of conforming to such product quality and production standards.... [Often] the inexperienced manufacturer of parts has had to learn the painful lesson that the end-product makers will soon cease to buy his output if it does not conform to the specific qualities and tolerance limits they require. A substantial number of Brazilian parts manufacturers have gone bankrupt or have been in serious financial danger through not learning this lesson in time. Nor is the lesson easily or quickly learned by a society emerging from centuries of accepting without question the lack of uniformity as a natural—in fact, usually desirable—characteristic of the output of handicraft forms of production.

From the first product it made in Brazil—incandescent lamps—to its present efforts to help Brazilian manufacturers learn to produce complex electronic tubes, GE has ceaselessly been disseminating high quality and production standards throughout the Brazilian economy. It has worked patiently with each new parts supplier, helping him to set up his production line, regulate his machinery, test his products, and eliminate unexpected irregularities in output. Where a producer has been slow to appreciate the importance of conforming to strict production standards, the Company has arranged for him and his engineer and chief foreman to visit its assembly lines so that they could see for themselves how and why each part fits into the finished product. . . .

As part of its efforts to promote quality standards in Brazilian industry, GE helped to found and has participated actively in several technical organizations and trade associations working in this field. . . .

Equally important, though more difficult to describe and document, has been GE's contribution to the dissemination in Brazil of the principles of high standards of business performance. The mutual trust and presumption of good faith required for reasonably efficient and profitable relationships between salesman and wholesaler, supplier and producer, retailer and consumer, banker and client are vital ingredients of any modern economic system.

Such standards of personal and business conduct are necessary not only between enterprises but also within them. Management must learn to conform to certain minimum standards of performance with regard to general business morality; basic respect for workers as individuals; socially responsible employee, labor, and community relations; cooperation with government agencies; etc. For their part, factory workers and office employees must be willing, and must learn, to achieve certain minimum standards of personal integrity, conscientious performance of the work task, regularity of attendance, responsible care of machinery and equipment, positive interest in the enterprise's productive performance, and so on. Without these and other norms of personal and business behavior, substantial economic growth is not likely to occur because the production process will remain too inefficient and economic relationships too undependable.

These standards of business performance are much less tangible and more difficult to inculate than are those relating to the physical characteristics of parts and finished products, for they are direct reflections of the most basic values and attitudes of a society. Preindustrial societies do not generally attach high value to productive labor per se, to disciplined, interdependent teamwork, to impersonal institutional loyalties, and to regularity of attendance at repetitive routine work tasks and their conscious and conscientious performance. The transition to the kind of "puritan ethic" required for a modern industrial system—whether capitalistic or socialistic—is neither easy nor rapid, as the industrializations of Western Europe, the United States, Soviet Russia, and Japan have each proved in different ways. Brazil as a whole is as yet in the earlier stages of this profound transformation, though it has already gone quite far in the industrially more advanced parts of the country.

. . . in Brazil GE was one of the pioneers and hence its influence in disseminating such standards of business performance has been of proportionately greater importance. In part, this effect has been the natural and inevitable result of GE's own operations. However, it has also been the result of a deliberate and conscious effort by the Company to set a good example.

. . . . .

Development of people. . . . In the writer's experience, there is no aspect of a U.S.-owned company's activities abroad that is more closely watched in lesser developed countries than its practice with respect to the training and promotion of the local people. Other considerations being equal, the degree of local acceptance of a foreign business firm varies directly with the extent to which it provides its local employees with opportunities to acquire technical and managerial skills and to rise to any position for which they can qualify. A foreign company may be making outstanding contributions in many other ways to the advancement of the host country; but unless it is also training the local people and promoting them to positions of responsibility, those contributions are likely to be overlooked or belittled.

While it is well known in Brazil that GE is U.S.-owned, only the rabid nationalists and crypto-Communists have tried—hitherto without much success—to use this fact as a means of attacking the Company. The vast majority of Brazilians regard GE as a Brazilianized —even if not a Brazilian—organization because, in their relations with it at whatever managerial level and on whatever technical or business problem, they deal almost exclusively with fellow countrymen who have the authority to make decisions and the competence to carry them out. And, because the Company is so regarded, its policies and practices are accorded a degree of respect which would otherwise be unattainable.

It was by no means easy for GE to implement its Brazilianization policy effectively. Considerable difficulties had to be overcome in developing local people capable of filling skilled and responsible positions. These obstacles are not simply the lack of education and training but, more importantly, they reflect more fundamental cultural differences, already noted, which affect local attitudes toward work and modern factory or office disciplines, the relative values attached to monetary and nonmonetary compensations and to material consumption as compared with other kinds of satisfactions, and the prevailing public, business, and personal moralities. . . .

For its part, the Company has obligations to its affiliates and shareholders in the United States which it cannot ever disregard. It must operate in an efficient enough manner to preserve the capital invested and sooner or later to earn reasonable profits. It must conform to the laws and regulations of the host country as well as to those of the U.S. government, where they apply. . . .

These two sets of considerations combine to complicate the adoption and effective carrying out of a policy of training local people for the higher-level technical and managerial positions. Nonetheless, many companies have successfully overcome the obstacles involved and more U.S. enterprises are now making determined efforts to do so. Among the former, General Electric has been one of the pioneers, not only in Brazil but in other countries where it operates. . . .

. . . . .

Another reason for GE's popularity in Brazil has been the fact that its solicitude for the development of its people has not been focused mainly upon the upper technical and managerial levels. The Company has been equally concerned to advance its unskilled and semiskilled workers—the great bulk of its employees. For example, after the factory at Santo André was completed, the unskilled and semiskilled construction workers who built it were offered the opportunity to stay on with the Company and learn to fill factory jobs in which their earning power would substantially increase. Many construction workers availed themselves of this offer and today constitute a higher-skilled and higher-income group than those who declined. Another example is the comparatively large number of blind and other physically handicapped Brazilians whom GE has deliberately hired and trained for skilled jobs. . . .

. . . . .

[The authors conclude with a discussion of the outlook for GE in Brazil. *Ed.*]

XV • ECONOMIC SYSTEMS AND IDEOLOGIES

Here is a document that changed world history. It was written for that purpose. Designed to foment revolt, it first appeared at the time of widespread social discontent that erupted into a series of revolutions in the Europe of 1848. Moreover, it was to remain a key element in the growing body of Marxian literature which finally helped bring the establishment of Communism in Russia. Though written long before Marx completed his Capital, *the massive work which embodied the results of decades of research, the* Manifesto *contains the major themes of Marxist ideology.*

78 • The Communist Manifesto

KARL MARX
FRIEDRICH ENGELS

A spectre is haunting Europe—the spectre of Communism. All the Powers of old Europe have entered into a Holy Alliance to exorcise this spectre; Pope and Czar, Metternich and Guizot, French Radicals and German police-spies.

Two things result from this . . .

I. Communismn is already acknowledged by all European Powers to be itself a Power.

II. It is high time that Communists should openly, in the face of the whole world, publish their views, their aims, their tendencies, and meet this nursery tale of the Spectre of Communism with a Manifesto of the party itself.

To this end, Communists of various nationalities have assembled in London and sketched the following Manifesto, to be published in the English, French, German, Italian, Flemish, and Danish languages.

I. Bourgeois and Proletarians

The history of all hitherto existing society is the history of class struggles.

Freeman and slave, patrician and plebian, lord and serf, guildmaster and journeyman, in a word, oppressor and oppressed, stood in constant opposition to one another, carried on uninterrupted, now hidden, now open fight, a fight that each time ended, either in a revolutionary reconstitution of society at large, or in the common ruin of the contending classes.

. . . . .

The modern bourgeois society that has sprouted from the ruins of feudal society has not done away with class antagonisms. It has but established new classes, new conditions of oppres-

---

KARL MARX and FRIEDRICH ENGELS, *The Manifesto of the Communist Party* (1848).

sion, new forms of struggle in place of the old ones.

Our epoch, the epoch of the bourgeoisie, possesses, however, this distinctive feature; it has simplified the class antagonisms. Society as a whole is more and more splitting up into two great hostile camps, into two great classes directly facing each other: Bourgeoisie and Proletariat.

. . . . .

The feudal system of industry, under which industrial production was monopolized by close guilds, now no longer sufficed for the growing wants of the new market. The manufacturing system took its place. The guildmasters were pushed on one side by the manufacturing middle class; division of labor between the different corporate guilds vanished in the face of division of labor in each single workshop.

Meantime the markets kept ever growing, the demand ever rising. Even manufacture no longer sufficed. Thereupon, steam and machinery revolutionized industrial production. The place of manufacture was taken by the giant Modern Industry, the place of the industrial middle-class, by industrial millionaires, the leaders of whole industrial armies, the modern bourgeois.

Modern industry has established the world-market, for which the discovery of America paved the way. This market has given an immense development to commerce, to navigation, to communication by land. This development has, in its turn, reacted on the extension of industry; and in proportion as industry, commerce, navigation, railways extended, in the same proportion the bourgeoisie developed, increased its capital, and pushed into the background every class handed down from the Middle Ages.

We see, therefore, how the modern bourgeoisie is itself the product of a long course of development, of a series of revolutions in the modes of production and of exchange. . . .

The bourgeoisie cannot exist without constantly revolutionizing the instruments of production, and thereby the relations of production, and with them the whole relations of society. Conservation of the old modes of production in unaltered form was, on the contrary, the first condition of existence for all earlier industrial classes. Constant revolutionizing of production, uninterrupted disturbance of all social conditions, everlasting uncertainty and agitation distinguish the bourgeois epoch from all earlier ones. . . .

The need of a constantly expanding market for its products drives the bourgeoisie over the whole surface of the globe. . . .

. . . It [the bourgeoisie] compels all nations, on pain of extinction, to adopt the bourgeois mode of production; it compels them to introduce what it calls civilization into their midst, i.e., to become bourgeois themselves. In a word, it creates a world after its own image.

. . . . .

The bourgeoisie, during its rule of scarce one hundred years, has created more massive and more colossal productive forces than have all preceding generations together. Subjection of nature's forces to man, machinery, application of chemistry to industry and agriculture, steam-navigation, railways, electric telegraphs, clearing of whole continents for cultivation, canalization of rivers, whole populations conjured out of the ground—what earlier century had even a presentiment that such productive forces slumbered in the lap of social labor?

We see then the means of production and of exchange on whose foundation the bourgeoisie built itself up were generated in feudal society. At a certain stage in the development of these means of production and of exchange, the conditions under which feudal society produced and exchanged, the feudal organization of agriculture and manufacturing industry—in one word, the feudal relations of property—became no longer compatible with the already developed productive forces; they became so many fetters. They had to burst asunder; they were burst asunder.

Into their places stepped free competition, accompanied by a social and political constitution adapted to it, and by the economical and political sway of the bourgeois class.

A similar movement is going on before our own eyes. Modern bourgeois society with its relations of production, of exchange, and of property, a society that has conjured up such gigantic means of production and of exchange, is like the sorcerer, who is no longer able to control the powers of the nether world whom he has called up by his spells. For many a decade past, the history of industry and commerce is but the history of the revolt of modern productive forces against modern conditions of production, against the property relations that are the conditions for the existence of the bourgeoisie and of its rule. It is enough to mention the commercial crises that by their periodical return put on its trial, each time more threateningly, the existence of the entire bourgeois society. In these crises a great part not only of the existing products, but also of the previously created productive forces, are periodically destroyed. In these crises there breaks out an epidemic that, in all earlier epochs, would have seemed an absurdity—the epidemic of overproduction. Society suddenly finds itself put back into a state of momentary barbarism; it appears as if a famine, a universal war of devastation, had cut off the supply of every means of subsistence; industry and commerce seem to be destroyed; and why? Because there is too much civilization, too much means of subsistence, too much industry, too much commerce. The productive forces at the disposal of society no longer tend to further the development of the conditions of bourgeois property; on the contrary, they have become too powerful for these conditions by which they are confined, and as soon as they overcome these limitations they bring disorder into the whole of bourgeois society, endanger the existence of bourgeois property. The conditions of bourgeois society are too narrow to comprise the wealth created by them. And how does the bourgeoisie get over these crises? On the one hand by enforced destruction of a mass of productive forces; on the other, by the conquest of new markets, and by the more thorough exploitation of the old ones. That is to say, by paving the way for more extensive and more destructive crises, and by diminishing the means whereby crises are prevented.

The weapons with which the bourgeoisie felled feudalism to the ground are now turned against the bourgeoisie itself.

But not only has the bourgeoisie forged the weapons that bring death to itself; it has also called into existence the men who are to wield those weapons—the modern working class—the proletarians.

In proportion as the bourgeoisie—that is, as capital—is developed, in the same proportion as the proletariat, the modern working class, developed, a class of laborers who live only so long as they find work, and who find work only so long as their labor increases capital. These laborers, who must sell themselves piecemeal, are a commodity, like every other article of commerce, and are consequently exposed to all the vicissitudes of competition, to all the fluctuations of the market.

Owing to the extensive use of machinery and to division of labor, the work of the proletarians has lost all individual character, and consequently, all charm for the workman. He becomes an appendage of the machine, and it is only the most simple, most monotonous, and most easily acquired knack that is required of him. Hence, the cost of production of a workman is restricted almost entirely to the means of subsistence that he requires for his maintenance, and for the propagation of his race. But the price of a commodity, and also of labor, is equal to its cost of production. In proportion, therefore, as the repulsiveness of the work increases the wage decreases. Nay more, in proportion as the use of machinery and division of labor increase, in the same proportion the burden of toil increases, whether by prolongation of the working hours, by increase of the work enacted in a given time, or by increased speed of the machinery, and so forth.

. . . . .

The less the skill and exertion or strength implied in manual labor, in other words, the more modern industry becomes developed, the more is the labor of men superseded by that of women. Differences of age and sex have no longer any distinctive social validity for the working class. All are instruments of labor, more or less expensive to use, according to their age and sex.

No sooner is the exploitation of the laborer by the manufacturer so far at an end that he receives his wages in cash, than he is set upon by the other portions of the bourgeoisie, the landlord, the shopkeeper, the pawnbroker, and so forth.

The lower strata of the middle class —the small tradespeople, shopkeepers and retired tradesmen generally, the handicraftsmen and peasants—all these sink gradually into the proletariat, partly because their diminutive capital does not suffice for the scale on which modern industry is carried on, and is swamped in the competition with the large capitalists, partly because their specialized skill is rendered worthless by new methods of production. Thus the proletariat is recruited from all classes of the population.

The proletariat goes through various stages of development. With its birth begins its struggle with the bourgeoisie. At first the contest is carried on by individual laborers, then by the workpeople of a factory, then by the operatives of one trade, in one locality, against the individual bourgeois who directly exploits them. They direct their attacks not against the bourgeois conditions of production, but against the instruments of production themselves; they destroy imported wares that compete with their labor, they smash machinery, they set factories ablaze, they seek to restore by force the vanished status of the workman of the Middle Ages.

At this stage the laborers still form an incoherent mass scattered over the whole country, and broken up by their mutual competition. . . .

But with the development of industry the proletariat not only increases in number; it becomes concentrated in greater masses, its strength grows and it feels that strength more. The various interests and conditions of life within the ranks of the proletariat are more and more equalized, in proportion as machinery obiterates all distinctions of labor, and nearly everywhere reduces wages to the same low level. The growing competition among the bourgeois, and the resulting commercial crises, make the wages of the workers ever more fluctuating; the unceasing improvement of machinery, ever more rapidly developing, makes their livelihood more and more precarious; the collisions between individual workmen and individual bourgeois take more and more the character of collisions between two classes. Thereupon the workers begin to form combinations (trade unions) against the bourgeois; they club together in order to keep up the rate of wages; they found permanent associations in order to make provision beforehand for these occasional revolts. Here and there the contest breaks out into riots.

Now and then the workers are victorious, but only for a time. The real fruit of their battle lies not in the immediate result, but in the ever-expanding union of workers. This union is helped on by the improved means of communication that are created by modern industry, and that places the workers of different localities in contact with one another. It was just this contact that was needed to centralize the numerous local struggles, all of the same character, into one national struggle between classes. But every class struggle is a political struggle. And that union, to attain which the burghers of the Middle Ages with their miserable highways, required centuries, the modern proletarians, thanks to railways, achieve in a few years.

This organization of the proletarians into a class, and consequently into a political party, is continually being upset again by the competition between the workers themselves. But it ever rises up again, stronger, firmer, mightier. It compels legislative recognition of particular interests of the workers by taking advantage of the divisions among the bourgeoisie itself. Thus the Ten-Hours-Bill in England was carried.

Altogether collisions between the classes of the old society further, in many ways, the development of the proletariat. The bourgeoisie finds itself involved in a constant battle—at first with the aristocracy; later on, with those portions of the bourgeoisie itself whose interests have become antagonistic to the progress of industry; at all times, with the bourgeoisie of foreign countries. In all these battles it sees itself compelled to appeal to the proletariat, to ask for its help, and thus to drag it into the political arena. The bourgeoisie itself, therefore, supplies the proletariat with its own elements of political and general education; in other words, it furnishes the proletariat with weapons for fighting the bourgeoisie.

Further, as we have already seen, entire sections of the ruling classes are, by the advance of industry, precipitated into the proletariat, or at least threatened in their conditions of existence. These also supply the proletariat with fresh elements of enlightenment and progress.

Finally, in times when the class struggle nears the decisive hour, the process of dissolution going on within the ruling class, in fact within the whole range of an old society, assumes such a violent, glaring character that a small section of the ruling class cuts itself adrift and joins the revolutionary class, the class that holds the future in its hands. Just as, therefore, at an earlier period, a section of the nobility went over to the bourgeoisie, so now a portion of the bourgeoisie goes over to the proletariat, and in particular, a portion of the bourgeois ideologists, who have raised themselves to the level of comprehending theoretically the historical movements as a whole.

Of all the classes that stand face to face with the bourgeoisie today the proletariat alone is a really revolutionary class. The other classes decay and finally disappear in the face of modern industry; the proletariat is its special and essential product.

The lower middle class, the small manufacturer, the shopkeeper, the artisan, the peasant, all these fight against the bourgeoisie, to save from extinction their existence as fractions of the middle class. They are therefore not revolutionary, but conservative. Nay, more; they are reactionary, for they try to roll back the wheel of history. If by chance they are revolutionary, they are so only in view of their impending transfer into the proletariat; they thus defend not their present, but their future interests; they desert their own standpoint to place themselves at that of the proletariat.

. . . . .

. . . The proletarian is without property; his relation to his wife and children has no longer anything in common with the bourgeois family relations; modern industrial labor, modern subjection to capital, the same in England as in France, in America as in Germany, has stripped him of every trace of national character, Law, morality, religion, are to him so many bourgeois prejudices, behind which lurk in ambush just as many bourgeois interests.

All the preceding classes that got the upper hand sought to fortify their already acquired status by subjecting society at large to their conditions of appropriation. The proletarians cannot become masters of the productive forces of society, except by abolishing their own previous mode of appropriation, and thereby also every other previous mode of appropriation. They have nothing of their own to secure and to fortify; their mission is to destroy all previous securities for and insurances of individual property.

All previous historical movements were movements of minorities, or in the interest of minorities. The proletarian movement is the self-conscious, independent movement of the immense majority. The proletariat, the lowest stratum of our present society, cannot stir, cannot raise itself up without the whole superincumbent strata of official society being sprung into the air.

Though not in substance, yet in form, the struggle of the proletariat with the bourgeoisie is at first a national struggle. The proletariat of each country must, of course, first of all settle matters with its own bourgeoisie.

In depicting the most general phases of the development of the proletariat, we have traced the more or less veiled civil war, raging within existing society, up to the point where that war breaks out into open revolution, and where the violent overthrow of the bourgeoisie lays the foundation for the sway of the proletariat.

Hitherto every form of society has been based, as we have already seen, on the antagonism of oppressing and oppressed classes. But in order to oppress a class, certain conditions must be assured to it under which it can at least continue its slavish existence. The serf, in the period of serfdom, raised himself to membership in the commune, just as the petty bourgeois, under the yoke of feudal absolutism, managed to develop into a bourgeois. The modern laborer, on the contrary, instead of rising with the progress of industry, sinks deeper and deeper below the conditions of existence of his own class. He becomes a pauper, and pauperism develops more rapidly than population and wealth. And here it becomes evident that the bourgeoisie is unfit any longer to be the ruling class in society, and to impose its conditions of existence upon society as an overriding law. It is unfit to rule, because it is incompetent to assure an existence to its slave within his slavery, because it cannot help letting him sink into such a state that it has to feed him, instead of being fed by him. Society can no longer live under this bourgeoisie; in other words, its existence is no longer compatible with society.

The essential condition for the existence, and for the sway of the bourgeois class, is the formation and augmentation of capital; the condition for capital is wage labor. Wage labor rests exclusively on competition between the laborers. The advance of industry, whose involuntary promoter is the bourgeoisie, replaces the isolation of the laborers, due to competition, by their revolutionary combination, due to association. The development of modern industry, therefore, cuts from under its feet the very foundation on which the bourgeoisie produces and appropriates products. What the bourgeoisie therefore produces, above all, are its own grave diggers. Its fall and the victory of the proletariat are equally inevitable.

II. Proletarians and Communists

In what relation do the Communists stand to the proletarians as a whole?

The Communists do not form a separate party opposed to other working-class parties.

They have no interests separate and apart from those of the proletariat as a whole.

They do not set up any sectarian principles of their own, by which to shape and mould the proletarian movement.

The Communists are distinguished from the other working class parties by this only: (1) In the national struggles of the proletarians of the different countries, they point out and bring to the front the common interests of the entire proletariat, independently of all nationality. (2) In the various stages of development which the struggle of the working class against the bourgeoisie has to pass through, they always and everywhere represent the interests of the movement as a whole. . . .

The immediate aim of the Communists is the same as that of all the other proletarian parties—formation of the proletariat into a class, overthrow of the bourgeois supremacy, conquest of political power by the proletariat. . . .

The proletariat will use its political supremacy to wrest, by degrees, all capital from the bourgeoisie, to centralize all instruments of production in the hands of the state—that is, of the proletariat organized as a ruling class; and to increase the total productive forces as rapidly as possible. . . .

When, in the course of development, class distinctions have disappeared, and all production has been concentrated in the hands of a vast association of the whole nation, the public power will lose its political character. Political power, properly so called, is merely the organized power of one class for oppressing another. If the proletariat during its contest with the bourgeoisie is compelled, by the force of circumstances, to organize itself as a class, if, by means of a revolution, it makes itself the ruling class, and, as such, sweeps away by force the old conditions of production, then it will, along with these conditions, have swept away the conditions for the existence of class antagonisms, and of classes generally, and will thereby have abolished its own supremacy as a class.

In place of the old bourgeois society, with its classes and class antagonisms, we shall have an association in which the free development of each is the condition for the free development of all. . . .

The Communists disdain to conceal their views and aims. They openly declare that their ends can be attained only by the forcible overthrow of all existing social conditions. Let the ruling classes tremble at a Communistic revolutions. The proletarians have nothing to lose but their chains. They have a world to win.

Working men of all countries, unite!

A group of economists from the United States visited Russia in the summer of 1960. Portions of the reports of two of them are given here. Professor Grossman teaches at the University of California and Professor Bond at Michigan State University.

79 · American Economists Report on Russia

GREGORY GROSSMAN

· · · · ·

The forces pressing for decentralization within the Soviet centrally directed (nonmarket) economy would seem to be strong and growing. They stem from successes so far attained as well as from a realization of past mistakes. Thus the very growth of the economy is continuously augmenting the costs of extreme centralization as it rapidly increases the range of choices to be made, the number of products to be considered, and the multitude of interconnections to be kept in mind by the central authorities. Greater reliance on indigenous technology calls for local decisions, while the rising level of competence of managerial and technical staffs renders it at once less necessary and more difficult to curtail their powers. And, lastly, the growing attention to the satisfaction of consumer needs, qualitatively as well as quantitatively, demands greater decentralization in this area, to provide better and faster transmission of consumer desires to the actual producers and prompter reaction by them.

Yet the centralizing forces continue to assert themselves too. While the military, economic, and political contest with the West continues at a high pitch, the Soviet economy's resources continue to be heavily committed and even over-committed (though less pronouncedly so than before), the strong central controls persist in order to insure their purposeful and priority-directed employment. Moreover, so long as the market is not given much play, central controls continue to be indispensable to maintain some correspondence between supply and effective demand.

· · · · ·

We had several discussions that threw light on the growing importance of consumer demand in the determination of production programs and in the thinking of managers and administrators. An official of the Moscow city *sovnarkhoz* [regional economic council] put it concisely when he said, with some emphasis, "Before, we simply distributed consumer goods; now we have to sell

---

GREGORY GROSSMAN, "Planning, Backbone of a Nation" and FLOYD A. BOND, "The USSR's Organization Man," from a symposium in *The Saturday Review* (January 21, 1961). Used by permission.

them." The same person told us that the *sovnarkhoz* would like to establish its own retail outlets for the marketing of its consumer goods, so as better to acquaint customers with its products and to sell them more effectively.

. . . . .

On several occasions we were told in some detail of the major role played by the Ministry of Trade or one of its wholesaling organizations in the determination of the assortment of consumer goods produced. This is not an entirely new role but it may well be rising in importance. It seems that Gosplan and other planning authorities set the factory's production plan in rather broad terms: so many tons of soap or of candy, or so many pairs of hose, for the year. These targets must be met, but within each category the detailed production program is largely determined by the quarterly orders submitted beforehand by the wholesale distributors. The exact assortment is apparently negotiated between the parent *sovnarkhoz* and the wholesalers' representatives, with only indirect participation by the factory. The individual factory's quarterly production plan is then adjusted to conform to the results of these negotiations.

Our attempts to have further light shed on this process were not very successful. To what extent is the *sovnarkhoz* active or passive in its negotiations with the wholesalers? One can easily imagine the distributors adjusting themselves to the producers' convenience, rather than the producers responding appropriately to demand; indeed, traditionally the former has been common in the Soviet economy, though some redressing of the balance may be under way. Other difficulties may be expected to arise from a hybrid process in which each element imposes its own—and often incompatible—incentives and criteria of success. The Soviet press continues to bear testimony that all is not working smoothly in this respect.

. . . . .

The *sovnarkhoz* is the closest thing to a "firm" in Soviet industry, although it is of course neither independent nor autonomous in any real sense. The individual factory (or "enterprise," as it is often called with dubious accuracy) is still limited in its powers largely to the technical side of production. The *sovnarkhoz*, on the other hand, not only has very broad powers over the same technical matters, but also appoints (or confirms the appointment of) the enterprise's top personnel; to a substantial extent determines its production program (though within the broad targets laid down from above); takes an active hand in the introduction of new products and processes, and in the setting of prices for new products; reshuffles funds, equipment, materials, and to some extent also personnel, within its jurisdiction; negotiates in a commercial way with other *sovnarkhozes* (city industrial administrations); arranges for the supply of scarce materials; conducts research and checks on the quality of products. It also takes an active part in long-term planning for the region—as for instance the long-term shift away from heavy equipment and toward precision equipment in the city of Moscow that was decided upon by higher authorities on the *sovnarkhoz*'s initiative.

Thus the *sovnarkhoz* exercises very close and detailed control over its enterprises, which it carries out primarily through its major subdivisions, the product-line "chief administrations." The range of industries under a *sovnarkhoz* is typically very wide, and the gross value of its industrial output is of the order of ten billion rubles per year on the average, with the largest regions accounting for many times as much. Consequently, even the hundred-plus *sovnarkhozy* in the country would not seem to be too many for the "span of control" of each, and it is not surprising that in the Ukraine, which accounts for about one-fifth of the USSR's industrial production but until recently had only one-tenth of the *sovnarkhozy,* their number was recently raised from eleven to fourteen.

The undependability of supply, especially in earlier years, has contributed to autarchic attitudes on all levels. But while the supply situation may have eased considerably in recent years—and we were so informed in a few places —the very growth of the economy leads, under Soviet conditions, to regional autarchy because it makes it increasingly difficult to plan and control the economic machinery from a single center. Willy-nilly the problem of central direction is being farmed out to the republics and provinces, in a process that can be better termed "deconcentration" than "decentralization." The republic becomes the main operative level in this connection, and its Gosplan the key organ. The relations among republics are beginning to resemble a system of multilateral barter, with the union (federal) Gosplan acting as the central clearing house and arbiter, and with a good deal of bargaining.

The process of annual plan construction was described to us by Mr. Ziiadullaev, the young and obviously able chairman of the Gosplan of Uzbekistan. His organization begins the formal annual planning process upon receipt of so-called Approximate Estimates (*primernye priderzhki*) early in June from Gosplan in Moscow. These indicate by way of first approximation the amounts of certain major commodities, some forty or fifty in all, to be produced by, supplied from the outside to, and (apparently) supplied to the other regions by Uzbekistan. This is followed by a meeting of the heads of all republic Gosplans at the union Gosplan, which our host openly described as a bargaining session. This in term is followed by a set of similar Approximate Estimates passed down by the Uzbek Gosplan to the Uzbek *sovnarkhoz* (there is only one for the republic) and to other economic-administrative entities. Presumably a bargaining session on this level takes place next. By July 1 the *sovnarkhoz* submits its draft plan for the next year to the republic Gosplan, and the latter submits its draft plan to Moscow by August 10. In September or October the republic's plan for the next year is supposed to be confirmed by Moscow, and the individual enterprise is to be informed of its annual plan in November, at least according to the timetable. Throughout the discussion our host stressed the key role of supply. The union Gosplan distributes allocations for scarce commodities to the republic Gosplans. These in turn allocate to the *sovnarkhozy* under them, and they allocate to the individual enterprises. One infers that the bargaining at all levels revolves largely around the supply allocations: "I can give more of this if you give me more of that."

FLOYD A. BOND

. . . . .

To provide effective incentives to management, a complicated system of monthly bonuses (called "premia") is used in addition to highly unequal base salaries.

Whereas the average monthly factory

wage is probably in the neighborhood of 800 rubles, plant managers normally receive from 3,000 to 5,000 rubles.

The manager of the Kirov "Electrosila" Works in Leningrad, which has about 10,000 employees, receives a base salary of 5,000 rubles a month. Judging from the data we received from the Leningrad regional economic council, which supervises more than 600 plants in the region, this would be at the top of their range.

To this would be added the bonuses for plan fulfillment, cost reduction, and the like, which could increase income by as much as 50 to 100 per cent.

In addition, a plant manager may live in a large apartment, have the use of a factory-owned automobile and the convenience of an expense account, possibly get part or all of his vacation free, and enjoy the prestige and other privileges that go with his position.

If, on the other hand, he fails to achieve the production goal set for him —and from one-fifth to one-third of the industrial plant managers do fail—he may be demoted, fired, or perhaps even prosecuted for "crimes" against the state, for which he may be imprisoned or suffer a worse fate.

Thus private economic gain is the main incentive to managerial efficiency in the Soviet Union.

But does this mean that the Soviet system has solved the problem of effective managerial incentives in the social interest in a society that does not permit private ownership of the means of production and that looks upon profits as arising solely from the exploitation of labor?

A negative answer seems inescapable. Bonuses based on plan fulfillment and similar "success indicators," even those adopted in the 1960 Soviet decree, are not adequate substitutes for the all-inclusive profit test. Whether the production target is set in terms of weight, volume, acres, value, or number of units, there is a strong incentive to fulfill the production quota in ways that are not socially desirable. It is easy to say that the product specifications will be controlled, but our own war experience indicates that this is easier said than done. And in any case such control takes resources away from other productive pursuits.

Perhaps the greatest social cost of this incentive system is the strong inducement to sacrifice quality in order to achieve greater quantity. This is a particularly serious problem in the Soviet system. In fact, since no bonus at all is paid top officials if output falls short of the mark even by as little as 5 per cent, a powerful stimulus often exists to reduce quality in order to increase quantity. This may be, and is, done in several ways. It is undoubtedly one of the reasons for the inferior quality of most Soviet goods.

Moreover, this incentive system may retard the rate of economic growth by holding down the rate of technological progress. Innovations are to be avoided unless they can be quickly adopted without disrupting current production. Long-run cost considerations are subordinate to short-run output considerations.

The incentive system also encourages falsification of records, the hoarding of labor and supplies, and numerous "unusual activities" such as "concealing" output one month to carry it over to the next, "borrowing" output that will be produced next month to meet this month's quota, working the employees on Sunday and giving them a day off during the month following, bribing the right people. The high premium placed on achieving the production goal is a strong inducement to breaking rules, cutting corners, even engaging in illegal activities, in spite of the danger of being caught and the severity of the penalties that may follow.

Yet, though they run risks and work long and hard, these men are not really the masters of their own souls. Herein, in my judgment, lies the greatest weakness of the Soviet system. People lack the basic security needed to liberate the spirit.

To be really free, and to exercise that freedom even in criticism of leading officials, one must have a status that cannot easily be destroyed by those officials. In our system, that security has rested upon at least two conditions: the ownership of property, and the existence of numerous employers—outside the control of the officials.

Without these two cornerstones of our civilization, I seriously doubt that economic and political freedom, as we know it, would and could exist. These freedoms have certainly given a quality to American life and culture which is strikingly absent in the Soviet Union. Americans value the spirit of life above the quantity of production—though the evidence does not yet indicate that a society needs to choose between them.

How could a plant manager operate efficiently in a tightly controlled, highly centralized, rigidly planned industrial system? Will not the surprises, the unforeseen contingencies, that are inevitable in the world of interdependent functions upset parts of every schedule, at least a little, creating ever more trouble for other managers? An economist who has specialized on Soviet affairs discusses these and other questions shortly after his return from an extended visit to Russia.

80 · How Soviet Industrial Managers Do Business

HARRY SCHWARTZ

Soviet industry is now going through the most massive reorganization of modern times. For three decades it has been a highly centralized organism. Now this vast enterprise is being changed over to a system of regional control which, the Kremlin hopes, will give much more room for initiative at the grass roots.

Anyone who has met typical Soviet executives, as has this writer, knows that they are not to be dismissed lightly. They are tough; they are smart; they get things done. We can understand why the Soviet press complains from time to time that they show little interest in Marxist theory. The niceties of dialectical materialism hardly touch the Soviet organization men, who have one harsh criterion: results.

. . . . .

The . . . vast majority of Soviet organization men . . . came from humble origins. Their decisive move forward

HARRY SCHWARTZ, "The Organization Man Soviet Style," *The New York Times Magazine* (June 2, 1957), pp. 9ff. Used by permission.

came when they received some kind of advanced technical or engineering training. They had little or no formal training in production economics or managerial skills, but learned on the job by watching their superiors operate. They won promotion by showing on the job that they could deliver on production assignments. And, although seldom active as political theoreticians, they have always been politically reliable.

In all this the production bias of the Soviet economy is clearly evident. One looks in vain among higher Soviet industrial executives for the lawyer, the salesman, the specialist in corporate finance, or the advertising or merchandising expert—types one meets so frequently among American executives. The typical Soviet organization man is an engineer or technician of some sort, one who knows how things are made and has been successful at making them. . . .

. . . . .

The fledgling Soviet executive may get on the first rung of the managerial ladder in a variety of ways. He may be a worker who shows more alertness and intelligence than his fellows so that he is promoted to foreman. If he is an honor graduate of the Bauman Technical Institute in Moscow—an institution which in practice has the combined prestige we attach to, say, the Massachusetts Institute of Technology and the Wharton School—many organizations will compete for his services. If his father knows the right people, that can be a big help in getting a good start. The Russians call the latter practice *semeistvenmost*—nepotism—and it is as ubiquitous in the Soviet Union as it used to be in Czarist Russia.

Mounting the rungs of the ladder depends, of course, on ability and performance, but having the right connections and being on good terms with your boss also helps, as in other societies.

The Russians use the term *Allilushchiki*, which means literally hallelujah-criers or more colloquially yes-men, to designate those who try to get ahead in the latter fashion. But there are limits to how far sycophancy alone can carry a man, for eventually the test of results must always be met.

The motivation of Soviet managers is also clear. It is the desire for power and for material comfort which moves men everywhere. In every plant this writer visited in Russia the power of top executives and the gap between them and the workers were immediately apparent. Walking through the Kharkov Tractor Factory with an assistant director, for example, I noticed that every worker we passed took off his hat or made a slight bow as a gesture of respect. . . .

The very dress of these officials—their relatively well-cut suits and the fact that they wore ties while workers normally do not—gave mute testimony in every plant that the *khozyain*, or boss, was a man apart, a figure respected and feared. . . .

. . . . .

For the past several decades, the typical Soviet executive—say, the director of the Magnitogorsk Iron and Steel Combine or the head of Kuibyshev Airplane Factory No. 1 has been the man in the middle. Above him has been the vast centralized directing and planning apparatus in Moscow, an aparatus which tried to bind him hand and foot, to give him orders on the most detailed matters. Below him have been his subordinate executives and his workers, over whom he has virtually absolute powers under the Soviet managerial principle of *edinonachalye*, one-man rule.

Before him always have been the planned production targets for his enterprise. If those targets were reached or exceeded, he received commendations, rich bonuses and promotion. If those targets were not reached, he received reprimands, faced the possibility of demotion or, in the Nineteen Thirties, even trial and punishment as an "economic saboteur." His has not been too enviable a position.

Looked at superficially, this harsh—and to American executives, strange—system has worked. Soviet production has grown enormously and is still growing. But, as Khrushchev has made clear in recent statements, it worked very inefficiently and in many respects even irrationally. . . .

It is no exaggeration to say that something approaching chaos is the reality behind the outwardly serene appearance of a smoothly functioning, planned Soviet economy. Plans often do not reach those concerned until weeks or months after they are supposed to, and then the plans are frequently changed with dizzying rapidity. Materials and parts often do not arrive in time. Labor is short. The harsh Russian winter often paralyzes the Soviet transportation system and makes mockery of earlier calculations. Yet none of these factors is acceptable as an excuse for not fulfilling the plan.

The only way out, Soviet executives learned long ago, is to break through the bonds of the formal system and operate in as free-wheeling a manner as the most resourceful entrepreneur of a capitalist society. It is the resourcefulness, the ingenuity and—not infrequently—the dishonesty of the Soviet organization man that makes the Soviet economy work despite all the blunders of the planners and administrators above him.

As his opening move, a manager may use what might be called plansmanship. This is simply the effort to get the lowest plan targets possible for his plant. An experienced plant director will calculate, say, that during the next year his factory can produce 1,000,000 ball bearings. He will then suggest that the plan be set at 700,000 units, hoping that in the ensuing bargaining and negotiations he will have his goal raised to only 800,000 or 900,000 ball bearings. . . .

How well a manager will do at plansmanship, as well as in many other areas of his job, depends on his *blat*. *Blat* is virtually untranslatable, but roughly it means influence or pull. A crude way to get *blat* is to do a discreet job of bribery. More usually, however, it is a matter of reciprocal favors, of getting one's superiors and equals obligated to one for past kindnesses.

Once the plan has been worked out and operations on it begun, the manager faces the problem of getting raw materials. He knows that he cannot count on deliveries always arriving on time, nor on the delivered goods always meeting specifications. Rather, he must be constantly on the lookout for emergencies caused by shortages which may halt the production line and imperil the plan.

To solve the problem of shortages, the manager has three weapons:

One is *blat*. If he needs a ton of copper urgently, for example, he may be able to get it from somebody whom he once helped out with a ton of aluminum. Or he may have a friend in the copper distribution apparatus who can be appealed to for help on the ground that the manager once gave the friend's brother-in-law a job. Or he phones his ministerial superiors in Moscow to get them to divert copper from another plant in the same ministry. . . .

But if *blat* cannot solve the problem, then perhaps the manager's *tolkach* can. Here is the indispensable man in the Soviet economy, though technically he is illegal. . . .

The *tolkach* is a fixer, a five-percenter, an operator. He knows where to find ten tons of natural rubber or a hundred essential spare parts when everybody who is legally empowered to supply such things swears on the works of Lenin that they are completely unavailable. The *tolkach* has friends in every factory that is likely to interest his clients.

He has mysterious ways of knowing when and where scarce goods arrive, when and where they are delayed en route. He knows where there is a surplus of this and a deficit of that, and who is willing to sell or swap at any given moment. In order to help bring supply and demand into balance, he sometimes executes deals of fantastic complexity, all outside the framework of the plan, which does not even recognize his existence. He is the free enterprise leaven in a chaotic "planned" economy, and he collects high fees for his services.

But neither *blat* nor the *tolkach* is infallible, so in self-preservation the typical Soviet executive behaves like a squirrel. He accumulates whatever he can—raw materials, parts, workers. He reasons that one can never have too much of anything, whereas a shortage can bring disaster. There are, of course, strict rules against such hoarding, but the smart manager has long since found ways to get around the rules, often by simply falsifying his records. In this he needs the cooperation of his chief bookkeeper, who must sign all financial and statistical reports.

The relationship between many a Soviet manager and his chief bookkeeper is suggested by a Soviet anecdote. A manager was interviewing three candidates for the bookkeeper's post and asked them how much two and two were. "Four," answered the first candidate. "Twenty-two," said the second. "How much do you want them to be?" asked the third. The third man got the job.

This instinct for executive self-preservation explains many of the ills of the Soviet economy about which Khrushchev has been complaining. Each Soviet ministry, he lamented, has behaved like an independent empire, taking care of the needs of its own plants and disregarding the needs of others. As a result goods are shipped needlessly thousands of miles, existing production facilities are not used fully while duplicating facilities are built nearby by some other ministry. The reasons, of course, is the fact that each minister also has his plan to meet, so his organization's activities are dedicated to assuring that his plants are properly supplied, regardless of what that means to other parts of the economy.

How will this picture of Soviet managerial operation be changed by the current industrial reorganization? Two factors at least are evident. The old ministries in Moscow have to a large extent been wiped out and are being replaced by ninety-two regional economic councils spread over the face of Russia. In addition, the powers of plant directors and similar executives are being greatly broadened and the old ideal of planning everything from Moscow has been abandoned.

Against the earlier background it is clear that in many respects this new organization simply legalizes what plant managers and other executives were already doing illegally on their own. The old network of informal *blat* relationships between plant executives in a given area is now in effect being formalized in the regional economic councils, which are supposed to secure maximum cooperation of all enterprises in each area.

. . . . .

But it seems probable that, even working at its theoretical best, the new system cannot change entirely the way in which the Soviet organiaztion man operates. The plan, and the compulsions associated with the plan, remain. Each factory director therefore must still put his own plant's interests first. Moreover, a new element that will encourage shady operations has been introduced; each economic region will be under inevitable pressure to put its own interests first, a tendency Khrushchev has already given a name—*mestnichestvo*—or localism.

Thus, it is unlikely that the new organization system by itself can remedy the basic defects of the Soviet system.

Future economic plans can hardly be perfect coordinators of an economy which scorns the market. The Soviet entrepreneur is still shackled by his bureaucratic role and will still lack the freedom that a Western business man has. And perhaps most important, the goal of the Soviet economy will continue to be the production of what Moscow wants it to produce, not what the Soviet consumers want, thus continuing to pose problems that no administrative reshuffle can ever solve.

One of the extensive investigations of the Joint Economic Committee of Congress has consisted of comparisons of our economy with that of Russia. Leading experts prepared detailed studies and discussed the facts and interpretations in testimony which ran to hundreds of pages. One of the experts, a professor at Massachusetts Institute of Technology, was asked to summarize the most significant findings. It is from his report that the points below are taken.

81 · Comparisons of the United States and Soviet Economies

WALT W. ROSTOW

An Overriding Conclusion

. . . . .

I believe I speak for virtually all the panelists who addressed themselves to the implications of their analyses for American policy when I say this: Our dangers do not lie primarily in the size of the Soviet economy or its overall rate of growth. Our dangers lie in a particular allocation of Soviet resources; in particular Soviet policies; in the way we Americans now conceive of our problems on the world scene; and, consequently, in the way we allocate our resources, human and material. . . .

. . . . .

A Summary of Findings

Doing some violence to the meticulously stated conclusions of the panel-

---

WALT W. ROSTOW, "Comparisons of the United States and Soviet Economies," papers submitted before the Subcommittee on Economic Statistics, Joint Economic Committee, Washington, 1959.

ists, the relative position and prospects of the Soviet and American economies may be summarized as follows:

1. Population and working force. Soviet war losses and recent fertility rates set against the rise in the American birth rate have yielded over the past generation a dramatic narrowing in the relative size of the Russian and American populations. Between 1939 and 1959 the Russian margin in population size over the United States decreased from 46 to 18 percent. Although significant shifts in the structure of both populations will occur over the next decade, the gap is not likely to open significantly during this period either for the population as a whole or in those categories most relevant to economic and military activity. . . . it is important for Americans to realize that the old historic image of Russia—as a nation where the population mass was vastly greater than our own—is no longer correct. We are, roughly speaking, two nations of about the same population size. With respect to the two industrial working forces, there is a similar crude equivalence brought about despite the higher participation of females in Soviet economic activity because of the much higher proportion of the American population in nonagricultural pursuits. In attitudes toward productivity, the Soviet Union has moved away from an earlier concentration on manipulating masses of unskilled labor, in a situation of relative manpower abundance, toward a concern with productivity per man more nearly like that which has historically characterized the United States. This shift is dramatized by the reduction in the role of forced labor in the Soviet economy in recent years, and by the emphasis now placed on mechanization and automation in industry.

2. Agriculture. After a long period of notably sluggish productivity in agriculture, Soviet policy has moved with some success to improve incentives and organization and to increase output of higher grade foods. In addition, a radical increase in the use of commercial fertilizers is apparently now under consideration. . . .

3. Capital. The rate of Soviet gross investment (about 25 percent of GNP) is likely to persist and to remain slightly above the American rate (about 20 percent of GNP including Government investment). Recent changes in investment criteria have probably improved somewhat the efficiency of Soviet investment; and the continued concentration of investment in industrial sectors—as opposed to services, transport, etc.—will probably continue to keep the Soviet rate of increase in GNP higher than the American rate.

4. Transport and power. Transport and power, representing two sectors on which the whole economic structure depends, are useful indexes for comparison. With respect to transport, Russia remains and is likely to remain for the next decade, more heavily dependent than the United States on the intensive use of its railway net. . . . Total American freight traffic is about twice the Soviet figure. With respect to energy, both nations are well endowed with resources sufficiently economical to justify only a relatively slow introduction of atomic energy. Both use hyrdo and steam power in the proportion of about 1 to 4; the United States generated in 1957 about $3\frac{1}{2}$ times as many kilowatt-hours as the U.S.S.R. On the other hand, the United States uses about half its electric power for industrial purposes, the Soviet Union perhaps 80 percent. . . .

5. Management and incentives. Over the past 30 years the Soviet Union has devised a framework of education and administration, compulsion and incentives which yield men and institutions capable of operating a modern, rapidly growing economy. The working norms and methods of this system differ both from the initial standards of egalitarian communism and from those which have emerged in contemporary American society. Recent efforts have decentralized some areas of Soviet administration, without diminishing the ultimate ability of Moscow to allocate resources. Soviet education for management has typically a higher technological component than the typically more humanistic American general education. Although, to a limited extent, interesting similarities can be noted between Russian and American modes and problems of administration, the Soviet industrialist operates in a setting where his relations to the working force, to the consuming public, to the political process, and to the law are radically different from those of his American counterpart.

6. Industrial output, productivity, national income, and growth rate. Despite enormous difficulties in useful comparative measurement, a high degree of consensus now exists among American experts on the Soviet Union with respect to the overall course and prospects of the Russian economy. In 1955, Soviet industrial output was not more than a third of American, perhaps substantially less; industrial productivity per man, certainly below one-third; and GNP, about 40 percent. Soviet industrial output is likely to continue to increase, despite some factors making for deceleration, at about 8 percent per annum, GNP at about 6 percent. Assuming optimistically a rise of 4.4 percent in the rate of increase of American GNP, the ratio of Soviet to American GNP would rise from its figure of 43 percent in 1958 to 48 percent in 1970, the equivalent per capita figures being 36 and 41 percent. A 3 percent U.S. growth rate would lift Soviet GNP slightly over 50 percent of the American figure by 1970.

Given the differences in growth rate this would mean that the Soviet Union would dispose for the first time of a larger annual increment in GNP than the United States, at the end of the coming decade.

7. Standard of living. International comparisons of living standards are the most difficult of all relative measurements. But something like the following appears to be true: Soviet housing standards per family are about a fourth of the American average; food consumption per head somewhat better than one-half; clothing, a bit less than half; medical services, public parks, etc., similar to American standards. In durable consumers' goods and travel, the Soviet standard of living is, as it were, just entering the competition. The prospects for a significant improvement in Soviet food, shelter, and clothing for the next decade are good; and certain types of durable consumers' goods are under rapid expansion. No serious effort is now planned to manufacture and diffuse the automobile on a mass basis; and new housing will remain principally large urban apartment buildings. Except in a few particular categories (e.g., fish, woolen fabrics, and butter) there is little likelihood that Soviet consumption per capita will exceed the American figures, down to 1965. Taken all-in-all, a rise in the Soviet standard of living from something like one-third to about 40 percent of the American level is to be anticipated over the next decade.

8. Military expenditures. When corrected for all the relevant factors, Soviet military expenditures are at about the same level as American outlays; that is to say, the Soviet Government is allocating more than twice the proportion of GNP to military purposes than the American Government.

9. Foreign aid. Although Communist bloc foreign-aid figures in no way measure the scale nor define the nature of the Communist threat in Asia, the Middle East, Africa, and Latin America, Soviet military and economic assistance to underdeveloped areas was about half the level of American assistance in the period 1954–59. In addition, Moscow may have granted important assistance to Communist China over these years, although it is not certain. In 1959, some 4,700 Soviet technicians were engaged on work in the free world, about 75 percent of the number of Americans.

. . . . .

The Stages of American and Russian Growth

To make sense of this broad picture, and to pose the questions it raises for American policy, it is important to look far back in the history of the United States and Russia. For in comparing the two countries, we are looking at societies at quite different points in their own evolution. . . .

In terms of these stages of growth, Russia is now roughly at the level of the United States in the first decade of the 20th century; but it comes to maturity at a different, more advanced level of technology. . . . But . . . let us look back at the principal differences between the evolution of Russian and American growth.

First, Russia faced a far more difficult problem than the United States in preparing itself for industrial growth. It began in the 19th century with a traditional form of autocratic monarchy which, in many ways, obstructed the road to modernization. It faced, as well, intractable problems of land tenure, an illiterate serfdom, overpopulation on the land, the lack of a free-wheeling commercial middle class, a culture which initially placed a low premium on modern productive economic activity. The United States was provided with vigorous, independent landowning farmers, and an ample supply of enterprising men of commerce, as well as a social and political system that took easily to industrialization, outside the South. Thus, in order to industrialize, Russia had to overcome the drag of a traditional society, whereas the United States had only to overcome the high attractions of continuing to be a supplier of foodstuffs and raw materials. Contemporary Russian society still bears the marks of this struggle.

Second, throughout this sequence, American consumption per head, at each stage of growth, was higher than in Russia. Basically, this resulted from a more favorable American balance between population and resources; but the tendency was reinforced in both Czarist and Soviet Russia by constraints imposed by the state on the level of mass consumption.

Third, the drive to maturity took place in the United States, after the Civil War, in a setting of relative political freedom in a society tightly linked to the international economy, at a time of peace, and, generally, with rising standards of consumption per head. In Russia it occurred in the three decades after 1928, in a virtually closed economy, against a background of war and preparations for war, which did not slow the spread of technology, but which did limit the rise of consumption; and it occurred with something over 10 million members of the working force regularly in forced labor down to very recent years.

Fourth, the Soviet drive to maturity took place not only with constraints on consumption in general but severe restraints in two major sectors of the economy, not fully represented in indexes of industrial production—agriculture and housing. In housing, the Soviet Union lived substantially off the Czarist capital stock down to recent years, minimizing housing outlays, letting space per family shrink; in agriculture it invested heavily, but within a framework of collectivization that kept productivity pathologically low, once Lenin's N. E. P. was abandoned in 1929. In addition, Russia has invested very little indeed in a modern road system, which has drawn so much American capital.

Thus, the statistical equality in historical pace between Soviet and American industrialization, which Professor Nutter has so well dramatized, has been achieved by a radically higher proportion of Soviet investment in the heavy and metalworking industries than in the United States, imparting a major statistical advantage to Russia in comparison of indexes of industrial growth. And this difference in the pattern of investment was reinforced by the following two further quite real technical factors enjoyed by any latecomer: The ratio of net to gross investment during the industrialization drive was higher in Russia than in the United States, and the pool of unapplied technological possibilities was greater than in the United States. Both of these latter advantages are, essentially, transient; that is, as Russia has come to maturity, it must allocate increased relative proportions of its resources to meet depreciation; and, as it catches up with modern technology over the full range of its resources, it can enjoy, like the United States and the other mature economies, only the annual increment to technology, as it were, rather than a large unapplied backlog.

Nevertheless, as several of your panelists have strongly emphasized, on the eve of the 1960's we must assume that the Russian rate of growth will be higher than the American. This difference stems primarily from the way that Soviet Government has decided since Stalin's death to balance its choice among the three postmaturity alternatives.

Since 1953, the Soviet Union has, to a degree, reduced the harshness of police state rule and cut down on forced labor. To a degree it has increased the level of consumption of the Russian peoples. But its basic decision has been to use the annual increments in production to maintain a very large military establishment and to continue pressing for enlarged power on the world scene. Quite consciously, Soviet policy is postponing the age of the mass automobile and the single family house—the revolution which seized the United States in the 1920's, Western Europe in the 1950's—in order to make a bid for primacy in world power. Technically, this has meant that a much higher proportion of Russian investment than American has continued to go into manufacturing sectors rather than into construction and services. It is this relative concentration of Soviet investment in manufactures—and especially in industry related to military potential—which largely explains the higher Soviet than American rate of growth—now and for the next decade.

In historical terms, the challenge posed for the United States is whether a nation which has gone beyond the age of the automobile and suburbia and is concerning itself with larger families, travel, the refinement and differentiation of consumption, and the various uses of leisure can cope with a nation now arrived at technological maturity, pressing out on the world scene with high ambition, to see how far it can go, even at the expense of postponing the satisfactions (and problems) of the mass automobile and the single family house.

. . . . .

The Multiple Dimensions of the Soviet Challenge

To understand the real nature of the Soviet challenge—and what the Soviet

Government evidently means by "competitive coexistence"—it is necessary now to go beyond economic analysis and consider what Moscow is trying to accomplish.

Although Soviet policy objectives are primarily military, political, and psychological, they are based on an economic fact: the arrival of Russia at technological maturity. This means that the Soviet Union has the resources and technological capacity to mount a wider variety of military and economic programs than in the past. . . .

Here one specific aspect of the Soviet growth rate should be noted. A 6 percent rate of increase in Soviet GNP means that the Government disposes each year of something like the equivalent of $12 billion for whatever purposes it chooses. Althought the level of American gross national product is more than twice that of the Soviet Union, an average growth rate of 3 percent means that the American economy as a whole —not the Government—disposes of an increment of, say, only some $15 billion. . . .

1. The threat of major war. The main weight of Soviet policy is being articulated to the Russian peoples and to the world in terms of a nonmilitary struggle, which is, indeed, being energetically and frankly pursued. But there is no evidence whatsoever that the Soviet military effort is being reduced; and there are no grounds for building American policy on the assumption that if the Soviet Government believed that it enjoyed a sufficient advantage in nuclear weapons to take out American retaliatory power at a blow, it would not do so. Inhibitions may well exist in the Soviet political system against such a course of action; but there is no objective basis for believing that the United States would be safe should the gap in military capabilities be permitted to open to such an extent. Put another way, we Americans have no right before man or God to tempt Moscow's planners with this possibility. . . . Although it is evident that the Soviet Government is not building its policy on the certainty or even likelihood that it will get far enough ahead of the United States to take out our retaliatory power at a blow, its allocations for military purposes (including air defense) and the military doctrines now developing within the Soviet military establishment are wholly consistent with a missile salvo being regarded as one among several possible routes to world primacy—coexistence or no coexistence.

2. The threat of limited war. Similarly, there is no evidence in Soviet military allocations nor in Soviet military doctrine that the use of arms short of an all-out atomic war has been ruled out. On the contrary, the evidence remains that the Soviet Union has continued to modernize its ground force in ways which would make possible combat with either conventional or tactical atomic weapons. . . .

. . . . .

3. Diplomatic blackmail. Since the early months of 1956 down through the Berlin crisis, the Soviet Union has on a number of occasions used the threat of its missile capabilities to strengthen the hand of its diplomacy. Again, this is a form of threat which cannot be defined with reference to economic analysis. It comes, in the end, to a simple test of nerve and will.

4. The political penetration of the underdeveloped areas. Soviet policy in Asia, the Middle East, Africa, and Latin America is increasingly discussed under the heading of "The Economic Offensive." This leads to complicated efforts to compare the scale of Soviet and American aid on a quantitative basis. And, indeed, it is quite clear that Soviet technical and economic assistance to underdeveloped areas in the free world as well as Soviet trade policy have been significant forms for creating areas of political influence and sympathy in various parts of the world. But analysis confined to these familiar dimensions misses the main point and the fundamental nature of the Soviet threat. It is quite evident from Communist thought, writing, and policy that their goal in Asia, the Middle East, Africa, and parts of Latin America is a repetition in some form of the story of China from, say, 1927 to 1949; that is, Soviet analysts look to a progressive failure of the non-Communist regimes in these areas to solve the problems of modernization and economic growth, leading to frustration, internal turmoil, and to acceptance of the Communist alternative as a way of organizing these transitional societies. Thus, the central challenge confronting the United States and the Western World in the underdeveloped areas is not, somehow, to outstrip Russian loans and technical assistance. The challenge is to mount our own positive long-term policies designed to maximize the chance that these transitional societies will emerge into modernization without losing their independence and without foreclosing the possibility of progressively more democratic political development. Additional American and free world resources are required in this effort; and Soviet aid and trade policies play some role in the mounting of this challenge—which is, I believe, the route to world power that Moscow now regards as most likely. . . .

5. *The fragmentation of the Atlantic alliance*. It is clear that Soviet policy is immensely alert to the possibility of exploiting schisms as among the Western European nations and as between Western Europe and the United States. Offers of East-West trade play some part in this Soviet policy; but its primary tools are military, political, and psychological—combined with the fact that Moscow controls Eastern Germany and, therefore, the possibility of German unity. . . . the American response lies in the area of new ideas and institutional arrangements within the Western Alliance—which is now very rich—rather than in new American expenditures.

6. *The psychological image*. In support of these various efforts to achieve or to prepare for a breakthrough to world primacy, the Soviet Union is mounting a remarkable and sustained effort to project to the external world and to the Russian peoples a quite particular image. That image is of an ardent, energetic, and technically competent competitor closing fast on—and preparing to supersede—a front runner who has lost the capacity to deal with his problems and prefers to go down in the style to which he has become accustomed rather than to maintain his position. . . . this campaign has its foundations in three dimensions of Soviet policy: a somewhat dubious numerical approach to "catching up" with the American economy which, nevertheless, is rooted in the high momentum and technological maturity of the Soviet economy; an exceedingly solid set of Soviet achievements in missiles technology (military and nonmilitary) and a sporadically successful projection of the Soviet Union as the leader in the quest for peace. At home, the building of Soviet policy around the objective of catching up with the United States and with the American standards of living has proved an exceedingly successful device for unifying Soviet society, appealing as it does to three strong motivations evident in the Russian peoples: a deep nationalist pride, a desire for higher standards of living, and a passion for peace. . . .

. . . . .

The Allocation Problem

The root cause of our difficulty lies not in our income or our growth potential but in certain American habits of mind, carried over from earlier phases of our history, and in the workings of the political process, as they affect the allocation of resources. This interplay of intellectual conception and conventional politics conspire to make it difficult for Americans to increase the scale of public outlays except at moments of acute crisis. Here lies a danger to the national interest as well as a threat to the quality of American society.

Specifically, the working concepts of modern economics encourage the view that public outlays should be accommodated to the natural ebb and flow of the private sector, perhaps to be expanded at times of recession but certainly to be restrained when the private sectors exhibit high momentum. This perspective, carried over inappropriately from an era of depression and peace to a time of chronic cold war and secular expansion, constitutes a powerful deterrent to outlays in the public sector, especially at a time of chronic prosperity; for it renders difficult a rational choice between marginal outlays in the public and private sectors, without extraordinary exertions of political leadership. . . .

. . . Neither our concepts of political economy nor our notions of politics have made it possible to deal with threats to the national interest in a forehanded flexible way. We have shifted erratically from the moods and political economy of peace, to those of war. In the interval between, say, mid-1948 and the attack in Korea, for example, men in responsibility came to believe that a military budget beyond $15 billion was a threat to the American way of life. After the convulsive reaction to the Korean war had lifted military outlays more than threefold, this new range became again accepted as a line to be defended with a quite irrational ideological fervor.

The heart of the Soviet challenge lies, then, in presenting us with a situation where our interest may be eroded away, without palpable crisis, to a point where a traditional convulsive American response will no longer suffice. Our conceptions and methods of allocation to the public sector are inappropriate to a world caught up in a technological arms race and a slow grinding struggle for power and ideological conception in the underdeveloped areas. It is not the Soviet growth rate we need fear but a mode of American allocation which tends to imprison us at a level of public outlays determined by our arbitrary response to the last major crisis.

. . . . .

Can the Democratic Process Solve the Problems?

The burden of this argument is, then, that the challenges the Nation confronts, finally, have major economic dimensions: The challenges of adequate and forehanded allocation to the public sector; of dealing with inflation without damping the rate of growth; of creating an environment and a public policy which would accelerate the rise of productivity on a broad front. Each of these is a direct challenge to the vitality of the democratic political process in the United States. As members of the Joint Economic Committee are well aware, there are many Americans (including, I would surmise, certain of your panelists) who would take the view that efforts by the American political process to come to grips with them would inevitably result either in more economic loss than the gain sought; or, in political damage to our society which would outweight the possible economic gain.

. . . . .

The real case [for more determined U.S. action] must be negative on the one hand, positive on the other.

Negatively we know that four of our worst mistakes in modern history arose from a fear that our democracy could not deal with the problems it faced, without losing its essence. I refer, of course, to the belief of the Republican administration after 1929 that it could not deal with the great depression without risking unacceptable damage to capitalism; to the belief of isolationists in both parties that we could not deal with Hitler and the Axis without permanently damaging basic qualities in our society; to the belief of the Democratic administration before June 1950 that our society could not afford a military budget of more than $15 billion; and, I would add, the similar belief of the ... [Eisenhower] administration that its overriding mission has been to reduce the public budget it inherited, despite the accelerated challenge it has faced since 1953 in many dimensions.

The lesson of our recent history is that everytime the men in authority decided that some problem was too tough for democracy to lick, and that they had to evade the problem in order to save democracy, we have gotten into a quite deep hole; and in all but the fourth case, where the bill is still to be reckoned, democracy was in the end, much more searchingly and dangerously threatened than if the challenge had been accepted in the first place, at an early stage of the difficulty.

But there is a positive case as well. The positive case is not only that the democratic technique, energetically applied, has proved capable of handling such awkward problems as severe unemployment, major war, and limited war; it is also the simple faith that if any problem is soluble by human beings it is best solved, in the long run, by responsible freemen, subject to the mixture of freedom and self-discipline which is the essence of the democratic process when it works. Without that faith the struggle in which we are engaged lacks meaning.

. . . . .

A Conclusion

Now, a final word. Khrushchev's Russia is not the first nation to arrive at technological maturity, feel its oats, look over the field, and decide the old front runner was ripe for the taking. In our own time we have faced such moods and policies from Germany and Japan.

In the past these fast-closing nations have been persuaded to accept the fact that the world was not their oyster and to settle down as part of the international community only by defeat in major war. Major war was then necessary because the older powers did not so conduct themselves as to make major war a totally irrational undertaking.

In Russia we do not face a nation irrevocably committed to pursue power by major war unless we tempt it beyond endurance by our weakness during the period of the missile gap. The main hope for Soviet world leadership lies in various other dimensions, notably in their hope that the Western World and the democratic principle will fail in Asia, the Middle East, Africa, and Latin America. Moreover, I believe that there may well be men in Russia who already perceive that the rise of new nations, in the southern half of the globe, and in China, in a world of atomic weapons, may require a much higher degree of collaboration with the United States than even Khrushchev's challenge to compete peacefully would imply; they may begin to count not on burying us, but on making common cause with us over a widening range of problems. The discussions about ending H-bomb tests, with all they imply about Moscow's worries concerning the spread of atomic weapons, are a small beginning in this direction.

I doubt very much that Mr. Khrushchev is sure exactly where peaceful coexistence will end: in a missile salvo; in a protracted and dangerous struggle in the underdeveloped areas; or in a peace in which Russia accepts its destiny as a very great power, in a world of many diverse substantial powers. The answer lies not in the Kremlin's plans, but in what the free world does or fails to do, notably over the next decade. It it too much to ask of Russians at this stage of their history not to exploit every weakness we may offer. It is the strength and effectiveness of our response to the Soviet challenge—in all of its dimensions—which will determine the final meaning of peaceful coexistence.

. . . . .